RUDOLF STEINER
IN BRITAIN

Zur frdl. Erinnerung
herzlichst
Dr. Rudolf Steiner

Frontispiece to The Way of Initiation *(1909) and* Occult Science *(1914)*

RUDOLF STEINER IN BRITAIN

A DOCUMENTATION OF HIS TEN VISITS
VOLUME I, 1902–1921

CRISPIAN VILLENEUVE

TEMPLE LODGE

The Publishers wish to express their profound thanks to the Anthroposophical Society in Great Britain for their sponsorship of this work.

Temple Lodge Publishing
Hillside House, The Square
Forest Row, RH18 5ES

www.templelodge.com

Published by Temple Lodge 2004

A catalogue record for this book is available from the British Library

ISBN 1 902636 57 0

Cover by Andrew Morgan featuring a photograph of Rudolf Steiner visiting Anglesey in August 1923, with Marie Steiner and Harry Collison

Typeset by DP Photosetting, Aylesbury, Bucks.
Printed and bound by Cromwell Press Limited, Trowbridge, Wilts.

CONTENTS

	Preface	1
1	First Visit	15
2	Second Visit	45
3	Third Visit	69
4	Fourth Visit	85
5	Interlude (1905–12)	145
6	Fifth Visit	389
7	Interlude (1913–21)	439
	Notes	661

PHOTOGRAPHIC SOURCES AND CREDITS

Verlag am Goetheanum: Frontispiece to Vol. 1; 10, 12, 24, 30, 31, 32, 43, 48, 63, 75. Sylvia Cranston: *Helena Blavatsky*: 1. *The Lotus Journal*: 2. Isabelle de Steiger: *Memorabilia*: 3, 34. *The Theosophist*: 4. Clara Codd: *So Rich a Life*: 5. John Dummelow: (The British Westinghouse Company) *1899-1949*: 6. Ulick o'Connor: *Celtic Dawn*: 7. *The Bookman*: 9. Elizabeth Sharp: *William Sharp*: 11, 35. Uppingham School: 14. Merton College, Oxford: 15, 16, 17. *The Path*: 18, 19, 20, 21. Theosophical Society in Canada: 22. Mabel Collins: *Light on the Path*: 23. Edith Young: *Inside Out*: 25. The Word Foundation: 26. Matthew Wright: *Havelock North*: 27. Rex Raab: *Edith Maryon*: 28, 36, 38, 39, 40. A.E. Waite: *Shadows of Life and Thought*: 29. Anthroposophical Society in Great Britain: 37, 41, 44, 45, 52, 53, 54, 55. Thomas Meyer: *D.N. Dunlop*: 42, 46, 73. Rudolf Steiner Archiv: Frontispiece to Vol. 2; 57, 59a, 62, 69. *The Times*: 47. Heinz Herbert Schöffler: *Guenther Wachsmuth*: 49, 51. *The Correspondence of Rudyard Kipling*: 50. Albert Mansbridge: *Margaret McMillan*: 58. Archiv am Goetheanum: 64, 74. Anne Taylor: *Laurence Oliphant*: 65, 66. Philip Henderson: *The Life of Laurence Oliphant*: 67, 70. H.W. Schneider and G. Lawton: *A Prophet and a Pilgrim*: 68, 71, 72. Leathersellers Company: 77. Author's collection: 8, 13, 33, 56, 59, 60, 61, 76.

TO
OWEN BARFIELD
(1898–1997)

'How lovely is Thy dwelling place, O Lord of Life.' 'How lovely is Thy dwelling place.'

D.N. D., adapting Psalm 84:1

Those delicate wanderers,
The wind, the star, the cloud,
Ever before mine eyes
As to an altar bowed,
Light and dew-laden airs
Offer in sacrifice.

The offerings arise,
Hazes of rainbow light,
Pure crystal, blue and gold,
Through dreamland take their flight,
And mid the sacrifice
God moveth as of old.

In miracles of fire
He symbols forth His days,
In dreams of crystal light
Reveals what pure pathways
Lead to the soul's desire
The silence of the height.

AE

Preface

The present work may best be introduced by recounting something of its long and difficult history. In the year 1987 Joy Mansfield, already then at an advanced stage in her life, conceived the idea of writing a book about Rudolf Steiner's visits to Britain. She duly embarked on the project, over a number of years assembled some relevant material, and attempted more than one draft of an evocative period narrative. But this never reached a publishable state, and through failing eyesight she eventually found herself unable to continue. Accordingly Sevak Gulbekian, who had undertaken to publish it, asked me in 1994 to bring the project to completion.

Joy Mansfield then generously handed over her various drafts and papers. Although of course grateful for her initial labours, on perusing this material I was left with a strong impression that a fundamentally different kind of book needed to be produced on the subject from the one which had been attempted. What was called for above all was the inclusion of numerous primary texts, many in the German language, which had not previously been made available to an English readership. I then began to make searches, gather and—where appropriate—translate such documents, and in the process came to see that they ought to form the main substance of what would be in effect an almost entirely new work.

This resultant product has therefore turned into a quite different enterprise from Joy Mansfield's initial idea. Some of the material which she took pains to discover has also been included within it, but the volume of documentation now here presented has given the work the character of a source-book, in which manifold texts of direct or indirect relevance to the subject are marshalled in appropriate chronological order and largely left to speak for themselves, just interlinked with a kind of marginal commentary rather than incorporated into a full-blown authorial narrative. My belief is that this arrangement, although in a literary respect sanguine and even perhaps somewhat clumsy, is nonetheless the best way to reproduce the temporal evolution of the many-faceted subject matter and set out the sequential interrelations of its various parts. Moreover, it allows a reader the maximum freedom to form his own opinions and judgements on the questions presented by the given evidence. Perhaps this approach may best be summed up by saying that, despite its length, the present work is not intended as 'the last word' on the subject, but tries to give a textual basis for further appreciation of this same subject by other interested readers.

Credit therefore for the original conception of this book and for unearthing some of the material to be found in it belongs to Joy Mansfield.

But the main work of research, compilation and translation has been undertaken by myself and for the final text I am alone responsible.

★

Rudolf Steiner (1861–1925) lived for 64 years and one month. By far the greater part of his life, a period covering 63 years and eight months, was spent on the European continent, chiefly in the German-speaking lands of Austria, Germany and Switzerland, though with occasional visits to other outlying countries—Hungary, Czechoslovakia, the various Scandinavian lands, Holland, France and Italy. His Italian journey of 1910 even included a few days on the island of Sicily in the Mediterranean Sea.

The remaining period is formed by his ten visits to Britain, that western European island in the Atlantic Ocean. Taken altogether, these visits add up to about five months of his life. Relative to the rest, the period is therefore short. Nonetheless, in regard to Steiner's intention to transmit the impulse of anthroposophy to the world as a whole—rather than to Middle Europe in particular, or even continental Europe in general—it may be said to have an importance quite out of proportion to its length. His visits to Britain were more numerous than those to any other non-German-speaking country. Strictly speaking they were equalled by his Italian visits, but the latter were all contained within the years 1906–12, and several had to some extent the character of private holidays. His British visits were spread out over a period four times as long, and were more directly related to the central nucleus of his work.

This last point may be illustrated by citing a passage in a letter written by Steiner's close co-worker Ita Wegman on 3 June 1927 to George Adams, himself an important figure in the present story: 'There is very little value in having a large building here in Switzerland which is not supported by a sufficient number of people deriving from the West. And how can it be supported unless a feverish activity develops in England for anthroposophical work? Dr. Steiner said this often enough...' It is therefore quite understandable that the subject of Steiner's visits to England and Wales remains of particular interest to such people as have been led by destiny to incarnate into, to reside within, or simply themselves also to visit the British Isles during subsequent years.

What has chiefly been known in the English-speaking world hitherto about Steiner's visits to Britain are the contents of his various lectures and lecture-courses. Almost all of these have been translated into English at one time or another, and many are in print today and readily accessible. There is therefore no need to spend much time quoting from them. Rather, the main object of the present work is to provide a kind of background. Brief accounts of some lectures, penned either by Steiner himself or by other parties, have however sometimes also been included. An appendix supplies a complete survey of all lectures given by him in Britain, in the hope that this book, by providing an immediate historical context, will also inspire readers to further perusal and study of these various cycles.

★

The need to reconstruct the context arises from the fact that we are now separated from it by such a long period of time that even the oldest human memories can scarcely reach back so far. And a large number, perhaps even the majority of British persons who met and worked with Steiner also themselves passed away either before he did or within about 30 years of his death. Already in 1956 George Adams began his reminiscences of Steiner[1] by pointedly remarking: 'Many among his English friends who may have known him better than I did, and would have had quite other things to relate, have followed him into the spiritual world.'

Few of those departed English friends actually related much which had found its way into print. No doubt there were varied reasons. The task of doing and spreading anthroposophy in a pioneer situation must rightly have been judged more important than that of publicizing one's own memoirs. A related point was made by Christoph Lindenberg in the foreword to his *Rudolf Steiner: Eine Chronik* (1988):

> . . . Finally, it must be considered that Rudolf Steiner himself, despite his continuous lecturing activity, was unusually taciturn and discrete. Regarding his personal experiences, impressions, judgements and plans he mostly expresses himself in a very reticent and subdued form, and precisely the persons who enjoyed his confidence themselves protected this discretion.

One English person who during the last years of Steiner's life came to enjoy his confidence was Eleanor Merry, who died in 1956, just when Adams was bringing out his reminiscences. She indeed had quite other things to relate about Steiner from those related by Adams, but although during the previous 30 years she had authored all sorts of articles and books on a variety of subjects, she was sparing of personal records. Neither her account of her own meeting with Steiner in 1922 nor her description of the Tintagel visit in 1924, nor her memories of D.N. Dunlop written after his death in 1935, nor even her autobiographical *Life Story*, datable on internal grounds to 1954, were published during her lifetime. All four of these pieces were simply left among her papers after her death and brought out posthumously under appropriate circumstances. It is a revealing paradox that she had at different times committed her vivid accounts to writing, often with an imaginary reader very much in mind, but was not prepared for the public to peruse them while she was still alive. Doubtless this also reflected peculiarities of her own character. When a few months after her death the description of the Tintagel visit was published in *Anthroposophical Movement*, it was prefaced with a brief foreword from Mabel Cotterell which revealed that Eleanor Merry herself had incarnated 75 years too early:

> This hitherto unpublished article by Mrs. Merry recalls personal memories of her which reach back to over thirty years ago when we were together at the Summer Schools of Penmaenmawr and Torquay. After her death last June someone wrote to me that 'a great soul had left the Earth'. Certainly a very gifted soul too, gifted in painting, music, speaking. She felt herself to be a 'Platonist' soul, allied to the arts, rather than one of the 'Aristotelian' stream to which most of the anthroposophical members now incarnated belong. She once told me that Dr. Steiner had said she came down to Earth too soon, that she should have waited until 1951. She descended perhaps to combine her work with that of D.N. Dunlop, both of them filled with such a strong Celtic impulse.

Once Eleanor Merry had died and George Adams had brought out his reminiscences, which probably inspired Gladys Meyer to add hers as well, there were no further British anthroposophists left who felt inclined to set down their memories in print. In a recollection of Dorothy Osmond in the Winter 1978 issue of the *Anthroposophical Quarterly*, Charles Davy remarked:

> I often wished that Dorothy would write her reminiscences, going back to the First World War and beyond. There was much she could have told us about Rudolf Steiner's visits to England and the beginnings of the AS in GB, but to write personally for public reading would have been foreign to her nature.

As over the following years the remainder of Steiner's still surviving English friends departed across the threshold, ever less first-hand information about his visits to Britain could be supplied. When on beginning the present project Joy Mansfield attempted to make some enquiries at Dornach, she received in 1987 a letter from Robert Friedenthal of the Rudolf Steiner Nachlassverwaltung—editor of both the Penmaenmawr and Torquay courses as well as the entire cycle of karma lectures—which began as follows:

> Dear Mrs. Mansfield,
> I am afraid that you are too late with this enterprise. 15 years ago, when my old friends W.B. Paton and Dorothy Osmond were still alive, it would have

been easy to answer these questions, but now? I really don't see who could find out such details . . .

Readers may therefore imagine the sense of utter resignation with which the present writer, faced with an even greater lapse of time from the subject matter, finally found himself in the year 1994 embarking upon this still unfinished enterprise. By that time there was of course no one left who could still pass on significant oral memories, and there only remained the task of examining and collating written records.

In the event this task proved far larger than I had anticipated. The more I worked on it, the more it seemed to grow, and there were times when I seriously wondered whether I could keep up with the growth. Nonetheless I still feel that it was right both to undertake the task and to bring it to completion. The old maxim 'better late than never' surely also applies to the restricted but still legitimate field of historical investigation just as much as to any other realm of human life or activity.

*

The reason why this task naturally came into my direction goes back to the year 1987, just when Joy Mansfield took it up. For this was also the year in which Thomas Meyer published the first German version of his biography of D.N. Dunlop.

Meyer had been examining the archive of Walter Johannes Stein and, since what he found there aroused his interest, he made a variety of further explorations. In 1984 he drew attention to Dunlop when introducing a collection of Stein's essays under the title *Der Tod Merlins* (later translated as *The Death of Merlin*) for the first in a series of 'Pioniere der Anthroposophie' promoted by the Verlag am Goetheanum. In the following year, 1985, he brought out as a second number in this series a full scholarly version of the university dissertation written by Stein with Steiner's help and annotations during the First World War, now given the title *Dokumentation eines wegweisenden Zusammenwirkens*.

The original version of the Dunlop biography appeared in the same series in 1987. While visiting Rudolf Steiner House in London I noticed a copy in the bookshop, and bought it. Dunlop's name was recognizable as occurring here and there in the literature concerned with Steiner and his times, but I knew next to nothing about him.

To read this book was a most amazing experience. For it drew me straight into a living relation with the subject of the biography, at a depth which had never previously connected me to any figure from the then largely long-departed circles of Steiner's contemporaries. But the most extraordinary, indeed utterly paradoxical feature of this book was that although centrally concerned with the culture of the British Isles it was written in the German language!

Others in Britain who could read German were similarly affected. Owen Barfield, then in his ninetieth year and already the doyen of British anthroposophists, at once put a notice into the Society *News-sheet*:

> The number of those who remember D.N. Dunlop is rapidly diminishing. He was General Secretary of the Anthroposophical Society in Great Britain from 1930 until his death in 1935—a fateful and stormy period in the life of the Society as also in that of the General Society—though he had taken a leading part in its activities for some years before that. I am one of that dwindling band, because I was a member of the Executive Council throughout the years of his office. If it was impossible not to respect his dedication and ability and, yes, his essential geniality, it was quite possible to do all this while having only the vaguest idea of his background, and I think that was the case with most members of the Council. One knew that he had been a member of the Theosophical Society, one had perhaps heard that Rudolf Steiner had acknowledged a close affinity between them, one had heard also that quite outside his occult and anthroposophical interests, D.N. Dunlop had international standing in a wide circle of industrialists and economists as Director of the British Electrical and Allied Manufacturers' Association.
>
> What one did not have was any adequate notion, if indeed any notion at all, of the true stature, both spiritual and practical, of this remarkable man. And that is what is so abundantly demonstrated in Thomas Meyer's book *D.N. Dunlop: Ein Zeit und Lebensbild* which has just been published by the Verlag am Goetheanum. 'D.N. Dunlop: his Life and Times' will presumably be the title of the English translation which *must* surely be undertaken before long. Five hundred pages would never have been devoted by a German-speaking author to a Scottish anthroposophist (including seven photographs at different ages) were he not firmly convinced not only that Rudolf Steiner esteemed him to be, but that Daniel Nicol Dunlop actually was, in a special sense, a man of destiny. It is a conviction the reader soon finds himself sharing.
>
> Unfortunately I have no space to adumbrate the book's contents in detail, or indeed to do much beyond expressing my unbounded admiration for the painstaking research into biographical and other details and the skilful marshalling of its results that characterize this beautifully produced volume. Dunlop, the lonely child on a tiny Scottish island, Dunlop, the youthful friend of, among others, W.B. Yeats, of the poet AE, who dedicated to him his volume of poems, of Richard St. Barbe Baker, the 'Man of the Trees', Dunlop, the far-sighted and still-remembered founder of the World Power Conference, which under its new name of World Energy Conference still

> meets at intervals, Dunlop, the influential worker for Anthroposophy in the West, the only begetter of both the Penmaenmawr and Torquay conferences, to which Rudolf Steiner attached so much importance, the servant of Michael to whom Steiner once said 'We are brothers.' And round this central thread a clearer and clearer picture emerging of the Spirit at work, now hidden and now more apparent, now for the better and now for the worse, both within and without the Anthroposophical Movement during that fateful first half of the twentieth century; that is the generous gift for which anthroposophists, and surely not only anthroposophists, have to thank Thomas Meyer, and for which I thank him warmly on their behalf.

Taking up the challenge latent in these words, I tried to 'adumbrate the book's contents' for English-speaking readers in articles for *Anthroposophy Today* and *Camphill Correspondence*. On the Continent too, appreciative reviews were appearing in the anthroposophical and even the theosophical press. In one or other way, they could all be taken as tributes to the power of the written word to open up in the human mind completely new areas of historical awareness.

Now since Meyer had supplied his book in the usual scholarly manner with ample bibliographical references, I became interested enough to follow many of them up. This led straight into exploration, chiefly in London in the British Library and the library of the Theosophical Society, of large parts of the field out of which the biography had been written. When in these parts I started to make further relevant discoveries of which the author seemed unaware, I passed them on to him. We entered into correspondence, and subsequently met.

I also corresponded and was interested to meet with Alan Denson, the indefatigable pioneering scholar who had laid the foundations for all research into the work of AE. He possesses an excellent knowledge of the Anglo-Irish cultural scene of the early twentieth century, and had made personal acquaintance with many other figures like Clifford Bax associated with it. Most of Denson's investigations were undertaken decades before, his *Letters from AE*, referred to by Meyer with appreciation, having been published as far back as 1961. In the preface to this book, which presented merely part of what he had assembled, Denson reported that the original selection from the vast accumulation of letters and notes comprised more than 700 letters, and approximately 450,000 words. He added however: 'Among AE's correspondents some failed to preserve his letters . . . Daniel Dunlop is presumed by all his children to have destroyed all his correspondence.' For no less than 30 years between 1905 and 1935 the person closest to Dunlop on a daily professional basis both in the Westinghouse Company and later in the BEAMA was Charles Weekes,[2] who also maintained extensive correspondence with AE. But it is remarkable that any of AE's letters to him survived at all. In 1970, to fulfil a promise made earlier to Weekes's widow, Denson printed privately a selection of her husband's *Poems*, stating in the foreword: 'Weekes destroyed all correspondence he had received prior to his marriage (1901). In 1939 he destroyed most of his accumulated correspondence again, to avoid risk of dispersal during the War. W.K. Magee' (also known under the pseudonym of John Eglinton) and Weekes corresponded regularly throughout life. After AE's death'—in 1935—'they agreed to destroy their personal letters in which AE was discussed. Dr. Magee in 1950'—four years after Weekes's death in 1946—'expressed to me his regret at that loss.'

The destruction of correspondence by Dunlop and others of his circle, however regrettable it may have been, was nonetheless amply compensated by the wealth of printed material lying unexplored in relevant libraries, and as the idea of translating Meyer's biography into English was slowly carried forward the results of my discoveries were duly incorporated. I also assisted the translation of Meyer's related booklet *Ichkraft und Hellsichtigkeit*, published in 1988, which came out in English in 1991 as *Clairvoyance and Consciousness*.

By this time the original German edition of the Dunlop biography had anyway gone out of print, so when in 1994, with financial assistance provided by the Anthroposophical Society in Great Britain, the Michael Wilson Fund, and ASEE Exhibitions Ltd (a publicizing body linked to the BEAMA which Dunlop himself had founded), the English translation finally came out, with an afterword by Barfield, it was not only the better but indeed the only purchasable version.

The corrections and additions to this English translation were in their turn translated back for another German-language edition which Meyer published in 1996 in his own Perseus Verlag. He wrote a new foreword mentioning my discoveries and that my 'Dunlop researches' had been 'continued to the present day'.

Since my 'Dunlop researches' naturally overlapped with the story of Steiner's visits to Britain, I had by then already been engaged to undertake the present work, and eventually came to realize that this would also provide a suitable context in which to bring forward for interested readers further results of these researches.

*

In his further biography *Ludwig Polzer-Hoditz—Ein Europäer* (1996), Meyer recounts striking statements made by Polzer in the year 1936:

> In September he and Berta spent an important, eventful day at the Ausee in Salzkammergut. The couple visited Lili and Eugen Kolisko, who were on holiday there. 'We spent a whole day in their company,' relates Polzer, 'with interesting talks from morning to evening.' Around this time he wrote in a letter to Stein on the 22nd of September: 'I'm realizing ever more strongly that the so-called split of 1935 was a necessity. For there are now different tasks. R. Steiner's work in England & Holland during his last year simply had another purpose from what people at Dornach now believe. And the Christmas Foundation Meeting was so little understood.'

This passage raises interesting questions. What did people then, or do people today—whether in Dornach, Britain or elsewhere—believe the specific purpose of Steiner's work in England and Holland in 1924 to have been? How was that purpose related to the work he had already undertaken in those same countries during his previous visits? And has a greater understanding of the Christmas Foundation Meeting generally come about since that time? The present book does not provide simple answers to such questions. But it may help to open out the ground on which appropriate answers may be sought.

Although the complex story of Steiner's successive visits to Britain is a subject of which certain parts are quite well known, it has never received as a whole a really adequate survey. This story is here reconstructed out of a multiplicity of both contemporary and later documents. They include Steiner's autobiography and his various reminiscences in lectures, addresses or articles; letters, written both by himself and by others; newspaper reports; journal accounts; memoirs of one sort or another; obituaries of this or that person; and further miscellaneous sources. The documents have been fitted together in chronological order to create as full a picture of the subject matter as is reasonably possible to provide. Some have lain till now comparatively inaccessible in archives or specialist libraries, or—to many people—even more inaccessible by reason of foreign linguistic garb in the German tongue. Others have been published in English before, but not in a context that would enable a reader to gain an overview of the subject and follow the stages of its development on the scale here attempted. The present writer is naturally aware that in course of time further relevant material may yet emerge from the Dornach archives, if from nowhere else. Such material will serve to expand the story, may well qualify certain emphases, or even correct specific details. But the overall account here given will still retain validity for reference purposes.

In perusing the varied texts put forward within the compass of this work a present-day reader must of course exercise a degree of historical discrimination. While some of these texts were fully public from the start, others were only published much later than the events therein narrated. Still others were implicitly restricted, explicitly esoteric or—in the case of letters—frankly private and not written with any thought of future publication. Since these different types of writing are here juxtaposed without any such distinctions, the reader is faced with a constantly changing perspective which is taken to assume a certain sensitivity and understanding on his part.

In this connection it must be stated that I have made a radical break with the traditional anthroposophical practice of sidelining or surpressing any dissentient opinion, and have instead sought to provide in an objective and comprehensive manner the widest possible variety of British comment from the early 1920s about Steiner and his work. This ranges all the way from laudatory eulogy by intimate adherents, through perceptive or amusing accounts by observers of more or less neutral stance, to compositions of undisguised and sometimes spicy hostility penned by downright opponents. Compared with the organized enmity towards anthroposophy which came to manifestation in German-speaking parts of the Continent, that evidenced on the earthly plane in the Britain of Steiner's day appears a paltry and random affair, but nonetheless persons who expressed in print their discontent may well have been representative. So rather than leave them in vague abstraction or anonymity at the story's edges, I decided to reproduce in full their recorded statements in order that readers might see for themselves exactly what was being said, who—where discoverable—was saying it, and what kind of literary organs were taking responsibility for its dissemination in the English-reading world.

It must be admitted that the variety which this work contains has made it into something of a thematic medley, even a kind of historical anthology, and no attempt has been made to impose on all these documents any editorial consistency of style. My hope is simply that readers will find the anthology both instructive and enjoyable, if not indeed also in some way typical of the British character itself.

⋆

Although having a national subject matter, the present work has of course no nationalistic intent. The story it relates can only be properly viewed within the supra-national context which anthroposophy itself provides. Here it must be remembered that Steiner's visits to Britain form only part of his relationship to that country. The other part is contained in the numerous observations *about* Britain or this or that aspect of British spiritual life which are scattered in many places throughout his lecture-courses. Most of these observations, which are by no means always complimentary, were not addressed specifically to British people but delivered to quite other audiences—chiefly at Dornach. Physical distance from Britain doubtless itself endowed them with requisite objectivity. But speaking *about* a particular country is a different matter from actually *living within* that country oneself—or even just paying it a visit. The present work does not attempt to collate or examine Steiner's observations *about* Britain, but confines itself to recording the progress of his *actual visits* to this country. The distinction is not meant to imply that his other observations are unimportant. On the contrary, they too require to be specially considered by British residents themselves.

Nor does this work purport to offer any general account of Steiner's life, a subject with which the book-market is surely by now sufficiently saturated. I have naturally made use of Lindenberg's *Chronik* as a controlling work of reference, and some small corrections of detail which I have made to it are not intended to detract from its enormous overall value. The remark in his foreword about the danger of picking out details might be held to have striking application to the present work, and I do not deny this danger's existence. But a discriminating reader will perceive from its title that the work is only intended as a specialist study, a small contribution to the total organic panoply of the great Initiate's earthly life in the late nineteenth and early twentieth century.

★

Steiner's visits to Britain number ten in all. They may be schematically set out as follows:

1.	July	1902	London
2.	July	1903	London, Esher and Oxford
3.	May	1904	London
4.	July	1905	London
5.	April-May	1913	London
6.	April	1922	London, Kings Langley and Stratford
7.	Aug-Sept	1922	London and Oxford
8.	November	1922	London
9.	Aug-Sept	1923	Ilkley, Bingley, Penmaenmawr and London
10.	August	1924	Torquay, Tintagel and London

A glance at this scheme shows the chronological pattern of the visits. The first four come relatively close together. After a long gap, the fifth stands by contrast rather on its own, and is followed by another long gap. The remaining five—especially the sixth, seventh and eighth, made within the same year—are again comparatively close.

It is also quite evident that wherever else in Britain Steiner may have gone to, the predominance of London in the record of his visits is incontestable. Not only was he in the capital every time he came, but on five of the ten occasions he seems to have gone nowhere else. Its geographical location in the south-east of the island makes a stay in this history-laden metropolis a matter of course for a continental visitor. But in Steiner's day London was also the famed capital of an extensive empire, and by making it his chief British stop he was implicitly demonstrating an intention to bring anthroposophy not just to Britain itself, but also through the medium of that country to the whole English-speaking world spread out over various areas of the globe, and in the process to all other peoples making use of what had already become the world-language.

★

How should a book about particular visits which are topographically linked but separated sometimes by many years be sensibly constructed? The plan which the character of the present work suggested was to fill in the account of intermediary months or years by such material as seemed germane to the main theme, or to the scarcely inextricable ancillary themes of the life and work of Dunlop on the one hand and the general development of British Anthroposophy on the other. The earlier period includes contemporary English-language accounts of Steiner and his works, and some relevant passages extracted from Ekkehard Meffert's biography of Mathilde Scholl and Magdalene Siegloch's biography of Lory Maier-Smits. For the period of the First World War there was a dearth of written material, but a fair amount of information about Dunlop. For the post-war period the gaps are chiefly filled with relevant letters from Edith Maryon's correspondence, whose importance was indicated by Rex Raab in the course of his Maryon biography. It should however be added that no complete account is given of Maryon and her work, a topic which for an English-speaking readership both needs and deserves a further volume in itself.

In this perhaps rather unusual but I believe justifiable way, I have tried to give the present work such balance and proportion as could reasonably be achieved without wandering too far into related but separate fields.

★

The nature of the enterprise as above explained has also determined certain features of detail.

Names of cited sources, where published, are given in the text itself rather than relegated to endnotes. But the standard scholarly practice of providing exact page references appeared unnecessarily intrusive. Readers interested enough to consult further the works referred to should have little difficulty in locating for themselves the pages on which the cited passages may be found.

Sometimes quotations have been slightly abbreviated, often silently. In all such cases the omitted words, phrases or sentences either had no relevance to the present subject, or were factually incorrect.

All translations are my own, though where they existed any previous translations have also been examined and at times gratefully adapted.

The endnotes consider technical or ancillary matters, or in some instances explore later developments falling outside the period of time covered in the main text.

A variety of more or less appropriate photographs are added for illustration. In the group photographs, only such identifications have been made as are attested, either at first hand or by statements from one or more reliable sources who themselves knew the persons identified, apart from a few cases which are based on close comparison with other known photographs and/or reasonable deduction. (It must also be stated that married ladies are denoted by their married names even where their marriages took place after the date of the photographs.) Although absolute certainty cannot be vouchsafed for every single instance, the author remains confident that the vast majority of given identifications are incontestably secure. But should any readers have grounds to challenge any given case, or indeed be able to provide further identifications of their own, he would be very interested to know. In this connection it may be added that in a letter to him in 1988, Constance Winney remarked: 'There were some anthroposophists who objected to these group photographs on the grounds that they were not of importance to the conference and were egotistical, but I know that Dr Wegman never objected to being photographed, and most of the eurythmists seemed to like it!'

*

Nothing further need be said except to express heartfelt thanks to the many anthroposophists and others—on both sides of the spiritual threshold between life and death as also of the marine threshold between Britain and the rest of the world—who down the long and often weary years of its progress have shown their interest in this enterprise and given assistance or encouragement to either Joy Mansfield or myself. Human contacts made or further fostered in this process have been a valuable outcome of the work. Particular mention must be made of the friendly assistance regularly supplied by Margaret Jonas in the library at Rudolf Steiner House in London, and of the kindness of Eileen Lloyd in undertaking the heavy task of compiling an index.

Perhaps it is appropriate to end this preface by asking to what extent the enormous time and energy involved in the compilation of a work of this volume may be justified. Readers must answer this question for themselves.

For my own part, I can say that during the years of its progress I have found myself repeatedly pondering that undated scene recorded by George Adams in his article on 'Rudolf Steiner in England':

> On one occasion as I was saying goodbye to him he thanked me personally, adding with emphasis: *Es ist ein grosses Opfer*—it is a great sacrifice. Oh no, Dr. Steiner, I said, I do it so very gladly. But he insisted, and repeated more than once: *Es ist ein grosses Opfer.*

It can only be in the light of this anecdote that the present work is now offered to its readers.

Crispian Villeneuve
February 2004

1
FIRST VISIT

The Path to the Inner Life

In January 1902 subscribers to the British journal *The Theosophical Review*, jointly edited by two prominent theosophists, Annie Besant and G.R.S. Mead, and published in London on the 15th of each month, were able to peruse among other items a review-article entitled 'The Mysticism of the Intellect', written by another well-known theosophist, Bertram Keightley.

Keightley was born in England in 1860 and educated at Charterhouse and Trinity College, Cambridge. While still a young man he came across Sinnett's *Esoteric Buddhism* on its first appearance in 1883, and in the following year joined the Theosophical Society and made personal acquaintance with H.P. Blavatsky. It was indeed he who invited her to move to England in 1887 and prepared for publication the manuscript of her magnum opus *The Secret Doctrine*, published in 1888. At Blavatsky's request Keightley then departed in 1890 for India, where he stayed for a few years, becoming the founding Secretary of the Society's Indian Section.

One memorable incident in this part of his life came in 1893, when during a stormy night he was involved in a shipwreck a few hundred yards off the coast of Ceylon. All his baggage—including precious letters from the now deceased Blavatsky—was lost. He spent the whole night in a crowded lifeboat which was unable to cross the surf until dawn. When the boat finally did reach land, the passengers found themselves in a completely uninhabited spot. In order to get anywhere at all, Keightley had to walk barefoot for miles on end, across the sand and further through marsh, mud and jungle. It took him no less than four days before he reached Colombo.

Some time after this, he returned to England, and in 1901 became General Secretary of the Theosophical Society's European Section. He was a regular contributor to *The Theosophical Review*, and since he could read various foreign languages the books that attracted his attention were not confined to those written in English.

Keightley's article on 'The Mysticism of the Intellect' will now be reproduced in full.

> It is quite true that for each of us the path to the inner life is different, that each must find, nay, rather that each is, the path; and although the presence of certain common features and characteristics does make it possible to generalize in a measure and speak of the path of knowledge, the path of

devotion, and so forth, yet it is an effort of no small practical usefulness for the individual to strive to understand and appreciate roads other than his own, along which his fellow-pilgrims have trod the hidden way that leadeth to life eternal. Now over the gateway of one such path—some may say perchance over the gateway of The Path—stand inscribed the words: Know thyself. There are, however, at least two very different ways in which this injunction may be taken; not improbably, it seems to me, there may be many more than two. But for the present only two need be considered here.

The one, that most familiar to us from the *Bhagavad Gita* and the philosophies of Ancient India, may perhaps be characterized as the endeavour by man to know himself as distinct and separate from all phenomena and activities of the manifested universe. The process is a negative one. Man knows himself either in Samkyan phrase as the eternal, non-acting Jiva, the deathless witness over against a universe of ever-acting and ever-changing matter (Prakriti), or with the Vedanta as one without a second over against a universe of unreal mulitiplicity and separation (Maya). I am here speaking by the book, as it were, describing this path as given in the books, not as transformed and illuminated, as it may be, by the inner light of deeper insight into what those ancient thinkers and teachers really meant. But there would seem to be another method, or path, or line of approach to the Inner Mystery, into which this same gateway of self-knowledge admits a man, which—or at least so it seems to me—presents quite a different aspect from that just so briefly indicated. Perhaps the two are one and the same, only viewed from different points. I cannot yet tell. But at least it would seem worth while to try and understand something of this other aspect as it is presented in a series of addresses to the Berlin Theosophical Lodge, by Dr. Rudolf Steiner, just published in book form under the title *Die Mystik im Aufgange des neuzeitlichen Geisteslebens und ihr Verhältnis zu modernen Weltanschauungen* (Berlin: C.A. Schwetschke und Sohn; 1901. Price 2m.).

In his introductory lecture, Dr. Steiner presents what I take to be his own understanding of this aspect of the path—in the main an intellectual one—which in his view is that trodden by the great representatives of mysticism in Central and Southern Europe: Meister Eckhart, Johannes Tauler, Heinrich Suso, Johannes Ruysbroeck, Nicolas von Kues, Agrippa von Nettesheim, Theophrastus Paracelsus, Valentin Weigel, Jacob Böhme, Giordano Bruno and Angelus Silesius. How far the view Dr. Steiner takes of these mystics is adequate, to what extent it expresses the essential keynote of their lives and teachings, are wide questions, and into these I do not propose to enter here or now. We are rather concerned to try and understand what Dr. Steiner himself is endeavouring to express, and we shall be helped, I think, in doing so by following him briefly through what he has to say about these men, whose names should be so familiar to every close student of mysticism. But first let us set before our minds—and hearts—what he himself tells us of his own understanding of the mystic path. He strikes his keynote in the following words:

'All these thinkers (Hegel, Meister Eckhart, Valentin Weigel, Angelus Silesius, etc.) have in common a strong sense of the fact that in man's knowing himself (*in der Selbsterkenntnis des Menschen*) there rises a sun which illuminates something quite other than the casual separated personality of the beholder. That which Spinoza became conscious of in the ethereal heights of pure thought, viz., that the human soul possesses an adequate knowledge (*Erkenntnis*) of the eternal and infinite being of God, that same consciousness lived in them as immediate feeling; and the knowledge of self was to them the path leading to this eternal and infinite being. It was clear to them that self-knowledge in its true form enriched man with a new sense, which unlocks for him a world which stands to the world accessible to him without this new sense as does the world of one possessing physical sight to that of a blind man.'

And he quotes as a most admirable description of the importance of this new world, the following passage from J.G. Fichte's Berlin lectures (1813):

'Imagine a world of men born blind, to whom all objects and their relations are known only through the sense of touch. Go amongst them and speak to them of colours and other relations, which are only present for sight through light. Either you are speaking to them of nothing at all; and this is the more fortunate, if they say it, for thus you will soon see your mistake, and if you cannot open their eyes, cease your useless talking. Or for some reason or another they will insist upon giving some meaning or other to what you say; then they can only understand it of that which is known to them through the sense of touch. They will seek to feel, they will imagine they do feel light and colour, and the other incidents of visibility, they will invent for themselves, deceive themselves into perceiving something within the world of touch which they will call colour.'

The same thing applies, remarks Dr. Steiner, to what Eckhart and the others found in 'self-knowledge'. As they experienced it, the new sense which it gave them yielded conceptions and perceptions which simply do not exist for one who does not see in self-knowing that which distinguishes it from all other kinds of knowing. One in whom this new sense has not revealed itself believes that self-knowing or self-perception is the same thing as perception through the outer senses, or through any other means operating from without. He thinks 'knowing is knowing, perceiving is perceiving'. Only in the one case the object of perception is something lying in the world outside, in the other this object is his own soul. He hears words merely, or at best abstract thoughts, in what for those who see more deeply is the very foundation of their inner life—namely in the fact that in every other kind of knowing or perception we have the object perceived outside of ourselves, while in self-knowledge or self-perception we stand within the object perceived; that we see every other object coming to us as already complete and finished off, while in ourselves we as doers and creators ourselves weave what we observe in ourselves. This may appear as nothing but a mere verbal explanation, perhaps even a triviality; it may appear, on the other hand, as a higher light which illuminates every other cognition.

Elaborating and further expounding this inner sense, Dr. Steiner points out that the external, independent world exists for us by communicating itself to our consciousness; and what is so communicated must needs be expressed in the language peculiar to ourselves. Further, we hear from within ourselves the same speech as penetrates to us from external things. But in that case it is we ourselves speaking. And the important point is that we should rightly grasp the transformation which occurs when we close our senses and perceptions to external things and only listen to what then speaks from within ourselves. But to do this rightly needs this new sense. If it has not been awakened, then we believe that in what is thus told us about ourselves, we are having only communications about something external to and outside of us; we fancy that there is somewhere a something hidden which is speaking to us in the same way as external things speak. But if we possess this new sense, then we know that these perceptions differ essentially from those relating to external things; then we realize that this new sense, unlike our ordinary perceptions, leaves nothing outside of itself, but takes up its object wholly into itself without any remainder.

Dr. Steiner points out further that what we add to objects through this new sense is neither any new idea, nor any enrichment of their content; but a lifting of the knowing (*Erkenntnis*), of the perception, to a higher level, where everything is suffused with a new glory. It is thus in truth a new birth of the things of the world, a taking of them up into a new life, so that no unknowable 'noumenon' or 'thing-in-itself' is left as an unresolved surd outside of consciousness. Once this new sense is awakened, I am no longer a separated, isolated individual consciousness, but realize in myself the one consciousness, the one Self, the very inmost essence of the whole universe. And he goes on to point out how Fichte and Spinoza, Hegel and Paul Asmus, the *Bhagavad Gita* and Goethe, have one and all experienced and expressed the same thing, giving most pointed quotations in each case to illustrate the fact, which unfortunately are too long for quotation here.

In the concluding pages of his introductory essay, Dr. Steiner shows how the awakening of this new consciousness, this new sense, brings freedom to the individual and thus gives a solution of the old riddle of necessity and free will.

The whole essay is well worth most careful study, and the working out of its leading idea as exemplified in the lives and writings of the great chain of German mystics is most helpful and instructive. But considerations of space prevent the following out of these illustrations here for the moment, though

I hope hereafter to return to them. In the meanwhile it remains heartily to congratulate our colleagues in Berlin upon having heard and given publicity to such an admirable series of addresses, and to express the hope that Dr. Steiner will ere long make further contributions to an aspect of theosophical study which is all too little represented in our current literature.

Readers acquainted with Steiner's book *Die Mystik* will observe at once the peculiarity of Keightley's review-article. Although supposedly introducing a whole book to an English readership, he concentrated most of his attention on the introductory chapter. The rest of the book was perceived by him as simply working out the epistemology contained in this initial 'essay', which is ultimately derived from Steiner's *Philosophie der Freiheit* (mentioned in the book's introduction) and earlier from his *Grundlinien einer Erkenntnistheorie*. Indeed it may be noted that the one German word which Keightley quoted three times over was the word *Erkenntnis* ('cognition, knowledge').

★

In September 1900 Steiner had been invited by Count and Countess Brockdorff to give a lecture to the Berlin Lodge of the Theosophical Society. Soon after doing so he resigned his three-year editorship of the *Magazin für Literatur*, and in October began a cycle of lectures in the Theosophical Library on the subject of 'Mysticism'. Sometime in the last two months of this year, Marie von Sivers first made her appearance at these lectures.

The first recorded letter from Steiner to Marie von Sivers dates from April 1901, and in it he thanked her for forwarding a copy of *The Theosophical Review*. He was turning his lectures on mysticism into a book, and in August was still correcting the proofs. By October he had begun to give a new series of lectures on 'Christianity as Mystical Fact'. Towards the end of the year, when Marie von Sivers had left for Bologna to help found the Society's Italian Section, the Brockdorffs requested Steiner both to join the Society and take on the leadership of the Berlin Lodge. He declared himself willing on condition that Marie von Sivers became his co-worker.

The Brockdorffs persuaded her to accept this plan, so on 17 January 1902—a couple of days after publication of the issue of *The Theosophical Review* containing Keightley's article—Steiner joined the Theosophical Society. An official diploma was sent to him from England.

Just over a fortnight later, on 2 February, Count Brockdorff's daughter Edda wrote to Steiner from Ceylon:

I have just read in the *Theosophical Review* of the 15th of January a very appreciative article from the pen of Bertram Keightley about your new book *Die Mystik im Aufgang des neuzeitlichen Geisteslebens* etc.; it's on pages 45 ff. I am very pleased the English are giving appreciative emphasis to your book and especially that they do so in this particular way. Otherwise they are always saying 'Germany isn't yet mature,' or 'What good can come out of Germany?' In my opinion you have really shown the English not only your maturity but that you, or rather let us say German mystics and you with your conception of them, are far in advance of the English. I saw myself, when your book was coming into being, that you were speaking to us like a teacher to his men and women pupils, and I felt far more sympathy and understanding for your lectures than for the erudition in Adyar. The hours we spent with you in the library were more profitable to me than the ingeniously learned lessons of Mrs. Besant. I was amazed at her knowledge and ability, and admired it, but only with you did my heart come into its own. True knowledge or intuition is located in the heart and works onto the brain from there. But all the others are trying to work onto the heart and the reason from the brain.

Over here there are far more members of the Theosophical Society, indeed learned members, but I believe the Society as such has had its day. The best things are coming from people who are not members on paper, but are much nearer the truth without any diploma from Adyar or London...

Dr Steiner's Leading Ideas

Although no further writing by Bertram Keightley on the subject of Rudolf Steiner's *Die Mystik* appeared in the February number of *The Theosophical Review*, in the March number there commenced a whole series of follow-up articles.

The first was entitled 'Meister Eckhart'. It began:

In a recent article I gave an account of Dr. Rudolf Steiner's very able and interesting series of lectures to the Berlin Theosophical Lodge upon the 'Mysticism of the Intellect', and I promised to illustrate the account there given of his own views from his treatment of the great series of German mystics from Meister Eckhart to Angelus Silesius. This promise I now propose to endeavour to fulfil by giving a summary of Dr. Steiner's remarks upon the thought of each of these remarkable men. In the following pages, therefore, I shall try to present, as clearly as considerations of space will permit, Dr. Steiner's leading ideas, with only an occasional comment or remark of my own interspersed here and there.

The reader will recall that, according to our colleague's view, the objective world undergoes a veritable rebirth in the mind of the man who has acquired that new sense of the real significance of his own self, upon which the doctor lays so much stress. He therefore introduces us to his study of Meister Eckhart with the observation that Eckhart's conception of the world was saturated through and through with the feeling that the objects which make up the outer world are born anew as higher entities in the mind of man. Like Thomas Aquinas, Eckhart belonged to the great Dominican order—the most learned of all the orders—and was himself a thoroughgoing admirer of that great theologian . . .

★

What Keightley meant by 'an occasional comment or remark of my own' became evident in a further article which appeared in the April number, entitled 'Friends of God'. Here, after discussing for some pages the writings of Johannes Tauler, he went on to examine the anonymous *Theologia Deutsch*:

> . . . We can devote a few words in conclusion to speaking of a book whose authorship is absolutely unknown, but which forms a very remarkable commentary upon this whole movement, and embodies in a very striking form almost a systematic guide to that higher life which Eckhart and Tauler expressed. Curiously enough it was first printed by Luther—no very earnest friend of mysticism as one generally supposes—and is dominated throughout by the same thought we should now express in the phrase 'the elimination and dissolution of the personality is the key to the higher life'. Some of its phrases are very striking; for instance: 'When the "ego" knows itself aright, it is no longer "ego" at all'; and a sentence that must be quoted in the original, since no rendering can do it justice: 'Denn Gottes Eigenschaft ist ohne "dies" und ohne "das" und ohne Selbstheit und Ichheit: aber der Kreatur Natur und Eigen ist, dass sie sich selber und das Ihre, und das "dies" und "das" sucht und will; und in all dem, was sie thut oder lässt, will sie ihren Frommen und Nutzen empfangen. Wo nun die Kreatur oder der Mensch sein Eigen und seine Selbstheit und sich selbst verliert, und von sich selbst ausgeht, da geht Gott ein mit seinem Eigen, das ist mit seiner Selbstheit.'
>
> The analogies between the above and some of the teachings in *Light on the Path* cannot fail to strike the student, and perhaps it might be of interest to compare them in more detail. But that would take us too far from our present lines . . .

★

A few days after the appearance of this April number of *The Theosophical Review*, Steiner was asked in Berlin to take on the post of General Secretary of the Theosophical Society's German Section, the foundation of which had already been planned for some time. At first, however, he did not give this request any definite answer.

★

After another pause in the May number, the series of Keightley's articles was resumed again in the June issue with one entitled 'Cardinal Nicholas of Cusa'. It began:

> A certain additional interest may perhaps attach itself in the minds of our readers to the name of Cardinal Nicolaus von Kues, or Nicholas of Cusa, the next in order among the mediaeval mystics of Germany to engage our attention, from the fact that H.P.B. speaks of him as an 'Adept' (*Secret Doctrine*, vol. iii., p. 367), and though the editor of that volume remarks in a footnote that this term is 'very loosely used by H.P.B.', and appears to mean here an uninitiated disciple, yet personally I remember H.P.B. telling some of us that Nicholas of Cusa was an initiated adept who in that particular birth was to a certain extent resting and, so to say, taking things easy. However that may be, he was certainly a very remarkable man and we shall find, I think, that Dr. Steiner's treatment of his writings will help to throw light upon that special conception of the mystic path which Dr. Steiner himself has formed, the elucidation of which forms the guiding thread running through the present series of articles.
>
> Nicholas of Cusa, then, was born near Trèves in 1401, and according to some writers, H.P.B. included, was the son of a poor boatman ...

Keightley went on to discuss Cusa's life and writings, but entered into so much detail that he could not possibly cover Steiner's exposition of this author within the available space. The article therefore ended with the words 'To be continued.'

★

In about mid-June, just when the issue of *The Theosophical Review* containing this article was published, Steiner accepted the offer of the General Secretaryship of the Theosophical Society's German Section.

Arrived on English Soil

At this juncture Marie von Sivers made her way from Bologna to London. From there she wrote to Rudolf Steiner, who was still in Berlin:

20 Clifton Gardens,
Maida Vale, W.
18th June

Dear Herr Doktor,

It would certainly be very nice if you could already be here early on Sunday 22nd, as you then gain a more precise impression of Mrs. Besant. She is a unique and exceptional phenomenon, and one has to experience her as a speaker to do her any kind of justice. Unfortunately you are coming at a bad time because the Coronation days are falling in between, when everybody is celebrating and no lectures are being held. At 7 on Sunday 22nd Mrs. Besant is giving the last but one of her popular lectures 'The Divine Kings'. She is such a priestess in this lecture-cycle that I can only advise you to gain this impression—and there are not many who can give *you* anything. Tuesday 24th sees the last of another lecture-cycle before a smaller audience, 'Will, Emotion and Desire', where her logicality, scope and precision of thought have been completely developed. You must at least hear this last one. The most abstract and difficult cycle, 'Consciousness and its Mechanism', on Thursday evenings for members only, unfortunately finishes tomorrow. So you will not be able to hear any of it. Leadbeater will also be speaking on the 23rd in the Blavatsky Lodge, which perhaps will not be repeated either. So if you are not here on those three days, 22nd, 23rd and 24th, you only have one Sunday lecture and the Convention days; at least, we know of nothing else at the moment. Mr. Keightley, who is looking forward to meeting you and only asks me to excuse him just now because of his 'excessive work-load', lives at '30 Linden Gardens, Bayswater W'. Write it down exactly, in case you have to take a 'cab' by yourself. If you lose or forget it, of course, come to our guest-house. Anyway, I shall wait for a message, and want to be at the station to greet you, if nothing special prevents me.

Many greetings to you and your wife

M. v. Sivers

The Coronation referred to was that of King Edward VII, who had succeeded to the throne on the death of Queen Victoria in the previous year. But although the Coronation was indeed planned for June, the still uncrowned king fell ill with appendicitis, so it was postponed until August.

*

Apart from attending lectures, Marie von Sivers was also gathering appropriate knowledge in a more personal way, recalled by Steiner in his autobiography:

During our first visit to London together, Marie von Sivers had heard from Countess Wachtmeister, an intimate friend of H.P. Blavatsky, a great deal about her, and about the arrangements and development of the Theosophical Society. She was familiar to a high degree with the spiritual content once revealed to the Society, and with the way this content had been further cultivated.

★

Steiner was at the time working on the last chapters of his book *Das Christentum als Mystische Tatsache*,[3] and did not arrive in England until the beginning of July, as related in a letter to his wife:

Hanover,
Monday afternoon

My dearly beloved Anna,

I'm sending you from Hanover station my first heartfelt greetings. I've just come from Dr. Hübbe-Schleiden, where his Munich friend Deinhard was also present. I've become convinced that it's Hübbe-Schleiden who's in the right and that Bresch is a base fanatic. I'll see what'll happen. In quarter of an hour I'm travelling further. On Monday morning I hope to be in London. Once again, for the sake of every precaution, I'll write you the address:

C/o Mr. Bertram Keightley
30 Linden Gardens
Bayswater
W

Please put the enclosed letter in the letter-box, and keep me in your love. With heartfelt kisses,

Rudolf

Greet Geni.

The latter was one of his wife's daughters by her previous marriage to Eugen Eunike.

★

A couple of days later, having made a sea-crossing for the first time in his life, Steiner wrote to his wife again:

London,
1st July 1902

My dearly beloved Anna,

Well, I arrived here this morning. The train came into Vlissingen yesterday evening at about 12 o'clock. At Vlissingen you get on the ship. Travelling long distances is really not at the moment very pleasant at all, as the trains are overcrowded.—So I boarded the ship in the middle of the night. There was something to eat. All criminally expensive. Then you got allocated a sleeping cabin. Cabin 33 bed 4. When I came in, there were already three chaps inside. And of what sort! One of them was snoring so much that sleep was no way to be thought of. Before entering the cabin I wrote you a picture postcard. So there was no question of sleep. I got up as soon as light dawned. It was a glorious morning! Even if the weather wasn't exactly glorious. Mountains apart, there's nothing more beautiful in Nature than water and sky all round. A ship here and there, at most. It was really beautiful. I was always obliged to think: if only you could be here now!—For I wouldn't have wished you to have gone through the night.

Arrived on English soil at about 6 o'clock. There's then still a 2¼ hours railway journey to London.—There are meadows on the way, then London appears. I get out at 8.45. With my voluminous trunk it's all a real palaver. Finally I've got my 'cab', that's a carriage with driver in front and passenger sitting inside. It's an English speciality. So I've got my 'cab'. Suddenly Frau von Holten and Fräulein von Sivers turn up. Just in time before I leave. Frau von Holten then travels on to Brighton, to her daughter. Frl. von Sivers takes me to Mr. Keightley. A real blessing: in such houses in England you have to have a bath every morning. So first London experience: a bath. Then breakfast with Mr. Keightley. He's a very kind, really nice person. I didn't want to come to lunch today, as it seems best not to fix myself down in that way to times. So I'm sitting here at 2 o'clock in the afternoon—but in Berlin that's already 3 o'clock—and have just eaten 'stewed kidney lyonnais'. You'd call the dish roasted kidney. Then at 7 o'clock this evening I've a meeting with Keightley, at which he'll be hearing how matters stand with the German theosophists.

I want to use today to find my way around everywhere on my own. I think in that way you orientate yourself most easily in a strange town. From the very outset London anyway makes an essentially different impression from all other towns I've seen. E.g. I've already been along many streets, but so far haven't yet seen any electric trams. Instead, it's all a storming confusion of carriages and omnibuses. Even so, there's more order in evidence than on the Potsdam Square in Berlin. But as I said, I've anyway seen little as yet. Perhaps the worst is still to come.

Heartfelt greetings and kisses
from your

Rudolf

Of Great Interest to Me

'The visit to London was of great interest to me,' reminisced Rudolf Steiner in his autobiography. 'There I met important leaders of the Theosophical Society. I was privileged to stay with one of them, Mr. Bertram Keightley, and became very friendly with him. I met Mr. Mead, so commendable a writer in the Theosophical Movement.'

In a lecture given in 1911 he went into more detail about his meeting with G.R.S. Mead:

> In the very year I joined the Theosophical Society, and was made Chairman without any ballot—there was no such thing at the time—the Congress of European Sections took place in London; the German Section was now going to be added. In the presence of Mr. Keightley, I had a conversation there with Mr. Mead chiefly centering on my *Mystik* which he had come to know from Keightley's review. At the time Mr. Mead uttered these words—I have to mention them as a fact, as it is illuminating—'In your book lies the whole of Theosophy.' Now of course such a slim book does not contain the whole of Theosophy. That kind of statement means: from what is contained within it, the whole of Theosophy may consequentially arise. Basically everything is implied in my *Mystik* which has since been read out of it. The question I would like to raise is: did not such a statement give reason to suppose that this particular stream of theosophical spiritual life would be met with longing? For by saying 'In this lies the whole of Theosophy' one is stating an amazingly great deal. When this statement had been made, it was justifiable to assume that the Theosophical Society might slowly form a context for something of which it had been said in London that 'In this lies the whole of Theosophy'.

After quoting Mead's statement in this lecture on 14 December 1911 Steiner did so a second time on 14 March 1915, a third time on 27 October 1918, a fourth time on 16 November 1920 and finally a fifth time in chapter XXX of his autobiography. So it is quite evident that what Mead had said left a deep impression upon him.

★

'At Bertram Keightley's house,' continued Steiner, 'there were the most interesting conceivable conversations about the spiritual knowledge living in the Theosophical Society.

It was especially with Bertram Keightley himself that these conversations became intimate. H.P. Blavatsky came to life in these talks. In the presence of myself and Marie von Sivers, my kind host, who had experienced so much through Blavatsky, described with the greatest vividness her whole personality and its rich spiritual content.

Annie Besant I met more briefly, and likewise Sinnett, the author of *Esoteric Buddhism.*

Steiner's first meeting with Besant took place on 3 July, on the same day as he also attended a lecture in the Blavatsky Lodge. Since this was the first English lecture he ever heard, it was strangely providential that the identity of the lecturer had had to be quickly rearranged, as reported in *The Vâhan*:

On July 3, the Lodge hoped to have listened to a lecture from Mr. Leadbeater, but unfortunately he was not well enough to deliver his address, and his place was kindly taken by Mr. Keightley, who on short notice gave an interesting lecture in which he pointed out the value of the evidence collected by the Society for Psychical Research with regard to abnormal states of consciousness. The writings of the late Mr. Myers were pointed to as containing much that could be used in support of the theosophical teaching with regard to these states.

⋆

Rudolf Steiner and Marie von Sivers had come to London in order to attend a Theosophical Convention. Its 'Report of Proceedings' recorded what happened on the following day:

On Friday afternoon, July 4, a reception of members was held at 28, Albemarle Street from 3.30 until 6, and in spite of the hot weather the many who attended spent a most enjoyable afternoon.

Straight afterwards, Steiner penned another letter to his wife:

London,
4th July 1902

My dear good Anna,

I'm very worried this Friday afternoon to have still had no letter from you. I was quite definitely hoping one would arrive this afternoon. Mr. Keightley, with whom I'm staying, is an exceptionally kind person. On Tuesday and Wednesday we talked in the evening for several hours on very important questions. I very much enjoyed it. Yesterday evening Mr. Keightley gave a most interesting lecture. Otherwise I'm wandering round London during the free time, which from today onwards is very limited indeed. There was a big reception today in the Society's headquarters here. I've just come away from it. In a couple of minutes I'll be called down to

Keightley's supper; then at 8.30 there's a lecture by Mrs. Besant. Yesterday I met Mrs. Besant in person.

The Convention begins tomorrow quite early. In the afternoon I'm invited to a 'tea'; in the evening there are lectures. It goes on like this till Tuesday. I'll write more often, my dear good Anna, even if it's sometimes just a couple of words, between my walks, which anyway in London are all journeys. The distances are simply frightful. I'm always thinking about you. You just can't believe how much I'd like to have you here. I'm longing for you very much.

Please write to me a lot. Heartfelt greetings and kisses to you for the time being

from your

Rudolf

★

The lecture by Annie Besant was described in *The Vâhan*:

In the evening Mrs. Besant delivered a very powerful address in the Queen's Hall at 8.30, her subject being 'Theosophy and Imperialism'. It was throughout very evident, from the frequent applause, that Mrs. Besant's eloquent speech had the strong approval of all who had gathered to listen to her.

The Queen's Hall in Langham Place was one of London's foremost concert halls. Built in 1893, it had a classical exterior modelled on the Pantheon in Rome. Inside, there were actually two halls, a larger and a smaller. The whole building was destroyed by German bombing in 1941.

Steiner recalled this occasion in a lecture on 14 June 1923, during a discussion of different spiritual streams working in the Theosophical Society:

. . . The most varied factors were at work. One of these factors wanted to join India to Asia, in order to create an Asiatic-Indian dominion with the help of the Russian Empire. So this teaching received an Indian element, in order to conquer the West in a spiritual way. This, you see, is a one-sided, nationally egoistic element, which was inside it from the very beginning, and met one with symptomatic significance. The first lecture I heard by Annie Besant was on 'Theosophy and Imperialism'. Anyone wanting to answer the question 'Does the real basic impulse of this lecture lie in continuing Blavatsky's actual spirituality, or does this lecture's real basic impulse lie in continuing what had gone on beside this?' would have to say: the latter.

It was often the case with Annie Besant that she would say things of whose ultimate causes she was totally ignorant. She would stand up for something whose ultimate causes she simply did not know. You should read perceptively the lecture 'Theosophy and Imperialism', which is in print. Read it with all its undertones, and you will see that if anyone wanted to tear India away from England, in a sense tear it away spiritually, they might take a first unnoticed step with the tendencies this lecture contained.

Truly International

The 'Report of Proceedings' of the Twelfth Annual Convention of the Theosophical Society's European Section also recorded details of the business meetings:

> The Convention assembled on Saturday, July 5, at 10.45 a.m., in the Banqueting Hall, St. James's Restaurant, Regent Street, W.

This restaurant had been built in 1875 as an annexe to St James's Hall towards the east end of Piccadilly, a vast edifice of early Victorian date in which Charles Dickens had once regaled London audiences with readings from *Oliver Twist.* By the time of Rudolf Steiner's first visits to London the buildings were past their prime, and in 1905 the entire complex was demolished.

> Members were present from India, Burmah, America, Holland, France, Belgium, Russia, Canada and many parts of the United Kingdom.

Although the members from Germany were not mentioned here, they were nonetheless named in an appended list of branches and delegates. They included not only Dr Steiner, Frl. von Sivers and Frau von Holten from Berlin but also Adolf Kolbe from Hamburg and the old theosophist Ludwig Deinhard from Munich, who later received honourable mention in the last chapter of Steiner's autobiography.

> Mrs. Besant was elected to the chair, and Mr. Bertram Keightley and Mr. A.M. Glass were elected secretaries of the Convention.
>
> Mrs. Besant introduced the delegates of other Sections, who briefly addressed the meeting...
>
> Dr. Steiner spoke for the proposed Section in Germany, the application for which had been forwarded to the President-Founder, and Frl. von Sivers translated into English. He said that he had been sent over by the Berlin Lodge to learn something of the Theosophical Movement at its fountain-head. In Germany they were about to found a new Section, and he would endeavour to give an idea of the state of things there. They had but few people at present who had the least idea of theosophical teachings, but there were some diligent workers in several large cities, and there was much latent

power in Germany and a strong desire to seek for further spiritual understanding. Rationalistic philosophy possessed a great influence among the classes it was most desirable to reach, and this philosophy might be made the greatest enemy if not encountered properly, or, on the other hand, it could be of the greatest assistance if the foundation of Theosophy in Germany were laid on the writings of the great German philosophers. Such men as Leibnitz, Schelling, Fichte and Hegel were real theosophists and they should attach themselves to the teaching these men had left.

After other speakers had also had their say, the 'Report of Proceedings' added:

The following telegrams were received too late to be read at the meeting...

'Herzliche Glückenwünsche sendet die Deutsche Theosophische Gesellschaft und Loge Charlottenburg—Graf Brockdorff.'

Mr. Keightley then read his report...

The report was very extensive. Only one passage need here be quoted:

...Special notice must also be taken of the foreign literature published within the bounds of our Section. In Germany a valuable book on mysticism by Dr. Rudolf Steiner has been published...

When the report was finished, there was some further discussion, at the end of which a resolution was proposed:

'That this Convention recommends that a Federation of European Sections be formed and the General Secretary of this Section be instructed to submit to other Sections a plan to carry out this idea.'

Mr. Keightley suggested that as there were two foreign General Secretaries, the future General Secretary of the German Section, and also a leading representative of the Italian Section present, they should meet him after the Convention and discuss a scheme for carrying the resolution into effect.

The resolution was carried unanimously.

On Saturday afternoon there was another reception at 28, Albemarle Street, from 3.30 to 5.30, at which tea was served. The rooms of the Society were none too large for the number of members who attended.

Another account published in *The Theosophical Review* gives an evocative impression of the general atmosphere:

What a Babel of sounds greeted the ear at the receptions, dinners and teas—we were truly international! And pleasant was it to see the all-pervading brotherliness, the complete ignoring of all national differences. And one thought how happy H.P.B. would have been to have seen the strong trees which had grown out of the tiny root of the European Section that she planted. Great verily was the difference between the little band that surrounded her at the making of the Section twelve years ago, and the hundreds of theosophists who thronged the halls in 1902.

Among those milling hundreds were two other persons who later became prominent anthroposophists, namely, D.N. Dunlop, a founding member in October 1901 of the Battersea Lodge, and the visting Dutch theosophist Elisabeth Vreede. Both gave accounts of the occasion in a single sentence.

Vreede, on whom Steiner was to make a powerful impression at the next Convention in London in 1903, wrote in a footnote to her autobiographical account:

He had already appeared at the General Meeting in 1902, but having at the time no post in the Theosophical Society, held himself completely in the background, and I did not then consciously see him.

By contrast, the notes[4] made by Walter Johannes Stein from Dunlop's life-story told in 1934 at the Anthroposophical Summer School at Westonbirt indicate that the latter retained some consciousness of the occasion, for they include the entry:

1902 sees Steiner in London.

The Most Varied Impressions

The Convention's 'Report of Proceedings' continued:

On Saturday evening at 8.30 addresses were delivered in the Small Queen's Hall, by Mr. Leadbeater on 'Steps to First-Hand Knowledge', and Mr. Mead on 'Theosophy and the Higher Criticism'. Both speakers were heartily applauded for their most instructive discourses.

In his autobiography Steiner referred to the first lecturer as follows:

Mr. Leadbeater I did not meet. I only heard him speaking from the platform. He made no particular impression upon me.

This was the only occasion when the paths of Rudolf Steiner and Charles Leadbeater ever actually crossed.[5]

⋆

The 'Report of Proceedings' then added details of other lecturers:

On Sunday evening at 7 o'clock Mr. Keightley and Mrs. Besant were the speakers, the former on 'The Spirit of Theosophy', the latter on 'The Uses of the Theosophical Society', and they had a highly appreciative and attentive audience.

Further business on the Monday was described in *The Theosophical Review*:

The General Secretaries present and Mrs. Annie Besant met on July 7th in the offices of the General Secretary of the British Section, and drew up a scheme to be submitted to the Sectional Executives. It is proposed that an Annual Congress of the European Sections shall be held in connection with the Annual Convention of the Section that invites the Congress; that the General Secretaries shall form the Federation Council; that the General Secretary of the inviting Section shall be the Secretary of the Federation Council for the year, and shall be responsible for the organization of the Congress; that each Section shall arrange in its own way for the selection of papers to be read from it at the Congress . . .

It must have been in the course of this later meeting that Steiner made the statement reported in his autobiography:[6]

The first time I spoke at a Congress of the Theosophical Society in London in 1902, I said: 'The unity formed by individual Sections must come about through each Section bringing its own content to the centre.' I sharply stressed that this was above all the aim I had in mind as regards the German Section. I made it clear that this Section would never work as a bearer of fixed dogmas but as a place of independent spiritual research, and would want to communicate at General Meetings about the cultivation of real spiritual life.

The concluding event was related in the 'Report of Proceedings':

On Monday evening at 8.30 Mr. Mead closed the series of meetings with a lecture at Albemarle Street on 'Theosophic Christianity', which was listened to with great interest by a crowded audience.

★

Steiner ended the account of this Convention in his autobiography:

I was deeply moved by all the interesting things I heard; but they had no influence on the content of my views.

I tried to use the intervals I had left from attending the Conference meetings to make careful visits of the scientific and artistic collections in London. I may say that from these scientific and historical collections many ideas arose within me concerning the evolution of Nature and mankind.

His explorations of London were also mentioned in a final letter to his wife:

London,
10th July 1902

My dear good Anna,

I'm now leaving here with Frau von Holten tomorrow Thursday at 10 o'clock, having tried in these days to walk around as much as humanly possible to have as much of London as I could. So tomorrow off to Brussels, probably for just one day, so on *Sunday* I'll be in Paris . . .

Tomorrow or the day after I'll write to you about *whether*, when and where we might be able to meet on the way. I'd very much like to. Heartfelt greetings and a kiss for today.

Yours,

Rudolf

★

In his autobiography Steiner later summed up what the whole occasion had meant to him:

> This visit to London was for me a significant event. I left with the most varied impressions deeply stirring in my soul.

Best Wishes for its Future Success

A few days after Rudolf Steiner's departure from England, the July issue of *The Theosophical Review* came out. It contained the promised continuation of Keightley's article on Nicholas of Cusa, which came to an end as follows:

> . . . For the moment it only remains to add a few words in relation to Dr. Steiner's view of the mystic path as it emerges from his treatment of Cardinal Nicholas. In what precedes I have endeavoured to follow briefly, but as closely as possible, Dr. Steiner's own exposition; in what follows I shall venture to make an attempt to elucidate what appears to me to be the essence of his thought so far as we have gone.
>
> For Dr. Steiner, the keynote to the universe seems to consist in the clear separation of the worlds of consciousness and 'matter', or whatever name we give to the sequence of processes in time and space which take place equally within and outside our own organisms.
>
> On what to many, perhaps to most, is the all-important question of the relation or connection between these two worlds, Dr. Steiner so far does not seem to me to have expressed any clear or definite view in this series of lectures. What he repeatedly insists upon is that the two are radically distinct, and that—so far as I understand him—realization of this distinctness, coupled with equally clear and distinct recognition of the reality in itself of

the world of consciousness, forms the essential element in that inner awakening which raises man onto a higher plane of knowledge, in which his 'separateness', his existence as a 'thing amongst other things', disappears, and he knows that the one spirit, the one whole of consciousness, is himself. This would seem to come to much the same thing as that 'knowledge of Brahman' of which the Vedanta teaches, whereby man knows and realizes the 'one without a second', and wherein all separateness, plurality, 'otherness'—and with them all pain and fear—totally disappear.

How far this brief statement does justice to Dr. Steiner, I am not prepared to say. When we reach the close of these lectures, it may be that a fuller understanding of his thought will be possible, or if not, then that in some future work he will make the problem clearer. Meanwhile I must apologize for making such an imperfect attempt to focus what appears to me to be the view he holds, at this premature stage. But it seemed needful to do so in this connection in the hope of throwing some light upon his closing essays.

In the August issue a final article followed on 'Agrippa and Paracelsus', which brought to an end Keightley's lengthy exposition of *Die Mystik*.

★

Meanwhile, progress with the foundation of the German Section was slow. This can be seen from a letter written by Rudolf Steiner to Marie von Sivers, who had gone back from London to her home town of St Petersburg:

Friedenau-Berlin,
20th August
1902

Dearly gracious Fräulein,

Many thanks for your letter, which gave me great pleasure. *The Secret Doctrine* arrived safely and is lying on my desk, where it's of great use to me, especially at the moment, as I keep referring to it in my relevant studies . . .

The foundation of our German Section appears to face greater difficulties than I had in England imagined. On top of bad experiences I've had since my return journey, I've just received a letter from Miss Hooper where she writes that Olcott can't understand about the two 'applications' he's received. So we'll probably have to wait another 8 weeks for the Charter, as it'll take that long till Olcott has my letter and the Charter is then here . . .

When you arrive, my work *Das Christentum als mystische Tatsache* will be ready . . . Hopefully we may expect you in Berlin on the 15th of September.

My wife sends her best greetings, and likewise your

Dr. Rudolf Steiner

★

While Marie von Sivers was still in Russia, a first meeting took place between Steiner and the young Dutch lady Ita Wegman. The background to this meeting was described by Wegman in an address given in London in 1933:

> It was on a beautiful summer's day that as a young medical student I visited Rudolf Steiner at Friedrichshagen near Berlin. I had no other purpose than to enquire about theosophical work and gain a direct impression of Rudolf Steiner, who was said in Dutch theosophical circles to have paths of his own in esoteric matters, differing from those of Annie Besant.

What was being said in Dutch theosophical circles must have originated from Steiner's statement in London in July that the German Section would work as a place of independent spiritual research. In his documentation *Wer War Ita Wegman* (1990), J.E. Zeylmans van Emmichoven therefore concluded:

> Wegman, who had already been for several years a member of this Theosophical Society, heard in Holland during the summer of 1902 about the appearance of this Herr Steiner in London. He had made a speech there at the beginning of July from which it might be gathered that in esotericism he was going his own ways. This awakened Wegman's curiosity, and since he was taking over as leader of the German Section she paid him a visit.

Zeylmans further explained that the link was supported by a photograph of Besant in Amsterdam. In a personal letter to the present writer in 1997, he gave a summary of the whole matter:

> Besant visited the Netherlands on the 28th and 29th of August. A photo of Besant is to be found in Wegman's archive; Wegman wrote these dates on the back. On the next day she travels to Berlin and the first thing she does is to visit Steiner. Wegman was living in Haarlem with theosophists who would certainly have heard about the London Convention and have reported it. The question to be solved was: why does Wegman visit Steiner in Berlin? My solution was made on the basis of these assumptions.

★

In Britain, the September issue of *The Vâhan* published a notice entitled 'Foundation of the German Section':

> An application for a sectional charter signed by the officers of the German branches having been forwarded to the President-Founder and duly accepted, the German Section now exists as an independent organization.

The following is a copy of the executive notice issued by Colonel Olcott:

Theosophical Society,

President's Office,
Ootacamund,
India.
July 22nd, 1902.

The undersigned hereby gives notice that on the application of the officers of the branches of our Society at Berlin, Charlottenburg, Düsseldorf, Hamburg, Stuttgart, Hannover, Munich, Cassel and Leipzig, in Germany, and our German branch at Lugano, Switzerland, he has authorized them to form themselves into a body to be known as the German Section of the Theosophical Society, which shall include branches in German territory, and German branches in Switzerland, subject to the provisions of the Society's constitution and rules. In testimony whereof he has issued this day to the Presidents of the above-named branches a charter, and caused the Society's seal to be affixed at Adyar. The undersigned appoints Dr. Rudolf Steiner, F.T.S., 95, Kaiserallee, Friedenau, Berlin, General Secretary pro. tem., pending the formal organization of the Section and adoption of byelaws for its government.

H.S. Olcott,
P.T.S.

The new Section starts its career with the best wishes for its future success from the Section of which it lately formed part.

I. Hooper,
Acting General Secretary.

A Spiritual Centre

A brief glance will now be taken at another person who plays a small but interesting part in some of the next few chapters. This is Mathilde Scholl, whose life as a whole is anyway marked by Western connections.

Mathilde Scholl was born in 1868 in Mettmann, near Düsseldorf, as a tenth child. Her parents, relatively old at her birth, were both dead before her ninth birthday.

After being looked after for a few years by one of her sisters, Mathilde was put at the age of 13 into the care of a maternal aunt and uncle. The latter was an Englishman, Alfred Baskerville, director of a small private school in Godesberg for wealthy boarders from England and America. Mathilde was therefore educated in Godesberg where, in about 1886, she met and formed a deep friendship with the English-born Maude Capon, who was also resident in that town.

Having completed her education, Mathilde started a three-year teacher-training course in Wolfenbüttel, and then worked for several years in a private capacity as a language teacher in Godesberg.

When she reached the age of 30, she and her friend Maude decided on a complete change of scene. So in 1898 they travelled together to Italy, and stayed there for a couple of years. Here Mathilde came across books by H.P. Blavatsky, and after reading them immediately joined the Theosophical Society. In 1900, while Maude returned to Germany and settled in Cologne, Mathilde travelled westwards—first to France and then over to England.

She stayed for a time in London, then the European centre of the Theosophical Movement. Only in the following year did she finally return to Germany, settling at first in Bonn. By the beginning of 1902 she had read Rudolf Steiner's *Die Mystik*, and later in that year decided to attend the foundation meeting of the German Section.

She duly arrived in Berlin on 19 October, the day the meeting was starting. In her memoirs, written down in about 1930, she recorded:

> Although this was the first time I saw Dr. Steiner and Marie von Sivers, they were not strangers to me.

★

The foundation meeting of the German Section took place from 19 to 21 October. Among those elected to its *Vorstand* were Rudolf Steiner as General Secretary, Marie von Sivers (Schlactensee), Wilhelm Hübbe-Schleiden (Hanover), Ludwig Deinhard (Munich), Günther Wagner (Lugano), Adolf Kolbe (Hamburg), Ludwig Noll (Cassel) and Richard Bresch (Leipzig). Annie Besant was also present and handed over the charter from Colonel Olcott.

In the evening of the 20th Steiner tried to give a lecture on 'Practical Karma Studies', but found most of his theosophical audience quite unprepared for this particular subject.

Scholl's biographer Ekkehard Meffert adds the following observation:

> During the foundation meeting of the Theosophical Society's German Section, Annie Besant gave on the evening of the 21st of October her first public lecture in Germany ('Theosophy, its meaning and objects'), which Rudolf Steiner introduced by drawing an absolutely astounding parallel with Giordano Bruno. The report in *Der Vâhan* states:
>
> 'Many people, he said, might have been surprised when he openly bore witness to Theosophy in the Giordano Bruno Union about a fortnight ago.

But just as Giordano Bruno, basing himself on Kepler's discoveries, called for acceptance of a new conception of the world, so too Theosophy was bringing a new conception of the world today. Exactly like then, we were now standing at a turning point in the history of the world. The German Section had today been founded and the most outstanding representative of the Theosophical Movement had therefore come here to speak the first words in public.'

Since Rudolf Steiner had spoken in an internal lecture the previous evening about practical karma exercises, should not these words be read as the expression of quite real karmic knowledge?

★

A couple of days later, on 23 October, Steiner was admitted by Besant to the Theosophical Society's Esoteric School. He explained in his autobiography:

This 'Esoteric School' went back to H.P. Blavatsky. She had created a place for a small inner circle of the Society where matters were communicated which she did not wish to tell the Society at large.

Blavatsky's inner circle lived on in the 'Esoteric School'.—I had placed my anthroposophical activity into the Theosophical Society. I therefore had to be informed about everything taking place in it. I had myself admitted into the 'Esoteric School' for the sake of such information, and because I considered that a more restricted circle was needed by those advanced in anthroposophical spiritual knowledge. My more restricted circle, however, was to have a different purpose from this School. It was to present a higher department, a higher class for those who had absorbed sufficient elementary knowledge of Anthroposophy.

★

From the very start, it was hard to make progress in the German Section. In his autobiography Steiner set out the impressions he was left with at this time:

I have spoken about the fact that in the Theosophical Society people could be found who wanted to listen to communications from the spirit-world. This does not mean that enrolled members of the Theosophical Society came primarily into consideration as such people. But many of these soon showed themselves to be full of understanding for my kind of spiritual knowledge.

A large proportion of members, however, were fanatical followers of individual leaders in the Theosophical Society. They swore by the dogmas given out by these leaders, who were working in a highly sectarian manner.

The work of the Theosophical Society repelled me by the triviality and dilettantism concealed within it. Only among English theosophists did I find an inner substance which still derived from Blavatsky and was at the time properly cultivated by Annie Besant and others. I could never myself have worked in the style these theosophists were working in. But I regarded what was living among them as a spiritual centre to which a person who in the deepest sense took seriously the spreading of spiritual knowledge might worthily be linked.

A Deep Sense of Portals Opening

On 7 July 1935, an unsigned obituary of D.N. Dunlop was published in *The Electrical Review*.

It stated:

The electrical industry has been deprived of the services of one of its most distinguished representatives by the death of Mr. Daniel Nicol Dunlop . . .

Mr. Dunlop was born . . . He was attracted to the United States . . . and at the works of the American Westinghouse Electric Co., and at its New York offices, he had experience of the production of electrical machinery and of methods of accounting. He returned to this country (in 1899) as an employee of the Pittsburgh firm, and the Westinghouse works at Trafford Park were erected. He acted as Assistant Publicity Manager here both for the English and the other European branches of the company.

At about this time we first made his acquaintance in a small office in Norfolk Street, Strand, London, where he and Mr. Warren, who had had wide electrical publicity experience in the States, were beginning activities. We little dreamt then how large a place Mr. Dunlop was destined to fill in connection with the organization of the great British electrical and allied industries . . .

In the course of 1902, the Westinghouse Company promoted Dunlop to Publicity Manager. But it was not only electricity that he was publicizing. For towards the end of the same year, the November issue of *The Theosophical Review* included an article by him, the first one he contributed to that journal. It was entitled 'A Deep Sense of Portals Opening':

These words of Mr. Laurence Binyon's are at once the most accurate and the most poetical description of a vital characteristic of the age. Everywhere, in all departments of life, the doors are being flung wide; currents of fresh air rush in upon us, bewildering in their exhilaration; our eyes are dazzled by the light of new landscapes; we divine in imagination vistas reaching far beyond our power of vision. In medieval days these doors were locked, and as a rule no troublesome access of curiosity assailed the dweller within the walls: for him, certitudes lay on the other side—a concrete heaven and a concrete hell, which would, in God's own time, be reached through the gateway of death. But we have broken through some of the barriers, and some have crumbled away, and the other side is strange and vast and vague, unlike all the stories we had heard of it. Those who first looked out shivered, afraid at the infinity they might never hope to penetrate, and longed for the old screen of beliefs to protect their naked souls against the blasts from the unknown.

In whatever direction we turn our eyes today, we find ourselves surrounded by the inexplicable, the mysterious. There was never an age in the history of man when he was more poignantly aware of the moving of strange presences in his midst. The door that opens on the material world reveals a multitudinous throbbing of life, from the minutest particle of dust to the remotest planet that strikes the soul with awe. New discoveries follow one upon another, but their explanation is lacking, and in the interim they flash with untold possibilities. Spiritual terms, we learn, are derived in the first instance from concrete objects; but the results of recent scientific experiments are so unprecedented that we are forced constantly to reverse this order, and describe them in spiritual terms.

The dazzling imagination of the Orient has never exceeded, in its catalogue of magic gems, the wonder of the newly discovered metals—radium, uranium, and others of their kindred—'that radiate light all around them, continually, indefinitely, and yet are not consumed.' The analysis of these emanations shows them to be composed of particles that are not ordinary atoms or molecules at all, but something very much smaller; and we are confronted with a new kind of matter, containing particles having a velocity about one-third that of light. And so, through a newly opened door, new mysteries of matter come pressing in upon us. The man of science recognizes that to give a name to these indwelling oceans does not imply that they have been explained or fathomed. The power we call electricity is as marvellous and inexplicable as the goddess named of old Diana of the Ephesians, and Professor Karl Pearson has written: 'Force as a cause of motion is exactly on the same footing as a tree-god as a cause of growth.'

This deep sense of portals opening is not confined to the poet and the scientist. It is a common experience of the ordinary man in his more gracious moods when he walks with Nature. The silence of a starry night has speech for him, and underneath the sound of ocean he perceives a silence. But weak souls are afraid alike of the silence and of the still small voice: and they seek relief from tension in the clamour of the market-place, today more raucous and persistent than ever before. They wrap themselves in fold upon fold of luxury and raise thick superstructures above them: for the materialism of which we hear so much is in truth nothing but a barricade erected to keep out the terrible unknown which has assumed proportions that at times threaten the reason, the emotions—the very soul.

And yet this mystery that we recognize round us is kinder to her votaries than she was in primeval and classic times. It is instructive to compare the modern attitude of man towards Nature with the ancient one. Mighty presences, when the moon was full, shook the Druid wood with awe; the Greek youth followed, through dappled tangle, the shine of Dryad limbs, snow-white, divine. Today we neither worship the god nor pursue the goddess. For we ourselves are the gods and goddesses. No one who has given careful attention to the trend of modern experience but is aware that we pass constantly, in the very streets, mortal creatures that have for brief moments tasted immortality. The annihilation of time is already accomplished; the armies that shall annihilate space are on the wing.

Fiona Macleod hears the grasses whisper, and the green lips of the wind chant the blind, oblivious rune of time: 'Time never was, time is not.' Emerson bids us live like the roses, above time. The annihilators of time have recently been reinforced by valiant champions who have endeavoured, from different points, to undermine that convention which we are used to call the past. Mr. W.B. Yeats seeks his inspiration out of olden times; but only because the Idea lived then a fuller life, and it is his will to reimbue it anew with vitality. But that the past is not past to him is exquisitely shown in these lines:

> When my arms wrap you round, I press
> My heart upon the loveliness
> That has long faded from the world.

Maeterlinck is still more emphatic on this point. Few utterances in modern times have been more pregnant with suggestion than his little essay on 'The Past.' 'So long as the life in our mind and character flows uninterruptedly on,' he says, 'so long will the past remain in suspense above us . . . and, like the clouds Hamlet showed to Polonius, adopt the shape of the hope or fear, the peace or disquiet, that we perfect within us.'

Not only, therefore, can we hold a living past in our arms; not only can we shape and change events that have happened, and so count ourselves, to some extent, kings over time; but the penalty of age, the ancient tragedy of so many lives, is removed every day farther away from us. Most of us number among our acquaintance some of those who can never grow old, because they live close to that which is eternally young, and even the most blasé have the secret of growing young with every spring.

This new attitude of man towards Nature has prompted a new method in literature for its expression—the method of identification. Where sympathy is intense, the sympathizer becomes one with the object of sympathy; and we are gods today because we have learned how to absorb ourselves completely in the mystery of the world, the immortality of the seasons. Formerly the manifestations of Nature were regarded as satellites circling round a human centre of things; now our whole endeavour is to break bonds, and leaving our personalities aside, to enter into a larger, wider existence. So T.E. Brown writes:

> Do ye not understand
> How the great Mother mixes all our bloods?
> O breeze! O swaying buds!
> O lambs! O primroses! O floods!

The waterfall no longer haunts us like a passion; but we are ourselves become the passion of the waterfall. Marvellous inspiration awaits poetry along these lines, but its flight is yet too tentative to have given life to more than passing flickers of expression. These flash out in all manner of unexpected directions. 'I am a bit of the shore,' says Edward Carpenter in his strangely unequal book *Towards Democracy*, 'I am a little arm of the sea ... Suddenly I am the ocean itself; the great soft wind creeps over my face.' Matthew Arnold reserves the identification till after death. 'How sweet,' he says,

> My sister, to maintain with thee
> The hush among the shining stars,
> The calm upon the moonlit sea.

This ecstasy of absorption in Nature is a new feature in literature, as in life. The Celtic poets approach it with a consciousness and a comprehension lacking in the work of other races. To them it is a mystic union—not the mere transference of self from one material plane to another, but the bringing into harmony of the material and the spiritual plane. Fiona Macleod expressly states that all that is best in modern poetry is due 'to the spiritual identification of the two worlds—of the outward mortal, and the spiritual immortal.' She listens, for the wisdom that is beyond all books, to the words of those who live very close to the core of the mystery; some of her wonderful lyric runes are translations from the songs of the fisherfolk of the Hebrides, and her tales are strange and lovely with Gaelic lore. Mr. W.B. Yeats tells us, in verse, in lecture, in essay, of the inner vision of the peasants in remote parts of Ireland; vision, which sees through the deception of the material object to the spirit it hides. 'Those that are blind have a way of seeing things,' said a native to Mr. Yeats, 'and have the power to know more, and to do more, and to guess more, than those that have their sight.' Not long ago an emphatic enunciation, by several voices, of the supreme importance of spiritual emotion in poetry was prompted by Mr. Stephen Phillips's article in *The Dome*, wherein he makes complaint of the materialism of present-day poetry, attributing it to the lack of 'some great compelling thought—some rapturous and passionate purpose'.

Poets thus strive to penetrate the mystery that is round us by listening to catch a murmur from the lips of those who live near its source; or by projecting themselves into the mystery—identifying themselves with it, that in intimate communion they may surprise its secrets.

There are some, however, who hold that we cannot master the hidden things of Nature by enlarging the circumference of our personality to embrace it; but that the function of both science and poetry is, by figure, and cipher, and formula, and metaphor, so to diminish Nature that it becomes easily manipulated. Mr. Collin, in his interesting paper in *Ethical Democracy*, is the best exponent of this view. 'Foreshortening,' he says, 'is our only weapon of defence against the enormity of time and space.'

Against this it should be urged that figure, cipher, and formula, though supremely useful up to a certain point, leave out the living factor that permeates every atom of the universe; and that metaphor, though often flashing in its insight, must be, to a large extent, inexact. We find in Mr. Collin's essay a reversion to the old error that strove to fit all the phenomena of the universe into human dimensions.

Many aver that the function of the man of science is to specialize, that of the poet to generalize. The one gives the patient research, the careful examination of detail, the weighing and testing of minute evidence; the other approaches the facts illuminated by a sense of their awe and mystery, and with his gift of insight groups and interprets them. 'Original research,' says one writer, 'is practically incompatible with great and comprehensive thought.' It is of course a commonplace to point out that all important discoveries have been the result of the laborious following-up of daring dreams; but it is only fair to add that in most cases the man of science has contained within himself the poet; and that the poet's most marvellous deductions have so far been drawn, not from the facts of original research, but from the facts of the universe—the times and the seasons unrolled before his eyes.

The discoveries of science are nonetheless justly obtaining more and more place in poetry. Among modern poets, Mathilde Blind has dealt extensively with evolution, and both Francis Thompson and William Watson find hurtling words to describe the wonders of the sidereal universe. But there is no revelation here, no new light; they only say beautifully and with ornamentation what has already been baldly stated.

Maeterlinck is perhaps the foremost example of the poet whose generalizations may materially assist the progress of knowledge. His hand has opened to us the portals of the hive, and he has revealed with delicate intuition and all the cautious hesitation of wisdom, mysteries as strange, as incomprehensible, as beautiful, as any that wait by the gates of our life. No formal analysis, we feel, could come so near the absolute truth as this fervid observation, conducted with a transcendental sympathy, and yet in its development kept within the rigid bounds of fact. Science will surely follow along the path of this insight; and yet perchance the deepest riddles of human existence may yield up their secrets in the honied byways of the hive.

Ruskin is another instance of one who approaches fact from its poetic side. His statements are steeped in emotion, and glow with that passion for righteousness that possessed his soul. He is more tumultuous, more magnificent than the Belgian, less exquisite, less quiet, and diametrically opposed to him on certain points of philosophy. For Ruskin states, with almost unnecessary emphasis, that it is our bounden duty to make up our minds concerning the mystifications that surround us. He says, for instance, with reference to immortality: 'Man must either hereafter live or hereafter die; fate may be bravely met, and conduct wisely ordered, on other expectation; but never in hesitation between ungrasped hope and unconfronted fear.' Surely this is an untenable position. There is no data to go on that can absolutely convince the reason; and many lack the sense of certitude that brings conviction to the soul. Maeterlinck's attitude is far more logical. He says in effect: these subjects are mysteries; infinite patience may disclose little by little glimmers of meaning to future ages; but it is not for us to say either yea or nay. 'In all questions of this kind,' says Maeterlinck, 'it is far less important to prove things than it is to awaken and inspire in men a certain grave and courageous respect for all which remains still inexplicable in their common human action, in their subjection to what appear to be general laws, and in the ensuing results.'

We hear from various quarters lamentations for the barriers that are being broken down, for the prop of old faiths removed, for all anciently accepted certainties that are gone forever. But here indeed is no cause for sorrow, but instead for exultation. On all sides the portals opening let in great draughts from the unknown, that intoxicate us with the thought of the strange lands and seas they have traversed, that stimulate to exploration, that throb with remote possibilities. For to live with an ever-present sense of the mysteries about us is both humbling and elevating, giving us kinship with the minutest atom, and raising us to the stature of gods.

2
SECOND VISIT

The Right Moment

The December issue of the Madras *Theosophist* included a short note by Colonel Olcott about the 'German Section':

> Mrs. Besant, who was present at the inaugural meeting of the new Section, writes that Dr. Rudolph Steiner has been elected General Secretary. This is an excellent beginning and we anticipate that under his able direction the Section will be a perfect success.

At the Annual Convention in India at Christmas, Olcott was even more enthusiastic, making significant remarks in his presidential address:

> In Germany we have chartered a Section with Dr. Rudolf Steiner, a man of high scholarly and literary abilities and a profound thinker, as General Secretary. What it would mean to the world if the seed-corn planted at the centres of dense population and in the soil of the educated class of Germany should take root, is easy to forecast. I have strong hopes that this may prove the case, and my prayer is that I may live to see Germany leading the van in this, as she has in so many previous religious, scientific and social movements for the betterment of mankind.

★

Throughout 1903, Steiner continued to lecture in Berlin, but as General Secretary of the German Section he began to extend his field of work to other towns as well. In February he lectured in Düsseldorf, and in April travelled to Weimar, a place well known to him from long residence there several years previously.

During this time Marie von Sivers wrote him a letter:

> Schlactensee,
> 18th April 1903
>
> Today you're now being attacked by Deinhard. I'm sending you the latest issue of *Der Vâhan*, which has just arrived. There are a number of interesting things in it. Bresch is noticeably improving. He's moderate and firm, and the couple of allusions to Hübbe-Schleiden are as correct as they're appropriate.
>
> Deinhard is certainly alarmed by your progress and has turned our poor

Frau Carola Mayne crazy, since she's not replying to me. You should tell him to leave her in peace.

I gather from the same report that Olcott is in Europe. Left on the 5th of March, so he's already here. Perhaps for the last time, with his advanced age. We have to see him, don't we? Perhaps he'll come to us. It's all the same if Hübbe-Schleiden and Deinhard resist it. It would be a sanctioning of our newly founded Section by the honourable first President. And it would be a fresh current and incentive for the members. The best thing would be for him to stay long enough to come to the festival and be my guest in Berlin. But if he had to leave earlier, it should also be possible to announce a lecture-evening in the summer when you would both be speaking together, and he'd perhaps stay a day or two in Schlactensee. If he can't manage all that it would perhaps be quite nice for us to go to London, preferably now rather than for the Convention.

I'll try at once to find out more details. I'd like best to send some words of greeting straight away, and in your name too, and also express the hope of seeing him step onto rugged German soil. Shall I? Also, if possible, let me know fairly quickly something of your talk with Deinhard, so that I've knowledge of the facts as regards Carola.

I seemed today to understand for the first time the nature of meditation on a deeper level. It's more creative than re-flecting, re-praying and re-feeling. I also wanted to preserve it, but then morning work intervened and now letters, and I fear it's dispelled. Probably you'll say I ought to have preserved it in spite of interruptions. But the calm of soul one has absorbed—a basic requirement—is lost, because of what hasn't been done.

By the way, that was something I realized particularly clearly today while meditating. The main obstacle for me was disorder. Also it gave me both a heightened feeling of being in a rush and a guilty conscience, and so what hadn't been done in daily life, but omitted, was always intruding into my devotional and mental images. This is a deeper reason for my slow progress, and as long as this vice isn't pulled out by the roots things won't go well. One has to start with small things.

There you have my freshly acquired insight.

But thank you a thousand times, you dear, best person, for the sea of light you give me, and your spiritual help.

How are you? Marie

If we did have to go there, or even on my own, I'd like best the 8th of May, Madame Blavatsky's death-day. Last year I was deeply sorry I couldn't be there, and since even this year we can't yet have a serious celebration, I'd like to make up for it.

Consider all this when arranging the finer details of your lecture tour, particularly Munich. Don't you want to suggest at once to Deinhard a lecture in Hanover, by you of course?

★

On the very next day Steiner replied:

Weimar,
19th April 1903

Dearly trusted sister,

At present Deinhard hasn't yet appeared. So probably he'll only come today. Yesterday the lodge of the Weimar branch was constituted. Besides the two lectures we also met twice in a more restricted circle—with those who are going to join. I've long been feeling that our presence in London will soon be needed. Now that Olcott is in Europe it's probably unavoidable. But we must consider everything well and choose the right moment for the purpose. I believe I can tell you that this coming period won't be bringing us unimportant things. In *no matter* ought we now follow our *immediate* impulses. What you've just sent me—in *Der Vâhan*—is just a symptom. Various things are at work against us. At present Bresch has the right instinct. What he is himself saying is just now perhaps more significant than the writer is himself aware of. Incidentally, on Tuesday I'm most probably travelling via Leipzig to Berlin. Right now it seems to me I must speak to Bresch.—When I'm with you again we can discuss everything about Olcott's presence. Frau Lübke, who in three years of work with London theosophists has learnt to see things quite differently from the old members in Germany, agreed with me the day before yesterday when I indicated how important it now was to approach Olcott *in person*. The feeling I have here is that what we've started to do is right. It isn't a question of how much we achieve here or there at the first attempt, but whether we're doing the right thing—what the karma of the times demands. As soon as I arrive in Berlin, my three lectures have to be printed. There's probably no better time for *Luzifer* to appear than when it's actually due to.

You'll readily admit that Deinhard's talk with me can't be significant if we want to make progress. The important thing for me won't be what he says but what he doesn't say. Also in Hübbe-Schleiden's latest letter, the most important thing is what isn't in it at all. During the next few days I'll speak with you about several matters which will make a lot clearer to you. For today just one guideline: we remain loyally together; and both do everything in completest loyalty to Mrs *Besant's* intentions, *even in face of possible misunderstandings, which might soon arise.*

I'm pleased by what you say about your meditation. I know you'll come further. I also know that the best powers are guiding you. So carry on. It's so nice that you wrote to me yesterday as well: I received your letter this morning . . .

In trust and brotherliness

R.St.

⋆

The allusion to *Luzifer* is explained in Steiner's autobiography:

> As soon as the German Section of the Theosophical Society was founded it seemed to me that we needed to have our own periodical. So Marie von Sivers and I founded the monthly magazine *Luzifer.* At the time, of course, the name was in no way associated with the spiritual power I later denoted as Lucifer, counterpart of Ahriman. The content of anthroposophy had not yet developed to the extent that these powers could already have been spoken about.—The name was meant simply as 'Light-bearer'.
>
> At first it was my intention to work in accordance with the leadership of the Theosophical Society. But right from the start I had a feeling that in anthroposophy something had to arise which should develop out of its own seeds, without making itself somehow dependent for its content on what the Theosophical Society allowed to be taught.—I could only do this through such a periodical. Anthroposophy as it is today has actually grown from what I wrote in that periodical . . .

In the Innermost Connection

The first number of *Luzifer* appeared in May 1903, as seen in a letter written by Rudolf Steiner at the beginning of the month to Mathilde Scholl: (E.S. = Esoteric School. T.S. = Theosophical Society)

> Schlactensee,
> near Berlin.
> 1st May 1903.
>
> Dear Fräulein Scholl,
>
> I ought to have written long ago. On top of all else, my obligations in respect to *Luzifer* have had for a time a rather oppressive effect. At last it will now be coming out in a couple of days' time. Hopefully I shall be coming into fairly regular activity too. Anyway, in future I shall not wait so long to reply as I have unfortunately done till now.
>
> It would be very nice if the more recent members of the E.S. in Germany would in some way come closer together. Precisely in Germany we need this. The E.S. must become the soul of the Theosophical Society, especially in Germany, because for a long time we can probably only hope for deep and inwardly collaborative work on the part of individuals, and larger circles will just be joining outwardly. It is precisely individuals who will form a more loyal, reliable and powerful base. This is what we need, as so much here is in a muddle.
>
> Everything in Weimar went very well. We now have a lodge there too.

Lectures were exceptionally well attended.—For the most varied reasons I should like to come to Cologne to lecture there as well. Please could you perhaps smooth the ground a little. A lot—a great lot—depends on our creating new centres. So far almost all German theosophists have sought much too loose a connection to the English mother-movement. Only out of this latter must we now work, in the innermost connection to it. There has been in Germany too much tendency to dogmatism and merely intellectual grasp of doctrines, while for living spirituality no proper understanding can be found. Only if we awaken this and open people's eyes to the fact that the progress of a theosophical stream does not just involve learning dogmas (Hartmann), but having a spiritual connection to central individuals from whom the wisdom comes, and with whom it has its continuously welling source—only then can we come forward. We have to make it clear—not through words, but through imponderables—that it is a matter of T.S. bearers being continuously fructified by central individuals. Only those who work esoterically will fully understand these things, so they must keep together in a clearly conscious, secure and powerful manner, and be awakeners for the others.

It was deeply satisfying for me to spend a few hours with you in Düsseldorf. That is the satisfaction we have when seeing another on a path where signposts are always 'forwards'. There's a gateway through which a theosophist should only pass once, i.e., forwards, and not go through again backwards.

We have in Germany only four or five absolutely reliable people. This is why we have to be intensely working. If we are, we shall find ways and means of coming forward. Unless we find these ways and means in Germany, we shall certainly fail now to do something which cannot quickly be made good.

My next exoteric task is to spread the teaching as much as I can.

Hopefully you are settling down well in Cologne, dear Fräulein Scholl, and can work there both for our cause and to your own satisfaction. How are the people you are looking after?

Hoping to hear from you again soon,

Yours with heartfelt greetings,

Rudolf Steiner

Frl. von Sivers sends heartfelt greetings.

★

In his biography of Scholl, Ekkehart Meffert explained:

The outward reason for transferring domicile to Cologne was that a relationship of destiny had meanwhile formed between Mathilde's friend Maude Capon, with whom she had lived for 14 years in Godesberg and Italy, and Eugen Künstler from Mulheim on the Rhine (today Cologne-

Mulheim). In 1903 the connection between Maude Capon and Eugen Künstler led to their union in marriage. Eugen Künstler, his wife Maude and her close friend Mathilde Scholl moved into 9, III, Haus Belfortstrasse, not far from the banks of the Rhine.

With this house a place had been spatially found and a sheath prepared into which Theosophy and Anthroposophy could incarnate. The Künstlers' dwelling is as significant an earthly spot for Cologne and the Rhineland as 54a Kaiser-Friedrichstrasse and 17 Motzstrasse were for Berlin.

★

The second number of *Luzifer* appeared already at the end of June. Issues were posted to various friends, as shown by two further letters from Steiner.

The first was to Wolfgang Kirchbach, a member of the Giordano Bruno Union:

Seestr. 40,
Schlactensee,
near Berlin.
30th June 1903.

My dear Herr Kirchbach,

Presuming you have returned again from your journey, I am sending you the two first numbers of *Luzifer*. Perhaps you will soon give me the pleasure of carrying out your promised collaboration. *Luzifer* however pays only 6 marks a side. Perhaps later on it will improve.

Heartfelt greetings!

Yours,

Rudolf Steiner

★

The second was written in some haste to the poetess Maria Stona:

Schlactensee,
near Berlin.
30th June 1903.

My esteemed and gracious lady,

The 1st number of my enclosed *Luzifer* will explain my bad manners in being silent. I beg your forgiveness a thousand times. I am absolutely delighted with the poetry collection, about which I shall write in detail on my return from London. I cannot today, I have to depart in two hours. Everything is pressing.

Your ever devoted

Dr. Rudolf Steiner

On Behalf of the German Section

This time accompanied by Marie von Sivers, Rudolf Steiner made his way again to the British capital. On the day after his arrival, he sent a card to his wife:

London,
2nd July 1903.

My dear good Anna,

I wanted to write you a letter today; but it's getting too late. I've just had a talk with Olcott. In the evening is a lecture. By the way, the journey was exhausting, but the sea-crossing wonderfully beautiful. Sea as smooth as glass for seven hours. Esher lies as far from London as Schlachtensee from Berlin. We arrived at 10 o'clock yesterday evening; at 9 o'clock this morning I was already going back to London. I only come out again in the evening after the meeting. Frl. v. Sivers arrived shattered and couldn't come into London today at all. If Geni still comes to London while I'm there she should certainly arrange for a rendezvous with me. Most heartfelt greetings from

your

Rudolf

*

In his autobiography, Steiner recalled his first impressions of Henry Steel Olcott:

> In 1903 Marie von Sivers and I again took part in the Theosophical Congress in London. Colonel Olcott, President of the Theosophical Society, had also turned up from India. A lovable personality. With his energy and extraordinary gift for organization, one saw how he could be a partner to Blavatsky in founding, setting up and guiding the Theosophical Society. Outwardly this Society had in a short time become a large body with an excellent organization.

Other details of his first meeting with Olcott were given in a lecture on 14 December 1911:

> . . . Take the situation of the Theosophical Society as it was when I became General Secretary of the German Section. At that meeting in London I also met Mrs. Besant, and at the second Convention a year later I met Colonel Olcott. The reason I mention this is because one needs to emphasize that nothing resulting from any event then happening did anything but confirm the idea of representing Theosophy in our way. Olcott said at the time that he was really astonished to see me. This fact at once made me reflect. He

said that after knowing about me for a year and a half he had expected me to be at least as old a man as himself...

...I always used to say to people: '...I do whatever seems to me right.' In my first conversation with Colonel Olcott—even at the risk that he might have preferred to hear this from a person of the same age—I told him I would be proceeding in that way, so as not to leave him in the dark. I have always spoken of Olcott with great warmth, as he was really the ideal founder for such a Society. He understood at once any stir of freedom and would never rebel against such a thing; it would never have occurred to him...

★

The lecture on Thursday, 2 July to which Steiner referred in the card to his wife was given in the Blavatsky Lodge by Bertram Keightley, and was entitled 'What is a Monad?'

Further events over the following days were described in the Convention's 'Report of Proceedings':

Associated with the Convention were the meetings of the Federation of European Sections, including, in addition to the British, the Dutch, French, Italian and German. A preliminary business meeting was held at 28, Albemarle Street, on Friday, July 3rd, at 3.30 p.m., to settle the method of meeting for the future. It was decided to hold the meetings annually in different countries, the meeting for 1904 to take place in Amsterdam.

On Friday evening, July 3rd, at 8.30 p.m., there was a reception of members at 28, Albemarle Street, the rooms being crowded to excess.

The Convention assembled on Saturday, July 4th, at 2.30 p.m., in the Banqueting Hall, St. James's Restaurant, Regent Street, W. Members were present from Holland (14), France (6), Belgium (9), Germany (2), and from many parts of the United Kingdom.

An accompanying list of branches and delegates shows that the Battersea Lodge was represented on this occasion by D.N. Dunlop.

The 'Report of Proceedings' continued:

Colonel Olcott, as President-Founder of the Society, took the chair, and Messrs. Bertram Keightley and A.M. Glass were elected secretaries of the Convention.

Then came addresses from various foreign visitors, including this one:

Dr. Steiner spoke on behalf of the German Section, Fräulein von Sivers translating his remarks, and said that it was the first time he had been present as General Secretary of the German Section to greet this Convention. They had the great pleasure for the first time of receiving Mrs. Besant, who gave them much help in their work. It would be their task to forward the work of the great international Society in the manner appropriate to the German nation, and they had tried during the past year to work in this manner. Those able to see only outer success might not observe any rapid advance, but those able to judge more fully might have greater hope. On one side there was the mystic nature of the German character, and on the other the critical, and they would like to use both qualities. He hoped to return each year to these meetings, as he knew they had much to learn from them.

The General Secretary was instructed to send greetings to those Sections represented.

Mr Keightley then read his report...

From the Very Depths of the Spirit

The Convention was continued:

> In the evening at 8.30 speakers representing the different Sections addressed a meeting in the Banqueting Hall, St. James's Restaurant, Colonel Olcott taking the chair. Mr. Mead spoke for the British Section, Capt. Terwiel for the Dutch, Mrs. Cooper-Oakley for the Italian, and Dr. Steiner for the German.

At this evening meeting Rudolf Steiner was first seen by Elisabeth Vreede, who recorded her impressions in an account found among papers left behind at her death 40 years later. It was finally published in the collection *Elisabeth Vreede: ein Lebensbild* (1976).

> For some years I used to go during the summer to General Meetings in London of the 'European Section of the Theosophical Society', as it was then still called. It was there in July 1903 that I first saw Rudolf Steiner. Through his activity as a lecturer he had a short time previously been voted General Secretary of the Theosophical Society's newly founded German Section. It may be said—without of course in any way wishing to extend the comparison—that basically Rudolf Steiner had just as little liking for his relation to the Theosophical Society as I did for my entry into it. But as an occultist and a person with knowledge of karma he accepted the fact that only in that Society had any understanding and readiness until then been shown to take up both his spiritual knowledge and his will. Elsewhere, he had in fact met either rejection or silent denial of his own spiritual striving. On this point one only needs to read his *Course of My Life*. Later on he once described his previous experiences with the most varied circles of people in the words: 'Here and there I threw spirit in—and was myself thrown out!'—By the time he said this, however, he no longer excepted the Theosophical Society.

I shall never forget the impression made on me by this first meeting. A gathering was just about to begin when a man entered the room: dark, slim, upright, lean, wearing a long, almost priestly black jacket—a face filled with inner fire, the closest attentiveness and a controlled will—this is how the picture rises from my memory. I was so impressed that I nudged my neighbour: 'Look, who's coming in there?!' In the strength of this impression everything which then led to my own further destiny already lay hidden in seminal form.

My ignorance of the identity of this impressive person was soon to be made good. During the meeting Colonel Olcott, the Theosophical Society's President and Founder, introduced him to the Society as General Secretary of the recently founded German Section. Rudolf Steiner climbed onto the platform and gave a welcoming address in German. Even his words imprinted themselves deeply into my memory. Not because at the time I particularly approved of them! On the contrary, I disliked the whole style of the speech. In those early years Dr. Steiner would speak with exceptional force and a temperamental power which even far exceeded the fiery strength we were later to experience in him. As if in every sentence he wanted to tell the world about the whole power and significance of his mission—from the black hair flying around his narrow head to the exceptionally lively play of gestures in arms and hands, and with the immensely powerful and emphatic utterance of his words, he seemed to make himself the bodily incarnation of what he had to say. This tremendous speaking power, which he as-it-were allowed to seize hold of his basically delicate bodily structure, Rudolf Steiner in later years more and more subdued into a fire of conviction blazing outwards from inside. The hallmark of his lecturing was always this power of conviction, which neither suggested anything, nor inwardly attacked any listener, and yet called forth in the soul a perhaps unconscious living feeling that he was speaking from the very depths of the spirit.

Nor did the content of what he was saying arouse my youthful approval. Rudolf Steiner himself later recounted: 'During these first years of working in the Theosophical Society I was really always saying the same thing, but some people didn't actually understand it, and others were peeved by it!' He was saying that there could not be any uniform or abstract Theosophy, but each folk had to develop this in its own way, and especially in Germany a connection had to be made to the great spirits of history: Goethe, Schiller, Herder etc. In these words Rudolf Steiner was depicting his own path, which had nothing to do with the customary dogmas and traditions in the Theosophical Society. He was so-to-speak developing a programme according to which he wanted the German Section to be led. To me this appeared simply 'nationalistic', and I was 'peeved', as I did not 'understand'!

So what remained was just the exceptionally powerful impression of this first 'meeting'.

A further detail was recorded in an article by D.J. van Bemmelen also included in the same collection:

> Elisabeth Vreede was one of the oldest members of our Society. I heard Dr. Steiner himself saying this in 1922 when the anthroposophical scientific course was being given in the Hague. As a member of the preparatory committee I could take my meals at the dinner-table with Dr. Steiner and other speakers. At table Dr. Steiner had a habit of telling jokes and anecdotes. He found this better for digestion than profound conversations. Once he told how he had already met Elisabeth Vreede as a young theosophical member in 1903. She was then wearing, as he recalled, a green dress. He was amused to see her baffled face and hear her calling out: 'Yes, yes, I was wearing something of the kind!'

Contemplation of Art and Culture

Social aspects of the 1903 Convention were related in another theosophical magazine, *The Lotus Journal*:

> The Convention did not spend all its time in business meetings, for on two or three occasions the London Headquarters at Albemarle Street were thrown open to the members, who had opportunity for many pleasant chats with fellow members in other places, to the accompaniment of tea. The rooms were decorated with flowers, and through the open windows the sunshine from outside came pouring in to augment the sunshine of cordiality and brotherly feeling which was everywhere in evidence within.

This was the convivial background against which Rudolf Steiner, a few days after his address in St James's Restaurant, penned a letter to his wife:

> London,
> 7th July 1903
>
> My dear good Anna!
>
> Only today are the Convention's first strenuous days somewhat coming to an end, and it's getting calmer.—During this time I've had meeting after meeting. In between, my dear good Anna, I'm worrying about you. I know you're seeing all sorts of things which don't exist at all. I also know it doesn't now help me much if I try to reassure you. It'll certainly be different again soon. You'll come to see that I'm very, very fond of you, as before.—At the moment I do ask you to have a little rest. It has been so difficult for you. I quite recognize all that.—I intend to be home straight after the 20th; but under the obtaining circumstances this can't be stated today with complete certainty.—At the moment it's even more animated in London than usual,

as Loubet is here, the President of the French Republic, and the streets are not just decked with flags, but so full of carriages and people that now and then a complete human knot builds up and one doesn't get further for half an hour.

Perhaps in the meantime you've already written to me. If you perhaps write to Geni, you can tell her that if she comes she should arrange a rendezvous in the Café Verrey, Regent Street, in case I'm still in London.

Hopefully you're very much better than when we parted.

Heartfelt kisses and greetings from

your

Rudolf

Address: Dr. Rudolf Steiner,
C/o Mrs. Bright,
The Lodge,
Esher,
near *London*,
England.

★

A couple of days later, on 9 July, Steiner may also have attended a lecture in the Blavatsky Lodge given by G.R.S. Mead, 'Concerning the Concept of the Logos'.

Be that as it may, this seems a suitable place to set out general remarks made by Steiner in a lecture at Dornach on 15 June 1923:

> ... There was at first a hope that the Theosophical Movement, united as it was in the Theosophical Society, might actually become entirely anthroposophical. Circumstances which made this hope appear justified included the fact that the particular way investigations were made in the Society brought about great disappointments among discriminating people. I have to say that on coming to London for the first and second times, I experienced the leading personalities as basically people who met one another with great scepticism. They felt themselves on completely uncertain ground, which however they did not wish to abandon since they did not know where to search for any security.
>
> Among the very leaders of the Theosophical Society were many disappointed people who were full of misgivings...

★

After a few more days, Steiner wrote another letter, this time to Wolfgang Kirchbach:

London,
12th July 1903

Dear Herr Kirchbach,

Please accept my greatest thanks for your postcard. I am very pleased that you want to write about Hegel's philosophy of the spirit. On receipt of the article you will of course receive the royalty at once. But perhaps I may ask you not to exceed the space of 10 pages. Not that I would be ungrateful for a longer article as well, but because I should like to bring precisely this article in one issue. I only return home on the 23rd of July at the earliest and request you to take care that the article only arrives then. Before then nobody is in my house, and confusion could easily occur with things arriving earlier. I am very pleased your son found something in my Tegel speech. At the time everything lay in the intent; and I wanted to say various things 'between the lines'.

Heartfelt greetings from your home town.

Yours very devotedly,

Rudolf Steiner

★

This was followed on the next day by a further letter to his wife:

Esher,
near London,
13th July 1903

My dear good Anna,

I'm writing you this letter here in Esher on Monday morning. Esher is a little place near London, where the Brights live in the summer. Most unfortunately everything in London this time had to proceed without Mrs. Besant. She's in India. I'm staying myself in the room she always occupies when recovering in Esher from her many exertions. The Brights are probably Mrs. Besant's best London friends. When she's in London they always put their town residence at her disposal, or their country residence here in Esher. The Bright family consists of the old mother, 68 years old, and daughter, who is at present living here with her. A son of this old mother lives with his family all year in the house next door. Old Mrs. Bright is the widow of a famous Member of Parliament, Jacob Bright. She used to be very much concerned with politics herself. But for many years she's been devoted to the Theosophical Movement. She's an unusually sprightly woman, who tells a lot of stories and is very energetic.—The two ladies are now living in the beautiful country house (The Lodge).

I'm very pleased you've travelled to Weimar. Hopefully you're recovering a little from your tiredness. We'll see each other again about the 21st. I'll still write to you with the details.

The Convention days were very strenuous, especially as from Esher to London is almost $\frac{3}{4}$ of an hour's journey, and also these days in London were very hot. Added to which was a visit by the French President, when one often couldn't cross the streets for hours on end.

I've received your second letter too, for which I'm very grateful. From now onwards everything should be left. I was particularly glad you sent me the card from Kirchbach, as I could reply to him from here. Kirchbach was actually born in London.

Between various business matters I've again seen several things of great interest, e.g. the old town of Oxford with its wonderful character and quite remarkable university.

Yesterday I was in the National Gallery, to have another look at the landscapes of Turner, that glorious painter who filled me with so much enthusiasm last year and seems to me even more significant than Böcklin.

Till we meet again, my dear good Anna, and many kisses and greetings from

your

Rudolf

★

The reference to a visit of the National Gallery may be amplified by a passage from Steiner's autobiography:

> On journeys undertaken in the interests of Anthroposophy I could immerse myself in the development of architecture, sculpture and painting.
>
> At various places in this description of my life I have spoken about the importance of art for a person who has experiences in the spiritual world.
>
> Before the time of my anthroposophical work, I was only able to study most art-works created during the evolution of mankind in reproductions. Of original works, those in Vienna, Berlin and some places in Germany were the only ones accessible to me.
>
> With journeys now being made on behalf of Anthroposophy and in company with Marie von Sivers, the treasures of museums all over Europe came within my reach. So from the beginning of the century onwards—that is, in the fifth decade of my life—I undertook an advanced schooling in the study of art. In connection with this I observed the spiritual development of mankind. Everywhere Marie von Sivers was at my side, entering with tasteful finesse into everything I was privileged to experience in this contemplation of art and culture, herself sharing and supplementing it all in a beautiful way. She understood how these experiences flowed into everything which then gave mobility to the ideas of Anthroposophy. What I brought to activity in lectures was permeated by what my soul received in the way of artistic impressions.
>
> In actually beholding great works of art, there came before us a world out

of which another soul-configuration is still speaking across to recent periods from older times. We were able to immerse our souls in the spirituality of art . . .

To observe architectural development was for me of special importance. In quiet contemplation of stylistic form there arose in my soul what I was then able to imprint into the shapes of the Goetheanum . . .

A Voyage of Discovery

Rudolf Steiner was still in London on 15 July, when the next issue of *The Theosophical Review* came out. Under the title 'Christianity as Mystic Fact', it included a review by B.K., recognizable as the initials of Bertram Keightley, of his own latest book:

Das Christentum als mystische Thatsache. Von Dr. Rudolf Steiner. (Berlin: C.A. Schwetschke und Sohn; 1902. Price 2m 50pf.)

It is by no means easy to sum up in clear and precise words exactly the line of thought which our colleague Dr. Steiner has aimed to suggest to the readers of the small volume in which he has published a series of lectures given in the Theosophical Library at Berlin. Still less easy is it to feel sure that one has rightly understood its significance. The best plan, therefore, will probably be to endeavour to give our readers an outline of its contents and leave the author himself to point the moral more precisely in subsequent works . . .

There followed a précis of the book covering three whole pages.

★

Further on in the journal came also a notice of a new publication:

Luzifer. Under this well-known title we have to welcome the new magazine edited by the General Secretary of the new German Section, Dr. Rudolf Steiner; a nicely-printed and got-up number in a convenient octavo size, avoiding at once poverty of appearance and also the needless luxury of print and paper which is the besetting sin of new publications. In his editorial Dr. Steiner takes to himself the example of Faust who, according to the old folk-tale, 'laid aside the Scriptures for awhile behind the door and under the bench, and would no longer be a theologian but a citizen of the world'. We must all agree, as he goes on to show, that the future of the world is with those who are willing to do this; reminding us that in all time, from that of the Egyptian priests onward, 'the ladder of knowledge led a student up from the crawling worm to his God', and that his 'faith' was only his 'knowledge' of the higher rounds of this ladder.

To restore this relationship between science and religion—the only one which can answer to the world's present needs—is the task of the Theosophical Society; and the new *Luzifer* promises thus by its learned editor: 'Lucifer will be no devil to drag the straggling Faust down to hell; he will be the awakener of those who believe in the wisdom of the world and who would bask in the golden light of divine wisdom. Lucifer will look boldly into the eyes of Copernicus, Galileo, Darwin and Haeckel; but also its gaze shall not falter and sink when the sages speak together of the home of the spirit.' A general review of literature under the heading 'Present-day Culture in the Mirror of Theosophy' is to form a regular feaure of the magazine, to which we heartily wish success and long life. The subscription is 6 marks for the year, and the publishers, C.A. Schwetscke und Sohn, Berlin, W.

★

According to the plans indicated in his letters, Steiner did not leave England until 20 July. By that time he had been in the country for almost three weeks, the longest period he was to spend there until the summer of 1922.

★

The next issue of *The Vâhan*, published on 1 August, included in its correspondence columns the following letter:

Dear Editor,

Come, let's reason together like good fellows. The old enthusiasm of the early days should surely be reawakened by the outgrowth of the Theosophical Movement in so many directions if we are not to become parochial. The literature of 'realism' may be useful to some, with its emphasis of detail, but there is another way of saying things which evokes and suggests. Let's go on a voyage of discovery.

I think *The Vâhan* capable of improvement. Has it grown with our organization? Does it become more and more interesting? If not, surely it is not for lack of interesting material. I would like to have heard the subject discussed at Convention, but with only one session there was no time for 'Reports and Suggestions'. I suggest, therefore, that you open your columns for discussion and begin by saying:

1st. That *The Vâhan* should represent more fully the international character and spirit of the Theosophical Society.

2nd. That the results of the labours and mediations of many students might be 'pooled' for the benefit of all, (a) by collecting references from many sources on many subjects, (b) by ventilating information on many subjects along lines allied to theosophical studies.

3rd. That by the assistance of Associate Editors you might give a resumé of advance in science, and the cream of mystical literature every month.

4th. That a subject-index to *important* books and articles interesting to theosophists and students of mysticism might be given monthly.

5th. That there should be a Correspondent appointed in each country in Europe, if possible, from among T.S. members to report briefly any important development along lines which interest theosophists, and may assist them in their work and studies.

Some improvement is possible, I believe, if members of the Theosophical Society are not too apathetic. *The Vâhan* should be looked for eagerly every month and welcomed gladly. Why not?

Yours sincerely,

D.N. Dunlop

*

The letter was followed by the editorial statement:

The Vâhan is very glad of such suggestions and trusts that this letter may lead to further correspondence which will be both interesting and practically useful. To that end correspondents are requested kindly to indicate in detail the practically available means of carrying out these and any other suggestions that may be made.

Theosophy and German Culture

Even after returning to Germany, Rudolf Steiner was still full of his impressions of the London Convention. On 8 August—almost three weeks after his return—he delivered a public lecture in Berlin entitled 'The Task of Theosophy at Present, with reference to this year's General Meeting of the Theosophical Society in London'.

He also wrote a report for the September number of *Luzifer*, under the heading 'The Theosophical Movement':

The 'Theosophische Gesellschaft' (Theosophical Society), founded in the year 1875 (with headquarters at Adyar in India), has the task of fostering a view of the world which this journal also brings to expression. In Europe it has a British, Dutch, French, Italian, and German Section. These five Sections form a Federation of European Sections. On Friday the 3rd of July talks about fruitful collaboration between these Sections took place in London, connected with the General Meeting of the British Section. These talks took on a significant character through being chaired in person by the founder of the Theosophical Society, who is currently also still its President, Col. H.S. Olcott (resident in Adyar). It was resolved to create a centre for

> the common work of European Sections at annual General Meetings held at different places in Europe. By kind invitation of our Dutch colleagues, Amsterdam was decided on as the venue for the General Meeting next year. The task of these meetings will be to deal with common concerns of the great Theosophical Movement in the world (so far as they concern Europe) and report on the progress and undertakings in individual Sections. The progress of the Movement will be given expression by its Proceedings, to be published annually. Mr. J. van Manen was elected editor of these Proceedings. On the 4th of July 1903 a second meeting took place where the state of the Theosophical Movement in particular regions of Europe was discussed. The speakers were: for the English Section: Mr. Mead; for the Dutch: Captain Terwiel; for the French: Monsieur Bernard; for the Italian: Mrs. Cooper-Oakley; and for the German: its General Secretary, Dr. Rudolf Steiner. Col. Olcott introduced the speakers to the meeting, and chaired. Dr. Rudolf Steiner spoke about the 'Relation of General Spiritual Life in Germany to Theosophy, and the Outlook for the Latter in the Future of German Culture'. The text of this speech will be given in the next issue; a report of the interesting General Meeting of the British Section, which took place from the 4th to the 6th of July, will then likewise be given in the next issue, since there is no room for it in the present one. (Inquiries about the Theosophical Society are answered by the General Secretary of the German Section, Dr. Rudolf Steiner.)

This was followed in the October issue by an article entitled 'Theosophy and German Culture', giving the text of the speech which had so peeved Elisabeth Vreede:

> Here will be reproduced in brief summary what was said by Dr. Rudolf Steiner (as General Secretary of the German Section of the Theosophical Society) on the 4th of July 1903 in London on the occasion of the first meeting of the Theosophical Society's Federation of European Sections (compare the previous article): 'The European Sections have agreed to meet every year for the common fostering of the Theosophical Movement. On these occasions there will take place a confluence of individual contributions which different regions of Europe are able to put forward towards our great international task. Representatives of individual Sections will take the stimulus of the Congress with them to their own home territory, to let it work on further. Our German Section is not yet even a year old. Naturally, therefore, it can only point to small success in the past. But we may be said to harbour the best hopes in regard to the future of Theosophy in Germany. For the whole being of the German folk-soul is pressing towards Theosophy. Wherever German spiritual culture has put forth its finest shoots, the bearers of this culture have been supported by a hidden but no less effective theosophical attitude. Not only has the deep mysticism of Meister Eckhart,

Tauler, Valentin Weigel, Jacob Böhme, Angelus Silesius and secret mystical Societies flowed out from this attitude and manner of thinking, but the way our more recent German thinkers—Fichte, Schelling, Hegel—contemplate the world also rests on this basis. What came to expression in these outstanding personalities is rooted in the depths of the German folk-soul. That is why the greatest of modern German poets, Goethe, was also imbued with this attitude and this type of picture-formation. Goethe is only fully known when the theosophical way of observing, which cannot be found on the surface but rather in the depths of his creations, is clearly seen. This side of Goethe's work has remained almost entirely uncomprehended. Once it is understood, what Goethe has created will give significant sponsorship to the Theosophical Movement in Germany. Goethe's entire view of Nature rests on a theosophical basis. Much of what, according to his own remark, he 'concealed' into *Faust* are theosophical truths. Besides, he also summarized his view of the world in his deeply symbolical 'Fairy Tale of the Green Snake and the Lily'. This fairy tale is really Goethe's 'secret revelation', and must be read in the way one reads esoteric writings. Its meaning must be studied as one studies the meaning in secret accounts of profoundly hidden truths. Nobody knows the whole of Goethe until they have done this. Under the influence of such a study, new light will also be thrown onto much else in Goethe's life and creativity. Above all, it will be proven that in him the Germans have a theosophical poet.—Consider Novalis, whose 'magic idealism' is indeed also theosophical. Lastly consider Schelling, who in his lectures on 'the Philosophy of Mythology' and 'the Philosophy of Revelation' at the University of Berlin appeared in the forties with views won through long and deep research. In all these theosophical endeavours by Germans only one thing is missing: a deeper understanding of the great universal laws of reincarnation and karma. Even if Jean Paul out of his intuition upheld the teaching of re-embodiment, it has never been organically joined to the previously mentioned streams. The Theosophical Movement will incorporate these comprehensive truths into German culture. It will thereby bring closer to the Germans their great personalities and indeed their own folk-soul. From this direction Theosophy itself will experience the most beautiful stimulus. While it is true that German life has much to expect from Theosophy, it is also true that German life has itself a good mite to furnish to the Theosophical Movement in the world.

With Much Interest

The September number of *The Vâhan* published the following letter:

I was glad to see in last month's correspondence issue of the *Vâhan* that Mr. D.N. Dunlop has given a lead in the matter of suggestions for the improvement of the Society's 'vehicle'. I have several times been on the point of writing to you myself to make similar suggestions, but I have always been deterred by the knowledge of the fact that I am, unfortunately, compelled to continue an unattached member in an isolated corner of the kingdom; and by the supposition that those who are at the centre should know better the needs of the Society at large than a humble member at the margin of its ever-widening circumference.

But now that the ball has been set rolling I should esteem it a favour if I might be allowed to give it a kick or two. I should like to say how heartily I endorse all Mr. Dunlop's suggestions, from firstly to fifthly, and if I might venture to add a sixthly it would be that the present method of question and answer be eliminated from the *Vâhan* in favour of (especially) Mr. Dunlop's first, second, and third. The penny post might be made the vehicle of the present method of conveying knowledge. The questioner should enclose two envelopes—one stamped but unaddressed, for the forwarding of the question from headquarters to the right answerer—the other stamped and addressed, in which to receive his reply.

May I give one more 'kick' to the rolling ball in the name of the unattached members? We have voted, by a substantial majority, to be assessed at a higher rate than lodge members when subscriptions next fall due, though some of us can ill afford the increase. By that vote we have shown our desire to help our beloved Society, and Convention has kindly acknowledged our desire. But we want work! We want to be allowed to *do* something for the cause we have at heart. For instance, if any member who has the wonderful gift of being able to write books or articles has also a knowledge of Pitman's shorthand I would undertake to transcribe his notes—with pen or typewriter. I could undertake a preliminary correction of proofs for the printer. I could give assistance to any member who desires or needs a knowledge of physiology, or any other subject a medical man may be supposed to know something of.

Any faculty that the Builders have built into my economy, and which I have learnt to use reasonably well, I should be only too thankful to be able to place at the disposal of my friends and fellow-members. This, I fully believe, is the desire of many an obscure and unattached member, and is undoubtedlty a line along which a good deal of latent energy might, with profit, be set free.

F. Leonard Sessions

★

The correspondence was continued in the October number with a long letter from G.R.S. Mead:

Dear Mr. Editor,

I have read with much interest the vigorous letter of our colleague, Mr. D.N. Dunlop, in the August issue, in which he puts forward a number of suggestions for the improvement of our sectional periodical. I was in hopes that this important letter would have been followed up with a large batch of correspondence, as indeed you were yourself, as stated in an editorial paragraph; instead of which in the September issue we have to thank Mr. Sessions alone for (in continuation of his own metaphor) keeping the ball rolling. As an old editor of *The Vâhan*, I have much sympathy with you, Mr. Editor, in what I know to be the difficulties of making such a restricted and official periodical *interesting* to such a mixed and critical body of readers as we are who receive it, and I know therefore how pleased you would be to adopt any practical suggestions for the improvement of our sectional paper. There is also another reason why I am interested in Mr. Dunlop's suggestions; for it stands to reason that what the readers of *The Vâhan* would appreciate the readers of *The Theosophical Review* would in every probability peruse with equal pleasure. I therefore venture to hope that this correspondence may not be allowed to drop, but that we shall have other useful suggestions brought forward, and a full discussion of ways and means, in order that they may speedily be turned to practical account. In bringing, however, the name of the *Review* into this correspondence, I need hardly assure you that I do so, my dear colleague, without the slightest wish to divert a single line of copy from *The Vâhan*, but with the sole object of pointing out that should any suggestion appear too ambitious for the space at the disposal of our 'vehicle', there exists a supplementary area for its development.

Many and many a time have I pondered over the amount of good that could be got out of our 'pooling' the results of our individual reading and study, as Mr. Dunlop so well puts it. We have potentially, so to speak, 'eyes on all sides'. How can we best utilize the results of their observations? How can this at present wasted energy be stored for the common good? How in brief can we organize the forces at our disposal? Yes, organize is the word; the genius that we specially require for such an opportunity is a skilful organizer; the bearer of the magic wand that brings all to life. And if we have not got a heaven-born organizer ready materialized, then we must do the best we can and create one for ourselves—by the mutual sacrifice of co-operation. We should ask the question: what is the reason for a theosophical periodical becoming lacking in interest? Though there may be a number of subsidiary reasons in any given case, dare I suggest that one of the principal reasons may be that *we* generally do not take sufficient interest in *it*? There is an editor; there are a few on whom he depends for regular copy; everyone else naturally supposes that it is all right; there is no difficulty, it goes on from month to month; no one realizes the danger of the thing becoming mechanical until too late; and then we yawn over the efforts of our colleagues. And this is an especial difficulty in the case of *The Vâhan*, where apart from the 'Activities' it is a question solely of writing answers to a kaleidoscopic examination paper, and most people are only too glad to feel that they *have not got* to do so. But let us take a case in which practically one of Mr. Dunlop's suggestions has for long been in operation; I mean the 'Watch Tower' matter in the *Review*. When I am myself editing, I not infrequently find that as a practical fact I have to hunt up the major part of the material myself; this is of course not stated by way of complaint, for it is naturally part of my work; but I am always being haunted with the feeling that in every probability what may interest me and *I* think suitable may by no means prove interesting to the majority of my readers, and remember, it is just this problem of interest which we are discussing.

But why is it, someone may ask, that the editors of *The Theosophical Review* are not always overflooded with material for the 'Watch Tower' notes? It is certainly not because of any lack of good will on the part of their readers; there is an abundance of good will. It is simply because of the great difficulty of *remembering*, even when one knows how a magazine is edited, or from the persuasion that there is always a plethora of material (for is there not always a full 'Watch Tower' every month?), or that what may interest us may probably be of no interest from the editorial point of view, or that the editors must have already come across the subject themselves.

Now how can this difficulty be overcome in the case of *The Vâhan*, for the general success of most of the suggestions put forward depends precisely on this widespread co-operation? May I suggest as a start that the best *remembrancer* for all of us who desire to make our theosophical periodicals interesting—or rather to help in this, no matter what our culture or literary ability may be—is that we should keep a *notebook* in which to note down (*correctly and with proper references*, my editorial and critical soul would add) any fact or short passage in our reading *which appears of special interest to us individually*; of this we might from time to time send a transcript to the editor of *The Vâhan*.

When the material comes in, it will be possible to arrange it, digest it, and use it. Meantime what we want is a supply of material. Let us make a start at once; should by chance *The Vâhan* be found too small to hold it all, there is the *Review* as an overflow. But think what could be done if this scheme could only be got into working order. If nothing else came of it, what a splendid collection of fine paragraphs, high thoughts, and wise sayings, of concisely stated strange facts, could be amassed by the numbers of readers of occult and theosophical literature we have in the Section! We are blasés like our age; let us then try the paragraph-system! Theoretically I might deprecate it in good conservative style, as too highly seasoned nutriment; practically I like it, because . . . well, because I suppose my appetite *is* jaded. On the other hand the gathering together of 'chaplets of pearls' has ever been regarded as a meritorious industry. Either way, many of us seem likely to like the scheme, and so there should be a very good chance of the material being forthcoming.

Yours expectantly,

G.R.S. Mead

★

Mead's letter was followed by a notice from A.P. Cattanach, one of those who with Dunlop had in October 1901 founded the Battersea Lodge.

> If *The Vâhan* is to be made more serviceable to members it rests with them to make it so, by taking advantage of the open door the Editor has given them. The invitation is—'Step in, and if you don't see what you want, ask for it!' Mr. Dunlop suggests: 'That the results of the labours and meditations of many students might be "pooled" for the benefit of all by collecting references from many sources, on many subjects.' And Dr. Leonard Sessions has expressed what must be the desire of many other well-read members, away in isolated corners, the wish to help. This is the help we want for Battersea Lodge just now. We have it in our minds to issue a neatly printed circular (*not* done by the local plumber, nor the man who mends bicycles) telling about the Society, its objects, and our meetings. When the first object is read by some thoughtful people, it generally satisfies them that they have run up against another crowd of cranks. Perhaps they have, but we want to show them, by quotations from sources they recognize as worthy of consideration, that the idea of 'Brotherhood' has been written and sung about by others outside the Theosophical Society, and that we are simply trying once more to get it recognized amongst the sons and daughters of men. Also that the second and third objects may not be unworthy of their consideration. To illustrate what we want we would print the first object in bold type, followed by illustration, thus:
>
> First: 'To form a nucleus of the Universal Brotherhood of Humanity, without distinction of race, creed, sex, caste or colour.'
>
> Then let us pray, that come it may,
> As come it will for a' that,
> That man to man the world o'er
> Shall brithers be for a' that.
>
> Burns.
>
> Second:—'To encourage the study of comparative religion, philosophy and science.'
>
> 'The true goal of religion is not mystery, but science—a science dealing with a strictly verifiable order of facts, though an order transcending that

with which physical science, whose professors wrongfully limit the generic term, is concerned.'

Theosophy, Religion and Occult Science—Olcott.

Third:—'To investigate unexplained laws of Nature, and the powers latent in man.'

'For so strange a compound is man, that one and the same individual may hold, at one and the same time, the most sublime views on some subjects, and the most absurd opinions on others.'

The Gospels and the Gospel—Mead.

Also we print on our syllabus illustrations concerning Theosophy, thus:—

Theosophy means divine wisdom.

'Wisdom is the principal thing; therefore get wisdom; and with all thy getting get understanding.'—Solomon the King.

Quotations illustrating the importance of wisdom would also be acceptable. This may serve to begin a series of most generally useful and serviceable queries in the interests of lodge work.

3
THIRD VISIT

The Spreading of Anthroposophy

In November 1903, Rudolf Steiner first visited Cologne. Mathilde Scholl invited her friends the Künstlers to hear him speak. They were so impressed that they too immediately joined the Theosophical Society.

Scholl had recently translated into German Annie Besant's *Esoteric Christianity*, and when a few months later, in February 1904, Steiner came again to Cologne for the foundation there of a theosophical lodge or 'branch', it was at Scholl's request called the Giordano Bruno Branch.

In a letter to her written in April, Steiner expressly stated: 'I am of course in agreement with the name you have given to your lodge. As far as I know there is nothing to be said against this name.'

★

> *Luzifer* was soon enlarged [continued Steiner in his autobiography], in so far as a Herr Rappoport in Vienna, who edited a journal called *Gnosis*, suggested that this publication be amalgamated with mine. So *Luzifer* then appeared as *Luzifer-Gnosis*. For a time Rappoport also undertook some of the distribution.
>
> *Luzifer-Gnosis* made the most splendid progress. The journal circulated most satisfactorily. Out-of-print issues even had to be reprinted. It did not 'collapse'. But in a relatively short time the spreading of anthroposophy took on the form of my being personally called upon to give lectures in numerous towns. In many cases single lectures turned into lecture-courses. At first I tried to keep up the editing of *Luzifer-Gnosis* as well as this lecturing activity. But the issues could no longer appear on time, and were sometimes months late . . .

The new development of the journal was noted in the April 1904 number of *The Theosophical Review*:

> We are glad to find from a parcel just received that *Der Vâhan* is not the only German representative of the Society, but that *Luzifer* continues to be regularly published. The beginning of the present year is marked by a change of form, the magazine being amalgamated with *Die Gnosis*, of Vienna, under the title of *Lucifer mit der Gnosis*, in larger form and printed in Roman letter instead of the old German type. We cannot trace in the two numbers before us any further signs of alteration; Dr. Steiner and Herr

Deinhard still furnish the groundwork, and there are in addition articles by Mlle. M. von Sivers on H.P.B. and Mrs. Besant; Ed. Schuré, 'The Theatre of the Soul'; and 'Aphorisms', by Fräulein Mathilde Scholl. We sincerely hope that in its new shape, and with the extension of its field by its South German connection, a long and prosperous future may open for it.

⋆

At the beginning of April, Steiner visited for the first time the lodge in Stuttgart. On the 7th he gave a lecture in the lodge, and on the 8th a public one.

The musician Adolf Arenson had a first meeting with him, and received a meditational exercise beginning:

> Every day a review is made of the personality's experiences on that day. One holds up before oneself the most important experiences one has had during that day, and the way one has behaved within them. All of this happens from the point of view of wanting to learn from life. How can I do better something I have done today? One puts such questions before oneself...

⋆

Another, rather older, couple who first met Steiner on this occasion were Franz and Doris Paulus. Like Arenson, they too asked him for esoteric instruction.

About a fortnight later, on the 21st of the month, when Steiner had travelled on to Munich and Switzerland, the Paulus couple wrote him a first letter.

The part written by Doris Paulus began:

> Dear Herr Dr.,
>
> Also heartfelt thanks from me for your letter from Zurich, you who are my leader. I am looking forward with great anticipation to the further communications you have promised. It was for me a very remarkable meeting, one which is still inwardly preoccupying me, though I am quite unable to call to mind your outer appearance. Who are you? This is still making me seek and grope—remarkable! And in the process I am speaking with you so much...

To this letter Steiner did not at first reply. His silence must have come to embarrass Doris Paulus, for a further letter she wrote to him twelve days later, on 3 May, includes a passage stating:

> ... My second misgiving is whether my question 'Who are you?' in our letter to Munich perhaps gave you offence, and for this reason you could not yet write to us?...

★

On 5 May Steiner was back in Berlin, lecturing to members there about H.P. Blavatsky. Two days later he wrote to his wife:

Berlin,
7th May 1904

Dear Anna,

In the couple of days I've been here in Berlin I've had a lot to do. I'm now leaving in $1\frac{1}{2}$ hours for London. I'll write to you from there. It's no longer possible from here. Just this, that I'm only coming back on May the 17th.

Heartfelt greetings,

Rudolf

With Full Authority

It is evident from her letter of 18 April 1903 that Marie von Sivers had wished to be in London for White Lotus Day, 8 May, but in the event Rudolf Steiner preferred to attend the Theosophical Convention in July.

The idea of going to London for White Lotus Day was therefore postponed to the next year, 1904, when they now arrived from Germany just in time for the celebrations. This must have been a memorable occasion for the two foreign visitors, since from then onwards Steiner celebrated this day for all the remaining years he spent in the Theosophical Society.

The Vâhan reported:

> At the commemoration meeting on Sunday, May 8th, at 28 Albemarle Street, Mrs. Besant was in the chair, and concluded the meeting with an address on the work which had been done by members who had passed from this life. Mr. Mead and Mr. Keightley gave short addresses, and Mrs. Hooper and Major Lauder read passages from *The Light of Asia* and the *Bhagavad Gita*. A telegram was received from the members of the Cologne branch assembled to celebrate White Lotus Day, sending greetings to the meeting.

★

The Cologne members were not the only German theosophists whose thoughts had accompanied Steiner to London. On the very next day, Adolf Arenson wrote to him from Stuttgart:

9th May, 1904

Dear Dr Steiner,

In accordance with our arrangement I am giving you today a report of how things fared in regard to my attempts at meditation . . .

Then I would like to ask you to have me nominated to the Esoteric Society; for when you were present here I expressed the wish to join. I do not however know what conditions are made, or what obligations are involved. But whatever may be required, I feel that even if I do not possess the strength, I have nonetheless a sincere will to strive incessantly for it.— Do I have to ask for admission directly? I would be most grateful if you would send me a line in reply to this question.

In grateful admiration,

Yours,

Adolf Arenson

*

The subject broached in this letter, the 'Esoteric School', was discussed by Steiner in his autobiography:

> Now I always wanted to link on to what was in existence, what was given historically. As I had done this in respect to the Theosophical Society, I also wanted to in regard to the 'Esoteric School'. Therefore my 'more restricted' circle first came into existence in connection with this School. But the connection lay only in *arrangements*, not in what I imparted as communications from the spirit-world. So in the early years my more restricted circle appeared outwardly as a section of Mrs. Besant's 'Esoteric School'. Inwardly it was not that at all . . .
>
> There was no possibility of my having been able to learn anything special in the 'Esoteric School' of Mrs. Besant for the simple reason that right from the start I took no part in events of this School, except for a few which were for the purpose of informing myself about what was going on.
>
> In any case there was at that time no other real substance in the School than what stems from H.P. Blavatsky, and that indeed was already in print. Besides this printed matter Mrs. Besant gave all kinds of Indian exercises for making cognitional progress, but these I rejected.
>
> So in regard to the arrangement, my more restricted circle was connected up to 1907 with the circle of this sort fostered by Mrs. Besant. It is however quite unjustified to make out of these facts what was made out by opponents. The utter absurdity was maintained by some that only through Mrs. Besant's Esoteric School had I been led to spiritual knowledge at all . . .

The reason for Steiner's visit to London on this occasion was to make official arrangements in relation to the Esoteric School. These were formalized in a document:

31, St James's Place,
London, S.W.
May 10, 1904

To all members of the E.S. in Germany and Austria

I hereby appoint Dr. Rudolf Steiner as Arch-Warden of the E.S. in Germany & the Austrian Empire, with full authority, as my representative, to call meetings of the School, to organize groups & appoint Wardens, & to do all else necessary for the welfare of the School, remaining in direct communication with myself.

Annie Besant

With Inward Delight

The address on the document giving Rudolf Steiner his esoteric authorization was 31, St. James's Place. It is recognizable as the London home of the Brights, later described in Esther Bright's autobiography *The Ancient One* (1927):

> St. James's Place was at that time very quiet and secluded—an ideal, peaceful spot in the midst of the great city. We could get through to the Green Park by a little passage; on one side of this stood the old home of the poet Rogers, where Byron, Tom Moore and many others had spent merry evenings. We used to think our little house the pleasantest in the place, for it looked out across the square and courtyard of Spencer House onto the Green Park. The balcony was ever gay with flowers and plants . . .

In his autobiography Steiner devoted a whole paragraph to the Bright family, in connection with Annie Besant:

> For a short period Marie von Sivers and I came into closer contact with Mrs. Besant through the fact that she used to stay in London with Mrs. Bright and during our later London visits we were also invited into this lovable home. The household consisted of Mrs. Bright and her daughter Miss Esther Bright, people like the very embodiment of kindness. I recall with inward delight the time I was privileged to spend in their home. The Brights were loyal and devoted friends to Mrs. Besant. They attempted to form a close bond between her and us. When in certain matters . . . it then became impossible to place myself at Mrs. Besant's side this also caused pain to the Brights, who uncritically held fast—with bonds of steel—to the spiritual leader of the Theosophical Society . . .

Steiner's account finds confirmation in reminiscences made by Esther Bright in her volume *Old Letters and Memories of Annie Besant* (1936):

> I had a sincere and affectionate friendship for Dr. Steiner. He was a most lovable man, a great orator, and a deep mystical student. I knew him well and often heard him lecture. His knowledge of Goethe was profound, and to hear him speak in his rich, eloquent German on this subject was a real delight.
>
> It was a grief to me when later Dr. Steiner and the Germans separated off from the Theosophical Society. For it was I who introduced him to A.B. and acted as interpreter between them. He spoke no English, and she but little German. I was very keen that he should understand her and work with her, but it became impossible. He was a fine soul; communion with him was full of life and deep interest.

Another passage in the same volume gives a further picture:

> Steiner was a remarkable individual in many ways. He had a wonderful power over his body. He ate hardly anything. He stayed with us for some time, and I tried to make him explain to me how he managed to live. For he lived on salad and a little bread and coffee—hardly anything else—and only slept two or three hours at night. He was very thin, but full of rich life and vitality. In reply to my smiling questions and curiosity he kept a smiling silence. But I know from a few words he said to me one day that he had trained himself in his own peculiar methods and could nourish his body in ways not known to the rest of us.

★

During this visit to England Steiner invited Besant to come on a lecture-tour to Germany.

In regard to Besant's own incarnational background it is of interest, and may have been noticed by Steiner and Marie von Sivers during their week in London, that in the issues from March to May 1904 of *The Lotus Journal* the transcripted text was then being published of a lecture Besant had given in London in 1898 about Giordano Bruno.

★

The Vâhan recorded a lecture held in the Blavatsky Lodge:

> On May 12th Mrs. Besant was welcomed with great pleasure by the Lodge, and delivered a most impressive address on the work of the Theosophical Society.

Although Besant was impressive as a speaker, there is one recorded anecdote which throws her in a different light. It was given by Hella

Wiesberger in the volume *Aus dem Leben von Marie Steiner-von Sivers* (1956):

> Marie von Sivers was at the time a great admirer of Annie Besant's brilliant personality. But her admiration suffered quite a blow from a small incident which Marie Steiner was fond of recounting in the last years of her life when speaking about this period. She once asked Mrs. Besant on a walk together through London: 'What do you think about Dr. Steiner?' and received the very sobering reply: 'I am not stupid enough to say what I think about people.'

★

As during his previous visits to London, so too on this present one Steiner wrote several letters. Some of them have survived, others not.

The first would probably have been the one he had promised before his departure from Berlin to write from London to his wife. This letter has not been preserved. It may however be noted that around this time Rudolf and Anna Steiner, after some four years of marriage, now separated.

Steiner also wrote to Adolf Arenson, whose letter to him he had evidently received. Again, Steiner's reply has not been preserved, but its existence is known by an allusion in a further letter from Arenson, to be given shortly.

One letter which has survived was written to the publisher Eugen Diederichs on the very last day of Steiner's London visit:

> 77 W. Portsdown Road,
> Maida Vale,
> London
> 14th May 1904
>
> Dear Sir,
>
> Some time ago you were kind enough to write about whether I might like you to publish a work on 'mysticism'. Today I would like to return to your question, since the matter is now definite. In 1 to 2 months I will have completed a work on 'mysticism' covering about 14–15 printed sheets. This will *not* be a historical work, but a thoroughly original one and despite the mystical standpoint will meet all scientific requirements of the present day. I would indeed be most gratified if the book were to appear from your publishing house, which I hold in high esteem. Might this be possible? Sales would already be guaranteed by the fact that I am General Secretary of the Theosophical Society's German Section and my books are read by members.—This book would at the same time have a generally comprehensible character.
>
> I have reviewed in *Luzifer*, edited by myself, the work on 'Gnosis' by

Eugen Heinrich Schmitt. Should you not have been sent a specimen issue, I would forward one straight away. In n.11 of *Luzifer*, which has meanwhile been amalgamated with the Viennese journal *Gnosis*, I have included the essay which precedes your Swedenborg edition by Brieger-Wasservogel. I would also be pleased to review in this journal your other mystical books, and so am requesting review copies.

Hoping soon to receive a reply to my above question, I am

With the deepest respect

Your most devoted servant,

Dr. Rudolf Steiner

From the 17th of May onwards I am back home at 17 Motzstrasse, W. Berlin.

★

The work referred to must have been an early version of the *Geheimwissenschaft*, the book later translated into English as *Occult Science*, which however was not published in its final form until six years later (and by a different publisher). It is interesting that the work is characterized as being on 'mysticism'. This seems to indicate a connection in Steiner's mind with his previous book *Das Christentum als mystische Tatsache*, the 'moral' of which Bertram Keightley had suggested in the previous year should be pointed more precisely.

Standing in the Spiritual Life

Another letter written on the last day of Steiner's visit to London was addressed to Doris and Franz Paulus:

London,
14th May 1904

Strictly confidential

Dear Frau and Herr Doctor,

A great amount of work and travelling have made it impossible for me to reply to your kind letters in full. I am especially pleased by your last letter, as I see you have continued the meditational work, and I beg you always to maintain it in this way. You may be assured of always receiving from me at the proper time whatever is needed. Precisely on account of our esoteric work in Germany I have had to spend the last few days here in London with our spiritual chief Mrs. Besant, in order to obtain from her a full esoteric authorization for everything I am doing in this field. You may be assured that in esotericism every instruction and piece of advice is given in the most careful way, and under actual guidance of the great spiritual leaders of the human race. Have no doubt that by meditational work you will sooner or later find the way to these leaders yourselves. Whoever has experienced what I have experienced may speak as I do. Now in the next few weeks I ask you also to meditate the parts of the *Voice* which precede the seven voices. In the next few days I shall interpret these seven voices under authority and you will then receive a first copy of the interpretation. This will have much more value than if I had given it to you a fortnight ago without complete authority. For only in the last few days has my esoteric work received full sanctification.

I now turn to your questions, dear Frau Doctor. If I were not an esotericist and standing in the spiritual life, I would perhaps say that your questions in Stuttgart and later on by letter astonished me. But through these stated capacities I was fully prepared for knowledge of your profound psychological insight. I can only tell you that you have good psychic gifts, and just as fine a precondition for spiritual knowledge as for activity from spiritual planes in the physical world. What you experience simply shows that you have a connection to the world's spiritual powers, and your whole nature just shows that you are called on to apply these spiritual gifts in a noble way for people's support. Among other things you have repeatedly asked me who I might be. A time for us to discuss this subject will perhaps also come. Today I will just tell you that I am justified in believing you to have once done me a really great service in a former life. Do not misunderstand me. Even in spiritual observations mistakes are of course not ruled out. But I am not a person to live in illusions. In spiritual realms I am among those considered cautious and perhaps even 'down-to-earth'. I may therefore speak of a justified belief. In my previous life centuries ago a person was instrumental in wresting me out of a certain family sphere and making possible at that time the paths needed for my then profession of Catholic priest. In those times the Church was not yet in complete decline like now. You then demonstrated that freedom from prejudice which also appears to me so great in you today. In addition you certainly created then the conditions of your present life. These are indications which I ask you to accept as critically as possible; but I can only tell you that I hold them with reason as fully justified. If what I am saying seems plausible, it will also be clear to you that you are called to a psychic life. Do not be afraid of this tendency. We must regard such gifts as sacrosanct, and live with them with as much familiarity as we do with the tables and people of our physical environment. We have to accept them quite objectively, and always maintain our 'ego' intact, as a firm central point.

Never should we make ourselves unfree by such influences. They are bestowed upon us; but never with the purpose of overwhelming us. Whatever else may come, hold fast to the principle that in the world's present evolutionary epoch all the powers of the world, spiritual as well as physical, are there in order that man, as a free, self-conscious, thinking being, self-supported, may first fulfil his task here on this Earth. Spiritual powers and influences should only lead him to find the correct pathways here. Woman especially is called upon today both to find and assert herself. Everything happening in this field will contribute to the well-being of mankind.

I am probably back in Berlin on 17th May and will then continue this letter. From here I send both of you heartfelt greetings for today.

Yours faithfully,

Rudolf Steiner

Serious words

By the next day, 15 May, Rudolf Steiner was back in Germany, giving a lecture in Hanover. On his return to Berlin a few days later he composed another long letter, this time to Mathilde Scholl in Cologne (in reply to one of hers which has not survived):

Berlin,
18th May 1904

Dear Fräulein Scholl,

I have just returned from London. During the journey I also gave a lecture in Hanover.

I must above all go into your meditational work. Your letter on the 15th of this month expresses a feeling you have about your inner experience. You say: 'I am no longer in despair if at times I sense the spiritual life less strongly.' This is the right mood of composure, which should increasingly govern a person doing inner work. The more one comes into a mood of accepting everything in silence and devotion, whatever may arrive, the more does proper progress take place. One should not wish to force anything at all, but wait composedly for what comes. However it may appear to you: you have come further, and will come further still. I have also spoken about you to Mrs Besant in this respect. For my recent mission in London was in essence to speak with Mrs Besant about the E.S. and its task in Germany. Mrs Besant was already able to appoint me 'Arch-Warden of the E.S.', the intention being that what I do is done in her own name. Among the first things I then had to discuss with her was admitting you into the School as really a member 'of the first degree'. In a few days I shall send you the 'rules' of the 'first degree', and you will then tell me how you stand.—But for the time being I must tell you that by admission to the 'first degree' the E.S. members come into real occult connection with the spiritual current issuing from the Masters, and in course of time this comes more and more—if also perhaps slowly—into consciousness. I can plead fully before the 'blessed Masters' that you have reached the stage of admission. What I have to tell you orally I shall tell you when we meet next—probably in Amsterdam. The success of the German Theosophical Movement depends upon our having a foundation of theosophists working esoterically. It is above all in this direction that you are chosen to give help. These are serious words which I am addressing to you, but you are always ready to give seriousness serious acceptance.

I shall soon be writing even more to you about everything else in this regard.

Above all do not allow yourself to be frightened by such things as—according to your letter—you have experienced. These are repercussions (reactions) on the ethereal—and thereby the physical—body by the astral body engaged in meditation. What you see are firstly physical and ethereal processes, which are jointly founded in your own physical organs. The causes of them lie in your astral body, which is stimulated by meditation. All this will be overcome. In place of these things there later enters the embodiment of real supersensible experiences. For everything has to be undergone. In repose.

I enclose the diploma for Frl. Dessauer—Settle everything else about it, please, with Frl. von Sivers.

So in Cologne things are certainly progressing well.—In Düsseldorf too the formal merger would really need to take place extremely soon.

Heartfelt greetings to your companions in the house, and heartfelt greetings to yourself from

Yours,

Dr. Rudolf Steiner

17 Motzstrasse,
Berlin W.

Ancient Wisdom

Most of chapter XXXVI of Rudolf Steiner's autobiography will be reproduced in the course of the present book, since it is of particular relevance to British developments.

It begins:

An arrangement came about within the Anthroposophical Society which does not actually belong in the framework of this account, as originally no connection with the public was intended at all. But it will now be characterized because the content of attacks levelled against me has been taken from this.

Some years after activity had started in the Theosophical Society, a certain source offered Marie von Sivers and myself the leadership of a Society of a still existing kind which preserves the old symbolism and cultic ceremonies embodying 'ancient wisdom'. I did not have the remotest thought of working in the spirit of such a Society. Everything anthroposophical should and must originate from its own source of knowledge and of truth. There was not to be the slightest deviation from this aim. But I always respected what has arisen in the course of history. The developing spirit in mankind's evolution is living within it. I was therefore in favour of linking, whenever possible, what is coming into being with what exists historically...

Exactly when or where Rudolf Steiner and Marie von Sivers were first approached by the source referred to, a Czech named Franz Zavrèl, is not known. But it must have been by this time at the latest, since on 23 May, less than a week after returning from London to Berlin, Steiner gave a first lecture concerning the 'ancient wisdom'.

A few weeks later, there followed a second lecture on the same subject. These two lectures now open the volume *Die Tempellegende und die Goldenelegende* (GA 93).

★

In the meantime, Adolf Arenson replied to Steiner's (no longer extant) letter from earlier in the month:

27th May 1904

Dear Herr Doctor,

Your friendly communication from London has given me much joy and pleasure. I am grateful for the trust you have in me—I shall quite certainly show myself worthy of it, even if my attempts to meditate should perhaps not meet expectations. This partly depends not just on my will. Already now I feel this daily composure influencing my character and making me stricter with myself. On one hand I feel more sensitively than ever my own shortcomings, but on the other hand I have more calm in myself, as I know I am on the right path.

This is all I have to tell you. In heartfelt devotion,

Yours,

Adolf Arenson

★

The June number of *The Theosophical Review* reported:

In Germany the inflow of spiritual life through the Society has become a necessity. The idealism represented in the first half of the nineteenth century by the great philosophers Fichte, Schelling, Hegel, Schopenhauer, and nourished by the religio-philosophical studies of Schlegel, Gorres, and others, was almost pushed into the background in the second half of the century. In the minds of the scientific and the majority of the cultured, naturalism, or simple intellectuality, took its place. Jacob Boehme and Angelus Silesius, highly valued during the first half of the century, were forgotten. The theosophical movement in Germany has as its mission the renewal of the spiritual life of the people. Owing to the facts above mentioned, many difficulties were experienced in its early days, and the noble efforts made in '80 and '90 failed of success. In 1902 was formed the German Section, with Dr. Rudolf Steiner as General Secretary, a man prepared as a channel for a truly spiritual efflux by twenty years' study of Goethe's esoteric teaching, and by his efforts to revive German idealism in his various books, notably his *Philosophy of Freedom,* published in 1894. He has now entirely devoted his life to this aim. From Berlin, where he works in collaboration with Miss von Sivers, the theosophical movement is spreading over Germany slowly but surely. Theosophical lectures in Berlin attract ever-increasing audiences. In Weimar, the town of Goethe and Schiller, where Mrs. Helene Lübke displays a beneficent activity, Dr. Steiner has given a series of theosophical lectures. During last winter he has also given similar courses in other German towns: Hamburg, Cologne, Düsseldorf, Stuttgart, Munich, Lugano, Nuremberg, Hanover. In Leipzig, Herr Richard Bresch has worked hard for the spreading of theosophical ideas. In Hamburg and Cologne energetic work is done by Herr Bernhard Hubo and Fräulein Mathilde Scholl. In the South of Germany the theosophical movement shows hopeful progress, and in Switzerland (Lugano) good results are obtained by Herr Günther Wagner's quiet activity. Theosophical ideas find a medium for propaganda in the magazine *Lucifer-Gnosis*, edited by Dr. Rudolf Steiner, where the necessity of spiritual life is insisted upon, as well as the harmony between theosophical views and modern science. The essays of Herr Ludwig Deinhard help for the spreading of occultism; those of Dr. Steiner for the knowledge of mysticism, philosophy and esotericism. *Der Vâhan*, edited by Herr Richard Bresch, busies itself with Theosophy and the Theosophical Movement in a more special way. A new book by Dr. Steiner under the title of *Theosophy, an Introduction to a Supersensual Knowledge of the World and the Destiny of Man*, will soon appear. Well-directed and energetic activity will certainly do much in Germany in the coming time for a deepening and expanding of spiritual life.

The Positive Answer

The Theosophical Congress in Amsterdam took place in late June. It was attended by hundreds of theosophists, chiefly of course from the Dutch Section. Among foreign visitors were 18 members from the still relatively new German Section, including Rudolf Steiner, Marie von Sivers and Mathilde Scholl, and 73 members from the long-established British Section, including Annie Besant, Esther Bright, Bertram Keightley, and D.N. Dunlop.

A lecture by Steiner, delivered as always in German, on 'Mathematics and Occultism' was one of several contributions by various speakers which were on offer simultaneously.

★

As indicated in *The Theosophical Review*, Rudolf Steiner's book *Theosophie* had just come out in the previous month. On its front page it bore a printed dedication 'To the Spirit of Giordano Bruno'.

In a lecture on 14 June 1923 the author recalled the origin of the book:

> . . . These questioning souls were present, and it was possible to know their questions. They believed their questions might be answered through something like what was contained in Annie Besant's *Ancient Wisdom*. Of course it would have been foolish to tell people that this or that in the book *Ancient Wisdom* was no longer suitable. That would not have offered these souls anything, but merely deprived them of something. It could only be a matter of really answering their questions, as they were not gaining any clear answer from the other direction. The real answer came about in this way: I did not concern myself much with *Ancient Wisdom*, which was a so-to-speak dogmatic book for such people, but wrote my book *Theosophie* and gave answers to questions I knew were being asked. That was the positive answer. One did not have to go any further. People had to be allowed complete freedom: do you want to go on taking up *Ancient Wisdom*, or do you want to take up *Theosophie*?'

After the end of the Amsterdam Congress Steiner presented various people with signed copies of the book. Inside Besant's copy he wrote these words:

> To Mrs. Annie Besant, a much-loved teacher and treasured leader. 22nd June 1904, Dr. Rudolf Steiner.

Inside Scholl's copy he put down a lengthier inscription:

> The task of man is to build up strength in himself to work for the All, and thus recognize the part apportioned to him. To his dear co-worker

Mathilde Scholl. Amsterdam, 22nd June 1904. Dr. Rudolf Steiner.

In the light of all this, another relevant passage may here be reproduced. It comes in a letter from Scholl written about a month later, towards the end of July, to Marie von Sivers:

> ... If you are now travelling to the Harz via Braunschweig and passing by Wolfenbüttel, please have a think about various things. In the ducal library in Wolfenbüttel lies an original letter from Giordano Bruno, written in Helmstedt on 6th October 1589. Bruno's letter can be shown to you—after some grumping by the librarian, my dear old teacher Geheimrat Otto von Heinemann. There are also some original editions of Bruno's works ...

4
FOURTH VISIT

Restoring a Spiritual Nobility to Life

The Fourteenth Annual Convention of the Theosophical Society was held in London on Friday, Saturday and Sunday, 1–3 July 1904. Here are some paragraphs extracted from the 'Report of Proceedings':

> The Convention assembled for its business meeting on Saturday, July 2nd, at 2 p.m., in the Small Queen's Hall, Langham Place, W. Owing to the Congress of the Federation of European Sections which had been held in Amsterdam in June, the number of foreign members who attended the Convention was much smaller than usual, but a few came from Holland, France, Germany, Belgium, Italy and Russia.
>
> Mr. Sinnett, Vice-President of the Society, took the chair at 2.15 p.m. Mr. Bertram Keightley and Mr. A.M. Glass were elected Secretaries of the Convention.
>
> The roll-call of branches was read ...
>
> Representatives of other Sections were then invited to address the Convention.
>
> Mrs. Besant spoke as representative of both the Indian and Italian Sections, and said that they might be regarded as related to each other...
>
> Mr. van Manen for the Dutch Section brought a message of goodwill and expressed the great interest taken in the affairs of the British Section...
>
> Monsieur Charles Blech brought warm greetings in the name of the French Section. They would never forget their close and intimate connection with the British Section to which they owed friendship and gratitude...
>
> Mrs. Lübke, on behalf of the German Section, brought cordial greetings and said that they were cultivating friendship for the English. The books they published were mostly translations from the English and it was the British Section which had afforded them most help. Their sincere wish was for its increased welfare.
>
> A resolution of thanks from the Convention to the Sections represented was proposed from the chair and the General Secretary was instructed to send greetings.
>
> It was proposed from the chair and adopted unanimously that the report of the General Secretary, which had been printed and distributed, should be taken as read. The adoption of the report was then moved and carried...
>
> Mr. Dunlop proposed:

1. That a Committee be appointed to consider the advisability of improving *The Vâhan*.

2. That this Convention empowers the Committee to carry out whatever improvements they may unanimously consider desirable, subject to the approval of the Executive Committee.

He had started a correspondence last August in *The Vâhan*, and as a result 'Stray Notes' was added, which he did not think much of an improvement. He had safeguarded the resolution by making the recommendation of the Committee unanimous and subject to the Executive Committee. He thought the international character of the Movement should be represented in *The Vâhan*. It should deal with all the interests of the Section, and might have a column treating of the mystical side of art, one dealing with literature and one with science. He thought that this should be possible with the aid of sub-editors. He would suggest Miss Spink, Mr. Orage and Mr. Mead as a Committee, with Mr. Keightley as chairman.

Mr. Lorimer Thomson seconded and thought that in any case no harm could be done by such a proposal.

Mr. Cuthbertson did not desire to oppose the motion but could not agree with the lines of improvement suggested. The main purpose of *The Vâhan* was a news-sheet for the Section, and it would be a pity to make it into a magazine.

Mr. Dunlop explained that his scheme did not aim to cut out the news or the 'Enquirer'.

Mr. Mead said that as a former editor he found the real want was copy, not schemes. He did not think it possible to make *The Vâhan* a general magazine, and no ambitious scheme would do. Any who would contribute either answers or 'Stray Notes' would be welcomed by the editor with open arms.

Mr. Glass remarked that the result of the invitation to members to contribute to the 'Stray Notes' column was a supply of three paragraphs since it had started, and when Mr. Mead, as editor some years before, began a column dealing with current literature, not a single contribution had come in.

Mr. Dunlop said his resolution simply opened the question, and settled nothing. He thought the Committee was the best method of dealing with the matter.

The chairman then put the resolution, which was lost by a large majority . . .

Mr. Keightley said that the London Federation had suggested that the Convention might be held in other places than in London, but he thought in view of the International Federation of next year this question might be postponed.

Mrs. Besant then proposed that the invitation given by Mr. Keightley to the Federation of European Sections for their next Congress be ratified by the Convention and that the Executive Committee be empowered to take all necessary steps and to contribute from the funds of the Section such money as may be needful to ensure the success of the Congress. The Convention would, she said, probably be aware that at the very successful Congress just held in Amsterdam an invitation was given to meet next year in London. The first meeting taking place two years ago in London could hardly be considered a meeting of the Congress. We must not fall below the standard of this year, but there was a danger of slipping into a national idea instead of emphasizing the international. Several committees were wanted, an art committee, a music committee, a committee to deal with the papers to be chosen, and a reception committee preferably of people who could speak other languages. Any who had ideas on the subject should send them in soon.

Mr. Keightley seconded, and said that he entirely agreed with Mrs. Besant as to the lines of work. He was glad to be able to say that Mrs. Besant had consented to return from India in order to preside over the Congress. The Executive Committee would welcome suggestions of all kinds, and after the holidays it would start upon the organization. The art and music sections would require as much time as possible, and he was therefore immediately going to ask the Committee to sanction the appointment of Miss Gertrude Spink as organizer of the art section.

Mrs. Besant's resolution was carried unanimously.

Mr. Dunlop then proposed the following resolution of greeting:

'The British Section of the Theosophical Society in Convention assembled sends fraternal greeting to all Sections of the Theosophical Society and all students of wisdom religion, to all mystics and mystical societies, to men of science and scientific societies, to scholars and societies for research and learning, to men of letters, to artists and musicians, to all Churches and religious organizations who sincerely seek to bring forth in the common life the dim and hidden beauty, it extends the hand of fellowship and invites their co-operation in restoring a spiritual nobility to life.'

The Chairman asked if it was expected that the Secretary should communicate with all these people.

Mr. Dunlop said that it might be dealt with in any way thought proper.

The Chairman thought the suggestion was met by bringing the matter before the Convention without passing it as a definite resolution . . .

The Reception of High Mysteries

By this time an issue of *Luzifer-Gnosis* had appeared in Germany containing the first instalment of a series of articles by Rudolf Steiner entitled 'How does one attain Knowledge of the Higher Worlds?' A following issue also contained the beginning of a another series, appearing anonymously, under the title 'From the Akashic Record'. In his autobiography Steiner recalled:

> In *Luzifer-Gnosis* I could first publish the material which became a basis for anthroposophical work. In it first appeared what I had to say about the effort a human soul has to make in order to gain its own perceptive grasp of spiritual knowledge. 'How does one attain Knowledge of the Higher Worlds?' appeared in instalments from one issue to another. Similarly, the ground was laid for anthroposophical cosmology in the ongoing articles 'From the Akashic Record'.
>
> The Anthroposophical Movement grew out of what was given here, and not out of anything borrowed from the Theosophical Society. If I thought about the Society's usual teachings when composing my works on spiritual knowledge it was only in order to confront and rectify one or other thing in these teachings which seemed to me erroneous...

Steiner also continued with his lecturing activity. On 1 July—just when the Convention was beginning in London—he was giving a lecture to members in Berlin. Here are some passages from it:

> It is quite especially interesting to put forward again that period in Europe's spiritual development which we considered a week ago. I mean the period from the 9th to the 13th, 14th, 15th centuries. If one has attained this selflessness in relation to thought content and thus united oneself with a proper sense of reverence, of devotion, which a mystic must also possess, then the time when great spirits appear in world history often looks quite different from how it does in profane historical writing. By looking in the Akasha Chronicle towards this time, our gaze falls onto a great figure, who can teach us much about the time. An observer perceives his greatness, and an occultist sees him as even more tremendous: Wolfram von Eschenbach.
>
> Wolfram von Eschenbach worked over German, Romance and Spanish sagas. He belongs among the great initiated poets, who were selfless enough to work over given material and did not believe they had to find it for themselves. Great poets like Homer, Sophocles, Euripides, Aeschylus have never had to search for material. To these poets belongs also Wolfram von Eschenbach...
>
> The Great White Lodge had to send out its messengers, to prepare and instruct human beings, that they could become organs to carry out the will of the Masters. So it was too with Wolfram von Eschenbach. In the Middle Ages it was known that there was a White Lodge. At the time it was called the Grail Castle...
>
> In such a way did Wolfram von Eschenbach consider and present history. A person who knows how to read between the lines in Richard Wagner's

Lohengrin will find that Wagner, if not in understanding, but in feeling, intuitively felt that there was something great there. He therefore believed in a renewal of art by making a link to the superhuman. In the Middle Ages this was presented in such a way that when Elsa von Brabant wanted to captivate Lohengrin in this world, he withdrew, as Wolfram von Eschenbach says, to India. The Grail Castle is finally presented as lying in India . . .

A fortnight later, on the 15th, Steiner gave another lecture in Berlin. Here is a passage from this one:

The saga of King Arthur and his Round Table was gradually united to the saga of the Holy Grail. This union is brought about in the 13th century by a real initiate, Wolfram von Eschenbach. Siegfried's initiation was still an old initiation. Worldly knighthood and the danger of betrayal through an element of selfishness still played a role. Only when this element has been overcome, when one has thrown it off and risen from the principle of worldly knighthood to that of spiritual knighthood could spiritual initiation be attained. This is presented by Wolfram von Eschenbach in Parzival . . .

It is interesting to compare this with the content of an article by D.N. Dunlop, published exactly one month later, on 15 August, in *The Theosophical Review* as part of a regular series 'From a Student's Easy Chair':

I walk through the German fir forests, one after the other, apparently infinite in extent; the stems, neutral coloured, dim in twilight, rising to vague heights, make an effectual barrier against the world; they seem rather the abstractions of trees than trees, and follow one another with a loveliness and rhythm of monotony which stills the whole being and makes it ready for the reception of high mysteries. Here is the very atmosphere to nourish mysticism; here is the strange pale quiet, the aloofness, the soil wherein, as Swinburne finely says in his last poem, 'The Altar of Righteousness', springs and strives 'from the root that is man, from the soul in the body, the flower that is God.'

The mystics, those seekers of the unity which underlies all diversity, are very close to us here. When the trees move under the impulse of the storm, we think of the figures in Blake's drawings, swayed all one way by some overwhelming emotion of terror or of joy; and the gnarled roots of the firs, clawing at precipices, are grotesque with the distortion of an extreme asceticism. A phantom procession of the German mystics, and singers, and dreamers flits across the vistas of the glades—men who had attained that ecstasy in which state alone, as Plotinus holds, the soul of man can become one with the divine. The Meistersingers pass on their way to the Wartburg to take part in the great competition of 1207; with them is Wolfram von Eschenbach, meditating, perhaps, his poem on Parzival: he sees between the framing fir stems visions of blue distance, and the goal of all dreams, the

Holy Grail, symbol of supreme aspiration and mystical union, glimmers, it may be not so very far away. Wagner's exquisite modern interpretation of the Grail legend is based, Mrs. Cleather and Mr. Crump tell us, partly on Wolfram von Eschenbach's poem, but the fir forests were no doubt as direct an inspiration to Wagner's philosophy and Wagner's music.

Thuringia may claim as hers the greatest of all mystics next to Plotinus, for Eckhart was born in this district in the year 1260. If any book is appropriate to these woods, it is the selections from the German mystics of the Middle Ages entitled *Light, Life and Love* (Methuen), among which Eckhart's writings stand first. Surely the absolute identification of the soul with the Godhead has never been more wonderfully expressed than by the priest whose writings after his death were condemned by a Papal Bull enumerating seventeen heretical and eleven objectionable doctrines in them. 'The eye with which I see God,' writes Eckhart, 'is the same with which he sees me. Mine eye and God's eye are one eye and one sight and one knowledge and one love.'

In brooding over the works of these mystics, the fir forests vanish away, and we see behind all their teachings the dazzling infinitudes of Eastern skies. Laurence Binyon, in an interesting article in the *Independent Review* shows the unexpected kinship of Blake with the Orient, and makes a curious comparison between his drawings and the work of the Chinese painters of a thousand years ago, pointing out among other things how both 'dwelt on rhythmically sweeping lines', and had for besetting weakness 'a tendency to distortion and grotesqueness'. So, too, the Grail legend is accounted by scholars mainly Oriental: in Wagner's *Parsifal* the permanent home of the Grail is on 'a lofty mount' in India. Eckhart's doctrines are writ large in the Upanishads: thus, in Sir Edwin Arnold's *Oriental Poems*, recently selected by J.M. Watkins, we read in his translation of the Eastern Scriptures:

The uttermost true soul is ill-perceived
By him, who, unenlightened, sayeth: 'I
Am I; thou thou; and life divided.' He
That showeth life undifferenced, declares
The spirit what it is, One with the All.

All this mysticism that is so old comes to us of this generation with the vigour and flush of immortality. The Church clamped the winged thing in iron bars; and Science, denying its existence, buried it alive. But it has escaped from its fetters and from its grave, from the dogmas of theology and science that sought to strangle it. 'To embrace a dogma,' says a recent writer in *Dana*, 'is an acknowledgement of intellectual failure.' The magisterial attitude of the age, attacked by a writer in *The Atlantic Monthly* as 'the great delusion of our time' is slowly giving way: the supreme value of 'supra-rational' ideals and inspirations is slowly gaining recognition. Science tends to become less insolently assertive, and even Theology ventures to shift its ground a little. Psychologists like Professor James help to remove mysticism from the sphere of disease and delusion: in the *Hibbert Journal* the Lord Bishop of Rochester enters into friendly controversy with Sir Oliver Lodge on the reinterpretation of Christian doctrine. Professor J.A. Coe states his belief before the Union Theological Seminary in America that the scientific spirit of the day, instead of destroying personal religion, will aid in removing outgrown forms and give it room for growth, and Maeterlinck's prose-poetry is the 'flowering tuft' of science. Everywhere there has been a great noise of the crashing down of barriers: man of science, theologian and poet alike are occupied with the mystical search for the unity that underlies diversity. Now there is margin of open space about our souls. And over this space there are coming to us the great Realities, the Brotherhoods of Wisdom: and there are voices in the firs.

The Outstanding Mason

In mid-September Annie Besant arrived in Hamburg for her German lecture-tour, accompanied by Esther Bright and Bertram Keightley. Steiner acted as her translator throughout the tour. For although he did not speak English at all, he did have a reasonable *understanding* of the language, whether in books or spoken by others on formal occasions.

The audiences were both large and appreciative. But during the tour there was also one awkward moment, recalled by Steiner in later years, when in one of her lectures Besant gave a historical survey of modern occultism in course of which she proclaimed to her German audience that 'the great wave of spiritual life has been conferred on the British people'.

When the tour reached Berlin, Keightley picked up the latest number of *Luzifer-Gnosis* and read an instalment of the anonymous series 'From the Akashic Record'. He asked Steiner what person they had among them whom they could use as a medium in this way. The author of the articles replied by referring to his own investigations, but Keightley failed to understand.

The tour went on to Munich, then to Stuttgart, and finally ended in Cologne. In her memoirs Mathilde Scholl reported on the Cologne part:

> Mrs. Besant's public lecture in the Casinosaal was well attended. At home there was also a lecture by Mrs. Besant for members and a meeting of the E.S. members: Mrs. Besant, Dr. Steiner, Fräulein von Sivers, Miss Bright, Mr. Keightley, M. Scholl in Mrs. Besant's room. Before leaving the room Mrs. Besant spoke with Dr. Steiner about study-material for E.S. pupils. She recommended Leadbeater's *The Christian Creed*. Dr. Steiner answered politely but firmly that he could not use this book for his pupils.

What astonished me at the time was that Mrs. Besant did not grasp the opportunity to speak with Dr. Steiner alone. It would have seemed natural to me that two such important people would have had a lot to discuss with each other. But unless Mrs. Besant was brought to other people through lectures etc. or meals, she mostly sat in her room working on her own.

The English guests then departed, and Steiner himself returned to Berlin. Here he picked up again his lectures on the 'ancient wisdom', giving one in September and another in October.

The third Annual Convention of the still youthful German Section has been recently held in Berlin [reported the *Theosophical Review*]. It abundantly proved that two years of incessant work have brought their due measure of results in spite of many obstacles that lay in the way. The number of members has more than doubled; six new branches and several new centres have added greater life and strength to the Section, and, most important of all, a strong tendency towards greater unity has shown itself, the essential need everywhere, but especially in this great empire but recently made out of many separate kingdoms.

The delegates, who had come from many parts of the country, expressed with warmest thanks their appreciation of the share their General Secretary had taken in this work, and of his untiring devotion and energy. Several delegates remained in Berlin for some weeks to take part in the life and work there, so that they might return to their own fields of labour with fresh stores of experience.

To his weekly lectures in the Architektenhaus Dr. Steiner draws an increasingly appreciative audience; his lectures on 'Theosophy and Tolstoi' and 'Theosophy and Darwin' being especially successful. On Mondays he treats of the mysteries of the Apocalypse in a series of well-attended public addresses, and he has been asked to lecture on mysticism to the Freie Hochschule. So that, however much materialism may have spread, there is little real cause for the student of mysticism to be pessimistic over the country of Jacob Böhme, Angelus Silesius, Cardinal Cusa, and many others. Their spirit has not died.

The next issue went on to review the current German journals:

Der Vâhan, November, contains the report of the Convention of the German Section, held at Berlin on the 29th and 30th October. The financial condition of the Section seems to be highly satisfactory, and membership has risen during the year from 130 to 251—very nearly doubled, though still a very tiny proportion of the German-speaking millions. But we know in England how far beyond the actual number of members the influence of Theosophy is felt, even when not acknowledged; and so we hope it will be in Germany. The contents of the number are Dr. Steiner's lecture on

'Clairvoyance'; 'Ernst Haeckel and his Monism' (unsigned); notices of the *Theosophist* and *Theosophical Review*; and original Questions and Answers, mostly as to how our doctrines can be harmonized with certain 'texts of Scripture'.

Luzifer, October. Here the first article is a very important study of 'Initiation' by Dr. Steiner himself. His explanation of the so-called trials of fire, water, air, etc., should be carefully studied.

The next issue continued:

Luzifer-Gnosis, November, is an interesting number and has several articles somewhat more approaching to what we English call 'light reading' than is usual with it, though still serious enough. I spoke last month of the value and importance of Dr. Steiner's own contribution, of which we have a further instalment; L. Deinhard's 'Sketches from Modern Spirit Life' and the anonymous 'From the Akasha Chronicle' should also be mentioned.

★

In November Steiner gave two more lectures about 'ancient wisdom', and another four in December.

In the course of these lectures he came to speak about the 'Grand Orient', and on 16 December stated that:

> Certain things will be ripening in the immediate future, and are therefore being spoken about, which makes it necessary to see how gradual progress in knowledge is needed. This gradual progress is thus rightly emphasized by those wanting to revive today the rite of Misraim and Memphis. Even if this is unsuccessful in the immediate future, one should not believe that failures in such things mean anything. At the head of the American Misraim movement stands a man whose significant character forms a certain guarantee for steadfastness in progress, the outstanding Mason John Yarker...

John Yarker was a leader in various alternative Masonic groups. Through the theosophical Mason Charles Sotheran he was brought into contact with H.P. Blavatsky, and in 1877, two years after the foundation of the Theosophical Society, he issued her with a Masonic certificate and was in his turn made an Honorary Fellow of the Society. Yarker was a well-travelled person, who also for instance formed connections in Italy with Garibaldi and Mazzini.

Bro. JOHN YARKER, P.M., P.Z., P.M.M., &c.

33° 90° 96°.

The family of Yarker is an old Yorkshire one, resident in the Parish of Wensley, N R, for 500 years, and Leyburn Hall is still in possession of what became the main line, and will die out with the present life.

In 1596, the holder of the estate from the Baronial family of Scrope died issueless, and left his lands to his youngest brother, the elder line from which our brother descends being then Recusant, or attached to the old faith, for which they were often persecuted, and were seated upon lands held from Streatlam and Raby Castles, in Co. Durham. A younger branch (Michael Yarker), about 1700, removed from Staindrop to Brough in Westmoreland, and his son John, in 1743, removed from Hartley Castle to Lowther. The subject of our sketch was born at Swindale, in the Parish of Shap, on the 17th April, 1833, and came to Manchester in 1849, since which time he has been engaged in commercial pursuits. We give herewith some particulars of his Masonic and general career.

Photo by Williams, West Didsbury.

Bro. JOHN YARKER, P.M. P.Z., &c.

Craft Masonry.—On the proposal of Bro. Richard Wood, W.M., of Lodge of Integrity, 189, now 163, Initiated 25th October, 1854; Passed 16th February, 1855; Raised 25th April, 1855. The Lodge then met at the Bush Hotel, Deansgate, and had a By-law requiring three months between each degree, but which was later expunged by desire of the P.G.L. Acted as Secretary in 1856, and on a vacancy arising, was offered the Senior Warden's chair in 1861, but being then a P.M. declined it. Joined a Lodge of Instruction, held at the Spread Eagle Hotel weekly, under sanction of the Lodge of Affability, afterwards transferred to the Integrity, but which ceased to meet 10th November, 1856, and there acquired by rote the whole 15 sections of the Lecture. In 1864 had the offer of A.P.G. Director of Ceremonies but declined it. Joined the Fidelity Lodge 623, now 430, Cheshire, 27th April, 1855; J.W. 1856, Installed W.M. 20th December, 1856, and Initiated, Passed, and Raised many new Members. This Lodge still possesses the fine old Integrity chairs bought in 1857.

Made an Honorary Member of Lodge 227, Dublin, in 1872; Past Senior Grand Warden of Grand Lodge of Greece, by patent, 1st July, 1874; Hon. Member and Medallist, Grand Lodge of Roumania, 22nd September,

The Masonic World

1881; and of the Ciro Menotti Lodge, No. 22, working in the Scottish Rite, 22nd November, 1882, Orient of Borgu Mozzano; also of La Verita Lodge, Italy, 7th January, 1883. Hon. Member of Thorne Lodge, No. 281, Orillia, Canada, 4th December, 1883. Member of the C.C. of Quatuor Coronati, No. 2076, May, 1887. Hon. Venerable of Lodge Giordano Bruno, Palmi, Calabria, 1st December, 1889.

Mark Master, &c.—Advanced 15th July, 1855, in the old time immemorial Cheshire Lodge that day meeting in the rooms of the Lodge of Loyalty, No. 402, now 320, Mottram, Ed. Bell, W.M. The Ark, Link, and Wrestle were afterwards added by its old P.M. Hill, the same having been discontinued prior to 1855.

Founded Fidelity Lodge, No. 31, under a warrant from Lord Leigh, G.M., and Installed W.M. 8th September, 1858, and admitted many Members including about six who founded the Union Lodge, No. 32, Manchester, and Installed their Officers at the Masonic Rooms, Cross Street, September, 1860. Offered Grand Office in that year but declined it. Hon. Member of the Wm. de Irwin Mark Lodge, and Prov. G.L. of Somerset.

In conjunction with Bros. Eichobz and Relph, revived the Fidelity, 31, for the Birkenhead brethren, 1896-7.

Royal Arch.—Early in 1856, the ancient Chapter of the "Garden of Eden," attached to the Integrity Lodge, was on the point of being erased, and sought to have it revived, but not then being Arched, and the old Members appearing to be indifferent, it expired. Exalted by Comp. Cornelius Goddard in the Industry Chapter, Hyde, 465, now 361, 6th April, 1856. In this year was present at the Eccles Chapter, No. 407, when the P.M. and the Veils were worked as preliminaries by Comp. Broadbent, P.S., year 1857; 3 P., 1858; 2 P., 1859; P.Z., 1860-1 (2 years).

Founded Fidelity Chapter, 623 Lodge, and Installed 1 P., 14th March, 1858.

During these years Exalted many brethren, and Installed Principals in Cheshire, and in Manchester, and Bacup.

Knight Templar.—Proposed by Sir Knt. Richard Wood in the Jerusalem Encampment, and Installed 11th July, 1856. C. of L., 1857; Registrar, 1858-9; 2nd Cap., 1860; 1st Cap., 1861. Installed E.C. in succession to Sir Knt. Wm. Romaine Callender, 16th Dec., 1862, by Sir Knt. W. H. Wright. In 1863 revived the degrees of Knight of Malta, and as Em. Prior, received many Members; also the degree of Templar Priest, Rosy Cross, &c., but this gave offence to certain Members.

After collecting the necessary documents wrote the history of the Encampment in 1869, and 1,000 copies were printed by the P.G. Conclave, which passed a vote of thanks. The Conclave or Preceptory also passed a vote of thanks, 13th December, 1869, and on the 14th March, 1870, the then E.C. presented a very handsome Sword in the name of the Prince Demetrius Rhodocanakis, a Scottish Templar then present.

Joined the Love and Friendship, Stockport, and Installed as its E.C., 20th March, 1861, and during the year 1861 and 2, Installed many Knights. Prov. Grand Chancellor of Cheshire under Sir Knt. W. C. Cruttenden, 17th April, 1861. Drew up a Code of Laws and received the thanks of the P.G.C., 23rd April, 1862; these now lost.

Appointed Grand Constable or Mareschal of England, by G. M. Stuart, May, 1864, and in that year visited America, West Indies, and Cuba.

Hon. Member of St. Amand Enc., Worcester, 15th June, 1870, and, pro-forma, Ordre du Temple; Templar Priest, 1st to 7th Pillar, 1865-71.

Joined the Antiquity Encampment, Bath, and all its high-grades in the Scottish and Mizraim Rites, 27th January, 1871.

Hon. Member of the various degrees, and of the Grand Cross of St. John, in the Royal Kent Priory, Newcastle, 16th December, 1895.

To give even a list of the several Rites in which Bro. John Yarker has held, and still holds high position, would take up more space than we can afford. He is a Member of many Learned Societies, is an Author of considerable repute, and has been the recipient of several Civil Decorations.

THE APRON.

By Bro. Wyndham M. Boyd.

The chief business of Freemasonry is to direct and guide the judgment to the practice of virtue, for it is chiefly by being able to distinguish clearly between *Right and Wrong* that depravity is avoided, and purity of mind cherished and insured.

In advancing through the different degrees of the Order, this object is enforced upon us by references to those symbols in which the knowledge of the Art lies embedded.

Among them we find the investiture with the Masonic Apron, a badge of high antiquity and unequalled honour, as also a bond of friendship.

Of high antiquity it most certainly is. We read in the Book of the Levitical law, of the investiture of Aaron, when he was consecrated as High Priest; and we know from the writings of many ancient authors, that the ceremony of investiture constituted an important part of all the mysteries of the days long since gone by.

Amongst the Greeks, the garment of initiation was *white*, because, says Cicero, white is a colour most acceptable to the gods. This robe was accounted sacred, and a never failing source of protection in every emergency.

Being and Shadow

One day in the spring of 1905 W.B. Yeats, at the time resident in London, opened his mail and found himself perusing the following letter:

Coole Park,
Gort.
Co: Galway
Saturday

Dear Willie,

Arrived here and found a wire for you from Dunlop asking if they could do *Shadowy Waters* (have mislaid it for the moment) but I suppose you have seen Mrs. Emery by this. It is cold and rainy here. It is a gr. nuisance being shut out of the theatre for so many days before *Kincora*...

Yours ever,

A.G.

★

The initials with which this letter was signed are recognizable as those of Yeats's friend and patroness Augusta Lady Gregory, and although the letter is undated the reference to her own drama *Kincora*, produced in Dublin in March 1905, indicates that it was written shortly before or perhaps at the beginning of that month.

What the letter makes apparent is that D.N. Dunlop, supposing that Yeats was in Ireland at the time, had sent to him at Lady Gregory's home in Coole a telegram with a request that his play *The Shadowy Waters* be produced at the forthcoming Theosophical Congress, hosted in London by the Society's British Section.

Mrs Emery, also mentioned in the letter, was an actress better known by her stage-name of Florence Farr. A close friend of Yeats, she was a theosophist—whereas he had resigned from the Theosophical Society in 1890.

★

The Shadowy Waters is a work with a long and complex history, deriving from imaginative visions formed by Yeats during his adolescence in 1883, and originally set in the form of a poem.

Some perceptive comments on this work and its author were made by his friend George William Russell, known as AE, in the very first chapter of his autobiographical study *Song and its Fountains* (1932):

> ... There grew up the vivid sense of a being within me seeking a foothold in the body, trying through intuition and vision to create wisdom there,

through poetry to impose its own music upon speech, through action trying to create an ideal society, and I was smitten with penitence because I had so often been opaque to these impulses and in league with satyr or faun in myself for so many of my days.

Yet this meditation, which discovers another being within us, unites us to it in some fashion, and in retrospect we seem to have lived two lives, a life of the outer and a life of the inner being. I do not know indeed, but I suspect of that inner being that it is not one but many; and I think we might find, if our meditation was profound, that the spokes of our egoity ran out to some celestial zodiac. And as in dream the ego is dramatically sundered into this and that and thou and I, so in the totality of our nature are all beings men have imagined, Aeons, Archangels, Dominions and Powers, the hosts of darkness and the hosts of light; and we may bring this multitudinous being to a unity and be the inheritors of its myriad wisdom.

As I tracked the congregation of desires in myself back to their fountains in childhood, I began to see too in those with whom I was intimate that each had some governing myth, that somewhere in their past, from the first bridal of soul and body, a germinal mood had been born which had grown to dominion over everything else in them. I can see today the central idea I surmised forty-five years ago in the young Yeats grown to full self-consciousness. I remember as a boy showing the poet some drawings I had made, and wondering why he was interested most of all in a drawing of a man on a hill-top, a man amazed at his own shadow cast gigantically on a mountain mist; for this drawing had not seemed to me the best. But I soon found his imagination was dominated by his own myth of a duality in self, of being and shadow. I think somewhere in his boyhood, at the first contact of inner and outer, he became aware of a duality in his being. In his earlier poetry one could pick out twenty lines showing how he was obsessed with this myth, how frequently and almost unconsciously the same idea recurs.

> Never with us where the wild fowl chases
> Its shadow along in the evening blaze.

or

> A parrot swaying on a tree
> Rages at its own image in the enamelled sea.

or

> Nought they heard for they were ever listening
> The dewdrops to the sound of their own dropping.

or

> The boy who chases lizards in the grass,
> The sage who deep in central Nature delves,

> The preacher waiting the ill hour to pass,
> All these are souls who fly from their dread selves.

> There are many such images in his early poetry. Then the mood ceased to haunt individual lines, but became the subject of a long poem. I remember, when we were walking along Leinster Road, his telling me the first conception of *The Shadowy Waters*. His hero, a world-weary wanderer, was trying to escape from himself. He captures a galley in the waters. There is a beautiful woman among the captives. He thinks through love he may have this escape, and casts a magical spell on Dectora; but he finds the love so created only echoes back to him the imaginations of his own heart of which he is already weary, and in the original form of the poem he unrolled the spell, and went alone seeking for the world of the immortals. I think when the poet came himself to love, the thought of that lonely journey to the Everliving grew alien to his mood; and the poem was altered, losing, as I think, the noble imaginative logic of its first conception, for in the new ending the love won by the magic art becomes an immortal love. Concealed or unconcealed, this preoccupation of the poet with that dualism of being and shadow is in much that he has written...

The Shadowy Waters was also elaborated into a play, which however did not reach printed form until 1900. Even then it had been revised several times before receiving its one previous public performance, in Dublin in 1904, at a time when Yeats himself was absent on a lecture-tour in America.

The Significance of the Congress

The March issue of *The Vâhan* stated:

> The Music and Dramatic Committees are very anxious to know exactly what help is available for the various functions at the Congress next July, so that their plans can be formulated accordingly.
>
> Will all those who can sing in a choir (or solos), play any musical instrument, or possess histrionic ability, kindly communicate at once with Mr. Bertram G. Theobald, The Hawthorns, Hornsey Lane, N.

The Dramatic Committee comprised Bertram Theobald, Florence Farr, D.N. Dunlop and I. Hooper.

In the April issue of *The Vâhan* arrangements for the Congress were the chief subject, filling several pages. The issue opened with an article by Dunlop on 'The Significance of the Congress':

In ancient days the mystic dwelt solitary. Shut in a monastery cell, he contemplated the divine, or chose some lonely and remote cave for his meditations. He walked the white roads of India, revered and aloof. Even when not specifically dedicated, even when pursuing the common avocations of life, the mystic still dwelt to a large extent solitary.

The little flame of mystical thought burns down through the ages: flashes in some quiet soul into clear light, or makes a smouldering way through the heavy lumber of useless dogma and unwise asceticism. The wisdom that illuminated Plato appears without intermediary in the cell of the nun at Norwich, and in the cobbler's shop at Görlitz; and today, when the crust of the creeds is breaking all around us, when the 'fierce misery' of materialism is no longer to be borne, this flame of ancient fires, freed from the formulae that choked its progress, is spreading from mind to mind, awakening the sense of kinship that lies deep below race and religion, giving impetus to new manifestations in the domain of art, and in the great sphere of practical endeavour supplying the courage of unfailing hope. For 'what a man has taken in by contemplation', says Eckhart, 'he pours out by love'.

It has been left to the present day to conceive of an International Congress of Mystics. Was ever Congress planned before that included such close kinship of spirit, together with such multifarious variety of its expression? For here would come the practical mystic, drawing out of his mysticism a consuming energy for the bettering, say, of the conditions of labour—the organizer of peasant industries and handicrafts. Here would come the mystics who, like Plotinus, desired to reach the good through the beautiful; and we should study their meaning through the pictures they have made, and listen to their plays, and their poetry, and their music. The scientific mystic would be there too, who objects to all beauty as irrelevant and, while allowing the overwhelming importance of imagination in science, would yet pursue his way in this strange land by laborious testing of every step.

Yet underlying all these divers opinions and varying methods, there would be a deep, immaculate sympathy, an instinctive bond, so that the gain of this free interchange of thought and experience would be as unique as it was incalculable.

Mysticism, to keep sane, must remain in contact with human things: strange punishments await those who cut themselves off from human weal, says Browning. History warns us of the dangerous paths into which mysticism may stray; efforts for others, however directed, and human companionship are its natural safeguards. Thus, from every point of view—from many points of view not touched upon here—such a Congress should be ardently welcomed, for it comes to bring life, and to bring it more fully.

After a plea for financial support, there followed details of 'The Dramatic Performance':

All members of the Society who contemplate attending the International Congress of the Society in July are specially requested to note the following announcement by the Dramatic Committee.

A performance of *The Shrine of the Golden Hawk*, an Egyptian play by Miss Florence Farr (a member of the Society) and *The Shadowy Waters*, a play in verse by W.B. Yeats, will be given at the Royal Court Theatre, on Saturday evening, July 5th, under the direction of Miss Farr.

In order to avoid disappointment, it is absolutely necessary that all applications for seats should be received not later than May 1st. They will be dealt with in order of priority.

Financial considerations make it impracticable that tickets should be given gratis, but the prices have been made as moderate as possible, viz:

			s	d
Stalls	(numbered and reserved)		5	0
Dress Circle	,,	,,	4	0
Upper Circle	,,	,,	3	0
Pit Stalls	,,	,,	2	6
Gallery	(unreserved)		1	0

Boxes will be £2 2s. and £3 3s. according to position.

Tickets are now ready, and all applications should be addressed forthwith to the Secretary of the Dramatic Committee, Mr. Bertram G. Theobald, The Hawthorns, Hornsey Lane, London, N.

Cordial Greetings

During the time when preparatory arrangements for the Congress were being made in Britain, Rudolf Steiner, on another lecture tour, wrote a letter to Marie von Sivers:

On the journey Freiburg-Karlsruhe.

My love, tomorrow you'll have to celebrate Lotus Day. In spite of what you've brought up against yourself recently, I know that what you're doing is good. This time too you'll find what's right, from your own fine being. I've just been writing down the enclosed thoughts in the railway carriage. Perhaps you can read them out. I'd like them to be seen as a kind of letter to the Besant Lodge. Afterwards you'll also be able to say some words about Annie Besant, H.P.B.'s greatest pupil.

Everything went well yesterday in Freiburg. But there was no end of questions. The Stuttgart people didn't find it right to have me this evening and have therefore cancelled. So I left Freiburg at 11.41 and arrive in Munich at 10 p.m. From 9 this evening onwards I had a talk with the

Freiburg people. How they stand in respect to the foundation we'll talk over on Thursday.

For now just heartfelt greetings, yours Rudolf

The train is rocking so much that it's quite impossible to write any further, and the compartment is full of the most prattling people.

Tomorrow I'm sending to London a greetings telegram for Lotus Day.

The thoughts of theosophists all around the world are united today in the name of H.P. Blavatsky. Even today only a few realize what our spiritual progress owes to the foundress of our movement, and those few only know it very incompletely. The profound wisdom lying in the *Secret Doctrine* unveils itself to a human being only slowly and gradually. Whenever a person has once again made a little progress on a path which to *every* human eye is lost from sight in dizzying heights, he discovers in this book new secrets to which formerly he was unable to find a right relation. So H.P.B. belongs to the individuals for whom respect grows as one's own development progresses. One has to experience this growth of appreciation for her if one wants to approach H.P.B. in the right manner. One must *learn* to honour her in the right way.

To begin with, people perhaps still ask about the externals of her life, in order to win a connection to her. But there comes a point where everything external recedes before the feeling of H.P.B.'s immeasurably important spiritual mission, and her great task in the present spiritual movement. If something of this spiritual mission is then truly observed, the result of such knowledge will be to recognize one's own position in relation to our great trail-blazer. One then learns to realize that someone with a mission of this kind will necessarily be subject to misunderstanding and even slander. Things of this kind belong to the sacrifices life demands of such a person.

H.P.B.'s work fell into a time when the materialistic way of thought and belief was engaged on an immense expansion. Science, life and everything else seemed to supply materialism with the bricks for a gigantic edifice. In such a time a personality who brought to mankind renewed awareness of the truth of a spiritual world had to be a complex one. It must be remembered that truth itself is not a sole determining factor of how it is transmitted to mankind, but human beings themselves play a part. To convey the truth to a materialistic way of thought and belief in such a manner that it might be understood was infinitely difficult. How H.P.B. had to appear was prescribed by the degree of understanding which the time was able to bring towards her. When an object is struck by a hammer, the hammer is not the only determinant of what happens. Glass shatters, but lead is beaten into a thin sheet. When a great spirit gives out great things, it still has to pour its gifts into the vessels held out by the recipients.—With

H.P.B. the distinction between the outer form and the inner value of her great gifts will only gradually be learned.—It was precisely the spirit of the times in which she had to fulfil her mission which made it an infinitely difficult one. That she took on this mission all the same shows the greatness of her personality to those who can recognize it. But it shows also the extent of this personality's readiness to make sacrifices connected with her mission.

There have been many objections to the genuineness etc. of H.P.B.'s achievements, especially from scholarly or would-be scholarly sources. Doubts have been expressed as to whether her revelations really came from the sources she described. But is that important? Is it not important in the first instance to understand the work and recognize its inner value? Many people, if they only studied it in sufficient depth, would have to admit that they could learn things at the source of H.P.B.'s writings which they would nowhere else find revealed. She is at any rate the intermediary. Does it really show great cleverness to receive from the hand of such a person truths about the highest concerns, and then start carping about the credibility of this same person in much lesser matters? Nothing would contribute more to turning H.P.B. into a miracle than if learned objections against her were to have any basis. Let us just visualize what conclusions would have to be drawn in such a situation. Assume someone doubts that the Stanzas of Dzyan are 'genuine'; this has been done and many still do it. That ancient source given by H.P.B. does not then exist. Very well; let us examine this position. One may argue about genuineness, but to argue about truth is preposterous. Everyone can convince themselves of the truth if they proceed towards it along the right paths. People who do this increasingly recognize in these stanzas the most profound truths. It is in fact the case that every advance in a person's own knowledge convinces him more of their limitless depth, and lets him see with increasing clarity things which even advanced knowledge can only *surmise*.—To one who really knows this, the accusation that H.P.B. invented the Stanzas of Dzyan loses all significance. The strangest thing would have to have happened: this woman discovers the most profound truths, and then makes up a silly fairy tale about their provenance. The conclusion is so implausible that it can only prove the illogicality of H.P.B.'s opponents; it certainly cannot be taken seriously by people with real understanding.

The accusers of this person, if they achieve even a moderate degree of understanding for her spiritual power and the nature of her mission, will find their whole house of cards collapsing. From the heap of accusations, misjudgements, etc. there will also gradually emerge an image of the woman who at an important time put her capacities into the service of a movement whose value will remain unrecognized only by those who have as yet no understanding for it.

We theosophists, however, will always observe Lotus Day as a day of remembrance for the moment H.P.B. left the physical plane, a day of celebration and also of love and gratitude towards the foundress of our movement. To those of us who do understand, H.P.B. is not an authority in the ordinary sense, for she does not need such authority. The correct, true authority which is her due will come about through knowledge of her work. A feeling of authority need only be *demanded* where it does not arise voluntarily. We respect and love H.P.B. because we would be unfaithful to the truth we have recognized were we to behave any differently. And we feel this respect of ours itself becoming an unfolding lotus flower. The more we ourselves grow in knowledge, the larger and more widespread the flower's petals will be. H.P.B.'s work provides a ladder which supports us in this growth. So gratitude must always be the response streaming from our hearts if Lotus Day is to be a living image of our growing knowledge.

⋆

The Theosophical Review later recounted:

White Lotus Day was celebrated at the Headquarters in May. There was the accustomed generous display of flowers, and H.P.B.'s portrait showed in the midst, the strong, undaunted face making a curious contrast with its environment of delicate blossoms. Mr. Keightley occupied the chair, and the Section rooms were filled with members. Following the custom of these gatherings, initiated at H.P.B.'s request, there were readings from *The Song Celestial* and *The Light of Asia*, by Mrs. Hooper and Miss Lloyd. Mr. Mead said that although the ground had doubtless been prepared by spiritualists, the Theosophical Society had done more than any other movement to destroy the fear of death. They had met to commemorate, not to commiserate. Our White Lotus Day should be a day of cheerfulness. Why was 8th May named 'White Lotus Day'? Surely it was because the lotus flower reminds us of the blossoming of a life-flower—the unfolding of the inner self from the mud and water of the lower nature.

The Rev. Dr. Currie followed the thought suggested by Mr. Mead. This day was to remind us of the success, the culmination, the glory of those whom we have known in their previous humanity. They have moved forward. Those who have passed on are endeavouring to lift the world to the place where they stand. Just as the Church when it thinks of its saints does not think of them as they were in their ordinary lives, but thinks of them in their glorified state, so do we remember our brothers who have passed on to the work unseen.

Mr. Keightley closed the meeting with some stirring words. We were engaged in weaving a web of comradeship. There were many threads in this weaving. Struggle and strife had their place; blood and iron were not necessarily excluded. Our ties must be of strength, not wholly of gentleness.

> By such means only could be welded the great instrument which was to be formed for the raising of humanity.

To this account *The Vâhan* added a further little detail:

> The following telegram from Germany was received at the meeting:— Cordial greetings for Lotus Day. Rudolf Steiner and Munich Lodge.

A Word of Advice

This story related in the present book will now turn to the figure of Clifford Bax. An account of his early years is found in his autobiographical *Inland Far* (1925), from which several passages will be quoted.

Clifford Bax was born in 1886, as the younger son of Alfred Bax. Alhough the family was English, he had a German connection through his uncle, Ernest Belfort Bax, who had studied German philosophy and in 1880–1 worked as a journalist in Berlin, meeting Eduard von Hartmann and later translating into English Kant's *Prologomena.* Ernest Bax went on to write a number of books, such as *German Society at the Close of the Middle Ages* (1894) and *The Peasants' War in Germany* (1899), and in collaboration with William Morris *Socialism, its Growth and Outcome.*

On reaching the age of puberty in the year 1900 Clifford's consciousness began to be stimulated by reading poetry:

> When first a boy realizes the power and beauty of words, and sees dimly before him the immaterial universe of literature, it is as though a new dimension were added to his existence.

In the spring of 1902, his elder brother, the musician Arnold, came across a copy of *The Wanderings of Oisin* (1889) by W.B. Yeats. Arnold Bax too wrote an autobiography, *Farewell, my Youth* (1943), where he described what Yeats's poetry meant to him:

> His was the key that opened the gate of the Celtic wonderland to my wide-eyed youth, and his the finger that pointed to the magic mountain whence I was to dig all that may be of value in my own art. Neither does my debt to that great man end there, for his poetry has always meant more to me than all the music of the centuries. All the days of my life I bless his name.

Arnold must have communicated this discovery to his younger brother Clifford, who reminisced with similar enthusiasm:

> When I was sixteen I discovered a living poet who had something to say upon the matters that excited me. Not only did he write about saints and fairy-women and the old gods of Ireland but, as I gathered from his 'Notes',

he assumed their reality, claiming that by vision a man might look upon beings of a super-physical order. Within a year I could have repeated every line that this poet had published. So completely was I enchanted by the iridescent loveliness of *The Wanderings of Oisin* and *The Wind among the Reeds* that I acclaimed the Celts as the chosen people, and regarded the English as a race of boors and boobies.

On leaving school at the age of 18, Clifford began to study art in London. And in the summer of 1904, his first year as an art student, while attending a performance in a London theatre he chanced during an interval to be conversing with the poet and editor Ernest Rhys. Rhys astounded him by offering to provide an introduction to meet Yeats himself on the following Wednesday.

Bax related:

Throughout that Wednesday I went about London in a dazed delight. 'I am a person who is going to meet Yeats'—that was the rhythm to which I worked at my drawing, and swallowed my exiguous lunch, and battled with humdrum humanity for a seat on the five-o'clock bus.

When at length I reached Woburn Buildings, a young man answered my knock: for Yeats had devised a rule that each visitor should go down to admit the next. I followed my guide up some narrow and ancient stairs. He brought me into a dusky room. It looked like a square black cave. A candle, stout as a lamp-post, threw an exaggerated chiaroscuro about the scene. Dim figures moved in its shadows; a dozen faces blinked and shone in its light. Yeats greeted me with a courtesy that would have befitted the palace at Urbino ... I was introduced to Lady Gregory ... For the rest, though I stayed for an hour, I remember little that can be recorded ...

When I had risen to go, I paused for a moment to look closely at four or five little pictures, visionary in subject and like enamel in the brilliance of their colour. 'I did them,' said Yeats, 'when I was at the art-school in Dublin.'[7] Then taking me to the top of the stairs, he observed: 'You are a young man. May I give you a word of advice?' 'Of course,' I answered. 'Always write,' he said, 'about what you know.'

Under the stars of a summer night I walked through the London streets. I felt like a man who has been upon a mountain. Perhaps I had touched the mood in which an Athenian youngster existed within an hour or two of his initiation at Eleusis. But 'write about what you know,' he had said: and in that sense I had known nothing. I wanted to write about nymphs in a forest, magicians who brewed philtres in lonely towers, or moon-worshippers riding ecstatically by the fringe of the sea. What did I 'know'? ... It might be that I should have to abandon painting ... I began to wonder how best I might equip myself as an author. 'The man who reads only one language,' I reflected, 'must always remain a parochial writer. Suppose I ... persuade my parents to send me to France and Germany? They may refuse, but at least I can put my project before them . . . A writer can get no outward help except by acquiring modern languages.'

During the winter my parents arranged that in the following May I should go to Munich, and enter the art-school there, and learn as much German as I could. Before this, however, I went with two cousins for a few weeks to Switzerland. In my bag I packed a *History of the Rosicrucians* . . .

Between his holiday in Switzerland and his sojourn in Munich, both of which took place in 1905, Bax discovered the poetry of AE.

AE presented, more definitely than Yeats, a picture of life as the adventure of a spiritual and immortal being. As I read his poems, my nebulous aspirations took form, and my hesitant thoughts expanded joyously. I had some acquaintance with the ideas of modern theosophy, but they had seemed to me cold and mechanical. Three ideas form the basis of theosophy—that behind the multitudinous and impermanent universe there is one eternal consciousness, that men live many lives upon Earth, and that the actions of one life determine the events of the next. AE invested this view with colour and reality. He wrote of it as though it were not a theory, but a fact. What though I might demand

in the mad pride of intellectuality,

that every philosophical proposition must be logically proven? What though I vaunted that I could prove any proposition to which I then subscribed? Poetry, like the sea, undermined those intellectual sand-castles; and when I read

Oh light our life in Babylon, but Babylon has taken wings,
While we are in the calm and proud possession of eternal things,

I might still have adduced objections to the theory of reincarnation, but something within me had apprehended that it is true. Something within me, again—some pioneer fragment of personality—had perceived that sexual love is among the least of love's manifestations, and I rejoiced that AE had written of

Love, a pearl-grey dawn in darkness, breathing peace without desire.

I recognized, as I read his heretical poems, that a kiss may sever and not unite two lovers, that

if from the light we part,
Only with clay we cling unto the clay.

Here, I found, was a poet who could enter a veritable world of vision—not a subjective state of fantasy, but as-it-were another dimension; to whom the beings of that incorporeal world were more lovely, wiser, and more significant than those whom he saw through his eyes; and who made that region of gods and angels in some way seem more desirable, and nearer to reality, than the London and the Munich that I knew.

For me, in Munich, wonder thronged upon wonder...

Bax's time in Munich in the summer of 1905 was spent studying German, and socializing in artistic, musical and theatrical circles. His account describes especially some young friends whom he made there, '... and every day, with the fire and faith of inexperience, we debated the riddles of life and the aims of art and the ideas of theosophy...'

One description of his friends is followed with this paragraph:

As I walked back to the lower part of the town, I felt a new lightness of heart. They had thawed the metaphysical snow with which the last years had covered my thoughts. The remembered sense of them glowed within me. Had I known them before? I wondered. And somehow the city of Munich appeared like the ghost of another city, and elusive sensations of life in a Greek colony during the later years of the Roman Empire drifted across my consciousness, like perfumes from far away.

Prosecuted with Vigour

In the period immediately preceding the Theosophical Congress in London, reports of work in the German Section given to readers of *The Theosophical Review* reached a level of detail never again repeated.

Here is what was contained in the May issue:

Theosophical work in Germany is being prosecuted with vigour, the branches displaying increased vitality. New Branches have been established in Berlin and Stuttgart, being in each case the second to be formed in these towns. Dr. Steiner is travelling continually from place to place, many of the branches having invited him to give courses of lectures at regular intervals, and he visits smaller centres en route. A lecture that is in great demand is 'Goethe and Theosophy'. Twenty years' study of Goethe and several years' work among the archives of Weimar, after the death of the poet's last surviving grandson, have made Dr. Steiner a well-qualified interpreter of Goethe's genius. Much theosophic teaching is to be extracted from this great writer, not only in essence, but even in minute detail, expressed in occult scientific terminology, and only covered with a light veil, easily uplifted by a cunning hand. Thus we find it in the fairy-tales, 'The Green Snake and the Beautiful Lily', 'Paris', and 'The Fair Melusina', and it gives, of course, the key to the second part of *Faust.* This initiation in occultism gives Goethe his profound knowledge of natural science, and makes him, in a way, the predecessor of Lamarck and Darwin, and a pioneer in the true science of colour. So that Dr. Steiner's lectures with their abundant proofs naturally strike those who would be otherwise antagonistic to Theosophy.

This is a year of festivities in commemoration of our other great national poet, and all over Germany lectures are given upon Schiller. Those delivered by Dr. Steiner in the Freie Hochschule disclose the deep sources of spirituality that fed the genius of this great man, whose art cannot be separated from the great problems of life and soul, fate and freedom, and whose real worth can only be appreciated by a humanity freed from the shackles of materialism.

In fact one has only to strike the rock of German thought in the past to cause the streams of spirituality to well up. But in the present day, the drought of materialism has almost dried up the source.

An attempt is being made to form a group of university students for the study of Theosophy. It is hoped that a series of lectures to be delivered in May and June by Dr. Steiner and dealing with the following subjects: 'Die theologische Fakultät und die Theosophie', 'Die juristische Fakultät und die Theosophie', 'Die medizinische Fakultät und die Theosophie', and 'Die philosophische Fakultät und die Theosophie', may help towards its realization.

In Munich a small nucleus has begun its work, and in Jena Dr. Steiner has been asked to lecture before the Philosophical Society.

The June issue added a further paragraph:

All over Germany there have been festivities in honour of Friedrich Schiller. The hundredth anniversary of his death has brought a revival of enthusiasm and of gratitude to the poet over which we theosophists have every reason to rejoice. For Schiller is amongst German poets the one whose work can least of all be separated from his conception of the universe and of the spirit underlying it. This is the reason why in our materialistic age he came to be a little underestimated by those who fancied they had outgrown his thought. This tendency, however, now seems to have made way for better insight, and all over Germany the thinker Schiller has received the warmest acknowledgement. Theosophists have participated in this commemoration. In Hanover, Düsseldorf, Cassel, Berlin and Nuremberg Dr. Steiner has lectured upon Schiller in the light of theosophy, and the lectures given by him in the course of the winter in the Freie Hochschule have been, at the request of many, issued in book form under the title of *Schiller und unser Zeitalter*.

During all this time Rudolf Steiner was also continuing his lectures on the 'ancient wisdom'. There were three in May and another one in June.

With Us Here Today

The time of the Theosophical Congress in London was now getting closer. All kinds of preparations were under way, as seen from a letter written by W.B. Yeats, who had just celebrated his fortieth birthday, to his wealthy American patron John Quinn:

18 Woburn Buildings
June 29, 1905

My dear Quinn,

I have been meaning for some days to write and thank you for your large share in the gift of the Chaucer. The book is a very great pleasure, coming as it does just when I am setting out to read Chaucer. I have always thought it the most beautiful of all printed books. The pictures have already raised images of stage scenery, and one of them has made an important change in the setting of the Deirdre play. I am busy rehearsing *The Shadowy Waters* for a performance under Mrs. Emery's direction at the Court Theatre. The theosophists are paying the piper as it is to be one of the entertainments at their annual convention. Of course, this does not identify me with them in any way. They get the play from me as might any other manager. Mrs. Emery is to be Dectora, and will play it very beautifully. The Forgael is Farquharson who made a success as Herod in Wilde's *Salome*. He is over-emphatic and shoots his voice up and down the scale in a perfectly accidental way. I long to get him by myself and make him speak on a note day after day till he has got rid of accidental variety, but I cannot do that as he is playing for nothing, or for the advertisement's sake, and would think he knew as much about it as I do. I have consented to the performance not because I think it a play I would like to be judged by, or because I think it can be well played, but because it gives me a chance of making a lot of changes and testing them. I missed the rehearsals of the play or most of them when it was done at first, through being in America, and besides I did not know as much then as I do now. I want to get it right for Brett's edition and for an edition here which I am trying to arrange.

Yours ever,

W.B. Yeats

★

Some five years before, in September 1900, Yeats had prefaced the text of *The Shadowy Waters* with a poem, printed in italics.

I walked among the seven woods of Coole,
Shan-walla, where a willow-bordered pond
Gathers the wild duck from the winter dawn;

Shady Kyle-dortha; sunnier Kyle-na-no,
Where many hundred squirrels are as happy
As though they had been hidden by green boughs
Where old age cannot find them; Pairc-na-lee,
Where hazel and ash and privet blind the paths;
Dim Pairc-na-carraig, where the wild bees fling
Their sudden fragrances on the green air;
Dim Pairc-na-tarav, where enchanted eyes
Have seen immortal, mild, proud shadows walk;
Dim Inchy wood, that hides badger and fox
And marten-cat, and borders that old wood
Wise Biddy Early called the wicked wood:
Seven odours, seven murmurs, seven woods.
I had not eyes like those enchanted eyes,
Yet dreamed that beings happier than men
Moved round me in the shadows, and at night
My dreams were cloven by voices and by fires;
And the images I have woven in this story
Of Forgael and Dectora and the empty waters
Moved round me in the voices and the fires,
And more I may not write of, for they that cleave
The waters of sleep can make a chattering tongue
Heavy like stone, their wisdom being half silence.
How shall I name you, immortal, mild, proud shadows?
I only know that all we know comes from you,
And that you come from Eden on flying feet.
Is Eden far away, or do you hide
From human thought, as hares and mice and coneys
That run before the reaping-hook and lie
In the last ridge of the barley? Do our woods
And winds and ponds cover more quiet woods,
More shining winds, more star-glimmering ponds?
Is Eden out of time and out of space?
And do you gather about us when pale light
Shining on water and fallen among leaves,
And winds blowing from flowers, and whirr of feathers
And the green quiet, have uplifted the heart?

I have made this poem for you, that men may read it
Before they read of Forgael and Dectora,
As men in the old times, before the harps began,
Poured out wine for the high invisible ones.

⋆

On 5 July, Rudolf Steiner once again set out on the long journey from Berlin to London. This time he was among a whole contingent of 13 German members coming to attend the Theosophical Congress.

The main part of the Congress took place in the Empress Rooms, which were situated on the north side of Kensington High Street, west of Kensington Palace Avenue. Most of the German party were allocated convenient lodgings, for Mathilde Scholl recorded that

> Dr. Steiner, Fräulein von Sivers, Countess Kalckreuth, Fräulein Stinde, Herr Kiem, Herr and Frau Dr. Peipers and myself all stayed in the hotel where most of the Congress events were also taking place, the Kensington hotel.

The reference is to the Royal Palace Hotel, an enormous Victorian building right beside the Empress Rooms, which overlooked Kensington Gardens[8] in general and the Palace in particular. It was finally demolished in 1965.

*

The Congress programme was a handsome little booklet of 48 pages, which opened with this item:

> Foreword
>
> When Olive Schreiner drew her Hunter after Truth, she drew him as a man who was to experience the uttermost loneliness. The market-places, where the birds uttered their luring cries, were humming with the crowds of men; but the heights over which the Hunter followed the gleaming wings of Truth were desolate and almost inaccessible, and death came in an awful solitude that had for sole consolation the dropping through the air of one feather—one single feather, the guerdon for a lifetime of painful pursuit.
>
> Was Olive Schreiner right in picturing for us a loneliness so terrible and so extreme? Were there no other Hunters that had attempted these heights before, and whose aspirations, soaring above their poor efforts, had reached even the peaks, and made them companionable? In other lands, were there no other climbers, strange of aspect and of speech, whose sympathy yet knew how to bridge space, and encourage by the kinship of a like quest? In the furthest solitudes of soul, indeed, no human companionship avails; but there a few of us may learn to find a deeper communion for which there are no words.
>
> Perhaps that Hunter of Olive Schreiner's did not die after all; perhaps he is with us here today—with us, the other Hunters of all nations, the swift and the slow, the intrepid and the faltering, whose feet are upon the same path, and whose faces are set towards the same goal. Perhaps he has brought with him that feather as earnest that the wings that have haunted our inner

vision are no mere phantasms of dream, those wings of the stork, and wings of the white merle, and wings of the dove.

Here, if he should come, he shall find companionship—companionship of aim, companionship of thought. Other explorers will show him different ways towards the goal—lines that they have traced from sacred writings, and short cuts that they have struck out for themselves. Investigators will bring the light they find in religions, in philosophies, in sciences, to bear upon the obscurities of the path. And the artist will shape into visible form the unbodied aspirations of which we are only dimly aware. Amid the symbols that surround him, unfamiliar though they may be—the Rose, the Cup, and the Flame—the Hunter shall feel himself at home; for the spirit that vitalizes them is all one. The music he hears will give voice to subtle emotions.

But, most of all, the Hunter shall feel the companionship of brotherhood—a brotherhood universal, comprehending every race and every creed. For those who are assembled here are not merely brothers-in-arms, united for the same struggle towards the same goal; brotherhood is with them more than a fact; it is the foundation of all religion. And so this Congress would aim at being a centre not only of thought, but of action; its members would walk not only among the seven woods of Coole, companioned by 'immortal, mild, proud shadows', but in the dark places of the earth, where evil things have sway. The Hunter to whom a single feather has floated down—the seekers who have followed the Bird with however stumbling feet—would point out its gleaming wings to those who have fallen far behind, and lie, in hopeless apathy, on the barren road.

D.N.D.

★

D.N. Dunlop was not the only theosophist attending this Congress who later played a part in Steiner's connection to Britain. The programme, which lists all members of the various Congress committees, includes in 'The Travelling Committee' the name of the London-resident Swiss, Max Gysi.

During this 1905 visit Steiner had a meeting with Gysi in a well-known vegetarian restaurant called 'The Apple Tree', situated in a quite different part of London from where the Congress was taking place, namely, on London Wall, to the north of the City. The buildings of the whole area where this street lies were later obliterated by some of the heaviest German bombing of London—in the Holy Nights towards the end of December 1939.

Gysi had formed a habit of meeting regularly at the restaurant with his friend George Coleman.[9] On this occasion, however, Coleman did not come; and the next day Gysi greeted him with the words:

You missed an historic occasion yesterday—Rudolf Steiner was here at 'The Apple Tree', and it was in your chair that he was sitting when he gave me permission to translate him into English!'

The Stirring of the Roots

Although the Congress proper did not begin until Saturday, 8 July, the first associated event took place in the afternoon of Thursday the 6th. This was the opening of the Exhibition of Arts and Crafts at 1, Tor Gardens, off Campden Hill, also in Kensington.

An account of the exhibition appeared in *The Theosophical Review*:

> Before visiting the Exhibition of Arts and Crafts I tried to define to myself what manner of subject and conception went to the making of a mystical picture.
>
> There is the picture of allegory and symbolism, the picture, for instance, that embodies some stupendous conception of the Deity under material form; William Blake's *Elohim Creating Adam*, or Watts's brooding figure of *The All-Pervading*.
>
> Then there is the picture which seems to make the material world a veil through which to look at the light behind. The Breton mystic, Henri le Sidaner, has painted many scenes of village streets, and passing along the empty ways we feel an exquisite companionship, which may be the ideal of gentle and simple life, or may be something more. Many of the Impressionists insist on the fluidity of matter, and their pictures should rightly be regarded as mystical.
>
> Then there is the picture of vision—the picture that would portray what the bodily eye has never seen. It is sometimes difficult to distinguish such a picture from the picture of imagination, but the appeal is different. Blake again is the one supreme exponent of this class—his *Nativity*, his *Morning Stars Singing Together*, and many other of his inspirations, reveal wonders and beauties far beyond the common reach.
>
> In the Exhibition shown at No. 1, Tor Gardens, there are pictures which belong to each of these groups. The Exhibition is interesting, but it is very small, and cannot in any way be considered as representative of mystical thought. There is aspiration, but little real achievement; we are aware rather of the stirring of the roots, than of the blossoming of the flower. The work that is most noteworthy is contributed by members of the Guild of St. Mâhel, and by George Russell (AE).
>
> The Guild of St. Mâhel, or Michael, the victor over the powers of darkness, is the name of a fellowship resident at Bushey, which possesses this striking distinction—the work of all its members is anonymous. It

contributes some very curious drawings done with charcoal on thick-ribbed paper, and reproduced by photogravure or lithograph. The effect is singular, and lends itself to interesting experiments in light and shade. In most of the drawings the whole surface is dark—in one a shrouded and kneeling figure emerges out of the gloom—*The Darkness Deepens, Lord, Abide With Me.* In *The Shadows* a partial light is introduced with excellent intention, where a chaos of titanic figures shuts out the Sun from a groping votary. But perhaps the most successful example of this method is an unnamed picture representing a crowned figure holding a flame whence stars arise. The figure is only vaguely seen against a dark mountain beyond, so that the whole attention is concentrated on the light of the flame and the stars. Another visionary figure is done in pastel of green and blue and violet, and represents a mysterious fairy apparition, almost without form, making a fairy ring. The colouring is strange, and suggestive of dim fairylands.

These pictures would all seem to fall under the head of allegory, with the exception of the last, which is rather a picture of dream.

There are some pictures shown that belong distinctively to the Impressionist School of landscape, and notably AE's *The Happy Valley*, but as these are not more mystical than the ordinary work of this school, they need not detain us. AE's *Changeling*, however, with its blue mountain, its purple-tinted foreground, and its mystery-charged atmosphere, is artistically the most successful of his exhibits.

AE has also given us some pictures that may be regarded as pictures of vision—*A Dragon Came Out of the Elf Mound, The Horn Blowers of the Sidhe*, and *The Thrones of the Sidhe*. In all these pictures the vehicle is imperfect to express the magnitude of the conception—you feel that the artist was a little dazed by the vision, and that his hand moved spasmodically. Only in *The Thrones of the Sidhe* does the whole grandeur of the idea struggle through. These crowned and titanic figures, seated on thrones that vanish afar into a blue mist, have vigour and glamour, and the memory of them lives.

The other pictures are some of them disappointing, poor both in thought and execution; and in the ambitious *Amour des Ames*, the floating bodies, though interpenetrated with light, are still too aggressively material to suggest a spiritualized love. One picture, however, must not pass unnoticed, *And the Twelve were Called to a Supper, and Behind Each Hung a Shadow*, by Miss Ethel Hastings. This represents monks in white praying in a church—and behind each monk hangs the dim whiteness of a crucified man. The picture is most impressive, and full of poetry and mystical meaning.

It has not seemed necessary to enter upon the crafts exhibited—the art jewellery, the pottery, the furniture, the book-binding, the hand-painted scarves, or the woven fabrics; because, lovely as were many of these, they did not differ from similar work shown in other exhibitions. Much exquisite success has recently been achieved in all these departments—and indeed perfection itself is not wholly unattainable here. The perfect chest, the perfect jar, even the perfect ornament, may reach accomplishment; but the perfect picture is beyond attainment. Our poor efforts to express the inexpressible have, however, profound pathos, and sometimes deep power of suggestion; and we venture to think that a large and wider exhibition of mystical pictures, embracing all times and all countries, would be of abiding value to the student.

Ian Mör

★

AE had first joined the Theosophical Society in 1889. Six years later, in the major split of 1895, he and all other Irish theosophists followed the lead of W.Q. Judge and the American Section. But Judge died in 1896 and although at first AE welcomed his successor Katherine Tingley, in 1898 he became disillusioned with her, resigned from the Society and re-established in Dublin the original Hermetic Society.

In 1899 his friend D.N. Dunlop also became disillusioned with Tingley, later in the year moved to London, and by 1901 realigned himself with the Theosophical Society (Adyar). In 1904, perhaps encouraged by Dunlop, AE also rejoined this body.

At about the time when he took this step, AE's artistic activities also took on a new burst of life.[10] His ideals in this sphere were once expressed in a letter to John Quinn:

> What I want to do is to paint landscape as if it had no other existence than as an imagination of the Divine Mind, to paint man as if his life overflowed into that imagination, and to paint the Sidhe as mingling with his life; indeed, the unity of God and man and Nature in one single being—an almost impossible idea to convey in paint.

The programme of the 1905 London Congress shows on the 'Arts and Crafts Committee' AE's Dublin friend H.F. Norman. Norman must have made the arrangements for AE's pictures to be brought over to England, though the idea of having them in the Exhibition at all might also be attributable to Dunlop. In his autobiographical *Struggling with Paint* (1956) the latter's artist son R.O. Dunlop recorded that

> Every year, almost without fail, my father journeyed to Dublin during Horse Show Week, and often came back with one of George Russell's canvases in his baggage. Our house and his office were decorated with these paintings by AE. I well remember them—vague yet romantic, full of rich overtones. I even remember some of the titles of those pictures—*Dancing on the Shore of Innisfree*, *The Little Creatures who live under Ben Bulben*, *The Spirits in the Rag-Weed*...

★

The name Ian Mör standing under the article about the Exhibition of Arts and Crafts is that of an old man who features in several tales by Fiona Macleod. Both the content and style of the article are sufficient to indicate that the name was being used as a pseudonym by Dunlop.

Fiona Macleod was itself the pseudonym of another Scotsman, William Sharp. Sharp first visited Dublin in the summer of 1897, shortly before Dunlop's departure to America in the autumn of that year.

Listed in the programme of the 1905 London Congress is also a 'Reception Committee' on which is found the name of Fiona's wife—another future anthroposophist—Mrs. W. Sharp, who became her husband's biographer. The Sharps indeed lived in Kensington, not far from the venue of the Congress.

One of Fiona's last poems, 'The Secret Gate', was first published in the August issue of *The Theosophical Review,* immediately following the article by Ian Mör. This was the only poem he ever contributed to that journal.

The Secrets of the World Invisible

The opening of the Arts and Crafts Exhibition was followed by other events. At 8.30 in the evening of the same day, Thursday, 6 July, Annie Besant gave in the Small Queen's Hall a lecture to the Blavatsky Lodge on 'Qualifications for Discipleship'.

During the Annual General Meeting of the German Section in the following October, Rudolf Steiner recalled the occasion:

> No one present will contradict me when I say that we spent together a time of deep theosophical life. One could take away a permanent impression both for heart and spirit. Seldom have I heard Mrs. Besant speaking in such an inward, heartfelt manner. I became convinced—not from any personality cult, but from the spiritual content of this personality—that what leads to higher spiritual worlds is living within her. Fifteen years ago I stood before H.P. Blavatsky as before a riddle, but through Mrs. Besant I have even found the way to H.P. Blavatsky.

★

On the Friday morning, there was a meeting of the Council of European Federations, followed in the afternoon by the Convention of the British Section. Its 'Report of Proceedings' gave an account:

> The Convention assembled for its business meeting on Friday, July 7th, at 2.30 p.m., in the Empress Rooms, High Street, Kensington, W. Owing to

the fact that the International Congress held its meetings during the following days, the business meeting was the only one arranged in connection with the Convention of the British Section, and at this a very large number of members from foreign countries were present, Holland, France, Belgium, and Germany being especially well represented, while members also attended from Scandinavia, Italy, Russia, Hungary, Spain, and Switzerland, and from America, India, and other distant parts.

Mr. Sinnett, the Vice-President of the Society, took the chair.

Mr Keightley and Mr. Glass were elected Secretaries of the Convention.

The roll-call of branches was read, and the representatives present responded, as shown in the following list . . .

Among many others present, the list shows D.N. Dunlop, representing the Battersea Lodge. His statement about Steiner in the autobiographical sketch written shortly before his death in 1935 may be recalled:

I had seen him about the year 1906 in a crowded Convention of the Theosophical Society and his face and bearing made an unforgettable impression. But his books and lectures were at that time unavailable in English . . .

Representatives of the various foreign countries gave short addresses recorded in the Convention's 'Report of Proceedings':

Dr. Steiner, on behalf of the German Section, remarked that it was, so to speak, the child of the British, which had always taken the greatest care of it and had given it much help. They would continue to work on in spite of all obstacles.

Mr. Keightley proposed and Major Lauder seconded, that the General Secretary be instructed to send the greetings of the British Section in reply to those received.

Carried unanimously.

⋆

In the evening, after an organ recital in the Queen's Hall, Annie Besant gave a public lecture on 'The Work of the Theosophical Society in the World'. *The Vâhan* reported that

Every seat in the Large Queen's Hall was occupied, and as Mrs. Besant's beautifully modulated voice thrilled through the great auditorium, the eager listeners sat as entranced, except when, stirred by some outburst of eloquence, silence gave way to thundering applause.

One passage in Besant's lecture—later published as a pamphlet—referred to the artistic elements in the Congress:

Turn from science to art. What has Theosophy to say to art? Theosophy declares that art ought not be the mere presentment of what is called the real, the objective, but the representation to us of the unseen, the ideal. There is much art greatly admired that simply gives us Nature back on a canvas, often very beautiful as a reproduction of Nature, but still, I think, not the highest type that art ought to be able to reach. For surely the artist, who is the man of genius, should make real to us the unseen behind the veil, should be able to show the hidden and make it manifest for the instruction of all men. And I see in art that tendency is coming; I see in art the ideal is being searched for more than it has been since religion dropped the pencil and the brush, and I look for a day in which again a mighty faith in the invisible will make an art worthy to be called an art. Only, instead of pictures of madonnas and children, we shall have some of the secrets of the world invisible throwing themselves on the canvas of the painter, or living in the music of the musician. The progress of art must be towards the ideal, to see more as beautiful and not less, and to show that even in things people think unbeautiful there lies a true beauty for the eye that can see . . .

Hail to the Day-Star!

The Congress proper opened at 10.30 on the morning of the next day, Saturday, 8 July, with a choir singing an ode, 'Hail to the Day-Star', specially composed for the occasion by L. Nightingale Duddington:

Hail! Thou Day-Star from on high,
Hail! Creation's Destiny!
Lowly sod and lofty soul
Upward climbing to their goal,
Lowly soul and lowly sod
Soaring surely to their God:
Hail! Thou Day-Star from on high,
Hail! Creation's Destiny.

Hail! Thou Universal Life,
Ruling o'er all forms of strife,
Soul of Nature, Fount of Light,
Shrine of Morning, veiled in Night,
Word of Power and Voice of Love,
Bid Earth's Mâya mountains move!
Hail! Thou Universal Life,
Pulse of God, beyond man's strife.

Hail! Thou Day-Star from on high,
Beauty, Wisdom, Destiny:
Let thy mystic waters flow,
Let thy hidden glory glow,
Till each life hath conscious part
In Love's ever-burning Heart.
Hail! Thou Day-Star from on high,
Beauty, Wisdom, Destiny!

This was followed with 'God is a Spirit' from William Sterndale Bennett's oratorio *The Woman of Samaria*.

Bertram Keightley gave an address of welcome, and then Annie Besant a presidential address. It will be seen that one passage in her address, later published in the Congress *Transactions*, particularly caught Rudolf Steiner's attention. In this passage Besant developed in more detail the artistic themes touched on during her public lecture the evening before:

Pass to the work that may be done by our movement in the great realm of art. Here it seems to me that Theosophy gives back to the artist a world that for a long time he has lost; opens up to him possibilities among non-human races of beings, whole series of new subjects for his pencil and paint-brush, and reveals to him new secrets of colour. For there are colours of the astral world rarer, finer, and more exquisite than in the physical; beings subtler and more beautiful. As art and philosophy join hands, these more delicate and exquisite beings will come down into the prepared sensitive brain of the artist, and to the vision of the sculptor, as new forms of beauty. So that there Theosophy may open a new gateway in the art world, and lead it onwards into realms unconquered yet.

I have come across cases of that among theosophical workers. I need only point to some of the strange effects of colour in the paintings of George Russell. You will find some in the Arts and Crafts Exhibition. See how he has struck new notes of colour, new combinations of colour.

I may tell you of another theosophist, a sculptor in Rome, who in his wonderful study 'The Dead Christ', now lying in the Memorial Chapel, Paris, built over the remains of those who perished in the fire at the charity bazaar, obtained the face which he has represented in a dream or vision, and carved it into living marble. The noteworthy fact is that this face is the face of the living Christ, and not the face of Christ symbolized in ordinary art. So that the theosophist, in following art, may bring to the knowledge of the world fresh forms of truth and beauty which the artist without that inspiration will be unable to achieve.

So too it seems to me that in the allied art of sound—music—the future lies along the lines of theosophic thought and ideals. Does not that great master of mystic music, Wagner, draw from mystic sources the most exquisite of dreams? I can, from time to time, amid his melodies, discern combinations found on the astral but not on the physical, showing that his ear had caught the sound of astral melodies, and materialized them into strains of physical harmony . . .

★

After this address, representatives from 13 different nations each gave short speeches in their own languages. In a lecture at Dornach on 27 November 1918, Steiner recalled:

> When first taking part in a Congress of the 'Theosophical Society' in London, I tried to put forward a certain point of view. I gave a quite short speech. It was the time when the 'Entente Cordiale' had just been concluded, and everything was standing under the impress of this recently agreed 'Entente Cordiale'. I tried to characterize the fact that in the movement represented by the Theosophical Society it cannot be a matter of diffusing something as theosophical wisdom from any random centre, but merely that the latest trends, the world over, should have a common meeting-place, a kind of focal point. And I then ended with these words: 'If we build upon the spirit, if we are seeking spiritual community in a really concrete, positive fashion, so that the spirit manifested here and there is drawn towards a common centre of the Theosophical Society, we shall then be building a different "Entente Cordiale".'
>
> I spoke in London about this other 'Entente Cordiale'. It was the first speech I had given in the Theosophical Society,[11] and I was speaking quite deliberately about this other 'Entente Cordiale'. Mrs. Besant indeed declared, to use her own expression—she would always add a few pompous remarks to everything that was said—that the 'German speaker' had spoken very elegantly. But the sympathies of the audience were not at all on my side. What I had said was drowned in a flood of words and clichés, while what the audience wanted was more in the line of the Buddhist dandy Jinarajadasa. At the time this too seemed to me symptomatic. Having spoken about something which was after all of historical significance for the world, of the other 'Entente Cordiale', I sat down again. The Buddhist dandy Jinarajadasa then came tripping and staggering down from his place somewhat higher up—I have to say 'tripping' in order to describe the matter quite exactly—stamping with his walking-stick on the floor. He gained the sympathies of the audience, but the impression I retained was like a torrent of words.

This judgement was doubtless perfectly sound. It may, however, be legitimate to observe that for most of the audience present, Steiner's own German would have been scarcely more comprehensible than Jinarajadasa's Singalese.

1. *Helena Petrovna Blavatsky (The famous "Sphinx" photograph, taken by Enrico Resta in his London studio on the 8th of January 1889, and autographed by him after Blavatsky's death in 1891)*

2. *Annie Besant*

3. *A.P. Sinnett*

4. *Bertram Keightley*

5. *G.R.S. Mead*

6. The British Westinghouse Publishing Department. Standing, left, D.N. Dunlop, right, Arthur Warren

7. *AE at his easel*

SECOND ANNUAL CONGRESS OF THE FEDERATION OF EUROPEAN SECTIONS OF THE THEOSOPHICAL SOCIETY

The Empress Rooms

KENSINGTON, LONDON.

JULY the 6th, 7th, 8th, 9th, 10th & 11th,

1905.

8. Title-page of London Congress programme

9. W.B. Yeats in 1905

10. Rudolf Steiner in 1905

11. Fiona Macleod

★

In the afternoon there was a meeting, reported in the Congress *Transactions*, about 'Theosophical Teaching for Children'. Those taking part in the extensive discussions included that former teacher Mathilde Scholl, as well as that parent of three children D.N. Dunlop.

Strange Enough

On Saturday evening came the theatrical performances, held in the Royal Court Theatre at the east end of Sloane Square in Chelsea. This was the original nineteenth-century theatre, destroyed by German bombing in 1940. The present theatre bearing an identical name was subsequently erected on the same site.

The Congress programme briefly explained the argument of *The Shrine of the Golden Hawk*, written by Florence Farr in conjunction with Olivia Shakespear. A more extensive note for *The Shadowy Waters* by W.B. Yeats made incidental allusions to Vedanta philosophy, Irish folklore and Swedenborg, and ended:

> The poet's endeavour has been to create for a few people who love symbol a play that will be more a ritual than a play, and leave upon the mind an impression like that of tapestry, where the forms only half reveal themselves amid the shadowy folds.

Also included was a programme of music by Handel, Dolmetsch, Rameau, Boccherini, Tchaikovsky and Grieg, for performance by a string orchestra.

★

The evening's plays were described in a lengthy column appearing a couple of days later in *The Times*:

> An invitation to the theatre from the Annual Congress of the Federation of European Sections of the Theosophical Society is almost a promise to the critic that he shall have no room for his usual complaint of the trite and the obvious; and the promise was fulfilled on Saturday evening. There was the audience, to begin with. It was a little uncanny to sit down, uninitiated, in the presence of who could tell what occult power and wisdom; and even the familiar figure of Mr. W.B. Yeats, prominent in a box, was not completely reassuring. It may be chronicled, however, that nothing uncanny happened in the body of the house; the strangeness—or most of it—was all on the stage, and there it was strange enough. The first of the two plays

performed, *The Shrine of the Golden Hawk*, by Florence Farr and O. Shakespear, took us to a cave in Mount Bakhua, near Sinai, in 4000 B.C. The great magician, Gebuel, has made a talisman in the form of a golden hawk (a small metal plaque in a frame) to the god Heru, in the hope of overcoming the power of Zozer, King of Egypt, a wise and beneficent monarch who has turned to good the various schemes for the destruction of Egypt which Gebuel's two attendant priests devised. Gebuel hangs up in Heru's shrine his talisman, and staggers out again, half blinded by the glory of the god. Then, in the guise of a seeker after wisdom, comes Nectoris, daughter of Zozer. If she can take this talisman from Gebuel her father has promised that she and her daughters shall reign over Egypt for ever. She has already the serpent-wisdom, and so impresses Gebuel with her desire for the hawk-wisdom that he leaves her alone to serve a novitiate by watching the shrine. So far from needing lessons from Gebuel, she is his superior; she has so far subjugated her flesh to her spirit (our language, we know, is crude, but it seems to express, in commmon terms, the authors' meaning) that heartened by the Ka (a very charming 'other self', who danced beautifully in strange raiment), she can face the god in his shrine, dance and sing in the rays of his glory, and take the talisman. Having won it and hung it round her neck, she persuades Gebuel, who returns surprised not to find her shrivelled, to follow her into Egypt, and bring the shrine with him. On the 'inner meaning' of it all we dare not touch. Seen from the outside, the little piece had the charm of strangeness and solemnity; to watch it was like watching the rites of a religion one does not understand.

In the second piece, *The Shadowy Waters* by W.B. Yeats, we were in a strange country still, somewhere in dreamland. We saw the deck of a strangely rigged ship, with a harp hanging on the mast; on the ship strangely dressed pirates, and beyond it a strange waste of waters. Forgael, the captain, lies asleep under the mast. His men are plotting to kill him, when he wakes and talks strangely. A Norse galley heaves in sight. It is taken by the pirates, who make it tow their own vessel, and bring aboard the Queen. All the others in the galley have been killed, and Forgael, standing alone on his vessel, has talked strangely as he watches their souls fly by him like grey birds. The Queen, promised by Forgael to his lieutenant, Aibric, tries to bribe the pirates to kill Forgael and bear her home. When they attack him he takes the harp from the mast; it turns to fire as he plays it, and the pirates slink away on to the captured galley. The spell of it sends the Queen to sleep. When she wakes she loves Forgael. They talk very strangely about love; the Queen unfastens the rope that binds the two ships together, and she and Forgael sail away alone.

That is what we saw—the plot, if we may use so inappropriate a word. What did it all mean? What was the ship, the sea, the harp, the love that was talked of so strangely? Who was Forgael and who the Queen? What were all the strange things mentioned—the red hound that fled from a silver arrow, the deer chased over the waters by white hounds, the Fool whom Forgael had seen in the forest, the quest the Fool sent him on? You may translate the symbols as you please or can. If you are up in your Vedas, your Irish folklore and your Swedenborg you will find in the acted play as much of the philosophy of love and life as the traffic of the stage gives you time to take in. If you are not, well, there is a strange ship on a waste of waters, a harp that flames, a Queen with wonderful red hair, a handsome Forgael, and some characteristic and beautiful poetry. You are probably better off so. It spoils a dream to worry about what it means.

The Search After a Far Ideal

Another assessment was given by D.N. Dunlop in an article appearing in *The Theosophical Review*:

The two plays produced at the Theosophical Congress have both for subject the search after a far ideal, and the crisis of each play deals with the final consummation of the search. The Egyptian princess in Miss Florence Farr's *Shrine of the Golden Hawk* goes to the cave of the metal-working fire magician to seek the wisdom that is beyond 'the sombre knowledge born of time', and reaches a union with the godhead so complete that it becomes identification. 'I look unharmed upon the face of the god because his eyes are my eyes, his power is my power, his spirit is my spirit. Whoso is made one with the gods makes their holy places desolate and himself becomes their sanctuary.' Forgael wanders over the shadowy waters in quest of the ideal love, the imperishable essence, 'the soft fire that shall burn time when times have ebbed away'.

And yet, though the themes of the plays are so closely akin, the atmosphere and treatment are startlingly different. *The Shadowy Waters*—one of the most exquisite things Mr. Yeats has done—pales in dramatic effect before Miss Farr's *Golden Hawk*, an interesting and original piece of work, written in strong and simple language, but wanting in the high inspiration and insight of the poet.

The reason is not far to seek. The dim charm of the shadowy waters depends upon their remoteness. They are farther away from our imagination than that magician's cave of years ago, and in his published book Mr. Yeats has prepared our consciousness to receive their vague lights by a proem haunted by strange and elusive beauty. No prelude of music can carry us so near the silent borders of these waters as the poet's own questioning of 'the immortal mild proud shadows':

And do you gather about us when pale lights
Shining on water and fallen among leaves,
And winds blowing from flowers, and whirr of feathers,
And the green quiet have uplifted the heart?

So the mind is made ready for the coming of mystery and inspiration: and though on the stage the deck of the galley with the great sail, and the blue waste of sky and water beyond, was a beautiful scene, yet no stage-craft could ever represent that dreamplace that Ailbric describes:

Our sail has passed
Even the wandering islands of the gods,
And hears the roar of streams where, druids say,
Time and the world and all things dwindle out.

So, too, they who float among these shadows, Forgael and Dectora, are too far removed from the everyday world to bear the impersonation of the full-blooded men and women who enact them. They are dreams, aspirations, desires, hardly materialized into human shape.

All that in Mr. Yeats's play is lovely indefinition becomes in Miss Farr's *Golden Hawk* concrete symbol.

She does not use an obscure symbolism, such as accompanies *The Shadowy Waters*, but builds her whole play on one definite image. The golden hawk represents the godhead, and possession of the enamelled pectoral of the hawk involves identification with the deity. This is clearly set forth—'Divine hawk, hovering in the blue light, dark as lapis lazuli! Immovable eye, in the midst of the wheel of the stars, send down a ray from thy splendid solitude upon this hawk—image of thee, thou solitary one, resting upon the empty air.' The plot therefore concentrates upon a line of action—the entry into the shrine and the taking of the pectoral. In *The Shadowy Waters* there is no action of this kind, but only dimly apprehended soul-changes. The moments that move in the reading—the flight of the souls as birds, and the playing of the harp without touch of hands—lose of necessity their thrill of mystery, because the stage is for the bodily eye, and these are for the inner understanding.

So it comes about that the lesser play has the greater power of stage-illusion—an illusion that is helped by the historic basis of thought and fact, and also by the admirable acting of Miss Italia Conti as the princess. Miss Farr has introduced with great skill much of the lore of the far past. Thus the character of the Ka, or other self of the princess, is excellently conceived. The Ka, Miss Farr tells us, is frequently represented on ancient frescoes as a smaller figure walking behind the king or queen. She also points out in an interesting note that the final ecstasy of the princess is quoted thought for thought from the earliest Egyptian texts that have yet been discovered. The invocations of the golden hawk and its prayers—its emotions of fear and ecstasy—are immediately apprehended and appropriate to the setting; while many of the most beautiful lines in *The Shadowy Waters*, spoken on the stage, are like wandering words that have lost themselves out of another region and die away in scarce-comprehended music.

In Sweet Music

The Congress continued on the morning of Sunday, 9 July, with a choice of 13 departmental lectures.

Rudolf Steiner probably attended the one by G.R.S. Mead, the theme of which was later described by him as 'interesting'. In the Congress programme, indeed, the title was formulated with such length that it might have been that of some German book: 'The Myth of Man in the Mysteries: A Hellenistic Source of Gnosticism Underlying Successive Jewish and Christian Overworkings, as Discovered by the Analysis of a Patristic Refutation of a Gnostic System'.

★

The afternoon was taken up by a *conversazione*, starting with madrigal renderings of Shelley's poem 'Music, when soft voices die' and the anonymous 'The Silver Swan', followed by two solos for cello by Hugo Becker, and a couple of German songs set to music by Brahms.

After an interval came further songs in Dutch, Flemish and Latin, and the piano prelude from Grieg's *Holberg Suite*. The programme ended with choral versions of three stanzas from Tennyson's *In Memoriam*, and of the song 'Orpheus with his Lute' from Shakespeare's *King Henry VIII*—an item for which Rudolf Steiner later drew a eurythmic form, for performance in violet robe and lilac veil:

Orpheus, with his lute made trees
And the mountain tops that freeze
Bow themselves when he did sing;
To his music, plants and flowers
Ever sprung, as sun and showers
There had made a lasting spring;
Every thing that heard him play,
Even the billows of the sea,
Hung their heads and then lay by.
In sweet music is such art,
Killing care and grief of heart,
Fall asleep or, hearing, die.

★

In the early evening there was another choice of twelve different lectures. Steiner may perhaps have attended the one on 'Astrology' by Alan Leo, who had given, he later reported, 'highly valuable information'.

The day was concluded with a lecture by Annie Besant on 'The Conditions of Occult Research'.

★

At 10.30 in the morning of Monday, 10 July came a further choice of 14 different lectures, including the one given by Steiner. It bore the German title 'Die Occulte Grundlage in Goethes Schaffen' ('The Occult Basis of Goethe's Creativity').

In her memoirs Mathilde Scholl recalled:

> Apart from Mrs. Besant, speakers were only allowed a limited time. So too Dr. Steiner. One of the gentlemen who were making sure the stipulated time was not exceeded sat beside him. He had a clock in his hand, and made signs that it was time to bring the talk to a close. This seemed to me very uncalled-for in regard to Dr. Steiner, who already then had of all speakers the most valuable things to say. In my opinion he should have been allowed unlimited time in which to lecture.
>
> I asked Dr. Steiner afterwards whether he would be prepared to give a longer lecture for our benefit. There were a number of other members besides myself who greatly desired to hear more from him. We wanted to arrange a special lecture by Dr. Steiner to be announced by the Congress Committee, and use a room in the hotel. Dr. Steiner asked us to refrain from this, but stated that for any members who were specially interested he was ready to give a special lecture in one of our private rooms. We chose the room of Fräulein Stinde and Countess Kalckreuth, and had there a stirring lecture on 'The Sin against the Holy Ghost'.

★

At 3.00 in the afternoon the official programme continued with a concert.

This began with a rendering of a dozen poems from William Blake's *Songs of Innocence*, set to music for four solo voices with piano accompaniment.

The first was sung by a tenor:

> Piping down the valleys wild,
> Piping songs of pleasant glee,
> On a cloud I saw a child,
> And he, laughing, said to me:

'Pipe a song about a Lamb!'
So I piped with merry cheer.
'Piper, pipe that song again.'
So I piped; he wept to hear.

'Drop thy pipe, thy happy pipe;
Sing thy songs of happy cheer!'
So I sang the same again,
While he wept with joy to hear.

'Piper, sit thee down and write
In a book that all may read.'
So he vanished from my sight;
And I plucked a hollow reed,

And I made a rural pen,
And I stained the water clear;
And I wrote my happy songs
Every child may joy to hear.

After an interval came the chaconne from the last movement of Bach's D minor suite for violin, various songs set to music by Glück, Spöhr, and several Dutch composers, and finally a Brahms quartet.

At 5.00 p.m. there took place a further meeting of the Council of European Federations.

At 8.00 in the evening, after some announcements by the secretary, G.R.S. Mead gave a lecture on 'The Gnosis of the Past and Theosophy of the Present', followed by a closing address from Annie Besant. A final *conversazione* at 9.15 p.m. brought the Congress as such to an end, though the Exhibition of Arts and Crafts remained open for a further day.

There seems to be no record as to whether Steiner stayed on in England a little longer, or returned to Germany at once. His next known whereabouts is in Berlin, but only on the 19th of the month, nine days after the end of the Congress.

With a Fresh Eye

W.B. Yeats had already returned to Ireland by about 11 July. From here he wrote in quick succession a spate of letters to Florence Farr about the performance of his play, and its effect on himself as regards the text.

Coole Park,
July 15

My dear Mrs. Emery:

I meant to write yesterday, for I have been afraid that I did not seem sympathetic enough about your accident. I had hoped to have some talk with you on Monday evening, or to get out to you on Tuesday and so learn how you were, but both became impossible. Please write and tell me, for it must have been a great shock and I have been afraid that you may have been more shaken than you thought. I brought the book of Johnson's poems with me that I might send it to you. Shall I send it while you are away from home or wait till you get there again? One of the covers has got a little soiled, on the journey as I think, but I shall get a vellum cover put on it when I get to London again. I am at work on *Shadowy Waters*, changing it greatly, getting rid of needless symbols, making the people answer each other, and making the groundwork simple and intelligible. I find I am enriching the poetry and the character of Forgael greatly in the process. I shall make it as strong a play as *The King's Threshold* and perhaps put it in rehearsal in Dublin again. I am surprised at the badness of a great deal of it in its present form. The performance has enabled me to see the play with a fresh eye. It has been like looking at a picture reversed as in a looking glass. When you went, Maclagan, after another thrust at Narcissus (who 'spoke the lines about holding a woman in his arms as if he were murmuring of his experiences in Piccadilly'), said 'it was worth while having the play done, well worth while, because Mrs. Emery was a delight. It was a great joy to hear her.' Or some such words, even stronger words I think, which I cannot remember. There is a good notice of the play—very well written—in *Today* where Synge and myself and Shaw are enumerated with Ibsen and Maeterlinck as great dramatists. You are commended for 'fine imaginative power' and after you, Jules Shaw is praised with evident enthusiasm for his Aibric. Lady Cromarty was I think really delighted with the Psaltery and when she comes here, which she does in August, I shall find if she could arrange for the Duchess of Sutherland to hear you.

Yours ever,

W.B. Yeats

★

Coole Park,
Wednesday

My dear Mrs. Emery,

I am glad you are so much better—you spoke to the Psaltery very well but I was afraid—not because you did not hide it—that you were worse than you pretended to me. I am changing *The Shadowy Waters* on almost every page and hope you will be able to play the new version—I think if you investigated however you would find that 'the beautiful poetry' was whenever you spoke and 'the irrelevant drama' whenever Farquharson did. The play as it was came into existence after years of strained emotion, of living upon tip-toe, and is only right in its highest moments—the logic and circumstances are all wrong.

I have sent the Johnson.

Yours always,

W.B. Yeats

*

Coole Park,
Friday night

My dear Mrs. Emery,

I was about to write to you today, when I was sent off to catch perch for some Catholics who are to dine here tonight—a fast day. Is not that a medieval way of getting a meal? I stayed out till I had caught six fish, enough for a dinner—and now the mail has gone. I am very sorry about your hurts—I am afraid you must have suffered a great deal and I think it was heroic of you to play the Psaltery that night. I am making a new play of *The Shadowy Waters*. It is strong simple drama now, and has actually more poetical passages. I wish you could get a good verse speaker who is a man. I wish I could persuade you that you are mistaken over Farquharson. I have been taken in in the same way more than once myself. When a young man has even a slight vulgar element—and it is not slight in Farquharson—one thinks it will leave him as he grows older. I thought that about Le Gallienne—who had what seemed like genius. It never leaves them, but when the enthusiasm of youth is over it gets much stronger till finally all else has left them. I have never known an exception. Apart from all else Farquharson is a man who always requires to be explained. Mrs. Shakespear for instance thought his manner was personally very offensive to you off the stage. He is really impossible as an artist. I had to use the greatest self-control over myself all through those rehearsals. Only my fear of making things difficult for you kept me quiet.

I want you to try and get me Paget's model for *The Shadowy Waters* scene. I will probably work out a scene for Dublin, which could be used by you if necessary. Our stage is nearly as big as the Court. I can probably get that harp made too—we have carpenters and so on of our own now. We are in all likelihood to have a large scene dock next door this winter and will be able to work things out very perfectly. You must come over some time and see our scenery, when the show comes off.

Yours ever,

W.B. Yeats

To Strengthen His Heart and Feeling

After returning to Germany, Rudolf Steiner for his part gave a detailed account of the Congress in a long letter to Günther Wagner:

Berlin,
23rd July 1905

Dear Herr Wagner,

Although it is only today that am I in a position to tell you this in a letter, I share with all my soul in the blow of destiny which has befallen you and your dear wife. My thoughts are often with you. We theosophists must also be ready to accept hard blows of destiny in a different way from how we could before our theosophical time. Our love and involvement cannot actually ever diminish through theosophical life, and our understanding and power to bear up become greater. Through theosophy we cannot lose out on anything, but we gain a great deal. We would be losing out if our feelings, which belong to life's greatest beauties, could to the slightest extent fade away. So I know what you are feeling, with your noble and glorious love. But I also recognize you as a really genuine theosophist. I know that to you karmic relationships are no mere doctrine: you live within them. Just now I would like to exchange some thoughts. One so easily takes everything fitted into our karma like the link of a chain to be karmic indebtedness. This is by no means always the case. True as it is that karma is a real all-embracing law, so is it also true that karmic blows can just be inserted initially into our causal relationship. Blows which befall us are not always compensation for the past. They are often first entries in our life's account, only finding in the future their corresponding balance. Just as a businessman has to make entries on one side for a first time, so is it too with the entries of our karmic account book. In recent weeks these thoughts were always passing through my mind when they turned to your lovely residence in Lugano; and within my field of vision the thoughts took on a character which shows that thoughts correspond to reality. You understand me, dear Herr Wagner, by the fact that I am writing to you about this inner experience—for such it is. Perhaps according to your own judgement you are also taking as reality what is such for me.

I am very much longing to greet both of you once again. And I hope it can be soon.

The celebrations at the London Congress, which unfortunately you could not attend, are over. In the nature of the case these kinds of festivities, even when arranged by theosophists, cannot go much beyond externalities. But I think a person who had a will to do so might nonetheless have taken things away to strengthen his heart and feelings. Mrs. Besant, for instance, gave lectures which were full of spiritual impulses. Firstly on Thursday before the Congress, about H.P.B.'s 'discipleship', in consideration of various attacks recently aimed at the Theosophical Movement's great foundress. It seems to me very important that this spiritually so advanced Mrs. Besant ever again refers so uncompromisingly to how H.P.B. was not for her like any other outstanding person who had entered her life but—as she said—the 'light-bringer' per se. She said, for instance, that spots should not be denied; but these spots are like sunspots, only existing where the Sun exists. I felt here the inner experiences of my own recent life really echoing on. The further progress I make, I must say, the more do I come to know what immeasurable power radiates out from H.P.B., and realize that I still have a great deal to learn in order to understand just a little part of H.P.B.'s work and creativity.

On Friday there was the Convention of the British Section. From what came up there, you will be interested that Bertram Keightley has resigned from the post of General Secretary, and in his place has come forward Miss Kate Spink. Keightley is first going for four months to India, and then wants to devote himself to the Theosophical Movement in a way made possible by his release from the official duties of General Secretary.

At this time there was also opened a Congress 'Arts and Crafts Exhibition'. Beside less significant things there were also some remarkable ones. I would just like to mention certain symbolic pictures by a painter, Russell. He tries to characterize inner processes of soul by symbolic colours in the picture (stars, rays etc., emanating from figures, symbolic representations in paint of outer natural objects, etc.). I can in fact say that nowhere was I able to grant to the pictures any real astral vision, and yet I was satisfied by the effort being made by a certainly talented painter.

The Congress itself was opened with a speech by Mrs. Besant on Saturday morning. It was one of those great panoramas of the aims and tasks of the Theosophical Movement which Mrs. Besant gives on such occasions. You will be interested that she mentioned a work by the Italian sculptor Ezechiel, a 'Christ', which she said in certain respects fits to the idea she herself has, as a theosophist, of the individuality of Christ. You will also be interested that Mrs. Besant referred on this occasion to Richard Wagner, in whose tones were audible the secrets of the astral world. For me this was particularly remarkable, as in the spring I was giving four lectures to Berlin theosophists on the spiritual substance of Richard Wagner's creativity.

Mrs. Besant's opening speech was followed by something of unusual diversity. Representatives of all theosophical regions of Europe gave addresses of greeting in their own tongue. So short speeches could be heard one after another in the following languages: Dutch, Swedish, French, German, Spanish, Italian, Finnish, Russian, Hungarian, Indian.

On the previous evening Mrs. Besant had given a comprehensive and wide-ranging speech to some thousand people in the Queen's Hall about the 'Work of Theosophy in the World'. She referred to the need of our time for a spiritual deepening, and to the work to be done for this in the most various parts of the world. Everything she said had a beautiful greatness and broad-mindedness.

On Saturday evening followed a theatrical performance. The good will prevailing there has perhaps to be especially taken into account. But particularly on that evening it became clear to me that the idea of these congresses will have to be extended if they are completely to fulfil their aim. What should be considered is not what the congress participants themselves find enjoyable, but above all that they find theosophical nourishment for their souls. They can then take this back to their theosophical homes for the greater benefit of those who are unable to take part in these communal gatherings. Congresses should be a centre of spiritual life from which currents then proceed everywhere into the world.

There followed the departmental sessions. I am sending you a programme by parcel post, from which you can at least gather the titles of the varied riches on offer. I would also particularly like to mention the lecture on Sunday by Mrs. Besant about methods of occult investigation. That was something quite magnificent. She set out in a most beautiful way the requirements for occult research in the West, and what has to be observed in such research by way of precautions etc.

On Monday morning I myself gave a small contribution on the 'Occult Foundations in Goethe's Creativity'.

I am sorry not to be able to write in greater detail; but lying before me are the final pieces of work for *Lucifer* Nos. 24 and 25. You can appreciate that this is preoccupying me. I have to publish these spiritual-scientific things which *Lucifer* has recently brought. The mere responsibility weighs heavily upon me. I must consider every line and turn of phrase ten times over, in order to reproduce as exactly as possible the spiritual content I have to give, which is itself transmitted to me in a quite different form and language.

Heartfelt greetings to your dear wife and yourself from

Your ever faithful

Dr. Rudolf Steiner

Motzstrasse 17,
Berlin W

Theosophical Nourishment

There are three matters which are particularly notable in Rudolf Steiner's letter to Günther Wagner.

Firstly, the admiration which Steiner even now retained for Annie

Besant. In his autobiography he formed a final appreciation of this complex woman by placing both her and the Theosophical Society in the context of the evolution of human consciousness:

> By reason of certain qualities Mrs. Besant was for me an interesting personality. I noticed that she had a certain right to speak about the spiritual world from her own inner experiences. An inner approach of the soul to the spiritual world—that she did have. Only later did this become overgrown by the external aims she set herself.
>
> I was necessarily interested in a person who spoke about the spirit from out of the spirit.—But on the other hand I was strictly of opinion that in our time insight into the spiritual world must live in the consciousness soul.
>
> I perceived mankind's ancient spiritual knowledge. It had a dreamlike character. Man beheld pictures in which the spiritual world was revealed. But these pictures were not evolved by any desire for knowledge in full clarity of mind. They arose within the soul, given from the cosmos like dreams. In the Middle Ages this ancient spiritual knowledge was lost. Man came into possession of the consciousness soul. He no longer has cognitional dreams. He calls up ideas into the soul in full clarity of mind through a desire for knowledge.—This ability first comes to expression as knowledge of the sense-world. It reaches its peak as sensory knowledge in natural science.
>
> The present task of spiritual cognition is, through desire for knowledge, to bring to the spiritual world one's experience of ideas in clarity of mind. The content a cognizing person then has in his soul is experienced as though it were mathematical. He thinks like a mathematician. But he does not think in numbers, or geometrical figures. He thinks in pictures of the world of spirit. In contrast to the waking dream of ancient spirit-knowledge, this is to stand fully conscious in the spiritual world.
>
> People in the Theosophical Society could not gain a proper relationship to this newer spiritual cognition. As soon as full consciousness wanted to approach the spiritual world, they were suspicious. They only knew full consciousness for the world of the senses, and had no proper feeling for going on to develop it into spiritual experience. By suppression of full consciousness they actually attempted to revert once again to ancient dream-consciousness. This reversion also existed in Mrs. Besant. She had hardly any possibility for grasping the modern type of spiritual knowledge. But what she said about the spiritual world was indeed taken from that world. So to me she was an interesting personality.
>
> Since this aversion to fully conscious spiritual knowledge was present in other leaders of the Theosophical Society, I could never feel at home in the Society as regards spiritual matters. Socially it was a pleasure to be in these circles; but to me their states of mind towards the spirit were alien.
>
> In my lectures at the Society's Congresses I was therefore disinclined to speak from my own spiritual experience. The lectures I gave could also

have been given by someone without any spiritual perception of their own.

★

Secondly, the letter shows that Steiner's attention had been especially caught by Besant's remarks about the arts, and by the paintings of AE.

In his autobiography he stated:

In the Theosophical Society artistic interests were hardly cultivated at all. From a certain standpoint this was at the time quite understandable, but it could not stay that way if a proper spiritual attitude were to flourish. Members of a society like this have at first every interest in the reality of spiritual life. In the sense-world the human being only appears to them in his transitory existence, severed from the spirit. Art seems to them to apply to this severed existence. So it appears to stand outside the spiritual reality which is sought.

Because of this situation artists did not feel at home in the Theosophical Society.

To Marie von Sivers and myself it was important for an artistic element to come alive in the Society. If knowledge of the spirit becomes experience it takes hold of the whole man. All powers of the soul are stimulated. When this experience is present, the light of spiritual experience shines into creative fantasy.

But here arises something which creates inhibitions. An artist has a certain anxious mood about this illumination of fantasy by the spirit-world. He wants unconsciousness regarding the spiritual world which holds sway within the soul. If it is a question of fantasy being 'stimulated' by the consciously considered element which has dominated cultural life since the start of the Consciousness Age, he is quite right. This 'stimulation' by man's intellectuality has a deadening effect on art.

But just the opposite occurs if fantasy is illuminated by a spiritual content which is really beheld. This brings about a resurrection of all the pictorial powers which have ever alone led to art in the life of humanity.

★

And thirdly, the letter shows that on the very evening of the performance of *The Shadowy Waters*, Steiner realized that the idea of the Congresses would 'have to be extended if they are completely to fulfil their aim', the extension consisting of 'theosophical nourishment' for participants to be carried out into the theosophical world at large.

Here can be observed the seeding of an impulse in his mind which in course of time, and translated into the medium of his own German language, would develop into the novel configuration of the 1907 Munich Congress, where a dramatic performance was made the centrepiece.

★

Some ten days after Steiner's letter to Günther Wagner, W.B. Yeats wrote another letter, this time to the writer Arthur Symons. It was still concerned with the results of his recently performed play:

Coole Park,
August 3, 1905

My dear Symons,

I have been awaiting with a great deal of expectancy your Wagner Essay, and would be very much obliged for the proofs if you still have them.

I am rewriting *The Shadowy Waters*, every word of it. I let them play it in London (and an execrable performance it was except for Mrs. Emery, and another) that I might find out what was wrong. Farquharson who seemed good in Herod was unendurable as Forgael.

I believe I am making a really strong play out of *The Shadowy Waters* and am certainly losing no poetry. It is the worst thing I ever did dramatically and partly because it was written when I knew very little of the stage and because there were so many old passages written or planned before I knew anything, that the little I did know could not pull it into shape.

Yours always,

W.B. Yeats

A Noteworthy Congress

Reports of the London Congress appeared in various theosophical journals, such as that in the August *Vâhan*:

In these troublous times, when everywhere there seems to be restlessness, sentiments of hostility, and even open warfare amongst nations, the Congress of the European Section of the Theosophical Society is to be deeply congratulated. It has given definite proof that the objects for which the Society was founded have become living realities. For here, in London, representatives from nearly every country on the globe met in that spirit of good fellowship and camaraderie which bespeaks the firm establishment of that 'nucleus of the universal brotherhood of humanity without distinction of race, creed, sex, caste or colour'. The papers read gave evidence that the 'study of comparative religion, philosophy, and science' has been most fruitful and the 'unexplained laws of Nature' and 'powers latent in man' have been well investigated.

In a short space it is impossible to give full details of such a delightful mental feast as was prepared for us. Fortunately the proceedings will be printed, and there we can have a leisurely survey of the immense work done, and enjoy over and over again the efforts of our members, coming from all the European countries, from Asia and America, and speaking in a dozen or more different languages.

★

Editorial comment was also provided by *The Theosophical Review*:

The theosophical event of July was the International Congress. It was marked throughout by warmth of brotherly feeling. All apparently heterogeneous elements formed one harmonious whole, and felt no walls of racial division, no strangeness among themselves. All seemed conscious of the peace, and it is noteworthy that in the musical events the audience seemed to give more to the artistes than is usually given by listeners, so that the effect on the inspiration of the artistes themselves was marked. Truly a noteworthy Congress. May all, returning to their several lands, carry with them the inspiration there found, and may the Society flourish the more vigorously in each land by the strength indrawn.

Another page gave a more detailed report:

So short an account as this of the Congress just held in London, where were gathered together theosophists from many lands, cannot give more than a mere impression, with here and there a mention of some special incident or name. As to numbers, some 600 members were present, and of these about 200 were non-British; so that this year's Congress has been in a sense even more international than last year's, for though the number of friends from other countries was not much greater, the nations represented were more numerous and wider apart. From India came a representative of Ceylon, a Mahratha brother, and a Panjabi; from farther East, an Anglo-Indian from Burma, a Dutchman from Java and a Japanese brother from Dai Nippon. Australia, New Zealand, Canada and the United States sent their groups of members, while nearer home Finland, Russia, Poland, Bulgaria, Hungary, Sweden, Norway and Spain added to the number of friends; as was to be expected, Belgium, France, Germany, Italy and Holland, still nearer neighbours, sent larger groups of representatives. Many of those present in London had already become friends in Amsterdam last year, so that a hearty and genuine feeling of good will and comradeship prevailed throughout the meetings and contributed largely to their value and effect.

The Congress itself lasted three days, but many preliminary and after proceedings lengthened it in reality to a week. For this year the Congress idea had grown and expanded, and new branches of work had been included in its programme. As was the case last year, so there was this year an

Arts and Crafts Exhibition, mainly of the work of members, but this year it was work from members of many nations and not from only one or two. A new departure was the performance of two mystical plays—one with its weird and entrancing plot laid in ancient Egypt, the other showing Celtic dreams of shadowy, strange shapes and elusive ideas. This dramatic experiment—for it was an experiment—was successful beyond expectation, not only on account of an appreciative audience that filled every seat in the Court Theatre, or of the favourable press notices, but as an indication of a line of mysticism and an expression of wisdom hitherto neglected by the Theosophical Society.

Musical and social meetings again formed a happy part of the programme and lightened the regular departmental work.

Without a shadow of doubt it was due to the President of the Congress—Mrs. Besant—that so much life, so much sincere spiritual enthusiasm, could find such harmonious expression as they did during every meeting. The President, indeed, put most of the members to shame by the completeness of her devotion to the Congress, its work and its members during the long busy days. Her opening and closing speeches with their friendly spirit and beauty of expression were gladly heard, and her address in the department on 'Occultism' was undoubtedly the *pièce de resistance* of the Congress, full of dignity, strength and beauty, and of great value. No wonder a vote of thanks to her at the close of the meetings evoked a thunder of applause.

Mr. Mead's interesting paper on the 'Myth of Man in the Mysteries' was listened to with great appreciation by a very large audience, and Dr. Steiner's paper on Goethe's occultism aroused much interest.

In the departments much good work was done. Some forty papers on the most varied subjects had been contributed, chiefly in French, German and English. In all its branches the Congress has well fulfilled its purpose, and will prove to have added strength to the movement in Europe and not only to the Section in which it was held.

Improving What Needs to be Improved

These English reports may be compared with an account of 'The Theosophical Congress in London' composed by Rudolf Steiner for the German readership.

The account appeared in the latter half of August, in an issue of *Lucifer-Gnosis* also containing an instalment in his series 'How does one attain Knowledge of the Higher Worlds?' about 'The Division of the Personality during Initiation'.

This year (1905) the Federation of European Sections held its Congress in London at the beginning of July (6th, 7th, 8th, 9th, 10th). The manner and organization of events at this second gathering was in its way generally similar to that held last year in Amsterdam. This time too, a beautiful feeling of belonging together streamed again through the participants. They had come from the most varied domains of theosophical work to exchange thoughts about methods of activity, testify to the progress of theosophical ideas in particular countries, and receive stimuli for work in their homelands. Just as last year the Dutch friends shunned no trouble or sacrifice to make the course of the Congress both worthy and fruitful, so too this year with our members in London. Anyone who can gauge the time and devotion which the organizing and preparatory work of such a gathering requires will be filled with warm gratitude towards our English friends.

Mrs. Besant undertook to be Congress President. The day before the gathering actually started, attending guests could come to a meeting of the Blavatsky Lodge to hear a significant lecture by Annie Besant about 'Requirements of Discipleship'. The speaker took up various recently published observations about all kinds of little weaknesses and mistakes of the Theosophical Society's great foundress, H.P. Blavatsky. She spoke with a feeling of deep gratitude about a person who was a light-bringer for her on the path towards truth and peace of soul. It is not a question of seeing little spots and weaknesses, but rather the great impulses emanating from such personalities. These we should abide by, and through them find our own pathway. If we hear much about the lives of 'initiates' which we say we had not expected, perhaps our expectations are just resting on misunderstandings. Wherever the Sun is, there may also be sunspots; but despite these spots the beneficial power of the Sun is still at work.

On the same day (Thursday, 6th July) Annie Besant opened the Exhibition of 'Arts and Crafts', which then remained open through all the days of the Congress. Such an exhibition, whose purpose is to bring to members' knowledge artistic achievements influenced by theosophical ideas or stemming from theosophists, cannot of course be absolutely perfect in respect to the choice and value of individual items. It is nonetheless a highly valuable addition to the Congress, and anyone seeking the tasks of the Society not in the mere spreading of theosophical thoughts but rather in building up theosophical life on all sides will surely not dispute its justifiability. Because of the abundant wealth of what was exhibited, it is quite impossible to go into details. Let it just be pointed out that in the pictures of G. Russell an interesting attempt could be observed to render astral reality both in symbolic coloured portrayals around figures represented in the picture and also in the colour of the landscape in which these are placed. To what extent this was achieved is another matter, which actually does not yet come into consideration today. Works by our member Lauweriks may be especially pointed out. Formerly he belonged to the Dutch Section, and since he has been active for some time as teacher of the Arts and Crafts

School in Düsseldorf he now belongs to the German. His art and craft works show everywhere a sensitive mind and a superb artist. Of German works, an interesting picture was exhibited by the President of our Düsseldorf Lodge, Otto Boyer, the *Alchemist*, and a portrait study by this same superb artist. He had also taken trouble to participate in the work of the Art Committee as German representative. Our active Munich member Fräulein Stinde made a contribution from the abundant wealth of her landscapes. There was also a picture exhibited by our member Fräulein Schmidt from Stuttgart.

On Friday evening Annie Besant gave a lecture to thousands of people in the large 'Queen's Hall' about the 'Work of Theosophy in the World'. She characterized in broad yet succinct terms the task possessed by the wisdom-teachings of theosophy in modern life today. To fulfil their mission they must be shown to advantage not simply as a creed, but through all domains of life, science, art and so on. What has been achieved in recognition of pioneer theosophical work even by artistic and scientific circles distant from the Theosophical Movement was excellently presented.

On Saturday evening the actual Congress proceedings were opened with some vivid words by Annie Besant. She referred to the need for nations to be acting together in urgent yet brotherly work towards their great aims, and characterized the starting points which existed here and there for a deepening of spiritual life. She alluded for instance to a work by the Italian sculptor Ezechiel, a 'Christ', in which a theosophist might see his own picture of Christ. It will be particularly interesting for Germans to hear that Annie Besant referred to the art of Richard Wagner, in whose tones were to be sensed influences of the astral world.—What now followed gave beautiful symbolism to the Society's international and brotherly character. Following a Committee resolution, individual representatives of different countries gave short addresses of greeting in their national languages. One speech after another could be heard in the following tongues: Dutch, Swedish, French, German, English (for America), Italian, Spanish, Hungarian, Finnish, Russian, and also an Indian dialect. Finally, Mr. Mead spoke for England. The morning gathering closed with business communications from the Congress Secretary J. van Manen.

In the afternoon began individual lectures and departmental proceedings. Here works are brought forward by individual members who volunteer from the most various working domains: philosophy, science, folklore, methods of theosophical work, art, occultism, and so forth. It is quite impossible even to indicate the abundant wealth here on offer. Lectures are held in various premises about the most diverse matters, followed by discussions. Let just some be mentioned: Mr. Mead spoke on an interesting Gnostic theme; Pascal, General Secretary of the French Section, gave a contribution on the 'Mechanism of Clairvoyance with Animals and Men'. M. Percy Lund contributed some work on 'Physical Evidences for Atlantis and Lemuria'. In the Department for Occultism Annie Besant spoke in a most illuminating way about the requirements and difficulties in methods of occult research. She demonstrated what caution—and reserve, even with the greatest caution—an occult investigator has to make, and how his results, despite the greatest conceivable conscientiousness, are to be taken with exactly the same caution.—Dr. Rudolf Steiner spoke in the 'Science' Department on the 'Occult Bases of Goethe's Life-work'. M.P. Bernard gave a contribution on 'Instinct, Consciousness, Hygiene and Morality'. The 'Foundation of Theosophical Morality' was set out by M.H. Choisy. Mr. Leo gave highly valuable information on 'Astrology'. Mr. Mead also spoke in a final meeting about Gnosis in the past and present and from there threw light on the correspondence of all Mystery-wisdom.—On Saturday evening a theatrical performance took place: two symbolical dramatic works, the first attempt in our Congresses to foster this particular art. On Sunday and Monday afternoon there were musical presentations: singing performances in various national languages once again gave beautiful symbolic expression to the principle of brotherhood.—On Monday evening Annie Besant ended the Congress with a short final speech. From Germany were present: Fräulein Scholl (Cologne), Frau Geheimrat Lübke (Weimar), Countess Kalckreuth, Fräulein Stinde, Herr and Frau von Seydewitz (Munich), Countess Schack (Doringau), Dr. H. Vollrath (Leipzig), Herr Kiem, Fräulein von Sivers and Dr. Rudolf Steiner from Berlin, Herr and Frau Dr. Peipers (Düsseldorf).—Special thanks are owed to our members J. v. Manen and Miss Kate Spink, who arranged all the secretarial work of the Congress.—It has already been mentioned that Otto Boyer took part in the work of the Committee for fine arts. Adolf Arenson (Stuttgart) undertook to represent Germany in the Committee for musical performances.

The lectures and all reports of proceedings of last year's Congress of the Theosophical Society's Federation of European Sections will shortly be appearing in a substantial volume, the 'Yearbook of the Congress'. It is quite understandable that publication of this book in the same year posed a big task to the collectors and directors (J. van Manen, Kate Spink) and therefore it is only now able to appear. The lectures and proceedings for this year will be completed in a shorter time. The publishing firm of Max Altmann in Leipzig has undertaken to sell the 'Yearbook' in Germany; and one may turn to them for purchases.

The Annual Meeting of the Theosophical Society's 'British Section' took place on 8th July.[12] On this occasion Mr. Keightley resigned from his office as General Secretary, and Miss Kate Spink was elected in his place. Dr. Rudolf Steiner greeted the meeting in the name of the German Section.

⋆

This careful and appreciative report shows that Steiner's first reflections about the London Congress in his July letter to Günther Wagner had already developed further. Two small but tell-tale details may be instanced.

Firstly, he now placed the Arts and Crafts Exhibition in relation to the task of 'building up theosophical life on all sides'. The enigmatic remark about AE's paintings, that the degree of success in his attempt to portray astral reality 'actually does not yet come into consideration today' may even be taken to imply that the matter might well come into consideration in another context at some future time.

Secondly, the dramatic performances of *The Shrine of the Golden Hawk* and *The Shadowy Waters*, however inadequate they may have been, were described as 'the first attempt at our Congresses to foster this particular art', thus placing them into a history of theosophical drama within a numerical order open to future extension.

The Sweet Sound of the South

In late autumn, addressing the Convention of the German Section on 22 October, Rudolf Steiner once again put before his listeners certain features of the London Congress held three months previously:

> . . . Everything depends on our cultivating not simply theosophical teachings but theosophical life. Only when theosophy rays out from art, science and all other branches of life has it completely grasped its mission.
>
> A Congress in London of the Federation of European Sections again finely showed what the Theosophical Movement signifies. Any such objections to these Congresses can be made as one might wish; perfection did not fall from Heaven. But here it is a matter of intentions. We must put before ourselves the ideal of improving what needs to be improved, of working together, and not criticizing.
>
> The Congress proceedings were as usual. There was an exhibition of art and craft works, by our own members in particular. Mention should be made of pictures by the Irishman Russell, who in his landscapes and human figures tries to express inner astral life in the environment and in symbolism . . .

⋆

During the month of October when Steiner was speaking these words, the 50-year old and already ailing William Sharp and his wife Elizabeth left Britain for the Continent. They travelled towards Switzerland, went on down to Italy and then across to Sicily—in Goethe's words 'that unique and beautiful island, which is clear, authentic and complete'.

After some time in Taormina they made for Castel Maniace, near Maletto, up on the western slope of the shoulder of Mount Etna.

Fiona Macleod caught a chill and died here in Elizabeth's arms on 12 December 1905, at about 3 o'clock in the afternoon. This is the very time of day when, in the words of Luke's Gospel, 'the veil of the Temple was torn right down the middle, and when Jesus had cried out in a loud voice, he said: "Father, into your hands I commend my Spirit." With these words he breathed his last.'

★

An Iona cross carved in lava was set above the Scotsman's grave, in a little woodland buriel ground within sound of the Simeto—rather like 'the sweet sound of the South' in his poem 'The Bandruidh'.

Many years later, Steiner set this poem to eurythmy, with green lighting for first verse, red for second, and both colours alternating fast for third.

My robe is green,
My crown is of stars—
The grass is the green
And the daisies the stars:
O'er lochan and streamlet
My breath moveth sweet...
Bonnie blue lochans
Hillwaters fleet.

The song in my heart
Is the song of the birds,
And the wind in my heart
Is the lowing of herds.
The light in my eyes,
And the breath of my mouth,
Are the clouds of spring-skies
And the sound of the South.

Grass-green from thy mouth
The sweet sound of the South!

In Britain, *The Theosophical Review* published an obituary of Macleod by G.R.S. Mead, who stated that

'... those of us who knew him in friendship, and still more, those who had met him in the intimacy of his inner belief and knowledge, have lost a source of great joy and refreshment; and the Theosophical Movement has lost a great sympathizer, for though he never actually joined the Society, he was with us in heart, and the 'Stanzas of Dzyan' were the subject of his constant contemplation; indeed, at our last parting he had promised us his notes on them for publication.[13]

5
INTERLUDE 1905–12

A Symbolic Cultic Activity

A report in the November 1905 *Theosophical Review* kept British readers informed about continuing events in the German Section:

> Dr. Steiner has just completed a lecturing tour in Switzerland and South Germany, visiting St. Gallen, Zurich, Basel, Freiburg i. B., Stuttgart, Nuremberg, Heidelberg, Frankfurt, Cassel and Weimar. After his public lecture in each town he had a meeting for questions and discussions. A new branch has been formed at Freiburg, and two more are in process of formation. The weekly public lectures in Berlin have begun in an overcrowded hall. Their subject is 'Haeckel, the World-Riddle and Theosophy'.

Steiner was also giving other internal lectures in Berlin on quite another subject, namely Freemasonry. These lectures are included in the volume *Die Tempellegende und die Goldenelegende* (GA 93).

Towards the end of November, through the mediation of Franz Zavrèl who had joined the Theosophical Society's Berlin Lodge, Steiner entered into negotiations with a German representative of John Yarker's Grand Orient rite. On 3 January 1906 he was officially empowered to form his own temple under the title 'Mystica Aeterna', and given the rank of Grandmaster.

Within this temple Steiner began to hold the cultic rituals to which he referred in chapter XXXVI of his autobiography:

> ... So I accepted the diploma of the Society in question, which belonged to the stream represented by Yarker. It had the forms of the so-called higher degrees of Freemasonry. I took nothing, absolutely nothing from this Society except the purely formal right to institute in historical succession a symbolic cultic activity.
>
> Everything contentually represented in the 'services' conducted within the arrangement I made was *without historical dependence* on any tradition. Although I was in possession of a formal diploma, the *only* matter fostered was what portrayed anthroposophical knowledge. And this was done to meet members' needs. Besides working on ideas which gave clothing to spiritual knowledge, people were searching for something speaking directly to perception and feeling. Such needs I wished to meet. Had I not been

approached by the Society referred to, I would have instituted a symbolic cultic activity without historical connection.

But a 'secret society' was *not* thereby created. Anyone approaching the institution was told in the clearest way that he was not joining an Order, but would experience, as a participant in ceremonial services, a kind of sense-perceptible demonstration of spiritual knowledge. If some of this took on forms in which members of existing Orders were admitted, or promoted to higher grades, there was no intention of organizing such an Order, but only of illustrating in sensory pictures the experiences of a soul in spiritual progress.

All authentic records of ritual texts, or fragments of such, used in the Mystica Aeterna are now presented in the volume *Zur Geschichte und aus den Inhalten der erkenntniskultischen Abteilung der Esoterischen Schule 1904–1914* (GA 265). Interested readers must therefore study the totality of what this 526-page volume contains.

Within the context of the present work there is no intention of reproducing the major texts contained in this volume. At the present point and at two subsequent points, however, certain shorter texts will be extracted for purposes of illustration.

Here is a text for admission into the third grade, as subsequently written down by a participant:

After the strokes of the bell had sounded, this is spoken:

(To the Masters present):
'Let us now seek the grave of Hiram Abiff.'
(There follows a procession.)
'Here is the grave of Hiram Abiff. An acacia branch do I plant upon this grave as a sign that your higher self rises alive out of your lower self, as this acacia branch out of your grave.'

(A person then speaks):
'Memento mori! Think on death, think that everything mortal in you is not yourself.'

(The General Grandmaster thereupon speaks):
'He shall be newly born as once Hiram Abiff.'
(This is repeated by one of the Masters standing at the North altar.)

(The General Grandmaster speaks):
'Light shall shine upon him from the East, as once for Hiram Abiff.'
(Again repeated by one of the Masters standing at the West altar.)

(The General Grandmaster speaks):
'He shall be a victor over death, as once Hiram Abiff.'
(Again repeated by one of the Masters standing at the South altar.)

(The General Grandmaster now approaches the coffin; this is opened and the General Grandmaster speaks):

'With the lion grip of the Master do I lift thee out of this grave.'

(He lifts him out and utters to him in a quiet voice the Masterword):

'M(ach) b(en) a(ch).' The bones are released from out of the flesh—with the Mastergrip.

A Good Deed for Many Participants

The account of the Mystica Aeterna given in Rudolf Steiner's autobiography continued:

> There was no question of activity in any existent Order, or of transmitting things which were transmitted inside such Orders. The proof is that members of Orders from the most different streams took part in the ceremonial services arranged by myself and found *something quite different* in them from what was in their Orders.
>
> A person who had taken part for the first time in one of our services once came up to me straight afterwards. This person had risen to high rank in an Order. Under the impression of what he had experienced he wanted to hand over to me his Order's insignia. His opinion was that after experiencing a real spiritual content he could now no longer partake in what remained a mere formality. I brought the matter into order. Anthroposophy should not tear anyone out of the life-connections they are in. It should add something to these connections, but not take anything from them. So the person in question remained in his Order and continued to participate in our symbolic services.

Reproducing this passage in the volume *Zur Geschichte und aus den Inhalten der erkenntniskultischen Abteilung der Esoterischen Schule 1904–1914*, Hella Wiesberger inserts here a footnote:

> The reference can only have been to Hermann Joachim (son of the famous violinist Joseph Joachim and godson of Hermann Grimm), who held one of the highest leading offices in the Grand Lodge of Freemasons of Germany.

Steiner continued:

> It is only too comprehensible that misunderstandings creep in when institutions like the one described become known about. For there are many people to whom the external fact of belonging to something seems more important than the content they receive. And many participants spoke about the matter as if they belonged to an Order. They were unable to distinguish that with us they were shown things *with no relation to an Order*

which were otherwise only given within the connections of such an Order.

The fact is that in this sphere too we broke with old traditions. Work was carried out as it must be carried out when a spiritual content is investigated in an original way out of conditions of fully conscious soul-experience.

Later on, people wanted to use the certificates signed by Marie von Sivers and myself when making a link with the historical Yarker institution as a pretext for all kinds of slanders. This is just treating risible things with a serious grimace for the purpose of forging such slanders. Our signatures were given as 'formulae'. The usual practice was maintained. And as we gave our signatures, I made a point of saying that it was a formality and the institution I was bringing about would take over *nothing* from the Yarker institution.

It is of course easy to make observations afterwards about how much 'cleverer' it would have been not to link onto institutions later used by slanderers. But I would like in all modesty to remark that in the period of my life coming under consideration here I still belonged to those who assume uprightness and not crookedness in the people with whom they have to deal. Nor did spiritual perception alter this trust in people. It should not be misused to investigate inner intentions of one's fellow men unless such investigation is desired by the person concerned. In other cases the investigation of another person's inner soul is just as forbidden to a spiritual researcher as is the unauthorized opening of a letter. One's relation to others is thus the same as for someone who has no spiritual knowledge. The difference is that one must assume people to be upright in their intentions until the contrary has been experienced, or be distrustful of the whole world. In the latter mood it is impossible to work with people in social partnership, for this can only be based *on trust, not on mistrust.*

This institution, which gave out a spiritual content in cultic symbolism, was a good deed for many participants in the Anthroposophical Society. As in all realms of anthroposophical activity, everything was excluded which did not fall within the sphere of clear consciousness. So there was no question of unjustified magic, suggestive influences and the like.—Members received something which spoke, on one hand, to their ideational views in such a way that their feelings could go along in direct perception. For many people this was also something which led them into a better formation of ideas. The possibility of continuing to foster these arrangements then ceased with the outbreak of the War. Although there was no question of any secret society, the institution would have been taken as such. And so this symbolic cultic section of the Anthroposophical Movement was put to rest in the middle of 1914.

The fact that persons who had taken part in this section—to which no one who considers the matter with good will and a sense for truth could raise any objection at all—became slanderous accusers, is one of those abnormalities in human behaviour which arise when people who are not inwardly sincere enter movements with genuine spiritual content. They expect things which accord with their trivial soul-life, and since they naturally do not find them, they turn against the institution to which they had—with unconscious insincerity—previously turned.

A Quite Particular Hope

Although the four visits Rudolf Steiner had made to Britain up to this point were of some importance in his own life, their effect on the spiritual life of Britain was by contrast fairly negligible. The main reason was of course that none of his addresses, pronouncements and lectures had been given in the English language.

For the German-speaking Steiner, as stated in a letter written by Marie von Sivers on 12 February 1906 to the Alsatian writer Edouard Schuré, did not wish to speak any foreign languages:

> He reads them, but he never speaks them.

★

In Britain meanwhile, readers who for their part never spoke the German language could still follow in *The Theosophical Review* the activities in the German Section.

Here is a report from the May 1906 number, in what proved to be the last of the series 'From Other Lands' which had been running in the journal for some three years:

> The Theosophical Movement in Germany is progressing favourably, thanks to the numerous lectures Dr. Rudolf Steiner has given this winter. Since the Annual Convention, in October 1905, more than a hundred new members have joined the German Section, and to the eighteen branches then existing four new ones have been added. From October 1905 to the beginning of May 1906, Dr. Steiner will have given twenty-four public lectures in Berlin and eighty-nine public lectures in other cities of Germany and Switzerland, namely, at Basel, Bonn, Bremen, Cassel, Colmar, Cologne, Dresden, Düsseldorf, Elberfeld, Frankfurt a.M., Freiburg i.B., Hamburg, Hanover, Heidelberg, Leipzig, Lugano, Marburg, Munich, Nuremberg, Regensburg, St. Gallen, Strassburg, Stuttgart, Weimar, Zurich. Besides the public lectures Dr. Steiner has given almost daily lectures for the branches in Berlin or the cities he has visited.
>
> In November there appeared the first number of an official journal for this Section. Its editor is Fräulein Mathilde Scholl. At present only two

numbers have been issued, for it is not intended that it shall appear regularly but only when there is sufficient news of importance.

★

In a lecture at Dornach on 15 June 1923, Steiner made some general comments about the first period of anthroposophical development:

> ... In this period, up to the year 1905 or 1906, there was some justification for a quite particular hope. This hope was that the content of anthroposophy might slowly become the living content of the Theosophical Society as such.
>
> Up to the year 1905 or 1906 the Theosophical Society could be said to have been growing into an anthroposophical one—slowly and through a quite natural development. What made this hope possible was the fact that Annie Besant, one of the Theosophical Society's most influential personalities, showed at the time a certain tolerance in her outer bearing, and really tried to allow different directions to work beside each other. This was entirely the case until about the years 1905 and 1906.

The latter year was singled out in Steiner's autobiography as a time when matters in the Society took a sharp turn for the worse:

> Already from 1906 onwards phenomena began to occur in the Theosophical Society which indicated its deterioration to a frightful degree.

The reference here was to activities of the prominent English theosophist and writer Charles Leadbeater.

In the spring of 1906 it became known throughout the whole Theosophical Society that Leadbeater's particular brand of occult experimentation had led him not only into the personal practice but even into the educational advocacy of sexual misbehaviour.

As a result of the ensuing scandal, he resigned from the Society.

United with the English

With the departure of Charles Leadbeater the air seemed—for the moment—to be somewhat cleared. Under the Society's ageing President, Colonel Olcott, the next European Theosophical Congress took place in Paris, at the beginning of June.

Members attending from Britain included Bertram Keightley, G.R.S. Mead and D.N. Dunlop.

The Congress proceedings show that besides giving a lecture of his own, Rudolf Steiner also acted as chairman of the 'Philosophy Department', which had as secretary Max Gysi. In the previous year he had given Gysi permission to translate into English his own Congress lecture, though even by 1906 the Transactions of the 1905 Congress were not yet published. It may be deduced from the sequel that at the Paris Congress in 1906 Gysi was allowed to make further translations.

★

The Theosophical Review took stock of the event in its July issue:

> Yet another Theosophical Congress to add to the long list! The recent Paris Congress of the Federation of the European Sections of the Theosophical Society has come and gone, and left a pleasant memory of the warm hospitality of our French hosts, of splendid weather, a charming place of meeting, and excellent arrangements. The Congress was a truly international gathering. Russians, Swedes, Czechs, Italians, Spaniards, Swiss, Belgians, Dutch, English, Germans, Americans, a Hindu and a Parsi mingled together and regretted the consequences of the Tower of Babel incident. A 'universal language' was badly needed; Esperanto, it is true, was on the programme for discussion, but the theosophical Greeks are as yet shy of its barbarisms. How many of each nation there were I do not know exactly. There were many English and Dutch (perhaps some hundred of them) and no less than fourteen Russians. The Germans, too, were numerous, and Dr. Steiner, in the days preceding and following the Congress, gave a series of instructive lectures in German to crowded audiences. In our opinion the main educative value of the Congress was precisely this mixture of races. The object-lesson of passing three or four days in the midst of such a Congress is, one may almost say, of equal value to years of private study or of constant attendance at the meetings of some provincial branch. Most of us have not sufficient imagination to realize theosophy beyond the limits of our immediate personal experience. We listen to our own lecturers, read our own magazine (some of us at any rate do) and glance at the report of our own Section. But how many ever look at the General Report of all the Sections, so as to realize that the Society is truly without distinction of race and creed and sex . . . ?

★

By the beginning of July Steiner was back in Germany, giving a cycle of lectures in Leipzig, and probably from here he wrote to the Annual Convention of the British Section held in London on July 7. The 'Report of Proceedings' records this letter being read out:

> In the name of the German Section I am sending to the Convention the most fraternal greetings. May the meeting of members on this occasion carry the best results for theosophical work, in which the German members of the

Theosophical Society feel united with the English. Only the impossibility to make twice a long journey, so soon after the Congress in Paris, hinders me from bearing these greetings personally to your Convention.

Respectfully,

Dr. Rudolf Steiner,
General Secretary,
German Section Theosophical Society.

★

At the end of the Paris Congress it was decided that the next year's Congress would be hosted by the German Section. Steiner left Paris with this already in mind.

What Dunlop had in mind on leaving Paris is not specifically known. But his daughter Edith Young (born in January 1892) recorded in her autobiography *Inside Out* (1971) going as a 14-year-old on a summer family holiday to Llandudno, with her Irish grandfather also present.

This seaside resort on the North Welsh coast must have provided an attractive family meeting-point about halfway between London and Dublin. The date was then in the summer of 1906.

Her father would already have travelled this way quite a number of times. The first occasion was when he came over from Dublin to attend the Theosophical Convention in London in the summer of 1893. Further journeys along this route took place after his return from America to Ireland and subsequent move to England at the end of 1899, for his daughter recorded being soon taken by him to stay with her maternal grandparents near Dublin, even specifying that the journey was by the Holyhead-Kingstown crossing, and that by this crossing her father brought her back to London some while later. It has further been seen that Ronald Dunlop recorded his father travelling to Dublin almost every year during Horse Show week.

These continual journeys between London and Dublin cannot have failed to open Dunlop's eyes to the scenery and atmosphere of the North Welsh coast. And in the summer of 1906 he was holidaying at a seaside resort which lies on a promontory a little eastward and in sight of the great headland of Penmaenmawr.

Climbing to the Stars

After his six months' stay in Munich, the 19-year-old Clifford Bax returned to Britain in November 1905.

His account in *Inland Far* reads:

> During the long journey to England I remembered the mood in which I had lived when I set out six months before. I must have been the same person? But life seemed now a far lovelier experience...

Scarcely was he back in England than Bax decided to set off again, but this time, at the suggestion of a friend he had made in Munich, on a far longer journey that would take him around the whole world.

He embarked at Southampton on a German liner, which at first headed south, and then through the Pillars of Hercules into the Mediterranean.

Here is a passage from his account of the sea voyage:

> I laboured to strengthen my power of concentration. Having determined to realize myself as a spirit, invisible, and my body as something not less external to me than my clothes, I attempted to gather up my consciousness behind my eyes in order that I might look upon the objective world not with but through them...
>
> Even in the Bay of Biscay the sea had not been rough. In the Mediterranean it was quiet as a lake. And there was romance in moving across those waters that had floated the navies and the merchantmen of so many vanished peoples. Day after day I read, in *Isis Unveiled*, of poetic rites and imaginative beliefs which the world had long since outgrown and, looking up from the page, beheld the blue miles of the inland sea flowing past the ship like those centuries of time through which my thoughts were speeding...

The ship travelled on eastwards, passed through the Suez Canal and out into the Indian Ocean. After visiting Australia, New Zealand, New Guinea, China and Japan, Bax travelled across the Pacific and landed on the coast of California, made his way over the American continent—not omitting to view the Niagara Falls—and finally to New York. Here he found a further passage across the Atlantic, and arrived back in Britain in May 1906, six months after his departure.

As soon as he returned from this lengthy voyage, he joined the Theosophical Society.

Not that *Isis Unveiled* was the only book he had taken with him all around the globe. Describing his world tour in his autobiography *Inland Far* (1925), he also mentioned that on the journey he read poetry by AE.

★

Bax next went on to relate a visit to Ireland during that same summer of 1906:

> For long I had sojourned alone on my intellectual hilltop, enveloped by an inhospitable mist of metaphysics, and not for some time did the mist begin

to disperse, and I to seek humanity. Once or twice in each year my brother and I now visited Ireland, going to Connemara, Galway, the Aran Isles, and Donegal; and I see clearly that although he knew nothing of mystical cosmogonies and did not hanker after that state which Plotinus touched three times, he was far more richly influenced than I by the beauty that awaited us . . .

I had met a romantic fellow, some four years my senior, a talented Irish poet named Maurice Joy. He was exclusively concerned with literary craft, and since we were much together I began to realize my crudity and ignorance as a writer. In consequence I was looking forward eagerly, when I set out for Dublin, to those technical talks with a fellow-artist and a superior from which a young craftsman most quickly learns to improve his work. And Joy had promised, too, that I should meet a new Dublin poet, his intimate friend, one Padraic Colum.

My brother and I arrived in Dublin on an August evening—Dublin 'miserable and wildly gay; always talkative, sometimes cynical, sometimes idealistic; uncomfortably honest, indecently corrupt; ineffective and yet affecting everyone' (Douglas Godring). On the next day my brother departed for Donegal; and a few minutes after he had rattled away to the station, Joy called for me at the hotel. We set off down Sackville Street, and continued to walk for a long time, seemingly without aim; for Joy was in one of his introspective moods and was following only 'a spirit in his feet'. As for me, the bright and buoyant life of the city was pouring into my senses, and on the supposition that my friend was taking me somewhere I was content to marvel at the breakneck career of the jaunting-cars, to observe the high spirits of the barefoot urchins, to note how many of the passing faces were keenly mentalized, and to hear my companion murmuring abstractedly, 'You must meet Colum, and Edward Martyn, and Tom Kettle, and Seumas O'Sullivan, and AE.'

'AE?' said I. 'Do you know him?'

'Everyone knows him,' replied Joy. 'He lives in Rathgar, and his door is open to the world on Sunday evenings. If you care, we will go next Sunday—'

'If I care!'

Bax was first taken to meet Padraic Colum, with whom he recorded having a long conversation.

Here is how it finished:

'. . . Instead of taking Athens as the antithesis of modern Europe,' resumed Colum, we should take England and France of today and compare them with England and France in the eighteenth century. We must say that the average person has now the possibility of a richer life. In Athens, culture only covered a pin-point; in our society, it covers a dining-table.'

'Perhaps,' I admitted. 'But does it cover anything else?'

Colum laughed. 'Well,' said he, 'maybe my metaphor was wrong; for culture certainly covered the dining-table in Plato's *Symposium*. Y've read that, of course?'

'I've hardly read Plato at all,' I said.

'Then y'must,' cried Colum. 'He was a great boy. Now, what do y'say to coming out with me, and buying a copy? Will y'do it?'

'Of course,' I said, 'and I'll read the book when I join my brother in Donegal.'

My new friend's invigorating companionship sped the days of the week as a yacht springs forward when the right wind catches her sails, until at last it was Sunday, until at last it was Sunday evening when I should become acquainted with AE. Joy took me to Rathgar upon one of

the glittering galleons of the street,

and with the liveliest anticipation I followed him up the steps of AE's house and in through the open door.

As Joy and I advanced up a narrow passage, we heard the sound of many animated voices in a room to the right. We entered and found ourselves among twenty persons. A light haze of tobacco-smoke clung to the ceiling. A track of spent matches connected the door with the fireplace. An easel or two out-topped the heads of the talkers; and the walls of the room were luminous with small pictures of visionary subjects. AE, a large, loose-built, shaggy-bearded figure, advanced to us, peering steadily with long grey shining benevolent eyes; and having accorded me a chair, seated himself cross-legged on the floor, and in answer to my hesitant questions extemporized with an eloquence that has been often and justly praised.

'Perhaps you can resolve,' I said, 'a problem that has annoyed me many times. It is this: how did the Egyptians come to worship cats and bulls and birds? For I am assuming that they were wiser than their modern exponents admit. Do you think that, under these images, they represented the various passions and powers of the soul and the outside world?'

'The learned,' replied AE, 'would probably tell you that the animals which the Egyptians worshipped were totems: each tribe in the early days, before their civilization consolidated, having one of these creatures for its guardian. In my view, that is a shallow explanation. I think that by giving honour to these different manifestations of life they were recognizing and adoring the mystery that is concealed within all things. They worshipped the One in the Many.'

'I see. I must think that over. In the meanwhile, will you tackle another of my difficulties?'

'I will say what I think.'

'Then tell me, AE, why is it that when a seer beholds a god or a fairy or any creature that is not physical, he sees it as, in general, a human form?'

'I don't quite understand your question.'

'No. I suppose it is as though someone were to ask me how I manage to breathe. I will put my point again. Here on your walls are pictures of spiritual personages—invisible entities that dwell among woods or on the mountains or within lakes. They are not human, yet they appear to you in human forms. I should have expected them to have forms as little like ours as the forms of animals and birds.'

AE stroked his long beard. He began to speak with more energy. 'I do not feel,' he said, 'that we ought to be surprised if the gods, the devas, reveal themselves in forms that are approximately human. Are you not thinking too poorly of the vestures that we wear? The truth is that you may give five different explanations of the form that a vision takes, and all may be correct for certain cases. I always regard the matter in this way. Everything on the Earth tends to be human. We ourselves are, among visible things, the nearest to the true divine human form, but one has only to compare the noble splendour of the visionary forms with those that clothe men and women in order to understand that we are but imperfectly human and are ourselves only reaching out to a higher form. The amoeba life tends to begin that way. We are halfway to it. The deva has achieved it—and is trembling on the verge of no form.'

By some forgotten transition we began to discuss my project of starting a magazine that should revitalize the arts by attaching them to the deep thought of theosophy, and should redeem theosophy by giving it aesthetic form. 'My dear man,' said AE, 'don't ask me to write anything. If you knew what it means to write about fifteen columns of journalese every week, you would understand how one loathes the sight of a pen. You see, I earn my living in two ways—by agricultural journalism and by painting. Out of the seven days I spend five and a half at the journalism; and I have always a headache, and I am always wondering how long I can go on.'

'Well,' I said, 'if I can't get a poem from you, perhaps you'll let me reproduce one of your paintings?'

'By all means. I am trying to work now on an initiation scene, and you could have that, if you like it. But I cannot get the legs right of a demigod, and I won't let the world suppose that the demigods have uncomely members.'

'Splendid! Let me have it as soon as you can,' said I. 'Perhaps, though, I ought to warn you that my magazine is likely to be a hole-and-corner production. I don't know any big men in the literary world, or a single reviewer.'

'You needn't bother about that,' replied AE. 'I have been trying, all my life, to help what you call hole-and-corner papers. I hate the prosperous kind, for I have always been on the side of the outcasts, and I hope I always will be. You have my sympathy,' he continued, 'in your desire to irrigate the Theosophical Society with beauty; and you may succeed; but I have begun to despair of any genuine love for mystical art or poetry or for any kind of spiritual imagination among theosophists. They are in a mental state which I can only describe as the devachan of a secularist lecturer, wherein all things heavenly are judged by reason and morality, and the flagging horses of emotion are whipped up to duty after every moral pronouncement. It's dreadful, after old H.P.B. But perhaps it's alright. There are as many ways of climbing to the stars as there are people to climb.'

'A moral enthusiast,' I said, 'may be climbing to the stars, however onerous he makes himself; but I must admit that I was surprised when I heard that you put so much effort into political enterprises. I don't seem to feel that they ever terminate among the stars.'

'You are somewhat mistaken about me,' responded AE. 'I care very little for what we mean usually by politics. But I am greatly interested in building up a rural civilization in Ireland on the lines of the old communes; and if you knew what this meant, you would be just as interested as I am. It is always better to work in life than in phantasy.'

I quoted his own lines:

> He who might have wrought in flame
> Only traced upon the foam.

'That is my feeling,' said AE, 'and I apply it also to the arts. So many people care for one's work only because of the art in it, that it is a real joy to find now and then someone who is more concerned about the life than the form. I have no interest in people who find in literature anything but an avenue to life. Every thought or mood is the opening or closing of a door to the divine world, and who is there that we would not laugh at if he went to a door, and only admired and looked at it, forgetting its uses? Art for art's sake is considering the door as a decoration, and not for its use in the house of life. English poetry, for all its splendour, moves in a world of illusion, because of its lack of fundamental ideas.'

'You would admit a few exceptions, wouldn't you?'

'I would. Shelley, Wordsworth and Blake. Myself I prefer Sufi poetry to any because of its intoxication with divine things; because romance and beauty and love, which in our literature move on a path of their own, are in Eastern mystical poetry rapt up into eternal things. For years, when I was young, I read hardly anything but Eastern literature, and I have never since been able really to enjoy the literature of Europe. When I was young, I thought I would be able to bring into our literature in Ireland that interior life, but it needs a much bigger nature than mine and a better artist to do this.'

The simplicity and sincerity with which AE spoke these words—AE who was then, as I believe him still to be, the counsellor and inspirer of all that is finest in the intellectual life of Dublin—impressed me so much that for a moment or two I was silent. Our conversation might have taken us into many high places of thought had it not been abruptly broken by the arrival of a visitor from the United States who, advancing across the room with open hand, strode up to AE, now risen from the floor, and gripping the poet's hand remarked: 'When I left New York I said to the folk at home: "I'll see AE. I'll not come back across the water till I've pressed that man's flesh!" ' The fulfilment of his vow occupied him for the length of a minute; and seeing that I had lost AE, I found Maurice Joy, and by him was introduced to Seumas O'Sullivan. For a time we all talked about books and the bright particular stars of the period, but AE's personality had struck so deeply into mine—always abnormally sensitive, perhaps, to the radiations of a new acquaintance—that I now remember nothing of what we said, but only that the Irishmen left me marvelling at the precision of their theories and the abundance of their vocabulary. When we rose to leave, a lady who had been talking with us produced a small parcel and said: 'Mr. O'Sullivan, *would* you mind posting this on your way home? I'm sure Mr. Joy would forget it.' We left AE's house, and at a noisy corner that was illuminated by a gin-shop we climbed up the stairs of a tram. 'She gave it to me,' said O'Sullivan sardonically, 'as to the least of poets.'

A few days afterwards, I joined my brother at a village on the roughest part of the Donegal coast. We put up at a small farmhouse, and were attended by a large, sweet-natured, guileless girl. She gave us eggs for breakfast, eggs for lunch, and eggs for supper; but who cares, at twenty?

Each day had more beauty than the senses could exhaust—the beauty of the sun-sculptured cliffs, the shimmering, beaten silver of the immense ocean, the bloom of colour on the inland mountains, and the forlorn stretches of peat and water—but even more memorable to me are the evenings of that remote holiday when, with a small oil-lamp on the table, my brother would read the miraculous legends in *The Lives of the Saints*, and I the first of the Platonic dialogues that I had ever read entire. I have known no joy, no joy of any kind, to surpass the glory of delight with which I discovered Plato. The man who believes himself to have found a lover in whom there is no alloy will marvel that life, in a world that has croaked so much, can contain a happiness that makes a pale shadow of all that he has hoped or imagined; and I, who loved ardently both literature and philosophy, found in those dialogues a complete assuagement of my thirst, and felt the Platonic view expanding my half-shaped thoughts with an almost alarming speed, and knew, by imaginative parallel, the experience of one who after many years of exile returns to the empire and the country and the city and the home in which alone he had ever been wholly glad.

Nearer to Human Life

In October 1906 *The Vâhan* published in its correspondence columns a letter on 'The Work of Theosophical Lodges':

> The question of lodge work is one which is daily becoming more difficult of solution, especially in the older branches of the Society. So far as an elementary knowledge of modern theosophical writings is concerned the majority of the members are now fairly familiar with them, so that little interest is shown in the study of such books as the manuals. Close and detailed study of the more abstruse works is, of course, not possible in the lodge, and must needs be left to the private effort of those who have the desire for such work. The ordinary lecture, although suitable enough for the general public, is almost useless to the lodge member, who already is acquainted by his own reading with nearly all the lecturer can say. This applies even to new members, who nowadays, as a rule, only join after having read a great part of the literature.
>
> What then remains to be done in order that the lodges may be kept alive? In rare cases, perhaps, the lodge may become a mutual admiration society, or may worship at the feet of some oracular personage within its ranks, but pleasant illusions like these cannot last very long. A few members may and do earnestly devote themselves to propaganda work, and thus find a most suitable field for their energies. The majority of members, however, after a time take but a very languid interest in lodge studies and lectures, and consequently derive little or no real benefit from them. The fact is that most members have absorbed as much theosophical teaching as they are able to take in for the present—they have reached saturation point. The question thus arises: what is the next step? I would suggest a perhaps obvious answer. Let the knowledge attained be crystallized out in action. In other words, let more definite attempts be made by individuals or groups of individuals to apply the principles they have accepted to the concerns of daily life. For years we have been garnering, let us now sow. In many of the existing social, municipal, political, scientific and religious institutions there is ample scope for the introduction of ideas and principles generally received as theosophical, and to these some of our members might give their special attention. Where suitable organizations do not exist, thought should be given to the introduction of new movements likely to be of general service. The knowledge we have gained is, I take it, for the use of men, in a world of men.
>
> Another and equally important matter for consideration is the need for more definite and systematic attempts to carry out the second and third objects of our Society. This is however much more than a mere lodge matter, it concerns the Section, if not the Society as a whole, and should be

dealt with as such. Nevertheless the lodges might become important factors in any scheme for better attaining the objects referred to, and it would be well if attention were directed to the whole subject with a view to common action later.

In conclusion, may I suggest that the pages of *The Vâhan* might, with advantage, be devoted to a consideration of the question of the better working of the lodges and of the Society.

W.H. Thomas.

★

In the November issue this correspondence was continued:

Friend Thomas raises a most interesting question for our consideration. To keep theosophical lodges alive he suggests introducing theosophical ideas into existing institutions, and where such institutions do not exist he suggests our starting organizations likely to be of general service to our fellows. This would no doubt be valuable work, but how would it keep theosophical lodges alive, as such?

The fact of the matter is: the Theosophical Movement has outgrown all Theosophical Societies, and no genuine effort has yet been made to unite the various Theosophical Societies. Our methods have not appreciably altered to suit the changed conditions. Our propaganda is carried on on the old lines. Our annual Conventions afford us an opportunity to consider our work—our real work—but we spend the time discussing paltry rules and regulations. How can the Spirit descend among us? Our cut and dried programme will not admit of it. Could we not, at least, change this and come together for the consideration of real and vital issues affecting the life of men and our relation thereto as a Society? *The Theosophical Review* is beyond the scope of our deliberations and we can give no consideration to any suggestions for its improvement! *The Vâhan* must go on as it has from the beginning! Our meetings must be carried on exactly on the old lines!

Well, if we cannot change these activities we can change ourselves. In the end it all comes back to each of us individually. One of my most excellent friends in his own inimitable way recently made some excellent suggestions in relation to work of another kind. Let me briefly summarize what I think applies to ourselves. We have surrendered to books much other activity associated closely with the life of men. Spiritual culture in the old time came 'as an exaltation of life itself'—not at the expense of life. In our lodges we should stir up the old imaginative life. The true philosophy of *life* is seeking its masters again. We must get nearer to human life till religion grows 'like a flower out of the stem of life'.

Specialized energy is not life, and 'life forgets what is self-sufficient'.

In our lodges, in our Conventions, and in all other institutions, we should appear as messengers who carry great news—interesting and even exciting.

> We should speak 'of far-off things' with animation. The ways are endless, but the messengers—what of them? Are they not at fault? Do they not speak with sleepy voices and give utterance for the most part to second-hand platitudes? Do we think to find the shining soul by psychical research or through some spiritualistic séance? I think, my friends, we lose our life among the tombs. The old enchantment thus forsakes us, and we look weary. Life will return to our lodges when the spring awakens in our hearts the magic of the first days. Be of good cheer! The greatest sinners among us (I wish we loved sinners more) may become the magicians and builders. Let us meet the Master in our own hearts, and He will restore memory of our powers and show us again the plans of the great building.
>
> D.N. Dunlop

★

A passage in John Dummelow's history, *1899–1949* (1949), of the first 50 years of the Metropolitan-Vickers Electrical Company (successor to the British Westinghouse Company) reads:

> More intangible but no less important than technical and commercial efficiency was the spirit prevailing in the works. The greatest benefits were obtained from social activities, which appeared at an early date in sporadic outbreaks of departmental picnics and hot-pot suppers, and these were strongly reinforced in 1905 by the formation of the British Westinghouse Engineers' Club, chiefly of engineers and apprentices. The object of the Club was 'to provide a means of transmitting to younger employees of the firm, apprentices in particular, knowledge possessed by older members'. There were two sections, general and technical: one covered cricket, tennis, and association football, and the other held weekly meetings where papers were presented by leading officials on some aspect of the Company's activities, discussions following.
>
> It flourished exceedingly. A great success of the second year was a 'parliamentary debating society' with A. McKinstry as Prime Minister, A.P.M. Fleming as Foreign Secretary, J. Bissett as Chancellor of the Exchequer, F. Crompton as Chief Government Whip, and D.N. Dunlop sitting on the cross benches where he could be relied upon to keep the proceedings interesting. New social sections developed quickly, chess enthusiasts being early in the field, and an annual dinner for the staff became an established function. Altogether the Club played a great part by instilling a habit of co-operation among its members and bringing into the organization a democratic spirit, then very unusual but an asset to the whole company.

In Freemasonic Terminology

In February of the next year, 1907, Colonel Olcott died at Adyar in India. The circumstances of the last fortnight of his life included spiritualistic manifestations during which directives were received from the other world, or at any rate from a certain part of the other world, to the effect that Annie Besant should be the Society's next President, and Charles Leadbeater be readmitted as a member.

All this gave rise to extensive controversy throughout the whole Theosophical Society. Nonetheless Besant won by a substantial majority the ensuing election to the Presidency.

★

In the middle of May the International Congress hosted by the German Section was held at Munich. Its major importance for the historical development of anthroposophy during this period is well known.

At around the same time there also occurred another event which is less well known but of equal or perhaps even greater significance in regard to the dissemination of anthroposophy in the world at large, namely, the first appearance in the twentieth century of a complete piece of work by Rudolf Steiner in English translation. This was the lecture he had given at the 1905 London Congress, which appeared in the Congress *Transactions*, finally published in the spring of 1907.

In its printed form the lecture began as follows:

> The Occult Basis of Goethe's Work
> Dr. Rudolf Steiner
> (from the German)
>
> Theosophy will only be able to fulfil its great and universal mission in modern civilization when it is able to grasp the special problems which have arisen in every land by reason of the intellectual possessions of the people. In Germany these special problems are in part determined by the inheritance bequeathed to her intellectual life by the men of genius living at the close of the eighteenth and beginning of the nineteenth centuries. Anyone who approaches those great minds, Lessing, Herder, Schiller, Goethe, Novalis, Jean Paul and many others, from the point of view of theosophical thought and attitude towards life, will have two important experiences. The first being that, as a result of this profoundly spiritual attitude, a new light is thrown upon the working and work of those men of genius; the second that through them Theosophy receives new life-blood, which must, in some way as yet not clear, produce a fructifying and strengthening effect in the future. It may be said without exaggeration that the German will understand

> Theosophy if he only brings his mind to bear upon the highest conceptions for which the leading spirits of his land have striven, and which they have embodied in their works.
>
> It will be the task of future generations to reveal the theosophical and occult basis of the great advancement in the intellectual life of Germany during the period in question. It will then be shown what an intimate knowledge and understanding of influences at work during this period is obtainable by regarding things from a theosophical point of view. It is only possible on this occasion to make a few references to one man of genius who was the leading light of this age of culture, namely, Goethe . . .

These 'few references' to Goethe were elaborated over the next 14 pages, which British theosophists would have been poring over at the very time when the Congress was being held in far-distant Munich.

One may perhaps wonder whether their attention was especially held by statements Steiner had made in London about the relations of man to the three worlds, physical, astral and spiritual, as illustrated by Goethe's *Märchen*:

> . . . Here again we can only point out a few short passages; it would need a large book to show how Goethe's theosophy is concealed in this poem. The 'three worlds' are here represented as two regions separated from one another by a river. The river itself stands for the astral plane. On this side of it is the physical world, on the other side the spiritual (Devachan), where dwells the 'beautiful lily', the symbol of man's higher nature. In her kingdom man must strive if he would unite his lower with his higher nature. In the abyss—that is in the physical world—dwells the serpent which symbolizes the self of man. Here too is a 'temple' of initiation, where reign four kings, one golden, one silver, one bronze, and a fourth an irregular mixture of the three metals. Goethe, who was a Freemason, has clothed in Freemasonic terminology what he had to impart of his mystic experiences . . .

Goethe was admitted on 23 June 1780 as an Apprentice to the 'Amalia at the Three Roses' Lodge in Weimar. In 1781 he was advanced, and in 1782 rose to Master. During this latter year he joined the inner Order of Strict Observance. And in February 1783 he even entered the Order of the Illuminati.[14]

A Memorable Gathering

Ever since the London Congress of 1905 Rudolf Steiner had been 'building up theosophical life on all sides' and 'improving what needs to be improved', to use the phrases from his report of that occasion. The result was that at Munich in 1907 the artistic, musical and dramatic elements presented—however inadequately—two years previously in London were put into central place. This centrality, according to the account in Steiner's autobiography, radically distinguished the Munich Congress from the three preceding ones (listed by him, it may be noted, not in chronological order but in one which gave priority of mention to the London Congress of 1905):

> The Theosophical Congress to be arranged in 1907 by the German Section took place in Munich. These Congresses, previously held in London, Amsterdam and Paris, included arrangements for dealing with theosophical problems in lectures or discussions, and were modelled on scholarly gatherings. Even administrative questions in the Theosophical Society were dealt with.
>
> In Munich much of all this was modified. We—the organizers—furnished the big concert hall serving for the conference with an interior decoration reproducing in both form and colour the prevalent mood in the content of the case we were presenting. The artistic surroundings and spiritual activity in this space were to form a harmonious unity. I placed the very greatest value on avoiding abstract, inartistic symbolism and letting artistic feeling speak for itself.
>
> An artistic offering was included in the programme of the Congress. Marie von Sivers had long since translated Schuré's reconstruction of the drama of Eleusis. I gave it a linguistic arrangement for performance. We included this drama in the programme. A connection, in however weak a form, was thus established with the ancient mysteries. But the main thing was that the Congress included artistic work—an artistic element indicating a will no longer to allow in the Society any spiritual life without art. In her performance Marie von Sivers, who had taken the role of Demeter, already gave clear indications of the nuances which dramatic art in the Society was to attain.—Besides, we were at a point where the art of declamation and recitation, by working out of the inner power of the word, had through Marie von Sivers come to a decisive stage from which further fruitful progress in this realm might be made.
>
> A large proportion of older members in the Theosophical Society from England, France, and especially Holland were inwardly dissatisfied with the innovations brought to them by the Munich Congress...

⋆

In view of this last sentence, coming as it does in the autobiography's final paragraph and written at the very end of Steiner's life, it is curiously ironic that the report of the Congress published for British readers in *The Vâhan* was not composed by an 'older' member of the Society at all. Its author was a certain James Wedgwood, who plays in the story of the present book an interesting but ultimately tragic role.

Wedgwood came from the famous potting family in the Midlands. He was born in 1883, educated in Nottingham, and on leaving school first found work as a chemist. While still quite young he soon however became attracted to the vocation of priest in the Anglican Church, for which he started to train in York. It was here in 1904, at the age of 21, that he heard a lecture by Annie Besant which drew him at once to theosophy. Forthwith abandoning his ecclesiastical training, he not only joined the Theosophical Society but soon started to become active within it.

At the time of the Munich Congress Wedgwood was no more than 24 years old, and having only joined the Society three years previously could not in any way be described as an 'older' member.

Here in full is Wedgwood's undeniably appreciative account, which would have been perused by the British theosophical readership of the day:

> The Congress of the Federation of European Sections held at Munich in May was not only a most successful gathering, considered from all points of view, but one of peculiar interest. The membership numbered perhaps some five hundred, towards which the British Section contributed twenty-seven. Representatives of the French, Dutch, Scandinavian, Italian, and the newly formed Hungarian Sections were present. From India came Mrs. Besant, Mrs. Russak, Miss Appel and Mr. and Miss Arundale; and one member hailed from America. Mr. Keightley and Mr. Mead, whose presence had at one time been expected, were both prevented from coming, the one remaining in India, the other in England. Officially present on behalf of the British Section were: Miss Spink, the General Secretary; Mr. Wedgwood, the Hon. Secretary of the Congress Committee; and Mr. Wallace.
>
> Two circumstances combined to render the Congress an occasion of more than ordinary interest; the first was, of course, the appearance amongst us again of Mrs. Besant, but this time as our President-nominate, the other was the opportunity of making the acquaintance of Dr. Steiner and his band of co-workers, amidst their own surroundings. The arrangements of the Congress were in the hands of the German Committee, and were drawn up so as to provide for the meetings a characteristic environment, intended to express the spirit of the traditional mid-European occultism. In Dr. Steiner our Society possesses a worker of many-sided attainments, a hard thinker, well versed in philosophy, an authority on Goethe's works of no mean renown, an occultist, himself the possessor of psychic faculties—such is the able Secretary and leader of the German Section. Dr. Steiner is a specialist in Rosicrucian lore; and it was this branch of occultism which was put before us with such ability and force in his lectures, and in the decoration of the

Congress hall. The room was draped all over in red, surrounded with shields and other decorative devices which represented great cosmological truths according to Rosicrucian symbology. At the front of the hall stood the two pillars of the Masonic and Kabbalistic lore, and zodiacal signs adorned the platform. Much music, rendered according to the true German spirit, and some admirable recitations regaled us; and the contemplation of some powerful sculpture by Dr. Ernst Wagner, one of the members, bewailed our scanty leisure moments. Nor, in sooth, should be omitted mention of an excellent vegetarian restaurant, opened by members of the Munich Lodge.

Dr. Steiner welcomed Mrs. Besant as President of Honour of the Congress, recalling her splendid work for the Society. What above all else, he said, constituted her chief claim on our gratitude was the fact that to so many of us she had been the portal to the spiritual life. He next passed an eloquent testimony to the work of Col. Olcott, the Congress standing the while. Col. Olcott's service to the Society he had helped to found would ever remain deep in our hearts. What had so crowned his labours with success was his devotion and enthusiasm, and his recognition of the treasure of individual liberty.

Mrs. Besant delivered three addresses, all of which were profoundly impressive—an opening address, and two lectures on 'The Place of Phenomena in the Theosophical Society', and 'The Relation of Masters to the Theosophical Society'. As these form the substance of lectures given at the Northern Federation Conference, and now being given in London, no attempt need here be made in the brief space available to indicate the nature of their contents.

Two lectures were given by Dr. Steiner, each lasting for an hour and three quarters, delivered with great force and rare eloquence. The first dealt with 'The Initiation of the Rosicrucians'. The seven stages of progress were symbolically expressed, he said, in St. John's Gospel, which was an initiation book, a picture of the spiritual life; and the Rosicrucian tradition was a Christian one. Taken in its entirety, the sevenfold initiatory scheme constituted a colossal moral lesson, which carried us up to the threshold of the spiritual world. The second lecture was entitled 'Planetary and Human Evolution'. Dr. Steiner dealt first with man's origin and aim, and the constitution of his nature, and pointed out that man was more evolved on the physical than on any other plane. Man's planetary evolution consisted in the unfoldment of different stages of consciousness. Dr. Steiner treated his subject from the Rosicrucian standpoint, advancing the idea that the planet on which we evolved was but one and the same planet, in different states or conditions, known as the Saturn, Sun and Moon state or influence in the past, the Earth state in the present, and the Jupiter, Venus and Vulcan states lying yet in advance. He spoke also of human conditions in Atlantis. Occultism was the supreme science, and he maintained that the dissemination of occult knowledge and research was the main purpose of the Theosophical Society, its first two objects being dependent on its third and most immediately important object.

Mr. Alan Leo read a paper on 'Astrology and Personal Fate', taking astrology along its esoteric side as dealing with influences and occult forces operating through planetary bodies. The burden of the paper was a masterly discourse on the age-old problem of free will and fate, showing how esoteric astrology illuminated the subject. Dr. Pascal contributed a well-reasoned paper on 'Unity and Hierarchy'. Herr Michael Bauer spoke on the unity of Nature, and drew an analogical representation of human progress by a study of natural progress. Mr. Wedgwood followed with a paper on 'The Value of the Theosophical Society' from a synthetic standpoint. He maintained that the study of occultism was most valuable in that it displayed to us the divine purpose, and enabled us to become conscious co-operators with the divine will. Dealing, as occultism did, with cosmic processes, the study of it should tend to instil into us wide-mindedness.

Mdlle. Kamensky traced the stream of theosophic thought in Russian literature, and referred to the vast stores of esoteric wisdom embedded in the rites and ceremonies of the Greek Church and preserved amongst hermits and monastic orders. Mr. Arvid Knös sounded a metaphysical note in his paper on 'Absolute and Relative Truths'. Frau Wolfram contributed an interesting paper on 'The Occult Basis of the Siegfried Myth', pointing out its Atlantean origin, and its application as an allegory of the relations of the higher and lower self.

On the last day of the Congress the proceedings took the shape of a discussion on 'The Necessity of supporting Occultism within the Theosophical Society'. It developed into what was virtually an interesting discussion on the value of spiritualism. Herr Agoston, of Budapest, started the ball rolling with a plea for the organized experimental investigation of psychic phenomena within the Theosophical Society. The following took part in the discussion: Messrs. Hubo, Deinhard, Unger, Bauer, Van Ginkel, Dezso, Wedgwood, Miss Severs and Frau Wolfram. Mrs. Dunglass spoke on 'Fellowship with Christ', dealing with the new theology, and there was a discussion on the education of children. Dr. Carl Unger, in addition, read a paper dealing with some philosophical aspects of theosophical teachings.

In conclusion, mention must be made of one most interesting and enjoyable event—the performance of a mystery play by M. Edouard Schuré, entitled *The Sacred Drama of Eleusis*, and translated from the French. The production and representation was undertaken entirely by amateur members, under the personal direction of Dr. Steiner, who worked out the scenic effects to the smallest detail. Musical interludes of an impressive character were written specially for the occasion by Herr Bernhard Stavenhagen. The performance, which was divided into a prologue and three acts, was greeted with prolonged applause, the dramatic power of Fräulein von Sivers, who took the part of Demeter, receiving special recognition. At the conclusion a telegram of thanks and congratulation was sent in the name of the Congress to M. Schuré, who is a personal friend of Dr. Steiner.

This rough sketch of a memorable gathering must suffice, for—one may say with St. John—were the many other doings of the Congress to be chronicled, even the whole of *The Vâhan* itself would not contain what could be written. Two years hence the Congress is to meet at Budapest, as the honoured guest of the newly formed Hungarian Section.

The many other doings of the Munich Congress have since been extensively chronicled in the 207-page volume *Bilder Okkulter Siegel und Säulen* (GA 284), which includes all official reports in German about the Congress, but makes no mention whatsoever of the report in the world-language.

Full of Life and Reality

Now the report of the 1907 Munich Congress written by James Wedgwood shows that although a relative newcomer on the theosophical scene, he had not failed to notice the Masonic significance of the two pillars decorating the Congress hall.

It is therefore especially striking that the only other published English reminiscence of this Congress, in Esther Bright's *Old Memories and Letters of Annie Besant* (1936), also relates to Masonic affairs:

> May 1907. My mother and I left London to meet Mrs. Besant in Munich early in May to attend the German Congress. I quote from my diary of that date:
>
> 'A.B. came on straight to us at Munich. The Congress a great success. Steiner impresses her favourably; I am glad. His Masonic ceremonies are full of life and reality and he looks fine in his black robes and brilliant red decorations.'

This diary entry reveals that during or around the time of the Munich Congress its authoress attended one or more cultic rituals conducted by Rudolf Steiner within the context of the Mystica Aeterna.

At this point a second text will consequently be brought forward from the volume *Zur Geschichte und aus den Inhalten der erkenntniskultischen Abteilung der Esoterischen Schule 1904–1914*. It is a fragmentary text by Rudolf Steiner preserved in the handwriting of Marie von Sivers. The precise context of its use is not known.

The Rosicrucian Mason in the soul of his spirit promises to his God to make himself into a bearer of *Wisdom*. A temple of this God does he behold in the human sheath of his being. He promises to make himself into a builder of this temple. Nothing will he think, which would put wisdom to shame. There hovers before his eyes the motto:

My thinking shall everywhere seek thee, divine spirit.

The Rosicrucian Mason would make himself into a servant of *Beauty*; he pledges himself to beauty, because in her womb alone may flourish the life of the God in his soul. The Rosicrucian Mason avoids a semblance which contradicts being; he seeks true incarnation in the semblance of being. There breathes in his breath the motto:

My speech shall reveal thee, divine soul.

The Rosicrucian Mason would make himself into a sheath for *Courage*; he pledges himself to courage, because only through *its* fire may ripen the being of God in his heart. The Rosicrucian Mason seeks to flee cowardice, which only lames the progress of all healing; he seeks courage, which paves the way for all progress with a sharp two-edged sword. There beats in his heart the motto:

My heartbeat shall affirm thee, divine will.

★

When the Congress was over, Besant stayed on in Munich for another week. Discussions took place between her and Steiner in the course of which a decision was made to separate off that part of the Esoteric School led by him, as a Western body distinct from the main Eastern part.

On her return to England, Besant penned a letter from the Brights' London home to Wilhelm Hübbe-Schleiden, explaining her view of the situation:

31, St James' Place,
London, S.W.
7/6/07

Dear Dr. Hübbe-Schleiden,

Dr. Steiner's occult training is very different from ours. He does not know the Eastern way, so cannot, of course, teach it. He teaches the Xtian & Rosicrucian way, & this is very helpful to some, but is different from ours. He has his own School, on his own responsibility. I regard him as a very fine teacher on his own lines, & as a man of real knowledge. He & I work in thorough friendship & harmony, but along different lines.

Yours ever sincerely,

Annie Besant

★

While Besant had gone to London, Steiner for his part returned to Berlin, where he wrote up an extensive report of the Congress for *Lucifer-Gnosis*.

He also sent off a telegram received at the Annual Convention of the British Section held in London on 6 July:

> Hearty congratulations from the German Section to the British one and fraternal wishes for prosperous work.
>
> Dr. Rudolf Steiner,
> General Secretary, German Section.

★

The Vâhan soon announced the formation of a new lodge in the British Section:

> July 28, 1907. Charter issued this day to Mrs. S.M. Sharpe, S. Ransom, M. Gysi, J.I. Wedgwood, Mrs. J. Ransom, Mrs. F. Faulding, A.J. Faulding, Miss C.E. Woods, Miss Esther Bright, Mrs. U.M. Bright and D. Besant to form a Branch of the Theosophical Society at London to be known as the H.P.B. Lodge.
>
> Kate Spink
> General Secretary

★

In the autumn of 1907 various further works by Rudolf Steiner came out in English versions. The October issue of the international journal *The Theosophist*, published in Madras, India, and edited now by Annie Besant, included a little editorial note:

> It is with the greatest pleasure that I present to the English-speaking world, through *The Theosophist*, some of the work of the well-known Dr. Rudolf Steiner, General Secretary of our German Section, T.S.

This was followed by the first instalment, 'The Superphysical World and its Gnosis', of the series 'How does one attain Knowledge of the Higher Worlds?' The translation, which continued through several further issues until completion in June 1908, was stated in a footnote to have been undertaken 'by some members of the H.P.B. Lodge, London'.

Translation of Dr. Steiner's Works

Other translations also began to appear in Britain. In October 1907 *The Theosophical Review*, now edited by G.R.S. Mead alone, brought out an article entitled 'Blood is a Quite Special Fluid', which was 'translated and summarized by B.K.', recognizable as the initials of Bertram Keightley.

The article began:

> The development of the Theosophical Movement in Germany, and the special form which it is there assuming under the able and untiring hands of Dr. Rudolf Steiner, cannot fail to be of interest to all whose attachment to the Society is deep, and whose love of Theosophy is earnest.
>
> It may therefore prove acceptable to readers of the *Review* if from time to time an endeavour is made to put before them some of Dr. Steiner's ideas, some of his somewhat unfamiliar views of Theosophy, even though this is done in a loose and quite unsystematic form, the object aimed at being rather clearness of presentation than logical sequence or structural coherence.
>
> The issue in printed form of one of his recent lectures, the title of which, 'Blut ist ein ganz besonderer Saft', is taken from Goethe's *Faust*, gives a welcome opportunity of doing this, as it brings out very pointedly some of his leading conceptions; and I shall therefore in the present article confine myself to a close, though abbreviated, rendering of its contents...

The lecture in question had been given by Steiner in Munich in November 1906.

It was followed in the December issue by 'The Lord's Prayer Esoterically Considered. Summary from a Lecture in German. By B.K.', rendering a lecture Steiner had given in Berlin in January 1907.

Also published in late 1907 were the *Transactions* of the 1906 Paris Congress, which included Steiner's lecture on 'Theosophy in Germany a Hundred Years ago'.

★

These various translations, appearing as they did in a variety of books and journals, gave evidence of an incipient interest in Steiner's work within English-speaking theosophical circles. It may however also be noted that they did not show much coordination between the different translators.

The situation was ordered at the end of December 1907. Steiner was then staying in Cologne, where, next to a decorated Christmas tree in the Künstlers' home in Belfortstrasse, he was giving a cycle of lectures on 'Occult Signs and Symbols'. According to a report in the *Mitteilungen*, guests were present from several foreign countries, including England. Discussions must have taken place with these English friends, as a result of which Steiner composed a short notice for British readers.

For reasons unknown the publication of this notice seems to have been deferred, since it only appeared in *The Vâhan* a few months later, in April 1908, under the title 'Translation of Dr. Steiner's Works':

> It has happened on several occasions that an article or book of mine has been translated into English by more than one person at the same time. In order to avoid a recurrence of such duplication of labour, I have appointed as my representative in England for this purpose Mr. Max Gysi, c/o the General Secretary, 28 Albemarle Street, London, W., and request all persons who contemplate translating into English any of my writings to communicate their intention to Mr. Gysi, who will be glad to give any information that may help them in their work.
>
> Rudolf Steiner,
> Cologne.

★

In May *The Vâhan* made a further announcement about 'Lectures by Dr. Steiner':

> The General Secretary of the German Section, Dr. Rudolf Steiner, will give a series of fourteen lectures in Nuremberg on 'Theosophie an der Hand der Apokalypse' ('Theosophy in the Apocalypse'). The lectures, for members only, begin on June 18th and continue till July 1st. Members desirous of attending should write in good time to Mr. Michael Bauer, Wunzelburg-strasse 3, Nuremberg.
>
> Those members who had the privilege of attending the last Congress in Munich will, no doubt, gladly avail themselves of this opportunity of hearing Dr. Steiner again.

Practising Meditation

Clifford Bax, whose early autobiography *Inland Far* was published in 1925, became in course of time a prolific writer in a whole variety of fields. And in later years he went on to bring out further essays of memoir character.

Rosemary for Remembrance (1948) was composed in chapters devoted to specific people, one of which was headed 'AE'. Describing once again, with a few different details, his first meeting with AE in August 1906, he ended:

> . . . It is astonishing to hear that at one time he was a tongue-tied loon, for there can seldom have been a more copious talker since Coleridge. On this occasion he said, I recall, that you could see a visionary form whether you had your eyes open or shut. You were seeing with a different sight.
>
> Soon after this exciting encounter I met an early friend of AE, an

engineer called Daniel Dunlop. They had lived—and others with them—in a community studying *The Secret Doctrine* and practising meditation...

Bax's meeting with Dunlop probably took place in London in the context of the Theosophical Society in 1908. By this time the enthusiastic 22-year-old had started to bring out the art magazine named *Orpheus*, which he had discussed with AE.

The reference to the 'community studying *The Secret Doctrine* and practising meditation' is to the 'Household' which lodged from 1891 to 1897 at 3 Upper Ely Place in Dublin. Since 'Meditation' was indeed a subject to which AE came to devote a whole chapter in *The Candle of Vision* (1918), this seems a quite appropriate context in which to reproduce it.

There is no personal virtue in me other than this: that I followed a path all may travel but on which few do journey. It is a path within ourselves, where the feet first falter in shadow and darkness, but which is later made gay by heavenly light. As one who has travelled a little on that way and who has had some far-off vision of the Many-Coloured Land, if I tell what I know, and how I came to see most clearly, I may give hope to those who would fain believe in that world the seers spake of, but who cannot understand the language written by those who had seen that beauty of old, or who may have thought the ancient scriptures but a record of extravagant desires.

None need special gifts or genius. Gifts? There are no gifts. For all that is ours we have paid the price. There is nothing we aspire to for which we cannot barter some spiritual merchandise of our own. Genius? There is no stinting of this by the Keeper of the Treasure House. It is not bestowed but is won. Yon man of heavy soul might if he willed play on the lyre of Apollo, that drunkard be god-intoxicated. Powers are not bestowed by caprice on any.

The formulae the chemist illustrates, making exposition before his students, are not more certainly verifiable than the formulae of that alchemy by which what is gross in us may be transmuted into ethereal fires. Our religions make promises to be fulfilled beyond the grave because they have no knowledge now to be put to the test, but the ancients spake of a divine vision to be attained while we are yet in the body. The religion which does not cry out 'I am today verifiable, as that water wets, or that fire burns. Test me, that ye can become as gods'—mistrust it. Its messengers are prophets of the darkness.

As we sink deeper into the Iron Age we are met by the mighty devils of state and empire lurking in the abyss, claiming the soul for their own, moulding it to their image, to be verily their own creature and not heaven's. We need a power in ourselves that can confront these mighty powers.

Though I am blind, I have had moments of sight. Though I have sinned, I have been on the path. Though I am feeble, I have seen the way to power. I sought out ways to make more securely my own those magical lights that dawned and faded within me. I wished to evoke them at will and be master of my vision, and I was taught to do this which is as old as human life. Day after day, at times where none might interfere, and where none through love or other cause were allowed to interfere, I set myself to attain mastery over the will. I would choose some mental object, an abstraction of form, and strive to hold my mind fixed on it in unwavering concentration, so that not for a moment, not for an instant, would the concentration slacken.

It is an exercise this, a training for higher adventures of the soul. It is no light labour. The ploughman's cleaving the furrows is easier by far. Five minutes of this effort will at first leave us trembling as at the close of a laborious day. It is then we realize how little of life has been our own, and how much a response to sensation, a drifting on the tide of desire. The rumour of revolt—the spirit would escape its thraldom—runs through the body. Empires do not send legions so swiftly to frustrate revolt as all that is mortal in us hurries along nerve, artery and every highway of the body to beset the soul. The beautiful face of one we love, more alluring than life, glows before us to enchant us from our task. Old sins, enmities, vanities and desire beleaguer and beseech us. If we do not heed them they change, they seem to be with us, they open up vistas of all we and they will do, when this new power we strive for is attained. If we are tempted down that vista we find with shame, after an hour of vain musing, that we were lured away, had deserted our task and forgotten that stern fixity of the will we set out to achieve.

Let us persevere in our daily ritual and the turmoil increases; our whole being becomes vitalized, the bad as well as the good. The heat of this fervent concentration acts like fire under a pot, and everything in our being boils up madly. We learn our own hitherto unknown character. We did not know we could feel such fierce desires, never imagined such passionate enmities as now awaken. We have created in ourselves a centre of power, and grow real to ourselves. It is dangerous, too, for we have flung ourselves into the eternal conflict between spirit and matter, and find ourselves where the battle is hottest, where the foemen are locked in a death struggle. We are in grips with mightier powers than we had before conceived of.

What man is there who thinks he has self-control? He stands in the shallow waters, nor has gone into the great deep, nor been tossed at the mercy of the waves. Let him rouse the arcane powers in himself, and he will feel like one who has let loose the avalanche. None would live through that turmoil if the will were the only power in ourselves we could invoke, for the will is neither good nor bad, but is power only, and it vitalizes good or bad indifferently. If that were all, our labour would bring us not closer to divine being, but only to a dilation of the personality.

But the ancients who taught us to gain this intensity taught it but as preliminary to a meditation which would not waver and would be full of power. The meditation they urged on us has been explained as 'the inexpressible yearning of the inner man to go out into the infinite'. But that infinite we would enter is living. It is the ultimate being of us. Meditation is a fiery brooding on that majestical Self. We imagine ourselves into its vastness. We conceive ourselves as mirroring its infinitudes, as moving in all things, as living in all beings, in earth, water, air, fire, aether. We try to know as it knows, to live as it lives, to be compassionate as it is compassionate. We equal ourselves to it, that we may understand it and become it. We do not kneel to it as slaves, but as Children of the King we lift ourselves up to that Glory, and affirm to ourselves that we are what we imagine. 'What a man thinks, that he is: that is the old secret,' said the wise. We have imagined ourselves into this pitiful dream of life. By imagination and will we re-enter true being, becoming that we conceive of.

On that path of fiery brooding, I entered. At first all was stupor. I felt as one who steps out of day into the colourless night of a cavern, and that was because I had suddenly reversed the habitual motions of life. We live normally seeing through the eyes, hearing through the ears, stirred by the senses, moved by bodily powers, and receiving only such spiritual knowledge as may pass through a momentary purity of our being. On the mystic path we create our own light, and at first we struggle blind and baffled, seeing nothing, hearing nothing, unable to think, unable to imagine. We seem deserted by dream, vision or inspiration, and our meditation barren altogether. But let us persist through weeks or months, and sooner or later that stupor disappears. Our faculties readjust themselves, and do the work we will them to do. Never did they do their work so well. The dark caverns of the brain begin to grow luminous. We are creating our own light. By heat of will and aspiration we are transmuting what is gross in the subtle aethers through which the mind works. As the dark bar of metal begins to glow, at first redly, and then at white heat, or as ice melts and is alternately fluid, vapour, gas, and at last a radiant energy, so do these aethers become purified and alchemically changed into luminous essences, and they make a new vesture for the soul, and link us to mid-world, or heavenward where they too have their true home.

How quick the mind is now! How vivid is the imagination! We are lifted above the tumult of the body. The heat of the blood disappears below us. We draw nigher to ourselves. The heart longs for the hour of meditation and hurries to it; and, when it comes, we rise within ourselves as a diver too long under seas rises to breathe the air, to see the light. We have invoked the god, and we are answered according to old promise. As our aspiration so is our inspiration. We imagine it as Love, and what a love enfolds us! We conceive of it as Might, and we take power from that Majesty. We dream of it as Beauty, and the Magician of the Beautiful appears everywhere at its miraculous art, and the multitudinous lively creatures of its thought are busy moulding Nature and life in their image, and all are hurrying to the Golden World.

This vision brings its own proof to the spirit, but words cannot declare or explain it. We must go back to lower levels, and turn to that which has form from that which is bodiless.

Brotherly Spirit

In the year 1908 Annie Besant decided to reinstate Charles Leadbeater as a member of the Theosophical Society.

This decision gave rise to great controversy throughout the Society, especially in the British Section. The tensions can be perceived in the 'Report of Proceedings' of the Eighteenth Annual Convention held that year, as published in *The Vâhan*:

> The Convention assembled for its business meeting on Saturday, July 4, at 2.30 p.m., in Essex Hall, Essex Street, Strand, W.C., a large number of British members attending but very few foreign members.
>
> Miss Ward was elected to the chair and Mr. Glass and Mr Shindler were elected Secretaries of the Convention . . .
>
> The Roll Call of Branches was read by Mr. Glass . . .
>
> The minutes of the last Convention were taken as read, and adopted.
>
> Letters and telegrams of greeting were received from the German and French Sections, the Brussels Branch and a group at Liège, and the General Secretary was instructed to send the greetings of the Convention in reply.
>
> The Report of the Executive Committee was taken as read. Mr. Thomas moved and Mr. B. Theobald seconded its adoption. Adopted unanimously.
>
> Miss Ward spoke on the accounts . . .
>
> Mr. Dunlop moved and Mrs Sharpe seconded the adoption of the report.
>
> After some questions, replied to by Miss Ward, the report was adopted . . .
>
> Mr. Dunlop then proposed the following, seconded by Mr. Ransom:
>
> 'The British Section of the Theosophical Society by its delegates and members in Convention assembled:
>
> '(a) Affirms the right of each individual member to hold and express any belief or disbelief concerning any psychic phenomena, or any other matter of philosophical belief, without question from any member of the Society, official or otherwise.
>
> '(b) It declares further that the Section as a whole should not have less than the generous spirit of its units, that it should exercise the same brotherly spirit alike to those of good or evil fame, expressing the love which rejects none.'

This second clause reproduces statements made by AE in an article 'On the Spur of the Moment' written with reference to W.Q. Judge and published in *The Irish Theosophist* in February 1895.

'(c) And it takes this opportunity of expressing on behalf of all members love and gratitude to the President of the Theosophical Society for the help received from her in the past, and the desire to unite with her in furthering the work of the Theosophical Society in the world, relying upon the laws of life to justify and sustain every true theosophical effort.'

The discussion on this resolution was continued at two adjourned meetings, on the Saturday evening at 7.30 and Sunday morning at 10.30.

The clauses were voted on separately, clauses (a) and (c) being passed *nem. con.*, and clause (b) amended.

A special report of the proceedings in connection with this resolution is being prepared for members of the Theosophical Society only. A committee was appointed by the Convention to settle this report, the Committee consisting of Miss Ward, Mrs. Sharpe, Mr. Burrows, Mr. Mead and Mr. Whyte. Difficulties having arisen in connection with its preparation, its issue is delayed.

Mr. Dunlop moved, and Mr. Old seconded:

'That in view of the Treasurer's letter in the May *Vâhan* a Committee of three be hereby appointed to investigate the financial affairs of the Section and make such recommendations to the Executive Committee as they may think desirable to put its finance on a sound basis.'

Mr. Twelvetrees agreed to withdraw the resolution standing in his name, urging the removal of Headquarters to a less expensive position, on the understanding that it should be a recommendation to the Committee.

On Mr. Mead's proposal Mr. Dunlop accepted a Committee of five instead of three, and on Mr. H. Sidley's suggestion included power to add to their number.

The resolution put to the meeting therefore stood:

'That in view of the Treasurer's letter in the May *Vâhan* a Committee of five, with power to add to their number, be hereby appointed to investigate the financial affairs of the Section and make such recommendations to the Executive Committee as they may think desirable to put its finance on a sound basis, having especially the consideration of the question of Headquarters.'

This was carried *nem con* . . .

The proceedings were then brought to a close.

Of Very Great Utility

The September 1908 issue of *The Vâhan* included this announcement:

> Battersea Lodge.—The Lodge continues its Order of Service to the Society, on the same old lines—weekly public meetings from October till the end of May. The attendance equals our accomodation, as a rule. Study is continued with the Adelphi Lodge, and taken fair advantage of by the members. It is with great regret that we have to record the loss of our beloved and genial President and his wife, Mr. and Mrs. D.N. Dunlop, who have had to leave London for Manchester.

Regret for another event was expressed 27 years later, in an obituary published on the 5 June 1935 by *BEAMA News Sheet*:

> It is with deep regret that we record the death of Mr. D.N. Dunlop . . .
>
> Daniel Nicol Dunlop was born . . . attracted to the United States . . . He was returned to this country as an employee of the Pittsburgh firm, and he saw the Trafford Park works go up. England was then, so far as the electrical industry was concerned, rather the Cinderella among the competing nations, and his job here was the somewhat onerous one of Publicity Manager for the great Pittsburgh firm. The A.E.G. was then at the top of its form and was actually installing a single-phase high-tension system on one of our suburban lines, an enterprise which Westinghouse publicity failed either to avert or modify, Trafford Park not having yet got into its stride. The arrival of Newcomb Carlton, the distinguished protégé of George Westinghouse, as Managing Director for the British Company, gave him his first big chance here, for to Dunlop's department Carlton, fresh from the United States, looked for most of his information about the English scene. One of Dunlop's rewards was his appointment as a Sales Manager in addition to his management of publicity . . .

The year of the appointment was specified in a biographical notice about Dunlop published on 4 April 1934 in *Electrical Industries*:

> In 1908 he was chosen by Mr. Carlton, Managing Director of the British Westinghouse, to be Sales Manager of the Supply Department, in addition to his publicity work. It was here that he had occasion to study closely the economic and selling problems of the British electrical and manufacturing industry.

On this new appointment Dunlop was transferred from the Westinghouse Company's London office to an enormous factory-complex which the company had erected on an American scale in the then still rural surroundings of Trafford Park, west of Manchester.

Although he was only to spend three years here before leaving the Company altogether in 1911, it is revealing that after Dunlop's death no less than 24 years later, *The Metropolitan-Vickers Gazette* published in July 1935 an editorial which stated:

> The short obituary notice on the late Mr. D.N. Dunlop has been written with a view to recalling memories of Mr. Dunlop when he held an important position at our Trafford Park works. As still quite a few of our readers will remember, he was Sales Manager of the Supplies Department. In addition to this he was head of the Publishing Department.

The obituary, which included a photograph, stated:

> It is with much regret that we chronicle the death of Daniel Nicol Dunlop. We feel that the readers of this *Gazette* (which was once the *British Westinghouse Gazette*) will be interested in his work at Trafford Park. He was Sales Manager of the Supplies Department, which then included transformers, switchgear, control gear, meters and instruments, lamps and accessories.
>
> Mr. Dunlop was a man of wide culture, and made a special study of Eastern religions.
>
> There are still quite a few of his old colleagues at Trafford Park who feel his death as the passing of an old friend and a great personality.

★

Returning to 1908, plans were being made to collect and publish in book form the whole translated series by Rudolf Steiner on 'How does one attain Knowledge of the Higher Worlds?'

Annie Besant composed a foreword:

> I am very happy to recommend this valuable little work to English readers, having already circulated the articles comprised in it in the pages of *The Theosophist.* Dr. Steiner's views, representing a deeply mystical Christian Theosophy, are of very great utility, supplying a side of theosophical thought which might otherwise miss fitting recognition. He is the natural heir of the great German mystics, and adds to their profound spirituality the fine lucidity of a philosophic mind. Under his guidance, German Theosophy is taking its right place in European thought, and is becoming a real force. If English readers find herein presentments of great truths that seem somewhat unfamiliar, let them remember that in this difference lies their specific value, and let them seek to gain new views of truth by studying it from another standpoint. If they read sympathetically, seeking to understand, rather than in the spirit of antagonism, seeking to criticize, they will find many a gem of value, many a pearl of price, among the thoughts herein

presented, and Theosophy's jewelled diadem will be the richer for their insetting.

Annie Besant,
President of the Theosophical Society.
Adyar,
17th September, 1908

★

As soon as the Dunlops arrived in Cheshire, they lost no time in forming a new Branch, notified in *The Vâhan*:

> A charter dated September 22 was issued to D.N. Dunlop, Sidney Ransom, W. Owen, Alice A. Owen, Josephine Ransom, Elinor Dunlop and Annie Larmuth to form a Branch of the Theosophical Society at Hale, Cheshire, to be known as the Hale Branch.
>
> S. Maud Sharpe,
> General Secretary

The Canadian Connection

From 1892 until 1897 D.N. Dunlop was editor of *The Irish Theosophist*. In May 1895 this journal published a report 'from a correspondent' (unnamed) about the First Annual Convention of the Theosophical Society in America.

The report included the following paragraph:

> One of the best addresses was made by Mr. Smythe, of Dublin, now resident in Canada. It was markedly quiet and restrained where all were so, but had great force about it. This gentleman asked me to give to the Dublin Lodge 'the Irish wit and the Irish heart'. I've a mind to keep them for myself!

Almost two years later, in April 1897, Dunlop himself crossed over the Atlantic to attend further Theosophical Conventions in New York and Philadelphia under the leadership of Katherine Tingley, newly appointed head of the American Society. But on his return to Ireland he wrote a short article, published in the June number, stating that he had been 'in the United States and Canada'.

Although nothing further is recorded about where in Canada Dunlop may have gone to, the probability is that he travelled north-west from New York towards the border town of Buffalo—he may have visited the adjacent Niagara Falls—and passed between the Great Lakes round to Toronto, where since 1891 a theosophical lodge had been in existence. For he must have been invited to Canada by Albert E.S. Smythe, now a leading member of the Toronto Lodge.

After his return from the American continent, Dunlop was among the theosophists who greeted Tingley in June 1897 when her 'Crusade' arrived in Ireland. And three months later, in September, he and his family moved over to America altogether, settling in New York.

Here Dunlop found employment in the sales department of the Pierce and Miller engineering firm, and also took on a secretarial post for Tingley which involved writing articles for *The New Century* and other theosophical journals. In February 1898 he was present at the Convention in Chicago when a constitution was drawn up for the 'Universal Brotherhood' founded by Tingley two years before. With many other theosophists he then made his way in April 1899 across the breadth of the continent to attend another Convention at the chosen site of the 'School for the Revival of the Lost Mysteries' at Point Loma, on the Californian coast. After this Dunlop returned to New York, and although for some months he continued writing articles for *The New Century*, his disenchantment with Tingley had set in.

The sequel was related much later, in an obituary which appeared soon after Dunlop's death in the July 1935 issue of *The Canadian Theosophist.* The obituary was unsigned, but its author was certainly the editor of that journal, Albert E.S. Smythe.

> Intelligence has come to hand of the death of Daniel Nicol Dunlop at the age of 67 . . .

At the time of his death, to be precise, Dunlop was in his sixty-seventh year, so aged 66.

> . . . Mr. Dunlop was an old-time theosophist, but withdrew from the English Society in dissatisfaction with the drift towards Leadbeaterism and allied himself with the Anthroposophical Movement of Rudolf Steiner. He wrote that he found this in entire harmony with Madame Blavatsky's Secret Doctrine. He first became a member of the Theosophical Society in Dublin and was one of the group associated with George W. Russell, W.B. Yeats, Charles Johnston, Claud Falls Wright and others of the Society which gave its impetus to the Irish Literary Renascence. He contributed to the *Irish Theosophist*, and his wife Ella also wrote with exquisite taste. She sent us some poems a few years ago, before her death, and one of these was printed in our March issue, with her pen signature, Freida Dunlop . . .

The previously published poem, headed 'Venus-Aphrodite', read:

> Draw nearer, artist-soul, be not afraid!
> I long to clothe thee with my perfect beauty
> Woven strand by strand thro' age-long suffering.
> Once I was Aphrodite, foam of life's

Surging sea, cast up to Heaven, upon
A tidal wave of passion—passion pure
As is the deep red rose of sunset.

'Twas there that Eros came—pouring the wine
Of true compassion into my fragile cup
He bade me drink, e'en to the bitter dregs.
Drinking—as I was bidden by my Lord
I became the Venus—Aphrodite—
A fount of love and inspiration
In the artist-soul of man.

Therefore it is I love thee with that divine
Compassion, which is eternal justice.
Thou art Prometheus—foreseer
And foreknower, prophet, priest and king
Of this wide universe, which is thy home.
I hold life's living water to thy lips,
Drink deep, beloved, this is thy heritage.

Smythe's obituary in the July issue went on:

> ... Mr. Dunlop was associated with Mrs. Tingley as her secretary for some time after her return from the World Crusade, and his intimacy with her methods and practices caused him to change his opinion of her at the time when in 1899 he was at Point Loma. With the present writer he was reported expelled from the Universal Brotherhood at that time, though now it is stated that no such action was taken. We were certainly reported as 'black magicians', as 'the faithful' of those days can testify ...

In the issues for September and October 1899 of the theosophical journal *The Lamp*, edited by Smythe and published in Toronto, are found articles over the signature Ian Mör.[15] Further articles openly signed by Dunlop, soon named as associate editor, are found in the issues for November and December, and even after his return to the British Isles and re-establishment in London, in a few more issues until discontinuance of *The Lamp* in May 1900.

Charles Lazenby

The present chapter will examine the biographical background to the association between D.N. Dunlop and another Canadian—Charles Lazenby.

Charles Lazenby was born on Saint George's day, 23 April 1878, in the small village of Brussels, far out in the south-western part of the province of Ontario. He was a half orphan, since several months previously his father, a newly ordained Methodist minister, had drowned—six weeks after his wedding, and within sight of his newly married wife—while trying to rescue a child from a river.

Soon after the baby's birth, the widowed mother moved several hundred miles east to the town of Guelph, a little west from Toronto. She found work to support herself and her child, and lodgings in the home of a poor and elderly couple. But only three years later the mother died as well, leaving her now wholly orphaned child to be brought up by this couple in conjunction with her brother, a noted homoeopathic doctor in Toronto.

The little boy slowly grew up, and in due course went to school in Guelph. A major influence was exercised by an English master, who taught the language rigorously. Every child was made to read aloud 'as though they meant it'. Each syllable was gone over and enunciated carefully, before the sense was explained.

Holiday periods were spent with the uncle in Toronto. When the boy was no more than seven years old, his aunt would read aloud to him from the dialogues of Plato.

On reaching the age of 13, the boy was converted to Methodism, a faith held by his late father. A year later he caught typhoid fever. His uncle, when sent for, found him in a coma, but gave medical help which enabled him to recover. From this time onwards, he began to take an interest in history, literature and comparative religion.

The teenager was now moved from Guelph into Toronto, in order to attend the High School. For a few years he made good scholastic progress.

At the age of 17, however, he suffered a major accident in the school. Being fond of acrobatics he used to practise flying somersaults, and one day made a disastrous landing which broke his coccyx. He managed to struggle home, but there collapsed on his back. In addition abcesses broke out all over his body, which his uncle was at first unable either to diagnose or to cure.

The uncle however would neither give him painkillers nor put him in braces. On finally discovering that the abcesses were caused by mercury poisoning, he prescribed an antidote which cleared them up. But the painful spinal problem healed only very gradually, and for the next four years the youth was obliged to remain on his back.

Although he profited from his enforced inactivity by reading voraciously on all manner of subjects, the prime of his youth slowly passed away, and by the time he recovered and learnt again how to walk, he had reached the age of 21. This would have been in the spring of the year 1899.

★

Now the Toronto Lodge of the Theosophical Society had been in existence since 1891, when Lazenby was aged 13. At some point during his youth his aunt took him to this lodge, where he borrowed a copy of *The Secret Doctrine*. He went on to attend lodge lectures in a wheelchair, which would have been after his accident in about 1895, and must have come into contact with Albert E.S. Smythe. It is therefore quite possible to suppose that Dunlop during his visit to Canada in the spring of 1897 could already have met the young invalid who was then just turning 19, the more so since Lazenby's aunt held in her home a kind of salon frequented by travelling luminaries. It is equally reasonable to imagine that after his move to America and the eventual debacle with Tingley and her Universal Brotherhood in the autumn of 1899, Dunlop made a further visit to Toronto to make arrangements with Smythe about editing *The Lamp*.

There is no record of what exactly Lazenby was doing during the years 1899–1901, except that he wanted to make up for his so-to-speak 'lost' years by going to study at university. His kind uncle duly raised the necessary funds, and in 1901 the 23-year-old enrolled in the University of Toronto.

Already by 1902 this rather mature undergraduate began giving lectures to first-year students on the subject of psychology, as well as publishing articles and poems in the university's magazine, *Varsity*. And together with some friends he founded two university clubs, significantly named the Heretics and the Iconoclasts.

During university vacations Lazenby took different kinds of casual work. Once he was employed as a kind of linesman by the Canadian railways. On four occasions, to further his studies in psychology, he crossed just over the border into the States and worked in an asylum for the mentally disturbed in Gowanda, 30 miles south of Buffalo. In this situation he managed so well that after only a month's training the warden of the asylum put him in charge of a whole floor.

On another occasion he travelled much further east, into Connecticut, and found work at Elbert Hubbard's little town of Roycroft in East Aurora, practising pottery, bookbinding and publishing. This is of particular interest since Dunlop contributed an article about this establishment to an English quarterly named *The Shrine*—edited by his Irish relative R.H. Fitzpatrick—in its issue of May–July 1902.

Alongside other extracurricular activities Lazenby maintained his interest in theosophy, and after graduating in 1904 formally joined the Theosophical Society, his diploma bearing the signature of Colonel Olcott.

The 26-year-old graduate was at once employed as an assistant in the Psychology Department of Toronto University. But he soon desired a further expansion of his horizons, and on several occasions worked his way across the Atlantic.

So even if Lazenby had not met Dunlop before, he must during these years have been put into contact with him by Smythe. *The Vâhan* shows indeed that on 6 October 1907 Smythe was on a visit to England, lecturing to the Battersea Lodge—whose President was Dunlop—on 'The Theosophic Attitude'.

★

Sometime during 1908 Lazenby took a working passage on an Italian ship going from England to the Mediterranean. The ship called in at Malta, and here he obtained a visa to enter Egypt. On arrival in that country, he had no money, and little to eat or drink. But he was able to visit the pyramids, and even read aloud to the Sphinx from Blavatsky's *The Voice of the Silence*! (Presumably he read in the way he had learnt at Guelph, with careful enunciation, and as if he meant it.) He also spent a night inside the so-called King's Chamber of the Great Pyramid, where he had an experience which profoundly affected him.

He then tried to work his way back to England, but at first could find no passage. Finally, however, he boarded an Orient liner which was just about to sail, and before the mate could be found, the gangways were withdrawn and the liner left the quay. Technically, he was a stowaway, and was at once put to work, which he did cheerfully, and quickly made friends among the crew.

During the journey, one of the passengers became mentally disturbed and dangerous, and no one was able to control him. Lazenby volunteered to look after him, explaining that he was familiar with that kind of responsibility. The man went for Lazenby with a jackknife, but after a tussle the strong Canadian managed to subdue him. There was no further trouble, and for the rest of the voyage Lazenby simply had the task of keeping an eye on him.

When the liner reached England the captain thanked Lazenby, and said that any time he wanted to travel he would find him a job on his ship. One of the crew laughed, 'Well, this is the first time I ever heard of a stowaway being asked to come again!'

The Joyousness of Life

The biographical account of the early life of Charles Lazenby given in the preceding chapter may be supplemented by more characterological descriptions, drawn from obituaries and reminiscences.

Since most of those who knew Lazenby came from the American continent, these descriptions are of course written in an American style and idiom.

★

The strong moral purpose which drove his Primitive Methodist grandfather and self-sacrificing father—as well as his mother, whose devotion was to what she wrote of as God's 'only way'—might have made the boy solemn and the man narrow-minded. But it was far otherwise. He was a laughing, light-hearted person who spoke to each man and woman in his or her own way. Nor did he vaunt his erudition, but responded to questions with answers he believed truthful and understandable. He was an artist in words, and used them as pigments in the representation of the truth he was determined to let people see—and they did see.

He was a fighter of the Jeffersonian tradition for freedom of speech and thought. As he saw it, the theosophical platform was open to any question regarding race, creed, sex, caste or colour.

Taking the long view of the individual's innumerable incarnations, and the functioning of the law of karma, he considered ultimate perfectibility as a practical ideal in each case. This view was far from what is seen as rosy-visioned optimism by self-styled realists. He considered himself a realist rather than an idealist, seeing suffering, hatred, malice and fear, even despair, present in most of humanity. He aimed at making these conditions more intelligible, and more bearable. He loved humanity. There was never anyone with such a spring of grateful love.

★

Lazenby is a regular. I was shipmates with him on and off for twenty-five years—some outlandish voyages. I will say this for him: he was never more than a point off his course, and his day's work went down in the log and on the chart exactly as it was run.

Those who knew him will appreciate why I cannot speak of him as 'the dear departed' and 'what a loss' and so on. He would laugh—laugh the way he does, like a good eagle, suddenly shot full of tickly electricity. The Lazenby I knew is here now. When he left his rickety flivver of a body in the ditch at last, after driving it up and down all the roads of the world, it was only to lie-in for a time.

He was a crusader for talking the way you live—no use bluffing about occult knowledge and mystical experience, if you are not living up to what you know. No use giving out heavenly messages if you are oblivious to what's going on here below—gang wars, unemployment, the prison situation. Lazenby fought false pretences wherever he found them, even in the admiration and adulation of people who wanted a free ride to some spiritually illuminated country on his running-board. He was certainly a life-long pest to those who liked best to live in the warm marshes of inertia.

Lazenby crusaded through a world which, in spite of war and struggle, was still getting by, and which went to hear his lectures of an evening and went back to its own immediate affairs the next day indifferent and unaffected. He was not concerned with the result of his work, only with doing it day in and day out.

He had a lot of fun doing it because he felt that mankind and the world and the stars were all spinning along the right road and that there could be no such thing as failure in any aspect of the big job.

★

A long ago night; folding doors flung open between the front and back parlours; a crowd of people packed in, even sitting on the piano and on the stairs. In the midst, a bushy-haired pockmarked man began to talk. He talked of gods and men, myths and mannikins, love here, love there. Gradually he worked himself loose; his skylight flung open, the earth parted at his feet. He was a living conduit between spirit and matter. Uprush and downpour met in his body and the crowd basked in the fused radiance. That was the first time I ever saw a man come to life. Leaning over the banister, I saw what a man should be; that anything else was a walking dead man; that, other than that, nothing under heaven was worth going after. I snatched the seeds of the mystery—not of a serpent on the rock, but of a serpent risen from the rock. Man alive . . . I chased him for weeks afterward, but it didn't happen again. He would give me the laugh—and Lazenby could laugh—but he knew what had taken place.

★

While friendship was his watchword, and dharma in its fullest sense the substance of his teaching, his gospel was the joyousness of life. Laughter! Rapture! The ecstasy of rippling blue water and pine-perfumed wind in the warm sunlight—these were the things to which Charles Lazenby pointed those who came to him seeking for light on the path. All the philosophies and religions of the world were so clearly co-ordinated in his mind as to be literally at the tip of his tongue, but at the end of a lecture, or a class, which might have ranged all the way from Thales to Bergson, he would suddenly throw all the music of his voice into the recitation of a poem. One of his best loved and most often quoted was that exquisite lyric of Noyes:

> Come down to Kew in lilac-time,
> In lilac-time, in lilac-time . . .

And it seems, to those who knew him best, that he so loved humanity that to him it was always lilac-time.

I Found It Everywhere

In the course of research undertaken by the present writer there came to light among papers of Charles Lazenby a remarkable letter written to him by D.N. Dunlop. It dates from 1908—probably soon after the visit to Egypt made by the then 30-year-old Canadian. Dunlop at the time was aged almost 40.

The letter refers in passing to the troubles in the Theosophical Society connected with A.B. (Annie Besant) and C.W.L. (Charles Webster Leadbeater). It may be relevant to note that some of the latter's mis-deameanours had taken place on a visit to the Toronto Lodge.

An intriguing reference to the 'dear Doctor at Carlsruhe' remains obscure. This is certainly not Rudolf Steiner, who was still living in Berlin, had not been present in Karlsruhe since a brief two-day visit in early February of that year, and with whom Dunlop would not at this time have been in epistolary contact.

Ashdale,
Warwick Drive,
Hale,
Cheshire
Oct 4/08

My Companion beloved! I thank you for your letter.

When I come to write I find I'm a man of few words. I find myself in agreement with you re C.W.L. & A.B. They both occupy little space in my mind.—I cannot say of either as I can of you 'What a nature!' 'How much abundant life!' That love which is the forgiveness of sins helps us to understand folk, no matter how little they conform to our expectations—is it not so? The character who delights us 'may commit murder like Macbeth, or fly the battle for his sweetheart as did Anthony, or betray his country like Coriolanus, and yet we will rejoice in every happiness that comes to him, and sorrow at his death as if it were our own'. It is not life in a mirror we want, my friend; it is life—not picture-making. When Lucifer stands among his friends, we feel no sorrow, for life herself has made one of her eternal gestures, has called up into our hearts her energy that is eternal delight. The tide of life is rising! I think this is chaotic Celticism!

My mood changes; its sombre aspect falls away. The Sun, the trees, all Nature calls me out of doors to frolic & play & gamble with you in the fields—to laugh loud & long; to compare notes & joke, but above all to laugh with the laughter of children. Well, come, let's go.

Now we breathe deeper & free. There is little need now to say anything from this greater mood we understand & understanding, how joyously we can laugh, & smoke, & talk.

The publishing matters have not yet assumed definite shape. I have written to the *Vahan* to see what support, if any, would be forthcoming for the little monthly sheet on simple Theosophy for the masses, localised through branches, with the back page reserved for syllabus & announcements of each. It will appear probably in this month's issue which should be published tomorrow. If this suggestion evokes no response I will see what can be done with our Bibelot scheme. There is no need to hurry overmuch, I feel. I will write the dear Doctor at Carlsruhe as soon as I have something definite in my mind on this matter.

I am being pulled everywhere, have others to talk, lecture etc. etc. but I am one who sits pretty tight & calm & smiling. Why shouldn't I? It's the first day & there is only one day & it's the first, & there is no other time than now & never will be. They are all in a damnable hurry running away from God & get to God. I will go out one day & shout—Stop! Stop! Stop!! Ye people, stop. God is here—right here. Draw in your chairs round His table & be partakers. I went to sleep last night in a perfect delight over these words: 'How lovely is Thy dwelling place, O Lord of Life.' 'How lovely is Thy dwelling place.'—Then I went on to think of His dwelling place & I found it everywhere & I was mighty glad. Say, isn't it lovely? My love to you as always,

Daniel

They are squabbling away here yet about C.W.L. but I simply have not got the least interest in the thing. It might be a little show on some other planet & I am inclined to think that's what it is. It hasn't yet reached the planet I'm on.

The Internalization of Ancient Clairvoyance

The letter written by D.N. Dunlop to Charles Lazenby on 4 October 1908 may inspire various kinds of commentary.

Already as a boy the Scotsman was told by his strict Quaker father to read the Bible day by day, beginning with the creation of the world and finishing up with the Apocalypse, and for the rest of his life he would read daily as much as five chapters. Edith Young described her grandfather Alexander Dunlop expounding in a Quaker meetinghouse the Song of Songs, and it is most appropriate that his

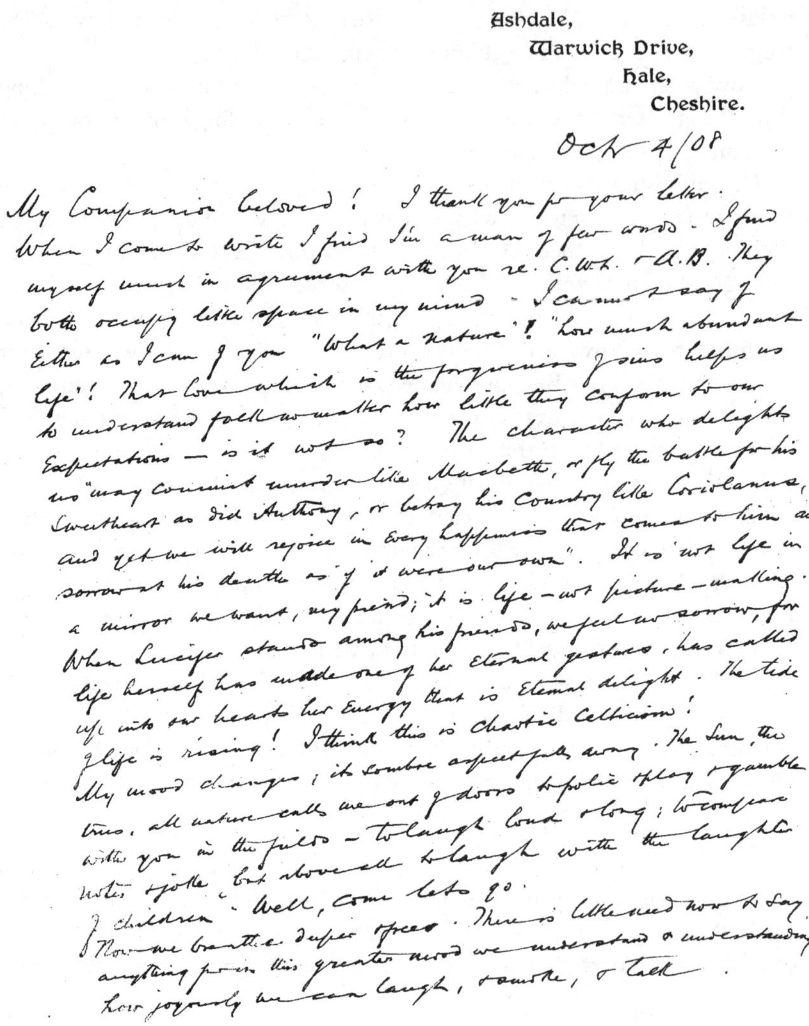
Ashdale,
Warwick Drive,
Hale,
Cheshire.

Oct 4/08

My Companion beloved! I thank you for your letter. When I come to write I find I'm a man of few words. I find myself much in agreement with you re. C.W.L. & A.B. They both occupy little space in my mind. I cannot say of Either as I can of you "What a nature"! "How much abundant life"! That love which is the forgiveness of sins helps us to understand folk no matter how little they conform to our Expectations — is it not so? The character who delights us "may commit murder like Macbeth, or fly the battle for his Sweetheart as did Anthony, or betray his Country like Coriolanus, and yet we will rejoice in every happiness that comes to him and sorrow at his death as if it were our own". It is not life in a mirror we want, my friend; it is life — not picture-making. When Lucifer stands among his friends, we feel no sorrow, for life herself has made one of her Eternal gestures, has called up into our hearts her Energy that is Eternal delight. The tide of life is rising! I think this is Chaotic Celticism! My mood changes; its sombre aspect falls away. The Sun, the trees, all nature calls me out of doors to frolic & play & gamble with you in the fields — to laugh loud & long; to compare notes & joke, but above all to laugh with the laughter of children. Well, come let's go. Now we breathe deeper & freer. There is little need now to say anything from this greater mood we understand & understanding. How joyously we can laugh, & smoke, & talk.

son should in this letter adapt a passage from one of the Psalms, the most poetic part of the whole Bible.

Here is a passage of relevance from the chapter on 'The World of the Psalms' in Emil Bock's *Könige und Propheten* (1936):

> Especially in the spiritual development of Israel, the sound of psalmic poetry has the magic of a new beginning. The world of the Old Covenant possessed to start with a basic attitude deliberately alien to beauty. Israel's inner task of distilling out from human nature the old twilit soul-forces and replacing them with clear thinking in a consciousness arising within man himself had necessitated renouncing art, in ancient humanity a fruit of

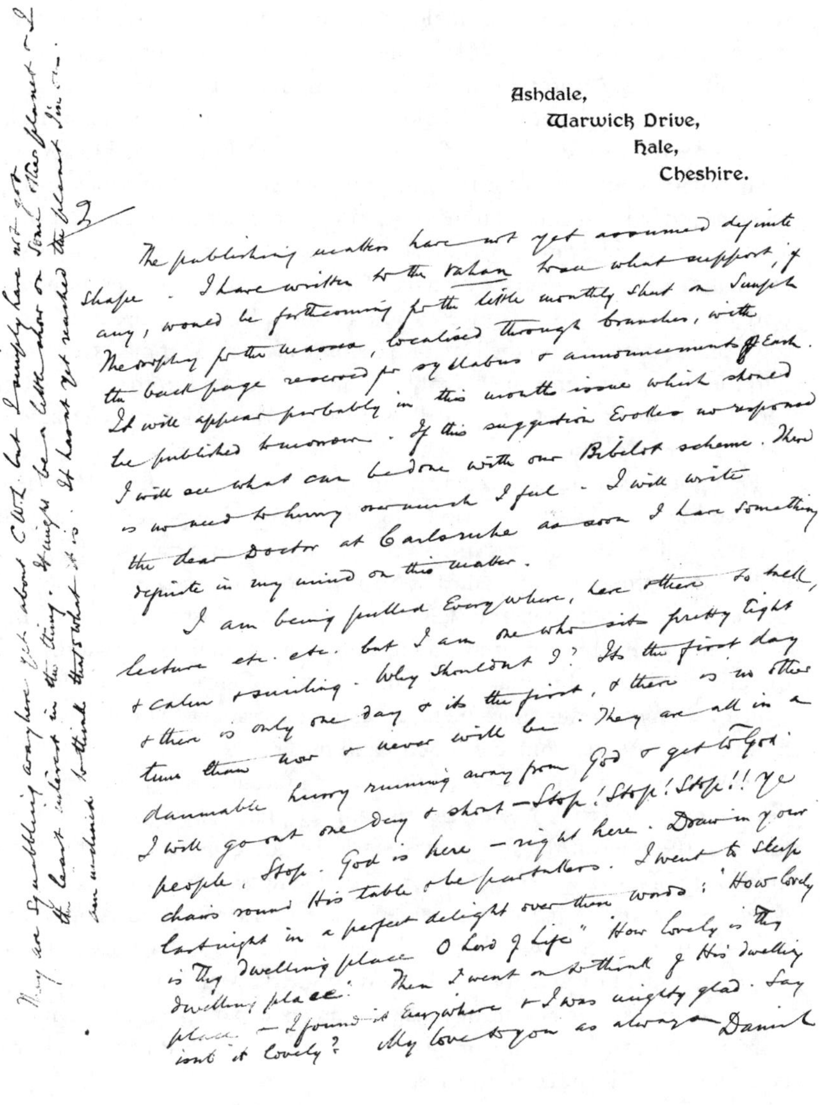
Ashdale,
Warwick Drive,
Hale,
Cheshire.

2

The publishing matters have not yet assumed definite shape. I have written to the Vahan to see what support, if any, would be forthcoming for the little monthly sheet on Sunfish Theosophy for the masses, localised through branches, with the back page reserved for syllabus & announcements of each. It will appear probably in this month's issue which should be published tomorrow. If this suggestion evokes no response I will see what can be done with our Bibelot scheme. There is no need to hurry overmuch I feel. I will write the dear Doctor at Carlsruhe as soon as I have something definite in my mind on this matter.

I am being pulled everywhere, here there & to hell, lecture etc. etc. but I am one who sits pretty tight & calm & smiling. Why shouldn't I? It's the first day & there is only one day & it's the first, & there is no other time than now & never will be. They are all in a damnable hurry running away from God & get to God! I will go out one day & shout — Stop! Stop! Stop!! Ye people. Stop. God is here — right here. Draw in your chairs round His table & be partakers. I went to sleep last night in a perfect delight over those words: 'How lovely is Thy dwelling place O Lord of Life.' How lovely is thy dwelling place. Then I went on to think of His dwelling place — I found it everywhere & I was mighty glad. Say isn't it lovely? My love to you as always — Daniel

They are squabbling anyhere yet about CWL but I simply have not got the least interest in the thing. It might be a little show on some other planet & I am inclined to think that's what it is. I haven't yet reached the planet I'm on.

clairvoyance and clairaudience. The stern law at Sinai had even expressly forbidden any pictorial art as transgressing against the Yahweh deity. But in the Davidic Age we now perceive on that tree of harsh sternness the flower of art coming to bloom. Admittedly there was no breaking of the commandment which excluded all sculpture, painting and architecture. But something of immaterial substance, namely word and sound streaming forth out of man's inner being, becomes an artistic medium. A marvellous inward union arises of poetry and music, poetry which through the vowels in its words brings to expression the melody for intoned singing, since the vowels in the Hebrew text of the psalms, when included in the writing, are at the same time notes. An art is born which is distinguished from that of the great magic cultures of Egypt and Babylonia by not being brought down from superterrestrial spheres through clairvoyant faculties, but instead blossoming forth out of youthful inwardness in human feeling, out of a personality seeking and finding itself. Humanization of consciousness creates its own artistic and poetic expression. Poetry and music appear on the scene as the internalization of ancient clairvoyance. The ecstasy of Saul, either prophetic or demonic, which bade farewell to the divine sphere and tore itself loose towards humanity, has in the Davidic psalms really arrived at man's level and into the sphere of humanness. Only as a distant memory of the stormy ups and downs in the soul of Saul do we see in the psalms an alternation between songs of suffering or repentance and songs of praise.

The poetic and musical element in the psalms is the fruit of a new relationship in which the human being, now becoming personal, stands to Nature. As long as man was inwoven as a member into natural life, like a child at its mother's breast, psalms of Nature like those contained in the Old Testament psalter did not arise. The human being had first to lose something of his old attachment to Nature and feel himself cut off from his Mother, so that he could marvel in praise over the wonders of creation. The yearning which resounds in this amazement, to experience anew the old unity and fusion, is an essential source of poetry and music.

David's relation to Nature presents a significant central point in the development of Israel. Moses, by his song of praise at the Sea of Reeds, stands as the poet of the first psalm. He is still looking into the elemental kingdom as if into a wide-open sphere of divine revelation. Nature's fire and clouds of smoke at Sinai are his element. Later, under the leadership of the Judges, a stream began which turned away from Nature. Divinity must no longer be sought outside, but exclusively inside the soul. Already Elijah on the slopes of Mount Horeb or Sinai no longer experienced the divine in elements of earthquake, fire and windstorm, from which it had still clearly been perceived as speaking to Moses.

David forms the midpoint between Moses and Elijah, between 'Moses and the prophets'. He is no longer so closely united and connected to the divine element in Nature as the Hebraic primeval age. But he is also not yet so separated and withdrawn from Nature as the Jewish prophets. The internalization of Nature poetically expressed in the psalms lies on a path beginning with an experience of Nature saturated with revelation and culminating in an extreme inner devoutness. Nature and the inner world find a balance in the art of David, the singer bearing the harp.

Here we also come closer to solving a remarkable historic riddle encountered in the heading of many psalms. We find there, not David, but the 'children of Korah' designated as poets and singers. Does it fit to the dark role played by the circle of Korah-people in wandering around Sinai that we now meet them again as singers of the very psalms we would count among the most beautiful and melodious? To the songs of Korah belongs the psalm of longing: 'As the hart longs for fresh water, so longs my soul for thee, O God. My soul thirsts for God, the living God' (42). The song of faith of Psalm 46, which Martin Luther composed into his song of refuge 'Ein fester Burg ist unser Gott' belongs to the children of Korah.

And finally the 84th psalm, the song of love for the Temple, is a song of Korah: 'How lovely are thy dwelling-places . . . My soul yearns and longs for the courts of the Lord.'

Did not the Korah gang once rise up in the desert against Moses, presumptuously laying claim to carry out the sacrificial service, and the Earth's depths open beneath them to swallow them up? How can it be that the former malefactors are now standing in such glory beside David as creators of the most inwardly divine songs?

In the age of Moses, the spiritual manner of the Korahites represented a historical element far ahead of its time. Bearing a principle of personality not nearly yet valid, they took offence at Moses and Aaron for leading the people instead of granting the same rights to every individual, above all for performing the sacrificial service. Just this abstract anticipation of an egohood to which mankind could only later mature also deprived them of a living relation to Nature, as other Israelites at their time still possessed. So by complying with them and letting them actually perform the burnt offering, Moses was able to confront them with the cosmic effects of their own abstract spiritual manner. The flames enkindled in the censers awakened into horrific activity forces of fire and smoke slumbering in rocky clefts of the wilderness at Sinai. The Korah-people saw themselves helplessly abandoned to the spirits they had called forth. They no longer possessed an instinct leading them to conduct themselves properly in relation to forces of Nature. That the Biblical report of a yawning abyss having swallowed up the Korah gang is meant imaginatively, not to indicate their physical destruction, is made clear from the sons of Korah being named in the Bible again, as psalmists along with David. In the age of Moses they were rejected. In the Davidic age the spiritual manner which had brought about fatal consequences during the period of wandering around Sinai was now reached, and became timely. The age of the sons of Korah had arrived. We must probably picture them as a progressive community, like an Order, who placed themselves in the service of artistic and cultic life. In David and the culture inaugurated by him a stream of Israel's spiritual life formerly experienced as standing under the ban of unrighteousness found its redemption. The relation—already becoming abstract—in which man stands to Nature by becoming an individual personality was now justified.

In David, who could be called the 'true Korahite', as well as in this whole group, it became the source of a rich artistry, a music and a poetry lending wings to spiritual and religious life.

Song Over the Winepresses

The letter from D.N. Dunlop to Charles Lazenby dated 4 October 1908 was written during the autumnal, Michaelmas season.

An article on 'Autumnal Song of Pilgrimage and Home' by Rudolf Frieling, first published in *Die Christengemeinschaft* in September 1956 and reprinted in Frieling's books, is of specific relevance to the psalmic quotation in Dunlop's letter.

When summer is ending, darkness and cold slowly come to mind again. At first unnoticed, but with gradually increasing insistence. A human being feels more strongly his need of a home, to shelter him for the winter. 'Weh dem, der keine Heimat hat' says Nietzsche's autumnal poem 'Vereinsamt'.

The more modern man comes to feel the uprootedness and homelessness in his outer existence, the more he should feel called upon to seek his true home in a higher world. If he succeeds in inwardly moving there, such homecoming then helps him to take up with new courage the destiny of his insecure and uncertain earthly pilgrimage.

These two things, finding a home in the eternal, and courage for the earthly path, have found wonderful expression in the 84th psalm.

The inscription characterizes it as an autumnal song; for as already set out in regard to psalm 8, the Hebrew text does not mean a song 'on the zither' (as Luther translates), but 'over the winepresses'. An autumnal mood is thus given, though in a different way from psalm 8.

A Song over the Winepress, by the Sons of Korah

How love-awakening are thy dwelling places,
Thou Lord of the resplendent hosts!
My soul is longing, yea is consumed
For the forecourts of the Lord.
My heart and my fleshly body, they thrill
In God who is Life.
The bird found its home, the swallow her nest,
In which to shelter her young:
Thy altars! Thou Lord of the resplendent hosts,
King and God of my ego-being!
Blessed they who dwell there in thy house.

They sing thee praise at all times.
Sela
(v. 1–5)

Even for us today these verses may still be a valid expression of cultic devoutness. We can also make them our own in respect to the sanctuaries of Christian sacramentalism. For we too know the feeling that wherever our altars are standing is our home.

God, quite certainly, is everywhere. But it is a fact of ancient experience that man's earthly environment may become quite specially permeable, as though transparent to that presence of the supersensible, in places underlying cultic arrangement. Earthly spatiality then stands as though inside a higher space of soul and spirit.—The psalmist is conscious of how the whole human being is addressed in this sensory and supersensory event: not just the soul, but the heart too, as the actual centrepoint of the ego, and even the 'flesh' as well. The earthly body has its share in the perceptible streams of life issuing from the Godhead (v. 3).

Various commentators have already noticed how finely in this psalm a trustful feeling of being at home with the divine is balanced with a reverent shyness. The idyllic, confidential picture of the swallow which has found a place for its nest is followed by an upward glance to the sublimity and majesty of the divine: 'my King and my God!' (v. 4).—The 'Lord Zebaoth' is, verbally translated, the Lord of the 'resplendent hosts', by which we may think of the visible star-worlds just as much as of the heavenly hosts of angelic realms belonging to them.

The first strophe of the psalm ends with the word 'Sela'. It is not quite clear what that means. The Greek translation says here 'Dia-psalma', which would indicate a musical interlude, where what has gone before finds an echo.

★

The first strophe closed with a blessing on those who dwell constantly near to God. At the beginning of the second strophe the blessing is taken up again (in the Greek stands here the word 'makarios', which we know from the beatitudes of the Sermon on the Mount). But now it applies to the human being striding courageously forward on the paths of his pilgrimage. Here a 'Michaelic' tone resounds powerfully into the psalm.

Blessed the man who has his strength in Thee.
Highways in heart, they pass through the valley of tears.
They turn it into a place of springs—
Full of blessings is he who points the way.
They go from strength to strength, to the sight of God in Zion.
Lord, Thou Godhead of the resplendent hosts,

Listen to my prayer, incline Thine ear, Thou God of Jacob.
Sela

(v. 6–9)

Whoever has found in his heart the 'ways leading upwards' (the Greek translation speaks of the 'anabaseis', the Latin of the 'ascensiones' in the heart) does not shrink back from the necessary paths of destiny through the 'vale of crying'. Luther uses here the word 'Jammertal'. For a certain religiosity fleeing the Earth this phrase 'valley of wailing' has not always had a healthy effect. But as regards the psalm it must be seen that in no way is expression here being given to a cowardly flight from the world. For the psalm is saying: Whoever bears in his heart the possibilities for rising higher will transform the earthly valley of wailing into a place of blessing. In the comfortless waste and desert he can open up the springs of the eternal (v. 7). Just as Christ told the Samaritan woman that the water He would give would become a spring in man welling up into eternal life.

For a pilgrim, the painful and dangerous earthly pilgrimage thereby becomes precisely a 'going from strength to strength' (v. 8).—

Then the text is not quite definite. What may be meant is: 'one is seen by God in Zion', or also: 'one sees God in Zion'. But however it may be understood, in the end both versions come to the same thing, the old mystical truth experienced as 'knowing even as I am known'. The vision of God is at the same time a being seen by God.—At the end of the pilgrimage stands therefore the vision of God 'from face to face'.

★

From this prospect the psalm then leads back once more to the feeling of at-home-ness in the consecrated place. The prayer 'Behold, O God!' again does not imply that the Omnipresent did not anyway see everything. But the sight here is probably felt not so much from the aspect of perception. It was still known that the seeing eye is not just a passive receiver of impressions, but a centre of light-ether which also itself sends out fine rays of light. The eye does not merely see, it also radiates. Hermann Beckh has pointed out that this very radiance of light is aurally stamped upon the Hebrew word for 'seeing' ('raah'). The prayer 'Behold' therefore means the divine light-ray becoming revealed. Then follows the further request: 'Brighten the countenance of Thine Anointed!' At the time, the singer of this psalm may have been thinking of the King in Jerusalem, or the High Priest. But these after all were only representatives of Him who in the fullest sense is then called 'the Anointed'. In the face of Messias, of Christ, the countenance of God becomes visible to us. 'He who sees Me, sees the Father.' God's creative ray of light finds its highest revelation in the Saviour's face.

Once again the psalmist is overcome by the consciousness of how infinitely valuable is that cultic experience of God: *one* day in the forecourts of the Temple outweighs a thousand other days (v. 11). Again there resounds the Michaelic tone of the autumn festival season: in the motif of 'Sun and shield' (v. 12).—The subsequent words, 'grace and honour', should not be understood as just generally edifying. They refer to concrete and distinct experiences. The human being, as he has been going around on the Earth till now, is not yet complete. 'It has not yet appeared what we shall be' (1 John 3:2). There is still a cloud of unexhausted future higher possibilities over our heads. What is one day to become our personal being, our innermost possession, is still above us. When something out of this creative cloud sinks down into man, that is then 'grace'.—The 'glory' (Hebrew 'kabôd', Greek 'doxa', Latin 'gloria') is a radiance of light perceptible to higher organs. In the Old Testament it sometimes appears precisely as a kind of 'member' of man's being. 'Wake up, my glory!' (Psalm 57:9). It is somewhat like a fine supersensible organism of radiance, which stirs inside man when he takes part in the grace streaming into him from above.

The psalm then ends with a third and last blessing.—

Thou our shield, send Thy ray of light, O God!
Enlighten the countenance of Thine Anointed!
One day in Thy forecourts is more precious than a thousand others.
Rather would I stay on the threshold in the house of my God
Than dwell in the tents of distance from God.
Yea, Sun and shield is the Lord God.
The Lord bestows grace, and light of glory.
He does not refuse bounty to those who walk in devotion.
Thou Lord of the resplendent hosts—
Blessed the man who founds his trust upon Thee!

The Doorway for the Truth

The other letter which D.N. Dunlop stated he had written to *The Vâhan* did not appear either in October 1908 or in any subsequent issue.

Meanwhile, one of the early French renderings of Rudolf Steiner's works received an appreciation by G.R.S.M., recognizable as the initials of Mead, in *The Theosophical Review*:

> We are glad to see that Dr. Steiner's *Das Christenthum als mystische Thatsache* ('Christianity as Mystic Actuality'), which was reviewed in our pages when it first appeared in 1902, has been translated into French by the able pen of M. Edouard Schuré. Our distinguished colleague, the General Secretary of the German Section, has in recent years inaugurated a movement of great vitality in Germany, which is now spreading to Austria, Holland, Sweden

> and Russia. Dr. Steiner is a born mystic, and widely read in many fields of research; his eloquence is great and his enthusiasm and earnestness contagious. The line he follows may be best described as Rosicrucian, and the end of all his teaching is the elucidation of the Christian Mystery, which he holds to be the highest of all.
>
> It will therefore be of interest to our readers to set before them some passages from his remarkable study on Christianity as the consummation of the ancient Mystery-teaching, a point of view which has our sympathy, in so far as we hold, as we have repeatedly stated, that by the authority of the Christ the essentially spiritual Mysteries were thrown open to the world, and that an understanding of the Mystery-teaching of antiquity is a prerequisite to a proper understanding of the Christ-Mystery . . .

There followed a detailed review of the French version, covering no less than four pages.

★

It was not however a historical treatise of this kind but a work on a more practical subject which was really to initiate anthroposophy in Britain. For in September 1908 *The Theosophist* had begun to publish in instalments another of Steiner's writings, 'The Education of Children', a printed version of a lecture given in January 1907 in Berlin. Translation of this work was continued in further instalments until the end of 1908.

The very first instalment made a strong impact on a particular English reader, though he seems not to have come across it until the winter. Herbert Heywood-Smith was a theosophist of about a year's standing, having joined on 14 November 1907 the then recently founded H.P.B. Lodge. Probably he came to learn that other members of this lodge were engaged in translating Steiner's writings, and decided to peruse the results of their labours.

Reminiscing about him in a 1970 issue of the *Anthroposophical Quarterly*, Dorothy Osmond recalled:

> Mr. Heywood-Smith was an austere, grave personality, one who gave the impression of a certain asceticism, and perhaps a rather excessive one-pointedness of outlook. It is difficult to visualize him living in the world of today, but what an example of devotion to Anthroposophy he was to us all, and how we can rejoice that, as his account tells, destiny led him one unexpected day to the place where he was to find the doorway for the truth for which he was seeking, and which through his insight was to be made accessible to numbers and numbers of his countrymen. The brief story of the work he then began and sustained until the end of his life is a record which no true history of the Anthroposophical Movement and Society in

this country could omit.

The story is contained in a typescript written by Heywood-Smith in December 1925, and found after his death in 1951 among papers bequeathed to the Anthroposophical Society in Great Britain. It describes his first discovery of Steiner's writings in the then rooms of the Theosophical Society in London.

These were the very rooms at 28 Albemarle Street where Steiner himself, on one of his early visits, had been borrowing books from the theosophical library. Evidently he had left something of his spirit behind in the library premises . . .

Heywood-Smith's story begins:

> During the winter of 1908/9, when one day I was in the rooms of the Theosophical Society in London, I read a translation of the first part of Dr. Steiner's 'Education of Children', which was appearing in instalments in *The Theosophist.* This delighted me very much, and after learning it almost by heart I hurried home to tell Mrs. Heywood-Smith of my discovery. She too was extremely interested in it, and together we set to work to find out more about Dr. Steiner. We were directed to Mr. Max Gysi, who was then responsible for translation of the books, and was publishing the first in English, *The Way of Initiation.*
>
> I interviewed Mr. Gysi in his pleasant home in Hampstead and he told me that there were many books and cycles of lectures by Dr. Steiner. This was exciting news, but the excitement was somewhat abated by the fact that everything was in German! Still, there was nothing to be done but to obtain what we could and begin translating. Mr. Gysi provided me at once with the cycle on St. John's Gospel which had been given by Dr. Steiner in Hamburg a short time before, and from that time onward Mrs. Heywood-Smith and I spent our days, and a good part of our nights, translating.

At this time Herbert Heywood-Smith did not himself know any German at all, but his wife Mabel, who had been to a Moravian school and was therefore fluent in the language, slowly taught it to him as they embarked on their translational work.

The Way of Initiation

The Way of Initiation was the original title of the volume reproducing the first half of the series 'How does one attain Knowledge of the Higher Worlds?' At about the time when he was interviewed by Herbert Heywood-Smith, Max Gysi composed for the volume a translator's note:

Being deeply interested in Dr. Steiner's work and teachings, and desirous of sharing with my English-speaking friends the many invaluable glimpses of truth which are to be found therein, I decided upon the translation of the present volume. It is due to the kind co-operation of several friends who prefer to be anonymous that this task has been accomplished, and I wish to express my hearty thanks for the literary assistance rendered by them—also to thank Dr. Peipers of Munich for permission to reproduce his excellent photograph of the author.

The special value of this volume consists, I think, in the fact that no advice is given and no statement made which is not based on the personal experience of the author, who is, in the truest sense, both a mystic and an occultist.

Max Gysi.
Belsize Lodge,
Belsize Lane,
London, N.W.
3rd November 1908

★

The book came out in late November, in a print-run of 1500 copies. Its spine, outside cover and title-page were decorated with Rosicrucian motifs. Peipers's photograph of the author was placed as frontispiece.

After the translator's note and Annie Besant's foreword, the text was further prefaced by Edouard Schuré's introduction to the recently published *Le Mystère Chrétien et les Mystères Antiques*, which after briefly describing Rudolf Steiner's life, ended with more personal impressions:

> ... He is equally skilled in the deduction of ideas in philosophical order, and in rigorous analysis of scientific facts. And when he so chooses, he can give a poetical form to his thought, in original and striking imagery. But his whole self is shown only by his presence and his speech, private or public. The characteristic of his eloquence is a singular force, always gentle in expression, resulting undoubtedly from perfect serenity of soul combined with wonderful clearness of mind. Added to this at times is an inner and mysterious vibration which makes itself felt by the listener from the very first words. Never a word that could shock or jar. From argument to argument, from analogy to analogy, he leads you on from the known to the unknown. Whether following up the comparative development of the Earth and of man according to occult tradition, through the Lemurian, Atlantean, Asiatic, and European periods; whether explaining the physiological and psychic constitution of man as he now is; whether enumerating the stages of Rosicrucian initiation, or commenting on the Gospel of St. John and the Apocalypse, or applying his root-ideas to mythology, history and literature,

what dominates and guides his discourse is ever this power of synthesis, which co-ordinates facts under one ruling idea and gathers them together in one harmonious vision. And it is ever this inward and contagious fervour, this secret music of the soul, which is, as it were, a subtle melody in harmony with the Universal Soul.

Such, at least, is what I felt on first meeting him and listening to him two years ago. I could not better describe this undefinable feeling than by recalling the saying of a poet-friend to whom I was showing the portrait of the German theosophist. Standing before those deep and clear-seeing eyes, before that countenance hollowed by inward struggles, moulded by a lofty spirit which has proved its balance on the heights and its calm in the depths, my friend exclaimed: 'Behold a master of himself and of life!

★

The Way of Initiation was reviewed in the December issue of *The Vâhan*:

For some years we have heard of the splendid work being done in mid-Europe by the indefatigable Secretary of the German Section; some members will recall his one or two visits to this country, especially in 1905, at the Congress in England. Under his inspiration a strong Theosophical Movement, with Germany as its centre, has struck deep roots on the continent, and we notice as an indication of its vitality that some three hundred members assembled in the summer in Stuttgart to hear Dr. Steiner's lectures.

The many English-speaking theosophists who could not read Dr. Steiner's own German words will be extremely grateful to Mr. Max Gysi, who has devoted much self-sacrificing labour to presenting us with this first volume of Dr. Steiner's writings, himself shouldering the financial responsibility. We must show him that his work is appreciated by ensuring a good sale for the book and so pave the way for more.

★

Like Herbert Heywood-Smith, Clifford Bax too must have entered the H.P.B. Lodge, for although he was only in his early twenties, the records show that during this year 1909 he was its President.

In his collection *Rosemary for Remembrance* (1948), after recounting his meeting with D.N. Dunlop, Bax went on to state:

. . . one afternoon Dunlop told me about certain 'very beautiful' essays by AE which had appeared long ago in *The Irish Theosophist*, and when I had read them, I suggested that Dunlop and I should set up as publishers and reprint the best of the essays . . .

In February 1909 *The Vâhan* therefore publicized 'A Suggestion from the Art-Circle':

> It is proposed in connection with *Orpheus* (the magazine published by the Theosophical Art-Circle in London) to reprint some of those papers which appeared in various theosophical magazines that are now out of print or difficult to procure. These papers will be printed as pamphlets (to be named 'the Orpheus Series') and sent out at the charge of 6d. a copy to the general reader and at 3d. a copy to those who already subscribe to *Orpheus* (the editor of this paper feels that subscribers do not at present receive their due, and is therefore loth to ask them anything but a nominal sum for the series of reprints).
>
> In all probability the first numbers will be formed from certain papers of a beauty rare and perhaps unique, which were contributed some years ago by the poet AE to *The Irish Theosophist*. For these I shall be indebted to Mr. D.N. Dunlop, who is associated with me in this scheme.
>
> The publication of the proposed series will depend on the support promised, and I would therefore request any persons who are interested in the project to communicate with me, that I may note their names as subscribers to the first number. Perhaps it is as well to indicate that the papers reprinted will be selected principally on account of the element of beauty.
>
> Clifford Bax.
>
> Ivy Bank, Hampstead, N.W.

★

The still ongoing controversy about the reinstatement of Charles Leadbeater ended in early 1909 with the resignation from the British Section of some five hundred members.

Various members of other Sections also departed. In Ireland for instance, AE finally resigned from the Society, and re-established in Dublin his Hermetic Society. Even in India, Bertram Keightley withdrew support from the Theosophical Society's leadership.

Among the most prominent resignations from the British Section was that of G.R.S. Mead, who went on to found in London the Quest Society. And Mead's resignation had an important publicational consequence. It is interesting to recall here what he had written six years before, in that letter to *The Vâhan* of October 1903:

> ... There is an editor; there are a few on whom he depends for regular copy; everyone else naturally supposes that it is alright; there is no difficulty, it goes on from month to month; no one realizes the danger of the thing becoming mechanical until too late ...

These words now came true. For on Mead's departure from the Theosophical Society, *The Theosophical Review* which he had for many years edited—and which had carried numerous reports of activities in the German Section as well as abridged English versions of Steiner's writings—ceased publication altogether with the issue of February 1909.

For the Good of Humanity

Those who chose to remain in the British Section of the Theosophical Society were now only kept informed about what was happening in the German Section through *The Vâhan*. This was originally the British news-sheet, and in regard to other countries naturally did not provide more than brief announcements of forthcoming events, and the occasional book-review.

The only exception was in April 1909, when *The Vâhan* published a long item entitled 'The Way of Art':

> We are indebted to Mr. Max Gysi for the translation from the *Mitteilungen,* No VII, from which the following account is taken:
>
> For some time past an attempt has been made by the Munich Lodges to interest the working classes in art; and the theosophical reading room in the Damenstiftstrasse has been thrown open to the public every Sunday evening with this end in view. It was soon found, however, that the space was too small to accomodate the numbers who availed themselves of the opportunity offered them, and it was felt by those interested in the scheme that a large hall would have to be provided. As is usual in such cases, the difficulties in following up the idea seemed at first almost insuperable; but doubts and difficulties alike were dispersed by Dr. Steiner, who in an inspiring speech dwelt upon the thought that it was the duty of those who aspired to the high title of occultist to see that the working people were not shut out from the refining and uplifting influences of art and beauty. A place must be found where these things could be brought to the people; where they might come in their working clothes, attracted by illuminated programmes in the windows or by strains of music sounding from within, and enjoy a period of rest and quiet with artistic influences all around them.
>
> After some search, a good sized house was found and pronounced suitable; cleaning and furnishing were put in hand without loss of time, and in a fortnight the hall of art was ready to be opened. A piano was procured, and a good harmonium given by a member of the Lodge; the room was artistically decorated with plants and flowers, and oil paintings by members and copies of well-known pictures adorned the walls.
>
> Outside the door was placed a notice-board with the inscription 'Hall of

Art and Music, Entrance Free'. In one window the programme for the week was exhibited on a transparent sheet; in the other that for the day. The hall is open every evening except Monday, and three times during the day as well. Three members have undertaken the musical part of the enterprise, and one of them is always present to arrange for performances. On Wednesday and Saturday afternoons a younger member tells a fairy story to children, and the attendance numbers some hundred and fifty. Old tales with an occult background, such as Grimm's, are almost exclusively chosen. These 'story-tellings' are opened and closed with music and singing. It has been found that this part of the work is well worth the trouble, for children go home and enthusiastically repeat what they have heard to their parents and younger brothers and sisters. On Wednesday evenings, and on Sunday mornings from 9 to 12, works of art are exhibited, and many members help by explanation and by keeping order. It is a fruitful field of work. On Fridays is an introductory lecture on Theosophy for those who know little or nothing of the subject, and at the conclusion of a course of six or eight lectures a new course, somewhat more advanced, is begun, so that those who have attended the first may pass on. Dramas and plays of all kinds are also read; the *Nibelungen* was the first to be given.

It is very cheering to see the love and devotion with which members of the Lodges work in the hall of art, and so freely give the time and energy needed for such an undertaking. More than twenty members are helping in the music room, and many of their friends occasionally or permanently. Such work in common for the good of humanity binds members and lodges together by the strongest possible tie. It is hoped that by means of this hall of art, theosophical thought may be spread, and the gulf bridged between theosophists and those who are working without the light of its teachings. More recruits are daily being found, and it is probable that before long other centres of the kind will be opened in different parts of the city.

The Greatest of All Things

Clifford Bax, referring in *Rosemary for Remembrance* to his association with D.N. Dunlop in publishing 'The Orpheus Series', stated: 'My colleague insisted that I should write a preface for the first of the booklets.' This booklet brought together under the title *The Hero in Man* three essays written in 1897 by AE.

Here is the preface:

λαμπαδια ἒχοντες διαδωσουσιν ἀλληλοις—Plato

We who live in the great cities could not altogether avoid, even if we would, a certain association with the interests of our time. Wherever we go, the minds of men are feverishly debating some new political measure, or some new scheme for the reconstruction of society. Now, as in olden times, the rumours of an impending war will engulf the subtler interests of men, and unless we are willing to forego all intercourse we find ourselves involved in a hundred sympathies. A friendly group will gather one evening and open their thoughts concerning the experiences of the soul; they will often declare that only these matters are of profound interest, and yet on the morrow most of them regard enthusiasms of the mind as far away, unpractical, not of immediate account. But even at noon the stars are above us, and because a man in material difficulties cannot evoke the highest experiences that he has known, they have not become less real. They pertain to his immortal nature, and if in the circumstance of life he loses memory of them it is because he is likewise mortal. In the measure that we develop our interior selves philosophy becomes the most permanent of our interests, and it may well be that the whole aim of man is to acquire an unbroken and ever-broadening realization of the Supreme Spirit, so that in a far-off day he may become the master of all imaginable conditions. He therefore who brings us back to our central selves, and shows us that however far we may wander it is these high thoughts which are truly the most real—he is of all men our greatest benefactor.

Now those who care for the spiritual aspect of life are of two kinds—the intellectual and the imaginative. There are men of keen intellect who comprehend some philosophic system, who will defend it with elaborate reasonings and proclaim themselves its adherents, but the Earth at their feet, the stars in the firmament, man himself and their own souls have undergone no transfiguration. Their philosophies are lifeless, for imagination is to the intellect what breath is to the body. Thoughts that never glow with imagination, are never applied to all that the sense perceives or the mind remembers—thoughts that remain quite abstract—are as empty husks of no value.

But there are those who have studied by the light of imagination, and these know well that the inner life of thought, though it may often be overclouded, is the only life which can henceforth give them content. They know that it was not when they were most immersed in the affairs of the day, but rather when the whole world appeared for a little while to be pulsating with an almost uncontainable splendour, that they were most alive. For the best mood we have ever known, though it be lost for long, is yet the clearest revelation of our true selves, and it is then that we learn most nearly what marvels life may hold.

If we read with imagination the dialogues of Plato we dwell for a while among those ardent Greeks for whom the universe was changed by the words of the poet-philosopher. So too when we read the letter that was written by Plotinus to Flaccus, perhaps the serenest height the human soul has ever attained, we become ourselves the recipients. In either case we feel that we have lived in the presence of a princely soul. It is an inspiration to realize that we are of the one race with these, and may look out on the same beauty of Earth and Heaven.

Yet the magic of the mind is not enduring, and to dream overlong of a bygone beauty is to make sorrowful the present. What imaginative reader of Plato but has desired with ardour that he might in truth have been numbered with those who walked on the daisied lawns of the Academy, might in truth have heard the voice of the hardly human Initiate, have seen him face to face, have responded to the influence of his presence? Who would but willingly translate his life to another century if he could but hear Plotinus endeavouring to describe in human language an ecstasy which makes of man a god?

I know that one may easily injure whatever one most loves by speaking of it in superlative praise to those who as yet remain aloof with interest unaroused, but for me it is hard to refrain from an expression of that admiration, and I would fain say also that affection, which burns up within me when I read the writings of AE. For they cause me to think of him as one of those rare spirits who bring to men the realization of their own divinity, who make the spiritual life seem adventurous, attractive and vivid, so that we go forth into the world with a new interest and a new joy at heart. That, as I have sought to show in the opening of this note, is the greatest of all things that anyone can do. The life of such a man makes beautiful the generation with which it coincides. If we penetrate the human words and inhabit, so far as we are able, the mood which was passing in the soul as it shaped them, we may learn from the reveries that are here reprinted how to the mystic of this material age the world remains equally wonderful, and human life equally holy, as either seemed in the far-off days when beauty was more greatly desired. For of deeper value at all times than any particular thought is the pervading mood. Perhaps the reader will remember here the following passage by Robert Louis Stevenson:—'Such are the best teachers. A dogma learned is only a new error—the old one was perhaps as good; but a spirit communicated is a perpetual possession. These best teachers climb beyond teaching to the plane of art; it is themselves, and what is best in themselves, that they communicate.' To read the essays that follow, or the three volumes of poetry that AE has published, is to recognize one who has endeavoured always to communicate the 'best in himself', and the mood which they induce is a mood from which we may see the world once more in its primal beauty, may recover a sense of the long-forgotten but inextinguishable grandeur of the soul.

Clifford Bax

April, 1909.

*

Almost 30 years later, in *Rosemary for Remembrance*, Bax added:

The reader may be amused by AE's dismayed protest against my extravagant hero-worship. He wrote:

'I like your preface, all except the references to myself. My dear man, you must tone these down. You cannot compare me with Plotinus and Plato, and the last paragraph must go. Why cannot you say that *in my degree* I am trying to do in my time what greater mystics and greater writers did in their time? And if you must conclude with a peroration in praise, why not say that in all I have published I have had only one aim. Tone it down like a dear fellow. I could not face the publication of essays of mine with so much praise, and yet I like your proem otherwise and think it ought to go in. You write very good prose indeed, beautifully balanced: let it stay there, but wipe out the passages I have marked on the proof, which would make it impossible for me ever to give a copy of the essays to anyone, as it would be like handing them in praise of myself. Leave it to the critics...'

The Work of Theosophy

Towards the end of April 1909, over in India, the now reinstated Charles Leadbeater first discovered the 14-year-old Jiddu Krishnamurti.

News of the discovery, however, did not arrive in Europe before the next international Congress had taken place in May, this time in Budapest. *The Vâhan* printed only a brief report, by S. Maud Sharpe, the new British General Secretary (Kate Spink having resigned from the post in the previous year). Altogether about two hundred members attended. How many came from Britain was not stated, but almost certainly the number was even smaller than had gone to Munich in 1907.

At the Congress Annie Besant awarded a medal to Rudolf Steiner for *The Way of Initiation*. In Britain the book, which had already gone out of print, had just been republished, in a further print-run of 1500 copies.

But by this time the differences of opinion between Steiner and Besant in the field of Christology were slowly coming to the fore, though friendly relations were still outwardly maintained. During the Congress discussions took place between them which ended in 'an amicable comparison'. Besant tried to embroil Steiner in the incipient Alcyone affair, which had already started in principle even before Leadbeater's discovery of Krishnamurti. Steiner also recorded that in Budapest

there was formed what I would like to call an international society of honest people. Among others it involved Mr. Keightley, who formerly had always corrected scientific mistakes in Mrs. Besant's books. This international society made a proposal from India that I should become its president. And in 1909 I told Mrs. Besant in Budapest: 'There is no question of my ever wanting to be anything at all within an occult movement except in relation to German culture.'

★

Meanwhile, British culture moved towards further development when the June issue of *The Vâhan* carried an announcement headed 'Proposed Theosophical Summer School':

Arrangements can be made with the Weybourne Springs Hotel for the holding of a Theosophical Summer School for five or six days, immediately following the Convention in London (July 3 and 4), if a sufficient number of members and friends will signify their willingness to attend. The hotel is in a beautiful and healthy part of the country, close to the pines and heather of Kelling Heath. Amongst the attractions of the neighbourhood are the ancient villages of Blakeney and Clay, with their wonderful churches and curious legends, and the ancient British Camp of Boadicea. The sea is a little over a mile away, and it is only a few miles by rail to Sheringham and Cromer. The hotel provides accomodation for sixty to sixty-five guests. Lectures and addresses, with discussions, would be arranged probably for mornings and evenings, and the afternoons devoted to excursions, boating, driving, and other outdoor recreations. The inclusive charge (without excursions) would be at the rate of 30s. per head per week.

If a sufficient number of friends (say thirty to forty at least) will at once communicate with the undersigned, indicating their intention to be present, arrangements will be completed without unnecessary delay, and an attractive programme of discussions, etc., prepared. Suggestions to this end will be gladly received and much appreciated.

This Summer School will afford a more excellent opportunity for friendly and profitable intercourse (under almost ideal conditions) than is possible at the Convention in London. Similar schools in connection with other organizations have been most successful, and there seems no reason why the Theosophical Summer School should not develop into an annual occasion for bodily and spiritual refreshment for members of the T.S. and their friends, while affording an opportunity for considering the best means of furthering the work of Theosophy in every direction. I shall be glad if all who are interested will communicate with me as soon as possible.

D.N. Dunlop

Ashdale, Warwick Drive, Hale, Cheshire.

The Best Occult Development

The Business Meeting of the British Convention took place on 3 July. *The Vâhan* reported:

Our Convention this year was dignified and inspired by the presence of our President, and and it may be truly said that it was characterized by a greater harmony and fuller sense of freedom than ever before. Both these qualities were very marked. The Saturday afternoon meeting was a happy augury for the years's work, started freshly on that day.

A considerably fuller report than usual is given of the whole proceedings, hoping that it may induce members to take a keener interest in the work of our National Society.

After the President had taken the chair, Mr. A.S. Banks and Mr. H. Shindler were elected Secretaries to the Convention . . .

The following representatives from other National Societies were then called upon by the President, and briefly addressed the meeting:

Mr. Lazenby (Canada): I have no message except what I give from comrades everywhere. We are in the T.S. to serve it, not to take for ourselves, and the Convention can only be a power as we take a message forth into the world. We have had a rough shaking, but we are far stronger than before, and we are here to take forward the message of Theosophy. That is my message from Canada.

Mrs. Windust (Holland): It is a very long time since I last had the pleasure of representing Holland at one of your Conventions . . .

Mlle Blech (Paris): I bring the greetings of the French General Secretary and Section, and tell you that all goes well there and that we are full of hope . . .

Mme Kamensky, General Secretary of the Russian Section: Today I have the joy of greeting you in the name of the Russian Section . . .

M. van Haeften (Belgium): The situation of the T.S. in Belgium is very much the same as before . . .

The General Secretary, Mrs. Sharpe, pointed out that the yearly report had already been published in the *Vâhan* . . .

Mr. Leo moved, and Mrs. Betts seconded the adoption of the report, and it was carried unanimously . . .

The Treasurer's report had also been published with the *Vâhan*; its adoption was moved by Mr. Dunlop, seconded by Miss E.M. Mallett, and carried unanimously.

The Treasurer thanked Mr. Tovey for his work in auditing, and in the preparation of the balance sheet, and proposed his re-election as auditor; this was seconded by Mr. Dunlop and carried unanimously.

Mr. D.N. Dunlop moved the following resolution:

'That the British Theosophical Society in Convention assembled hereby expresses its satisfaction with the declaration of principles embodied in the resolutions passed by the General Council of the Theosophical Society in December last, and desires, by fully endorsing them, to annul the resolution moved by Mr. Burrows, and irregularly passed at the last Convention of the British Section of the Theosophical Society.

'The Convention takes this opportunity of expressing its fullest confidence in the President of the Theosophical Society and desires to thank her, and through her the General Council, for the generous provision made for those who desire to be associated with the work of the Theosophical Society while differing in matters of detail and organization.

'The Convention at the same time desires to express its goodwill and fraternal greetings to all members of Theosophical and kindred societies, under whatever name they may be known, in the hope that (to use the words of our President) all "may labour together in the name of Theosophy for the peace of nations and the enlightenment of the world".'

Mr. Dunlop, in moving the first part of his resolution, said that it seemed to him desirable that we should put a finishing touch to what had taken place during the last twelve months. It was just a year that day since he had last stood there. He had then intended his resolution to be taken as one and not as three. But for the convenience of some it was divided, although he had protested, and instead of the clause 'It declares further that the Section as a whole should not have less than the generous spirit of its units, that it should exercise the same brotherly spirit alike to those of good or evil fame, expressing the love which rejects none', the resolution moved by Mr. Burrows was substituted. That resolution was objectionable in many respects. It should not have been taken as an amendment, but as a substantive resolution. As an amendment, however, it was voted on and carried. In his opinion, and in that of Mr. Mead, it was irregular.

Circulars had recently been issued, and statements made which called for our attention, and the answer he proposed we should give was this resolution, which counteracted the one passed last year.

Mr. Burrows's resolution was expressly sent to the President and General Council, and they had drafted two resolutions in reply. It was fitting that we should acknowledge and endorse those two resolutions, and so finish the business.

(Here the resolutions of the General Council were read.)

Referring to the second clause of his resolution, Mr. Dunlop said that there had been differences of opinion with regard to the generous provision of the General Council, and he thought we should express our thanks for a proposal that was even more than generous. Some thought it was unnecessary to express full confidence in, and thanks to the President; such expressions were too often left till White Lotus Day, but it was not necessary to be so shy about our feelings. It was wise to put on record that we had confidence in our President, and that we were not afraid to put our confidence on record. We were not living for today, nor working for today; we should think of the future. What we did today might appear to be insignificant, but might be seen to be very necessary in the future. And so he had no hesitation in expresssing his fullest confidence in the President. It had been said that he that would be greatest among us must be the servant of all. In that sense Mrs. Besant was the greatest.

Turning to the third clause, Mr. Dunlop said he thought everyone would agree that it was only proper to say what we felt to those who had left us. There were many points on which we could unite, and he had no doubt a day would come when all the Societies who honoured the name of H.P.B. would be united, and all their work be brought together. The opinion seemed to be held today that it was quite easy to form a Society; but our Society was a living thing, and had required an Initiate to start it, and that was why the T.S. was a living Society. It had been said that we had lost many of the cultured and educated people, but H.P.B. had said in a letter to Mr. Judge that the work of the T.S. in the twentieth century would be to make Theosophy known to the masses of the people. We wanted scholars, but as Mr. Judge had said: 'When trouble comes, watch them fly.' If we were not thinking all the time of what we could do for others, we also should fly quickly. We were in the Society for what we could give, and for what we could do, and that spirit would ultimately produce the best occult development possible.

Mr. Ransom, in seconding the resolution, said that it expressed a year's thought on the subject.

Miss Hope Rea asked if Mr. Dunlop made a point of the three parts being voted on as one resolution. She had instructions from her lodge not to vote for the first clause, as it had been considered unwise to reopen the question. Delegates from three other lodges stated that they were in the same predicament. Mrs. Betts, President of the Blavatsky Lodge, said that, though she also had been similarly instructed, after hearing Mr. Dunlop's able explanation, she would take the responsibility of assuming that the members of her lodge would now see the wisdom of the resolution, and would act accordingly.

The President said it would be better, in the circumstances, to separate the resolutions ... The voting was: for the first clause 43, against 2; the second and third clauses were carried unanimously.

Mr. D.N. Dunlop moved:

1. That the work of the Art Circle be recommended to the attention of members.

2. That methods of propaganda and the need of lecturers be considered.

3. That recommendations be considered, and made to the Executive Committee, as to change in next year's Convention.

Mr. Dunlop, in speaking upon these three suggestions, said that it was especially desirable that we should encourage *Orpheus*, the publication of the Art Circle. We should consider how much of our energies in the past had gone along scientific lines, and should encourage the art movement, and identify our Movement with all the arts. This would be more and more necessary for the T.S. in the future. People were of different types, and we should be able to feed all movements and thus encourage these young artists, who associated the Society with what was beautiful and would endure.

Referring to the subject of propaganda, Mr. Dunlop said that this subject was now really being considered in a very practical way. He was glad to see Mr. Bell's scheme for a propaganda fund in the *Vâhan*, but if it were to succeed it must not be a paper scheme only. Unless this were a national movement, and advantage were taken of the impetus given, it would fail. It was absolutely necessary that everyone should make up his mind to contribute to the fund. If this appeal were responded to, we should have something tangible to show for it at the next Convention.

Miss I.M. Pagan (Edinburgh) said that good propaganda work was to be done by means of the drama, and it was a way to interest others outside the T.S. When *Peer Gynt* was performed in Edinburgh, there were thirty-nine actors and thirty in the orchestra; only about twelve of them were theosophists. Yet all worked with enthusiasm, and the majority of those not in the Society were to be seen listening to the President when she came to Edinburgh. We knew that the drama was used among the Greeks as a religious training to get the mind and body to work together. If we looked at the dramatic movement, we should see that the demand for religious and mystery plays was great...

Mr. Sidney Ransom, Miss E. Severs, Mrs. Leo, and Miss Hilda Hodgson Smith also took part in the discussion.

Mr. Dunlop spoke in favour of holding our Conventions from time to time in other parts of England, and gave suggestions for making them of greater and more national importance. Our Convention should be far more than a business meeting, though the business part was a necessity also.

The business of the Convention being disposed of, the President gave her concluding address...

Towards the Future

The Vâhan also carried a report of 'The Summer School', signed by the initials H.R.

> The Summer School, suggested by Mr. Dunlop in the *Vâhan*, came into being in due course, and, as I write, has just dissolved, its members scattering to the four corners of the kingdom and carrying with them what will probably be a lasting impression and a high inspiration.
>
> The place selected for the experiment was a summer season hotel, built at the feet of low wooded hills, a mile from the little Norfolk village of Weybourne and but slightly further from the pebbly coast-line which, running east and west, is better known in connection with Cromer and Overstrand. The spot was ideal for the purpose, in a space of unspoiled country, open to sea and sky and surrounded by woods and heath.
>
> The company numbered from forty to fifty persons, comprising almost as many types, grades and callings—a gathering which at first appeared a baffling tangle of interests and character, but, as day followed day, the apparent confusion resolved itself into a human web of definite if complex pattern, the unifying design to which all conformed being desire of service.
>
> Our programme was simple and elastic; each morning and evening were devoted to lectures or discussion, the afternoons being left free for rambles or less formal interchange of thought. Throughout, Mr. Dunlop was the Chairman—an excellent arrangement, giving unity to the whole week's proceedings, and establishing in them that character of sweet reasonableness which was the distinguishing note of our first Summer School.
>
> The principal speaker during the week was Mr. C.A. Lazenby, B.A., of Toronto University, a man of original mind and untiring energy; bringing with him the freshness of the new world, yet with no lack of reverence; his treatment of those aspects of the 'Ancient Wisdom' upon which he touched was both illuminating and inspiring. Mr. Lazenby lectured on the 'Origin of Religion', the 'Theory of Reincarnation' and the 'Philosophy of Jesus', while with less formal discourse he filled any vacant interval that occurred, ranging from Faust to Lao Tzu, from Omar Khayyâm to psychology, or to the basis of symbolism, with almost equal suggestiveness. Those of us who had read *Leaves of Grass*, as the poems of a representative American, now began, perhaps for the first time, to understand the significance of Walt Whitman's message, which will not be fully understood until the sixth sub-race has become the dominant power of the new age of freedom. During three sessions Mrs. Ransom led a conference on Mrs. Besant's St. James's Hall Lectures, preceding her review by an introduction to theosophical ideas, for the benefit of those of our number who were not as yet members of the T.S. Mr. Robert Gardner, author of *In the Heart of Democracy*, a

thinker who has drawn forth from the background of experience vital truths of daily life, lectured on the 'Socialism of the real Christ'; Dr. Louise Appel led a conference on the 'Theosophical Order of Service' and Miss Bothwell Gosse one on 'Mystic Masonry and the Co-Masonic Movement'. Another session was arranged to consider the 'Influence of the Imaginative Arts on the Theosophical Movement', to be opened by Mr. Clifford Bax; in Mr. Bax's unavoidable absence the discussion turned on the play as a means of theosophical propaganda, and on the possibilities of a new field for painting being opened up by the development of astral vision. A short Mystery Play was read in illustration of the first suggestion, and one of the company, Madame Pogosky, spoke of remarkable paintings she had seen executed by an artist possessing clairvoyant vision. Madame Pogosky brought into our Summer School the spirit of Russia—a link with H.P.B. Her presence was a distinctive element which none of us would willingly have missed. She was impressed with the loving comradeship which united us together as one happy family, and as proof of her goodwill and her interest in Theosophy, she joined the T.S. and the H.P.B. Lodge on her return to London.

Valuable and illuminating as were the different sessions held, yet even more valuable was the spirit generated in them all. One felt on every hand the strong endeavour to throw aside for the time being the limitations and barriers incidental to the personality, and to speak from the depths of the individuality those thoughts and aspirations which were nearest the heart. The outlook maintained was one of hope directed towards the future; very seldom, and then only incidentally, was reference made to what is now the past. The number taking part in the discussions from first to last was large, comparatively few refusing to contribute something to the exchange of thought. Another interesting feature was the prominence given to music; every evening the lecture or conference was preceded by a violin solo, with piano accompaniment; sometimes a second piece was called for and readily given; sometimes a song was substituted. A delightful spontaneity prevailed. One thing only was invariable, that in one form or another we had music first, and then, attuned and harmonized, we turned to the subject chosen for the evening's considerations. Our musicians earned and had our hearty thanks.

The weather during the School was extremely variable, one or two days of summer glory lay between days of exceptional fury; during one of these a gloom was cast on the neighbouring villages by the loss at sea of two young fishermen, each leaving behind them a wife and child. The School attempted to relieve the darkness by sending a combined thought of help and peace to those left behind, as well as to the two souls so suddenly flung into the life beyond. A material collection of coin of the realm resulted in a substantial sum, which was sent, accompanied by a letter from our Chairman, to the district coroner, to be handed to the widows. An official

> acknowledgement 'to the Theosophical Summer School' showed that our presence in the neighbourhood was realized, and that in a way entirely to be desired.
>
> In recalling the general impression of the School, perhaps these summer gales will be among the deeper lines of the picture. None will be likely to forget the gatherings in the gaunt bare billiard-room, where we sat, as best we could, around the oil-cloth-covered table, the air vibrating with the last notes of the violin, and gathering a finer intensity of vibration, as our thoughts went out in high aspiration towards the Wisdom, while outside the storm from time to time forced itself upon our consciousness, as the rain lashed the uncurtained window-panes, and the booming of the wind rose and fell.
>
> At the close of Sunday evening, when we were all gathered around the fire which the weather's inclemency rendered attractive, the opinion generally expressed was that the Theosophical Summer School had proved itself an unqualified success, and must be built up into an institution of the Society. Many proposals of a most practical character were made, and noted by the Chairman for careful consideration, and the result, we all confidently hope, will manifest itself in the summer of 1910.

It need only be added that at this Summer School Charles Lazenby first met a Scottish lady by the name of Margaret Clark.

Sprung from a Western Source

Despite the defection of large numbers from the Theosophical Society's British Section in 1909, those who remained were still sufficiently numerous that in the further course of that year it was decided to divide this Section into two, on a geographical basis. The larger part was renamed the 'Theosophical Society in England and Wales', while the 'Theosophical Society in Scotland' was separated off as an entirely new Section.

★

The Vâhan continued to provide announcements of forthcoming events in the German Section:

> Members will be interested to hear that a Mystery Play, entitled *The Children of Lucifer*, will take place in Munich during August, and lectures by Dr. Rudolf Steiner will be given during the following months at the following places: Cologne, Düsseldorf, Christiania, Budapest, Cassel, Munich and Basel. Further information can be obtained from Miss M. von Sivers, 17 Motzstrasse, Berlin.

A further issue added:

Those who take an interest in the activities of the T.S. in Germany and the teachings of Dr. Rudolf Steiner will be glad to hear that during his visit to Munich (August 22–31) special facilities will be made for visitors who do not know the German language. Dr. Steiner will lecture on 'The Orient in the Light of the Occident, the Children of Lucifer and the Brothers of Christ'; should it be desired, a resumé of each lecture will be given on the following day in English. A course of lectures will be given, also in English, on 'The Evolution of the World and of Man', as contained in Dr. Steiner's 'Akashic Record'. Another course will be arranged on the esoteric meaning of the Gospel of St. John, a subject to which Dr. Steiner has given much thought, as all his readers know. The same arrangements and facilities will hold good in Basle (Sept. 15–26), where Dr. Steiner will lecture on 'Occult Teaching in St. Luke's Gospel, and its relation to the other three Gospels'. All inquiries concerning these conferences may be addressed to I.M.M., Königinstrasse 83, Munich, Bavaria.

*

Max Gysi brought out a further book by Rudolf Steiner, *Initiation and its Results*. He composed an extensive foreword, laying more stress on the Western character of Steiner's teachings:

The widespread interest taken in the first volume of this series (entitled *The Way of Initiation*) and its success, have encouraged me in the present volume to place before English readers a translation of the articles written by Dr. Steiner as a sequel to the above series, and originally published in *Lucifer-Gnosis* (Nos. 20–28), a theosophical magazine published by M. Altmann, Leipzig, and edited by Dr. Rudolf Steiner. The same magazine is now bringing out a series of articles entitled 'The Theory of Cognition according to Occult Science', which when finished will conclude these very important communications from a source of genuine occult wisdom. When completed, I propose to publish them as a third volume of this series.

To save disappointment to some readers into whose hands this book may chance to fall, let me frankly state at the outset that neither this nor its companion volumes are intended for people who deny the possibility of attaining knowledge by other means than their physical organs of sense. Belief in, or at least hypothetical acceptance of, the reality of the unseen world and of forces not perceptible by our physical senses is therein taken for granted. For those unable to accept these premises there exists a vast literature which, if approached with an unprejudiced mind and carefully studied, will convince them of all that is here postulated.

These volumes might be called advanced text-books of occultism, and those to whom the subject is repellent had better not read them, because they are written by an occultist of a very high order for those really interested in the subject, and desirous of advancing in their self-development to a point hitherto unattainable by them, since it has not until now been deemed expedient openly to publish such far-reaching revelations of the occult. The book is intended for those only who will use every power gained for the helping of their fellow-pilgrims, and who place self-sacrifice and unselfish devotion to the best interests of mankind above all other virtues.

On the other hand, there is a large number of people, deeply interested in the subject, who were under the impression that there is only the one occultism whose home is in the East, and who now eagerly welcome a teaching sprung from a Western source, which shows them that they need not go beyond Europe in their search either for genuine occult knowledge, or for teachers competent to instruct those willing to fulfil the conditions necessary for the safe treading of the narrow path leading up to the feet of the One Initiator.

There are few leaders of thought at the present day who have a larger following than Dr. Steiner in the German-speaking part of Mid-Europe, and I know of no other teacher able to gather around him from 500 to 600 cultured people who will eagerly travel any distance and stay for two or three weeks wherever he may choose to lecture. During his recent courses of addresses on the Apocalypse, the Gospel according to St. John, 'From Buddha to Christ', on Cosmogony, etc., etc., held in Berlin and Basle, in Christiania and Budapest, in Munich and Rome—to mention only a few of the cities visited by this indefatigable worker for the good of humanity—students were gathered together from all parts of Europe; from Hammerfest in the North and Palermo in the South, from Eastern Siberia, and from France and Spain.

That we are living at present in a wonderful time of transition, when 'the old order changeth, yielding place to new' may be gathered from the fact that a very large number of those most eager to welcome these wonderful teachings are recruited from highly cultured classes, whose predecessors of but two decades ago would have scoffed at the whole subject.

In conclusion, I should like to draw attention to the close and wonderful relation which the careful student may trace between the 'exercises' and 'trials' set forth in *The Way of Initiation* and the means of vivification of the astral organs (chakras) described in this volume. After the success of the first volume, we are satisfied that there is a widespread demand in English-speaking countries for the teachings of Theosophy as enunciated by Dr. Steiner, and we shall try gradually to make accessible to English readers all the more important works of this truly great mystic and occultist.

For those who are fully satisfied with the exoteric teachings of the day this volume is not intended, but it is earnestly hoped that it may bring light and peace to serious seekers after truth.

Max Gysi
Belsize Lodge,
Belsize Lane,
London, N.W.,
31st August 1909.

A Transforming Power

The first part of AE's *The Hero in Man* reproduced an article which originally appeared in November 1897 in *The Internationalist*—into which *The Irish Theosophist* was amalgamated after D.N. Dunlop's departure in October of that year to America.

There sometimes comes on us a mood of strange reverence for people and things which in less contemplative hours we hold to be unworthy; and in such moments we may set side by side the head of Christ and the head of an outcast, and there is an equal radiance around each, which makes of the darker face a shadow, and is itself a shadow around the head of light. We feel a fundamental unity of purpose in their presence here, and would as willingly pay homage to the one who has fallen as to him who has become a Master of life. I know that immemorial order decrees that the laurel and the crown be given only to the victor, but in those moments I speak of a profound intuition changes the decree, and sets the aureole on both alike.

We feel such deep pity for the fallen that there must needs be a justice in it, for these diviner feelings are wise in themselves and do not vaguely arise. They are lights from the Father. A justice lies in uttermost pity and forgiveness, even when we seem to ourselves to be most deeply wronged. Or why is it that the awakening of resentment or hate brings such swift contrition?

We are self-condemned; and the dark thought which went forth in us brooding revenge, when suddenly smitten by the light, withdraws and hides within itself in awful penitence. In asking myself why it is that the meanest are safe from our condemnation when we sit on the true seat of judgment in the heart, it seemed to me that their shield was the sense we have of a nobility hidden in them under the cover of ignoble things; that their present darkness was the result of some too weighty heroic labour undertaken long ago by the human spirit; that it was the consecration of past purpose which played with such a tender light about their ruined lives, and it was more pathetic because this nobleness was all unknown to the fallen, and the heroic cause of so much pain was forgotten in life's prison-house.

While feeling the service to us of the great ethical ideals which have been formulated by men, I think that the idea of justice intellectually conceived tends to beget a certain hardness of the heart. It is true that men have done wrong—hence their pain. But back of all this there is something infinitely soothing, a light which does not wound, which says no harsh thing, even although the darkest of spirits turns to it in its agony. For the darkest of human spirit has still around him this first glory which shines from a deeper being within, whose history may be told as the legend of the Hero in Man.

Among the many immortals with whom ancient myth peopled the spiritual sphere of humanity are some figures which draw to themselves a more profound tenderness than the rest. Not Aphrodite rising in beauty from the faery foam of the first seas, not Apollo with sweetest singing, laughter and youth, not the wielder of the lightning could exact the reverence accorded to the lonely Titan chained on the mountain, or to that bowed figure heavy with the burden of the sins of the world. For the brighter divinities had no part in the labour of man, no such intimate relation with the wherefore of his own existence so full of struggle. The more radiant figures are prophecies to him of his destiny, but the Titan and the Christ are a revelation of his more immediate state. Their giant sorrows companion his own, and in contemplating them he awakens what is noblest in his own nature. Or, in other words, in understanding their divine heroism he understands himself. For this in truth it seems to me to mean: all knowledge is a revelation of the self to the self, and our deepest comprehension of the seemingly apart divine is also our furthest inroad to self-knowledge. Prometheus, Christ, are in every heart. The story of one is the story of all. The Titan and the Crucified are humanity.

If then we consider them as representing the human spirit, and disentangle from the myths their meaning, we shall find that whatever reverence is due to that heroic love which descended from Heaven for the redeeming of a lower nature must be paid to every human being. Christ is incarnate in all humanity. Prometheus is bound forever within us. They are the same. They are a host, and the divine incarnation was not spoken of one, but of all those who descending into the lower world tried to change it into the divine image, and to wrest out of chaos a kingdom for the empire of light. The angels saw below them in chaos a senseless rout blind with elemental passion, forever warring with discordant cries which broke in upon the world of divine beauty. And that the pain might depart, they grew rebellious in the Master's peace. And descending to Earth the angelic lights were crucified in men; leaving so radiant worlds, such a light of beauty, for Earth's grey twilight filled with tears, that through this elemental life might breathe the starry music brought from Him. If the 'Foreseer' be a true name for the Titan, it follows that in the host which he represents was a light which well foreknew all the dark paths of its journey; foreseeing the bitter struggle with a hostile nature, but foreseeing perhaps a gain, a distant glory o'er the hills of sorrow, and that chaos, divine and transformed, with only gentle breathing, lit up by the Christ-soul of the Universe. There is a transforming power in the thought itself. We can no longer condemn the fallen, they who laid aside their thrones of ancient power, their spirit-ecstasy and beauty, on such a mission. Perhaps those who sank lowest did so to raise a greater burden, and of these most fallen it may in the hour of their resurrection be said, 'The last shall be first'.

So, placing side by side the head of the outcast with the head of Christ, it has this equal beauty—with as bright a glory it sped from the Father in ages past on its redeeming labour. Of his present darkness what shall we say? 'He is altogether dead?' Nay, rather with tenderness forbear, and think that the foreseeing spirit has taken its own dread path to mastery; that that which foresaw the sorrow foresaw also beyond it a greater joy and a mightier existence, when it would rise again in a new robe, woven out of the treasure hidden in the deep of its submergence, and shine at last like the stars of the morning triumphant among the Sons of God.

Clifford Bax, referring in *Rosemary for Remembrance* to publication of *The Hero in Man*, stated:

AE had refused to claim any advance or any royalty on the booklet, and in lieu of them I sent him fifty copies. In September 1909 he wrote:

'I have just come back from wilding it in Donegal for a month and I find what seems a whole edition of *The Hero in Man*, and copies of a new and more expensive edition. The firm of Dunlop and Bax are certainly the most generous publishers, and they have my blessing. Oh that Lane were like this or that the hard heart of Macmillan might be pierced through with contrition, for they only send me six copies. And Mosher in America imitates their low ways. A new era is dawning, and the publisher of the Golden Age coming will give all the edition to the author to dispose of as he will—at least, given Lane as the first step and Dunlop and Bax as the second step, that is the logical conclusion of the matter.'

★

In September there also appeared *Initiation and its Results* by Rudolf Steiner, in a print-run of 1500 copies. The outer motif on spine and cover was an encircled swastika.

The book received an appreciative review in the October issue of *The Vâhan*:

The success which attended Mr. Max Gysi's translation of Dr. Steiner's *Way of Initiation* (now in its second edition) has encouraged him to go further with his good work of making accessible to English-speaking students the writings of our German General Secretary. No theosophical student reading these books can fail to see that we have here a genuine well of occult knowledge, and to perceive by the nobility of thought which permeates it and the loftiness of the goal of unselfish labour for the world which it sets before us that Dr. Steiner's teaching comes from the one deep Source of Wisdom whence come all great and good things.

Mr. Clifford Bax, who has done the work of translation, is to be congratulated upon the clear, smooth way in which he has 'Englished' Dr. Steiner.

In the Light of Theosophy

On Tuesday 12 October 1909 a debate was held in Bath, in the south-west of England. Reports of the occasion given in two local weeklies were so extensive that they must have been made by stenographers. 'A Heated Discussion' appeared on the front page of *The Bath Herald* on the 13th, and 'Strong Words in Lively Debate' in *The Bath Chronicle* on the 14th. The present account conflates the two versions.

> Considerable public interest was taken last evening in a debate on 'Theosophy', with which the Bath Y.M.C.A. Debating Society opened their winter session. The Jubilee Hall was crowded, and at times considerable heat was shown in the discussion. Amongst those present were many holding orthodox religious views, many theosophists and many socialists. A large proportion of the audience were ladies.
>
> The debate was opened by Mr. D.N. Dunlop (Theosophical Society lecturer, of London), the principal speaker in opposition being the Rev. W.P. Hanks, M.A., F.R.S.L.

Since Dunlop was not at the time living in London at all, but in Cheshire in the north of England, he must have been asked to step in for this occasion by the Executive Committee of the Theosophical Society at its London headquarters.

> Mr. George E. Fyson, who presided, congratulated the society on having arranged such an interesting debate and on having secured such a magnificent attendance. On behalf of the Rev. W.P. Hanks, the Chairman asked Mr. Dunlop to give some definition of Theosophy in his address. According to the rules of debate the opener was given 20 minutes to move a resolution, and the opposer a similar time to reply; then the meeting was thrown open for discussion and the two speakers were afterwards given 10 minutes to reply.
>
> Mr. Dunlop said in opening that a businessman was at a slight dis-

advantage in a debate, and he hoped they would follow him sympathetically. Theosophy was a rather large order for him to define in the scope of 20 minutes. Someone had said that Theosophy was an ocean, which was deep enough to lose oneself entirely in, and at the same time one could paddle about in it. The fundamentals of Theosophy were to be found in all the world's religions. There was nothing more ancient. It was believed by theosophists to be the basis of all religions, and that all religions were the same in essentials. In his opinion the study of Theosophy made Christians better Christians. The study of Theosophy had given him a better outlook on Christian doctrines. He did not say for a moment that all would find it so, but in his case it had thrown new light upon the subject, and he spoke for himself alone. Theosophy began at the beginning, if there was such a thing as a beginning. But as far as their own planet was concerned, it was quite sensible to his mind to talk of a beginning, and they were all familiar with the term which was given to that great fundamental intelligence that was behind all manifested life, the name of God. He would accept the word, but it was almost blasphemy to define it in human terms at all. It was all about them. There was no place anywhere where God had not been. The first differentiation, as the mystics called it, was the world of the spirit, where they found the models for all others to come. Proceeding from that, they had what theosophists called the psychic world. There they found etherial forms far more definite than in the realm of spirits. Then they came to the grossest form of all, the physical. There they had a manifestation so great that there was no disputing the fact that they had physical bodies. Man was essentially a spirit, he had also a psychic nature, a physical body, and an animal nature. Mr. Dunlop quoted Genesis, which stated that God breathed into man and he became a living soul. That was the battleground they found between higher and lower things. It was upon that battleground that all struggles had taken place. There was a fight going on between the lower animal nature and the higher spiritual nature. Which would gain the victory? Theosophy took them over a vast field of time and a vast sweep of evolution, comprehending everything, he believed, in its grasp. That was one of the objections raised against Theosophy—it was too wide-sweeping. People wanted something much more concrete. ('Hear, hear.') They could limit themselves to their own satisfaction. They could confine themselves immediately to the points which interested them most. In the world of science great improvements were going on. There was a revolution since the discovery of X-rays, radium, radioactivity, etc. In the works of Mdm. Blavatsky they would find the prophecies made of what had since then taken place with regard to radium, and so forth. They would also find the whole world of psychic phenomena dealt with there, if they wished it. Many people today interested themselves in the psychical nature of man. There was a great world to be investigated there. Theosophists considered nothing to be outside the scope of their investigations, and Theosophy certainly assisted investigations. Dealing with physical life, Mr. Dunlop said that the first object of the Theosophical Society was the Universal Brotherhood of Man. (Applause.) Man was a brotherhood throughout the entire world, without distinction of race, sex, caste or colour. (Renewed applause.) They had however fallen out with each other, like the members of some family, and according to Theosophy they required the Elder Brothers to come and tell them how to get home. The theosophist believed that man started sweet, pure, noble, godly, and, plunged into the experience of man, his soul came through this great psychical evolution, but at the present moment had reached a point in the ascending road and was going back on his homeward journey. They would find in the study of the subject the idea of reincarnation, which had caused so much discussion. This taught that man had an immortal soul. He had never had a beginning, but when he began to be associated with the body forms of the lower elements had associated himself with that body throughout the ages since, for the purpose of garnering experience. That was the law of psychic progression throughout all Nature. Each period produced its elect, its perfect man; these formed the teachers, guides and seers to the humanity that followed. The world had never been without some manifestations of these Masters. Jesus was perhaps one of the last, and perhaps the same as he who appeared in the East as Buddha. Why should it not be so? There was Jesus appearing in Galilee and teaching the old teaching that Buddha taught, called by a new name. If they lived up to the teachings of Jesus the world would be an entirely different place. The civilization of today stood condemned by the teachings of Jesus. (Applause.) Why had they had all this confusion of thoughts with regard to the various doctrines of Christianity? Why, theosophists asked, were there so many sects founded upon the teaching of the simple Nazarene? It was so simple that they could not live up to it. It was not difficult for any man or woman studying Theosophy to get to the kernel very quickly when they began to realize that all religions were similar in essentials, when they realized that there was no need for intolerance to any other religion or sect. Mr. Dunlop concluded by quoting the principles of Theosophy from a treatise written by himself. Finally he moved a resolution in the following terms 'That Christian doctrines can only be truly interpreted in the light of Theosophy'.

The resolution was formally seconded by a lady in the audience.

The Rev. W.P. Hanks then rose to oppose the resolution. He said he had been hoping to get at close quarters with Theosophy. Through the Chairman he put out a feeler to try to secure a definition of Theosophy, but they were told that it was a subject wide and deep as the ocean. Evidently it was deep enough for a man to drown in. He had discussed Theosophy with many of its leading exponents, and he was still as much at sea as regards the tenets and authority of this strangely uncertain and insane creed. If Mr. Dunlop had come to them with a philosophy which would meet the difficulties of life, and help men and women to lead better lives, they could have taken Theosophy at its own valuation, and argued whether or not it did cast any light on great problems, but he had given in a resolution so arrogant and insulting—

A good deal of uproar interrupted Mr. Hanks. There was considerable hissing, and loud cries of 'No! No!' 'Hear, hear!' 'Shame!' 'Apologize!' 'Rats!', and a voice 'Calm your temper for a Christian!'

'It is not I who am losing my temper,' was Mr. Hanks's retort. 'I am perfectly calm.' He again endeavoured to make himself heard, but there were renewed demands on the speaker to withdraw, accompanied by such remarks as 'Disgraceful!' and 'That's the Christian Church!'

Once more Mr. Hanks tried to finish his sentence. 'Withdraw!' shouted a section of the audience. 'Most decidely not,' was Mr. Hanks's emphatic reply, and encouraged by cries of 'Go on,' he yet again essayed to make himself heard, urging his audience: 'Hear what I have to say before I withdraw.'

After a time Mr. Hanks was able to continue, and speaking with some heat, he said: 'The resolution says the Christian doctrine can only be truly interpreted in the light of Theosophy, and I say it is not only insulting to me—' (Loud applause.) 'I say it is absolutely insulting to the Christian Church—' (Hisses.) '—insulting to us all.' (Applause, and more hisses.)

'I appeal to the chair that I have a right to speak,' continued the reverend gentleman, when there seemed signs of the uproar being renewed. 'I am asked by a Young Men's Christian Society to come and speak in defence of Christianity, and surely I have a right to be heard.' (Applause.)

A voice: 'He is as much entitled to speak as you.'

The Chairman: 'Mr. Hanks is in possession of the house.' (Applause.)

Mr. Hanks, warmly: 'Do you want me to speak or go home?'

A voice: 'Go home!'

Mr. Hanks expressed the hope that an allowance of time would be made for the interruptions, and repeated that the resolution was insulting to the Christian Church, adding 'If I am asked by a Christian Association to come here as a Christian minister and debate the question, then I must debate it with the gloves off, and in earnest.' (Applause.)

The speaker was then able to continue his speech without further interruptions. He declared with emphasis that he wanted to discuss the question most calmly and equably. He was still calm and equable, except that he did not like being hissed at. ('Hear, hear.') But to come and tell them Christian doctrines could only be interpreted in the light of Theosophy, and to back it up by such a speech, seemed to him the utmost limit of mental audacity—he said no more. ('Hear, hear.') Who, and who alone could interpret the doctrines of the Christian Church? The Church itself. ('Hear, hear.' A voice: 'True,' and some ironical laughter.) Suppose he said that the Christian Church alone had the right to interpret the doctrines of Theosophy—what would they say to him? They said they who taught Theosophy had a right to teach Christians. (Applause.) He contended that the resolution cast dirt in the face of the Christian Church, of its Great Founder, of the Twelve Apostles, and of the martyrs and saints of the Church who for 2000 years had lived and died for Christianity, by a new-fangled sect with Madame Blavatsky at its head—Madame Blavatsky, who was declared by the Psychical Research Society to have been an imposter and a fraud. ('Hear, hear,' and dissent.) Madame Blavatsky had written their theosophical Bible. Who were their accredited teachers? To whom were they to go when they wanted to know the true meaning of our Christian doctrine, which had been so terribly misapplied and misunderstood through these two thousand years of Christian history? He listened patiently until the end of Mr. Dunlop's speech, and then they knew, for Mr. Dunlop then read from his own book. Did Mr. Dunlop, on his own authority, claim that only he was able to tell the true meaning of the almighty revelation which had saved the world, and was in the van of civilization today? If that was not an insult to the Christian Church he did not know what was.

'No hissing, sir!' exclaimed the speaker, as there seemed a tendency in that direction. 'Don't keep me silent in the face of an insult so profound and so disgraceful!' (Applause.)

The speaker hoped still that some sort of definition of Theosophy would be given. So far as Mr. Dunlop went, he denied a personal God; and Theosophy, denying a personal God, was going to interpret for them the Christian doctrine of the God-Father! The theosophical idea of God was the negation of everything—the last refuge of intellectual despair. To whom did theosophists pray? To the great void, to the great Causeless Cause, the First Intelligence, to Pure Thought? Christians prayed, and to a Father. (Applause.) They believed that Christ was God. What would Theosophy tell them of their Christ? Was he God or man? Theosophists talked about the 'Brotherhood of Man', but that was simply, of course, the Christian doctrine. Theosophists borrowed half their teachings from India. Pick and choose—that was the new Theosophy. 'Eat, drink and be merry, for tomorrow you die!' Theosophists were simply plagiarists. They took a bit from one religion and a bit from another, and showed that they did not understand any. Anything they did not like they did not take: and that was the method of the New Theology today. ('Hear, hear,' and dissent.) How could anyone put forward the argument that the teaching of Jesus and of the Buddha was the same? Buddhism was the very incarnation of despair. Mr. Hanks ridiculed the doctrine of reincarnation, which would teach that a man was suffering today for what he did in past lives, and yet he did not remember those lives. What was the good of suffering for the sins of a man one never knew, who lived a thousand years before? The doctrine seemed, too, to limit God's whole plan simply to the present world, whereas we knew there were myriads of worlds. He wished people, before they turned theosophists, would study Christian theology with the same ardour and earnestness that they studied the doctrines of Theosophy: they would never turn at all. (Applause.) But the great critical queestion was this—if they claimed to interpret Christian doctrines to them, what did they say about Christ? Mr. Hanks condemned the theosophist view of Christ as a mere teacher of right conduct, and defended the view which regards Christ as God and the Saviour of the world.

'Choose between Mr. Dunlop and your Christ,' were Mr. Hanks's final words before moving as a direct negative: 'That this meeting utterly repudiates the claim of theosophists to interpret Christian doctrines.'

The meeting was then thrown open for discussion, and among those who contributed were Mr. Councillor John, Messrs. Hector Sants, Whiting, G. Hayward, Orchard and Reynolds, and several ladies.

By one speaker it was urged that there had been some misunderstanding, while another (a lady) pointed to degrading social conditions, and inquired where was the justice of this? Theosophists could explain it by reasonable hypothesis, but she had not heard it explained in any Church she had been to.

The next speaker was a clergyman, who introduced himself as a stranger to Bath, and as one who had come to close quarters with Buddhism in inland China. He spoke of the degradation of life, the cruelty to animals, the appalling sin out there, and criticized the lives that Buddhist priests and nuns are living. Christian missionaries had been thanked by the Chinese authorities for the uplift they had given the Chinese nation. He had spent 22 years out there, and during that time 224 of his fellow-missionaries had been massacred. He was going back there to preach a living Christ, a living Saviour, for whom he was not afraid, if need be, to give his life. (Loud applause.)

The next speaker was a lady, who explained that Theosophy takes in the fundamental bases of all religions. The fundamental principles which had been preached or taught through the ages were exactly the same, and that was why they had been accused of stealing. She told the audience how Theosophy had solved for her difficulties in relation to much apparent injustice.

Another lady, a theosophist, referring to the remarks of the Rev. W.P. Hanks, suggested that the idea of Christianity, illuminated by the light of Theosophy—divine wisdom—was nothing to cavil at. They did not come there to fight. They came to help each other find a little more of what they were all looking for. (Applause.)

Mr. Reynolds, who wore the flaming tie of the Socialists, and who declared that he was pleased that he was not a Christian, expressed admiration of the moral teaching of Christ, but strongly criticized organized Christianity, accusing it of tolerating present social conditions, of despising the child born in the slum, and of supporting a social system which allows a man to corner God-given food. He pointed to the slums and the distinction there was between rich and poor as 'the things I want to bring home to prick your conscience' he said, addressing Mr. Hanks. 'Look at yourselves, you Christians, and be Christians.'

Another Socialist followed in the same strain, but when he was declaiming against the masses being bled to death so that a few could pile up wealth, he was called to order by the Chairman.

The next speaker defended Christianity. He had yet to learn that Christianity was in any way responsible for the cornering of wealth. (Applause.) Referring to the degradation of women in China, he spoke of the high position held by women in England, and asked how many English women had to do work fit only for animals. (A voice: 'Thousands.') He said there were none. (Applause.) Who was it that built our hospitals—Christians or theosophists? (Applause, and a voice: 'All sorts.')

A lady member of the Theosophical Society informed the meeting that the last three speakers did not belong to that Society. She pointed out the teachings of Christianity which Theosophy embraced.

Another lady theosophist having spoken, Mr. Orchard, a Socialist speaker, declared that when he had been to theosophist meetings he had found there the elect of society, and precious little of the feeling of the 'brotherhood of man'. So long as people groped after intangible ideals, so long they would miss the ideal of human brotherhood. Mr. Orchard did not think Christianity could stand against Theosophy, because the Church upheld a system which said 'Each man for himself and the devil take the hind one.' (Cries of 'No.')

The next speaker, a man, declared that anyone who took up Theosophy in a sympathetic spirit would find it a great blessing.

Then came a passionate speech on the vagueness of Theosophy and the reality of Christ—a speech that was much applauded.

Mr. Councillor John said he came to learn and not to take part in the debate on either side, but he should like to say, as one more in sympathy with the proposer than the opposer, that he certainly could not congratulate the champion of orthodox Christianity upon his temper or method in debate. (Applause.) He believed theosophists might be good allies to the Christian Church. At times in a man's life other explanations and views than the traditional and orthodox must operate if they were to keep the man anywhere near the realm of Christian society. Had Theosophy such explanations to offer? Mr. Hanks had spoken of the Church as the true interpreter of the Christian doctrines, but he did not know that he had proved it. It was a tremendous assumption. (Applause.) Mr. Hanks must know that within the ranks of his own Church there were many who put many different interpretations on the creeds they were all supposed to hold in common. At the same time he (Mr. John) was not quarrelling with them. He believed it was necessary, but so long as it was possible for any system of thought to help a man in his course through life, whether by opening larger vistas, or by offering explanations more satisfactory than the old ones, surely that was something not to be railed at. (Applause.) If he might be allowed to say so without offence, railing they had had that night and not argument, and he was sorry for it.

'I believe,' said Mr. John, 'that everything a man needs is to be found in the Christian religion, but not as interpreted by the Church, and not as exemplified by some Christians.' (Applause.)

The Rev. W.P. Hanks, replying in his subsequent 10 minutes' speech, said that some of the arguments brought forward had been something in the nature of a personal attack upon himself. He stood there without any consciousness of having offended against the rules of public decency, good manners, courtesy, or debate. (Applause.) People in that room who took him for an exponent of official and orthodox Christianity did not know him. But to return to the definite charge which had been made against him—the charge of railing and so forth. He submitted that he was in the most unmannerly manner interrupted by hissing and other remarks, absolutely unparliamentary, undignified and indecent, in the middle of a sentence the meaning of which no one took the trouble to understand. He did not say a word about the speaker or the words he used; he spoke absolutely of this resolution—arrogant, insolent, in his opinion—and simply said the terms of the resolution were arrogant and insulting, and then was interrupted and had to conclude—'to the Christian Church'.

'Have I not a right as a Christian minister to say that?' asked the speaker warmly. (Applause.) 'Should I not be false to my trust, to the responsibility laid upon me here tonight, if I failed to say it?' (Applause.)

He submitted he was within his rights. He acknowledged that the speech was in absolute good temper and good form and said he had nothing to complain of in any single word spoken, except this argument in the resolution. Mr. Hanks went on to say that the careless way in which people who took no trouble to acquaint themseves with the matter discussed these great questions and poured out a farrago of nonsense fairly made his blood boil. What certainly made him lose his temper was when he was interrupted by hissing and groans. He hoped to answer one or two of those ladies who had with such distinguished calmness, sobriety and reasonableness put forward their arguments. One lady had quoted as doctrine 'an eye for an eye and a tooth for a tooth'. Those words were not the teaching of the law of karma but, as far as he remembered, occurred in a text pointing out the old idea of revenge. It was not the teaching of Christianity today. What struck him most was the material view their theosophist friends had taken. One would think the whole idea was that this world was an unequal world, unjust of God because people were put into different positions, the poor and the rich, some into a slum, others into a palace. Christians worshipped the child which was born, not in an inn, because there was no room for him in a common inn; not in a hotel, but in a stable. (Applause.) The whole teaching of Christianity was that this world was physically impossible. It was not spiritually imperfect. Through suffering and pain the spiritual man fought upward, and by the very means of poverty and temptation he won his eternal triumph. As if life could be measured by these sordid material things, by sordid materialism! They did not teach that this world was perfectly physically ordered. They did teach that it was created by God. Their speaker that evening had said man was equal to God, and had never had a beginning. He made God and man one, as did the Rev. R. J. Campbell and the New Theologists. Several ladies had told them that the teachings of Theosophy and Christianity were exactly the same. Then what was the good of Theosophy? Was it borrowed from Christianity? All they had to rely on that night was the authority of Mr. Dunlop and his teachings. They asked what the Church was. He would tell them from the sacrosanct prayer offered at Holy Communion. It was 'the blessed company of all the faithful'. Let them follow it if they would. (Applause.) He did not come there as a foe to Theosophy, but as a friend. He came there to find some common meeting ground, to find in what way they were agreed, and he was met with that resolution. How could he turn his back to everything he held dear to him, to which he had put his name, or have remained a true Christian minister if he had not opposed that resolution with all his might and strength? He could only repeat the appeal he had made before, that people should study something about the history and ancient meaning of Christianity before they flew elsewhere for food for their souls. (Applause.)

Mr. Dunlop, on rising to answer the opposition in the debate, said that first of all he wanted most heartily to apologize for any implied insult that might be found in the resolution. He had become so used, when seeing 'Theosophy', to reading it as 'Divine Wisdom', and he intended his resolution to mean that Christianity could only be interpreted in the light of divine wisdom. Theosophy was not antagonistic to any system of religion, and he was certainly not putting up Theosophy against Christianity. Theosophy embraced the truths found in the religions before Christ as well as the truths of Christianity, and they could not blot out all the ages before Christ. Referring to the debate, he pointed out that there were a good many things in existence before Christianity. Surely they were not going to leave all those things out of consideration. He disliked debates because Theosophy was always put in antagonism to something. It was not antagonistic. He had found all he desired in Christianity, but he found Theosophy of value in interpreting that Christianity. Mr. Dunlop showed that the philosophers, down from Confucius, had all known the golden rule, in one form or another, 'Do one to another as ye would have others do unto you.' In that debate he had not been able to give them Theosophy as he should have liked to, and Mr. Hanks had not been able to give them Christianity properly. Speaking about the Christian Church, he said that it had always persecuted reformers. (The Rev. W.P. Hanks: 'Jesus included.') The churches, abbeys and cathedrals were shut up most of the time; they ought to be wide open. Christ, he said, was a god incarnate, he was a great teacher. He repudiated the statement that Madame Blavatsky was a fraud; the man who was supposed to expose her was afterwards a psychist himself, and remained so till his death. Mr. Dunlop said the Psychical Research Society had gone a long way since they condemned her. Mr. Hanks had referred to the Holy Spirit of the Church as being the interpreter of Christianity. He agreed with him there. The Holy Spirit was the authority for Theosophy. Mr. Hanks did not seem to have grasped the most elementary theory with regard to the matter of reincarnation. They were not to think that Theosophy was set up as a religion against Christianity.

In face of Mr. Dunlop's interpretation of his resolution, Mr. Hanks withdrew all he had said about the resolution.

Afterwards the resolution was read out in an altered form. It was about to be submitted with 'Divine Wisdom' substituted for 'Theosophy', when Mr. Hanks objected, pointing out that they could not vote on something that had not been discussed.

Mr. Dunlop suggested that they should not vote, to which Mr. Hanks agreed. No vote was taken.

The meeting concluded with a vote of thanks to the principal speakers, proposed by the Chairman.

Lift the Stone and Thou Shalt Find Me

In his letter to Charles Lazenby on 4 October 1908 D.N. Dunlop had mentioned the idea of a 'little monthly sheet on simple Theosophy for the masses, localized through branches, with the back page reserved for syllabus & announcements of each', adding however that 'there is no need to hurry overmuch I feel'.

Since that time, especially with the demise of *The Theosophical Review*, the need for such a publication had increased, and during the following summer, in the Convention on 3 July 1909, Dunlop referred to a statement by H.P. Blavatsky 'in a letter to Mr. Judge, that the work of the T.S. in the twentieth century would be to make Theosophy known to the masses of the people'.

There may well have been a connection between Dunlop's performance three months later in the debate on 12 October organized by the Debating Society of the Bath Young Men's Christian Association and the appearance of just such a news-sheet in mid-December. For it took the form of a monthly supplement to the well-established weekly newspaper *The Christian Commonwealth*.

The title of the news-sheet was *Theosophy*. No newspaper library today has preserved a copy of the first issue, but the second, dated 12 January 1910, consisted of a single sheet of small-newspaper size identical to that of *The Christian Commonwealth*, fully printed on both sides.

In the top left-hand corner was a notice giving details:

> *Theosophy*. A monthly supplement to *The Christian Commonwealth*. Edited by D.N. Dunlop, Ashdale, Warwick Drive, Hale, Cheshire, who will be responsible for unsigned articles, and to whom all communications are to be addressed. The next supplement will appear in February.
>
> Contributions should not exceed 750 words in length.

This last instruction was scarcely being followed, since of the three articles on the front page, the principal one, on 'The Objects of the Theosophical Society', was about twice that length. The other two articles were by Robert Gardner, who had been present at the Summer School five months previously, and Clifford Bax, who had intended to be present.

On the reverse side were three shorter items, including a 'Bibliography', signed with the initials E.W., which listed and commented on elementary theosophical works and gave information about where to obtain them. Two whole columns provided details of the Theosophical Society, and especially of public lectures on a variety of theosophical subjects being given by different speakers during the following month at named addresses in central London, west London, Bath, Brighton, Glasgow, Hale, Harrogate, Liverpool, Manchester and Southampton. This was followed by a 'Directory of Meetings' spelling out for interested or even just curious readers the addresses and regular meeting-times of theosophical groups in Birmingham, Blackpool, Bolton, Bournemouth, Bradford, Cardiff, Cheltenham, Clifton, Derby, Dover, Edinburgh, Folkestone, Forfar, Golborne, Greenock, Leeds, Letchworth, London, Merthyr, Middlesborough, Norwich, Nottingham, Oxford, Plymouth, Portsmouth, Sheffield, Stoke-on-Trent, Sunderland, Surbiton, Tyneside, Wakefield and York. A further statement added: 'Secretaries are requested to inform the Editor of all changes in address, etc.'

★

The third issue was published on 16 February. It was twice the size of the previous one, a full double-sheet, and this size was maintained in subsequent issues. At the top of the front page, so-to-speak instead of a headline, was the motto 'Not to repel or destroy so much as to accept, fuse, rehabilitate'.

Articles included the second instalment—presumably the first one had appeared in the issue of December 1909—of a series entitled 'Elementary Theosophy' which reproduced an anonymous series on 'Theosophy in Plain Language' running in *The Irish Theosophist* from December 1892 to March 1894, as well as an article by AE also from that journal. There were articles by Lazenby and other named or initialled writers on 'The Lodge', 'Meditation', 'Karma', 'The Brotherhood of Religions', 'The Perfect Way', 'The Mystic, Mythical and Historical Christ', a poem by Walt Whitman, and an updated list of public lectures. E.W. gave a second instalment of his or her bibliography, mentioning various works by H.P. Blavatsky, Mabel Collins, G.R.S. Mead, Annie Besant,

> . . . and for those who prefer the line of more purely Western and Christian occultism, there are two excellent treatises by Dr. Rudolf Steiner of Berlin, which have been recently translated into English. These are *The Way of Initiation* and *Initiation and its Results*. The price of each is 3s. 6d. net.
>
> As before, it is only necessary to add that all these works can be obtained from any bookseller or direct from the publishers—The Theosophical Publishing Society, at 161, New Bond Street, London, W.—who will send catalogues on application. A lending library is also to be found at the same address.

★

The March number of *The Vâhan* included the following three items:

> It is proposed to hold the second Summer School following the Convention in July. Arrangements, to be satisfactory, have to be made well in advance. I shall therefore be glad to hear from members and friends who intend being present so that a place may be found which will afford adequate accomodation. The first school was a great success, and the second promises to be better. An excellent programme is now in course of preparation. Suggestions as to place of meeting will be thankfully received; also suggestions for increasing the attractiveness of the School in any direction.
>
> D.N. Dunlop
>
> Ashdale, Warwick Drive, Hale, Cheshire

———

The Hale Lodge has been an active theosophical centre during the past three months. Theosophical friends from Paris, London and Toronto have foregathered with us, and their presence at the study class every Saturday evening added greatly to the interest of the discussions. Mr. Lazenby, late of Toronto University, has been with us all the winter, and we have been greatly stimulated by his activity. His conduct of the *Secret Doctrine* class has been quite masterly, and his series of public lectures in St. Baldred's Hall, Ashley Road, are being well attended and create interest in matters theosophical among a wider circle of people. Altogether the Hale Lodge has had a gladsome time.

D.N.D.

I have been asked to say a few explanatory words about the theosophical supplement to the *Christian Commonwealth* for the benefit of readers of the *Vâhan*.

1. The cost is met by the generosity of a few theosophists. Would any others care to share in the expense? It is intended to keep the supplement going for twelve months. It is published about the middle of each month.
2. Copies are printed separately from the *Christian Commonwealth* for the benefit of lodges who want copies for propaganda purposes.

★

The fourth issue of *Theosophy* came out on 16 March. The motto at the top was 'Train yourselves for service by doing your duty where you are at the moment'. Both the series on 'Elementary Theosophy' and 'The Lodge' were continued—also into further numbers—and there were articles on 'Freedom', 'The Tree in Myth and in Tradition', 'Prayer', 'Reincarnation' and 'Kshanti'. The list of public lectures was updated, and the directory of lodges reissued with additional details concerning Bath, Burton, Glasgow, Leicester, Maidenhead, Manchester, Nelson, Plymouth and Wimborne.

The fifth issue appeared on 13 April. Its motto was 'Lift the stone and thou shalt find Me; Cleave the wood and there am I'.[16] There were articles on 'Concentration', 'The Three Paths', 'My Contact with Theosophy', 'The Unity of Religions', 'Brotherhood', a further poem by Whitman, and an updated lecture-list and directory of lodges.

The sixth and final issue was published on 11 May. It repeated the same motto from the previous issue: 'Lift the stone and thou shalt find Me; Cleave the wood and there am I'. Possibly the repetition indicated that after experimenting with other mottoes the editor intended to retain this one as a regular headline. There were articles on 'Why our Past Lives are Forgotten', 'How a Soul Grows', 'The Masters' Methods' and 'Practical

Brotherhood'. The directory of lodges was again reproduced, but instead of the former lecture-list there was an item on 'Second Theosophical Summer School':

> The experiment made last year by several members of the Theosophical Society to run a Summer School met with such a hearty response and proved so successful that it has been decided to repeat it this summer, extending the period during which the school shall be open from a week to a fortnight. Weybourne Springs Hotel, the scene of last year's activities, is again available, and many are in favour of a return to the same spot, it being eminently adapted for the purpose. Arrangements to this effect are therefore now in hand, and the Second Theosophical Summer School will be open from the evening of Monday, July 4, to the morning of the 18th.
>
> Weybourne Springs Hotel is charmingly situated in a retired position about a mile from the village of Weybourne and two from Sheringham, in Norfolk. From the front of the building there is a fine panoramic view over the village to the sea, above which it is elevated some 200 ft., while pine-woods and heather-clad hills form a delightful background. The well-known Kelling Heath and Boadicea's Camp are within a short walk, and the whole district is full of historic interest. There is accommodation for about seventy in the hotel itself, but there is every probability of the party being larger than this, many already having applied for particulars. Every effort will be made to find beds in the village or at Sheringham for any overflow after the rooms at the hotel have been allotted. It has also been suggested that some may like to camp out, and inquiries as to the possibility of pitching tents in the hotel grounds are being made. Mr. Hugh Mapleton has undertaken the catering, which will be entirely vegetarian; and it is hoped that members of the school camping or sleeping out will be enabled to take their meals at headquarters with the rest of the party.
>
> An interesting and varied programme of lectures, dealing with Theosophy, the theosophical life, and literature of a theosophical order is being prepared, and musical and dramatic friends will contribute to the enjoyment of the meetings. Discussion and questions are invited at all times. A committee will be formed to organize excusions to places of interest in the vicinity.
>
> The inclusive charge per week for those sharing rooms will be 35s. per head, and will cover all incidental expenses, such as printing, stationery, conveyance of luggage, tips to servants, etc. There will be a 5s. premium on single rooms, which are limited in number.
>
> All interested in Theosophy, whether members of the Society or not, will be cordially welcomed.
>
> Applications for copies of the prospectus and preliminary syllabus of discussions should be addressed to the Summer School Secretary, Miss W.A. Parley, Temples Croft, Upton, near Aylesbury, Bucks. Any suggestions

which may add to the interest and success of the Second Theosophical Summer School will be gratefully accepted by the organizer, D.N. Dunlop, Ashdale, Warwick Drive, Hale, Cheshire.

Harry Collison

In January 1910 *The Vâhan* stated:

> Readers will be interested to know that at the request of theosophists in Sweden Dr. Rudolf Steiner will be giving a course of lectures in Stockholm from January 2–16. The subject will be 'The Gospel of St. John in relation to the other three Gospels'. The fact that this subject was specially requested by the Swedes themselves is but one of many proofs of the deep and lasting interest aroused by the courses of lectures already given by Dr. Steiner on the occult significance of the Bible. During last summer, courses were held on the Gospels of Mark and Luke, three courses having been previously given on the Gospel of St. John and two on the Book of Revelations. In Munich the subject was 'the Children of Lucifer and the Brothers of Christ; from Buddha to Christ; or the Orient in the Light of the Occident'.
>
> It may be useful to some of the widely scattered readers of *The Vâhan* in Europe to know that from February 19–28 inclusive, Dr. Steiner will give lectures in Cologne and the neighbouring towns of Elberfeld, Bonn, Düsseldorf, and Coblenz. In March a course of lectures will be given in Vienna, and in May one in Hamburg. A course will be given in Christiania during the summer.

Even these indications did not represent the whole of Steiner's lecturing programme. The March lecture-course in Vienna only formed part of a lengthy tour taking him and Marie von Sivers as far afield as Sicily. On his way south through Italy he was lecturing in Rome, and here took place a first meeting between him and an Englishman named Harry Collison.

The part played by Collison in the subsequent story of this book is of such importance as to justify a description of his life, which for long was poorly recorded. Towards the end of the twentieth century Rex Raab tried to rectify the situation by giving an account in the course of his Maryon biography, but although he began by stating that misjudgements of Collison have to be corrected, it must be said that his own account was neither adequate nor itself free from errors. In the compilation *Anthroposophie im 20. Jahrhundert* (2003), Philip Martyn has provided a more satisfactory picture, if also not flawless.

The present account is reconstructed from a variety of sources, of which the two principal ones were published in the *Anthroposophic News Sheet*, firstly the tribute by Marie Steiner on the occasion of Collison's seventieth birthday in 1938, and secondly the article by Elsie Armour 'In Memory of Harry Collison' from 1946. These have been supplemented by further information partly provided by Collison himself, notably in his posthumously published *Commentary on Rudolf Steiner's Four Mystery Plays* (1949), and partly also gathered by the present writer in other appropriate places.

★

Harry Collison was born on 5 March 1868 into a well-to-do evangelical family originating from Norfolk, but at the time living in Wimbledon. His father already had a German connection, having been educated by Moravian Brethren at Neuwied, on the Rhine near Coblenz. His mother's family was Catholic and ultimately of Irish ancestry, but she converted to Protestantism on her marriage to Henry Clerke Collison, which took place in 1863 at St Martin-in-the-Fields in London. Two children were born to them, a daughter and a son, who was named Harry after his father. It must be added that the son's connection to his parents, especially his mother, was to remain exceptionally strong. Steiner is said to have commented on this and explained the significance of it, though his explanation has not been recorded.

In 1872, when the boy was aged only four, the family sailed away to South Africa. For several years they lived in Cape Town. (They were indeed the family of 'Collison's South African Gin'!)

During this time at the Cape his mother would often tell her son stories from Greek myths or Nordic legends. Fed on these tales, little Harry would go out alone on explorations, riding over the slopes of Table Mountain among the ferns, the arum lilies, the apricot and silver trees—and also among the gnomes and other nature spirits, whose language he seemed to understand.

After some years in South Africa, the family returned to England. Back on native soil, the father formed the intention of sending his son to Winchester College, but an illness to which the boy succumbed prevented this plan from being realized.[17] Throughout his whole life he was often to fall ill; in this connection Steiner is again said to have remarked that Collison's sensitive and delicate constitution was a necessary condition for the fulfilment of his special mission.

So instead of proceeding to Winchester College the 15-year-old youth was admitted in May 1883 to West Deyne, a boarding house at Uppingham School in Rutland, then being formed by its famous headmaster Edward Thring into one of the foremost public schools in the country.

Harry's time at Uppingham, however, did not go well, for though admiring Thring he disliked the compulsory sport, and became indeed so unhappy that in April 1885, when he had spent only two years at the school, his father withdrew him.

To prepare for an intended diplomatic career, the 17-year-old was sent to continue his education in Paris, where he stayed for a whole year. He seems to have spent much of this year in attending theatrical performances, for with regard to his interest in drama he later recalled that 'my experiences in Paris at the time of the greatest achievements of the Théâtre Français implanted in me a sense of impartial criticism and a certain artistic standard'.

Harry then proceeded to the University of Bonn (not so far down the Rhine from his father's old school at Neuwied). Here he studied languages and acquired a good command of German, though for the next 24 years he was to have no further occasion to use this language. He then spent some time in Berlin—presumably in early 1887, still several years before Steiner first arrived in that town—and also visited Dresden, where he received a very powerful impression from the sight of a painting by Raphael: the famous *Sistine Madonna*.

On his return to England, the 19-year-old matriculated in Michaelmas Term 1887 at Merton College, Oxford, where he proceeded to study classics and history. He joined the Myrmidons, a dining club in the college.

And it was here in Oxford, at the age of 21, that Harry first joined a Masonic lodge.[18] This was the Apollo University Lodge No. 357—founded in 1818 and reputed to be the premier university lodge in the world. He was initiated into it on 28 May 1889 at the Masonic Hall which then stood in Frewen Court, off the Cornmarket. He passed on 6 November, and was raised on 25 February 1890.

He remained a faithful member for the rest of his life.

On the Search

While still an undergraduate at the University of Oxford, Harry Collison in 1890 obtained by patrimony the freedom of two medieval London guilds, the Grocers Company and the Leathersellers Company. In 1891, when he gained his degree and was already elected to the Livery of the Leathersellers' Company, he was admitted to one of the inns of court in London, the Inner Temple, to train as a barrister.

In 1892 he joined another Masonic body, the Earl of Sussex Lodge No. 2201 in Brighton, recently founded in the famous Royal Pavilion (built earlier that century in Oriental style for the then Prince of Wales, later George IV). This did not however imply any lessening of his university connections, for at Oxford in 1893 he was exalted to Apollo University Chapter, of which he also remained a member for the rest of his days. On 6 April 1894 he went on to join in London the distinguished Westminster and Keystone Lodge No. 10. This lodge, founded in 1722, had in the late nineteenth century come to acquire a strong Oxonian connection. Collison gave as address his father's house: Newlands, Weybridge, Surrey. Considering that as an undergraduate at Merton College he had joined the Myrmidons, one may even wonder whether in July 1894 he may have taken part at Richmond in the summer banquet held by the Westminster and Keystone Lodge. Be that as it may, towards the end of the year he obtained professional qualifications by being called to the Bar at the Inner Temple. Later he was to state: 'I shall never forget the legal training in sifting evidence and gaining a sense of proportion.'

In November 1895 Collison was installed as Junior Warden of the Earl of Sussex Lodge, and a year later, in November 1896, advanced to Senior Warden. Perhaps his Masonic commitments were becoming too numerous, for on 3 December he resigned from the Westminster and Keystone Lodge. However, in the following year, 1897, at the age of 30, he was appointed Worshipful Master of the Earl of Sussex Lodge.

It must have been around this time that he was commissioned in the 3rd Oxford Light Infantry, and soon promoted to Lieutenant, for in 1899 he took part in the British campaign in the Sudan. But when in March 1900 he joined another Masonic body, the Oxford and Cambridge University Chapter No. 1118, in London, he gave his profession as barrister. He had chambers at 2 Dr. Johnson's Building, and later at 1 Temple Gardens, both in the Inner Temple, and practised on the Northern English Circuit. According to Elsie Armour 'his work in the law courts gave him an insight into the shadow side of life, which deepened his understanding and widened his sympathies'.

By now, however, Collison's secure family background was collapsing around him. Not only had his sister died some years before, but in 1901 his father died as well. Soon afterwards his own home was destroyed by fire, and he himself suffered a lapse of health. In October of that year, probably as a result, he resigned from the Earl of Sussex Lodge, and in 1902 also resigned from the Oxford and Cambridge University Chapter.

Somewhere around this time, under the inspiration of Edouard Schuré's book *Les Grands Initiés*, he undertook a prolonged journey around the world, visiting the scenes of ancient civilizations. He set off in an easterly direction, stayed in both Greece and Turkey, and then journeyed southwards to Egypt. In remarks on the eighth scene of *Der Seelen Erwachen* in his later published *Commentary on Rudolf Steiner's Four Mystery Plays* are found references to the Sphinx near the Great Pyramid, and to the tombs at El Amarna.

Greece and Egypt are lands associated with the figures of Orpheus, Plato, Pythagoras, Hermes, Moses, to each of whom were devoted specific chapters of *Les Grands Initiés*. Another chapter was concerned with Krishna, with a footnote elaborating on the greatness of Buddha. And proceeding further in an easterly direction, Collison travelled across to India.

Having immersed himself in ancient civilizations of both Europe and Asia, he continued eastward, right over the Pacific to America, always on the search for something unknown which he seemed unable anywhere to find.

Despite interesting sights in the countries he had visited, the negative result of Collison's journey in regard to his present existence was strikingly shown when after travelling across America, taking ship over the Atlantic and finally regaining England, he simply tried to pick up once again the threads of his legal occupation. But this did not prove successful, and he suffered a further collapse of health.

In order to restore his well-being he then put his legal career somewhat into abeyance, and took up painting instead. He prepared himself thoroughly for this new pursuit by studying in London—under Frank Brangwyn—in Paris and especially in Rome, to which he and his mother would travel regularly every year. They stayed in No. 14 Via Quattro Fontane, and in that vicinity came into contact with entirely new circles of people.

In England meanwhile, Collison's spiritual loyalty to Freemasonry was again renewed. In June 1908 he entered another Chapter of the elite Royal Arch: the Westminster and Keystone Chapter No. 10, in London. Once more he began a swift rise up the echelons of the Masonic hierarchy: only a few months later he was installed as 3rd Principal, a post known in the craft by the initial J. ('Joseph'). In the following year he advanced to 2nd Principal, known as H. ('Haggai'). And as a freeman of long standing he was also elected to the Livery of the Grocers' Company.

His new career as a landscape- and especially portrait-painter became moderately successful. From 1909 onwards over the next 27 years he had one painting exhibited at the International Society, two in the New English Art Club, three in the Walker Art Gallery in Liverpool, another three in the London Salon, six in the Royal Academy, and no less than 91 in Walker's Gallery, London. This was an average of about four paintings on exhibition every year.

The Roman Lectures of 1910

Now in this same year, 1909, when Harry Collison's activity as a painter was just starting to flourish, his mother died. Owing to the strong connection between them he experienced this event as a shattering blow—'the saddest moment in my life'.

Soon after his mother's death, on one of his still-continuing visits to Rome, he came across a copy of Rudolf Steiner's *The Way of Initiation* (whether in the original German or in English translation is not known). He read the book three times, and after the third reading began to have a feeling of beholding his own self in every person whom he met on the street!

In the spring of 1910 Steiner himself then arrived in Rome on his lecturing tour. From 11 to 13 April he was giving three semi-public lectures—to members and guests—in the seventeenth-century Palazzo del Drago, which is situated at the very crossroads of the Quattro Fontane. In his book *Rudolf Steiners Erdenleben* (1951) Guenther Wachsmuth stated that these lectures were attended by 'a large circle of Italian and foreign guests'. Among the latter was Harry Collison.

Even in the original German these Roman lectures of 1910 were not published until 1965, 20 years after Collison's death, when they appeared in a volume of the Gesamtausgabe entitled *Das Ereignis der Christus-Erscheinung in der Ätherischen Welt* (GA 118), the third of them being related to the main theme of that volume. Since however the surviving transcript, which does not derive from a professional stenographer, is fragmentary by comparison with those of other lectures in the book, the Roman lectures were relegated to a kind of 'appendix' at the back.

Incomplete as it may be, the transcript is nonetheless moderately extensive, and the resultant text presents the characteristic thematic complexity of most of Steiner's courses. And anyone reading these Roman lectures today with the person of Harry Collison in mind can hardly fail to observe certain small but arresting points of contact with specific countries, or specific events, relevant to his biography.

The first lecture, 'The Being of Man', discusses different forms of initiation, firstly modern and then ancient, for most of the lecture in a quite general kind of way. Towards the end of the lecture, however, and almost as an afterthought, Steiner brings forward a particular example of ancient initiation by making a reference to Egyptian Mysteries.

The second lecture, 'Higher Worlds and their Connection with Our Own', treats the given theme from various angles. Here is a passage:

> We then have to grasp the meaning of death with the whole strength of our feelings. With what different feelings will we then approach the deathbed of a person we love! This does not imply that we should suppress grief over a separation, for a soul which felt suffering no more would wither away. But we ought to regard life from a higher standpoint on which spiritual science puts us and say to ourselves: 'Seen from below, death appears painful and dreadful, but seen from above it presents itself quite differently to our spiritual gaze.'

In the further course of the lecture, Steiner goes on to examine the vision of a Rosicrucian pupil, comparing it with that of a 'botanist, lyricist or painter'. He also refers to his own book *Wie erlangt man Erkenntnisse der höheren Welten?*

The third lecture, 'The Christ Impulse and its Great Proclaimers', was given in Italy on the very same day, 13 April, when in Britain there came out the fifth issue of *Theosophy*, introducing the motto 'Lift the stone and thou shalt find Me; Cleave the wood and there am I'.

This lecture begins by explaining the nature of the Bodhisattvas, and discussing in particular the figure of Gautama Buddha as a forerunner of the Christ.

> Only during his incarnation as the Indian Prince Siddharta did he rise to the level of a Buddha. His mission was to prepare the teaching of compassion and love. It might be objected that Christ did this. But Christ did not only teach it; he poured love and compassion themselves into the heart of mankind.
>
> Between the teaching of Buddha and the power of Christ there is a difference like that between an art connoisseur before a painting by Raphael and Raphael himself...

Reference is subsequently made to the Vedas of ancient India. Buddhistic teaching is carefully explained, and put into proper context from a Christian perspective.

> ...This development in the spirit, as taught by Christianity, contains infinite comfort, and makes separation from those we love less painful. For we know that separation is only necessitated by physical barriers, and we can find a way to our loved ones in the spirit.

The 42-year-old Harry Collison, doubtless absorbed by the main content of these lectures, must also have felt personally addressed by such allusions and observations. He realized that he had discovered here what he had been searching for all his life.

Robert Felkin

Now that Harry Collison has entered the present story, it is time also to introduce a completely different person, who in contrast to Collison will play a role of only tangential and even questionable character, but nonetheless one which cannot be entirely overlooked, namely, Robert Felkin.

Felkin's life may be reconstructed partly from an obituary published for the Royal Geographical Society in the 1927 number of the *Geographical Journal*, and partly from accounts of 'The Havelock Work' appearing in *Te Mata Times* on 9 September 1983 and in the compilation *Havelock North*. Passages from these various sources are here combined.

★

Robert William Felkin was born in March 1853 at Beeston, Nottinghamshire. His father was a Baptist, but his mother a Congregationalist, so when a son was born to them they compromised by having him brought him up as an Anglican. He always went to chapel on Sundays, and his father—a lace manufacturer—often entertained the local ministers. The boy was educated at Wolverhampton Grammar School.

At this time a great topic of interest in the British press was provided by the disappearance and eventual rediscovery deep inside the 'Dark Continent' of the pioneering African explorer David Livingstone. It was Livingstone's subsequent death in 1873 which really opened the floodgates to the complex process of European exploration, conversion and colonization of Africa, and the young Felkin was among those caught up in this flood. At the age of 23 he decided to set out for Africa as a missionary. The Christian Missionary Service, however, considered him still too young, and sent him first to study medicine. Two years later, although not yet fully qualified, the young man was then accepted for work in Uganda.

> On the foundation of the C.M.S. Mission in Uganda as a result of Stanley's appeal, expeditions were sent both from the East Coast and by way of the Nile, Felkin, who went out as a medical missionary, being one of the party which took the latter route, starting in 1878 and reaching Mtesa's capital in February 1879. The journey had been delayed somewhat owing to the obstruction of the bed of the Upper Nile then existing. He was the first Englishman to set eyes on both the great lakes of the Upper Nile.

Both lakes were discovered by Englishmen, Lake Victoria in 1858 by John Hanning Speke, and Lake Albert in 1864 by Samuel Baker. The American explorer Charles Chaillé-Long was the first to cover the ground between the two lakes and thus factually confirm the long-standing supposition that the Nile flowed from one into the other. Henry Stanley in his

1874 expedition was unable to do so because of warring tribes in the vicinity, so in 1879 Felkin became the first Englishman to follow in Chaillé-Long's footsteps.

> After many adventures, and suffering great hardships, the party at length reached Uganda, where Felkin was soon commandeered by the local king as his personal physician. He became an expert on tropical diseases, being one of the first to recognize the link between the mosquito and malaria. He is said to have been the first white man to measure the pygmies of Central Africa.
>
> Unfortunately his own health suffered and he was obliged to return to England. The king, who had earlier, for no good reason, threatened to have him killed, in the end was loath to let him go, and only agreed on condition that he take with him three envoys whom he was commanded to present to Queen Victoria.

> Circumstances compelling his return after a stay of three months only, he again took the northern route, but the river being still blocked, he and his companion, the Rev. C.T. Wilson, made an important journey overland across the whole breadth of the Bahr-el-Ghazal region, then most imperfectly known, from south-east to north-west, striking the Upper Bahr-el-Arab, the main western feeder of the Bahr-el-Ghazal, on its upper course, and continuing north to Dara in Darfur (reached on 31 December 1879), and so to Egypt. Both travellers gave an account of their experiences at an evening meeting of the Geographical Society in April 1880. The journey across the Bahr-el-Ghazal was for the greater part over new ground, and a route-survey carried out by the travellers was worked up in Germany by Dr. Hassenstein and published in *Petermanns Mitteilungen* in 1881, with accompanying letterpress.

In Britain, the three Ugandan envoys whom Felkin had brought

> created a great sensation. We dressed them in blue dressing gowns, edged with red, and red fezzes. We had to present them to Queen Victoria, who received them in the throne room in Buckingham Palace.

> Felkin resumed his medical studies, first in Edinburgh and then in Germany, where he qualified as a Doctor of Medicine. He practised as a physician in both Edinburgh and London, and lectured extensively on tropical diseases, not only in Britain but also on the Continent.

In 1882 he married, and had one daughter, Nora Ethelwynn.

> Felkin was joint author with Wilson of an important work, *Uganda and the Egyptian Sudan*, which appeared in two volumes in 1882, and was one of the editors of the *Collection of Letters and Journals of Emin Pasha* (translated from

the German by Mrs. Felkin), which came out in 1888. He also contributed various papers on medical and ethnological subjects to scientific journals, and in 1895 published a small book on the *Geographical Distribution of Tropical Diseases in Africa.*

On a further African trip, the Felkin family settled for some time on the island of Zanzibar, off the east coast. They must also have travelled onto the mainland, for at some point Felkin attempted to establish a trading company in the Congo. When however the British Government withdrew its support, this venture was abandoned, and they returned again to Britain.

★

After his return, Felkin found a new interest supplementary to his medical profession. In the year 1894 he joined the Order of the Golden Dawn.

Only a brief account of the Order's history can be given here. It was founded in 1888 by William Westcott, Secretary of the Societas Rosicruciana in Anglia (the Rosicrucian Society of Freemasons), with the help of the aged William Woodman, Supreme Magus, and of Samuel 'Macgregor' Mathers. Gradually other members then also joined during the following period.

Woodman died in 1891, and a few years later Westcott, by profession a coroner, was obliged to resign from all offices in the Order by reason of Home Office disapproval. So by 1897 the Order was effectively left under sole control of 'Macgregor' Mathers. He soon also founded an inner group, the Rosae Rubeae et Aureae Crucis.

As time went on Mathers became ever more eccentric and autocratic. In 1901 a rebellion broke out against his rule, with the result that the Order split into three parts, of which only a small minority—the Alpha et Omega—remained faithful to him. The vast majority of members re-aligned into two new Orders. One part joined the Independent and Rectified Rite, led by the prolific occult writer A.E. Waite. Others—including W.B. Yeats—joined the Stella Matutina under the leadership of Robert Felkin. It may be added that despite this split, there still remained some intercommunication between the three separate parts.

Members of the Golden Dawn or its derivatives were required on admission to select a motto, preferably in Latin, which should 'express the candidate's highest occult aims or aspirations'. On Felkin's admission in 1894 he had chosen the motto 'Finem Respice'.

★

In 1903 when Felkin reached the age of 50, his first wife died. A few years later he married again. His second wife, Harriot, a graduate of Aberdeen University, was 20 years his junior and probably younger than his own daughter Nora.

Now during the opening years of the twentieth century Felkin was also travelling extensively on the Continent, with a particular hope of meeting genuine Rosicrucians. His efforts in this direction led him in 1906 to some Freemasons living near Hanover. Whether or not these Freemasons were also theosophists, it was in this same year that Felkin first tried to make contact with Rudolf Steiner.

In his book *The Magicians of the Golden Dawn* (1972), Ellic Howe took up the tale:

> Felkin was in Germany again in 1910, staying with a certain Dr. Marcus at Bad Pyrmont, a spa not far from Hanover, at the end of June when he received a postcard from Dr. Wilhelm Hübbe-Schleiden, who wrote from Göttingen and regretted his inability to meet Felkin at Hanover on Thursday 30 June.
>
> Since a meeting with Hübbe-Schleiden was impracticable, Felkin must have asked him for Dr. Rudolf Steiner's address, because Hübbe-Schleiden wrote to Felkin on 30 June and gave him detailed instructions for finding Steiner's residence in Berlin. He explained that Steiner could never be seen at short notice. 'Perhaps it might facilitate matters if you mention my name, for when he is in Berlin for a day or two there are always dozens of persons, mostly his disciples, who are waiting for hours at his door hoping to catch him for a short hearing.'
>
> It is evident that Felkin visited Steiner in Berlin or elsewhere in Germany in 1910 and was greatly impressed by him.

A Common Search for Truth

A certain Irving S. Cooper contributed to the August 1910 issue of *The Vâhan* an article on 'Some Weybourne Impressions':

> 'May the Summer School be granted many incarnations' is the terse wording of the oft-expressed wishes of nearly everyone who spent the fortnight at Weybourne Springs Hotel. Despite many little inconveniences and most ungracious weather, the gatherings of the 'faithful' in the assembly-room every morning and evening were marked by an exceptionally fine spirit of friendliness and tolerance. It was really remarkable how the eighty-odd members of the School lived together so harmoniously without feeling it their imperative duty to discover all the weaknesses in

their neighbours' characters, when many of them slept three or four in a room in the hotel, or walked nearly a mile to the village where they worried away the hours between midnight and dawn upon a village bed. The nationalities represented were significant: Russian, German, Dutch, Scottish, Irish, English, Danish, American, French and Belgian. And the temperaments! Artists were present gazing with seraphic vision upon the symbolic beauties of the world of form; scientists were there who thought in terms of molecules and ions; others quivered with quick sympathy when the fire of spiritual *abandon* flashed through the words of an inspired speaker; still others, astrologically inclined, became more and more convinced, as day after day rich with theosophic thought passed by, that the destinies of man bore witness to the silent influence of those mighty celestial bodies that wing their endless way across the sky. Some were philosophically inclined, others yearned for immediate action, for propaganda, for service; some loved the poets, while others loved palmistry, yet amid all this diversity unity arose in the fair form of a common search for truth tempered by willingness to listen thoughtfully to each other's ideas. The members did not all think alike. Frequently, diametrically opposed opinions were expressed, usually with the vigour of conviction, but always with gentleness and tolerance. At times, especially when the subject discussed dealt with things eternal, it seemed as if the various personalities were merged in one common life, that swept through the room and whispered in every heart.

It is not wise to hold such rich theosophical feasts for a period longer than two weeks; mental indigestion is apt to result. One needs time for reflection after a steady diet of the 'Fundamentals of the *Secret Doctrine*', 'Initiates', '*The Voice of the Silence*', 'The Rosicrucians', '*Isis Unveiled*', 'The Races of Men', 'The Upanishads' etc. It may be well to mention while touching on the subject of diet that even in the dining-room good-fellowship prevailed. What greater miracle could we ask than this? Even nut-mixtures—may karma deal lightly with the person who invented them—of unknown potencies, powers, proportions and probabilities were enthusiastically greeted and occasionally sampled upon their arrival.

It should not be supposed, however, that the members were always brooding over serious problems of this description. Many were the delightful walks across the moors, purpled with sweet-scented heather, and many the evening rambles down to the restless sea after the lecture and discussion of the evening were over. Those who loved thrills visited the ancient churchyard and listened to stories of vapoury ghosts. One can shudder so easily at the appropriate moment when mouldering tombs and crumbling arches are near at hand. If you do not believe this just ask the opinion of one young lady who visited the School and heard a well-ornamented tale one evening in the churchyard.

One day the School 'boiled over' and the neighbouring town of Cromer suffered. Amid much enthusiasm enough money was raised to give four public lectures in the town hall. So on a Saturday we invaded the place, sixty strong, and presented the truths of Theosophy through the media of four different personalities. The audience in the afternoon (including members) numbered about 145, while that in the evening did not exceed 110. Those present were urgently asked to hand in their names if they wished to join a study-class, and I am glad to say that one lady responded. A half-dozen lads from a local school were there an hour ahead of time in the evening to listen to the lecture on 'Some After-Death Conditions'. We were told afterwards that they came to see some ghosts, and were very much disappointed because none appeared.

It is safe to prophesy that the Summer School will be a permanent and needed feature in our theosophic development. In time it should become closely identified with the life of each national Society, and would then be attended by hundreds, where now only scores come. Our deepest students and most brilliant talent would deem it a duty to be present and give to the members some of the thoughts and treasures they have found during the preceding year. Dramas might be given, propaganda methods discussed, principles for handling classes elaborated, and in a thousand ways forces set going which would work out for the benefit of the Society. We need such a 'clearing-house for ideas' to stimulate the interest and ability of the members and to build up a closely knit organization. The present Summer School has been potent with suggestions for the future and we should make good use of them.

A New Fire

The new Scottish Section of the Theosophical Society began to produce its own journal, *Theosophy in Scotland*. One of the first issues also carried a report on 'The Summer School':

The Summer School which was instituted for the first time last year has once more been held at Weybourne in Norfolk. Mr. Dunlop, the moving spirit of the whole venture, again chartered the Weybourne Springs Hotel, which is situated in as delightfully retired a spot as could anywhere be found, and any person who enjoyed the immense privilege of forming one of the party will, I think, never forget the experience.

At first it was difficult fully to comprehend the reason that had led to the choice of the word 'School' to designate the institution; but it was not long before one discovered that 'School' and none other was the right word to employ. The delightfully refined unconventionality of all the proceedings, the power of the meetings, and the pervading spirit of good fellowship and brotherhood all combined to sandpaper over any unpleasant 'angularities' of individual members in an incredibly short space of time.

Those present formed a representative gathering. There were members from Russia, Holland, France, England, America and Scotland, and when we mention the names of Mrs. Despard, Mrs. Windust, Mr. Lazenby, Mr. Dunlop, Mr. Cooper (America), Mr. and Mrs. Bell, Mme. Pagosky, and state that most of these spoke at nearly every meeting, the power generated during the first week, when we were happy to be present, may in some small measure be realized.

The 'writings of H.P.B.' and 'Brotherhood' were the foundations and keynote of the lectures of the first week, and the way in which Mr. Lazenby and Mrs. Windust treated the subjects and warmed up to their work will not be forgotten for many a year.

We look forward to another Summer School next year, and hope for the time when such an institution will be a recognized factor in the yearly life of every National Society throughout the world, for a better means of arousing the practical realization of the liveableness of brotherhood could not be devised.

★

There was a further unsigned account in a supplement to the August issue of *The Path*, a new journal initiated in July, at the very time of the school, and edited by D.N. Dunlop and Charles Lazenby.The identity of the author is easy to guess.

The teachings of Theosophy are reiterated over and over again, and yet when a practical demonstration of the truths is presented, even old students are surprised.

We are accustomed so often to the saying of the Master of Judea—'Where two or three are gathered together in my name, there am I in the midst'—that we have lost all sense of its meaning, and yet it is the simplest statement regarding all Nirmanakayas. When any group of comrades meet together and put all carping criticism of each other out of their mind and unite in thought of mutual love and sympathy, they form by this very unity a body into which a great invisible being may enter, and connect Himself for the time with the group who have formed this body for His use. He is no 'spook' shadow of the astral plane, though even on that low level he may form a Mayava Rupa for the clairvoyants and psychics who require a special shape in order to sense his presence.

The spiritual body interpenetrates the whole assembly, and unconsciously every mind present enters into and is coloured by the glory of His presence within it.

'What is happening?' we ask in bewilderment. 'What is this wonderful upwelling within us? Why do the world and our comrades appear so beautiful? What is this far sweep of consciousness into worlds of which we never dreamed?'

It is all very simple. The Nirmanakaya is waiting and His love to us rushes forth to strengthen our love and sympathy for each other.

So it was at Weybourne Springs.

Many diverse elements, many strong idiosyncrasies, many firm conceptions of personal antipathy, but with all these there was in every heart the desire to learn truth, and devotion to the Masters of Wisdom and Compassion.

And so within two days the antipathies had melted, and love and comradeship shone forth. We became a united family, and our faces shone with the joy of human beings. Steadily ever brighter grew the flame, and although some of the most loving personalities left us at the end of the first week, the oil of their love continued and continues to feed the flame of the Weybourne fires.

Only those who were present can know the power and beauty of the Summer School, only those who entered into the body of the Great One can know the joy of His presence. But there were ninety-two of us there, and each one of us is a witness to the reality of the *exaltation*, each one of us has come forth with the reality of the inner worlds strong in our hearts.

And what are the lessons we carry with us from this school? The first and most important one is that where a group of comrades united in the common purpose of human service will put aside their personal antipathies and strive to help the best in each other to shine forth, they will be aided and strengthened and made joyful by a presence much higher and more beautiful than any one of the group could call up for himself.

The second lesson is the proof to our minds of that reality, of which until we have to some measure experienced it, we only talk as theory.

The third lesson is the strengthening of our faith in the greatness of H.P.B. as a messenger to man from the Masters of Wisdom, and a more clear comprehension of the wonderful intellectual world portrayed in her works.

The fourth lesson is that we should strive to turn the attention of our comrades as strongly as possible to the *Key to Theosophy*, *Isis Unveiled*, and the *Secret Doctrine*.

The fifth lesson is to insist that for those ignorant of the dangers of the lower psychic faculties, there is no book in civilization for the Psychical Research Society or Stead's Bureau or the abnormal psychologist to compare in worth and value with *The Voice of the Silence*. There are other lessons also, for each one present taught and learned from each other one.

Ninety-two earnest souls drawn more closely to H.P.B., and determined to find out, according to their capacity, the truth she came to give the world, this should mean something for the cause of truth and man's freedom.

Ninety-two men and women who will put power into their efforts to serve mankind, and who have learned the reality of their strength to create through love and sympathy for each other a body from the group for a Nirmanakaya to enter and teach them.

But they have learned also that the Nirmanakaya will not enter into a group where they are met to learn for themselves. Love to mankind and the desire to learn those lessons helpful to their fellows, this is the power which through the group creates the body to be used by the Great One.

The Weybourne Springs Summer School was wonderful, but its power has not ceased; it will go on down the centuries, for it unbound in each of us some trammels, and gave to each of us a new fire and clearer vision.

Drama in a Foreign Tongue

After listening in Rome to the three lectures given there by Rudolf Steiner in April, Harry Collison decided a few months later to travel up to Munich.

In Munich he had a first interview with Steiner. He asked to become his pupil, but added that he found it impossible to join the Theosophical Society, towards which he felt a certain aversion. Steiner made arrangements that Collison, though not a Society member, could nonetheless attend the theosophical events then taking place in Munich.

These events included a performance of Edouard Schuré's play *The Children of Lucifer*, as reported by Isabella Pagan in *Theosophy in Scotland*:

> Half-past nine in the morning is a somewhat unwonted hour to visit a theatre, but those who arrived later than that at the Munich Playhouse, taken by theosophists for the Munich performances on the 14th and 15th of August, had to content themselves with back seats. The best places were all reserved for those who failed to answer the question 'Sprechen Sie gut Deutsch?' in the affirmative, and we consequently found ourselves surrounded by a Babel of tongues—Scandinavian, Italian, Russian, French and English—and were not long in recognizing several familiar faces, and exchanging polyglot greetings like the rest. Presently we had an opportunity of introducing the Norwegian and English translators of Dr. Steiner's works to one another; and the latter pointed out to us, among various prominent theosophists, the commanding figure of M. Edouard Schuré, the Alsatian poet, whose drama *The Children of Lucifer* we were about to witness. Later on we were introduced to him and were interested to learn that this play, which has never yet been performed in the original French, had been the means of bringing him into touch with the Theosophical Movement, and also that its production in Germany was entirely due to the energy and enthusiasm of its translators. (Fräulein Sivers undertook the first literal

rendering in German, which was turned into sonorous and psychically appropriate language by Dr. Steiner—i.e. such language as called up the same colour forms before the listening clairvoyant as were aroused by M. Schuré's beautifully melodious French prose.) The action of the play takes place in Asia Minor, in the reign of Constantine, and the setting is elaborate and beautiful, so that those responsible for its fitting production had an onerous task. The dresses were designed and made by theosophists, the scenery was painted by theosophists, the music was composed and rendered by theosophists. 'Hard work for you all,' we said to the secretaries sympathetically. 'No, no, not hard,' was the bright reply. 'It was beautiful work, happy work; but of course there was a good deal of it.' We subsequently heard that for weeks on end the speaker and many of her assistants had been on short allowance as regards sleep, and sometimes could scarcely even find time to eat. The actors and actresses—some of them professionals—were all gladly giving their services, members of the Society too; and although naturally there were technical imperfections—certainly the less experienced players failing to find the correct pitch of voice for the delivery of lines in so large a building—there was so much vitality in the rendering, and such sympathy and understanding on the part of the audience, that the fatigue of listening to a drama in a foreign tongue—with only one brief adjournment for light refreshments—was marvellously lessened.

On the following day, 15 August, came the premiere performance of Steiner's first Mystery Play, *Die Pforte der Einweihung*.

When reviewing in the Michaelmas 1926 number of *Anthroposophy* a second edition of the English translation of the Mystery Plays, Collison included what are obviously his own reminiscences, though he fictionalized himself into the third person:

> I may mention how the performance influenced the life of a friend of mine, a man of middle age, a sceptic, who found himself in Munich during the performance. He had had great trouble, his life had become disillusioned, he was tired of people and of things. Shy and reserved, he avoided crowds; but it was a hot August when he found himself in the early morning standing in a queue waiting to hear a play in a language which he had in great measure forgotten. He had a ticket by favour, for the audience was restricted to members of the then Theosophical Society. He had a great personal dislike to theosophists and all such 'cranks'. Still he went, he was jostled by the crowd, had to fight for a seat. He managed to get one, and there he sat with the exception of a short interval for a hasty meal of an apple and a bit of bread. He sat there from 10 a.m. to 6 p.m., when the play finished. He was not exhausted, his interest had been maintained throughout, he felt refreshed and wanted to see and hear more. What was the power? The play could not be called dramatic. The actors were amateurs. There was nothing

> during these eight hours to appeal to the reason or the senses. And yet the man became a changed being. Undoubtedly a spiritual force had filled him, turning him to life with a broader outlook; his lassitude and weariness he felt transformed to vigour and cheerful hope, and he has ever since been a stronger and happier man—happier in the knowledge that he can bring happiness to others, interested in all men and all things, no longer living in an isolated attention to his own grievances. It is certainly one of the instances when a direct vision or a spiritual picture or great work of art has had its effect, more than an appeal to reason or sentimental mood.

The reference to 'direct vision' will remind those who know this play of Theodora's speech in the first scene, which gave dramatic expression to what Collison had heard in Steiner's third lecture in Rome some months previously. And from his account one can also hardly help wondering whether Collison, as a painter, may have seen both professional and personal features of himself in the character of Johannes Thomasius.

Similar Aims and Ideals

Harry Collison stayed on at Munich for the lecture-cycle on 'Secrets of the Biblical Story of Creation', which in the next issue of *Theosophy in Scotland* received a further report from Isabella Pagan:

> To attend a theosophical Congress anywhere on the Continent—and even sometimes in London itself, is apt to make one long exceedingly for the apostolic gift of tongues. Our great wealth of literature, together with our geographical position, tends to make us feel that our mother tongue is sufficient, for even those who travel a good deal are apt only to supplement the smattering of French and German acquired at school, by a set of tourists' phrases, chiefly concerned with immediate needs of the physical body—sleep and rest and food; and too many of us would find ourselves sadly at a loss at these gatherings abroad, but for the fact that our continental brethren give a different place to the study of languages, and are consequently able to speak their warm fraternal greeting, and play the gracious host or hostess, without feeling handicapped by the necessity for the use of an alien speech; which is a matter worth our serious consideration, for until we can do likewise, we can hardly hope to have our British Conventions attended to any great extent by the ever-welcome foreign guest. And yet it is astonishing how the consciousness of similar aims and ideals helps to bridge the gulf, and how much of the thought and feeling of a meeting can be gathered by means of some sort of telegraphic or psychic communication! Had we realized how far a very imperfect knowledge of German could be made to carry us towards a sympathetic understanding of the lectures and dramas

given at the Munich Conference, we should have arranged the date of our visit there so as to include the whole course. As it is we are more than thankful to those members who so warmly exhorted us to go for at least part of the time, and cordially recommend our fellow-members in this part of the world to go and do likewise as speedily as possible, choosing by preference the country where the speech is most familiar, and also giving extra time to the reading of theosophical books by the lecturer in his own language, so that his pet idioms and characteristic turns of phrase may not be altogether new. This is especially desirable in the case of Dr. Rudolf Steiner, who declines to borrow any ready-made words and phrases—Sanscrit, Latin or Greek—and speaks out his message in absolutely pure German; a practice strongly to be commended, as it certainly makes the teaching a living reality at once even to those utterly unfamiliar with Eastern ideas. The unwary foreigner, however, who is accustomed to the use of a large number of technical terms, and expects to hear them Germanized, finds himself face to face with the unknown, in the shape of interminable compounds such as *nacheinanderfolgende*, which as far as we can remember was part of the Teutonic substitute for 'reincarnation'! Even the familiar word 'Theosophy' was avoided, and we had, instead, the rendering *Geisteswissenschaft*. In addition to many German cities, London, Amsterdam, Brussels, Christiania, Copenhagen, and Budapest have all been visited by Dr. Steiner, and wherever he gives an important course of lectures, scores of members flock from all countries to hear him. He is not only the most prominent among our German theosophists, but is distinguished in literary and scientific circles as well, and the publication of his more recent books on initiation and spiritual evolution have attracted a great many truth-seekers to his lectures; membership is going up by leaps and bounds, and his recent courses have generally been attended by five or six hundred members—many of whom have only recently heard of the Movement—and at this most recent conference the numbers rose to over 700. The rapid growth of lodges and the consequent multiplication of activities has been tremendous, but willing hands were always to be found, and the organizing work was carried out with an enthusiasm and energy delightful to witness. The subject chosen by Dr. Steiner for this course of ten lectures was the first chapter of Genesis, and the preface to the opening lecture was a silent one—the projection on a screen of photographic reproductions of Michelangelo's Great Days of Creation from the Sistine Chapel in Rome. Then followed a magnificent analysis of the Hebrew text—syllable by syllable—and a comparison of that wonderful presentment with the stanzas in the *Secret Doctrine* . . .

There is not in fact any mention in these lectures of *The Secret Doctrine*. Perhaps the misstatement simply reflected the authoress's lack of understanding of the German language!

... The breathless interest of those present, and the eager discussion—in many tongues—in which various groups of students engaged after the meeting was over, testified both to the excellence of the teacher and the enthusiasm of the students.

The cycle ended on 26 August.

At seven o'clock in the evening of the following day, the 27th, Collison had a second interview with Steiner. During this interview, Steiner asked him whether his aversion towards the Theosophical Society extended also to the German Section, and when Collison assured him it did not, had him admitted to that Section.

The Magic of the Spoken Word

In August, *The Vâhan* stated:

We have to announce a series of lectures on the Gospel of Saint Matthew, to be given by Dr. Rudolf Steiner under the auspices of the John Lodge, Berne, of the Theosophical Society in Germany, during the first fortnight in September. The ticket for the course is 10 Mks. (10s.), and application should be made to the Secretary, Die Loge Johannes, Theosophische Gesellschaft, Junkerngasse 57, Berne.

★

The September issue included a notice on another subject:

To answer a number of enquiries from T.S. lodges will you please announce that:

1. *The Path* was started in response to a demand, fairly general, from readers of the *Christian Commonwealth* supplement, notice to discontinue the latter having been received from the editorial board of the *C.C.*, owing probably to a change in policy.
2. It consists of twenty pages and cover, and is published monthly at the modest price of 2d., or 2s.6d. per annum post free in the United Kingdom.
3. A monthly calendar of special interest to theosophists and mystics generally is published as a supplement without extra charge.
4. T.S. lodges can be supplied with fifty copies at 4s. each for sale at meetings or for free distribution. At this price no copies unsold can be returned. Less than fifty copies may be obtained on sale or return at 25% off published price. The back page of cover can be used for local announcements of lectures, etc., at the bare cost of printing.
5. *The Path* contains elementary articles on Theosophy in addition to special articles for students, and a 'Corner' for children.

6. May I express the hope that T.S. members will support *The Path* whole-heartedly.

D.N. Dunlop

★

In his letter to Charles Lazenby of 4 October 1908, Dunlop had stated that he would '. . . see what can be done with our Bibelot scheme. There is no need to hurry overmuch I feel . . .'

It was indeed almost two years later when an announcement in the September 1910 number of *The Path* stated:

> The first number of the Theosophical Bibelot will be published at the beginning of October. Price 1/- per copy. Orders now being booked. Be one of the discerning.

The first number of this series was the *Letters to a Lodge* by Jasper Niemand—pseudonym of Julia Keightley—which had appeared in 1894–5 in successive instalments published in *The Irish Theosophist.*

The second number, brought out in 1911, was *The Lodge* by Ordion, which had also appeared in instalments in *Theosophy* and *The Path.* Ordion was a pseudonym of Charles Lazenby, used sparingly and only for those of his writings he believed were inspired from his highest spiritual consciousness.

The Bibelot booklet series does not appear to have run any further than these two numbers. 'The Orpheus Series' also brought out a further impression of AE's *The Hero in Man.*

★

In the meantime, alongside Charles Leadbeater's sensational 'Lives of Alcyone' series which had begun to appear in *The Theosophist*, Annie Besant was producing in the same journal a series on 'Theosophical Worthies', giving pen-portraits of prominent theosophists of the day. A different person was selected for each issue, and that of October 1910 featured Rudolf Steiner. Reproducing Peipers's photograph and some of Schuré's biographical account, Besant added a few extra comments of her own:

> Dr. Rudolf Steiner, the able and much-beloved General Secretary of the Theosophical Society in Germany, is hardly as widely known in the Society as he should be, from the fact that his literary and oratorical activities are all in the German tongue. Anyone who has listened to his powerful and moving eloquence will know how much those lose who are unacquainted with the virile language of the Teuton. His books are many, and blend into

one harmonious whole a spiritual philosophy and a reasoned science, peculiarly suited to the Western mystic and idealist; and they are finding a large public, though naturally without the magic of the spoken word which draws great audiences around him in the largest cities of the continent.

Long may he live to guide the people whom he enlightens, and to carry his message through Europe.

Pure Experience

At this very time 'the magic of the spoken word' was also drawing an audience around one particular lecturer in a northern British city. There was a report in *The Path*, co-edited by D.N. Dunlop, who was living nearby.

Mr. W.B. Yeats, the poet and playwright, gave the first of a series of three lectures in the Memorial Hall, Manchester, on Oct. 31st. His subject was 'Contemporary Poetry'.

Mr. Yeats began by explaining why he came to lecture. 'If one only tells of one's own search for truth in one's own craft (he said) it necessarily has a meaning for others whose craft and whose way of life are quite different. We all founded our lives (he continued) on certain values—on certain things we had made up our minds were good and certain things we had made up our minds were bad. We generally began by defying the generation that went before.' Drawing a comparison from painting Mr. Yeats said: 'You have in Manchester an exhibition of painting of the modern school. You have work there by Mr. Augustus John, and it is probably puzzling you very much. Many of you perhaps are experiencing for the first time how great is the revolt of the young painters against academic form . . .

'In poetry (Mr. Yeats continued) we have had an exactly equivalent revolt. Side by side with the discovery of academic form was the discovery of classic morals. I think perhaps Seneca was the principal influence in bringing them into English literature, but the first notable expression of them was in Milton. Milton is the Raphael of traditional morality. It passed on to many poets. Sometimes you find it in Wordsworth, noble and beautiful, and sometimes very dull indeed. It passed on again and got to Tennyson. It touched that supreme genius and it chilled the 'Idylls of the King' and it made him less than Nature meant him to be. After Tennyson's death it becomes fainter still until you get all that group of poets who write for the exclusive delight of what R.L. Stevenson used to call "the egregious spectator".

'Then came the revolt (Mr. Yeats said) of my own fiery generation. The man who first proclaimed it was the younger Hallam, who invented the phrase "the aesthetic school in poetry". A poet of the aesthetic school is a man who writes out of his own impression of the world. He simply gives you the sight and the hearing of the world as it comes to a man of very delicate senses. He does not wish to teach you; he does not think he knows better than other men. He only knows that he hears and sees and feels very intensely, and he always tries to give you his vision. He is always unpopular because there is nothing familiar about him. He has to be a long time in the world before people come to understand him . . . '

Mr. Yeats told the story of how the revolt came to himself, and of how he began to realize that 'we have thrown away the most powerful of all things in literature—personal utterance'. Later, he discovered that what he thought was his own thought was the thought of his generation. 'It is always wonderful,' he added, 'how a generation has come to think the same thought.' He and kindred spirits formed the Rhymers' Club. 'One thing I had not foreseen (Mr. Yeats proceeded), and that was that if you make your art out of your personality you will have a very troubled life. Goethe said: "We know ourselves by action only; never by contemplation." The moment you begin the expression of yourself as an artist, your life in some mysterious way is full of tumult. To me it meant Irish leagues and movements and all kinds of heterogeneous activities which were not good for my life, as it seemed to me at the time. To the others it meant dissipation; that generation was a doomed generation, and there is hardly one of them still alive. I believe it was that they made their natures passionate by making their art personal.'

The examples of the new poetry Mr. Yeats gave were taken from the works of Lionel Johnson, Ernest Dowson and Sturge Moore. Speaking of Johnson, Mr. Yeats said that a poet gave to the world not his defeat but his victory, and Johnson out of his strange life full of gloom, created happiness and the happiest and most ecstatic poetry of our time. The art of Dowson was curiously faint and shadowy. 'I believe (Mr. Yeats said) that the art of any man who is sincerely seeking the truth, seeking for beauty, is very likely to be faint and hesitating. The art that is entirely confident, or the speaking or writing entirely confident, is the work of the kind of man who is speaking with other men's thoughts.' Another comment Mr. Yeats made on Dowson's work was that 'if you express yourself sincerely I don't think your moral philosophy matters at all. The expression of the joy or sorrow in the depth of a spiritual nature will always be the highest art. Everything that can be reduced to popular morality, everything put in books and taught in schools can be imitated. The noblest art will always be pure experience—the art that insists on nothing, commands nothing—an art that is persuasive because it is almost silent, and is overheard rather than heard. And when I think of that doomed generation I am not sure whether it was sin or sanctity which was found in their brief lives.'

The Moving Finger Writes

Here is the editorial from *The Path* in November 1910:

> We are often asked what the word 'Lipika' means, and why we have chosen it as the name of our press.
>
> Briefly then, the 'Lipika' are the recorders of karma, the book-keepers of the gods. (Karma—'Whatsoever one sows that also must he reap'.) Their function is not the carrying out of karmic decrees, but the placing on record the movements of the life of man in evolution. They are impersonal, unbiassed recorders of all action and thought in the consciousness of man, and are also the order of gods who record the will of the Manu in the projection of future types of humanity. The August number of *The Path* describes the Manu in his work of world-building. H.P.B. in the *Secret Doctrine* says: 'The "Lipika" from the word *lipi*, writing, means literally the Scribes. Mystically these Divine Beings are connected with karma, the law of retribution, for they are the Recorders or Annalists, who impress on the (to us) invisible tablets of the "astral light" the great picture gallery of Eternity—a faithful record of every act and even thought of man; of all that was, is, or ever shall be in the phenomenal universe. It is the Lipika who project into objectivity from the passive universal mind the ideal plan of the universe, upon which the "Builders" reconstruct the kosmos after every Pralaya, and thus it is they who are the direct amanuensis of the Eternal Ideation—or as Plato calls it, the Divine Thought. The Eternal Record is no fantastic dream, and the Lipika are not deities connected with death, but with Life Eternal.'
>
> There are four great immortals who preside over the four corners of the great cosmic square, and these are the ones mentioned in Ezekiel's vision (ch. 1.). They are great overlords of the tabernacles for man's thought, and, again quoting H.P.B.—'These four are the protectors of mankind and also the agents of karma on Earth, whereas the Lipika are concerned with humanities hereafter.'
>
> That is, having recorded the present moment, they hand the book over as it were to the agents of karmic judgement, the executors of the righteous law. They have only to do with the coming event. No projected ideal for man's well-being can reach the material world without passing first through their books. Hence it is said they are concerned with humanity's future.
>
> Omar Khayyam describes them in their function in that stanza:—
>
> The Moving Finger writes, and having writ
> Moves on, nor all your piety and wit
> Can lure it back to cancel half a line,
> Nor all your tears wash out a word of it.

But the reader must bear in mind that 'writes' is in the ever-present tense and that there is no fatalism in the present moment, though we are inexorably bound by the karma of the past.

Each one of us is free to have what we will written by the Lipika for the future, though we have to bear our past now, as we will have to bear our future when it becomes the present, and merges into the past of some distant tomorrow.

Our little magazine being devoted solely and fundamentally to the cause of human evolution and the sowing of the true seed of life for humanity's future harvests, we have no hesitation in taking this symbolic name for our press nor any fear of breaking the great Lipika law, 'Thou shalt not take the name of thy Lords, the Gods, in vain.'

The next number of *The Path* carried an article signed by W.W.L., the initials of Mrs Winnifred Leisenring, secretary to D.N. Dunlop.

An event significant in the Theosophical Movement has occurred in the inauguration of the Blavatsky Institute, the first college to be named after Mme. Blavatsky. The group who are preparing the building and organizing for carrying on the work of publishing, lectures and classes invited comrades to join them in dedicating this Institute to the service of humanity in its higher evolution. Between fifty and sixty responded and on Saturday Nov. 5th gathered in the lecture-room to join in a programme of readings from a few of the world's great scriptures. Music from Beethoven and Wagner increased the pervading unity.

The members of the Institute feel that they have found a building eminently suited in every respect for the purposes of study and initiation into the higher mysteries of human experience. The building is simple and solid as a Greek temple on a small scale. The long oak-panelled hall is lit from above and out of it open lofty rooms, also panelled in natural woods on ceilings and walls, long windows look upon quiet woods and fields, and a peace and dignity pervade the place and seem to bespeak the true serenity of man's higher self. The personality faces itself here and sees that pride and desire must give place to a love of learning, to a contemplation of the truths which the great philosophers have uttered and which we find confirmed within ourselves.

Mr. Dunlop pointed out in his concluding remarks that the Institute would be sacred to the spiritual mysteries, and that those who sought the psychic realms instead of the realm of the true Psyche would be disappointed. For here will be no revelling—only a revel with the real Comrade, the spiritual One who teaches us what the sacrifice of the personality really is. Many schools are already established in England, as well as in other parts of the world, for the development of pseudo-occultism, but this spot will be protected as a centre for the promulgation of those truths which are always in danger of being swamped in the lower astral waters at certain critical periods in man's evolution.

Telegrams of greeting, wishing success to the Institute, were received from several comrades, including Mrs. Sharpe, the General Secretary of the T.S. in England.

In the evening Mr. Lazenby spoke on Madame Blavatsky's work, *The Secret Doctrine*, and an interesting discussion followed.

On Sunday evening Mr. Dunlop conducted a reading and discussion on the first chapter of St. John's Gospel, which brought all to a wonderful sense of spiritual kinship.

On Monday evening Mr. Lazenby lectured on 'The Blavatsky Movement in the World', and showed the pinnacle of knowledge and insight from which Madame Blavatsky viewed the problems of science, religion and philosophy. Her influence has been felt in all the sciences and arts, and has brought to the world, both within and without the T.S., a wonderful unifying standpoint for comparison.

Announcement was made that classes and public lectures would be free to all, but that a minimum of five shillings per week would be asked from students to help meet the expenses of rent, lighting, heating and general upkeep of the building.

Our Good Wishes

In *The Magicians of the Golden Dawn* (1972), Ellic Howe continued the story of Robert Felkin, who by this time had established spiritualistic contact with a discarnate 'Arab Teacher':

> Since Felkin could not remain in Germany to receive whatever teachings Steiner might have to offer, he decided to send a certain Neville Meakin as his representative. Meakin, who lived at Ringwood in Hampshire, was in his forties and must have had sufficient private means for a lengthy absence from England. Before he departed the Arab Teacher was consulted. On 7 November 1910 Felkin asked 'Shall Shemseddin' (i.e. Meakin) 'go to Berlin and is it advantageous to see Steiner?' The answer was 'Yes (decidedly).'
>
> So Meakin went to Berlin. The length of his stay there is unknown. In 1911 he began a longer journey intended to repeat Christian Rosenkreutz's legendary travels in the Middle East. The purpose of this symbolical pilgrimage is obscure.

Felkin also wrote his own account (F.R. = Finem Respice, his motto; E.O.L. = Ex Oriente Lux, Meakin's motto):

> Frater F.R., 1910, was able to introduce E.O.L. (who was abroad seeking health) to the members of the Order in Germany. These Fratres then said

that in order to form a definite link between themselves and Great Britain it was necessary for a Frater from Great Britain to be under their instructions for a year. Frater E.O.L. decided that he would place himself under the instruction of the Order. After residing for some time in North Germany and Austria, he was sent to Constantinople, and finally returned to Germany, where, having passed his tests, he was initiated by special dispensation into the first few grades of the Rosicrucian Society, corresponding to our 6 = 5.

★

While Neville Meakin was on the Continent making suitable occult progress in Berlin, Harry Collison had returned to England and was making further Masonic advancement in London. On 21 November 1910 he was appointed to 1st Principal of the Westminster and Keystone Chapter, a post known in the craft as M.E.Z. ('Most Excellent Zerubbabel').

★

Rudolf Steiner's book *Theosophie*, which in 1908 had gone into a second edition—silently dropping the dedication 'to the Spirit of Giordano Bruno'—then went into a third.

And towards the end of 1910 it first appeared in English translation, receiving an appreciative review in *Theosophy in Scotland*:

> So carefully has Dr. Steiner worded his new book that the title *Theosophy* is the only term that can be considered by any means outside the vocabulary of the ordinary and general reader. For this reason alone, the book must be called unique among expositions of theosophic doctrine, although the extraordinary clearness of thought and originality of statement upon subjects usually regarded as most obscure must also give it a place by itself. Anyone, however new to the doctrine of man's various vehicles of consciousness, for example, or to the idea of his recurrent incarnation in them, will find here, if he can read at all and keeps an open mind, an exposition of these teachings that is incapable of misconception. The English version is from the third German edition, translated by Mrs. Douglas Shiels.

The book was also reviewed in *The Vâhan* by James Wedgwood, who had reported on the Munich Congress in 1907.

> The circle of English readers of Dr. Steiner's writings has become a large one, since Mr. Max Gysi first did the service of beginning their systematic translation. The present book has achieved a wide reputation in Germany, and consequently will be welcomed by serious students over here.
>
> Dr. Steiner is a man of wonderfully magnetic personality, able to evoke great enthusiasm and devotion from his followers. There is often behind

what he says a power and spiritual stimulus which make his utterances living. He has a peculiar way of quickening the mystical and intuitive perceptions in his audience. Having known and loved the man, it is hard to be content with a book—and that a translation.

To translate Dr. Steiner is no light task, because English does not lend itself happily as a vehicle of transcendental thought. There are certain word-values and subtleties of expression in German which have no apt English equivalent—the words *uralt*, *Weltanschauung* are cases in point. None the less, this particular translation is well done, and those who know the especial difficulties which have had to be faced will be the less inclined to criticism.

We believe that a reflective study of Dr. Steiner will prove very useful to students. His method seems to be specially directed towards expanding the powers of the consciousness through the spiritual imaginative faculty (‘*imaginative Erkenntnis*’—vide p.376 of his latest work *Die Geheimwissenschaft im Umriss*). There is a rich charm and suggestiveness about Dr. Steiner's thought which is very stimulating to higher mental processes. This book is a fine study in consciousness, and regarding its writer we always call to mind the phrase applied to him, ‘Behold a master of himself and of life.’

The Vâhan further reported:

Dr. Rudolf Steiner, General Secretary of the T.S. in Germany, still continues with unsparing energy his lecture tours. A brief list of his December engagements will leave some of us sufficiently breathless. December 2 and 3 he lectures at Cassel, on the 4th at Eisenach, the 5th at Weimar, the 8th at Berlin, the 9th, 10th, 11th and 12th at Munich (this will probably be a series and therefore doubly interesting), the 15th at Berlin again, and the 27th finds him at Stuttgart giving a course of lectures on ‘Historical Events and Personalities in the Light of Occult Science’, which continues into the new year. January's list is even fuller, but we can follow Dr. Steiner no further for the present except with our good wishes.

The Face of the True Sun

The December engagements of other lecturers were meanwhile described in *The Path*:

The Blavatsky Institute is gradually forming on the physical plane. The different members of the group are taking their places in the picture, and the purpose of group education is assuming definition.

Though formally opened a little more than six weeks, several courses of lectures are well under way. Brother Atisha has introduced the subject of higher Buddhism for three or four successive Friday evenings. At the last meeting a very vital view of Nirvana was presented, including the interpretation given the subject by eminent western scholars. Those in attendance felt the great privilege of being able to gather in this quiet centre and discuss with those who have thought and realized the eternal themes of our salvation.

Quite a different aspect is presented when the *Secret Doctrine*, under Mr. Lazenby's direction, is being discussed on Saturday evenings, and again a contrasting phase is shown on Sunday evenings when Mr. Dunlop deals with the truths expressed in the Christian religion. One week the subject is treated from the devotional standpoint, and the next a more manasic discussion of the symbols is usually led.

The morning and afternoon lectures are in competent hands, and after Christmas lectures on theosophical psychology and symbolism in literature will be undertaken.

On alternate Monday evenings an excellent series of public lectures are being given by Mr. Lazenby, which are well attended.

At the time of going to press we are about to begin the Christmas programme, and many comrades are coming for this season and the opening of the New Year. All comrades, and especially those who have written of their sympathy with our gathering, as well as all readers of the *Path* will be welcomed into the consciousness of the group. 'For I love Thee, Oh Eternity.'

★

Of the many obituaries of D.N. Dunlop which appeared after his death in 1935, that by Albert E.S. Smythe in *The Canadian Theosophist* was the only one to say anything about Dunlop's wife, Eleanor (a name sometimes spelled Elinor), who had died in 1932. A long time previously, she had indeed contributed an article to Smythe's previous journal *The Lamp*, in the issue of March 1900.

The December 1910 number of *The Path* included 'A Legend of the Polar Stars', signed with the initials E.D.

Countless are the legends woven like silver nets to catch the mysteries of the stellar universe, which o'ershadows mortal life with life immortal. The legend appeals more intimately to the child-heart of humanity than does any other form of teaching. Legend, myth, saga and rune are the wellsprings of the gods from whence perennial waters flow for the refreshment of mankind.

Every European land has its own version of the Arthurian legend, for this hero soul is claimed by all who realize the divine power inherent in man. 'Arthur, that vast shadowy figure whose only kingdom may have been the soul of primitive races, and whose sword may have been none other than the imagination that is for ever on its foolish and perilous quest.'

In this legend of the polar stars, adapted from one of Fiona Macleod's beautiful essays in *Where the Forest Murmurs*, we find the early myth identifying the great Celtic champion with the chief constellation of the North.

At sunset the young son of the great King Pendragon came over the brow of a hill. All day he had been wandering alone, his mind heavy with wonder over many things. He knew a great destiny awaited him, when into his keeping should be given the vision and knowledge which belonged to the ancient kingly race. He came over the brow of the hill, and being tired lay down among the heather, gazing out across the grey wilderness of the sea until the stars climbed out of shadowy abysses, and the great chariots of the constellations rode from west to east, and from north to south. His eyes closed, but when he opened them again he saw a kingly figure standing beside him. So splendid was this mysterious one that he thought this must be one of the gods. 'Do you know me, my son? I am your father Pendragon. But my home is yonder, and there I go before long, that is why I come to you now.' And as he spoke, he pointed to the constellation of the Arth, or Bear, which nightly prowls about the vast abysses of the polar sky.

When the boy turned his gaze from the constellation he found he was alone. Then he became like a cloud, and as a cloud rose beyond the brows of the hills, ascending the invisible stairways of the sky . . .

It seemed to him that he had passed beyond the far-off blazing fires of innumerable suns—until he stood on the verge of Arth-Uthyr, the Great Bear. There he saw with immortal eyes a company of nobly majestic figures seated at a circular abyss which had the semblance of a vast table. Each of these seven great kings had a star upon his forehead; these were the stars of the mighty constellation of the Bear, which the boy had seen night after night from his home by the sea. It was with a burning throb of wonder that he recognized in the King of all these kings no other than himself. While he gazed in amazement he saw this mighty Self rise towering over all present, and heard a voice as though an ocean rose and fell through the eternal silences. 'Comrades in God,' it said, 'the time is come when that which is great shall become small.' When the voice was silent, the mighty figure faded into the blue darkness. Only the great polar star shone where the uplifted dragon-helm had touched the roof of heaven. One by one the white lords of the sky followed in his mysterious way, till once more only the seven stars of the Bear were to be seen.

Then the boy dreamt that he fell as a falling meteor upon the hills of his own land. When he awoke he found himself on the same heathery slope looking out on the eternal mysteries of sky and sea. Then he remembered. Slowly the boy king went down the hillside, his mind wrapt in thought. When he was come to the home of his father, Pendragon, the king came forth to meet him, for the Archdruid had foretold that the great king to be had received his initiation amid the holy silence of the hills.

'I am no longer Snowbird the child,' the boy said, fearlessly. 'Henceforth I am Arth-Uthyr.' (Pronounced Arth-ur in Ancient British. Arth means Bear, and Uthyr, great, wondrous.) 'For my place is in the Great Bear which we see yonder in the north.' So all there assembled acclaimed him as Arthur, the wondrous One of the stars.

'I am old,' said Pendragon, 'and soon you shall be king, my son. Ask a boon, and it shall be granted.' Then Arthur remembered his starry vision. 'Father and King,' he said, 'when I am king after you I shall make a new order of knights, who shall be strong and pure as are the Immortal Ones, tender as women, and simple as little children. Now I ask of you seven flawless virgin knights to be of my chosen company. Tomorrow let the woodwrights make me a round table of a size whereat I and my chosen knights may sit at ease.' 'So be it,' said Pendragon the king.

Arthur having chosen the seven flawless virgin knights, spake these words unto them. 'Ye are now children of the stars, Comrades of Arthur, who shall be King of the West. Ye shall be known as the Knights of the Round Table. No man shall make a mock of that name and live. In the end that name shall be so great in the mouths and minds of men that they shall consider no glory of the world to be so great as to be the youngest and frailest of that knighthood.'

That is how Arthur the son of Pendragon, who three years later became King of the West, read the rune of the stars that are called the Great Bear, and took their name upon him, and from the strongest and purest and noblest of the land made knighthood, such as the world had not seen, such as the world since has not known.

★

Charles Lazenby preserved a letter written to him from Elinor. It bears no date, but above the letterhead has been pencilled '1910'.

The Blavatsky Institute

Hale,
Cheshire
Christmas Eve—

Beloved Comrade, may the Face of the True Sun shine upon you, calling forth those unseen Powers of the Soul. We are so glad to have you amongst us dear old Friend I thank you at the close of this year of inner struggle & pain for your faithful love—nothing have I done to deserve such love but as the days pass bye, & the work grows, that love will return to the Lover. Keep a firm strong hand upon the reins of your emotional & sensual nature & all will be well. Yours all the way.

Freida

1910

The Institution of the dear love of Comrades.—*Walt Whitman*

THE BLAVATSKY INSTITUTE

Departments.—The Lipika Press, Literary and Publishing. Correspondence Bureau—Lessons on Theosophy for Beginners and Advanced Students. Lectures, Classes, etc. Dramatic and Musical Departments. Arts and Crafts Fellowship.

Telegraphic Address: "LIPIKA, ALTRINCHAM."
Secretary: Mrs. WINNIFRED W. LEISENRING, B.A.
Telephone

HALE, CHESHIRE

Christmas Eve—

Beloved Comrade,—may the Face
of the True Sun shine upon
you,—calling forth those unseen
Powers of the Soul. We are
so glad to have you amongst
us dear old Friend. I thank
you at the close of this year
of inner struggle & pain for
your faithful love—nothing
have I done to deserve such

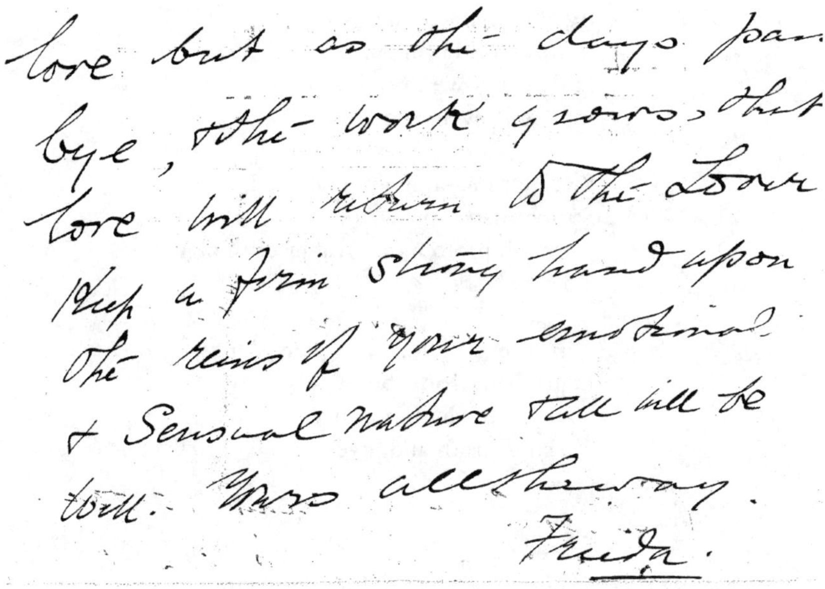
love but as the days pass
bye, & the work grows, that
love will return to the Lower
Keep a firm strong hand upon
the reins of your emotional
& Sensual nature till all will be
well. Yours all the way.
Frieda.

★

In this same month *The Path* published a poem by Lazenby entitled 'The Christmas Babe'.

Baby Christ, to Thee we bring
All we have and are,
Wise men journeying from the East,
Guided by thy star.

Laying humbly at thy shrine
Gems of precious worth,
Brightest jewels of the world,
Honouring thy birth.

Each one bearing as he comes
His immortal soul,
Placing in Thy baby hands
Absolute control.

Let us leave our ancient lies,
All our words uncouth,
Let thy holy purity
Guide us into truth.

Aged, ancient though we are
In this world of men,
Little babes we must become
In Thy heavens ten.

Sweetest infant, Thou shalt lead,
Strong men thou we be,
Through profoundest realms of thought
To simplicity.

Take then, Child, Thy servants' gifts,
Light them from above.
Give to us Thy innocence,
Teach us truth and love.

★

Early in 1911 *Theosophy in Scotland* published a letter:

Dear Mr. Editor,

Having spent Christmastide and New Year at the Blavatsky Institute, Hale, Cheshire, and found there so much, I feel it incumbent on me to call the attention of any possible and earnest students in our Society to that truly unique 'place of learning'.

Those who read *The Path* and have seen the little syllabus booklet with its photographs of the Institute will already know something of it, but not till they actually set foot within its walls will they experience the influence and the meaning of it as a training ground, spiritual and mental.

Why an old gentleman, unknown to the T.S., should have spent £10,000 on a building of this nature, palatial in space and in other ways (e.g. floors, ceilings, walls, even in the kitchens, are of panelled and finely polished wood), and dying, so fetter the place with conditions as to make it useless to the ordinary tenant but ready for the purposes of the ardent founders of the Blavatsky Institute is a problem worth thinking over.

Here in Scotland our propaganda work is growing apace. We are in need of a greater number of cultured exponents of Theosophy. Minds of various types are found in our audiences, whose questions have to be satisfactorily answered. I would urge then any who have it in their power and would fit themselves to teach others something of those truths which have been of such infinite blessing in their own lives to take a course of study at this Institute, if not of months, even of a few short weeks. I was impressed with the great fact that students there would of necessity learn *how* to *think*. I ask that we send loving and helpful thoughts to this brave band of workers. May their efforts indeed be blessed!

I may add that a comfortable boarding-house, 'The Guest House', at some minutes walking distance, is conducted by theosophists.

Ever yours sincerely and fraternally,

Isabel Stead

★

The Vâhan also published a notice by Eleazer ben Mosché:

For one who has chosen the Path of Service, the Blavatsky Institute may prove a veritable Mecca full of power and inspiration. After a short sojourn in Hale one returns to the 'outer world' as a giant refreshed, and it is long before the coldest student loses the helpful influence of the Institute. Adyar is of course *the* centre, but for the most part Adyar is but a name, physically at least. The Institute on the other hand is within easy reach, and herein lies its great utility.

Apart from the unmistakable feeling of real brotherhood and perfect toleration both at the Institute and Guest House, one soon finds something indescribably beautiful in the aura of the Institute. 'A quiet dignity,' it has been said, 'pervades the whole.' This statement, far from exaggerating, hardly serves to describe the wonderful effect experienced by many within the portals.

It was the writer's lot to arrive on a winter's evening, and in approaching the Institute down its narrow, dark country lane he was forcibly reminded of the narrow ancient way leading to the inner temple. In the darkest part of the path one seems to be enveloped by flowing streams of force which leave a curious effect, difficult to describe. Few who approach the Institute can fail to be affected, and one enters into silent communion with Those who have the directing of the T.S. The power is truly great, and one realizes that if the Brothers are anywhere they are here.

We Will Enter the Fold

Around this time in early 1911, at the other theosophical centre of Adyar, Annie Besant, Charles Leadbeater and George Arundale dramatized their sensational claims for Jiddu Krishnamurti by founding around his person the 'Order of the Star in the East'. The foundation was trumpeted by literary publicity in theosophical journals, chiefly in the English-speaking world.

The present work ignores this publicity and highlights instead the—relatively very small—amount of English-language matter relating to Rudolf Steiner and his work, alongside accounts of the contemporaneous impulse emanating from D.N. Dunlop. A reader must however remember that everything presented here was being written against a theosophical background where quite different views on Christology from those of Steiner or Dunlop were being suggestively disseminated, and receiving extensive support.

It was now a couple of years since Herbert Heywood-Smith had first come across Steiner's writings and begun to make private translations of the then still unpublished lecture-cycles. His account continues:

> Of course we could not keep our treasure to ourselves, and so we invited a number of friends who came regularly each week to study Dr. Steiner's work together.

This may already have happened by 1910. Be that as it may, one spring day in 1911 Heywood-Smith opened his mail and found himself perusing the following letter:

> Teosofisk Samfund.
> 115 Nyelandsvej,
> Steiner-Logen.
> Kjobenhavn.
> March 25, 1911
>
> Herbert Smith Esqre.
> London
>
> Dear Sir,
>
> Some time ago I wrote to Mr. Max Gysi, at the wish of Dr. Rudolf Steiner, and asked about the possible chances for a series of lectures on 'Rosicrucian Theosophy' in London.
>
> I received this morning a very kind reply in which he says that in his opinion 'a course of lectures on Rosicrucian Theosophy would be welcomed by many people in London and, if properly arranged, they could be made to pay.'
>
> Mr. Max Gysi regrets that he could not possibly find time to arrange the thing for me, and continues: 'You might write to my friend Mr. Herbert Smith etc. who may be able to advise you further in the matter'—and here I am!
>
> I am not in a position to make any pecuniary sacrifice, but I should on the other hand be willing to take a reasonable risk.
>
> I think the lectures should be public, though of course principally with a theosophically interested public in view.
>
> The lectures are without any necessary connection with each other. I mean that there would be no inconvenience in hearing one single lecture. Titles, for instance:

The Christ-principle and Evolution.
The Lucifer-principle.
Christ then and now
The Importance of our Earth-life.
The Mission of Truth.
,, ,, ,, Wrath.
,, ,, ,, Devotion.
What ought we to learn from Theosophy?

I suppose I have to praise myself in telling you that I have had great success as a lecturer in this country and in Sweden.—Hoping to hear from you,

I remain very sincerely yours,

C.A. Walleen

★

As a result of this letter, Heywood-Smith tried to arrange for Baron Walleen to come over to Britain and give lectures in London. In the event, however, this did not prove possible until much later in the year, in November.

★

The March issue of *The Path* opened with a poem by AE, first published in *The Internationalist* in October 1897.

Lord of the Wand, draw forth from the darkness
Warp of the silver, and woof of the gold.
Leave the poor shade there bereft in its starkness:
Wrapped in the Fleece we will enter the fold.

There from the many-orbed heart where the Mother
Breathes forth the love on her darlings who roam,
We will send dreams to their land of another,
Land of the Shining, their birthplace and home.

A note in this issue stated that the Summer School would be held 'probably at Penmaenmawr'.

★

The May issue of *Theosophy in Scotland* included an editorial note from D. Graham Pole:

To any who wish to spend a few days or more in a delightful theosophical atmosphere I recommend a stay at the Blavatsky Institute at Hale, Cheshire. I had the pleasure of spending two days there at Easter on the invitation of

Mr. and Mrs. Dunlop, and the spirit of brotherhood simply permeates the place. One has, in addition, the benefit of the *Secret Doctrine* and other classes that are continually going on there, and one feels that to stay there is to grow.

The Path gave a fuller account of these Easter festivities:

The activities at the Institute were increased during Easter week by a large number of visitors from a distance who came to attend the special lectures given at that time to celebrate the festival.

At the opening gathering, Thursday April 13th, Mr. Dunlop in his welcome referred to Wm. Q. Judge, whose birth anniversary it was, and told briefly of his work in organizing the Theosophical Society. Selections from *Letters That Have Helped Me* were read, also from Walt Whitman's *Leaves of Grass*.

An interesting feature of the lecture on 'The Path of the Pilgrim' was the use of the stereoptican lantern in showing slides of diagrams that indicated in various ways the evolution of consciousness.

The lectures in a general way suggested the vast fields that open to the student of Theosophy, and all were pleased with Mr. Lazenby's treatment of his subjects as he pointed out the fundamental philosophical conceptions underlying the Easter Festival.

Sunday morning the Lotus Circle gave their contribution of a short programme which ended with the acting of part of Act IV of *The Blue Bird*. The natural mysticism of 'the little child' was so beautifully expressed that all were lifted to a mood receptive to the teaching from the Master. Indeed His presence was realized in the consciousness of the group on several occasions, and, for all, sectarianism, separateness, personalities vanished into nothing, and the ideal of union in one work for one humanity became for a time genuinely vital. There was given a vibrant incentive to enter 'the great within', the abode of *our*, the one, Master and from that stronghold to resist all desires of self, which always ultimately lead away from and obliterate the ideal of service.

Sunday evening Mrs. Dunlop gave a most illuminating address on 'The Robe of Glory', giving a hint of that wonderful world of beauty where one dons the garment of service. The necessity for union in this ideal, for individual effort, was inspiringly pointed out at the last meeting, Monday evening, by Mr. Dunlop, who also explained that the realization of the object of the Theosophical Society depended entirely on the individuals in the Society. The Masters cannot be said to be responsible for any mistake of the members which may lead to schism. *They* have given the initial impulse, and the future will tell whether we can live up to the ideal and carry on the work of the T.S., which is to bring into active realization *their* own unchanging love and tolerance.

The music contributed so excellently by Miss Beatrice Grania and Mr. Conal Quirke, from London, aided in maintaining the spirit of unity, and the final gathering was concluded by a recital of German Lieder and Italian and English songs.

It was announced that the members of the Institute would have the pleasure of a visit from Mrs. Annie Besant, the President of the Theosophical Society, in May, when, as she says in her letter to Mr. Dunlop, 'I shall have the pleasure of seeing your good work.' She will be accompanied by the two young Indians, Alcyone and Mizar, and the party will remain over the night of May 22nd.

Tidings of Good Cheer

Around this time there appeared among the publications of the Blavatsky Institute a booklet which collected the series of articles on 'Theosophy in Plain Language' brought out in 1892–4 in *The Irish Theosophist* and reprinted in 1909–10 in *Theosophy* and *The Path*. It was entitled *In the Light of Theosophy*—a phrase recognizable from the resolution moved by D.N. Dunlop at the debate in Bath on 12 October 1909, 'that Christian doctrines can only be truly interpreted in the light of Theosophy'.

The booklet was brought out anonymously, 'by a Fellow of the Theosophical Society'.

★

In the chapter on AE in his *Rosemary for Remembrance*, Clifford Bax continued:

> Dunlop and I did bring out a second booklet—*The Renewal of Youth*—and of this venture he ('AE') wrote:
>
> 'I have looked over some old essays and patched them together, leaving out certain references in them to affairs in the T.S. at the time. It is the best I can do. I have selected passages which had a kind of unity of cheerfulness. I am trying to bring tidings of good cheer. I think it would make a booklet about the same size as *The Hero in Man*. I hope if you think these good enough to print you will have pages the same size, so that people who like them can bind them together in one book. I am glad to think people like what I write. If the essays come out this way, nobody after I am dead will go back to the old *I.T.* and print them with all their errors and obscurities from the pages of that paper, but will have them in the form I choose now. That is, if anybody will ever want to read what I have written when I have gone back to myself. You are a kindly angel, and it is a pity you don't live in Ireland.'

The Renewal of Youth came out in May 1911. It brought together three articles from *The Irish Theosophist* of 1895–7.

Here is the last one, which originally appeared in October 1895:

Who are exiles? As for me,
Where beneath the diamond dome
Lies the light on hills or tree
There my palace is and home.

We are outcasts from Deity, therefore we defame the place of our exile. But who is there may set apart his destiny from the Earth which bore him? I am one of those who would bring back the old reverence for the Mother, the magic, the love. I think, metaphysician, you have gone astray. You would seek within yourself for the fountain of life. Yes, there is the true, the only light. But do not dream it will lead you farther away from the Earth, but rather deeper into its heart. By it you are nourished with those living waters you would drink. You are yet in the womb and unborn, and the Mother breathes for you the diviner airs. Dart out your farthest ray of thought to the original, and yet you have not found a new path of your own. Your ray is still enclosed in the parent ray, and only on the sidereal streams are you borne to the freedom of the deep, to the sacred stars whose distance maddens, and to the Lonely Light of Lights.

Let us therefore accept the conditions and address ourselves with wonder, with awe, with love, as we well may, to that being in whom we move. I abate no joy of those vaster hopes, yet I would pursue that ardent aspiration, content as to here and today. I do not believe in a Nature red with tooth and claw. If indeed she appears so terrible to any it is because they themselves have armed her. Again, behind the anger of the gods there is a love. Are the rocks barren? Lay your brow against them, and learn what memories they keep. Is the brown earth unbeautiful? Yet lie on the breast of the Mother and you shall be aureoled with the dews of faery. The Earth is the entrance to the Halls of Twilight. What emanations are those that make radiant the dark woods of pine! Round every leaf and tree and over all the mountains wave the fiery tresses of that hidden Sun which is the soul of the Earth and parent of your soul. But we think of these things no longer. Like the prodigal we have wandered far from our home, but no more return. We idly pass or wait as strangers in the halls our spirit built.

Sad or fain no more to live?
I have pressed the lips of pain:
With the kisses lovers give
Ransomed ancient powers again.

I would raise this shrinking soul to a more universal acceptance. What? Does it aspire to the All, and yet deny by its revolt and inner protest the justice of Law? From sorrow we shall take no less and no more than from our joys. For if the one reveals to the soul the mode by which the power overflows and fills it here, the other indicates to it the unalterable will which checks excess and leads it on to true proportion and its own ancestral ideal. Yet men seem forever to fly from their destiny of inevitable beauty. Because of delay the power invites and lures no longer, but goes out into the highways with a hand of iron. We look back cheerfully enough upon those old trials out of which we have passed. But we have gleaned only an aftermath of wisdom, and missed the full harvest if the will has not risen royally at the moment in unison with the will of the Immortal, even though it comes rolled round with terror and suffering and strikes at the heart of clay.

Through all these things, in doubt, despair, poverty, sick, feeble, or baffled, we have yet to learn reliance. '*I will not leave thee or forsake thee*' are the words of the most ancient spirit to the spark wandering in the immensity of its own being. This high courage brings with it a vision. It sees the true intent in all circumstance out of which its own emerges to meet it. Before it the blackness melts into forms of beauty, and back of all illusions is seen the old enchanter tenderly smiling, the dark, hidden Father enveloping his children.

All things have their compensations. For what is absent here there is always, if we seek, a nobler presence about us.

Captive, see what stars give light
In the hidden heart of clay:
At their radiance dark and bright
Fades the dreamy King of Day.

We complain of conditions, but this very imperfection it is which urges us to arise and seek for the Isles of the Immortals. What we lack recalls the fullness. The soul has seen a brighter day than this, and a Sun which never sets. Hence the retrospect: 'Thou hast been in Eden, the garden of God. Every precious stone was thy covering, the sardius, topaz, and the diamond, the beryl, the onyx, the jasper, the sapphire, emerald ... Thou wast upon the holy mountain of God. Thou hast walked up and down in the midst of the stones of fire.' We would point out these radiant avenues of return. But sometimes we feel in our hearts that we sound but cockney voices, as guides amid the ancient temples, the cyclopean crypts sanctified by the mysteries. To be intelligible we replace the opalescent shining by the terms of the scientist, and we prate of occult physiology in the same breath with the most Most High. Yet when the soul has the vision divine it knows not it has a body. Let it remember, and the breath of glory kindles it no more; it is once again a captive. After all, it does not make the mysteries clearer to speak in physical terms and do violence to our intuitions. If we ever use these centres, as fires we shall see them, or they shall well up within us as fountains of potent sound. We may satisfy people's minds with a sense correspondence, and their souls may yet hold aloof. We shall only inspire by the magic of a superior beauty. Yet this too has its dangers. 'Thou hast corrupted thy wisdom by reason of thy brightness,' continues the seer. If we follow too much the elusive beauty of form we will miss the spirit. The last secrets are for those who translate vision into being. Does the glory fade away before you? Say truly in your heart: 'I care not. I will wear the robes I am endowed with today.' You are already become beautiful, being beyond desire and free.

Night and day no more eclipse
Friendly eyes that on us shine,
Speech from old familiar lips,
Playmates of a youth divine.

To childhood once again. We must regain the lost state. But it is to the giant and spiritual childhood of the young immortals we must return, when into their clear and translucent souls first fell the rays of the father-beings. The men of old were intimates of wind and wave, and playmates of many a brightness long since forgotten. The rapture of the fire was their rest; their outgoing was still consciously through universal being. By darkened images we may figure something vaguely akin, as when in rare moments under the stars the big dreamy heart of childhood is pervaded with quiet and brimmed full with love. Dear children of the world, so tired today—so weary seeking after the light. Would you recover strength and immortal vigour? Not one star alone, your star, shall shed its happy light upon you, but the All you must adore. Something intimate, secret, unspeakable, akin to thee, will emerge silently, insensibly, and ally itself with thee as thou gatherest thyself from the four quarters of the Earth. We shall go back to the world of the dawn, but to a brighter light than that which opened up this wondrous story of the cycles. The forms of elder years will reappear in our vision, the father-beings once again. So we shall grow at home amid these grandeurs, and with that All-Presence about us may cry in our hearts 'At last is our meeting, Immortal. O starry one, now is our rest!'

Come away, oh, come away;
We will quench the heart's desire
Past the gateways of the day
In the rapture of the fire.

Rank Materialism

The background to the foundation of the British Electrical and Allied Manufacturers' Association was explained in the obituary of D.N. Dunlop published on 7 June 1935 in *The Electrical Review*:

> During these years many efforts were made to adopt group plans for preventing disastrous undercutting. They were not successful. Later a number of leading electrical manufacturers definitely got together in London, and we were allowed to attend their meetings. For some years they continued to deal with various trade and other problems of common interest. The movement spread northwards, and as the electrical and allied engineering industries were becoming increasingly important the need for a larger and stronger organization conducted on more ambitious lines to deal with internal foreign competition and other matters was recognized. In 1911, therefore, the National Electrical Manufacturer's Association gave way to, or was absorbed in, the newly-formed BEAMA.

The obituary published on 5 June 1935 in *BEAMA News Sheet* stated:

> Dunlop had himself learned a good deal about the many defects of the British Cinderella, the chief of which was that her home market was entirely laid open to Germany, principally by reason, in those pre-tariff days, of the form of home competition known as 'cut-throat'. It looked to everyone an almost incurable position; but Dunlop saw that combination might save it. Convinced that the thing could be done, he found his vehicle in the little trade association then known as the National Electric Manufacturers' Association.
>
> Some intensive publicity and a good deal of quiet personal persuasiveness, of which he was past master, won him support from many of the more sober-minded firms, who had hitherto held aloof. In the year 1911, the BEAMA was launched with Dunlop as Secretary. The rest of his story is to be found not only in what everyone in the electrical world knows about the BEAMA, but in the council records of many other bodies, a few of which may be mentioned: the I.E.E., the F.B.I., the B.S.I. . . .

The last point was elaborated in *The Electrical Review*:

> Mr. Dunlop is credited with the original conception of the BEAMA organization as it has subsequently developed, carrying its influence in innumerable directions affecting electrical science and industry. He was prominently identified with all movements connected with electrical progress, education, research, standardization, &c. He found himself as time went on a member or chairman of a host of committees. He believed in committees heart and soul, and his tactfulness and conciliatory influence in

this connection are common knowledge among BEAMA members and their representatives.

The study of any annual report of the Council of BEAMA suffices to convey a general idea of the close relations into which he was brought with institutions, associations, conferences and committees in his continuous operations carried on in the interests of the electrical industry.

The obituary in *World Power* stated:

It is with profound regret that we announce the death of Mr. D.N. Dunlop, O.B.E., Director of the British Electrical and Allied Manufacturers' Association and editor of this journal...

For nearly a quarter of a century Mr. Dunlop had devoted his energies to the development of the BEAMA. One has only to look back to the desperate economic conditions of electrical manufacture in Britain twenty-five years ago to realize that the need for such an organization was urgent. The evils were obvious and widely recognized at the time; and it is largely due to Mr. Dunlop's belief in the principle of that form of industrial co-operation which would preserve individual initiative and enterprise of the member companies that the electrical manufacturing industry today has attained to its position of economic strength. This change, from threatened collapse, has rendered possible to an incalculable degree the collateral development of an unrivalled technical and engineering reputation throughout the world on the part of British electrical manufacture.

★

In June 1911, the pages of the wide-ranging *Occult Review* carried a lengthy article by Agnes Blake on 'Rudolf Steiner, Ph.D., Scientist, Mystic, Occultist', illustrated by the well-known Peipers photograph.

This began:

The subject of the present article may in truth be acclaimed one of the most remarkable men our generation has produced. Ours has been an age of brilliant achievement—an age of 'specializing', that practice whereof the greatly over-estimated value has been so persistently and blindly extolled. Hence a growing conviction is gaining ground that a certain one-sidedness has crept into almost every department of exact science, giving rise to a corresponding grooviness and lack of mental elasticity on the part of the majority of its exponents. It is in relation to all these outward signs of a materialistic age that Dr. Rudolf Steiner, of whom we would speak, differs so widely from the accepted man of science of the day.

Well able to hold his own with any whose work, be it in study or laboratory, entitles them to speak with authority, Rudolf Steiner's genius is yet so constituted as to render it impossible that it should rest satisfied within the limits of any one branch alone. It has often been maintained that the domains of science are now too vast for one human mind to comprehend them all. Yet we have in Rudolf Steiner one of those extraordinary minds which, like those of Leibnitz and Pascal, seem mentally able to assimilate not only the salient points but the intricacies of each and all, while the pursuit of material knowledge has but served to intensify his spiritual convictions as a theosophist, a mystic and occultist of the first order.

There followed a detailed sketch of Steiner's life based on Schuré's account, but supplying additional information.

The article was then concluded with some further remarks:

Before closing what we feel to be but a very inadequate sketch of one of the greatest leaders now among us, we should like to bear witness to the highly intellectual section of the public who form his audiences at public lectures held during the winter months in Berlin. It is no elementary Theosophy this, but a blend of metaphysics and science tempered with a dissertation on the higher ideals in art, an intellectual feast such as the German mind above all delights in. The hall, a vast one, is filled to its utmost sitting and standing capacity long before the Doctor mounts the rostrum, while the great percentage attending comprise professional men, scientists and students.

The writer of this article once enquired why the Doctor had chosen Berlin of all German cities as his headquarters, when there is not one that is not more spiritually and artistically attractive—and the answer given was: 'He chose Berlin because of its rank materialism'.

The Rosicrucian Lodge

The July issue of *Theosophy in Scotland* included a notice on 'The International Summer School.' It showed that the idea of having the venue at Penmaenmawr had been abandoned.

The School is promoted by the Blavatsky Institute, Hale, Cheshire, to promote unity in religion, philosophy and science, and its expression in all branches of social service, and will be held at The Hayes, Swanwick, Derbyshire. The station is Butterly (Midland Railway), and the dates from 11th to 16th August.

The preliminary list of lectures includes:—Greeting from Mrs. Besant, President of the Theosophical Society. Dr. Franz Hartmann, of the International Theosophical Brotherhood, Germany, will be present and lecture; also . . . Rev. K.C. Anderson, D.D., of Dundee, on 'The Cradle of the Christ'; . . . Mrs. Bell of Harrogate, on 'The Symbolism of the Path' (with stereopticon views); . . . Allen Upward, Esq., author of *The New Word*, etc., on 'The King of the Jews', ... and Mabel Collins, the writer of *Light on the Path*.

Arrangements are being made with other societies to send representative lecturers, and in addition to these, lectures and addresses will be given by other well-known lecturers, members of the Theosophical Society.

Arrangements have been made for chamber music for ancient and modern stringed instruments at all the sessions.

The buildings on the estate, surrounded by beautiful gardens and grounds, provide comfortable accommodation for 300 people, chiefly in small single bedrooms. There are spacious sitting-rooms, a lounge hall with pipe organ, reading and writing rooms, conservatory, committee room, large dining-hall and conference hall or marquee. The grounds contain five tennis and croquet courts; there is a swimming bath and fives court.

Vegetarian and ordinary catering has been arranged, and a large gathering is expected.

All applications for rooms should be made to the Secretary, Blavatsky Institute, Hale, Cheshire.

The very same issue held a competing announcement:

Dr. Steiner, the German General Secretary, announces that a series of Mystery Plays, acted by members of the Society, will be given at Munich, on 13th, 15th, and 17th August, in the Gärtnerplatz theatre. These will be followed by a cycle of lectures by Dr. Steiner himself, which will take place daily till the 27th, at 8 p.m. in the Prinzen-Sälen of the Café Luitpold. Scottish members who were present at the similar cycle last summer were deeply interested. Tickets can be had from Gräfin P. Kalckreuth, 55 IIIr Adalbertstrasse, Munich.

★

Theosophy in Scotland also reviewed a further work by Rudolf Steiner which had just come out in English, *The Education of Children*:

This short treatise will be welcomed by many others beside teachers. Dr. Steiner gives much valuable information about our development and the successive unfoldment of different vehicles of consciousness at the early stages of each incarnation ...

The work was further reviewed in *The Open Door*, a supplement to *The Path*, where it was described as

... a valuable book full of suggestions for anyone in touch with children and young people ... more original and suggestive than any work on education that has been published for a long time.

12. Rudolf Steiner and Annie Besant at the Munich Congress in 1907

13. Herbert Heywood-Smith (Oil painting by Nellie Heath)

14. At Uppingham School in 1884

15. As an Oxford freshman in 1888.

16. In 1889

17. In a Myrmidons group at Merton College in 1890

Harry Collison in early years

18. *Photographs from the 1910 Summer School at Weybourne Springs*

19. *A group of Kelling Heath during the Summer School. Standing under tree, near end of branch, Charles Lazenby. In centre at back, with hat and bow tie, D.N. Dunlop*

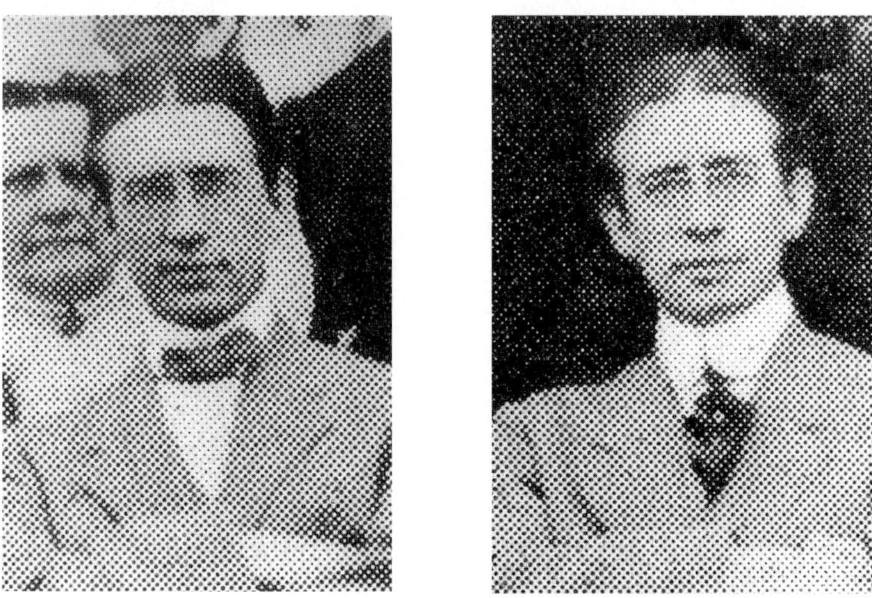

20. *D.N. Dunlop in July 1910, aged forty-one*

21. *The 1911 Summer School at Swanwick*

22. *Charles Lazenby and D.N. Dunlop at the Blavatsky Institute*

23. *Mabel Collins*

24. *Carl Alphonse Walleen*

25. *Eleanor Dunlop*

26. *H.W. Percival*

27. Robert Felkin

28. Edith Maryon in 1912

29. A.E. Waite

30. Alfred Meebold

The Vâhan reviewed another new book by Steiner, *Atlantis and Lemuria.* The reviewer was again James Wedgwood, who on the resignation of S. Maud Sharpe had now succeeded as General Secretary of the Theosophical Society in England and Wales.

His review commented:

> Much of what Dr. Steiner says is strikingly interesting, some of it exceedingly suggestive. But only a critic able to observe the Akashic Records for himself is competent to speak authoritatively on such matters, and we therefore content ourselves with recommending students to read the book and judge for themselves.

★

Although these published writings by Steiner were now appearing in English translation, his lecture-courses were still virtually unknown in Britain. Indeed, Herbert Heywood-Smith came to realize that they were meant to be restricted, and he should not have been imparting their contents to his circle of interested non-theosophical friends. His account continues:

> We then found that none but theosophists might read the cycles. I was the only one in the circle who was a member of the Theosophical Society,[19] and our friends, while desiring earnestly to study the cycles, did not wish to become members of the T.S. They agreed, however, that if I were to form a group of the T.S. for the sole purpose of studying Dr. Steiner's work they would join this group.
>
> Accordingly I wrote to Mrs. Besant in 1911 for permission to form such a group, bearing the name 'The Rosicrucian Group', and on 1 August 1911 received a letter in reply from Mr. J.I. Wedgwood, the Secretary, saying that permission had been granted and that the charter was in order.

The permission was published in the August issue of *The Vâhan*, which appeared that very same day:

> The Executive Committee have authorized the issue of a charter to the following London members to form the 'Rosicrucian' Lodge of the Theosophical Society: Miss A.L. Bowles, Mrs. C.W. Faulkner, Miss E.R. Haslehurst,[20] H.J. Smith, Mrs. H.J. Smith, Mrs. M. Stewart[21] and Miss V. Wakley. The officers are: H.J. Smith, President; Mrs. H.J. Smith, Secretary, and Mrs. C.W. Faulkner, Treasurer.

Membership diplomas had in fact been issued on 27 July not only to the one man and six ladies named in the announcement, but to five other ladies as well: Emily Allott, Charlotte Booth, Maude Haslehurst, Eleanor Latham and Alice Wakley. On 8 August, a diploma was further issued to another lady: Jessica Carr.

Evidently Heywood-Smith lodged an objection about the missing names, for he received in reply a further letter from Wedgwood. It was written from new premises, to which the London Headquarters had moved:

Theosophical Society in England and Wales

106, New Bond Street,
London, W.

Dear Mr. Smith,

Thank you for your kind letter. I am sorry the mistake occurred in the *Vâhan*: it was a clerical error on the part of the staff here (also the misspelling of the name Haslehust). The Charter form is all square!

Thanks for what you say about the *Vâhan*!

Very sincerely yours,

J.I. Wedgwood

★

Heywood-Smith continued:

We then wrote to Dr. Steiner informing him of what we were doing and told him that the group would meet for the first time on 3 September.

In Such an Atmosphere

The Vâhan stated:

In Munich theosophical events promise to be very interesting during the month of August. Three dramas will be given in the Gärtnerplatz Theatre: on the 13th 'The Eleusinian Mystery' by Edouard Schuré; on the 15th, 'The Portal to the Rosicrucian Initiation' by Rudolf Steiner; and on the 17th, 'The Proving of the Soul', also by Dr. Steiner. These will take place at 10 a.m. From August 18–27 Dr. Steiner will give a course of lectures on 'The Wonders of the Universe; Tests of the Soul; Revelations of the Spirit'.

Information and tickets, for members of the Society only, may be obtained from Gräfin Kalckreuth, 55, Adalbertstrasse, Munich.

★

Of those Britons who had attended events in Munich in 1910, Harry Collison was once again present there in 1911.

Isabella Pagan, by contrast, appreciative though she had been of the events at Munich in 1910, gave priority in 1911 to the Summer School at Swanwick. At the beginning of August, a notice about this 'International Summer School' appeared in *The Vâhan:*

> The promoters of the Summer School have pleasure in announcing that all Railway companies will give tickets for the double journey at a single fare and a quarter to members of the school who present a voucher signed by the Secretary of the Blavatsky Institute when purchasing tickets. Special through-carriages will also leave London on Friday the 11th, to accommodate visitors. Information regarding this will be sent to intending visitors later on.

After the School was over, *The Vâhan* published an account, signed by the initials H.L.

> The International Theosophical Summer School, promoted by the Blavatsky Institute of Hale, Cheshire, held its third session under the able leadership of Mr. D.N. Dunlop, at The Hayes, Swanwick, Derbyshire, from August 11 to 25. The size of the gathering was significant of the growing interest in Theosophy in the wider sense of that term, consisting as it did of more than three hundred persons.
>
> The Hayes, officially described as 'The First Conference Estate, Limited' is a country house standing in its own grounds of forty acres, to which is attached a large dining-hall and hostel, with the necessary accommodation. There is a particularly fine organ in the lounge, which is otherwise suitable for concerts, large rooms opening out of it. Excellent arrangements were made for providing good music every evening, and probably the feeling of harmony which has been such a distinctive feature of the present gathering may be partly attributable to this.
>
> The international character of the meeting was strongly marked, the distribution of races being roughly as follows: India 2%, Holland 5%, Scandinavia 2%, Austria 2%, England 74%, America 3%, Finland 1%, Scotland 5%, Russia 1%, Germany 5%.
>
> The School was opened by Mrs. Besant's address of greeting, read by the Chairman, the Theosophical Society in other countries being represented by the General Secretaries of Holland (Dr. A.J. Cnoop-Koopmans) and Scotland (Mr. D. Graham Pole). A telegram of greeting and wishing the Summer School all success was received from the General Secretary in England and Wales, who was unable to be present at the opening, being detained in London by theosophical work.
>
> As the lecture-platform was absolutely free, many different schools of thought were induced to send representatives. The mental kaleidoscope was consequently kept in continual movement, new combinations of ideas

constantly presenting themselves before the mind's eye. The spirit of criticism so prominent in the world today and only to be expected in such a vortex of conflicting opinions was kept employed in the most useful fashion possible, looking for differences in order to harmonize, not to accentuate them. Mr. Tudor Pole gave a most interesting account of his experiences in Persia in connection with the Bahais. Mrs. Despard lectured on 'The Religious Aspect of the Woman's Movement' and Mrs. Kirkwood dealt with the 'Prevention of Destitution'. Mrs. Dunlop's paper upon 'Celtic Traditions' and Mrs. Hunter's on 'Myth, Ritual and Drama' were greatly appreciated, as also was Mrs. Leisenring's on 'A Modern Philosophy'. Mme. Pogosky spoke on 'The International Fellowship of Workers', and Mr. Loftus Hare on 'Thoughts on Religion'. Mr. Oyler delivered an excellent lecture upon the education of children, outlining an idea which is to take shape in the form of a school, to be opened in the Hindhead district of Surrey. Mr. Charles Spencer, of the Higher Thought Centre, Miss Alleyne of the Liberal Christian League, and Professor Bickerton all gave interesting lectures upon their special subjects, while Dr. Khedkar explained the Adwaita philosophy of the Vedanta and held discussion thereon, answering questions after the Socratic manner. Mrs. Windust chose 'Theosophy and World Movements' as her subject; Miss Pagan, 'Reincarnation, with special reference to Plato's Vision of Er'. Mr. Sinnett, who was expected to lecture on the 21st, was unfortunately unable to be present. Theosophy in its many aspects was dealt with by Mr. Lazenby in his usual logical and luminous manner, sometimes in the spacious marquee, sometimes beneath the spreading oak tree, where groups frequently gathered to ask questions and receive instruction on knotty problems. Mr. Dunlop in his capacity of Perpetual Chairman was kept hard at work at a difficult task, ably and tactfully performed.

Amongst other attractions must be mentioned the exhibition of national and traditional handicrafts, chiefly Russian, presided over by Madame Pogosky, the Hon. Organizer of the International Fellowship of Workers for reviving ancient arts and crafts.

As the result of Mrs. Kirkwood's and Mrs. Despard's lectures a collection amounting to £25 was made on behalf of the women strikers of the Bermondsey jam factories. The glorious weather was a great encouragement to outdoor amusements, and enabled excursions to be made to places of interest in the neighbourhood. In spite of the many inconveniences resulting from the general railway strike and the exaggerated apprehension to which it gave rise, the School did not on the whole suffer as severely as was expected.

There can now be no doubt that the Summer School has become a permanent institution in our midst, and we look forward with keen interest to its future, with all good wishes for its continued success.

The Summer School was further reported in three successive issues of *The Christian Commonwealth*, from which are taken the following paragraphs:

> The opening of the school was preceded on Friday by the very successful performance of a play by W.B. Yeats, *The Land of Heart's Desire*, based upon the tradition that the 'faery people' may steal newly married brides upon May eve. It gave a tender picture of Irish peasant life, and a lovely glimpse of the beauty of Celtic folklore which many of us will be led to renew for ourselves by a closer study of its literature. The performers, who were all amateurs, acquitted themselves remarkably well.
>
> The wind blows out of the gates of the day,
> The wind blows over the lonely of heart,
> And the lonely of heart is withered away;
> While the faeries dance in a place apart,
> Shaking their milk-white feet in a ring,
> Tossing their milk-white arms in the air;
> For they hear the wind laugh and murmur and sing
> Of a land where even the old are fair,
> And even the wise are merry of tongue;
> But I heard a reed of Coolaney say—
> 'When the wind has laughed and murmured and sung
> The lonely of heart is withered away!'
>
> On the only wet evening in the whole fortnight we gathered in the large entrance-hall to hear Mrs. Dunlop's paper on 'Celtic Traditions'. Sometimes in the midst of a wonderful legend she would, in parenthesis, throw out a suggestion of how it might be translated into the formidable terminology to which most theosophists have grown accustomed. At the end of a description of the Celtic goddess Brig, queen of love and beauty, mother of gods and men, whose mantle of blue and silver is the mist and the twilight haze upon the hills, it was with something of a shock that we learnt that theosophists call her the Buddhic principle. But the lesson was not lost upon us. For those who have studied and lived Theosophy until the essence of its fundamental ideas, apart from any particular way of expressing them, has taken root in their souls, there is indeed a beauty and a significance in ancient legends . . .
>
> Mr. Lazenby works as hard as anyone here, and that is saying much. He is greatly in request for his stirring readings from Walt Whitman, his answers to questions, which are stimulating as well as satisfying, and above all for his masterly expositions of the teachings of H.P. Blavatsky as set forth in *Isis Unveiled*, *The Key to Theosophy* and *The Secret Doctrine*. There are times, of course, when we tire of these lofty themes, and long to relieve ourselves with a little wholesome frivolity. And it is to Mr. Lazenby

again that we turn in such moments, for his fund of humour is apparently inexhaustible.

How to express our love and appreciation for Mr. Dunlop in words that will escape his blue pencil is a formidable problem. But Walt Whitman swore that he would always leave the best untold, and this seems a good excuse for giving up the attempt.

The Dawn of a New Day

The Summer School of 1911 indeed gave rise to quite a number of different accounts. Here is part of a Dutch report appearing in *De Theosophische Beweging*:

> The principal aim of the School was to bring together all kinds of people who are working for the evolution of humanity along either scientific, philosophical or religious lines, so that uniting them in one centre, expression might be given to practically all phases of human thought.
>
> It was put forward that *that* should be sought after which *unites*, and not which *divides*, each person having the absolute freedom to express what in his heart he felt to be true, with the surety that his opinions would be impartially considered.
>
> Most varied subjects were treated, and underlying all the addresses and discussions was the idea of unity and brotherhood, in fact the whole atmosphere seemed permeated with the thought. Many who were not members of the Theosophical Society were agreeably astonished to find that such a feeling of oneness could possibly exist.
>
> Great interest was evoked by many whose thoughts were travelling along quite different lines from that of Theosophy; some were still guided by science, others by revelation and yet others by philosophical thought, yet all appeared to be of the opinion that a new effort was necessary for the uplifting of humanity, that the dawn of a new day was breaking through, and that brotherhood and tolerance were no longer to be allowed to remain mere words, but *must* and *can* become realities in our everyday lives.
>
> And during these fourteen days the collecting together of such heterogeneous elements has proved that the realization of that ideal is possible. The Theosophical Society has always put this idea forward in her organization, but I do not believe that ever such a convincing proof of the truth of it has been known as on this occasion. What has been done by a few shall be done in the future by the Theosophical Society at large, and it will be able to do so while retaining to the full the individuality of its members.
>
> Then of the dangers that threaten to turn the Theosophical Society into a sect or creed we need have no fear, but it will keep ever in view the great and eternal truths that called it into being.

We cannot conclude without a word of admiration for the two leaders, Mr. Dunlop and Mr. Lazenby. The former presided, opening and closing each meeting with suitable words, and often completing what the speaker omitted, or softening the sharp edges of the ideas put forward.

Sixteen members from Holland were present, and we hope that next year many more will be able to see with their own eyes the excellence of this work.

The Open Door contained an extensive account of the occasion, reportedly written by a 14-year-old named R. Butler Hunter, of Letchworth, who must have been a precociously literate child. It ended with these paragraphs:

> The last of the lectures I had the pleasure of hearing, for I had to leave on Tuesday, was by our friend Mr. Lazenby on 'The Skandhas'. 'Man, know thyself' was written on the doors of the Delphic oracle. Self-knowledge is the key to the drama of life. The great consciousness behind the drama is the mind. The Skandhas are the group of powers that make each personality. As we think, so we become. That which we desire we achieve. I left in the midst of an animated discussion to catch the train, Mrs. Dunlop holding forth a theory which was being discussed by many eager persons . . .
>
> Altogether the Summer School was wonderfully varied and included almost all possible types of mind and many different nationalities. All were ably provided for by the ever-working enthusiast and director, Mr. D.N. Dunlop.
>
> By no means the last to be mentioned is the music, which was provided by the skilled musicians Messrs. Van der Straeten, cellist and violist, Miss Holloway, violinist, Miss Beatrice Grania, vocalist, and Mr. Quirke, accompanist. Organ recitals given in the lounge by Mr. Frank Merry were much enjoyed.

⋆

The most numerous accounts of the Summer School at Swanwick were given by *Theosophy in Scotland*. The September issue opened with an editorial from D. Graham Pole:

> We are very happy to publish this month an account of the Third International Theosophical Summer School . . . promoted by the indefatigable workers of the Blavatsky Institute, Hale, Cheshire; and we feel that it would be difficult to estimate the far-reaching value of the work that this great gathering of members and sympathizers has accomplished. The first noticeable feature of the School was the complete harmony and brotherliness which prevailed among the students assembled; the second that of the large number of varying views of life and philosophy expounded by the numerous lecturers; and the third, the all-embracing note of tolerance and

freedom of opinion and expression accorded to every person who had the good fortune to set foot within the little community, and so ably maintained by the ideal permanent chairman, Mr. D.N. Dunlop.

And how refreshing it was to realize that our chairman's success in that capacity was very largely due to the fact that when introducing or thanking the various representatives of the many different schools of thought who addressed us, he simply gave his own honest opinion!—courteously, sometimes humorously—but always quite straightforwardly and fearlessly; taking for granted that no mere difference of intellectual opinion could ever possibly be a cause of quarrel, and that everyone present would look upon such variations in belief as perfectly natural and legitimate, and even desirable. In consequence of which the discussion that followed each discourse—whether formally in the lecture tent, or informally in little groups under the shade of spreading chestnut or stately oak, or on sunny banks by the tennis court—flowed on in the key he set. Earnest and keen the speakers might be; absolutely opposed in their views theological, philosophical, sociological or scientific; but their strenuous talk was broken by ripples of mirth, the speakers remained sunny and serene, and the groups formed and dwindled and broke and reunited like crystals in a kaleidoscope—ever varying, but with a symmetry of their own. Some of the lecturers came and went comet-like, and were therefore hard worked while with us . . . The permanents—there for the whole fortnight—naturally consisted of our own well-known lecturers, who were, as was to be expected, always ready to fill up a gap or resign an hour just as the organizers required. Mr. Charles Lazenby was, as the chairman observed, always 'on tap', and those who know his vigorous style, with its quaint Canadian flavour, and his magnificent clearness of thought, will not be surprised to learn that the particular 'brew' most often demanded by his hearers, whether members of the Society or otherwise, was a series of readings and commentaries on the great writings of H.P.B.

We were quite sorrowful when the fortnight came to an end, but this feeling was somewhat sweetened by the knowledge that we who met and conversed formed in some mystic way a Body free from the trammels of time and space, and that the ties which have been formed will persist as Summer School succeeds Summer School, ever becoming stronger and stronger, till we shall have realized and accomplished the great ideal 'institution of the dear love of comrades' partially foreshadowed in this Summer School that we have just left.

The published account, signed with the initial C., included this paragraph:

Throughout the fortnight there was an unfailing supply of mental food, and the lectures were as diverse as they were fine. Mr. C. Lazenby, B.A., was a constant fount of wisdom. He lectured upon 'The Gods', 'Theosophy', 'The Skandhas', and besides holding many and varied open-air classes, he was ever ready to expound the *Bhagavad Gîta*, or to recite Walt Whitman ... It seemed that every heart beat in unison, and that in truth the school formed some great, mystic body through which silent forces constantly poured forth and radiated. And ever watchful, balancing, moulding, the permanent chairman of the school, Mr. D.N. Dunlop, moved silently from group to group, a splendid example of optimism and good-will, and although as he said, the school would not have been possible without the untiring help of the many devoted, unobtrusive workers of the Blavatsky Institute, the great success and far-reaching results of the School are mainly due to his keen insight and practical power of organization ... We must close this brief reference to a gathering which was more successful than the most daring organizers could have predicted, and whose significance will only become apparent to such as were privileged to attend, in years to come when these milestones of progress will be seen in the true relationships that they bear to one another.

In the following month a certain J.H. Elder contributed a further account, 'Some Impressions of the Summer School'.

The growth of the capacity for voluntary co-operative effort is strongly shown in the increasing popularity of Summer Schools. These constitute not only a sign of conscious awakening to the great fact of brotherhood but also a valuable stimulus to the realization of that eternal fact. The astonishing number of comparatively useless and temporary little societies which multiply around us till it really seems as if we were incapable without their help of being kind to animals, or getting up in the morning, or reading solid literature, etc., have not for their real root the apparent purpose set forth in their names and rules but the unconscious need of evolving humanity for practice in collective thought and co-operative effort.

A great point about this Summer School, it seems to me, was the consciousness of this purpose. And that being so, it is intensely interesting to see how the ideal held by its promoters has worked out. They hold that one of the ways of helping the formation of that nucleus of brotherhood which is the first object of our Society is the provision of a free platform where all who are earnestly working for the uplifting of humanity shall find a place. All such should be welcomed, and in the limited time and space of this wonderful fortnight all those who have chosen to avail themselves of this opportunity have been welcomed, not necessarily among the lecturers only, but as members of the School.

In noting the various details of the working out of this grand ideal we find that a large proportion of the lectures were given by those who were not members of the T.S., and that few dealt with what are popularly called theosophic theories. No attempt was made to make the School an opportunity for consecutive teaching by means of elementary or graduated classes, for the daily lectures of one of our leaders of thought did not belong to that category. We were indeed fortunate in being represented by Mr. Lazenby, whom the consensus of opinion acclaimed as the most universally popular lecturer. His marvellous lucidity of expression, wide knowledge and breadth of view appealed to all, however widely they might differ from him in opinions. Most valuable was the demonstration given by his whole personality that there is no orthodoxy in the Theosophical Society. In this he was ably seconded by our permanent chairman, whose function in synthesizing the whole and constantly raising discussion to the level of the ideal was admirably performed. I think that no one present could but be impressed by these two theosophists, men who are not afraid of truth—that truth which we are all seeking but of which, for the most part, we are desperately afraid.

About one fourth of our number were not members of the T.S., and I think they felt they belonged quite as much to the life of the School as those who were. No one asked them to become members; their freedom of opinion was always respected. In such an atmosphere we grow . . .

The artistic element of life was not forgotten, and readings were given from Shakespeare. The music, the voluntary gift of talented artistes, played a large part in harmonizing the audience before every formal lecture. The beautiful trios of Beethoven may be mentioned as showing the quality of the music chosen. The great art of life was exemplified in the harmonious comradeship shown in work and play. It was remarked that as the days went on the spiritual quality of the various faces became more plainly visible, and maybe the ability to recognize that quality also grew.

The International Theosophical Summer School was not an official activity of the T.S. (It was warmly approved by our President, who sent a special letter of greeting to the School.) But it did owe its existence to the Society through which the perception of theosophical truth reached its promoters, and in which and for which they work. To them, and to all the willing band of unknown workers to whom members of the School owe so much—much gratitude!

The Most Extraordinary Event

The August number of *The Path* opened with an item entitled 'Friendship'. A footnote stated: 'From an address delivered at the Blavatsky Institute, June 18th, 1911, by D.N. Dunlop.' The text covered some six pages.

Comparison of the text shows it however to have been almost entirely drawn from a series of two editorials, similarly entitled 'Friendship', which had appeared some months earlier in the February and March numbers of *The Word*, an occult journal edited in America by H.W. Percival.

Percival's editorials in this journal came from this time onward to exercise such a strong influence over Dunlop that on certain occasions repeated at shorter or longer intervals over the following nine years he made from them extensive and largely unacknowledged verbal borrowings.

To any reader interested in Dunlop and his writings, this whole problematic matter seems worth examining in some detail, and an account will first be given of Percival's own life.[22]

★

Harold Waldwin Percival was born on 15 April 1868 at Bridgetown on the Caribbean island of Barbados—then British West Indies—where his English parents, James and Elizabeth Percival, owned a plantation. He was the third of their four children.

The foreword to Percival's work *Thinking and Destiny* (1946) included 'a sketch of some experiences of my early life'.

> Rhythm was my first feeling of connection with this physical world. Later on I could feel inside the body, and I could hear voices. I understood the meaning of the sounds made by the voices. I did not see anything, but I, as feeling, could get the meaning of any of the word-sounds expressed; and my feeling gave the form and colour of the objects which were described by words. When I could use the sense of sight and could see objects, I found the forms and appearances which I, as feeling, had felt, to be in approximate agreement with what I had apprehended. When I was able to use the senses of sight, hearing, taste and smell and could ask and answer questions, I found myself to be a stranger in a strange world. I knew I was not the body I lived in, but no one could tell me who or what I was or where I came from, and most of those whom I questioned seemed to believe they were the bodies in which they lived.
>
> I realized that I was in a body from which I could not free myself. I was lost, alone, and in a sorry state of sadness. Repeated happenings and experiences convinced me that things were not what they appeared to be; that there is continued change; that there is no permanence of anything; that people often said the opposite of what they really meant. Children played games they called 'make-believe' or 'let us pretend'. Children played, men and women practised make-believe and pretence. Comparatively few people were really truthful and sincere. There was waste in human effort, and appearances did not last. Appearances were not made to last. I asked myself: 'How should things be made that will last, and made without waste

and disorder?' Another part of myself answered: 'First, know what you want. See and steadily hold in mind the form in which you would have what you want. Then think and will and speak into that appearance, and what you think will be gathered from the invisible atmosphere, and fixed into and around that form.' I did not then think in these words, but these words express what I then thought. I felt confident I could do that, and at once tried, and tried long. On failing I felt disgraced, degraded, and I was ashamed.

I could not help being observant of events. What I heard people say about things that happened, particularly about death, did not seem reasonable. My parents were devout Christians. I heard it read and said that 'God' made the world; that he created an immortal soul for each human body in the world; and that the soul who did not obey God would be cast into hell and would burn in fire and brimstone for ever and ever. I did not believe a word of that. It seemed too absurd for me to suppose or believe that any god or being could have made the world or have created me for the body in which I lived. I had burned my finger with a brimstone match, and I believed that the body could be burned to death. But I knew that I, what was conscious as I, could not be burned and could not die, that fire and brimstone could not kill me, though the pain from that burn was dreadful. I could sense danger, but I did not fear.

People did not seem to know 'why' or 'what', about life or about death. I knew that there must be a reason for everything that happened. I wanted to know the secrets of life and of death, and to live forever. I did not know why, but I could not help wanting that. I knew that there could be no night and day and life and death, and no world, unless there were wise ones who would tell me how I should learn and what I should do, to be entrusted with the secrets of life and death. I would not even think of telling this my firm resolve, because people would not understand; they would believe me to be foolish or insane. I was about seven years old at that time.

Some three years later, when the thoughtful boy had reached the age of ten, his father James Percival died. This event marked the end of the outwardly idyllic existence on the Caribbean island, for the widowed Elizabeth Percival moved with her children not just onto the mainland of the American continent but indeed into the most urban environments conceivable of the United States, settling first in Boston, Massachusetts, and subsequently in New York City.

Nothing specific is known about the further course of Harold Percival's youth and early manhood, except that he was an avid reader, and largely self-educated. He developed a propensity for mathematics and for languages, especially Greek and Hebrew. His wide-ranging interests also included geology, history, economics, politics and current affairs, while his favourite practical activities were gardening and photography.

Hidden deep within him, however, the inner experiences of his early childhood still lived on. The next recorded event in his life, which took place around the time of his twenty-fourth birthday, was connected to them.

> Fifteen or more years passed [from when he was aged about seven]. I had noticed the different outlook on life of boys and girls, while they grew and changed into men and women, especially during their adolescence, and particularly that of my own. My views had changed, but my purpose—to find those who were wise, who knew, and from whom I could learn the secrets of life and death—was unchanged. I was sure of their existence. The world could not be without them. In the ordering of events I could see that there must be a government and a management of the world, just as there must be the government of a country or a management of any business for these to continue. One day my mother asked me what I believed. Without hesitation I said: 'I know without doubt that justice rules the world, even though my own life seems to be evidence that it does not, because I can see no possibility of accomplishing what I inherently know, and what I most desire.'
>
> In that same year, in the spring of 1892, I read in a Sunday paper that a certain Madame Blavatsky had been a pupil of wise men in the East who were called 'Mahatmas'; that through repeated lives on Earth they had attained to wisdom; that they possessed the secrets of life and death, and that they had caused Madame Blavatsky to form a Theosophical Society, through which their teachings could be given to the public. There would be a lecture that evening. I went. Later on I became an ardent member of the Society. The statement that there were wise men—by whatever names they were called—did not surprise me. That was only verbal evidence of what I inherently had been sure of, as necessary for the advancement of man and for the direction and guidance of Nature. I read all that I could about them. I thought of becoming a pupil of one of the wise men. But continued thinking led me to understand that the real way was not by any formal application to anybody, but to be myself fit and ready...
>
> From November of 1892 I passed through astonishing and crucial experiences, following which, in the spring of 1893, there occurred the most extraordinary event of my life. I had crossed 14th Street at 4th Avenue, in New York City. Cars and people were hurrying by. While stepping up to the north-east corner curbstone, Light, greater than that of myriads of suns, opened in the centre of my head. In that instant or point, eternities were apprehended. There was no time. Distance and dimensions were not in evidence. Nature was composed of units. I was conscious of the units of

Nature, and of units as Intelligences. Within and beyond, so to say, there were greater and lesser Lights; the greater pervading the lesser Lights, which revealed the different kinds of units. The Lights were not of Nature, they were lights as Intelligences, conscious Lights. Compared with the brightness or lightness of those Lights, the surrounding sunlight was a dense fog. And in and through all Lights and units and objects I was conscious of the presence of consciousness. I was conscious of consciousness as the ultimate and absolute reality, and conscious of the relation of things. I experienced no thrills, emotions or ecstasy. Words fail utterly to describe or explain consciousness. It would be futile to attempt description of the sublime grandeur and power and order and relation in poise of what I was then conscious. Twice during the next fourteen years, for a long time on each occasion, I was conscious of consciousness. But during that time I was conscious of no more than I had been conscious of in that first moment.

Being conscious of consciousness is the set of related words I have chosen as a phrase to speak of that most potent and remarkable event of my life.

Consciousness is present in every unit. Therefore the presence of consciousness makes every unit conscious as the function it performs in the degree in which it is conscious.

Being conscious of consciousness reveals the 'unknown' to the one who has been so conscious. Then it will be the duty of that one to make known what he can of *being conscious of consciousness.*

The great worth in being conscious of consciousness is that it enables one to know about any subject, by thinking. Thinking is the steady holding of the conscious Light within on the subject of the thinking. Briefly stated, thinking is of four stages: selecting the subject; holding the conscious Light on that subject; focusing the Light; and the focus of the Light. When the Light is focused, the subject is known...

Kindredness of Mind

In the context of the widespread turmoil in American Theosophy which followed the death of W.Q. Judge in 1896, H.W. Percival organized in New York a group called the Theosophical Society Independent. For a number of years he served as its President, both giving lectures and developing into a remarkable conversationalist. In 1904 he began to bring out an occult monthly named *The Word.* His Theosophical Publishing Co. of New York further reprinted various books on occult subjects.

He continued looking after his mother until her death in 1905. Three years later, in 1908, a group of friends to which he belonged acquired and began to work some five hundred acres of farmland, orchards and an associated cannery up the Hudson river about 70 miles north of New York.

★

Among Percival's close friends was a certain Benoni B. Gattell. Although the date of their first meeting is not recorded, it had certainly taken place by 1895 at the latest. From 1902 onwards they lived together in New York in the very same house, and continued doing so for the next 30 or more years.

On 2 January 1932 Gattell wrote a preface (in later editions reordered as an afterword) to a substantial work which Percival had been dictating to him at intervals over the previous 20 years, eventually published in 1946 under the title *Thinking and Destiny*. In the course of his preface Gattell stated:

> While Percival published the volumes of *The Word* from October 1904 to September 1917 he dictated some of the editorials to me, and the others to another friend. They were dictated hurriedly, to be published in the next issue of *The Word*...
>
> Percival at that time intended to tell enough to enable everyone who wished to find out something about who he was, where he was and his destiny. Generally, his chief object was to bring readers of *The Word* to an understanding of the states in which they are conscious...

D.N. Dunlop was just such a reader. When in February and March 1911 he read the editorials on 'Friendship' in *The Word*, they brought him—in the terminology used by Percival and Gattell—to an understanding of the state in which he was conscious of friendship. He became indeed so absorbed by these editorials that the first half of his address on 18 June (the half published in the August issue of *The Path*) was taken up in paraphrasing them. But he did not mention his source, simply presenting the paraphrase as if it were his own work.

He only made two original additions to the text of his paraphrase. One came about halfway through:

> ... Friends will be drawn together as naturally as a magnet attracts iron ... and sometimes, if friends part, although years may intervene between the parting and the meeting, they will experience this: that it is just as if they had parted an hour before, there is no need of any explanations or apologies, distance has made no difference in the relationship of friendship.

The other came at the very end. For towards the conclusion of his second editorial Percival stated:

> True mental friendships begin or are formed by the contact and appreciation of mind with mind. This may result from association, or without either one having seen the other. Some of the strongest friendships have been formed where neither friend had seen the other. A noted instance is that of the

friendship between Emerson and Carlyle. Kindredness of mind was recognized and appreciated by Emerson when he read *Sartor Resartus*. In the author of that book Emerson at once perceived a friend, and communicated with Carlyle, who had an equally keen appreciation for Emerson's mind. Later Emerson visited Carlyle. Their personalities did not agree, but their friendship continued through life, and it did not end.

Dunlop in the text of his address compressed this paragraph into a couple of sentences, and then went on:

> ... It was based on the enduring element in the nature of each, where spiritual friendships are formed—on the relationship between mind and mind, a calm, firm, deep-seated conviction as the result of experience. You may patch up a friendship on a false basis, and you will be perpetually in fear lest you may do something which will dislocate that friendship. But if it is based upon such a poor understanding of the very necessary elements of an enduring friendship, it is better disturbed. So also with the tenderness that will not disturb the peculiar bliss of another. You may not like to disturb that apparent peace, but if it is necessary for the continuation of a friendship that you should never express your own views upon any matter because they may be different from those of another, that friendship will not endure from life to life.(*To be continued.*)

★

In the remaining space at the foot of the page was reproduced W.B. Yeats's poem 'The Indian upon God':

I passed along the water's edge below the humid trees,
My spirit rocked in evening light, the rushes round my knees,
My spirit rocked in sleep and sighs; and saw the moor-fowl pace
All dripping on a grassy slope, and heard them cease to chase
Each other round in circles, and heard the eldest speak:
Who holds the world between his bill and made us strong or weak,
Is an undying moorfowl, and He lives beyond the sky.
The rains are from His dripping wing, the moonbeams from His eye.

I passed a little further on and heard a lotus talk:
Who made the world and ruleth it, He hangeth on a stalk.
For I am in his image made, and all this tinkling tide
Is but a sliding drop of rain between his petals wide.
A little way within the gloom a roebuck raised his eyes
Brimful of starlight, and he said: *The Stamper of the Skies,*
He is a gentle roebuck; for how else, I pray, could he
Conceive a thing so sad and soft, a gentle thing like me?

I passed a little further on and heard a peacock say:
Who made the grass and made the worms and made my feathers gay,
He is a monstrous peacock, and He waveth all the night
His languid tail above us lit with myriad spots of light.

From Life to Life

The continued text which printed the second half of D.N. Dunlop's address on 'Friendship' on 18 June 1911 followed in the September number of *The Path*. But in contradistinction to the first half, it was entirely his own original work.

> Friendship forbids the surrender of honour, it forbids the acquiescence to requests often made in selfishness and pettiness, it forbids blind folly, it requires one to follow his own beliefs, to be independent in thought and to offer reasonable resistance to all not believed right in the friend. Those who see into the spiritual nature of friendship are not influenced by the desires and emotions which may become manifest in friends. They have strength to stand alone if necessary. With strangers we cannot be ourselves. They will not let us; they do not know. With our friend we cannot help being ourselves; explanations are unnecessary. The true friend, differing widely in view, will tolerate with perfect joy and gladness the variety of expression in his friend, and the friendship will be far more likely to remain through all storms that may arise. So that we find how necessary it is that there should be this understanding between man and woman, between husband and wife, parents and children, as they agree to maintain the true recognition of the mental freedom of each, the freedom to think and act in accordance with what seems right to each. But remember you can never lose anything that is yours in another individual! What is kindred to you in another will always return to you. We must develop within ourselves a knowledge of our own nature, and then will come this absolute tolerance for the diversities of each other, this comprehension of the underlying and eternal bond which unites us all through the entire structure of life from top to bottom—the Jacob's ladder, the 'coat of many colours'. Nature is one great immortal fountain of eternal life and energy and we are expressions of that, and our friend has the same right as we to his expression of life in every direction. A recognition of this truth will eventually bring about a relationship between man and woman of which the world at present knows nothing. For when a man and woman rise above the realm of desire in their association and direct the energies for higher uses, there is no thought of sex. If man works with woman, linked in a common service, for a common need in the evolution of humanity, in any direction, the thought of sex is not present. That

element belongs to another level of consciousness, and it may enter only when the mind is taken away from that greater work which involves mental activity. But a knowledge of the nature of each will soon overcome the difficulties which may arise in that way. True knowledge of the nature of man, although it may be gleaned from books, does not really begin at all until you establish a pure relationship with another. That constitutes the book of life, that is the Secret Doctrine, the real Secret Doctrine. The tests that come to you in such relationships are the tests of the Mysteries. By knowing all the tests which Nature and experience can give you, you learn gradually how to overcome all the temptations of the lower nature. Men should, where possible, have the help of women who are above the level of the lower desires. Only so can a true balance be brought about between the sexes. Then man and woman, hand in hand, will stand complete in themselves, in one consuming flame of love. Their children will be children of the race, and they will seek no other expression of love than that which can be found in humanity. This expression begins generally with one or two. Where two or three are gathered together in the name of friendship, there is the Lord of Life in the heart of each, and all distinctions are risen above—sex distinctions, diversities of opinion, all fall to their own level. The united love of such friends and comrades will create a condition that represents the total consciousness of the whole. I cannot tell what experiences my brain has passed through, the ages of experience through which man has passed, but if I can unite myself in love and sympathy with one or two such comrades or friends, the experience is never to be forgotten. Through balance, patience, toleration and love we will meet at the trysting place where mind meets mind and finds the Master; and that is the kind of relationship between man and woman that will ultimately redeem the race. It is a foreshadowing of the love which the saviours showed. The experience between the Magdalen and the Master is one of the most beautiful known. There is nothing to touch it in its human purity and love. How she sprinkles the oil and the Master understands the act of recognition—the cry of the soul to the Master Soul in man!

Such recognition, such knowledge, must be learned through the diversities of the personality, and by the knowledge thus gained man *makes friends* and learns how to build abiding friendships which will last from life to life and from age to age. We can never lose that bond which is inherent in the true nature of man and exists between two comrades who understand. But it is well that some of the relationships of life should not be perpetuated. Why, it is impossible to conceive of it! They are not on a high enough level. And some relationships you will not wish to perpetuate, they belong to a different order and 'go to their own place'. They have done their work in furnishing the conditions necessary for a certain experience. We shall all be in physical conditions where certain trying experiences will arise, such as little explosions of temper, etc. I feel that is human, and we will be a part of humanity for some time to come. But I never like to see this disturbance wait long, because it reacts on the inner bodies and affects seriously the inner nature. Establish peace as soon as you can, and in that moment of equilibrium there will grow a greater love. You will swallow up all that temper in the emotion of love. That is how the chickens come home to roost. Do not regret. When you have lost your temper, lose it entirely and come back to the quiet place of peace in your mind, and there will flow out a love which will arise and burn out all differences.

I think it is one of the healthiest signs that women are learning to love women, to know the bond of comradeship between themselves, because if women begin to understand these things you can easily see that through the function they perform in building bodies they will have a tremendous effect on the evolution of humanity. In that wonderful way that she herself only knows, a woman has the positive and negative elements balanced in her own being—negative without, positive within, in order to build up and mould the structure in which a human mind and soul can incarnate and lead the involving life to a knowledge of itself.

I said an individual begins by having one or two friends, and finally becomes a friend to all. What better, what more wonderful expression would you find for anyone to attain to, 'He is the friend of all creatures'? He probably began by having one friend, that extended to two or three, and so on, until, through them, he knew all. Then linked with all other men he finally enters the world, a Master of Life, having complete control. But he has reached this because he has seen and known, through experience, that that experience extended to and included all, and this is what the world needs in a redeemer. He appears 'born in a manger', through humble parents. That is true spiritually. That is the method of appearance of one who is a Master of Life. He comes humbly, without any blare of trumpets, he comes because of his tremendous passion of love for humanity, because he knows through experience of life and love that it is by an understanding of that same experience that all men will be brought into the fold of love. We can call him the friend of all creatures, not only of men and women, but of the animal and the other kingdoms below. He sees this great creative thought and energy and love through all the mistakes and veils of time, and he makes no distinction, no explanations, but utters the laws of his being, because he knows they are the laws of all true being.

At the foot of the page where this conclusion stood, there was still some space left, which was filled by a poem from Walt Whitman:

I dream'd in a dream I saw a city invincible to the attacks of the whole of the rest of the Earth,
I dream'd that was the new City of Friends,

Nothing was greater there than the quality of robust love, it led the rest,
It was seen every hour in the actions of the men of that city,
And in all their looks and words.

My Best Thoughts

On 1 September 1911 *The Vâhan* published a small notice headed 'Rosicrucian Lodge':

> The opening of the above lodge will take place on September 3, at 11.15 a.m.; open to members of the Lodge only.

Herbert Heywood-Smith recorded:

> To our great delight we received on the day a telegram from Rudolf Steiner with the words 'My best thoughts are today with you'. This telegram remains one of our most treasured possessions.[23]

★

A week later, the next European Theosophical Congress, due to be held at Genoa, was cancelled at just a few days' notice. *Theosophy in Scotland* reported:

> The Federated Congress of European Sections had to be abandoned almost at the last moment owing to quarantine precautions at Genoa. Many members were actually on their way.
>
> Perhaps some of those who were thus disappointed may avail themselves of the opportunity of attending Dr. Rudolf Steiner's course of lectures 'From Jesus to Christ' from 4th to 14th inst., in Karlsruhe, Baden. Arrangements are made by English students enabling those visitors who desire it to hear a resumé of the lecture in English each following day. All information may be obtained from Herr Hugo Harden, Edelsheim Str. 5, Karlsruhe, Baden, Germany.

Many, if not most members who had been on their way to the Congress were from the German Section. They were hoping for a showdown with Annie Besant over the Alcyone affair, which she had been vigorously promoting in London.

The reasons for cancellation of the Congress gave rise to extensive and long-lasting controversy. This is what *The Vâhan* stated:

> We extend our cordial sympathy to our colleagues of the Italian National Society. At the eleventh hour the Congress, for which they had made such ample and well-planned preparations, had to be abandoned owing to the

prevalence of cholera in Italy. The actual danger from cholera itself in Genoa was not great, but the President and her party could not afford to run the imminent risk of quarantine, as this would have meant the loss of four passages to India, with boats so full that later accomodation was doubtful. As a matter of fact quarantine was being imposed at that time. The fear of infection was keeping many people away, and as the enforced absence of the President would have entailed a still more scanty attendance, it was wisely decided by the Italian General Secretary to drop the Congress. We note that the International Peace Congress, which was to have been held in Italy, was also abandoned.

★

With regard to forthcoming events at home, *The Vâhan* went on to include the syllabus of the Rosicrucian Lodge:

During the winter months lectures will be given by Mr. Heywood-Smith on various subjects connected with the Rosicrucian teachings based upon Dr. Steiner's lectures, commencing with a course on 'Rosicrucian Theosophy'. This will be followed by a course on 'Evolution', and afterwards by a course on 'The Gospel of John'. A Healing Class will be held in connection with the Lodge.[24] Lectures will be given on Thursday evenings during September at 8.30 p.m., at 37, Ridgmount Gardens, W.C.

As a result of the lectures two further members joined the Lodge, Vera Scott and Aimée Furnivall, who were issued with diplomas on 27 September.

So the Rosicrucian Lodge now consisted of Herbert Heywood-Smith and no less than 14 ladies!

★

The Rosicrucian Lodge was not however the only British theosophical group where Steiner's ideas were being examined. *The Vâhan* also published a notice headed 'Blavatsky Institute':

The syllabus of lectures for the session October to December 1911 has been arranged and includes several new features. On Sunday the 'Lotus Circle' will be continued and also the addresses at 7 p.m. by Mr. D.N. Dunlop. The usual classes for the study of the *Key to Theosophy*, *Isis Unveiled*, *Secret Doctrine* and *Modern Panarion* will be conducted by Mr. C.A. Lazenby, B.A., who will also lecture on philosophy and psychology and give readings from the World Scriptures.

The works of Mrs. Annie Besant, of Mr. C.W. Leadbeater, and of Dr. Steiner will be studied in classes conducted by Mr. F.S. Snell, B.A.

> The method of presenting Theosophy to the working class will be developed in a group under Mr. E.C. Reed.
>
> Theosophical psychology, based on the new book *In the Light of Theosophy*, will be presented by Mrs. W.W. Leisenring, B.A., who will also lead discussions on the recent philosophers William James, Bergson and Deussen.
>
> Mr. G.R.S. Mead's book *Echoes from the Gnosis* will be studied in classes under the direction of Mrs. Elinor Dunlop.
>
> Brother Atisha will continue his Friday evening lectures, taking as subject for this term Greek Theosophy. On Saturday evenings a general discussion of theosophical problems will be held, with different members of the staff in the chair. Beginning in November, the first Saturday evening in each month will be thrown open for social reunion with music, etc.
>
> The Secretary of the Blavatsky Institute, Hale, will send a syllabus of lectures on application.

But in the Blavatsky Institute there would only have been access to Steiner's published books and booklets—not to the lecture-cycles, which, even when they existed in translation, were still restricted, and probably not available at all outside the Rosicrucian Lodge in London.

Nor is there reason to suppose that Dunlop had at this time any particular interest in Steiner's work. The main substance of his thoughts was derived in these years not from Middle Europe but on the contrary from America. The October number of *The Path* reproduced an address he had given on 4 June entitled 'Individuality and Personality', which was almost entirely drawn from an editorial on 'Individuality' published some five years earlier by H.W. Percival in the January 1906 number of *The Word*.

★

Another book by Steiner newly brought out in English by Max Gysi was *Mystics of the Renaissance*. The translator was Bertram Keightley, who nine years previously had paraphrased it so extensively in *The Theosophical Review*. A note in *The Vâhan* stated:

> For a reviewer to try and summarize this highly condensed little work is like trying to give extracts of some essential oil.
>
> In a small compass we are given six essays on the most metaphysical of European mystics.
>
> The highest and deepest possibilities of the human soul are rapidly touched upon and a Herculean attempt is made to bring the greatest mystics face to face with the giants of German scientific modernism.

★

During this winter of 1911 the musician Arnold Bax came to live in Dublin. In his autobiography *Farewell my Youth* (1943), he recorded:

No sooner was I settled in than Clifford was invited to stay with me. He had known George Russell ('AE') for some years, and we lost no time in going round the corner to 17 Rathgar Avenue, that I might be introduced to the poet whose work I had always revered.

We were warmly welcomed, and whilst I prowled round the walls of the studio examining iridescent paintings of children playing or dancing by the sea's edge, or strange delineations of the sidhe, the fairies and elementals, I listened for the first time to one of those mellifluous if often almost incoherent rhapsodical monologues . . .

The pictures enthralling me, and finding myself a little out of my depth in the ethereal mists of that rarefied discourse, I was so silent that at last even my host noticed it, and asked if I were perhaps not interested in adventures of the soul. On my assuring him that I thought there was little else worthy of sustained consideration he looked quite relieved, and instantly invited me to come again with my brother next Sunday. It was his way to leave his front door ajar every Sunday evening, when he and his wife kept open house to his friends and any friends of theirs they might like to bring along.

At Home

The first chapter of Isabelle de Steiger's *Memorabilia: Reminiscences of a Woman Artist and Writer* (1927) opens:

I am beginning this on November 18th, 1911. I feel inclined to begin. I have put it off and off, and as I am seventy-five, I must start now or never.

I was born in 1836, February 28th, on a Sunday, in Liverpool, at number 2 Canning Street. Doubtless many other people started their lives on the same day, in the same city (it was called a town then), but I have not met any of them, so will confine myself chiefly to my own history, as it is the only one I really know much about.

I do not intend to be discursive about my childhood, for I do not think I was completely born until I was about thirty-six. This may seem an astounding statement, but probably many people will understand what I mean to express as my own experience. Have they not felt, seen and thought many things which did not seem related to their surroundings? Were they not also conscious of being unable to form a clear account of the vague inferences and deductions they intuitively drew from their surroundings? Did they not continue questioning—feeling, rather than noting, events and their consequences? Only observing people, and connecting them with thoughts and events somewhat as phantasmagoria passing slowly through their vision?

The mind is often unable to concentrate and fit itself into untried grooves, not from want of interest but from overmuch rush of interest when the brain is not as yet sufficiently developed to understand its duties and capabilities. I did not dream of evolution then!

I am now seventy-five, and just learning to regulate my enjoyment and interest in Nature and philosophy—also in interesting or uninteresting people. I like art, science, and chief of all, philosophy, more than ever.

Many people may here find that I have given a true reflection of their own minds. Those natures that are naturally critical, observant of details, with accurate memories for words rather than for ideas, noting most things from a predetermined point of view, usually grow up very quickly, and remain just as clever, or just as stupid as the case may be, all their lives. By nature they are Aristotelians of the modern school, which has so recently decided to search and research for the true meaning of Real and Ideal.

When I was about nineteen, I remember thinking to myself: 'If things were different, I could become a musician, a naturalist, a scientist, a doctor, a traveller, a writer or an artist.' The artist I put last, as I felt it included all the others, and it has proved to be the vocation for which I probably was born. But whilst I knew that art was my destiny, I felt a longing and capacity for all the others, and would like to have tried that of a naturalist. This may sound outrageously vain, but I now think it was merely the surging up of memories of past lives, though I then knew nothing of the doctrine of reincarnation. I think most artists have similar feelings—those who create pictures, who compose music—all who carry on their work in the world with an ideal beyond actual achievement, those who rarely reach their aim but keep the goal always in front.

These pioneers will follow my meaning, and understand that vanity and self-esteem cannot be implicit in such natures. I felt this to be so, and believe it to be characteristic of many. I have now after a long struggle modified my naturally very impulsive temperament, to which deliberate action was of all things the most difficult.

The very first thing I remember is standing at a big fireplace, with other people, in a great room at Steephill Castle. (A.D.1841). I fancy this was the name of a place at Ventnor, in the Isle of Wight, where I was sent by my parents from my home in Liverpool . . .

Although Isabelle de Steiger was already 75 when she began her reminiscences, she still had another 15 years of earthly life stretching away into the future. From time to time during these years she would return to her account and write a little more, not always in chronological order, but simply as things occurred to her. And rather like Rudolf Steiner in his autobiography, she interwove her memories with subsequent reflections.

She had started as a spiritualist, and in that capacity became one of the earliest British members of the Theosophical Society. Many of her memories concerned prominent theosophists from former times. One chapter began:

> London during the years from 1881 to 1890 was indeed a different place in every way from what it is now. It was very nice for the set of people in which I found myself...
>
> On one occasion, when Mr. Sinnett's *Esoteric Buddhism* and the subject of the Mahatmas were booming delightfully (Mrs. Kingsford's, Mr. Sinnett's and Madame Blavatsky's circles were not in any opposition) it was unanimously decided to join in a great 'At Home' in the large rooms of the Royal Institution in Piccadilly, where important picture exhibitions were held. Madame Blavatsky and Mrs. Kingsford with their male friends were the chief guests. There was a large crowd, and the meeting was a decided success. No entertainment was offered, and it was merely a conversazione.
>
> Madame Blavatsky's short fat form, heavily draped in black, was surrounded by her special coterie, from which she did not stir. She always received advancing neophytes with the same respectful princess-like manner, as well as the delightful and inquisitive ones, though merely visitors. She held a large fan, somewhat hiding her face, very quietly and steadily refusing all entreaties to address the audience. She always gave a decided 'No' before even being asked to mount any platform. On one occasion, in Avenue Road, when she was somewhat over-pressed to speak, I remember hearing her say, after she had consented to go into the large room for meetings, 'No, I am a pheelorsephor, noat a porleteecian,' and she hugged herself more deeply into her easy chair. She spoke beautiful English, but in short phrases, and sometimes dragged the syllables after the French manner.

Another recollection was:

> Madame Blavatsky called one day at my studio—I had one in Holland Park Road, Kensington. I remember I had no servant, and recall how with great difficulty she got out of a hansom cab unhelped, and laboured up my one flight of steep stairs. She was very bulky—shapeless, I should say—and dressed like any Victorian old lady, with no attempt at producing personal effect. Of that kind of vanity she was quite devoid, and she never impressed me with any feeling of awe or surprise, only with a cold, irritated feeling, my heart neither still nor palpitating. Of course, I was very desirous of receiving her with due honour, but we both felt mutually separate. She looked round intelligently, and I do not doubt she was of the artistic temperament. I respected her on those grounds, for she had no aversion to art, music, or Christianity as I sincerely felt Mrs. Besant had to an unusual degree. (As Mrs. Besant always had the great talent of feeling the public pulse, she was wise enough to keep silent—difficult, no doubt, but a wise policy.) H.P.B. did not stay long, just making a few sensible remarks, as many people do, of little

consequence. But she stopped before one picture, a life-size male head, and asked 'What do you call that picture?' 'John the Baptist,' I replied...

About the same time I was commissioned by Madame Blavatsky to paint a portrait of one of the two Mahatmas—of course, gratis. Mr. Schmiechen, a German artist very much in vogue for painting ladies of society in evening dress, was also commissioned to paint the other Mahatma...

The World of Truthfulness

In the same month of November 1911, the long-awaited Baron Walleen finally arrived in Britain.

At this very juncture, however, the Theosophical Society's London Headquarters were being moved yet again, into Tavistock Place. Because of the upheaval it proved impossible for Walleen to lecture at Headquarters, and he had to give his lecture elsewhere. However, he agreed to return to England again and give further lectures in the following year.

In the meantime, Herbert Heywood-Smith offered to lecture to theosophical audiences himself. *The Vâhan* announced that

> The president of the Rosicrucian Lodge, London, Mr. H.J. Heywood-Smith, is prepared to give lectures in the London district and the provinces on the following subjects:—1. The Rosicrucian Conception of Christ. 2. Rosicrucian Theosophy. 3. Cosmogenesis and Anthropogenesis. 4. The Gospel of John. 5. The Apocalypse. 6. Manifestations of Karma. 7. The Biblical Account of Creation.
>
> These lectures are based upon the Rosicrucian teaching given out by Dr. Rudolf Steiner, and are an expression of the Christian occult teachings of the West. Will those wishing to know more of these subjects please apply to the Secretary of the Rosicrucian Lodge: Mrs. H.J. Heywood-Smith, 37, Ridgmount Gardens, W.C.

★

Heywood-Smith's account continues:

> Early in December 1911 Mrs. Heywood-Smith and I journeyed to Berlin and paid our first visit to Dr. Steiner.
>
> How indelibly is everything connected with that visit imprinted in one's mind! The lodge-room in Geisbergstrasse where the group met and where we sat on 5 December, waiting for the moment when we should see our Leader for the first time in this life; how he came in, mounted the tiny platform and spoke of Death and the Mystery of Golgotha, and on a later occasion of Parsifal,[25] in words and tones that can never be forgotten.

Steiner was giving the final lecture of the course on 'Evolution from the Viewpoint of Truthfulness', and the words which Heywood-Smith could never forget were:

> If anyone comes to understand these things, to grasp how the development of Christ Himself goes forward and thereby the development of certain human faculties—grasps this through understanding spiritual science today—then when he has gone through the gate of death nothing prevents him from taking part in this event, when it really enters as a first shining of Christ into the world of men. Whoever prepares himself for this event in the physical body today can therefore also experience it in life beteween death and new birth. But those human beings who neither prepare themselves nor gain understanding of it in this incarnation cannot, in the life following on from this one, between death and new birth, know anything about what is taking place from our century onwards for the next three thousand years in regard to Christ. They have to wait till they are incarnated again, and make further preparation for it on Earth. So what had to take place as a cause of all subsequent Christ-development on Earth, the death on Golgotha and the results it created, can only be grasped inside a physical body. Among all the facts important to us for higher life, this is the only one which can only be grasped inside a physical body. It will then be further worked on, further built on in higher worlds. But we must first have grasped it inside a physical body. The Mystery of Golgotha could never have taken place in the higher worlds, nor does it have an archetype there. Since it involves death, it is an event contained within the physical plane. Understanding for it must therefore be gained here. Indeed it is actually among the tasks of a human being on the physical plane to gain this knowledge in one or other of his incarnations.
>
> We must thus say that we have also largely found something here which so-to-speak shows us direct reality on the physical plane, direct truthfulness. For what is then real on the physical plane? Death is real on the physical plane in such a way that we can stand by it and say 'Here we have something true!'—death in the world of human beings, not in other realms of Nature. And as for historical events taking place in course of earthly development, if we want to understand them we must proceed from each such historical event to a spiritual archetype. Only not with the Mystery of Golgotha. In that Mystery we have something which, just as it is, belongs directly in the world of truthfulness.

The Ideal of Cooperation

In December 1911 *The Open Door* published on its front page an item headed 'International Club'.

The editor grasped the opportunity of an interview with Mr. D.N. Dunlop when he was at the Blavatsky Institute during a weekend recently. Mr. Dunlop is a busy man and has, at present, very little time for writing. We therefore in the interests of our readers asked him several questions in regard to some phases of the many activities in which he exercises his organizing genius. We give the interview below as it was taken down by a stenographer.

'We have heard that you are planning the organization of an international club. Will you tell us something about it?'

'This club, as I am contemplating it, would be constituted of progressive societies and organizations. At present these organizations have each their definite objects, each their own system of organization, their own methods of propaganda. But many of these societies have fundamentally similar objects, and a certain amount of co-operation should be an advantage, along lines where they could unite their ideals. Nothing proposed in connection with this club would interfere in any way whatever with their individual efforts or initiative. One of the greatest of the advantages would be that these associations would have an international headquarters in London, which is still regarded as the centre of the world, where they would meet regularly and come more closely into contact with each other, each getting to understand the other's point of view. It would also be a rendezvous for thinking people from all parts of the world who visit London. They would find such a headquarters of great value, especially where they were interested in the ideas which are common to most of the societies associated with the club.'

'Would there be anything in this which has never been done before?'

'Yes, in many repects. The tendency of all progressive societies at the beginning is to segregate themselves out from the orthodox organizations, and while that is necessary in the beginning, the time is now arriving when the ideal of co-operation must be brought definitely before them so that they can unite together. Individuals who feel the significance of some one special phase of thought break away from an existing organization in order to make themselves separate from the general tendency, in order to emphasize one or two features which they consider absolutely essential to progress. In this way societies have increased very rapidly during the last few years, but I think the time has now come when they may be brought together for the advantage of each individual society.'

'You wish to promote a general feeling of universal brotherhood and understanding. But can you not give us a more definite idea of the advantages of this new club?'

'The club will answer a necessity which is universally arising. In the world today the ideals of co-operation are being fully recognized in every direction, in farming, in trade, in commerce generally, and in the conditions existing between labour and capital the absolute necessity for co-operation if satisfactory progress is to be made is now recognized. It is the tendency of the present age to co-operate for mutual advantage, in fact it is an absolute necessity. In the first place it is necessary for self-preservation, and also for mutual benefit. For example, most societies of the kind to which I have been alluding begin as a rule with a great wave of enthusiasm. Many societies enlist in their ranks at the beginning a large number of young men and women who have become weary of the older organizations, with all their limitations of creed and form and ceremony, and who realize how necessary it is to have a constructive programme. This is where the experience of some societies can be of considerable advantage to others, so that when the period of waning enthusiasm arises in one, as it is sure to do in the evolution of all organizations of this kind, there will be ready to hand the experience of men and women who have been associated with similar movements in the past and who are able to contribute to these various societies the results of their experience and thus tide them over this time of ebbing enthusiasm.'

'You are prominently identified with the Theosophical Society, I believe, Mr. Dunlop. Do I infer from your remarks that there is a waning enthusiasm there?'

'No, but the enthusiasm takes a different direction nowadays. Unfortunately the Theosophical Society, although it provides the broadest platform of any organization in the world, has become rather indifferent to the broader phases of thought outside the Society and has got into rather restricted lines of investigation. It attracts a certain type of student, especially those interested in psychic phenomena and research. But on the other hand the restrictions with which it is surrounded, in the minds of many other types of enquirers, make it impossible to regard the society as the only organization for this work of bringing together men and women of all shades of opinion who are seeking, like the members of the Theosophical Society, to bring about a nucleus of universal brotherhood, although they necessarily differ as to the means by which this is to be accomplished.'

'But this, I suppose, implies restriction only in the minds of those who do not properly understand the objects of the Society, not in the Society itself?'

'You speak as if there were but one Theosophical Society. A glance at the Directory of Societies on the back page of *The Open Door* will show that there are at least seven springing from the parent Society founded by Madame Blavatsky in New York in 1875. This fact is frequently overlooked. There is need for unity here as elsewhere. I look forward to the time when all can co-operate together again, without impairing their advantages as separate organizations in matters of government. I think all these Theosophical Societies are somewhat restricted—I think their methods necessarily imply restrictions. The Adyar Society tends to become identified exclusively with the views of its President. For instance, Mrs. Besant has lately launched a movement which has for its principal object the preparation for 'The Coming Christ' and in the minds of a great many people this is identified with the Theosophical Society (Adyar). Even in the publications of the Theosophical Society one repeatedly finds this confusion.'

'You conclude, then, that we need a fresh platform for the expression of the world's thought?'

'Personally, I think the Theosophical Movement includes all Theosophical Societies. I regard the Adyar Theosophical Society as being only one of the organizations within the Theosophical Movement. It is doing excellent work within definite channels. But we require a platform which will, to some extent, serve for the creation of a viewpoint that will embrace within its field all organizations which have aims identical with the Theosophical Movement. The idea of the second coming of Christ may be a good thing in itself, and I am not prepared to say that it has not great value for many, but all impartial students of philosophy and comparative religion will recognize at once that if it were to come about as prophesied, it will be only another of the systems of religion which they have to study and compare with existing religions, so that they may discover in what way it leads them closer to a realization of the Living Christ within themselves. The club would in fact encourage ideas of this kind being discussed, and welcome the exponents of all religions, old and new.'

'Might I ask what the name of the club is to be?'

'The name has not yet been decided. The first duty of the organization will be to call together a suitable number of the representatives of progressive organizations who have headquarters in London, with the object of starting a club on a broad basis, and to decide upon the name and various other necessary details of organization, rules of membership, etc.'

'Do you think many societies will come into this club?'

'Yes. I have been brought to realize the necessity for some effort of this kind through my experience with the International Theosophical Summer Schools during the last two or three years. For instance, at 'The Hayes', in Derbyshire, in August of this year, visitors to the Summer School came from England, Ireland, Scotland, Canada, United States, Russia, Germany, Austria, Denmark, Finland, Sweden, Norway, France, Holland, India, etc., and in various discussions I had with them during the School sessions they all said how very useful such an organization would be, especially with central premises as headquarters in London.'

'You propose, then, that your Summer School should be promoted by the Societies composing this club?'

'Yes, I believe that the Summer Schools in future will be organized by this international club. Already plans have been formulated for conducting next year's Summer School on broader lines than ever before, and efforts will be made to interest such men as Prof. Bergson, Prof. Thomson, of Aberdeen University, etc. There will probably be different departments, as a department of religion, a department of philosophy, ancient and modern, a department of science, of sociology and social service, of arts and crafts, of occultism, mysticism, spiritualism, etc. There would be certain general gatherings at which all the departments would be represented, but a good deal of departmental activity would be necessary to cover the field under each head satisfactorily and adequately. In my opinion, such an international gathering, representing so many phases of thought and human activity, will command the attention of the press and have a stimulating influence upon the minds of thinking people in all countries. It would also tend in a vital way to remove racial prejudices.'

'What will be the special activities of the headquarters in London? Do you expect to have a residential club, courses of lectures, etc.?'

'Yes, I think it will probably be more convenient to have it a residential club, although that may not be possible at the beginning. There would be courses of lectures arranged, and eminent men in their respective departments would be invited to lecture from time to time, and I believe it would be advisable to conduct classes occasionally for the study of subjects in which the various progressive organizations are interested.'

'Have you yet any idea as to the site of the building, or the district?'

'I can only say that it will be as central as possible, probably somewhere in the West Central district.'

'You have been an organizer and the Director of the Blavatsky Institute. Does this new club mean that the Blavatsky Institute will go out of existence?'

'No. I believe the activities of the Blavatsky Institute will go on and be more necessary than ever. In my opinion there is great need of an opportunity to study systematically and thoroughly the works of Madame Blavatsky.'

'Is that not being done anywhere at present?'

'I do not think it is being done anywhere in the way in which it ought to be done. In fact, I have heard some prominent theosophists refer to the *Secret Doctrine* as 'a much overrated book'. But I believe this statement to be due to the fact that such theosophists have not studied it.'

'Is this work not out of date by this time? When was it published?'

'In 1888, I believe, and it will never be out of date.'

'That is rather a sweeping statement! Scientific and philosophical books rapidly go out of date.'

'I am glad that is so. I think it is absolutely in the nature of things that such books should go out of date. The conclusions arrived at are, as a rule, based upon data which later discoveries alter, and therefore new statements are necessary. But the *Secret Doctrine* is a book in quite a different class. The statements and conclusions arrived at in it are based upon fundamentals, which are, practically speaking, unchangeable. I do not mean to say by this that the *Secret Doctrine* is an infallible book. I have no doubt there are statements in it that may be successfully controverted, but, speaking broadly, I think it is a book for the future, and that it will be studied more and more as the years go by. Personally, every time I go to this work to study any particular subject, I find more and more what an inexhaustible storehouse it is. Of course, in the Blavatsky Institute other books are studied. Thinkers of all schools are studied, but the Blavatsky Institute exists principally for the study of Theosophy as presented to the world through Madame Blavatsky.'

'Will the Blavatsky Institute remain at Hale?'

'No. It will be removed to some suitable place near London.'

'Will it be located at the headquarters of the international club?'

'No. The club will be an entirely separate organization. It will not be identified more with the Institute than with any other organization. The only requirement will be that the organizations associated together in the club will recognize the necessity for co-operation in forming a nucleus of the universal brotherhood of humanity, without any distinctions whatever.'

'Is not Mrs. Besant building a place in London which will practically serve the same purpose?'

'Yes. I believe it is intended that the new Theosophical Headquarters should be an international centre, but it will be some time before it is ready, and I do not think it will serve the same purpose as the club which I have described. I wish to emphasize again that the Theosophical Society is only *one* of the organizations making for righteousness in the world. And a great many people have prejudices against the name because it has become identified in their minds with sectarianism and psychism. I do not say that this is true, but this prejudice exists, and we have to recognize it.'

'I see you prefer to use the word "club" rather than some other, "association" for instance?'

'Yes. I think the various associations existing separately with their own rules and regulations and methods of activity will need a headquarters where they can all "club" together, so that the members will become better acquainted with each other, and this headquarters should have all the benefits which have become associated with the ideal club.'

'Then it would have reading-room and library?'

'Yes. Reading-room, library and other entertaining rooms.'

'Will you require a publication as an organ for this club?'

'Not at the beginning, certainly. That is an ideal for the future. At present a number of the organizations have small publications of their own, and it may be possible at a later date to amalgamate them in one representative organ, to the great advantage of all, but that is a matter for future development.

'I might say in conclusion that events of the last few months particularly indicate that the time has come for the crystallization of thought into the organization of a club of this kind. During last summer, we had the Universal Races Congress, the International Theosophical Summer School with its broad platform and varied activities, the visit of Mrs. Besant and the growing interest in her lectures, the visit of Abdul Baha and the great interest taken in the spread of the Bahai movement throughout the world, the visit of Prof. Bergson, etc. And on all sides we see evidences of general interest in the researches and discoveries of modern science, and their approximation to the position of the mystic and occultist. There is also a growing desire on the part of people of all countries for the settlement of disputes by arbitration, and progress is being made towards unity by the Churches of various denominations, so that the growth of brotherhood generally points to the necessity for a centre like that described by Walt Whitman:—

'Within their walls shall all that forwards perfect human life be stated,
None but shall here be honoured, helped, exampled.'

Not Present in Our Movement

Since the Heywood-Smiths stayed on in Berlin for several weeks, they were probably guests at the Annual General Meeting of the German Section on 10 December. They would certainly have attended Rudolf Steiner's next lecture-cycle, from the 12th to the 16th, on the subject of 'Pneumatosophy'.

Halfway through this cycle, on the 14th, came also a lecture from Baron Walleen, about 'Experiences on lecture-tours in Scandinavia and England'. Walleen described the hindrances which representatives of the spiritual stream issuing from Steiner's teachings were encountering in non-German-speaking countries. During a discussion on the next day, he went on to explain that theosophical friends from abroad who recognized Steiner as their own special teacher wished to create an independent union (in German *Bund*). A committee was formed to forward the work of this *Bund*.

*

On 16 December a class was held for the Mystica Aeterna. During such occasions notes were not permitted to be taken. Afterwards, however, one participant wrote down from memory what Steiner had said:

> It might be thought that the concern here is to establish what is generally called 'Freemasonry', but that is not so. However secretly Freemasonry may have been cultivated in former times, it has nonetheless always been something external. Freemasonry originally appeared in the world through a betrayal in the Mystery Schools, and it therefore comes about that many symbols found in Freemasonry are also found here. Through pupils who were not sufficiently penetrated by their value and meaning, these symbols from the Mystery Schools made their way into what for the outer world are secret societies. But secret societies, which are known under the general name of Freemasonry, have never been able to grasp and explain the symbols' real depth. The holiness of these symbols by itself brings about that they cannot be properly understood outside the occult temple.
>
> For the world at large, our occult stream has till now borne the name of Freemasonry, because from an occult standpoint one should always if possible link onto what exists. But as regards our temple this name will from now on fall away, and our arrangements will be called '*Misraim-Dienst*'. If wanting to indicate our occult service, one may abbreviate it with the initials 'M.D.' The term 'F.M.' should now finally disappear, and as far as the outer world and all arrangements on a Freemasonic basis are concerned, Freemasonry is thus not present in our Movement. If we are asked whether any Freemasonry also belongs to our Movement, it may be denied without expressing an untruth. What is established here is an occult service, called 'Misraim service', which is intended to mean: bringing about a union of the earthly with the heavenly, the visible with the invisible.
>
> Misraim service was already known in ancient Egypt and was among the most practised services in the Mystery Schools. In our temple this same service will now also be established, with the added expansions and reforms brought about by Mark. The Mark referred to here is that pupil of Peter, one of the twelve apostles, who wrote the Gospel of Mark while resident in Egypt as Bishop of Alexandria. Together with an Egyptian initiate he made new rules for the occult service (cult), which we now know as Misraim service.

★

Herbert Heywood-Smith concluded the account of his first stay in Berlin:

> We remained more than five weeks on that occasion, had our first audience with Dr. Steiner, and accompanied him to Hanover for the course of

lectures on 'The World of Sense and the World of Spirit'. Then we returned to Berlin for a few days longer before journeying home.

★

During the time when the Heywood-Smiths were in Germany listening to the spoken words of Rudolf Steiner, D.N. Dunlop was continuing to recompose under his own name the written words of H.W. Percival. In November and December 1911 *The Path* printed addresses he had given on 'The Law of Periodicity' and 'Breath' which in part related to a series of editorials on the zodiac in *The Word*, and in January 1912 a further address on 'Will' also paraphrased from an editorial of that title published in *The Word* almost six years previously, in March 1906, with merely a couple of original paragraphs added at the end.

★

Meanwhile, *The Vâhan* printed a further announcement about 'Dr. Rudolf Steiner's teachings':

> Baron Walleen, President of the Steiner Lodge, Copenhagen, will visit this country in the end of January and the commencement of February for the purpose of lecturing on the above.
>
> All arrangements have not been completed but full particulars will be sent to anyone interested on application being made to H.N. Croxford, 115, Riverview Gardens, Barnes, S.W.

In the next issue at the start of February, by contrast, theosophists were given an account of the Annual Convention at Adyar, India, which included an arresting extract from Annie Besant's Presidential address:

> It is no secret that the situation in Germany has caused much anxiety in more than one National Society. Fortunately the difficulty has not been so acute in this country as in some others; but we welcome with much satisfaction the following pronouncement:
>
> 'In Germany the movement goes forward energetically on the lines laid down by Dr. Steiner. These differ considerably from the generally accepted theosophical teachings by giving to Christianity a primacy which non-Christian nations could not accept, but which suits German ideas. The perfect freedom of thought within the T.S. secures full expression for schools of thought however divergent, but it should be remembered that non-German schools of thought have equally the right of free expression, and that a militant propaganda in other National Societies against the views of other theosophical exponents is not conducive either to liberty of thought or harmony of action. Even in Germany a growing number of theosophists prefer the older and wider teachings to the new, and while as

President I defend the right of every exponent to teach his own views, it is also my duty to protect as far as possible the holders of other opinions from undue interference. The General Secretary for Germany will, I am sure, assist me in smoothing the friction which is arising in other National Societies by the action of his more aggressive followers, so that all may pursue in peace the studies which they prefer.'

Endeavours for the Bund

'The work thus commenced in England grew rapidly,' continued Herbert Heywood-Smith. 'Our little flat at 37 Ridgmount Gardens, W.C. was soon crowded out, and when the number had reached about thirty we were packed so closely that there was little air-space and it became necessary to find larger quarters. With the need came the friend. Mr. Collison visited the Group one evening—he was a member then in Munich—and offered his studio for our meetings. From this time Mr. Collison became an indefatigable worker; he devoted his energies and material resources to the spreading of Dr. Steiner's teachings in England and to the publication of the books.'

Already towards the end of 1911 Collison had brought out an English version of Rudolf Steiner's latest book, *The Spiritual Guidance of Man and of Humanity*. The publisher was John M. Watkins in London.

Heywood-Smith went on:

> The work was also assisted very much by periodical visits from Baron Walleen, who gave lectures publicly. It was at the close of one of his lectures in Eustace Miles's Restaurant that a lady asked to be placed in touch with Dr. Steiner's workers in London; it was Mrs. Drury-Lavin, who became one of Dr. Steiner's best helpers in England. She entered enthusiastically into the work—it was in February 1912—and within a short time gathered together a circle of seventeen friends ready to hear lectures.

From this month onwards there survives some correspondence from Collison to Heywood-Smith, chiefly concerning various problems of their developing organization.

Here is the first letter: (E.S. = Esoteric School)

Windham Club,
St James's Square,
S.W.
13th Feb. 1912

My dear Smith,

People are asking me to form a lodge at the studio. There are too many lodges already; I do not want to do that. But I want you to help me in getting a large group together (not the Bund) or started before B. Walleen goes, & then that group can have its offshoots. At present we do not know what the other is doing & it looks as if we were all at war with one another. A little frankness, a little confidence is wanted. I see no reason for what looks like mystery, especially as the mystery is so soon exploded. I heard of a meeting that would take place under you at Eastbourne & another somewhere tonight, accompanied with the words 'Perhaps I ought not to say'. If it is an E.S. then they should be more careful. I am very glad to hear you have other groups, but it sounds so odd coming second-hand. If I do not know of your groups, however, & you will not tell me the members of your groups, we shall be continually clashing in our endeavours for the Bund. I think it would be easier to work if we worked together & got one large group. If you want to call it your group please do. It is you who started the first Steiner lodge, & I am the last person in the world to grudge you the honours you so well deserve.

It may be these groups are getting out of hand. It is high time they were controlled. The other day I found in the house of a lady I understood to be quite a novice (I now hear she is not, but it makes no difference) a whole series of the Doctor's lectures lying on the sofa!—The supply of Steiner literature ought to be kept very strictly under the control of Bund representatives; otherwise I see no reason for the Bund.

I suggest that you at once say you are going to do (this is for you to choose) one of these alternatives:—

1. Hold the lodge in my studio every Thursday evening & invite the whole of Baron Walleen's audience to come on payment of ? shillings a lecture.

2. Choose a day to lecture to the group now forming at the studio & invite the lodge & all your group to it.

In addition on one afternoon every week we will have a less advanced meeting at which people will ask questions.

We shall thus by either means get our big group together & then after a short time start dividing the group into sections & selecting our Bund people.

You really have no more room at present at 37 R. Gardens, so a lodge room will have to be got. Here you have one ready & to which people have got accustomed. I would not wait till B. Walleen's lectures are over; I would get people into the 'outer group' while they are warm to it. This will help in our selection. At any rate an announcement should be made at once, & by you. If you cannot come tomorrow, let me know by return post to the studio if you consent to my saying it, & if you consent to 1 or 2.

People are getting impatient & Baron Walleen expects to take away with him a prospective list of our Bund people here.

Yours very sincerely,

Harry Collison

Please answer this to the studio if you are not coming.

The Wish was Father to the Thought

A further letter examined the alternative ideas of erecting for Rudolf Steiner's work a purpose-built headquarters or of acquiring for the same purpose a house in Kensington:

Windham Club,
St. James's Square,
S.W.
21st February, 1912

Dear Smith,

It seems that some inaccuracies are flying about which may cause more mischief than intended. It is therefore as well that you should have a copy of what I said today at the meeting.

On Monday I said that as far as the building scheme was concerned I heartily agreed, but it could hardly come about just yet. I thought it a little premature to have mentioned it. I said however the wish was father to the thought.

I am still of the same opinion as I have always been.—I also said that my studio was a makeshift & a lodge room would have to be found.

It would have been unnecessary to have said anything had you not taken on yourself to speak for the whole house committee without asking my opinion or consent. I was therefore forced to speak for myself later; it would have created a disturbance if I had interfered. I was strictly loyal to what you said in the morning about expenses & subscriptions in England.

You will be good enough to take my retirement from the committee as addressed to you as well as to Mrs. Stewart.

Yours sincerely,

Harry Collison

Copy of my letter to Mrs. Stewart:—

I have never changed my opinion of the house scheme. I think the idea an excellent one, but as I have said before, it is no good taking a house until we know who are going to be tenants.

Then the landlord will have to be approached & there are many difficulties, of which in my profession I have had some experience. The difficulties will I think be surmounted, but until something more has been achieved I think it unwise to mention the matter in public.

It is most unfortunate to start with a misunderstanding & if Mr. Smith & yourself desire it I shall be happy to retire from the committee. Indeed I think it would be better to do so. At the same time I shall be ready to help if the little assistance I can give can be of any service.

Perhaps you will be good enough to show this letter to Mr. Smith.

verbatim H.C. 21.2.12.

Baron W. has kindly consented to give an extra lecture here on Saturday next at 4.30. This will be outside the course of lectures & open to anyone who can find sitting accommodation. A small collection will be made on behalf of the new Society; that is, towards the expenses at headquarters at Stuttgart, for I must remind you that all expenses in the first instance will be incurred there in starting the Society. The Society is international & exists in order to give facilities to anyone wishing to study Dr. Steiner's works, which till lately were only available for members of the T.S. There are no rules, no formalities, & no dogma.

Mr. Smith will tomorrow at 8. p.m. continue his lectures on the Gospel of Saint John. He has promised to give an afternoon's lecture in addition every Wednesday, after Baron W.'s departure. I hope Mr. S. may be induced to give more. He is the first to introduce Dr. S.'s lectures to us in England & we owe him a great deal. These lectures will be open to members of Mr. Smith's lodge & also to members of the new Society; the subscription to the latter being 10s/- till August. This 10s/- will be kept in hand for future requirements; the disposal of it will be settled by the members. Members of the lodge will no doubt make arrangements with Mr. S.

I would be glad if those who think of forming groups & who do not belong to Mr. Smith's lodge or who in any way wish to continue studying Dr. Steiner after Baron W.'s departure & think we could be of help to them will leave their names and addresses. Mr. S. & I can then go through them & propose arrangements.

★

Two further letters continue the story (A.B. = Annie Besant):

27 Clareville Grove,
29th Feb. 1912

Dear Mr. Smith,

I have run short of paper here, so forgive half sheet.

In this morning's letter from my club I forgot to send you the enclosed two letters which were here. Please let your lodge see them & then return them to me.

As regards the constitution of our new lodge, you will be President, & would Mrs. Smith consent to be Sect., as she has already been of the old lodge, & keep the books? We don't want a Treasurer at present; the fewer officers the better.

The official address pro. tem. 37 Ridgm. Gdns. please. You said that it would be here, but I may be away from time to time.

I have always understood that this new lodge will be what you originally proposed but postponed because of Walleen's coming. I suppose the lodge members understand that it is not a lodge under the A.B. rules. I think it would be as well to have this clear at the start. Otherwise there will be awkward questions from the many who object to the T.S.

Yours,

H. Collison

You should recommend people to buy the *Occult Review* of this month, where is a splendid article by Mabel Collins dealing with the Steiner work in England.

★

Windham Club,
St. James's Square,
S.W.
12th March, 1912

My dear Mr. Smith,

As you will be lecturing in Eastbourne next week, I shall be happy to take your place at my studio, so as to obviate a break in the course you have begun.—And if you like I would read out the lecture you would otherwise be giving.

Unfortunately Tuesday from 5–6 is exactly the one day & hour of the week upon which I am always engaged on the committee of my club, & next Tuesday some matters of especial importance are to be submitted.

Please be so good as to consult those you meet this afternoon & explain the awkward position I am in. I can give any hour & any day next week, either in the morning, afternoon or evening except Tuesday 5–6. That is an hour arranged years ago. Perhaps Tuesday morning would be a good time, but I can make any time convenient except the one mentioned.

Yours sincerely,

Harry Collison

(Friday 2–3 would be awkward.)

A Grand Ideal

The article by Mabel Collins, published under the title 'A Rosicrucian Ideal' in the March 1912 number of *The Occult Review*, began:

> In the teaching of Dr. Rudolf Steiner we have held before us a grand ideal, a superb conception of the Christ Spirit in its relation to man, and a lofty, pure, and true picture of the development of man as he enters into consciousness of this spirit. The ideal is one which those who look towards it must see as an uplifted cross held high above common life; and yet, by following the leader who carries it, every detail of common life is glorified and filled with meaning and dignity.
>
> There are many who will not be prepared to accept various points in Dr. Steiner's teaching, but none can fail to see how sublime the character of it is, and how it blends and perfects into a whole the highest doctrines of the great religions of the world. For Dr. Steiner's occultism is not a sectarian one. He claims to be in perfect agreement with all real occultists, both Western and Eastern. This must be so; it is the hall-mark of what is real. The truth which lies behind the physical world is one and can be obtained by duly developed initiates at any time and in any country. This he declares, and this is endorsed by all genuine students of the mysteries of life. Dr. Steiner's teaching in respect to the Christ is not a matter of defending Christianity or any other religion, but is given because he feels the necessity of proclaiming to the world the cosmic fact of Christ's deed of love 'which by and by will be acknowledged because it will be experienced by everyone, and humanity will be grouped in harmony round the central Sun of evolution: Christ'.
>
> Dr. Steiner writes and speaks in German only, and in this country we have but little of his more elementary teachings translated. There are volumes of his works in German, locked as yet to those who do not know that language. In Germany his following is great and ever-growing; he lectures continually and instructs pupils who are prepared to enter upon actual exercises of practical occultism. His followers are of all classes, rich and poor. In England no one has found out how to take theosophical teaching to the poor; but the poor in Germany come in numbers to attend Dr. Steiner's lectures, travelling long distances third class (an incredible hardship

in that country) and going without food all day in order to obtain spiritual bread. The need is felt here too. There are many who are not satisfied with a sectarian religion and seek something actual, real, to which the whole nature of man can respond, and by which it can be developed.

Dr. Steiner's great conceptions have been so far only available outside Germany to readers. A new international league is now formed for the study of occultism in the Western form as given by Dr. Steiner, and he has accepted office as its teacher, while the administration is to be in other hands. The form is hierarchic, higher power being vested in a central committee. Two men are responsible to this committee for carrying out the work of the league—Dr. Carl Unger for Germany, and Baron Walleen, of Stuttgart, for other countries. Baron Walleen has undertaken to travel and give lectures in various places, being able to render the teaching with equal clearness in French and English. He is President of the Steiner Lodge of the Theosophical Society in Copenhagen. Last November he came to London with the object of explaining the Rosicrucian conception of Christ to theosophical students and proposed to do so at the rooms of the London headquarters. But the arrangements for his doing so were delayed and became difficult, so that at much inconvenience he was forced at the last moment to give his lectures elsewhere. This last month he has come again to London with the same object, having been privately invited to lecture on the subject. The time and place of the lectures has not been made officially known among theosophists, but this has made no difference to the attendance at them, as the news that they were to be given has been carried about among those who are seriously interested in such matters. No doubt a great impetus will be given to the study of this Rosicrucian ideal, and representatives of the new league who will carry on the work will be prepared to form groups of students who can obtain practical guidance from Dr. Steiner's writings. The idea impressed upon his pupils is that since the coming of Christ the way, the truth and the life have been, and are, open to all. Before Christ only high initiates were able to get into touch with divinity. The divinity was outside man; now he is within man and the whole Earth; but 'has to be awakened by man's own effort without a school of initiation'.

Jewish initiates foretold that at a certain time a certain human being would have so purified his astral, ethereal and physical bodies that he would be able to receive within himself the Cosmic God, and from that moment a fresh impulse would be given upwards. This high being was Zarathustra, who incarnated as Jesus of Nazareth, and at the baptism of Jordan withdrew his ego; in its place came the cosmic Christ. At this moment, or rather, at the event of Golgotha, the Earth's aura underwent a change. The great Sun-being, Christ, had been approaching the Earth gradually, and many high initiates were forerunners of the great event. Zarathustra, the leader of the Persian epoch, was the one who naturally could realize best the great Sun-

God, the Christ. The old schools of initiation were broken up, and Christ gave to man the impulse to find him by his own endeavour. This seed was sown two thousand years ago, and Dr. Steiner's teaching is that it is but now springing above the surface.

The Buddhist uses his incarnations to purge his karma and escape from matter and the wheel of life altogether. Dr. Steiner points out that the man in whom the Christ spirit is awakened has to transform matter into spirit, not to get away from matter. In the lecture given on February 12, Baron Walleen gave this doctrine very definitely. As he expressed it (as nearly as I can remember) he said that 'We have to take the evil in the world and turn it into radiating, beautiful spirit, by the power of love.' This transformation of matter into spirit, of evil into good, has never been taught in this country or language before so far as I am aware save in my book, *The Story of the Year* (out of print). In this the mystic litany is given, the litany chanted at ceremonies attended by the spiritual entities of advanced disciples, in which is contained esoteric teaching as to transformation and transmutation. This was published in 1895. Much adverse criticism was directed against this profound doctrine in certain quarters; it now comes to us in a similar form from another country, from another recipient of occult truth. I have explained and amplified the teaching I have received in respect to this in a new volume now forthcoming, *When the Sun Moves Northward* (Theosophical Publishing Society), and I welcome this confirmation of its vital reality which has come to me from hearing Baron Walleen explain Dr. Steiner's doctrine.

The uselessness of spiritualistic seances, according to Dr. Steiner's teaching, formed part of the subject-matter of Baron Walleen's lectures. The view he takes is very different from that of some prominent London theosophists, who actually practise spiritualism and profess to receive messages from Masters through the agency of a medium. There is, to my mind, a sort of blasphemy in the mere idea of such a thing. I endorse to the uttermost and to the full, Dr. Steiner's positive teaching that all must be done, all knowledge obtained, all instruction received, in full consciousness.

There followed a detailed account of certain anthroposophical teachings, ending with this paragraph:

That there are dangers in the path of occultism is admitted by all teachers on the subject. That life becomes a more severe lesson, its hardships and trials accentuated, is a recognized experience. The idea of this deters many from venturing upon the path. Dr. Steiner declares that 'No one ought to hold back from occult education on account of dangers that confront him; rather should the very prospect form a powerful inducement toward the acquisition of those qualities which must be possessed by the genuine occult student.' And to one who holds the Rosicrucian conception of Christ there is no real danger. His power is a cosmic reality existing around us everywhere. We are in it and of it, even if we are not awake to the fact. Christ has given us the power to carry our karma; He helps us to carry it; He is with us always; He seeks the lost sheep; and there will be one herd and One Shepherd.

Conditions in England

Among those attending Baron Walleen's lectures was perhaps also Robert Felkin, as can be deduced from the content of a lengthy letter published by the pseudonymous 'Inquire Within' in *Light-Bearers of Darkness*[26] (1930). The letter has no date, but is stated to have been written in 1912, to 'Baron C.A.W.', the initials of Walleen, by Felkin's associate Neville Meakin. Since in the very first sentence it refers to 'the proposed International Bund', which to some extent had already become reality, it may reasonably be assigned to early in the year.

(Dr. S. = Dr. Steiner. Dr. F. = Dr. Felkin. T.S. = Theosophical Society. Mr. T.P. is unknown. Mr. S. = Mr. (Heywood-)Smith. Mr. C. = Mr. Collison. S.M. = Stella Matutina.)

Dear Sir and Brother,

I have heard from Dr. Felkin of the proposed International Bund, which seems in many ways an excellent scheme to which I wish every success. As Dr. Steiner's name is so potent on the Continent, it is bound to prosper there. In England he has a band of admirers, but his name is not so generally known. The conditions in England are also peculiar. Dr. S. himself said to me that he recognized the difference. Therefore I write to you, for we have a double tie—the Rosicrucian Fraternity both of the Continent and in England; we can speak freely. What I say now I wish to be laid before Dr. S. by you, and the risk is mine. For if I do not speak without fear or favour, no one else can.

Dr. S. is a statesman in his schemes. But a statesman, when enquiring into the condition of a country unknown to him, does not go only to the members of one party in it. For Austrian politics one would not consult only Magyars, nor for German, members only of the Catholic block. In England the few members of the Continental Order are all theosophists, i.e. members of the T.S. They are none of them members of the English Freemasons. They see things from the T.S. point of view, and they have to use their spectacles. I am the only member of the Continental Order who is not and never has been a T.S. member; I owe no allegiance to Mrs. Besant. I am, as the Doctor knows, entirely with him in the policy of abandoning Oriental or Indian for European or Kabalistic training; I am also an English Freemason, so I can give him the point of view of the other parties.

English occultism is roughly divided into (1) members of the T.S., i.e. Mrs. Besant's followers, headed by the Co-Masons in one sense; (2) members of the Hermetic Orders and Freemasons; (3) Independents, whether in small groups or individuals.

The first class is the only one really known to the Doctor. Of the second Dr. F. is very representative. Of the third Mr. T.P. . . .

Now when the Doctor comes to establish his Bund there are certain considerations of great importance. With regard to Group 1, the T.S. and its branches, I cannot pretend to say what will happen. Mr. S. and Mr. C. both know the T.S. people and its style of work—by lecture etc. The risk, however, is with regard to groups 2 and 3. The Bund will, unless carefully managed, be regarded merely as a schism of the T.S. It will command as much attention as the Quest Society of G.R.S. Mead, and it may arouse great prejudice, for many will take it exactly in the spirit in which England took the German telegram to President Kruger. I am quite serious when I say that to many the Bund will be thus considered—'We don't care for Mrs. Besant any more than we cared for Jameson and his raid, but after all, Mrs. Besant is English. Who are these Germans to interfere?' It may sound ridiculous, but I know my country.

The next point, a very serious one indeed, is the attitude of the Freemasons. This must be taken into consideration. Here for a moment I must apparently digress. I wish to contrast the working of groups 1, 2 and 3. Group 1 works on the familiar lines of lectures, magazine publications, etc. Dr. S. does much the same. Group 1 attracts a large number of idle women who have the leisure to take a little occultism with their afternoon tea. Practically all the members are people with time and money. It attracts members, but each lecturer is apt to get a personal following; hence schisms, i.e. the Quest.

Group 2 is small in numbers. It works by Lodges and circulates manuscripts. Its teaching is done by correspondence, by individual officers etc. It seldom has lectures. It taps a wholly different class, gets at more varied social strata, has a far larger proportion of men. Being highly organized, it has more coherence; at the same time each Temple is apt to be jealous of outside interferences. Most of its men are Freemasons. Some entire Temples are Freemasonic, e.g. the Societas Rosicruciana in Anglia. Now these people are busy. There are singularly few idle, moneyed or leisured women and men among them. They are very proud and independent. In course of time, if they can get teaching in their own manner, by MSS. in circulation, by visits of members from Lodge to Lodge, by or through their own Chiefs, I am certain they will all, given time, join your Bund. But they will not accept any T.S. dictation; they will not tolerate Chiefs whom they do not know; they will not care for attending cycles or lectures for which they have no time or inclination. These bodies are older than the T.S. and they do not forget it. Humoured they will help you. If they are not considered they will neither oppose you nor regard you. They will simply leave the Bund alone exactly as they leave the T.S. alone, the Co-Masons alone, etc. They must be got at from within, not from without.

The third group I can assist with in course of time. But how they will act now I do not pretend to know. Most of them will accept no authority over them.

Now I come to the Freemasonic point. Here I tread on very delicate ground. But I feel I must state the case, as I said, without fear or favour. The Doctor is too great a man to be vexed with me. After all, all I wish to do is to secure that the best teaching reaches those most fit for it in the easiest way.

At present to establish a definite branch of the Continental Order giving grades etc. in England will be a very diffcult matter. You are not yourself a Freemason. We sometimes call our Order, the Continental Order, Esoteric Masonry. The grades are closely akin to Freemasonry. Dr. S. indeed has some link with certain English or Scotch Masons—he gave me the name—from whom he derives a certain authority, a link in the physical.

Now English Freemasonry is not occult, though it has occult lodges, and most English occultists not T.S. are Freemasons, if men. English Masonry boasts the Grand Lodge of 1717, the Mother Lodge of the world. They are a proud, jealous, autocratic body. Co-Masonry derives from the Grand Orient of France, an illegitimate body according to English ruling. No English Mason can work with Co-Masons. Now the Masons who gave Dr. S. his link are regarded—you had better get Dr. F. to verify me here—as eccentrics who invent spurious grades. If the English Grand Lodge hears of anything called 'Esoteric Masonry' derived from such sources, under Chiefs once T.S. members, under a head in Berlin, it will not inquire who Dr. S. is or what is the nature of his work. It will simply say: 'No English Masons of the Free and Accepted Masons may join any society working pseudo-Masonic rites'; i.e. no one of ordinary accepted Freemasonry can attend any meetings or take any grades in this illegitimate body! Finis!

Then we who are members of Dr. S.'s Lodge and are Freemasons will be in a sad plight. At present this would affect only myself and, well, Dr. F. too. But if Esoteric Masonry is breathed of in England, and the fiat goes against it, no English Mason will wish to join the Bund.

After all this cold water, you will ask what useful suggestion do I imagine I have to make. Well, perhaps nothing very useful. Still, this is my practical suggestion. Let the Bund be started. Let Messrs. S. and C. get all the MSS. they can, and let them establish relations with the bodies in Group 2. Either let them supply such written teaching as can be given to the heads of the Lodges that will come in, and seek no interference with the Lodges, or let them form a definite committee under Dr. S. with representative people in it. All this must be done slowly.

The system of having people in the Lodges like Dr. F. to teach 'processes' within Group 2 is the most practical; and to have Bund officials like Messrs. S. and C., one of whom should join an English Lodge, to go between England and the Continent, and to get the written teaching will probably work well enough.

But if a Lodge of the Continental Order is to be established in England, Dr. S. will be faced with the Masonic difficulty. This is really serious, and no one of the T.S. will understand it, nor even any Continental Freemasons. Look at my position and again at Dr. F.'s—if we were banned from all association with Freemasons, i.e. from practically all Lodges in Group 2, or else from association from the Bund. Either we must be cut off again, or our usefulness for general purposes is gone. If Dr. S. would summon one or two non-theosophical persons to discuss with him, he would see this at once. The practical solution will be found in a compromise. If he avoids the name 'Esoteric Masonry' and allows perhaps a ritual like those used in the Societas Rosicruciana or in the S.M., and has for officers in England a mixed group, including the heads of the chief Hermetic Lodges etc.,—as well as T.S. people and a few who will join anything of Dr. S.'s—it will succeed. Otherwise I fear much that only a few T.S. people and a few whom Dr. F. and myself can influence directly will be all that will join at the outset. As a theosophist schism, and a foreign intrusive Masonic schism, the Bund will arouse every possible English prejudice against it. Devoted to the Doctor as we are, we should both regret it.

Yours fraternally,

(Neville Meakin)

The Masonic Examination

The April number of *The Path* included an article on 'The Masonic Examination', reproducing a lecture given by D.N. Dunlop at the Blavatsky Institute in January:

> The symbols of Masonry are suggestive of degrees, which can be obtained only by passing an examination. The symbolism of Freemasonry is the symbolism of Theosophy. Many Freemasons would deny this, but nevertheless it is true that theosophical symbolism and the symbolism of Masonry are practically the same, and I refer to it tonight because of the significance of examinations. There is a point in the life of all men and women when they have to go through a certain examination. Considering first the physical life, we know that when a young man or woman reaches a certain age, they have to examine themselves and decide what occupation they will follow. Especially is this the case with young men, and we all recognize this as a most important step in our physical life, since a great deal depends on

the decision that is made. Now in the life of the soul exactly the same thing happens. In some incarnation a man or woman must face the problem, must pass certain elementary examinations. In the Masonic ritual it is illustrated by a series of questions like the following:—'From whence came you?' is one of the questions. And the answer is 'From the West.' 'Whither are you directing your course?' 'To the East.' 'What is your object?' 'To seek a Master and from him to gain instruction.' 'Who are you that want instruction?' 'A free and accepted Mason.' 'For what purpose came you hither?' 'To regulate my conduct, correct my passions, and make progress in Masonry.' 'How do you know yourself to be a Mason?' 'By the regularity of my initiation, repeated trials and approbations, and a readiness at all times to undergo an examination, when properly called on.'

This examination which we all have to undergo is much more important than any other examination relating only to lesser phases of life or experience, because it prepares the way for an immortal and eternal journey—a path that stretches far away; and it is very necessary to prepare ourselves if we are not to lose the road. Now in passing an examination in the ordinary sense, thought is required. In our modern schools it is necessary to prepare for examinations by certain exercises, and though we do not approve of the cramming process we recognize the necessity for preparation. And in the same way it is necessary to make preparation by study and other methods to pass these examinations connected with the progress of the soul. The Christian scriptures would probably be suggested as one field of study, for the reading of great literature, of scriptures usually called holy, is part of the preparation necessary for the examination that comes later on. Through reading books of philosophy, through study of what the great ones of the ages have said about the constitution of man, what the teachers have laid down with regard to life, you come to understand your own nature. The fundamentals of all great teachings are exactly the same. All true teachers have taught that man is a spiritual being, that he contacts the physical world through the medium of a soul and finally through the medium of a physical body; that certain exercises are necessary in order to come to a realization of this spiritual life, in order to awaken the memory of the life associated with the spirit, and by the performance of these exercises you prove for yourself what is stated in these books. You cannot regard a statement as satisfactory until you have proved it for yourself. The statements made by Jesus or Buddha, or any teacher, have to be confirmed by each individual for him or herself. People differ in temperament, and it is necessary to remember that what is suitable for one may not be suitable for another. Some are satisfied with the New Testament, others are not. But the important thing is this, that in one way or another there must be a satisfactory preparation for the examination which life inevitably brings.

It should be noted, too, that until you make yourself proficient in one degree you cannot proceed to the next. That is why people have made so little development. They do not see the necessity for proficiency in the elementary stages. They have so strong a desire to know the whole at the beginning that they fail to realize how necessary it is to become proficient in the *first* degree before proceeding to the next. The true teacher suggests, and leaves the rest to the student. 'Think it over,' he says, 'and see if it agrees with what you yourself think.' For he does not wish to compel you to think as he does, but rather to put you in a position to arrive at conclusions for yourself. There is nothing to be gained by using any influence over other human beings. Each individual has to travel the path and solve the mystery of his own nature. And if you are assisted for the time being, in some way, on the path you are told to follow, without exercising your discrimination, you are simply acting by suggestion and are not building on sure foundations.

You will find that the relationship existing between a student and teacher grows more intimate and confidential as they proceed. This relationship is probably the only true brotherhood that man knows. Blood relationship is often a very feeble bond. It may happen sometimes that beings who enter the same family are bound together by many things mutually attracting them to each other, but very often this is not the case; and the most wonderful relationships that occur are between those who are following the path of spiritual unfoldment. They began in the beginning, and have been going on through all the ages ever since. That relationship, where one is the teacher in one incarnation and the pupil in the next, is characterized by an immortal sympathy which nothing can obliterate. Through all the mixture of blood, races, families, tribes, these kindred spirits find each other, and their relationships are not determined so much by degrees of knowledge as by the spirit of the work in which they are engaged. Pride and insincerity, it is needless to say, are enemies to such relationships.

Now in the preparation for this examination of which we have been speaking, there must be a basis; there must be some elementary preparation by the pupil himself. He must learn that all growth and development come from within. No one can reveal a secret to you: that is an absolute impossibility. What then is a secret? What is it takes place when secrets are really revealed? It is the unfolding of the life within yourself, and then only do you see what was hitherto secret. The child of God wrapped up in you, that divine seed of God in you and me unfolds, when nourished in the right way, and in the unfolding of that god-life one secret after another is revealed. Why then 'secret'? Because until they are unfolded in the consciousness, certain states and facts of nature are 'unknown'. But just as powers unfold as you grow from childhood to manhood through youth, so it is in the spiritual life. You may whisper all sorts of secrets, but it won't make a bit of difference. Wisdom only appears as the seed of understanding begins to grow. These secret orders that are springing up everywhere ensnare and delude people. We know perfectly well that it took millions of years to produce a daisy; how many more will it take to produce a perfect man or woman? Everything develops according to law. You only know that which you recognize in yourself. You can only know yourself, and the revealing of a secret can be of no value to you unless you have prepared yourself to that point of self-recognition; and then it does not matter whether you belong to a secret order or not. The circumstances combine, and the secret will be revealed in the heart. You hear much about the stone which the builders rejected, 'the lost word'. But do you not know that you pass through these ceremonies yourself? How many Masons know what is the stone which the builders rejected? I should like to bring men and women back to the recognition of the simplest and most fundamental elements, viz., that there is not a single fact or formula which is not to be found within your own nature; that by following along the line which you yourself know to be right at the time, and by being honest and straight with yourself, you will come to a point when secret after secret (which are only secrets because of your own ignorance) will be revealed. Only that which is spiritual in its essence can discern spiritual things. Locked up in the heart of the most degraded man or woman are all the secrets of the universe, and neither virtue nor vice can succeed in entirely concealing them.

On entering this path you enter a novitiate, and so it is necessary to begin by setting your house in order, to 'take stock' of your own being before you start, and I anticipate you will be discouraged by the time you get through. But remember, there are 'stocks' you cannot see yet because you have not the power of vision. As you grow and develop, you will say, 'I did not know before that I had this power,' and you may be tempted into pride of it, before you realize what is happening. But you will reach a day when there is no concealment, when you will know even as you are known. And though I say you must find the secrets in your own consciousness, I do not mean to suggest that there are no Masters to guide you. There are Masters. They are taking part in our evolution. They have attained, and what They have done all may do on the same terms.

The knowledge you gain will lead you to keep the law; and the law is to give freely, because you have received freely. Therefore we have to prepare to live freely and in freedom. But freedom does not mean licence. We hear of a free-woman, a free-lover, a free-thinker, and perhaps connect with these licence; but licence is the greatest slavery you can possibly conceive. When you begin to understand freedom, you begin to lead the life according to law; but if you run counter to the law you have no freedom. If you break the laws of Nature you lose your freedom, and finally you are broken by the law. By acting according to the law, with the law, you begin to live a balanced, ordered life. You defeat this often because you anticipate—it may be trouble, joy, pleasure—you run forward to meet it. It is better to live just from moment to moment, giving each one its due, not running forward and thinking what you are going to do the next hour, day, week, but having your full self present at every moment of time and space. So will you prepare for the Great Moment, when the examination may be passed with distinction. When the Master meets you, he sees you as you really are. When you begin to approximate to His ideal, everything fits into true place in your life. You find yourself at peace in the midst of 'warring elements'. The warfare does not cease, but your inner serenity is undisturbed, and you readily find the path to the centre, around which the whirling energies revolve. Every day will bring its own examination; where you fail today, you may 'pass' tomorrow. Never at any time does the Master lose His patience. Keep this in remembrance and all examinations, however severe, will find you well prepared. For our moods are the varying elements; in all degrees the law is the same.

Great and Fundamental Differences

At the beginning of April 1912, *The Vâhan* published two items of relevance to the present story.

One was entitled 'Fourth International Summer School':

> It is proposed to hold the fourth Summer School at Torquay—August 3 to 17 inclusive.
>
> Last year over three hundred people attended at Swanwick, Derbyshire, and it appears that a greater number are likely to attend this year. The School has outgrown the facilities of one place, and arrangements have been made with various hotels and boarding-houses close to the central headquarters and meeting-place to accommodate parties from twenty to fifty. The catering difficulties will thus be overcome, and it will be easier to suit the requirements of each individual. Reduced fares have been arranged with all railway companies, on lines similar to last year. Early booking is desirable. The lecture list is in course of preparation. Among theosophical subjects the following may be noted as of special interest:
>
> 'Socialism and Racial Changes', 'Woman and the New Cycle', 'The Value of Intellect in Occultism', 'Some Occult Schools and their varying Teaching'.
>
> Full particulars may be had on application to Oakley House, Bloomsbury Street, London, W.C.
>
> D.N. Dunlop, Director

*

The other item was entitled 'An Explanation'. It was a letter from Max Gysi, who also brought out in this year a translation of Rudolf Steiner's book *The Gates of Knowledge*.

Dear Sir,

I hear with great regret that the two lectures delivered by our President to the London Lodges on 'Variations of Clairvoyant Investigations' are being strongly objected to by some of our fellow-members, who are making a special study of Dr. Rudolf Steiner's teachings. As far as I can ascertain their objections chiefly centre round the second lecture, which was delivered on March 6, and which dealt particularly with the differences between the views held by our President and other investigators on the one hand, and those held by Dr. Steiner on the other.

Lest what I feel compelled to say in this letter should be taken as ingratitude for all I have learned and all the kindness I have received at the hands of Dr. Steiner in such large measure, I wish it to be clearly understood that I have the greatest admiration both for himself and his great work. Dr. Steiner himself does not quarrel—nor do those who understand him best. He only gives out the fruits of his researches to be accepted or rejected, and he has helped and brightened innumerable lives through personal service. I know as a fact that the unwise zeal and sometimes injudicious partisanship of some of his more enthusiastic followers have caused Dr. Steiner much grief in the past, and it is my hope in writing this open letter to be able to lead others to see how unnecessary and injurious is such a controversy to the realization of our ideals of brotherhood.

It seems that our honoured President is blamed most for having based her last lecture on notes which were taken in the usual way at Dr. Steiner's lecture to the Besant Lodge in Berlin on October 23, 1911, and circulated by and among his own followers. Moreover, they are only confirmatory of statements contained in lectures delivered by him during the last two years. I myself cannot see why it should be considered 'unfair' to quote from a lecture given by Dr. Steiner, least of all from this one, which states frankly his never-concealed position and which he gave for the express purpose of showing his pupils on what points the two Schools differ.

To anybody who has the privilege of knowing our President, the mere suggestion of her ever taking an unfair advantage of anyone—least of all of one of her co-workers—seems absurd, but as this criticism has been brought to my notice, I feel compelled at last to break the silence which I have observed since joining this Section eighteen years ago, and to trouble readers of *The Vâhan* for the first time with a personal explanation dealing with the same subject.

I have been blamed by some of my friends over here for bringing out Dr. Steiner's works in English, because they considered this as working against our President. On the other hand, some of Dr. Steiner's followers think that

I could serve our great movement better by accepting their particular views as regards evolutionary processes, Hierarchies and states of consciousness—views interesting in themselves, but far beyond our ken and affecting in no way either our daily life or our conduct. Any such criticisms are not in keeping with the noble ideals presented to us by Theosophy, nor with the broad toleration shown to us by the founders of the T.S.

It may interest some of my critics in this country to know that our President asked me herself to translate Dr. Steiner's works into English, and would have been glad to publish all our translations in the *Theosophist*, had not this scheme been partly frustrated, and the publishing of several important works by Dr. Steiner, which have been ready for some time, been unavoidably delayed, in consequence of the complicated copyright laws in the U.S.A. and the difficulty of finding suitable publishers in America.

Dr. Steiner's books contain, in my opinion, valuable independent corroboration of many of our teachings, for which we ought to be very grateful. Where they differ from the generally accepted views of others, they stimulate our own thought, and will always be valuable as coming from a great thinker and experienced occultist, one who presents us with first-hand knowledge.

I cannot understand why there should be any trouble on account of differences among our trained investigators, for our theosophical platform is broad enough to include many different views, if our members only show the good-will and the tolerant spirit of our leaders.

For the last six months we have received from the Continent vague and indefinite rumours of what some friends considered great and fundamental differences between the teachings of Mrs. Besant and Dr. Steiner. But it was difficult to gain any authentic information, especially as I have not been able to visit Dr. Steiner personally for over twelve months. It was not until the last days of February that I received the notes of Dr. Steiner's lecture mentioned above, and as it contained for the first time in a short compass the various points of difference, I translated the notes as quickly as possible and sent them to our President for her consideration. With the promptitude that is characteristic of Mrs. Besant, she answered within forty-eight hours of the receipt of the translation the various questions it raised; and at the meeting of members already referred to discussed them in so broad, tolerant and loving a spirit that I certainly thought it could not possibly give rise to any adverse criticism.

I leave the technical points of this controversy to be settled among themselves by the very few competent occultists or scholars. It is for them to determine the truth of Dr. Steiner's statements, which he himself propounds in many of his lectures, supported by elaborate investigations, to the effect that there lived about the year 100 B.C. a Jesus called Jeschu-ben-Pandira, in whom the Bodhisattva was incarnated; whilst at the beginning of our era, two other Jesus children were born, the parents of the one living in Nazareth, those of the other in Bethlehem. The child of the latter, at the age of twelve, took possession of the body of the Nazarene Jesus and in his turn gave up his bodies at the age of thirty to the Christ; who, according to Dr. Steiner, is quite another individuality from the Bodhisattva—He being a manifestation of the second aspect of the Logos, a cosmic being who descended once only to the physical plane, but cannot return again in a physical form.

It is of course impossible to give your readers in this letter all the details regarding the nature of the Christ according to Dr. Steiner's teachings, but in reading it and especially in hearing the remarks made by some over-zealous followers of his, we cannot help recalling the beautiful words which Mrs. Besant wrote in her *Theosophy and Christianity*, p. 8: 'All this must be an aspect of what men call God; all this but the burgeoning of that illimitable Existence. And then, when thought falls helpless, then, when mind sinks dumb, then remember that man, a half-evolved organism on a grain of sand in space, dares to anathematize his brother, because his conception of that ineffable Existence differs in human language from his own. What it is no human tongue may speak, no human mind may conceive. *Only we feel we dare not limit, we dare not use words of It which are taken from our petty attributes, our narrow limitations.* Not by the intellect may we know the Self of the universe, much less That of which the Self is but a fragmentary expression' . . . (Italics by M.G.)

Personally I am very glad to find that Dr. Steiner also affirms that during the present century the Bodhisattva will return in physical form. The problem as to whether this great Teacher of humanity is identical with the Christ, according to Dr. Steiner's definition, or not, does not in the least affect our lives or our conduct, and it is so far above the possibility of our common knowledge that it is useless for us to try to solve it, and most unseemly to quarrel about the highest Ideal of humanity.

In whatever way the points at issue may ultimately be answered, our belief in any one of the two opposing views does not really matter, so long as we live according to our highest Ideal.

How the curious position in the theosophical world in Europe has arisen I cannot explain, just as little as I can find an explanation of the equally puzzling situation in the world of politics, but that both exist is apparent to all students.—I write this letter in an appeal to my brother theosophists not to allow themselves to be drawn into a controversy which has in it all the elements of the religious quarrels with which history is replete; and which is full of the same misunderstandings and suspicions which have brought two great nations to the brink of war.

All-inclusive brotherhood is the one tie that binds us together, so do not let us become unbrotherly over a controversy in which the vast majority cannot take part through lack of understanding, but we each can help the President to keep the theosophical platform wide and tolerant and encircled with our love.

I think it is our duty as members of the Theosophical Society to support whole-heartedly our President in her noble work for humanity, and not to cripple her splendid endeavours with petty and academical dissensions among ourselves. I know of no nobler, more tolerant or more ideal leader than the one who at present guides so ably the destinies of our beloved Society, and I am content to serve her to the best of my ability. I hope that Mrs. Besant's helpful lecture on 'Variations in Clairvoyant Investigations' will soon be published in *The Theosophist*, so that all our members may be in a better position to judge for themselves of the tolerance she has shown in dealing with this difficult question.

After this lengthy letter I trust that I need never again trouble your readers. I for one am determined to follow in this (as in any other future difficulty) the admirable *con*structive policy which has proved so successful in the troubles of 1894 and 1907.

Yours, etc.,

Max Gysi

★

This letter was the most explicit account which British theosophical readers were ever to receive of the differences between the teachings of Rudolf Steiner and those of Annie Besant. Without going into full details, the letter seemed to imply that the differences lay in the field of Christology, of which it briefly publicized certain highly esoteric aspects. But in its final appeal for readers not to let themselves be drawn into any controversy, the letter also shows that by this time Gysi had become less perceptive of what was really going on, and of what was actually at stake, than the members of the Rosicrucian Lodge to whom he must have been initially referring.

Personal Confidence

While readers of *The Vâhan* were still mulling over the letter from Max Gysi, Harry Collison was typing out in his club a different sort of letter, for limited circulation only.

Windham Club,
S.W.
19th April, 1912

Dear

An international Society has been formed for the impartial study of Dr. Steiner's works. The reason is that several people wish to study Dr. Steiner without the restrictions existing in theosophical societies, and many people do not care to call themselves theosophists. The printed books are open to everyone in the world to read, but there are certain lectures which are of a more intimate character and which will never be put into book form. Hitherto these lectures and also admission to the performance of Dr. Steiner's wonderful Mystery Plays were available for members of theosophical societies only. These privileges will be extended to members of the new Society, and members will have every advantage that Dr. Steiner can give them. The lectures are typewritten and are from courses of private lectures delivered on the Continent. A course generally consists of about twelve lectures. There are thirteen of these at present and there will be more, and there are also single lectures on various subjects apart from the above.

The Society, so far as the non-German element is concerned, is presided over by Baron Walleen of Copenhagen, who will, it is hoped, continue to visit England and give us the English lectures we have so much enjoyed. Under Baron Walleen, the Society in England is represented by Mr. Heywood-Smith, whose understanding of Dr. Steiner's works is most complete, and by myself; and our duty is to explain these lectures as far as we can and facilitate study of them. For this pupose we shall gradually translate the lectures and lecture upon them. Mr. Heywood-Smith at present lectures twice a week at my studio in 27 Clareville Grove, near Gloucester Road Station. It is to be hoped that later on we will have a proper lecture-room and greater facilities.

The lectures on Tuesday afternoons at three o'clock are of a more elementary character than those on Thursday evenings at 8 o'clock and are advisable for those unacquainted with Dr. Steiner's phraseology. To those who wish to join the Tuesday classes and have therefore missed five of the course, I will give such a résumé as will help them to follow the remainder.

Mr. Heywood-Smith and I have fixed on a nominal fee of ten shillings until August. This fee will be inclusive and there is no liability whatever on anyone joining the Society. No promises are asked, except to keep the lectures private, and as far as possible the names of members are concealed. The reason that the month of August is chosen is that it is then the first General Meeting of the Society will be held in Munich. Till then arrangements can only be provisional, and by then Dr. Steiner will have given the Society a name.

The chief difficulty and our chief duty is to see that these lectures do not fall into the hands of those who would only take them up in a spirit of curiosity, or with the intention of opposing them and causing friction, or those who might be tempted to make commercial profit out of them. As it really has to be quite a personal matter, we act quite independently when anyone signifies a desire to become a member.

Joining the Society requires a certain amount of personal confidence on both sides. But there are no rules; there is no dogma. It is advisable, of course, to attend lectures, but not absolutely necessary. Dr. Steiner himself has no representative in England that I know of.

I am

Yours faithfully,

H. Collison

★

On the very next day, Colonel Webber sent a letter to Heywood-Smith:

58, Earl's Avenue,
Folkestone
April 20

Dear Mr. Heywood-Smith,

I have had a letter from Mr. Collison, of which I understand he has sent you a copy.

I am coming up to town, on Monday next, to 5 the Grove, the Boltons, & remaining until Thursday, proposing to attend your lecture at Clareville Grove on Tuesday.

If you would care to discuss any of your future arrangements with me, as I note that Mr. Collison says he 'must leave Mr. Smith to make what arrangements he thinks best' (until the General Meeting in Aug.) perhaps you would drop me a line to No. 5 the Grove saying what time you could call to see me, preferably before your meeting on Tuesday aft.

With kind wishes to Mrs. Smith & yourself, in which my wife joins,

Yours very sincerely,

J. Webber

Please reply to No. 5 the Grove, Boltons, S.W.

★

A further letter from the Colonel is undated but can probably also be assigned to this time:

58 Earl's Avenue,
Folkestone.
Tuesday

Dear Mr. Heywood-Smith,

I am sorry to see from the letter you forward to me that Mr. Collison appears to be not quite well. It will no doubt be a good plan to wait a few days until he is better, and if he comes to Folkestone perhaps he may settle something.

You may remember that when I was elected to the Committee I was authorized by Mr. Collison and the meeting to look out for a suitable house, for which Mr. Collison said the money would be forthcoming.

I found one 96 Redcliffe Gardens, which would be let on an agreement for £120 a year and is suitable—or if he prefers it, he could buy 26 Collingham Gardens, which has been offered him very cheap.—If Mr. Collison has since changed his mind about getting a house for the Society, I am afraid I cannot help it.—You and Mr. Collison are our Chiefs and I am only a recruit under your banner, though I hope a willing one.

I will write if I hear further, or see Mr. Collison.

With kind regards to Mrs. Smith & yourself,

Yours very sincerely,

J. Webber

★

Although Collison had stated in his letter that as far as possible the names of members were concealed, one of them by this time was certainly Baron Rosenkrantz. He was of Danish birth, had rather an international upbringing, and came to play such an active role in the development of anthroposophy in Britain that something must be said about him.

Arild Rosenkrantz was born in Denmark in 1870. His Danish father died when he was only three years old, and he was brought up by his widowed mother, the Scottish-born Julia Mackenzie of Tabat. After the death of her husband she often travelled to Scotland or Italy, taking her youngest son Arild with her. In 1886 she moved to Rome, and there became involved in spiritualism.

The 16-year-old Arild was taken on in Rome as a pupil of the fresco-painter Modesto Faustini, and three years later, in 1889, travelled to France to pursue his artistic education at the Académie Julian in Paris, where his teachers were J.P. Laurens and Benjamin Constant. Through his mother he was introduced to the French writer, art critic and mystic Sar Peladan, and in 1892–5 exhibited pictures of his own at the latter's 'Salon de la Rose-Croix' in Paris. He also had works accepted at the Royal Academy of Art in Copenhagen.

After a few years in the United States, where among other activities he worked with stained glass at the Tiffany Studios in New York, he moved in 1898 to Britain, where in 1901 he married a Scottish cousin, Tessa Mackenzie. In London he soon established himself as a portrait-painter, illustrator and teacher. During the years 1905–12 he gained many assignments in the decorative arts, painting for instance twelve large panels for the ceiling of the dining room at Claridge's Hotel in London, and making stained glass windows or bronze sculptures for a number of English churches and castles, e.g. Berkeley Castle. He also illustrated the Danish translation of Edgar Allen Poe's *Tales of Mystery and Adventure*, and other literary works.

In 1909 he visited his mother in Rome, at a point where she had just heard a lecture by Rudolf Steiner. By this time she was befriended with Collison's mother, and hence it came about that when in 1912 Collison started his group in London, Rosenkrantz joined it.

On a Good Foundation

The only recorded sequel to the letter from Max Gysi published in *The Vâhan* came from Germany. For at the end of the month, James Wedgwood wrote a personal letter to a Munich member:

Theosophical Society in England and Wales
Satyan Nasti Paro Dharma

19, Tavistock Square,
London, W.C.
Office of General Secretary
April 30th, 1912.

Dictated.

Dear Baroness Gumppenberg,

I return with this the copy of your letter to Mr. Gysi.

I am sorry, but it was quite impossible to include it in the *Vâhan.* The present number is 28 pages and I am supposed to limit it to 24. You say 'there is an impression afloat that letters emanating from Germany are generally refused insertion' and add that the *Vâhan* is the only periodical in which theosophists can exchange ideas. I think members would be living very much more in harmony with the theosophical spirit if they would not allow such rumours to spread. During the time I have been General Secretary I have never refused a letter from Germany, because I have never had one. There must be a limit to the length of articles or letters that we can insert. Mr. Gysi's letter was much longer than I liked, and I inserted it in full only because he is one of our oldest workers and explained that it was the first time he had ever thus written to the *Vâhan*. If you will state your points in a concisely worded letter of shorter length, my offer to insert it still remains open. You must remember that the *Vâhan* is not an organ for the T.S. generally, but specially for our Section, and I must therefore give precedence to its own affairs and business, and to matters in which our members are specially interested. This is my obvious duty and it cannot be altered by the fact (if it be a fact) that 'the *Vâhan* is the only periodical in which theosophists can exchange ideas'.

Of course truth ranks before tolerance—but are any of us sure that we possess absolute truth? Tolerance displayed towards another is a method by which he and ourselves are helped towards the appreciation of truth.

Are you coming to England again, and if so, won't you come and see me? Our last meeting was one of very cordial relationship, and I do not think that differences of opinion would in any way interfere with that.

Yours very sincerely,

J.I. Wedgwood

★

At the start of May, Marie von Sivers wrote to Herbert Heywood-Smith suggesting that English members travel to Germany in order to speak to Rudolf Steiner just over a week later: (R.C. = Rosicrucian.)

1/V 1912

Dear Mr. Smith,

Excuse the brevity of my letter, but only an absolute lack of time is the reason for it. I wanted to suggest whether if some of the English R.C. members would like to speak to Dr. Steiner or myself, you would think his visit to Cologne from 6th to 9th of May a good opportunity? It was scarcely possible until now to find a date in Berlin. He was always travelling, and for 3 weeks in Helsingfors and Stockholm. At Berlin only for lectures and overladen with pressing work that had to be finished for Easter: calendar, plans for the building, etc.—This could be a chance, but audiences would be best put on the 9th, as the days before are so filled with meetings. There was a lady especially who wanted to talk—could you ask her if she wishes to go to Cologne? Or would you or Mrs. Smith make it possible?

Yours sincerely,

M. Sivers

★

Heywood-Smith must have notified Collison, for both of them packed their bags and travelled out to Cologne. Steiner was staying there for a week, consecrating the new group room and giving various lectures. Presumably they were able to have an interview with him.

Heywood-Smith also took down some notes headed 'Business Arrangements in connection with the "Bund" agreed to in toto by Dr. Unger, Mr. Collison & H.J. H-S. at Cologne, May 7th 1912':

> In order to get Dr. S.'s work in England on a good foundation we must have Headquarters in England.
>
> We must have a Committee.
>
> All business to go through Committee.
>
> The English Committee arranges internal English affairs.
>
> No need to wait, go ahead at once. The Conference at Munich in August will not affect any of our working arrangements.
>
> We recognize Dr. S. as our leader and teacher.
>
> All official communications from Germany to be sent to both C. and H-S.

★

On his return to England, Collison decided to type an 'open letter' to Heywood-Smith, of which he also sent copies to such as Colonel Webber.

Heywood-Smith was somewhat taken aback by this action, as is shown by marginal annotations which he made on his copy of the letter. The letter is here reproduced with these annotations inserted in italics after the paragraphs to which they refer.

> Windham Club,
> S.W.
> 15th May, 1912.
>
> Dear Mr. Heywood-Smith,
>
> This open letter is hardly intended for those few members who have quite recently joined.
>
> *Who is it intended for, as all the members have joined within the last two months?*
>
> We should much appreciate their views but cannot ask them for promises.
>
> *Why not?*
>
> I am glad to have this opportunity of assuring you that there was no real reason for doubting that the scheme suggested by you is to be permanently connected with the Bund; and that the person to whom we are primarily responsible is Baron Walleen, with the right of appeal to the Head Central Committee.
>
> *There seems to be a certain amount of confusion about this word 'responsible'. It would be well to have Baron W.'s powers as regards the various foreign sections clearly defined.*

I see no reason why you should not at once proceed to make plans for the future of the Society—on a sound basis. But foundations must be firmly laid, and we must first see how much support, both moral and financial, we may expect from the members. The first step is to gauge the feeling of the present members; and as we have only ten weeks before dispersing, and in view of the condition of unrest that prevails in London during the summer season, I think we should set to work at once.

We are unable to ask our present subscribers for any further help until after August.

Why not?

But I think they should be reminded that on the 1st August the Society in England will cease to exist unless some effort be made to carry it on.

The Society in England will not cease to exist as long as I am alive.

They have now had the benefit of many of your lectures, and I think may well be invited to write to us and say what help, if any, they are likely to be able to give; and if they wish to make a donation, by what date we may expect to have it (the sooner the better).

Unnecessary.

At the same time I am convinced it would be the wrong policy to attempt to levy any particular sum; the gift and the amount of the gift must be quite voluntary. And I am sure it would be better for the Society if it were supported by the general body of its members than by two or three people only.

I suggest a Committee be formed to put the scheme in shape and arrange the business affairs of the Society, but they must have nothing to do with either the teachings or the subjects of the lectures. They will certainly be of the same opinion, only in this open letter it is as well everything should be clearly stated.

Unnecessary.

I must also inform the future Committee that many members on joining insisted their names should not be disclosed and I must ask the Committee to respect their wishes and make this a rule.

Confused!

Now as to our funds, Mrs. Heywood-Smith has a credit balance of over twenty pounds for the Bund (please inform members of the exact amount.) And the Bund at present has sixty-four members, I believe. In addition there is a balance from your theosophical lodge; how far members of the lodge think they would simplify matters by joining the Bund, I am unaware.

So am I. So far we have made the arrangement—which has worked very well—that the Bund members attend the lodge meetings, & vice versa. The members of the lodge will remain in the T.S. as long as Dr. S. does!

As soon as a fresh sum of £25 has been collected I am prepared to add £150 in furtherance of the above scheme.

What scheme?

This would give a comfortable balance of about £100.

There is another larger scheme of buying a house and with this in view a very suitable house has been seen, freehold and a great bargain.

Some idea of cost should be given.

But however nice and however cheap, it would in my opinion be of little use without the support, moral and financial, of the members. Therefore members might quite well be invited to express their views on this to the Committee. We can call this latter scheme Scheme No. 2. And the following questions might be put to each member:—

Question 1. Would you care to continue to belong to the Society on a subscription of one guinea a year from (say) 1st October?

Subscriptions. This is a matter for the Committee to settle.

Question 2. In addition to this subscription, would you be inclined to assist in any way towards (a) the hire and maintenance of a suitable lodge room or (b) the purchase or hire or mortgage of a house, and if so, to what extent?

In scheme (b) I am prepared to assist up to a quarter, or twenty-five per cent, but with a security proportionately equal to that required by the providers of the remaining three quarters, or seventy-five per cent.

Finally, it must be made clear to everyone who joins that the Bund though undogmatic has for its sole purpose the study of Dr. Steiner's works and is therefore in the truest and purest sense a Theosophical Society.

Unnecessary.

In England Theosophy at present seems to mean something different and I can understand the objection people have in England to the name Theosophy.

Confused.

The formation of the 'Bund' gets over the difficulty.

What difficulty?

Yours faithfully,

(Signed) Harry Collison.

Ten to Three

In his reminiscences, translated into German as *Verwandeln des Lebens*, the Russian writer Andrei Belyi described Rudolf Steiner receiving visitors in Berlin:

> . . . And past these involved, restless rooms there stream, stream and stream all those who have announced themselves for a consultation with Steiner . . . Occasionally the visitor is a foreigner and speaks not a word of German; then Steiner quickly fetches Marija Yakovlevna' [Marie von Sivers]. She

who speaks many languages is his constant translator. In French he can make himself understood only with difficulty and with a pronounced accent. He was not gifted in languages. This side of him moved me. I was almost glad of it. It was extremely difficult for him to learn foreign languages, and from this inability of his I gained a certain feeling of security. It would be terrible to associate with a person who knows no difficulties...

In May 1912, while Steiner was coming and going in Berlin, the poet Rupert Brooke, gifted in the English language, was also resident in that town.

At the Café des Westens, Brooke wrote down a nostalgic poem first entitled in his manuscript 'The Sentimental Exile'. Later he changed the title, and it has been known ever since as 'The Old Vicarage, Grantchester':

Just now the lilac is in bloom,
All before my little room;
And in my flower-beds, I think,
Smile the carnation and the pink;
And down the borders, well I know,
The poppy and the pansy blow.
Oh! there the chestnuts, summer through,
Beside the river make for you
A tunnel of green gloom, and sleep
Deeply above; and green and deep
The stream mysterious glides beneath,
Green as a dream and deep as death.
—Oh damn! I know it! and I know
How the May fields all golden show,
And when the day is young and sweet,
Gild gloriously the bare feet
That run to bathe...

Du lieber Gott!

Here am I, sweating, sick, and hot,
And there the shadowed waters fresh
Lean up to embrace the naked flesh.
Temperamentvoll German Jews
Drink beer around; and there the dews
Are soft beneath a morn of gold.
Here tulips bloom as they are told;
Unkempt about those hedges blows
An English unofficial rose;
And there the unregulated sun
Slopes down to rest when day is done,

And wakes a vague unpunctual star,
A slippered Hesper; and there are
Meads towards Haslingfield and Coton
Where *das Betreten*'s not *verboten* . . .

ἔτθε γευοιμηυ . . . would I were
In Grantchester, in Grantchester!—
Some, it may be, can get in touch
With Nature there, or Earth, or such.
And clever modern men have seen
A Faun a-peeping through the green,
And felt the Classics were not dead,
To glimpse a Naiad's reedy head,
Or hear the Goat-foot piping low:
But these are things I do not know.
I only know that you may lie
Day long and watch the Cambridge sky,
And, flower-lulled in sleepy grass,
Hear the cool lapse of hours pass,
Until the centuries blend and blur
In Grantchester, in Grantchester . . .

God! I will pack, and take a train,
And get me to England once again!
For England's the one land, I know
Where men with Splendid Hearts may go;
And Cambridgeshire, of all England,
The shire for Men who Understand;
And of that district I prefer
The lovely hamlet Grantchester . . .
There's peace and holy quiet there,
Great clouds along pacific skies,
And men and women with straight eyes,
Lithe children lovelier than a dream,
A bosky wood, a slumbrous stream,
And little kindly winds that creep
Round twilight corners, half asleep . . .

Ah God! To see the branches stir
Across the moon at Grantchester!
To smell the thrilling-sweet and rotten,
Unforgettable, unforgotten
River-smell, and hear the breeze
Sobbing in the little trees
Say, do the elm-clumps greatly stand

Still guardians of that holy land?
The chestnuts shade, in reverend dream,
The yet unacademic stream?
Is dawn a secret, shy and cold
Anadyomene, silver-gold?
And sunset still a golden sea
From Haslingfield to Madingley?
And after, ere the night is born,
Do hares come out about the corn?
Oh, is the water sweet and cool,
Gentle and brown, above the pool?
And laughs the immortal river still
Under the mill, under the mill?
Say, is there Beauty yet to find?
And Certainty? And Quiet kind?
Deep meadows yet, for to forget
The lies, and truths, and pain? . . . oh! yet
Stands the church clock at ten to three?
And is there honey still for tea?

Mental Science

In May 1912 *The Path* opened with an article on 'The Path of Discipleship', stated in a footnote to have been 'an address delivered at the Blavatsky Institute by D.N. Dunlop'.

It opened:

> I can claim no originality for what I am going to say to you on this subject. I can only give you the substance of what has been said in many places by many writers and thinkers, keeping as far as possible to what my own experience has to some extent justified.
>
> A disciple may be self-appointed to the School of the Adepts or the School of the Masters. In the former the senses are used as a means leading to the control of the mind. In the latter the mind is turned from the objects of the senses to the reality which these objects reflect. Yet the disciple does not despise the senses; he knows that he must, through them, learn what the experience teaches. In both schools the experiences may be similar in character. Here I will pass on to you what has been stated by another member of the same school . . .

The person referred to was to H.W. Percival, and not only the first five sentences of the second paragraph but indeed the entire remainder of Dunlop's address, which covered some nine pages, was simply copied out from an editorial published in *The Word* in February 1910 as part of an ongoing series on 'Adepts, Masters and Mahatmas'.

Over in America, Percival must have had access to *The Path*, for at this point he finally came to notice the unacknowledged borrowings which Dunlop had been making from his editorials. He wrote to Dunlop calling his attention to what he was doing and asking him how he could claim as his own what he had taken from *The Word*. Dunlop replied that what was written in *The Word* must have been taken by Percival from the *Secret Doctrine* and other well-known books which were accessible to everybody. Percival wrote back stating that the editorials published in *The Word* were not taken from the *Secret Doctrine* or any other book, and that there was no other from which what had been printed in *The Path* could have been taken. He asked Dunlop to give the sources from which he claimed to draw. On receiving another reply with what he considered 'contemptible excuses', Percival wrote to Dunlop again requesting him either to cease publishing his articles or else to give credit to *The Word* for what it published.

★

The May issue of *Theosophy in Scotland* announced:

> Arrangements have been made to hold the Fourth International Summer School at Torquay, for two weeks, 3rd to 17th August. The headquarters are to be in the Bath Saloons, and will comprise lecture room, visitors' room, sale library and business offices. The growth of the movement makes it impossible any longer to accommodate, as residents in one building, all who wish to attend. For general convenience arrangements have been made for parties of from ten to fifty visitors to be allocated to various selected boarding establishments and private hotels. The booking fee is five shillings per week and admits to all meetings. Board and residence can be had from thirty-five shillings a week. All communications to be addressed to the Secretary, 7 Oakley House, Bloomsbury Street, London, W.C.

★

In the June issue of *The Vâhan* appeared a report concerning matters in Germany:

> To the Berlin correspondent of the *Observer* we are indebted for the following interesting paragraphs.
>
> 'Plans have been completed for the erection of an imposing Temple of Theosophy at Schwabing, a well-known retreat near Munich. The temple is to serve the combined purposes of college, theatre, chapel, monastery and

hospital, and its dedication next year is to be made the occasion of a great gathering of theosophists. The official title of the temple will be "High School for Mental Science".

'Architecturally the new temple is to be an imposing creation, with two immense domes as conspicuous features. Music and drama portraying and idealizing theosophic doctrine are to be performed regularly in the theatre section of the temple, which will have room for nine hundred persons.'

We sympathize heartily with this project of our German brethren—except perhaps with the hospital if it is part of the one building, as that should be situated at some distance off, so as to isolate its influence. Some stress is inevitably being laid at present on the differences of belief which tend to separate off the followers of Dr. Steiner from the main stream of theosophic teaching. We therefore welcome the opportunity to say that any work done in the interests of Theosophy and the spiritual amelioration of humanity, even though we may differ on subsidiary methods and beliefs, has the cordial sympathy and respect of English theosophists. Our personal differences of belief count for little in comparison with the giving of Theosophy to a nation through the methods to which it is temperamentally drawn.

Towards the end of June, Rudolf Steiner made his way to Munich. He stayed there through the whole of July and further, busy with rehearsals for his next mystery play *Der Hüter der Schwelle*, which was going to receive its first performance in late August.

Now it was also in Munich during this time that Robert Felkin and his wife Harriot, together with Neville Meakin, attended a cultic ritual of the Mystica Aeterna. Their attendance was to become the source of much confusion in British occult circles.

The confusion seems indeed to be directly traceable to Felkin himself. His own account, quoted by 'Inquire Within' in *Light-Bearers of Darkness*, reads as follows: (F.R. = 'Finem Respice', Felkin's own motto, and Q.L. = 'Quaero Lucem', that of his wife.)

In June and July 1912 Frater F.R. and Soror Q.L. were able to go to Germany, and altogether visited five Rosicrucian Temples in different parts of the Continent, and were initiated themselves, Soror Q.L. obtaining grades equivalent to our 7-4 and Frater F.R. 8-3. The rituals not being in MS. form, they are memorized.

This probably indicates that the Felkins during their visit to the Continent came into contact with various groups of Freemasons. In their view, the Mystica Aeterna was simply one of these groups. And they imagined themselves to have received from Steiner some Masonic grades.

Each in Our Own Individual Way

The present chapter reproduces a series of letters which passed between Herbert Heywood-Smith, Colonel Webber and Harry Collison at the end of June and beginning of July.

Correspondence began with a letter from Heywood-Smith to Collison:

37 Ridgmont Gardens,
London, W.C.
June 29th 1912

Dear Mr. Collison,

Doubtless by this time you will have received a form from Col. Webber for you to fill in the amount of your subscription towards providing a home for the Rose Cross teachings in England.

However, since the forms were sent out I have decided that it would be more in accordance with the spirit of the Rose X to work not on a minimum subscription of 1 guinea but entirely on a voluntary basis. On a voluntary basis the hierarchical principle is the only one possible & in accordance with this there can be but one head to a group.

Would you therefore prefer to form your own group?

Please do not think this course is suggested from any spirit of antagonism. There is no reason whatever why we should not work harmoniously together with one another, each at the head of his own group.

On the other hand, supposing you do not care to work a separate group, it must be clearly understood at the outset that I work the group in the way I judge best. If you are willing to agree to this, then will you let me know as soon as possible what amount you are willing to subscribe yearly towards the work, so that we may find a room in accordance with our means.

Please do not misunderstand my motive in penning this letter. It is sent in the friendliest spirit, & only with the intention of providing a clear understanding of the base on which we wish to work. Please let me know as soon as possible the course you would like to take.

I hope that you are enjoying your holiday & will return much benefited by the change.

I remain

Yours very sincerely,
H.J. Heywood-Smith

★

On the very next day, Colonel Webber also wrote a letter to Collison:

5, the Grove,
Boltons,
S.W.
Sunday June 30th

Dear Collison,

I had written an answer to your letter & was going to post it when I had a letter from Mr. Heywood-Smith sending copy of a letter he was sending you, proposing that you should either each have a group or else there should be only one head, as he does not think the present way of working satisfactory.

I confess that having two heads (one away) is not a good plan. The number of heads should be either three or one, & the minority when three to abide loyally by the wishes of the majority.

I do not think matters are satisfactory as they are at present. Many people, including yourself, have not filled in & returned the papers the committee sent out, so as we do not know what funds we shall have, matters are in abeyance & appear according to present arrangements likely to remain so.

When we hear from you whether you intend starting a separate circle or not, we shall know much better how we stand & can get a house or rooms according to our requirements.

In reply to questions in your letter, the 'New Steiner Society' was a short name for the 'Bund' in England, which I believe I am responsible for. If a better name can be found we can alter it, but our circular had to be headed with some sort of title, our intention being to see the 'Bund' but with an English name.

The other points to which I replied do not now require reply on account of Mr. Heywood-Smith's making fresh arrangements.

I hope we shall see you in England soon refreshed by your travel.

With best wishes,

Yours very sincerely,

J. Webber

★

Collison replied to Heywood-Smith:

Poste Restante,
Marstrand,
Sweden.
6th July 1912

Dear Mr. Heywood-Smith,

Thank you for your letter. Believe me when I say that I sincerely reciprocate the kind sentiments therein expressed. The only reason for our temporary disagreement is that we are both terribly in earnest. This does not mean friction. I am glad you have decided that any connection with Dr. Steiner should be worked out entirely on a voluntary basis. It has always been my own idea & is more consistent with the principles of the Bund. I have written to Colonel Webber to say so.

I also agree that it would be better for each of us to form & work his own group.

As I do not think, however, that our ideas are quite the same concerning outer matters, & we are now starting afresh & on quite a new basis, I will not as yet contribute to any room in common. I have always considered the scheme a little premature.

Let us start in the spiritual way & it will grow into the organic form for which it is most naturally suited.

I think this is a happy solution & believe it will make us work each in our own individual way in harmony with one another & with the Bund.

With best regards,

Yours very sincerely,

Harry Collison

★

Colonel Webber wrote Collison a further letter:

5, the Grove,
Boltons, S.W.
July 8th 1912

Dear Collison,

Thanks for your letter. I got yours of 21st some days ago and had written you a reply when your Co. Representative showed me a letter written to you which altered matters, so I delayed answering until I had heard from you whether you would subscribe to Mr. Heywood-Smith's group, or start one of your own.

I think that any rate there should be only one head to a group, as no member can follow the leadership of two men who have sometimes possibly different views, which makes it unpleasant for everybody: and where there exists division of opinion, plans cannot be definitely formulated, settled and adhered to; and we want to start the 'Bund' in England on a clear and satisfactory basis & without any discussion.

Mr. Heywood-Smith announced a few days ago that subscriptions would be voluntary, and our committee, to give you both a free hand in your arrangements, resigned.—Mr. Heywood-Smith does not think a committee necessary for his group.—I still hold the funds collected as a temporary measure.

You mention your 'open letter' to Mr. Heywood-Smith and express regret that the views therein have been ignored. I do not see how this concerns me; it is a matter between you and Mr. Heywood-Smith, as it is not my province to give any directives or take any action on a letter one representative addresses to another.

Besides, the wishes therein were not, according to my idea, ignored. I read your open letter to the committee, and it was your suggestion mentioned in questions (1) and (2) that a guinea subscription should be fixed and a donation as well. This the committee sent out, but you yourself have not replied as yet, though you voluntarily promised £50 subs. when £25 had been collected—which it has.

I need hardly go into the question of whether any subs. may or may not be fixed for us by the 'Bund' Headquarters, as probably if we accept the teaching of the Bund, they may leave us to manage our own finances in accordance with local requirements.

A Society cannot be carried on without funds, which I presume Headquarters will expect us to find for our branch. Raising objections to the methods without suggesting other means is certainly not helpful, and causes much delay and uncertainty.

However, things will no doubt be much easier to manage when the sole head of a group can definitely settle matters his own way, in accordance with general directives from the Bund—and we can then work quicker and harmoniously.

I hope you are well & enjoying your trip.

Yours sincerely,

J. Webber

P.S. The name 'The New Steiner Society' I was responsible for, as we had to send out our circular with some heading or other. If this name is not approved it can be changed at Headquarters or otherwise.

★

Heywood-Smith replied to Collison:

37 R. G. London
July 10th 1912

Dear Mr. Collison,

Many thanks for your letter. I am glad you concur in the sentiments expressed in my last letter & will form your own group. This clears the ground a good deal & I am sure that we shall work in this way quite amicably & harmoniously.

With regard to the amount I hold, contributed by those who wished to hear the lectures until the end of July, together with the chairs purchased, if you are agreeable I propose to place this towards the expenses of my group, as you have been away and I have given all the lectures.

In forming my group of course I have not approached any of your

37 R. G. London
July 10th 1912.

Dear Mr Collison,

Many thanks for your letter. I am glad you concur in the sentiments expressed in my last letter & that you will form your own Group. This clears the ground a good deal & I am sure that we shall work in this way quite amicably & harmoniously.

With regard to the amount I hold, contributed by those who wished to hear the lectures until the end of July, together with the chairs purchased, if you are agreeable I propose to place this towards the expenses of my Group, as you have been away & I have given all the lectures.

In forming my Group of course I have not approach any of your people – those in the following list – so you will know who to write to in forming yours:—

Wilson. Parr. Blake. Halliday. Heriot. Loder. Hardy. Montag Bricka. Walker. Stuttaford. Brant. Riddel. Hamilton. Cull. McGill. Gray. Crawford. Richards. Thurburn. Studd. Villiers. Corbett. Hoare. Halse Cook. Congreve. Sir F & Lady Hogg. Bevan. Rosenkrang. Hughes. Morrison.

Several of the above, viz., Wilson, Parr, Blake, Halliday, Heriot, Loder, Montagu, Bricka, Walker & Stuttaford had promised donations while the plan was to carry on the Work as one grou To these I have written informing them that you intend formin a Group of your own & that if they wish to join yours then they are free as regards their promise.

I think that is all clear. If there is anything else later I will write again.

With all good wishes,
Yours very sincerely
H. J. Heywood-Smith.

people—those in the following list—so you will know who to write to in forming yours:—

Wilson. Parr. Blake. Halliday. Heriot. Loder. Hardy. Montagu. Bricka. Walker. Stuttaford. Brent. Riddel. Hamilton. Cull. McGill. Gray. Crawford. Richards. Thurburn. Studd. Villiers. Corbett. Hoare. Halsey. Cook. Congreve. Sir F. & Lady Hogg. Bevan. Rosenkrantz. Hughes. Morrison.

Several of the above, viz., Wilson, Parr, Blake, Halliday, Heriot, Loder, Montagu, Bricka, Walker & Stuttaford had promised donations while the plan was to carry on the work as one group. To these I have written informing them that you intend forming a group of your own & if they wish to join yours then they are free as regards their promise.

I think that all is clear. If there is anything else later then I will write again.

With all good wishes,

Yours very sincerely,

H.J. Heywood-Smith

P.S. Mrs. Cook has been elected a member of the Executive Committee of the T.S. Headquarters here. You may have seen this in the *Vâhan.*

A Decided Cosmic Sweep

The issue of *The Vâhan* to which Herbert Heywood-Smith referred also carried an announcement:

Light on the Path Lodge

This lodge is international. It invites to membership students of *Light on the Path*, or those who desire to become students. Persons who are not members of the Theosophical Society and who wish to join in the study undertaken by the lodge may become associates of the lodge.

The special work of the lodge will be conducted by means of question meetings, to be held at whatever place seems most desirable, and to be announced in the *Vâhan.* Questions must be sent in before the meetings, in writing, in order that their importance may be considered. Important questions and answers will probably be published in *The Path*, and afterwards sold separately to subscribers in all countries under the title of *Proceedings of Light on the Path Lodge of the Theosophical Society.* It is hoped that by this means there will be an increase of understanding in respect to this 'archaic writing', which has its students already in every country in the world.

All communications should be addressed to the President of the Lodge, Mabel Collins, 19, Tavistock Square, London, W.C., or to the Secretary at the same address.

A preliminary meeting of the above lodge will be held at 19A, Tavistock Square, W.C., on Friday evening, July 5, at 8.15. This meeting will be open to all F.T.S. who may be interested. Questions on *Light on the Path* will be answered and discussed. Questions should be sent in at once to Mabel Collins, 19, Tavistock Square, W.C., accompanied by the name and address of sender.

D.N. Dunlop,
Secretary.

★

On 17 July, *The Christian Commonwealth* carried a paragraph about 'The Summer School Habit':

> The promoters of the Fourth International Summer School have selected a beautiful locality for the gathering this year. Mr. D.N. Dunlop, the director of the school, writes that he has been down to Torquay, and is delighted with the environs for the purposes of the school. In such a place the 'outdoors' has a decided cosmic sweep, and the programme of lectures is so arranged that one may benefit by the attractions of land and sea, and enjoy a holiday, stimulating physically as well as mentally. New ideas are as much of a tonic as a change of air, and from the syllabus of lectures there promises to be plenty of suggestions and food for thought in the air at this summer school. All phases of thought must find their correlation one with another in the mind of the future humanity, and these summer gatherings from year to year, under the wing of certain idealists and mystics, realize to some extent the possibilities of a great synthetizing consciousness made up of many diversified individuals. In this way unity in religion, philosophy, science and social service is sought. Carefully arranged programmes of music will be provided by Miss Margaret Holloway (violinist), Mr. Van der Straeten (cellist), and others. A descriptive pamphlet and complete programme of lectures can be obtained from Department C., Fourth International Summer School, Oakley House, Bloomsbury Street, W.C.

★

The Summer School took place from 3 to 17 August.

One intending participant was again the old German theosophist Franz Hartmann, who it may be noted had been present in April 1897 at the Theosophical Convention in New York also attended by Dunlop. But once more Hartmann did not arrive. He had reached the end of his days and died on 7 August, as noted in a first instalment in September of his memories of H.P. Blavatsky, 'translated with Dr. Hartmann's permission, and corrections, for publication in *The Path*'. Further instalments followed.

Progressive March

Walter Johannes Stein's notes about the life of D.N. Dunlop state:

Mother † with 26 Dunlop only 5
from Arran
Mother in cave looking at the waves
like Iphigeneia

In his article 'An Appreciation of Daniel Nicol Dunlop' published in December 1935 in *The Present Age*, Stein expanded these notes.

> Mr. Dunlop's mother died when she was twenty-six, and the little boy was only five. The mother was born in Arran. Mr. Dunlop told me that his only memory of her was a little cave on the beach that was shown to him, where he was told that his mother had often sat deep in thought, looking at the waves. He often came to sit in this cave and gaze on the sea, and think about his mother whom he so much missed.

This can only be the Black Cave at Bennan Head, a few hundred yards west of the village of Kildonan on the south coast of Arran. On a clear day, Ireland is just visible from this cave on the distant horizon.

★

H.P. Blavatsky was another person with a connection to caves, shown especially in a book written in her native Russian and published in English translation in 1892 under the title *From the Caves and Jungles of Hindostan.*

In course of her introduction to the first volume of *The Secret Doctrine*, written in English and published in 1888, Blavatsky discussed the figure of Buddha. Here are some of her remarks:

> Indeed the secret portions of the '*Dan*' or '*Jan-na*' ('*Dhyan*') of Gautama's metaphysics—grand as they appear to one unacquainted with the tenets of the Wisdom Religion of antiquity—are but a very small portion of the whole. The Hindu reformer limited his public teachings to the purely moral and physiological aspect of the Wisdom-Religion, to Ethics and MAN alone. Things 'unseen and incorporeal', the mystery of Being outside our terrestrial sphere, the great Teacher left entirely untouched in his public lectures, reserving the hidden Truths for a select circle of his Arhats. The latter received their Initiation at the famous Saptaparna cave (the *Sattapanni* of Mahavansa) near Mount Baibhâr (the Webhâra of the Pali MSS.). This cave was in Rajagriha, the ancient capital of Mogadha, and was the *Cheta* cave of Fa-hian, as rightly suspected by some archaeologists. (Mr. Beglor, the chief engineer at Buddhagaya, and a distinguished archaeologist, was the first, we believe, to discover it.)

★

The reason why Dunlop selected Torquay in particular as the venue for the 1912 Summer School is shown by a quotation reproduced at the foot of a page in the August number of *The Path.* It is taken from a chapter on 'Esoteric Geological Chronology' found in the fourth section, 'Duration of the Geological Periods' of the third part, 'Science and the Secret Doctrine Contrasted', of the second volume, 'Anthropogenesis', of *The Secret Doctrine.*

The first half of the quotation reads:

> The Esoteric Doctrine teaches distinctly the risings and falls of civilizations ... The most interesting example of this progressive march is perhaps afforded by the celebrated Kent's Cavern at Torquay ...

In *The Secret Doctrine* itself, the quoted passage continues:

> In that strange recess, excavated by water out of the Devonian limestone, we find a most curious record preserved for us in the geological memoirs of the earth. Under the blocks of limestone, which heaped the floor of the cavern, were discovered, embedded in a deposit of black earth, many implements of the Neolithic period of fairly excellent workmanship, with a few fragments of pottery, possibly traceable to the era of the Roman colonization. There is no trace of Palaeolithic man here. When, however, we penetrate still deeper through the dense layer of stalagmite beneath the mould into the red earth, which of course itself once formed the pavement of the retreat, things assume a very different aspect. Not one implement fit to bear comparison with the finely-chipped weapons found in the overlying stratum is to be seen; only a host of the rude and lumbering little hatchets and scrapers of the Palaeolithic age, mixed up confusedly with the bones of species now either extinct or emigrated, driven away by change of climate.

The conclusion of the passage is reproduced in the second half of the quotation given in *The Path*:

> In all cases we meet with the same evidence that, from historic to Neolithic and from Neolithic to Palaeolithic man, things slope downwards on an inclined plane from the rudiments of civilization to the most abject barbarism—in Europe again.

Set in the context of *The Path*, this quotation may be said to indicate that the choice of Torquay as venue for the Summer School was meant to highlight the converse rising of civilization in Europe, its 'progressive march' from Palaeolithic through Neolithic and historical periods up to the present and on into the future.

With Hope to the Future

On the Continent in September, Rudolf Steiner gave to Lory Maier-Smits the first elements of the new art of eurythmy.

It is interesting to compare what was being attempted in August in the British Isles, as shown in a description of 'The Summer School at Torquay' contributed by J.H. Elder to *Theosophy in Scotland.*

> The ideal underlying the International Summer School is probably sufficiently understood by most of our readers: its aim is 'to vitalize all worthy ideals which shape the minds of men and women to a common end'. It is a great experiment, or rather a series of experiments (may they be many!) in co-operative thinking, in the use and organization of the collective mind, the shaping of minds to a common end. And how has it worked?
>
> Those who have had the advantage and pleasure of participating in more than one of the International Summer Schools begin to realize that there is here no question of stereotyped repetition, that its promoters do not live on memory, but turn the mind 'with hope to the future, hope in new possibilities without end, new ideas, new inspirations'—and that each successive manifestation of the underlying idea must be different in many details. Time alone—a brief fortnight—limits the might-have-been, ruthlessly excludes many aspects. But the briefness of its duration prevents the undue hardening of the form, and that also makes for good.
>
> No, Torquay was not too hot. And the scattering of members in various houses separated by some little distance from each other, if it made the preliminary task of welding the gathering into a living body more difficult, only showed that it could be successfully accomplished. The heart and centre was at the lecture-rooms, and the circulation was healthy throughout.
>
> Lectures took place morning and evening, and as the days proceeded nearly every lecturer gathered an extra group of people interested in their special subjects. These groups grew rapidly; it became more and more difficult to find time for all. Distracted enthusiasts waited outside lecture rooms to pounce on a spare room or hour, and still more distracted individuals tried to attend two lectures within an hour! Nothing more need be said concerning appreciation of the mental fare.
>
> The School was truly international—France, Holland, Denmark were represented, Russia sent us Madame Pogosky and also an artist, W. Wroblewski, whose ideals drew a large group around him; America gave us a poet, Charles Wheeler; Australia a mystic, Mr. Kroemer; and Scotland added a fresh element in the person of Professor Patrick Geddes, whose lecture on 'Greek Ideals' was warmly received. Religion, philosophy, theosophy, occultism, life and its problems, educational and otherwise, were

presented in various aspects, the breadth of the platform allowing the discussion of opposing points of view and helping to the realization that

> There are nine and sixty ways of inditing tribal lays,
> And every single one of them is right.

The President of the Theosophical Society sent a cordial letter of greeting to the Summer School, emphasizing the importance of freedom of thought and the value of differences in opinion. There is no doubt the position accorded to art by the organizers would meet with her warm appreciation. The high standard of the music supplied at the beginning or end of every formal lecture is a special feature. Painting had its exponent in Mr. Wroblewski, and poetry was represented in a new and interesting experiment. The School had the distinction of inspiring Mr. Wheeler with 'The Dance of Life', which the author recited to the accompaniment of a symbolic dance by Eleanor Elder, who represented 'Life'. The audience received the novelty of dancing to poetry instead of to music very favourably, and it is hoped that a repetition will take place in London. Dramatic art was also represented in readings from *Peer Gynt*, and in the beautiful rendering of Plato's *Gorgias* read in the open air.

It is hoped that it may be possible for Mr. Dunlop to hold the Fifth International Summer School in Scotland next August, and we are sure that as many of our members as can possibly attend will eagerly avail themselves of the great opportunity which will come to their doors.

Before the Voice Can Speak

An article contributed by Winnifred Leisenring to *The Path* stated:

> The International Summer School to promote unity in religion, science, philosophy and other branches of social service closed its fourth annual session on Friday evening, August 16th, at Torquay. The vitality of this movement is evident in the cumulating community of interest among members of the school. No two of these four annual gatherings have been alike. They have each been characteristic of some one phase of human consciousness as it labours for realization of itself. The call is sent out to bring together comrades who work in diverse spheres for the coming of divine humanity on Earth, and the majority of those who respond meet with a pure purpose, disinterested in persons and parties, but 'strong in will to strive, to seek, to find' the secret of beauty in life and work. The 'silent, cyclic chemistry' modifying humanity from moment to moment works towards a mysterious triumphant finale, and in its activities exercises a binding influence from which true comrades cannot escape. There is a tie

which, in our ordinary fearful conceptions of life, is not a tie. It is the tie inhering in each human being; it causes him to realize his common life with the Earth and its essences, which have been distilled from subtler substances and originated in that intangible 'seed perfection' hidden in every moment and motion of consciousness.

Religion, philosophy, science, art, are really artificial divisions of thought; they are different ways of examining and expressing life, and represent separate paths of discovery. We are at a time when, in bringing together thinkers on these different paths, we may see the similar state of consciousness underlying all sincere effort in these worlds of thought. The leaders of humanity are closing in around a common citadel; they have climbed the hill on which are the temples of the gods. And these temples are never entered by any partisan priest, for there is one law that the priests of all religions and sciences, of all philosophies and arts must find before they understand the gods. One finds this law frequently referred to in contemporary literature, whereas not so long ago there were only many special laws defined in the different departments as the law of gravity, the law of dynamics, etc. Man has found law operating wherever he has made investigations, and he is coming to the conclusion that all specific, differentiated laws finally merge into The Law.

This is the Law by which H.P. Blavatsky saw, rising out of all our modern researches in science, in archaeology, in myth and symbol, the Supreme, Self-Knowing Intelligence of humanity which she named the Master. This indeed is He—the Master-Mind in whom humanity is one. He is the humanity who never dies, but who ever seeks his own through all His different organisms, His nations and races of the Earth . . .

The article went on to describe the lectures, mentioning among others those of Wm. L. Hare, Sir Richard Stapley, W. Tudor Pole, Mrs. Cook and Charles Lazenby.

★

Mrs. Cook was better known by the name of Mabel Collins, who brought out in *The Vâhan* an article entitled 'Transactions of the *Light on the Path* Lodge (A Brief Extract from a discussion at the International Summer School in August)'.

Question.—'Kill out ambition.' Is that to be effected at the beginning of the Path?

Answer.—I understand it as only to be attempted after the first initiation is passed, that initiation which is defined and described in the first four rules of *Light on the Path*; an initiation which is not external and is not accompanied by any ceremonial, but is a change of spiritual attitude which places the ego in a new position towards life.

Question.—What then should be the attitude towards ambition of the person who has not passed this initiation?

Answer.—I think that ambition leads him to rise out of indifference and apathy, and approach the Path. It is a great strengthening quality. I regard the desire to enter on the Path as the highest form of ambition. After the initiation of which the 'four truths' are the expression, you work as those work who are ambitious, but without the thought of self-advancement which has previously been the incentive. The first two of these rules bring the neophyte to the 'harmlessness' of the Yogin. 'Before the eyes can see' represents the attitude of 'compassion' with which the student of *The Yoga Aphorisms of Patanjali* is acquainted, as being the first great step upon the Path. The personality is laid down, and then compassion arises, and the disciple can no longer fight against any other. The warrior in him from thenceforth fights against evil forces, not against other personalities. The next two rules refer to the Masters. 'Before the voice can speak' we have agreed to accept as meaning the opening of the soul towards the Master to receive the influx from Him. It is not speech in the sense of noise, but an 'asking'. 'Before the soul can stand in the presence of the Masters' could be expressed thus: 'Before the soul is perfectly steadfast, so that it cannot be shaken, or turned aside, or thrown down. It has no longer to decide upon direction: it has decided, and it remains steadfast whatever may happen.'

The Vision of the City Beautiful

D.N. Dunlop published a series of reflections in *The Path*:

The Fourth International Summer School has come and gone. The meetings at Torquay were a great success. In my opinion the lectures reached a higher standard than at any previous Summer School. The fact that members of the School were scattered about in different boarding-houses prevented to some extent the realization of social unity; it was more difficult to build a body for the 'Nirmanakaya' of the group. Those who attended our gatherings in previous years missed this fusing element. Notwithstanding this, interesting groups were formed for sustained study, and links were forged between comrades which will not soon be broken. Our experience at the 1912 Summer School taught us many lessons which will be valuable for the future. A strong 'nucleus' has been formed around which some permanent centre may be established for work along many lines, and in the fullness of time, when the right place is discovered, our Christmas and Easter festivals and our Summer Schools will succeed in building a home for comrade-pilgrims from many lands, where the invisible presence will descend, where the soundless voice will be heard in the stillness of the heart. This is our greatest need. Under such conditions all our ideals may be projected in a common ideal, and our most sacred aspirations invoke the 'mysterious visitor' who will express them in the miracle of love in which all personal elements are absent. Here the fragments of the bread of life will be gathered in baskets to feed the multitude. May we all learn to be obedient disciples of the Great One, to mount on the eagle wings of the imagination, to run with winged feet His errands, to walk with steady feet the path of light, and while in the wilderness of life, to faint not by the way.

The Temple of the love of Comrades is not easy to build; the work of the masons is often tedious, and 'weather' conditions delay the building operations. The plan of the Architect is in our hands, but trust and devotion are needed if the building is to be completed. The interest of each should be devoted to carrying out the plan to perfection, not devotion to any lesser light than the highest. Each 'stone' for the building must be chiselled by loving hands and adapted to its place in the edifice; the cement uniting all the stones must be love. Our song must be the song of the busy workers at their labour of love—the song of the builders—what a song! Sometimes when lectures were being delivered at the Summer School I heard it in the silence; others heard it too.

Not a few have had their lives made more significant, full and beautiful by the stimulus of the Summer Schools; they have been enabled to walk through the 'murky' cities with the vision of the City Beautiful before their eyes. The fire of comradeship glowing in the heart has warmed them through many a bleak hour, and made physical distance and separation as nought; the faces of distant comrades have glowed radiant in the fire, and all misgivings and distrust obliterated. What is the use of the Summer Schools? Have they not been more than justified by the results? The fire generated by 'the dear love of comrades' may flicker spasmodically sometimes in a few hearts, but it can go out no more; in others it grows steadily—brighter and brighter to the perfect flame, illuminating the future and giving a new significance and warmth to every human gesture, as we walk together by the way of life.

A comrade writes:—'Looking back on the great spirit of the Summer School, I begin to think that on that level where it met in the hearts of its children, there was a yawning crevice which yet has to be filled by something that the children failed to bring. Methinks it is not a holiday after a strenuous year of labour we had in view. All through the year, meeting daily fresh problems of life and feeling our own insufficiency, we longed for the comrades' meeting-ground where the soul could be unburdened, the sharp little pain removed, and we might feel whole again. It is not with frolics and lusty songs we should embark for such a goal! For him who seeks, for him who suffers this suggestive little pain in his heart of hearts, nothing less than a true pilgrimage will do; nothing less than a laborious march through the dusty roads, a hunger and a thirst of the body, a fixing of our thirsty wandering soul into the far-away Self that may bring us nearer. I believe in pilgrimages. Through thousands and thousands of years there have been human beings who undertook pilgrimages, who went through them unflinchingly and—perhaps—reached the far-away Self. Let us go to the next Summer School in the spirit of the ancient pilgrimages.'

'Cheerfulness, gaiety and the high heart' are required by the soul of man, and are as necessary to the growth of the soul as food is to the body. We go forward to the future with courage, gaiety, hope, preparing again for the pleasant meeting of friend and friend, of men and women together in mutual confidence and love for stimulation to service in innumerable ways. The love of true comradeship runs into many moulds, building up the arts, literature, sciences, industries and civilizations. With this vitality we shall attack great labours together cheerfully, for the work we are trying to do lies at the root of health, gaiety, courage and exuberant life.

D.N.D.

Out of the Great Unknown

Reaching the year 1912 in his biography of AE, *That Myriad-Minded Man* (1975), Henry Summerfield stated:

> AE had now become one of the greatest talkers of Dublin, a city famous for the quality of its conversation. He had only two rivals, James Stephens, the master of comic fantasy, and the scholar Mackenna . . . AE's own talk ranged over the whole field of his interests; he was as ready to launch forth on dairy farming as on the *Bhagavadgita* or the origins of the Abbey Theatre. Images, quotations and epigrammatic phrases flowed in a melodious stream that drew the listener into the speaker's own intellectual realm. While talking, he usually held his pipe, and from time to time he gestured with his hands. If he read a passage from a book, he would hold it close to his eyes on account of his shortsightedness. He spoke with a mellow Ulster accent, and the rhythms of his speech seemed to some inclined to become too pronounced; Yeats was once heard to protest: 'For God's sake get Russell a harp.' As he became older, the habit of the monologue grew on him. One of his friends noticed that his talk on Sunday was often repeated in his next leading article in the *Homestead* . . .
>
> James Stephens wrote: 'AE as a bulk was gay; he inclined to sit on the top of the morning all day.' When the conversation ran spontaneously, the

lighter side of his personality was given free rein. His humour, which delighted his friends, appears only occasionally in his writing. Teasing a visiting English lady, he warned her 'that she would never resist the Celtic atmosphere, struggle how she might, but would soon be wandering in the mountain mists with a fillet round her head.' When Yeats's sisters were at their wits' end trying to persuade their father to return from America, he suggested they cable: 'Family all dying. Come to receive last messages.' Dr. Gibbon recalls the gusto with which he parodied his own poetry, and he caricatured the style of Yeats's lyrics for Susan Mitchell's anthology *Secret Springs of Dublin Song*...

By this period the greatness of AE had become evident to his contemporaries. For many of them it lay in the rare perfection of his character, rather than in the sum of his varied achievement. The mystic, the poet, the artist, the practical man and the editor had coalesced in a radiant personality that communicated a zest for living, limitless compassion, an ardent love of beauty and an unquenchable optimism in the future of the universe to a wide circle of friends, acquaintances and readers. In articles and memoirs they recorded their wonder at finding a man who seemed to have recreated in himself the harmony that he had discovered in the universe, and to have opened up in some secret recess of his being a wellspring of the spiritual qualities that all religions praise. They felt intuitively that he had annihilated in himself every trace of hatred, greed and malice, and had almost succeeded in renouncing in his heart personal ambition and pride. He seemed to have transcended the egotism from which sprang the emotions that dominated normal life. Entering into his presence, the worldly glimpsed his serenity, and briefly escaped from their own self-centered emotional shells. In a country seething with many hatreds, men who were irreconcilable political enemies met peacefully in his home.

Katherine Tynan wrote of him: 'He is of the world, unworldly—the world's stain has never touched him; without religion, yet profoundly religious; the peace of God which passeth understanding lies all about him...There is no room in him for any of the small meannesses of humanity. There is something strangely benign about him. He keeps his image of God undistorted, undefaced, as few of us have kept it. When I am struck cold, remembering that such and such a one, something uniquely precious of God's making, is no longer of this world, I turn to think upon George Russell, that untroublesome genius. I am glad that in all probability he will survive me, for of him, more than anyone else I have ever known, I would say: We shall never look on his like again.'

Mr. Diarmuid Russell, who only came to know his father intimately in adult life, writes of the atmosphere that surrounded him: '...he possessed, more than any other person I have met, an air of spiritual power, an emanation of sweetness and tenderness that was almost as perceptible as the light from a lamp—and as hard to describe.' Wishing to evoke his presence, many resorted to the word 'goodness'—and felt its inadequacy. His friend Dr. Constantine Curran found a Franciscan quality in his life, and tried to define his effect on the authors he helped: '. . . during his life he was to these writers, and now in memory remains, part of their conscience, a tribunal before which the ignoble dwindles.'

Stephen Mackenna almost wept when AE, in a passing mood of despondency, wrote of his service in the Co-operative Movement as a desertion of his spiritual duty: 'I say to myself "It was done for the beloved motherland, this errantry of mine," but I know in my heart that the service I gave was an easier and lower service than doing the best and highest it was in me to do.' In his reply Mackenna declared: 'I have always thought of you, always in these long years, as one of the noble expressions of the divine mind . . .'

Carrie Rea, another friend to whom he was a spiritual guide, said after his death: '. . . I have always thought of him as one who came out of the Great Unknown, and who after a short period partially withdrew again. He might have had neither father, mother nor brother.'

Mr. Padraic Colum, too, sensed that there was a kind of homelessness about him, which yet was in no way melancholy. Many descriptions of AE recall the young George Richmond's feeling that talking with the elderly Blake was like conversing with the prophet Isaiah. Maurice Joy, at one time secretary to Plunkett, wrote: 'He could be the simplest and warmest of companions, and when one walked with him, all human as he was, along an Irish country road in the moonlight, one could at least understand why it was that on the road to Emmaus the hearts of certain fishermen burned within them.'

A Voice of Thunder from a Bygone Age

In his autobiographical sketch of 1935, D.N. Dunlop recalled his Irish years:

> At the end of the nineteenth century, the works of H.P. Blavatsky were making a greater stir in the West than is often realized. Her writings attracted around that strange, enigmatical personality minds of calibre and students of mystical and occult philosophy all over the world. The Stanzas of Dzyan seemed to be a voice of thunder from a bygone age, carrying their own conviction of spiritual reality, but remote and imperfectly understood. For years I was engrossed, in company with the Irish poet AE and others whose names have since become well known, in the study of H.P. Blavatsky's works . . .

The Stanzas of Dzyan were discussed by Blavatsky in her introduction to *The Secret Doctrine*, placed at the beginning of the first volume, on 'Cosmogenesis':

> One of the greatest, and, withal, the most serious objection to the correctness and reliabiliity of the whole work will be the preliminary STANZAS: 'How can the statements contained in them be verified?' True, if a great portion of the Sanskrit, Chinese, and Mongolian works quoted in the present volumes are known to some Orientalists, the chief work—that one from which the Stanzas are given—is not in the possession of European libraries. The Book of Dzyan (or 'Dzan') is utterly unknown to our Philologists, or at any rate was never heard of by them under its present name. This is, of course, a great drawback to those who follow the methods of research prescribed by official science; but to the students of Occultism, and to every genuine Occultist, this will be of little moment...
>
> Agreeably with the rules of critical scholarship, the Orientalist has to reject *a priori* whatever evidence he cannot fully verify for himself. And how can a Western scholar accept on hearsay that which he knows nothing about? Indeed, that which is given in these volumes is selected from *oral*, as much as from written teachings. The first instalment of the esoteric doctrines is based upon Stanzas which are the records of a people unknown to ethnology; it is claimed that they are written in a tongue absent from the nomenclature of languages and dialects with which philology is acquainted; they are said to emanate from a source (Occultism) repudiated by science; and, finally, they are offered through an agency incessantly discredited before the world by all those who hate unwelcome truths, or have some special hobby of their own to defend. Therefore, the rejection of these teachings may be expected, and must be accepted beforehand. No one styling himself a 'scholar', in whatever department of exact science, will be permitted to regard these teachings seriously. They will be derided and rejected *a priori* in this century; but only in this one. For in the twentieth century of our era scholars will begin to recognize that the *Secret Doctrine* has neither been invented nor exaggerated, but on the contrary simply outlined; and finally that its teachings antedate the Vedas. Have not the latter been derided, rejected, and called 'a modern forgery' even so recently as fifty years ago? Was not Sanskrit proclaimed at one time the progeny of, and a dialect derived from, the Greek, according to Lemprière and other scholars? About 1820, Prof. Max Müller tells us, the sacred books of the Brahmans, of the Magians, and of the Buddhists 'were all but unknown, their very existence was doubted, and there was not a single scholar who could have translated a line of the Vedas... of the Zend Avesta, or... of the Buddhist Tripitaka, and now the Vedas are proved to be the work of the highest antiquity whose 'preservation amounts almost to a marvel' (Lecture on the Vedas).

Rudolf Steiner, during a lecture given at Düsseldorf on 12 April 1909, stated that

> ... those Stanzas of Dzyan in *The Secret Doctrine* ... contain much of what has come from the teaching of the holy Rishis and flowed down through sanctuaries of the East ... Only gradually will a great deal found in the Stanzas of Dzyan be understood in all its depth.

★

Blavatsky's introduction to *The Secret Doctrine* was followed by the main text, which opened with a long 'proem':

> An Archaic Manuscript—a collection of palm leaves made impermeable to water, fire and air, by some specific unknown process—is before the writer's eye ...

At the end of this 'proem', some 20 pages further on, there was appended a 'note':

> The stanzas which form the thesis of every section are given throughout in their modern translated version, as it would be worse than useless to make the subject still more difficult by introducing the archaic phraseology of the original, with its puzzling style and words. Extracts are given from the Chinese Thibetan and Sanskrit translations of the original Senzar Commentaries and Glosses on the Book of DZYAN—these being now rendered for the first time into a European language. It is almost unnecessary to state that only portions of the seven Stanzas are here given. Were they published complete they would remain incomprehensible to all save the few higher occultists ...

Then began the first part, 'Cosmic Evolution', of the first volume, which opened with the first seven stanzas. All the Stanzas of Dzyan were printed in capital letters.

Here is the fifth stanza, 'Fohat: the Child of the Septenary Hierarchies':

> 1. THE PRIMORDIAL SEVEN, THE FIRST SEVEN BREATHS OF THE DRAGON OF WISDOM, PRODUCE IN THEIR TURN FROM THEIR HOLY CIRCUMGYRATING BREATHS THE FIERY WHIRLWIND.
>
> 2. THEY MAKE OF HIM THE MESSENGER OF THEIR WILL. THE DZYU BECOMES FOHAT, THE SWIFT SON OF THE DIVINE SONS WHOSE SONS ARE THE LIPIKA, RUNS CIRCULAR ERRANDS. FOHAT IS THE STEED AND THE THOUGHT IS THE RIDER. HE PASSES LIKE LIGHTNING THROUGH THE FIERY CLOUDS; TAKES THREE, AND FIVE, AND SEVEN STRIDES THROUGH THE SEVEN REGIONS ABOVE, AND THE SEVEN

BELOW. HE LIFTS HIS VOICE, AND CALLS THE INNUMERABLE SPARKS, AND JOINS THEM.

3. HE IS THEIR GUIDING SPIRIT AND LEADER. WHEN HE COMMENCES WORK, HE SEPARATES THE SPARKS OF THE LOWER KINGDOM THAT FLOAT AND THRILL WITH JOY IN THEIR RADIANT DWELLINGS, AND FORMS THEREWITH THE GERMS OF WHEELS. HE PLACES THEM IN THE SIX DIRECTIONS OF SPACE, AND ONE IN THE MIDDLE—THE CENTRAL WHEEL.

4. FOHAT TRACES SPIRAL LINES TO UNITE THE SIXTH TO THE SEVENTH—THE CROWN; AN ARMY OF THE SONS OF LIGHT STANDS AT EACH ANGLE, AND THE LIPIKA IN THE MIDDLE WHEEL. THEY SAY: THIS IS GOOD, THE FIRST DIVINE WORLD IS READY, THE FIRST IS NOW THE SECOND. THEN THE 'DIVINE ARUPA' REFLECTS ITSELF IN CHHAYA LOKA, THE FIRST GARMENT OF THE ANUPADAKA.

5. FOHAT TAKES FIVE STRIDES AND BUILDS A WINGED WHEEL AT EACH CORNER OF THE SQUARE, FOR THE FOUR HOLY ONES AND THEIR ARMIES.

6. THE LIPIKA CIRCUMSCRIBE THE TRIANGLE, THE FIRST ONE, THE CUBE, THE SECOND ONE, AND THE PENTACLE WITHIN THE EGG. IT IS THE RING CALLED 'PASS NOT' FOR THOSE WHO DESCEND AND ASCEND. ALSO FOR THOSE WHO DURING THE KALPA ARE PROGRESSING TOWARDS THE GREAT DAY 'BE WITH US'. THUS WERE FORMED THE RUPA AND THE ARUPA: FROM ONE LIGHT SEVEN LIGHTS; FROM EACH OF THE SEVEN, SEVEN TIMES SEVEN LIGHTS. THE WHEELS WATCH THE RING...

The Ring 'Pass-Not'

The commentary on the fifth Stanza of Dzyan begins:

> This is, perhaps, the most difficult of all the Stanzas to explain. Its language is comprehensible only to him who is thoroughly versed in Eastern allegory and its purposely obscure phraseology. The question will surely be asked, 'Do the Occultists believe in all these "Builders", "Lipika", and "Sons of Light" as Entities, or are they merely imageries?' To this the answer is given as plainly: 'After due allowance for the imagery of personified Powers, we must admit the existence of these Entities, if we would not reject the existence of spiritual humanity within physical mankind. For the hosts of these Sons of Light and "Mind-born Sons" of the first manifested Ray of the

UNKNOWN ALL, are the very root of spiritual man.' Unless we want to believe the unphilosophical dogma of a specially created soul for every human birth—a fresh supply of these pouring in daily, since 'Adam'—we have to admit the occult teachings. This will be explained in its place. Let us see, now, what may be the occult meaning of this stanza.

The Doctrine teaches that, in order to become a divine, fully conscious god—aye, even the highest—the Spiritual primeval INTELLIGENCES must pass through the human stage. And when we say human, this does not merely apply to our terrestrial humanity, but to the mortals that inhabit any world, *i.e.*, to those Intelligences that have reached the appropriate equilibrium between matter and spirit, as we have now, since the middle point of the Fourth Root Race of the Fourth Round was passed. Each entity must have won for itself the right of becoming divine, through self-experience. Hegel, the great German thinker, must have known or sensed intuitionally this truth when saying, as he did, that the Unconscious evolved the Universe only 'in the hope of attaining clear self-consciousness', of becoming, in other words, MAN . . .

The commentary on the sixth sloka reads:

The Stanza proceeds with a minute classification of the Orders of Angelic Hierarchy. From the group of Four and Seven emanates the 'mind-born' group of Ten, of Twelve, of Twenty-one, etc., all these divided again into sub-groups of septenaries, novems, duodecimals, and so on, until the mind is lost in this endless enumeration of celestial hosts and Beings, each having its distinct task in the ruling of the visible Kosmos during its existence.

The esoteric meaning of the first sentence of the Sloka is that those who have been called Lipikas, the Recorders of the Karmic ledger, make an impassible barrier between the personal EGO and the impersonal SELF, the Noumenon and Parent-Source of the former. Hence the allegory. They circumscribe the manifested world of matter within the RING 'Pass-Not' . . .

The Lipika separate the world (or plane) of pure spirit from that of Matter. Those who 'descend and ascend'—the incarnating Monads, and men striving towards purification and 'ascending', but still not having quite reached the goal—may cross the 'circle of the Pass-Not' only on the day 'Be-With-Us'; that day when man, freeing himself from the trammels of ignorance, and recognizing fully the non-separateness of the Ego within his personality—erroneously regarded as his own—from the UNIVERSAL EGO (Anima Supra-Mundi), merges thereby into the One Essence to become not only one 'with us' (the manifested universal lives which are 'ONE' LIFE), but that very life itself.

Astronomically, the 'Ring PASS-NOT' that the Lipika trace around the Triangle, the First One, the Cube, the Second One, and the Pentacle to

> circumscribe these figures, is thus shown to contain the symbol of 31415 again, or the coefficient constantly used in mathematical tables (the value of π, pi), the geometrical figures standing here for numerical figures...
>
> The chemist goes to the *laya* or zero-point of the plane of matter with which he deals, and then stops short. The physicist or the astronomer counts by billions of miles beyond the nebulae, and then they also stop short; the semi-initiated Occultist will represent this laya-point to himself as existing on some plane which, if not physical, is still conceivable to the human intellect. But the full Initiate *knows* that the ring 'Pass-Not' is neither a locality nor can it be measured by distance, but that it exists in the absoluteness of infinity. In this 'Infinity' of the full Initiate there is neither height, breadth nor thickness, but all is fathomless profundity, reaching down from the physical to the 'para-para-metaphysical'. In using the word 'down', essential depth—'nowhere and everywhere'—is meant, not depth of physical matter.
>
> If one searches carefully through the exoteric and grossly anthropomorphic allegories of popular religions, even in these the doctrine embodied in the circle of the 'Pass-Not' thus guarded by the Lipika may be dimly perceived. Thus one finds it even in the teachings of the Vedantin sect of the Visishtadwaita, the most tenaciously anthropomorphic in all India...

The present chapter may be closed with another passage from Blavatsky's introduction:

> To my judges past and future—whether they are serious literary critics, or those howling dervishes in literature who judge a book according to the popularity or unpopularity of the author's name, who, hardly glancing at its contents, fasten like lethal *bacilli* on the weakest points of the body—I have nothing to say. Nor shall I condescend to notice those crack-brained slanderers—fortunately very few in number—who, hoping to attract public attention by throwing discredit on every writer whose name is better known than their own, foam and bark at their very shadows.

That's My Sacrament

Elinor Dunlop contributed to the August 1912 number of *The Path* an article on 'Sacraments of the Mother'.

> Few have heard of the Sacrament which in Western Isles is known as 'the Mothering'. This simple nature-rite might well be restored in this twentieth century of godless cynicism, when to be pagan is to be considered an outcast. In olden days the first act of the mother after her safe delivery was an act of consecration. At noon, when the Sun was at her fullest glory, the

mother went forth carrying her babe to some spot endeared by memory. Kneeling on the Earth, she laid her new-born infant face downward on the grass asking Dana, the Great Mother, to protect her little one from danger, both by land and sea. This rite was performed by mother and babe unattended, save by the spirits of air, trees and wayside flowers. It is the most ancient of Celtic earth-rites and has been witnessed many a time by those who love the peasantry of Ireland and Scotland. 'The Mothering' is but one of these pagan customs. Another was to pass the new-born child from mother to father across a fire which burned in the hearth—'to get a turn through the smoke', as they call it in the Gaelic. Another was to lift the little human flower as high up as the mother's arms could reach, to be kissed by the Sun and the wind; this seems to me the most beautiful of these beautiful earth-rites.

Would it be possible to revive these ancient customs with any degree of their olden magic, a word whose potency is well-nigh forgotten? Faith may catch its meaning, but loses its fragrance, for the word *magic* enshrines for me both faith and elemental joy. Most of us know the healing power of Nature, the comfort and inspiration which flow from contact with her primeval wisdom. Is there anything in Nature which does not make for beauty? You may answer that the weeds, snakes and parasites are not beautiful, neither are the selfish desires and passions of human nature. But if the Earth could not produce weeds and pests, if man could not err and sin, existence would suffer from lack of that resistance which makes for strength. Loyalty, courage and patience would be lacking. The soul of man responds to the Mother-Soul when fighting against great odds. Nature has been man's nurse, asylum and friend from the beginning; now she waits to reveal to him that inner beauty which we call wisdom. We hear of God, immanent and transcendent, but through the gateway of a symbol a child may enter the mystery. Absorb the beauty of a new-blown rose until it enters the heart as symbol of the *immanence* of God. Inhale the fragrance of a thousand roses in one drop of perfume; that attar of rose is a symbol of that love which *transcends* and endures long after the forms which have enshrined it have vanished. Philosophies and metaphysics cannot satisfy the heart whose delight is ever to be found in unbounded and immortal joys!

Let me take you to a top back room in the East End of London, where a modern pagan strove to live the life of a good Christian. When quite a young girl I left my home in Ireland to work in a Christian Mission. In the home we held many classes for young and old; Tuesday and Friday nights were devoted to teaching 'grown-ups' how to read and write. It was wonderful to see what enthusiasm still smouldered in these tortured lives as they strove to 'keep up with the times' by learning to make decent pothooks and hangers. To be able to read the news was surely a high ambition. I became so fond of some of these good people that I was almost sorry when they graduated, which usually happened when they could write their names and addresses and were able to read a chapter of the Bible. One of my best pupils was a widow of about forty-five, a cook in a City restaurant. Mary wasn't a Cockney, you could easily tell that from her voice and the far-off expression in her blue eyes. One night, after I had read to her the account of the Lord's Supper, she said there was something on her mind which she wanted to tell me. Would I come and see her the following evening?

I found Mary in her top back room, which was very clean. The window looked out on a back yard in which some boys were playing pitch-and-toss. On the window-ledge was a box in which some scarlet geraniums were blooming. When I had enjoyed a cup of tea, Mary began to relieve her mind somewhat in this way. 'On Sunday I'm up by six o'clock, so as to get my bit of work done before the church bells ring. I don't go to church, Miss, not since I came up here to live. My clothes aren't decent enough. So I just sit down by these geraniums and read the fourteenth chapter of John.' (This chapter Mary knew by heart.) 'Then maybe I'll sing a hymn, and maybe I won't. I goes by the way I feel at the time. Then I get on my knees by the window and pray that God will let me die in the country where I was brought up, and where I married my man twenty-six years ago come Christmas. Then' (here Mary's voice sank almost to a whisper) 'I take the holy sacrament, and that's what is troubling me, Miss, for I don't know if I'm displeasing Almighty God by eating some of the earth in the box out there, and drinking a sip of water to wash it down. That's my sacrament. I take it because I love the earth and the water. Do you think I'm doing wrong?' Mary, looking into my eyes, saw there an understanding joy. Two pagans well met! Mary felt very happy when I kissed her. In my heart I sang a song of joy while descending the rickety stairs.

The remaining space on the page was filled with a quotation:

By conserving the natural and spiritual powers and retaining virtue, it is possible to escape dissolution.

By restraining the passions and letting gentleness have sway, it is possible to continue as a child.

By purging the mind's eye from impurity, it is possible to continue untainted.

By governing the people with love, it is possible to remain unknown.

By continual use of the gates of heaven, it is possible to preserve from rust.

By transparency on all sides, it is possible to pass unrecognized.

To bring forth and preserve, to produce without possessing, to act without hope of reward, and to expand without waste—this is the supreme virtue.

Lao-Tze.

Filled with Eternal Meaning

After the end of the Summer School on 17 August, there were at any rate some of its participants who stayed on in Torquay for a few more days.

Among papers of Charles Lazenby preserved in the Theosophical Society in Canada was found a typescript containing the following text:

MARRIAGE SERVICE.

Used by D.N. Dunlop in uniting Charles Lazenby and Margaret Clark at Torquay, on August twenty-first, nineteen hundred and twelve.

The Lord's Prayer.
Reading from *Bhagavad Gita.* (Chapter XIII.)

'One kiss of Nara on the lips of Nari and the whole universe awakes.'

Thus in an ancient scripture was symbolized the eternal duality entering into manifestation. Through the union of these eternal parents, Nature is preserved, and from age to age called back to life and action.

You, Charles Lazenby, and you, Margaret Clark, male and female, stand in the presence of the High Gods at this moment to proclaim this symbol and to enact in this Mystery the drama of eternal duality becoming one manifested unity.

In this rite it is my duty to explain to you some of the meanings and responsibilities to which as centres of Divine Life in this most sacred mystery you are called.

I must charge you first to reverence the bodies each of the other and of all mankind. You are to realize that the physical body is a temple of the Living God, sacred and holy, built under the Eye of the Supreme Architect for a divine purpose. I charge you that you do not degrade the human body nor any function of its noble economy by any unworthy thought or contempt of mind. I charge you to think with nobility of sentiment and clearness of vision upon the world of beauty round about you in Nature, and to realize that the forces of your manhood and womanhood are of the same character as you see manifesting in the glowing rose or the swaying pine. I charge you to be natural and unashamed as the acorn and the apple-blossom in your united life.

I charge you to remember always the perfect equality of the male and female. The male is not less than the female, nor more, but both are equal and necessary in the production and preservation of the forms on all levels to be filled with the God-Life. To each of you I say, 'Uphold and cherish the dignity and divergence of your mate, with no thought of inequality in your conception.'

I charge you to realize the power of thought and to know that as your male and female natures unite, you are producing on all planes. There is no

29 Three Dedications of Marriage
Child-giving
& Leave-taking

MARRIAGE SERVICE.

Used by D.N.Dunlop in uniting Charles Lazenby and Margaret Clark at Torquay, on August twenty-first, nineteen hundred and twelve.

The Lord's Prayer.

Reading from BHAGAVAD GITA. (CHAPTER XIII).

"One Kiss of Nara on the lips of Nari and the whole universe awakes".

Thus in an ancient scripture was symbolized the eternal duality entering into manifestation. Through the union of these eternal parents, nature is preserved, and from age to age called back to life and action.

You, Charles Lazenby, and you, Margaret Clark, male and female, stand in the presence of the High Gods at this moment to proclaim this symbol and to enact in this Mystery, the drama of eternal duality becoming one manifested unity.

In this rite it is my duty to explain to you some of the meanings and responsibilities to which as centres of Divine Life in this most sacred mystery you are called.

I must charge you first to reverence the bodies each of the other and of all mankind. You are to realize that the physical body is a temple of the Living God, sacred and holy, built under the Eye of the Supreme Architect for a divine purpose. I charge you that you do not degrade the human body nor any function of it's noble economy by any unworthy thought or contempt of mind. I charge you to think with nobility of sentiment and clearness of vision upon the world of beauty round about you in nature, and to realize that the forces of your manhood and womanhood are of the same character as you see manifesting in the glowing rose or the swaying pine. I charge you to be natural and unashamed as the acorn and the apple-blossom in your united life.

kiss or other caress between man and woman which is not a creative act. The thoughts in your mind at that moment become stronger and more defined. If in your thoughts you are degraded or mean or unworthy, the children in the thought-world will become a brood of hateful and ugly ideas round about you. Equally if you are loving and pure and kindly disposed to all beings in all worlds, you will fill your thought-atmosphere with beauty and your offspring will be children of light, blessing the parents and adding to the joy of the whole world. I charge you in all your love and joy in each other to know the above as a law of God, the Father-Mother, the Parent of all beauty and harmony.

I charge you to realize that in the union of your male and female natures you will deepen and widen your spiritual and mental comprehension, and that this fulfilment and power is not for yourselves alone, but that as you receive joy and strength you should use them for the well-being of your race. You should together think upon the intellectual and spiritual evolution of mankind, and stand united stronger in your union than apart, to aid the High Gods in their eternal task.

Charles Lazenby, you, the man, should bear in mind these charges and endeavour to fulfil them. It is your duty to honour and protect the woman with whose life you are uniting. You should find delight in making her path smooth and in bearing her burdens. You should strive to be her comrade and friend as well as her husband, and to realize as her protector that her future happiness through many lives depends to a large extent upon the unfoldment which will take place through your interest in her true welfare, and through your sympathy with her aims and ideals. You should try not to suppress her individual evolution nor make it subservient to your own. Realize at all times that you are children of God, equally loved of that Dear One. Reverence the divine liberty of your comrade.

Have you listened carefully to the charges I have put upon you and will you strive to fulfil and realize their meaning?

Answer—'I will.'

Margaret Clark, you, the woman, should bear in mind these charges and endeavour to fulfil them. It is your duty to honour and protect the man with whose life you are uniting. You should find delight in making his path smooth and in bearing his burdens. You should strive to be his comrade and friend as well as his wife, and to realize as his protector that his future happiness through many lives depends to a large extent upon the unfoldment which will take place through your interest in his true welfare, and through your sympathy with his aims and ideals. You should try not to suppress his individual evolution nor make it subservient to your own. Realize at all times that you are children of God, equally loved of that Dear One. Reverence the divine liberty of your comrade.

Have you listened carefully to the charges I have put upon you and will you strive to fulfil and realize their meaning?

Answer—'I will.'

Charles Lazenby, take now the ring in your right hand, remembering what it signifies.

The ring is the symbol of Eternity, and should convey to your mind that this is no light action, but is filled with eternal meaning, and the results of this union are destined under the Karmic Law to proceed down the centuries, affecting humanities yet unborn.

The ring is the symbol of the law by which all things return to their source. It is the ever-beautiful form which alone expresses the movement of time in its mighty periods through eternal duration.

You, the man, now place it on the finger of the woman to symbolize the Divine Will limiting itself in order that definition may arise and concreteness may result. Without limitation the Divine Will cannot manifest in form, therefore the Ring 'Pass-Not' is around every synthesized universe. It is this symbol you have just enacted.

And now in the presence of the High Gods I declare you united for the work your ideals shall inspire. May the Strength, Beauty, and Peace of the Great Trinity be with you and upon you both. May you be servants together of the High Gods and of the One Light that lightens the world.

AMEN

★

The August number of *The Path* reprinted 'The Two Trees' by W.B. Yeats.

Beloved, gaze in thine own heart,
The holy tree is growing there;
From joy the holy branches start,
And all the trembling flowers they bear.
The changing colours of its fruit
Have dowered the stars with merry light;
The surety of its hidden root
Has planted quiet in the night;
The shaking of its leafy head
Has given the waves their melody,
And made my lips and music wed,
Murmuring a wizard song for thee.
There the Loves a circle go,
The flaming circle of our days,
Gyring, spiring to and fro
In those great ignorant leafy ways;
Remembering all that shaken hair
And how the wingèd sandals dart,
Thine eyes grow full of tender care:
Beloved, gaze in thine own heart.

Gaze no more in the bitter glass
The demons, with their subtle guile,
Lift up before us when they pass,

Or only gaze a little while;
For there a fatal image grows
That the stormy night receives,
Roots half hidden under snows,
Broken boughs and blackened leaves.
For all things turn to barrenness
In the dim glass the demons hold,
The glass of outer weariness,
Made when God slept in times of old.
There, through the broken branches go
The ravens of unresting thought;
Flying, crying, to and fro,
Cruel claw and hungry throat,
Or else they stand and snuff the wind,
And shake their ragged wings; alas!
Thy tender eyes grow all unkind:
Gaze no more in the bitter glass.

White Lodge

On 24 August—three days after the marriage of Charles Lazenby and Margaret Clark at Torquay—the premiere of *Der Hüter der Schwelle* took place in Munich. Among the audience were Harry Collison, Herbert and Mabel Heywood-Smith and Ada Drury-Lavin. Certainly the Heywood-Smiths, and probably the others too, stayed on further for the subsequent lecture-course 'On Initiation'.

The original foundation of the Anthroposophical Society in England was recorded by Heywood-Smith in punctilious detail in the course of a letter written in May 1914 to Marie von Sivers:

> On the occasion of our visit to Munich in 1912 there was a Committee Meeting of the new 'Bund' on Friday, Aug. 30th at 7.00 p.m. At 7.55 p.m. Dr. Steiner gave it the name 'The Anthroposophical Society'.
>
> On our return to England we decided to found a branch of the newly named Anthroposophical Society in London.
>
> On Sunday September 15th 1912, at 11.15 a.m., we had our first meeting, at which 11 persons were present.

Heywood-Smith's typewritten account recorded the venue of the meeting, and made special mention of two particular people:

> At this time the movement in England enjoyed the support of a very active and valued member, Colonel Webber. It was due to his efforts that in

September 1912 the group found itself installed in commodious premises at 47 Redcliffe Square, S.W. We were also very much assisted by Captain Beauclerk. After this we had four lectures each week in the group.

★

During that same September the Blavatsky Institute in Cheshire as such closed down. For since the BEAMA needed to be located in London, its Secretary D.N. Dunlop was after four years in the North of England moving back to the British capital.

Here his impulses found expression under a new name. Around the time when the anthroposophical group found itself installed in commodious premises in Kensington, Dunlop's group moved into equally commodious premises in Wimbledon, as described by his daughter Edith Young in her autobiography *Inside Out* (1971).

Our next move was to a house at Wimbledon large enough to have a room for theosophical meetings on the ground floor. My father, with a further increase in salary, could afford to expand, to air his views in public, to pass on the message of the Mahatmas as it came to him through the work of Blavatsky.

He called the house White Lodge, after the Great White Lodge of the spiritual brotherhood of those who had the welfare of mankind at heart.

The Great White Lodge stood well back from a road encircling Wimbledon Hill, near the Common. Its front looked out on a shrubbery of evergreens. At the back was a wrought-iron balcony, draped by vines and wisteria, which was a haze of mauve in spring. A grand piano imported by a wealthy American woman who had offered her services as my father's secretary occupied a place of honour under the picture of Master K.H. and enlarged photographs of Blavatsky and Besant.

To help her run an establishment which was now more like an institution than a home, my mother had to rely on a daily char and the assistance of two of the more humble of my father's followers. One was the daughter of a country parson, who offered her services in return for her keep. She had a room in the basement next to the large, gloomy kitchen. When little red-haired Elsie upset my mother she would squeak an apology, blush to the roots of her hair, and scuttle away to her dark hole under the stairs. She seemed to take pleasure in effacing herself. My brother alone brought animation to her watery blue eyes. If he condescended to tease her, a sly smile crossed her freckled face. She was inwardly happy, it seemed, because to have become a servant in my father's house made her a bit of a martyr and so furthered her spiritual evolution . . .

★

The September issue of *The Vâhan* included these announcements:

The *Secret Doctrine* Group

Mr. Charles Lazenby will lecture on 'Walt Whitman and the Theosophical Society' in the Temporary Hall on Friday, 18th October, at 8 p.m.

As this will be Mr. Lazenby's last London lecture before leaving England to continue his work in America, the *Secret Doctrine* Group extend a very hearty invitation to all who may be interested, whether Fellows of the Theosophical Society or not.

D.O.

Light on the Path Lodge

Weekly meetings of the above lodge will begin on Friday, October 4, at 8 p.m. The meetings will be held at 19A, Tavistock Square, and will be open to all Fellows of the Theosophical Society. The book chosen for study and discussion is *The Yoga Aphorisms of Patanjali*. The President of the lodge, Mrs. Cook (Mabel Collins), will preside and conduct the discussions.

D.N. Dunlop,
Secretary.

The Theosophical Fellowship

Weekly meetings of the Theosophical Fellowship will be held every Saturday evening, beginning on 28th September, at 8 p.m. at The White Lodge, Sunnyside, Wimbledon, S.W. All Fellows of the Theosophical Society and their friends are cordially invited. H.P.B.'s works will be studied and discussed, beginning probably with *Isis Unveiled*.

D.N. Dunlop,
Secretary.

★

A couple of months earlier, in July, *The Path* had begun to reprint a series of anonymous articles on 'Proteus' taken from issues between May to August 1893 of *The Irish Theosophist*. The reprinted series was completed in the September number, and later in the year brought out in booklet form under the title *Protean Man*.

Dunlop's address on 'Friendship' (the first half adapted from editorials by H.W. Percival) in June of the previous year was also brought out as a booklet entitled *The Basis of Friendship*. 'Published at the request of many who found inspiration in the original article', it was attractively printed on good paper with an artistic cover, and Schmiechen's portrait of Master Jesus as frontispiece.

★

Max Gysi meanwhile published another work by Rudolf Steiner, *The Occult Significance of Blood*. It was reviewed in September in *Theosophy in Scotland:*

> If Dr. Steiner is right in what he asserts, there can be no doubt that he has made a discovery of the first importance, and one which must be of great interest to scientists. At any rate he has the faculty, rare in psychic investigators, of presenting his information in such a manner as to arrest the attention of even the most conventionally minded. Briefly put, Dr. Steiner's discovery is that blood is the expression of the ego, that the intellect was born as a result of mixing the blood through exogamy, and that only in so far as a quality is in the blood can it be said to be possessed by man. He then points out several directions in which these assertions have a practical bearing, showing that the subject deserves the careful attention of students.

★

In his autobiography *Farewell my Youth* (1943) the musician Arnold Bax recorded:

> I was in Glencolumcille in the autumn of 1912 when I received a postcard from AE suggesting I should join him for a week at Breaghy, near Dunfanaghy, where he went every September to paint. A day or two later, I set off on my bicycle for that faraway place at the other side of County Donegal. I toiled over the vast wilderness of high bogland between Glen and Glengesh, and pedalled into squalid Ardara and thence to Port Noo on the sea-coast.
>
> Next day I started again, riding now into the Rosses' country (with at first rather stiff thighs) over those strangely red roads that look as though dyed with ancient carnage. From Burtonport of the granite I took train to Dunfanaghy Road, and thence after picking up my suitcase went on to Breaghy by outside car. There at the door of a snug thatched cottage on a hill and surrounded by whin-bushes I descried AE's burly and bearded form, his kindly short-sighted eyes peering out in search of me. Within the house we were mothered by a simple apple-cheeked old lady, and fed sumptuously on freshly caught salmon, superb eggs, and a huge and rich home-made cake.
>
> It was an odd entranced week that I spent there, quite dreamlike in the guttering candlelight of memory. Close by our hillock were the fine house and estate of Sir Hugh Law, a Nationalist M.P. who, an old friend of AE, had loaned him a summer house in the wooded grounds above the sea in which he might paint on wet days.
>
> I have not met with many experiences which cannot be accounted for by

a rational explanation, but one of these occurred in that place in the dripping Breaghy woods.

My friend was painting at his easel in the middle of the floor, in his absorption allowing his pipe to go out every two minutes and having to cross to the mantelpiece for a light, so that between the easel and the fireplace there was a track strewn with dead matches.

I was reading in the window-seat near the door, and we had not spoken for perhaps a quarter of an hour when I suddenly became aware that I was listening to strange sounds, the like of which I had never heard before. They can only be described as a kind of mingling of rippling water and tiny bells tinkled, and yet I could have written them out in ordinary musical notation.

'Do you hear music?' said AE quietly. 'I do,' I replied, and even as I spoke, utter silence fell. I do not know what it was we both heard that morning, and must be content to leave it at that.

Intensely Interesting

Around this time a certain clergyman in the Order of the Stella Matutina, Revd. J. Fitzgerald, was visiting New Zealand, and staying with a friend in Havelock North who belonged to a group of spiritually interested people searching for esotericism. Fitzgerald put this group in touch with the chief of his Order, Robert Felkin.

The group sent Felkin and his family an invitation to visit New Zealand, even offering to pay their travel costs.

The enterprising Felkin—who had only recently returned to England from Germany—accepted the invitation. He decided to set off for New Zealand, with his wife and daughter, and stay there for three months. During his absence from Britain he arranged to leave Neville Meakin in charge of the Stella Matutina.

On the very same day, perhaps even at the same time, as the first meeting of the Anthroposophical Society was taking place in London, Felkin was writing to W.B. Yeats. (V.H. in the Latin address = Very Honoured. F.R. = 'Finem Respice', Felkin's motto.)

London,
15 September 1912.

Private

Care V.H. Frater,

We do not leave till October the 10th: so I hope we shall see you before we start. We had a very interesting time in Germany & got several grades.

I am sorry that you cannot come on the 21st: but be sure & let us know when you can come.

Fraternally yours,

F.R.

★

A few days after Felkin's departure in October for the antipodes, another member of the Stella Matutina, the 40-year-old sculptress Edith Maryon, wrote—in German—a first letter to Rudolf Steiner, enclosing a photograph of her recently-sculpted frieze 'The Seeker of Divine Wisdom'.[27]

58, Grove Park Terrace,
Chiswick,
London
16.10.12.

Dear Dr. Steiner,

Dr. R.W. Felkin (F.R.) told me to send you this and ask whether you would give me an interview. If I can arrange it I hope to spend a few weeks in Cologne, and if you would write and let me know when you will be in Cologne I shall try to plan my visit at that time. I must first find somewhere where I could live 'au pair' and give English lessons.

I can speak only very little German, but perhaps we could speak together in French.

Yours faithfully,

(Miss) L. Edith C. Maryon

★

There also survive from this time a couple of letters from Harry Collison to Herbert Heywood-Smith.

The first was written on the same day as Charles Lazenby gave his final lecture in London on 'Walt Whitman and the Theosophical Society', before returning with his wife Margaret to his native Canada.

Windham Club,
St James's Square.
S.W.
18th Oct. 1912

Dear Mr. Heywood-Smith,

Baron Walleen has arrived. He should like to be allowed to come and see you. Will Sunday (early afternoon) be convenient? If so, would you send a postcard to the studio? It would be very kind of you.

Yours very sincerely,

Harry Collison

★

The second was as follows:

Windham Club,
St James's Square.
S.W.
27th Oct. 1912

Dear Mr. Heywood-Smith,

I think it right to tell you that I have had a letter from an unknown person in Yorkshire—one S.C. Sharland—as follows:—'For the benefit of a friend of mine who is deeply interested in the writings of Dr. Steiner, may I ask for particulars of The Steiner Society, conditions of membership, etc.?'

I have answered to the effect that there is no Steiner Society that I know of, but there are various groups of people who study Dr. Steiner & have rules of their own, & in order to enter my group an introduction is necessary. I also suggest that if the friend were to make a personal application the reply might be more satisfactory.

Of course if you think this too strict or severe then I can write again & tell him to write to you.—I feel we have to be careful.

Yours sincerely,

Harry Collison

Have you one or two copies of *Weg zur Selbst-Erkenntnis* to spare, I mean that you could sell me?—I have in a weak moment given my own away, & have no copy for myself.

★

During the second half of October, Neville Meakin, who had previously written that long letter to Baron Walleen, and whom Felkin had in his absence left in charge of the Stella Matutina, suddenly died.

★

In the October number of *The Path* appeared the first instalment of an unsigned series of articles on 'The Zodiac'. An editorial footnote stated:

> I wish to take this opportunity of acknowledging my indebtedness to my friend H.W. Percival, editor of *The Word*, for the help received from him in the studies on the zodiac, and at the same time to thank him for his kind permission to utilize matter and illustrations already used in *The Word*.

These articles were a shortened version of a series of 13 editorials published in *The Word* between April 1906 and April 1907, which Percival had since brought out in book form under the title *The Esoteric Zodiac*.

The shortened version in *The Path* was continued, initially, through four successive numbers.

★

On 6 November, *The Christian Commonwealth* published a report signed by the initials W.A.R:

Mr. D.N. Dunlop's lecture to the City Temple Literary Society last Thursday dealt with evolution from the theosophical standpoint. Here was a system the very idea of which took the breath away. Not only was it unlike any other system, but it implied the best of all.

The universal spirit put forth evolves through seven periods, in which each individualized unit gathers experience. This might be called the descent of spirit into matter and its gradual ascent into its primary conditions, plus the experience gained in each of the periods. At present our humanity is in the fourth period, which is apparently the turning-point, the spirit ascending to complete the cycle of evolution. Each unit of humanity is invested with power to hasten or retard the evolution of humanity towards its glorious goal. It is scientifically true that a leaf fluttering down to the ground affects infinity. None the less true is it that every unkind thought or deed affects the march of evolution and is felt by the Higher Beings in the scheme of evolution, who superintend the actions of humanity. The lecture set forth a theory which a few ill-constructed sentences could belittle, requiring as it does unremitting study and enthusiasm. As expounded by Mr. Dunlop it was intensely interesting. Sir Richard Stapley presided.

Making a Fool of Himself

Edith Maryon wrote once more to Rudolf Steiner:

58, Grove Park Terrace
Chiswick,
London.
15.11.12.

Dear Dr. Steiner,

I venture to write to you again as I have had no reply to my letter of a month ago. At Dr. Felkin's (F.R.) request I sent you a photograph of my work 'The Seeker of Divine Wisdom'; & also asked if you could grant me an interview when you come to Cologne. Would it be possible for you to see me, & could you also let me know when you will visit that town? I shall come to Germany specially to see you & there will be a good many things for me to arrange beforehand, so that I should be very grateful if you could let me know soon.

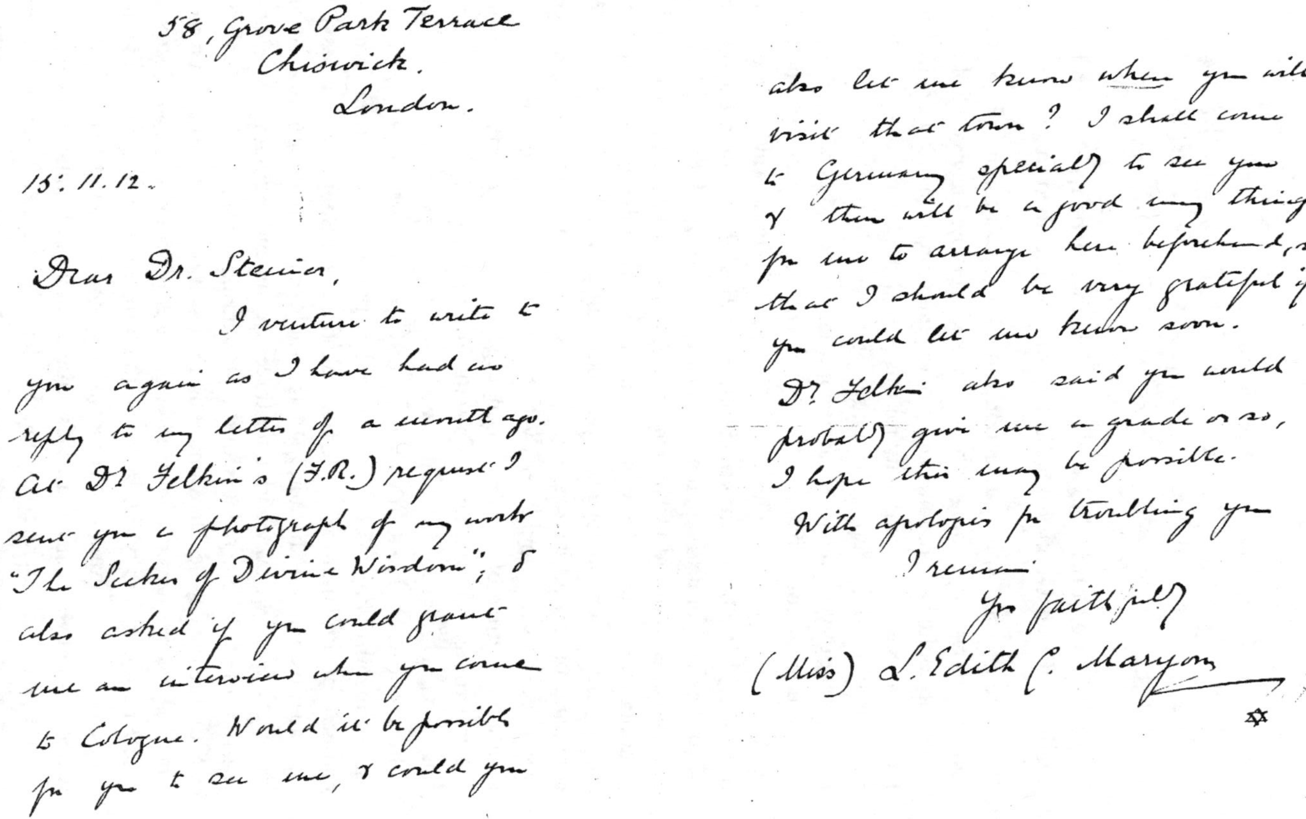
58, Grove Park Terrace
Chiswick.
London.

15: 11. 12.

Dear Dr. Steiner,

I venture to write to you again as I have had no reply to my letter of a month ago. At Dr Felkin's (F.R.) request I sent you a photograph of my work "The Seeker of Divine Wisdom"; & also asked if you could grant me an interview when you come to Cologne. Would it be possible for you to see me, & could you also let me know when you will visit that town? I shall come to Germany specially to see you & there will be a good many things for me to arrange here beforehand, so that I should be very grateful if you could let me know soon.

Dr. Felkin also said you would probably give me a grade or so, I hope this may be possible.

With apologies for troubling you
I remain
Yrs faithfully
(Miss) L. Edith C. Maryon ✡

Dr. Felkin also said you would probably give me a grade or so, I hope this may be possible.

With apologies for troubling you

I remain

Yrs faithfully

(Miss) L. Edith C. Maryon

★

Three days later, on 18 November, Elisabeth Vreede wrote from Berlin a long letter to her Dutch friend Li Content. It included this passage:

As for the aversion you write about, caused by bad intoning or pronouncing, it's anyway something to be got over. Otherwise I fear you'll also take exception to the Dr.'s pronunciation of foreign words—namely English and French. He hasn't any sensitivity for this at all. I don't take exception to it, and certainly could also explain how it comes about. I've really been thinking about you this week, as in connection with some unusual work I had the uncommon privilege of being for two days in succession the Dr.'s guest at lunch and afternoon tea. He was reading aloud to me a piece from the *Theosophist*, Mrs. Besant's magazine, in an English pronunciation which was more than comic. I could myself observe how painful it was to Fräulein von Sivers, as if she had a feeling that the Dr. was making a fool of himself in front of me. I didn't find anything funny in it, perhaps because I know how it comes about for someone to have a command of all the sciences and no command of foreign languages (at least as regards pronunciation). I once wondered how Li would get over something like this? But good pronunciation, either of your own language or of foreign ones, is just an external thing and nothing to do with inner gifts. Even in his defective English the Doctor has of course good intonation.

In recent weeks Fräulein von Sivers had a whole mass of typing—English—which had first to be dictated and then typed out twice over. Since it consisted of fairly intimate matters she asked me to help, perhaps also as the Dr. had spoken to me about it. I was again able to talk to him on Monday of last week. We were busy with it for three days on end—tiring work—but I was rewarded by being a lot with the Dr., during the first two days, at any rate; on the last day he left again on his travels. It was very pleasant at table. The Dr. was by turns deeply serious, or cheerful and witty. I also learnt a whole mass of things worth knowing. I felt lucky and really contented, in contrast to when sitting beside him on the ship travelling to Helsingfors, which I found very painful. But it's quite different in his home circle. You then relate to him as a human being. Incidentally I never face him except in a relation of pupil to teacher, a teacher in whom one feels superhuman powers at work.

★

On the very same day as Elisabeth Vreede was writing this letter in Berlin, Harry Collison in London was again writing to Herbert Heywood-Smith:

Windham Club,
St James's Square,
S.W.
18th Nov. 1912

Dear Mr. Heywood-Smith,

As the time draws nearer I am reminded that I ought not to accept your kind invitation for tomorrow. It is the anniversary of my father's death, & a day upon which I do not go out for pleasure.

In fact I make a journey into the country & see that everything is in order & properly kept.

My acceptance for the 19th was really an oversight, for which I must ask you to apologize and explain for me.

Yours sincerely,

Harry Collison

Baron Walleen tells me he is going.

6
FIFTH VISIT

We Open Our Hearts

On 14, 21 and 28 November, Baron Walleen gave three lectures in the Aeolian Hall in New Bond Street. They were probably semi-public lectures, to members of the newly formed Anthroposophical Society and their guests.

Further lectures by Walleen were given to the Theosophical Society's also recently formed *Light on the Path* Lodge, whose President was Mabel Collins, and Secretary D.N. Dunlop. These were announced in *The Vahan* (which now dropped altogether its circumflex accent).

> Under the auspices of the above lodge, Baron Walleen will give two lectures entitled 'Through Theosophy to Christ', according to principles put forward by Dr. Rudolf Steiner. The lectures will be given in the Headquarters Lecture Hall at 8 p.m. on Mondays, 2nd and 9th December, admission free.

On both occasions it was Dunlop who acted as chairman. He introduced the first lecture as follows:

> This meeting, as probably most of you know, is held under the auspices of the *Light on the Path* Lodge of the Theosophical Society in England and Wales. It is customary for the President of a Lodge to take the chair, but our President has asked me to take her place, as Vice-President of the Lodge, and as she is already so distinguished in other directions, I suppose she does not object to my shining on the platform.
>
> The opportunity was given to us of inviting Baron Walleen, who is a pupil of Dr. Steiner's teaching, to lecture to us on the subject which has been announced—'Through Theosophy to Christ'. The *Light on the Path* Lodge desires to be particularly associated with the broad platform of the Theosophical Society, and in inviting any distinguished representatives of any aspect of theosophical thought and teaching to come and present their views, which may be in some respects different in detail from the views presented, say, by Mrs. Besant or Mr. Leadbeater or Mr. Sinnett or any other distinguished theosophist—the fundamental idea being that Theosophy stands for freedom of thought and absolute toleration. We are particularly pleased, as a lodge, to afford an opportunity to a pupil of Dr. Steiner, because most of us in the Theosophical Society have not had the

> opportunity (at least, not the direct opportunity, apart from the published books of Dr. Steiner) of having a direct teaching on this important subject.
>
> Therefore, without any further preliminary remarks, I will ask you to give attention to Baron Walleen, whom we are particularly pleased to welcome among us. I hope that Baron Walleen will take an opportunity of assuring the members of the Theosophical Society in Germany, and Dr. Steiner in particular, that we welcome him, that we open our hearts to receive teaching from whatsoever source it may come, that we are willing at all times to have an open mind, to receive what is presented to us without partiality, and that we particularly would like, some day not very far distant, to hear that Dr. Steiner would condescend to visit England and come amongst us and tell us direct—even if it were through an interpreter—some of the things he has to say that are of such great importance. (Applause). I believe there is something to be gained by the direct influence of a teacher, whether you understand his language or not; there is something conveyed to an audience by the presence of a teacher which is not gained in any other way. And we must all recognize that Dr. Steiner is undoubtedly a teacher. Therefore I will ask you to give attention to what Baron Walleen will say this evening.

After the second lecture a week later, it was again Dunlop who added some closing remarks:

> I do not wish to detain you, as the time is already extended. But I would like you to unite with me and the members of the lodge in expressing our great thanks to Baron Walleen for his lecture to us. And while you are doing so in an emphatic way, I would also like to suggest that the *Light on the Path* Lodge would arrange one or two lectures from him again when he comes back in March. (Applause). At all events, I should like to say this: we should like him to tell Dr. Steiner that in England we are ready to receive his teaching with open arms, discuss it freely and consider it, find out what there is good in it and incorporate that into ourselves. And I do hope he will say that here there will always be a free platform for whatever aspect of the truth may be presented. I hope it may be arranged through Mr. Collison that he will lecture to us again. (Applause).

Walleen then travelled up to Scotland, *Theosophy in Scotland* reporting that

> Baron Walleen visited Glasgow and Edinburgh on 11th and 12th of December, and delivered lectures under the auspices of the Glasgow Lodge and Edinburgh Lodges.

Expelled from the Theosophical Society

By the time Baron Walleen's lectures were taking place in London, Mathilde Scholl in Berlin came to realize that Rudolf Steiner was expecting his followers to take initiative themselves in regard to the oppressive conditions which had arisen for his work in the Theosophical Society. She therefore summoned from all over Germany the Vorstand of the German Section to an Extraordinary Meeting in order to decide what to do. The meeting was held on 8 December, lasting from 10 o'clock in the morning until 10 o'clock at night.

A resolution was passed to the effect that membership of the Order of the Star in the East was considered incompatible with membership of the German Section. It was also decided to send a telegram to Adyar, where the Society's Annual International Convention was about to take place. The content of the telegram, duly sent on the 11th of the month, was a demand by the whole German Vorstand for Annie Besant to resign as President of the Society.

★

The idea of Steiner himself coming to lecture in Britain at 'some day not very far distant' had been suggested by D.N. Dunlop, at Baron Walleen's lecture on 2 December.

Harry Collison, who was among those present, evidently passed on the idea to Herbert Heywood-Smith, whose account continues:

> It now became our ideal to invite Dr. Steiner himself to come to England to lecture to members and also give other private meetings. We did this when in Berlin at Christmas 1912. He consented at once and arranged to come the following May.

★

By Christmas 1912, when Steiner accepted this invitation from his British friends, matters in the Theosophical Society were coming to a head. The Adyar Convention was taking place, and during its proceedings the Society's General Council asked Besant to withdraw the charter of the German Section. On 27 December, Besant delivered her presidential report, which included the statement: 'The German General Secretary, educated by the Jesuits, has not been able to shake himself sufficiently clear of that fatal influence to allow liberty of opinion within his Section.' The text of the report was included in the supplement to the next edition of *The Theosophist*, to be published on 13 January.

On the very next day, 28 December, Steiner made his way from Berlin to Cologne. Karl Künstler described the succeeding events:

> Arrangements had been made shortly before for a lecture-cycle to be given in Cologne. It was to take place in the hall of the Dreikönigs-Gymnasium on the Thurmchenswall, where however the school headmaster would not tolerate either social occasions or musical offerings. Some hundred members from both inland and abroad gathered on the 28th of December 1912 to attend the cycle 'The Bhagavadgita and the Epistles of Paul'. Before his first lecture, Rudolf Steiner portrayed the character of Annie Besant's untruthful teaching, and with the loudest vocal power at his disposal uttered the words: 'We have been expelled from the Theosophical Society!' He then explained that a new Society was now to be founded under the title 'Anthroposophical Society'. Whoever wanted to join the new Society should make their way to the teachers' room on the ground floor, where certificates would be given out. There, as well as Marie von Sivers, Dr. Carl Unger and Kurt Walther had taken places. Working together, they took on all the issuing of certificates, which was accomplished in a relatively short time. The Anthroposophical Society was thus founded, and the first lecture of the cycle given to members of the Anthroposophical Society only. This lecture-cycle was received by those present with an inner joyfulness and gratitude of a kind not previously experienced.
>
> A celebration took place in the Branch at 9 Belfortstrasse. Dr. Unger announced what the statutes were and explained their reasons. During this celebration, which was accompanied by musical offerings, Dr. Steiner gave a lecture on the theme 'There is No Esotericism Without Truth'.

⋆

On 30 December, Harry Collison tendered his resignation from the Westminster and Keystone Chapter, of which just a couple of years before he had been M.E.Z.

Since Robert Felkin was still absent in New Zealand, and Neville Meakin had died, it was Collison who arranged for Edith Maryon to have an interview with Steiner. This took place in Cologne on 31 December.

On the following day, Maryon wrote Steiner another letter:

> Baselerhof Hotel
> 1.1.13.
>
> Dear Dr. Steiner,
>
> I think you must be too busy to grant me another interview, but I do want to ask you two questions, so will write them.
>
> You said yesterday I was far more developed occultly than I can bring

through in this incarnation—does that mean in consequence of some fault I have committed or because there is some other kind of work for me to do?

Then for some years I have always felt there is something definite for me to do, & that sometime I shall meet the Master who will tell me what it is & explain some of the things which have puzzled me so much. For a long time I searched, at last I thought perhaps it was Abdul Baha who would be the right person, but when I met him although I liked him so much I knew he was not the person I was looking for. Then I thought it possibly might be you, & when I saw you in Berlin I knew at last I was right about the Master, there remains only the second part—is there really any definite thing for me to do, or do I only imagine it? If there is, may I know now what it is? I think the time has come for me to know if it is so, but I am quite sure you will know best, & if I may have some of my muddle cleared up or must still wait.

Believe me

Yours sincerely

L. Edith C. Maryon.

⋆

On the very same day, Felkin wrote from New Zealand to W.B. Yeats:

Havelock North,
New Zealand.
1 January 1913

Dear Mr. Yeats,

Your letter has only just come & you do not seem to have had the long letter I posted to you the day we left.

I had expected Mr. Meakin to have told you much but he died so very suddenly that I have to write you.

We are all well & hope to be back in April.

I must not write more as your letter only came just before the post leaves.

Every good wish for 1913. I wrote to you twice already with general matters of interest.

Yours always,

R.W. Felkin

Both Sides of a Question

Between Christmas 1912 when Rudolf Steiner agreed to come to Britain again and May 1913 when his visit took place, a separation was finally effected between the Theosophical Society and the Anthroposophical Movement. The present work brings forward such documents about this separation as were available at the time to an English readership, interspersing them with other background material. In regard to the chronology, it must be borne in mind that there was a certain time lag between the main events happening in Germany or India and subsequent reportage of these events in Britain.

⋆

At the beginning of January 1913 *The Vahan* published a long article by the Society's General Secretary for England and Wales, James Wedgwood. It was headed 'An Explanation':

> In the December number of *The Theosophist* is a report of a meeting held at Munich by some of Dr. Steiner's followers. Dr. Francke, of London, was reported to have made various allegations against officials of the T.S. in England and Wales. I at once wrote a letter asking him if he would have the kindness to justify to me four of his statements by giving chapter and verse for them, and assuming until he had informed me to the contrary that he was correctly reported in *The Theosophist.*
>
> I trust it will not appear discourteous if I say that his reply is somewhat discursive and much of it deals with his particular beliefs, with which, as an official, I am not concerned. He does not answer the questions. The following paragraphs appear to me to lend themselves to being extracted fairly from the rest of the letter.
>
> 'As to your questions, the speakers at Munich are neither responsible to their General Secretaries nor are they responsible for the reports.'
>
> 'What I have stated are facts, but the report gives a somewhat different meaning, not only to my own words, but also, as far as I can remember, to those of others...'
>
> 'Further, as a theosophist, I am free to have my own opinions.'
>
> The four statements, which are now again declared to be facts, are:
>
> 1. 'One lodge in London has decided not to lend out nor to buy any longer the books of Dr. Steiner.'
>
> 2. 'In *The Vahan* "Geisteswissenschaft" is translated as mental science, which translation is, of course, calculated to undervalue altogether the teachings of Dr. Steiner.'
>
> 3. '... a follower of Dr. Steiner was refused the permission of lecturing in the Headquarters...'
>
> 4. '... an advertisement of Baron Walleen's Rosicrucian lectures was suppressed in *The Vahan*, though it had been sent in time.'
>
> I will touch briefly on these four points:
>
> 1. I know nothing about this.
>
> 2. I do not know where the bad translation occurred, or who was responsible for it. *The Vahan* has published appreciative reviews of Dr. Steiner's books.

3. The use of Headquarters was not refused. A Steiner propagandist arrived in England just over a year ago, heralded about three days previously by a letter requesting permission to lecture at Headquarters on Dr. Steiner's teachings. I told him we were contemplating immediate removal from Bond Street, so that I could give no definite answer. We then decided to move, and did so within (I think) a week after this decision. A month or two later (I think) rumours of this supposed refusal began to reach me from Germany.

In November last, I was approached by the *Light on the Path* Lodge to ask if I objected to the same lecturer speaking under their auspices at Headquarters. I immediately consented, on the understanding that nothing showing want of proper tolerance to the beliefs of fellow theosophists was said. The Chairman assumed personal responsibility for this, the stipulation having been made in view of complaints which had previously reached me. The lectures took place at Headquarters.

4. One of the questions I asked Dr. Francke was: did he know the special circumstances governing this case, and did he narrate them at Munich?

These circumstances were: the notice was sent to *The Vahan* barely in time and leaving no interim for further discussion; the customary etiquette of notifying the General Secretary that a worker from another Section was coming to lecture had not been observed; I had just received word that the lecturer was engaged in founding a Society actively antagonistic to Mrs. Besant and had just been lecturing in this spirit at the Continental Headquarters.

I therefore said that, without prejudice one way or the other, it was clearly my duty not to grant the request until I had been able to enquire further into the matter, as I did not wish *The Vahan* to be used as a means of promoting disharmony. The applicant replied courteously that my points were well taken.

I have tried, as far as possible, to exclude controversy from *The Vahan*—much to the annoyance of a handful of excited folk who consider their grievances all-important.

I should not have thought it worth while to break through this practice in the present instance but for one fact—which it is no breach of confidence to mention in the abstract—that very serious difficulties in connection with the German Section are now engaging the attention of the General Council.

I have, personally, endeavoured to give every consideration and freedom to the various schools of thought in our midst. The T.S. is in its constitution an exoteric body, and has to be conducted as such. Therefore every fellow is free to derive his spiritual inspiration from whatever source he chooses, without being made to feel uncomfortable in the T.S. or any of its National Societies.

*

It was probably also in January 1913 that there appeared in Britain the first (undated) number of a new publication entitled *The 'Mitteilungen'*, which provided a complete English translation, undertaken by Harry Collison, of the German theosophical news-sheet edited by Mathilde Scholl.

This first number rendered the continuation of the issue for December 1912, prefaced by a translator's note informing readers that

> In view of the misstatements and inaccuracies allowed to stand in English theosophical papers with regard to Dr. Steiner and his theosophical work on the Continent, it is necessary to translate the *Mitteilungen* for the benefit of those English-speaking people who are willing to hear both sides of a question.

On the occasion of Scholl's seventieth birthday in 1938, Collison recalled in *Was in der Anthroposophischen Gesellschaft vorgeht*:

> During the Besant crisis I turned to Mrs. Besant and the editors of her journal requesting them in the name of fair play to accept my short report in the cause of Dr. Steiner. I received a very dry refusal with the words 'Impossible to make our journal an organ for different opinions.'
>
> I therefore sent a copy of the *Mitteilungen* in the English language to every branch of the T.S. in the world. I received only four acknowledgements. The others remained silent. Mr. Dunlop said it did not interest him.

The reason why Dunlop was not interested may readily be deduced from the motto he had put at the top of *Theosophy* on 16 February 1910: 'Not to repel or destroy so much as to accept, fuse, rehabilitate.'

★

One item published in an early number of *The 'Mitteilungen'* was 'A Letter from the Rosicrucian Lodge, British Section, T.S., London, to Adyar':

> At a special meeting of the above lodge on January 16th, 1913, the following resolution was passed to be sent to Adyar:—
>
> Having been made acquainted with the reasons for the action of the German Section of the T.S., the members of the Rosicrucian Lodge of the British Section unanimously endorse its action in sending the telegram of Dec. 11th, 1912, to the General Council at Adyar, in which it says that it 'can only see in the resignation of the President the possibility for further existence of our Society'.
>
> On behalf of the members unanimously,
>
> H.J. Heywood-Smith,
> President.

★

Heywood-Smith subsequently provided further details in his letter of May 1914 to Marie von Sivers:

> The Rosicrucian Lodge of the Theosophical Society, which had been formed for the sole purpose of studying the work of Rudolf Steiner, and of which I was the leader, ran alongside the Anthroposophical Society until Tuesday Jan. 21st, when we heard from Germany that Mrs. Besant had withdrawn the Charter from the German Section. The Charter of the Rosicrucian Lodge was at once returned to the Theosophical Society and the members transferred themselves to the already-existing Lodge of the Anthroposophical Society.

The news from Germany concerning the withdrawal of the German charter proved in fact to be somewhat premature, but this made little difference to the ultimate outcome of the matter.

Strange Books

Towards the end of January 1913, AE crossed over to Britain for the first time since 1896.

The 45-year-old Irishman was spotted in London by the 26-year-old Clifford Bax, who described the event in his autobiographical *Inland Far* (1925).

> ... So pleasant was the afternoon that I could not bring myself to go home. The light was still good, and I decided therefore to see if the Italian Primitives in the National Gallery would charm me as much as they had when I was a student at the Slade. To this end I boarded a bus, and lulled by its rhythmic jogging, fell into a day-dream ... I woke up to find, with surprise, that we were already in Trafalgar Square; and as I rose to get off, I looked down at the passers-by, and observed an unmistakable figure who, with forward-peering eyes and brown beard patriarchally flowing, strode somewhat forlornly through the preoccupied crowd. 'What can have brought him to London,' I mused, 'he who never leaves Dublin except for Donegal? Or can I be seeing only his astral form?' I overtook the tall apparition, and found that it was indeed no other than AE, AE in the flesh.
>
> 'My dear man,' he said, with his usual friendliness, 'I'm delighted to see you. But take me to some quiet spot. I haven't been in London for seventeen years, and I assure you that it's even more dreadful than it used to be. I feel as though I had lost my soul.'
>
> 'Well,' I suggested, 'we might go and see old Watkins, the bookseller. I expect you know him. He specializes in occult and mystical books, and has

read them all, and he'll be greatly interested to meet you. His shop is just down an alley, over there.'

'I know him very well by repute,' said AE. 'Let's do as you say. I'd like it.' And as we edged our way through the people, he murmured: 'Why don't you come to live in Dublin, near the mountains? The air in London is dead, exhausted, many times breathed. But all these people, I suppose, are immortal beings, if we could see through appearances.' I could not help smiling at the implication that immortality might be an exclusive endowment of the Irish, but I saw at once that AE had meant that there is no need to pursue the divine.

By grace of Mr. Watkins we spent an hour or more in examination of the strange books that lined his shop: Bibles composed by forgotten fanatics, much-thumbed astrological volumes that Sir Thomas Browne might have perused, treatises on serpent-worship, the poems of Hafiz that put into language the songs of the nightingale, the glowing revelations of Boehme, the dizzy soarings of Plotinus. The old bookseller acted as our guide in that world of silent shades, that bewildering assembly of distorted or magnificent ideas; and from time to time AE took down a book and commented upon its place in his mental history. 'Ah,' he cried, thus laying hand upon *The Algonquin Legends of New England*, 'here is a book that I read with delight in my youth. It contains a marvellous tale—yes, here it is—'The Invisible One'. I have no doubt that it comes from a great experience and refers to the Ancestral Self. Once I thought of trying to make it into a poem.'

'And here', he said, a few moments later, 'is a book that meant a great deal to me in the old days. But it all makes me realize that after a man is forty he doesn't read so much. At present,' he added, turning to me, 'you wouldn't feel that, I expect. You are still reading everything.'

This scene took place in Cecil Court, off the Charing Cross Road, in the occult bookshop of John Watkins, bookseller and publisher, the very person who two years previously had published the English edition, brought out by Harry Collison, of Rudolf Steiner's *The Spiritual Guidance of Man and of Mankind*.

⋆

On his return to Dublin, AE wrote to Charles Weekes:

Irish Homestead
Friday

Dear Charlie,

I have been caught into the usual vortex on my return. I don't know whether I have any sketches at present I would care to sign but will look up what I have on Sunday. You see I had neuritis in my painting arm, and did not do anything for three months and was only able to use my arm again at the beginning of this year. Anyhow I can use it now and if I have nothing I can *make* something to send you. I was sorry I could not see you again. I was so rushed with one thing or another. I concluded my last day in London Friday by lunching with Asquith and Birrell and dining with Arthur Balfour, sandwiching between these two a visit to Orage, Magee, and a long talk with Ralph Hodgson who is I think the best of the young poets on your side of the water. I felt like God, holding no form of politics but benevolently contemplating all. I am very sorry I missed Dan. I will write you again if I find a sketch or when I make one. I have to write a long Memo on Home Rule for a friend of mine who wants to try and influence some of the lords not to be foolish over the present bill. But it is much more difficult to be sure. I would like to wring the neck of the present Home Rule Bill.

Yours ever

AE

*

Another letter was written to John Quinn:

Irish Homestead
February 7, 1913

My dear Quinn,

I was over in London last week and saw a big post-Impressionist exhibition. I think it is the second childhood of art, with Noah's ark, trees, houses and animals, only rather more badly drawn than the Noah's Ark, trees and houses of first childhood. Gauguin and one or two others of the pioneers of this movement had a kind of talent, but now Picasso and Matisse have gone into a kind of hopeless drivel of line and colour and ideas which makes one feel unhappy as if one were in the society of lunatics. I saw a Conder exhibition—some lovely things there. He is of the same clan as Beardsley.

The New English Art Club was closed just the day before I got over. I had four good days, saw Moore, Steer, Tonks, McEvoy, Harrison, Ralph Hodgson the best of the younger poets, Laurence Binyon, and F.S. Oliver, who wrote the *Life of Hamilton*. I had two hours with Asquith and Birrell at Downing Street, at lunch, and had four hours with Arthur Balfour the same night, and sandwiched in between these two a couple of hours with the cleverest Socialist in England, probably in the world—a young fellow named Orage, half Irish by the way.

I came back to Dublin loving Ireland more than ever. The size of London is appalling. The more humanity crowds together, the more inhuman does it seem. I believe in the small communities. I think, with the Greeks, that a city should contain no more citizens than could be influenced by the voice of a single orator. I wish we could get self-government here, and be quit of all the big imperial rascalities, which draw us about like a small boat tugged by a rope after a mammoth liner. My ideal state would be about the size of County Sligo. But I am afraid I will never live to see Ireland divided up into independent county kingdoms, like the little Greek states. I believe in the intensive cultivation of humanity. But I won't go off into my special political theories. My writing is so bad I dare not inflict more of it on anybody than two pages.

Yours ever,

AE

The Gravity of the Situation

In February *The Vahan* published a notice stating:

The Charter of the Rosicrucian Lodge of the Theosophical Society has been returned, and the members of the Lodge have resigned their fellowship.

This announcement was followed by another long article from James Wedgwood, entitled 'Affairs in Germany':

The General Council, which is the supreme legislative body of the Theosophical Society, has by unanimous resolution requested the President to withdraw the charter of the German Section. We do not know if the President has yet taken this step or is still holding back.

This extreme measure, we can well understand, has only been taken under considerable pressure and in view of the gravity of the situation in regard to Germany. It is impossible to go into any detailed examination of the points at issue in *The Vahan*, for the documents are far too lengthy. Presumably a full statement will be printed in the General Report.

Dr. Steiner alleges continuous indifference on the part of the President to his communications, and attempts at spying on the internal activities of his Section from Adyar; and the German-Swiss lodges complain of the manner in which the French-Swiss lodges formed themselves into a Swiss Section (but now limited to French Switzerland) without consulting them.

My own feeling, after a close consideration of the correspondence, was that there was misunderstanding fostered by the barrier of language; and though I knew that the feeling in Germany was bitter and intense, I felt that so delicate a matter could better be handled by a meeting of General Secretaries in Europe than from Adyar. I voted more or less in that sense; but appointed Mrs. Sharpe as my proxy on the Council, giving her discretion to modify my voting and take further action in the face of fresh issues, recognizing that unforeseen emergencies are always likely to arise.

Such fresh issues arose when in December the Executive Council of the German Section sent the following cable:

'To the Recording Secretary, Mr. J.R. Aria, for the General Council of the Theosophical Society.

'The Executive Council of the German Section T.S. assembled in extraordinary meeting in Berlin on December 8th, 1912, recognizes in the proceedings of the P.T.S. a continual objective distortion and misrepresentation of facts contradicting the highest principle of the T.S., the demand of truthfulness.

Basing upon the recognition that the President has continually and even systematically violated this highest principle of the T.S., "No religion higher than truth", and has abused the presidential power in arbitrary way, thus hindering positive work, the Executive Council here assembled, after minutest examination of documents, can only see in the resignation of the President the possibility of further existence of the Society.

'The detailed documental proof will be sent shortly by the Executive Council of the German Section to the lodges.

'We beg to submit this telegram to the thirty-seventh Convention T.S.

'The Executive Council of the German Section here present, unanimously (here follows a list of names).'

The cable is signed by the chief German workers, excluding Dr. Steiner.

It is further alleged that members of the Order of the Star in the East in Germany had been expelled from the German Section.

Anxious that English F.T.S. should have the facts, I cabled (reply paid) to Dr. Steiner:

'Have Star members been expelled from German Section?' and received the following reply:

'Steiner absent, information given in next *Mitteilungen*. Scholl.'

In the foregoing remarks I have striven to give an impersonal and impartial record; but I am bound here to say that I consider this reply extremely unsatisfactory. If the Berlin officials do not care to say yes or no in response to a request for a plain statement of fact, it would surely have been possible to communicate with Dr. Steiner. The cable is merely an evasion, and it is scarcely fitting that an official communication from the T.S. in England and Wales should be treated thus.

Since writing the above, through the courtesy of a brother General Secretary, I have been able to secure a copy of the document printed below. It will thus be seen that the Executive Council of the German Section have officially brought forward a resolution for the expulsion of O.S.E. members. Whether this is now effective or has to be endorsed by a German Convention I am unable to gather.

'Copy of the Enclosure with the official invitation to the General Convention of the German Section.

'To the honoured members of the German Section of the T.S. who are members of the Order of the Star in the East.

'The undersigned are in duty bound to notify you hereby that the Executive Council assembled in extraordinary meeting on December 8th, 1912, has passed the following resolution. This resolution has not been passed on account of any existing differences of opinion or mutually conflicting standpoints, which, it goes without saying, can be represented in the Theosophical Society, but only on the ground that the attitude which the leaders of the "Star in the East" have taken up towards the German Section seems altogether irreconcilable with the first object of the T.S. If therefore it be said that the German Section excludes certain views and standpoints, this must be characterized as incorrect.

'The resolution above-mentioned runs: The Executive Council of the German Section of the T.S. regards membership of the "Star of the East" as irreconcilable with membership of the Theosophical Society, and requests members of the "Star of the East" to leave the Theosophical Society.

'The Executive Council of the German Section will consider itself compelled to exclude from the German Section members who do not fall in with this request.

'Proposed by the Executive Council of the German Section.

The General Secretary
The Secretary.'

F.T.S. who wish to acquaint themselves more fully with the German point of view may obtain information about this—and the newly formed Anthroposophical Society—from Mr. H. Collison, 27, Clareville Grove, Onslow Gardens, S.W., who is responsible for the English edition of the German official organ—the *Mitteilungen.*

I have received a long letter from Fräulein Mathilde Scholl, editor of the *Mitteilungen*, maintaining that the account of the Munich meetings given in the December *Theosophist* is incorrect and a breach of confidence. I declined to print the letter here on the grounds (1) that I should require it to be written in more tolerant and courteous language, and (2) that the *Theosophist*, not *The Vahan*, published the report. *The Vahan* has already given publicity to Mr. Francke's statement as to the alleged inaccuracy of the report, and only reproduced four passages (bearing on English doings) which were endorsed by him as true statements of fact.

Where the Difficulty Comes In

Mathilde Scholl's letter to James Wedgwood, rejected for publication in *The Vahan*, subsequently appeared in *The 'Mitteilungen'*:

Motzstrasse 17,
Berlin W.,
January 14th, 1913.

Sir,—

Will you kindly publish the following in the next issue of the *Vahan*:—

In the January number of the *Vahan*, 1913, you wrote an article under the title 'An Explanation' which chiefly refers to some remarks of Mr. Francke, which he is said to have made during a meeting held at Munich in August 1912. They are taken from a report containing a brief reference to several meetings in Munich, which report appeared in the December number, 1912, of the *Theosophist* under the title 'Three Public Meetings held at Munich in August 1912 establishing the necessity of the Bund'.

First of all, let me say that these meetings were not at all 'public meetings', but strictly private for members of the Theosophical Society only, and any reference to them in a public magazine attainable to everyone who subscribes to it and distributed in public libraries is a gross breach of confidence as long as such publication is not authorized by the Executive Committee of the German Section. This, however, has not been the case.

Second, I feel it a duty to inform your readers that the abridged form in which the speeches of the Munich meetings are reported contains incorrect renderings of what has been said, or such superficial report of the contents of the speeches that their true meaning is in several cases absolutely distorted.

Thus the speech of Frl. von Sivers contains numerous misstatements. Sentences are quoted which she never uttered. Important things are omitted, and mere details or illustrating examples have been given an importance which they never had.

Here let me mention a sentence from a paper sent 'To Presidents of Lodges and Centres,' London, Jan 4th, 1913, by yourself, p.1: 'It is above all desirable that whatever information is given to lodges should be trustworthy, and this is precisely where the difficulty comes in.'

Yes, here the difficulty does come in!

It is high time that every member of the Theos. Soc. should feel it his or her absolute duty to ask whether what he reads in theosophical papers and pamphlets is true and proven as fact; and that where objective distortions of truth are found to be written and published and addressed not only to members of the Theos. Soc., but to the public at large, it is contradictory to all feeling of honour and honesty to be silent or to bow before the man or woman who spreads such objective untruth in the most abominable way.

Above all, General Secretaries ought to use discrimination with regard to what is published month after month and year after year at Headquarters, as it is an entanglement of objective distortions of facts and objective veiling of truths. Such duty has been conspicuously neglected, in a most deplorable way, except by a few.

A long chain of false ideas and misrepresentation of facts has been engendered by the objective distortions in the report of the Munich private meetings. With regard to my own words, let me mention that no one who heard them would recognize any of the chief points dwelt on in my speech.

The whole report touches the main points of importance only upon the surface, and is far from illuminating the depth of what was really expressed in those private meetings. Truly, no earnest member having been in touch for some time with the most serious and conscientious positive work in Germany would be otherwise than disgusted at the scale on which those most important and serious gatherings, provoked and quite unexpectedly made necessary by the undermining agitation-work of representatives of the Star in the East in Germany, have been dealt with in that unallowed report. Only an outsider to the true spiritual movement could have written this. At the head of the report stands 'By one who was there'. It may be 'by one who was there' physically, but decidedly not by one who was there with the spiritual understanding necessary to grasp the depth of the actual happenings and the true meaning of the words spoken.

Yours sincerely,

Mathilde Scholl.

The Present Moment

On 2 February, a gathering was held in Berlin in place of the previously announced Annual General Meeting of the Theosophical Society's German Section.

Before this gathering proceeded to more contentious matters, Rudolf Steiner began on a quite different subject:

I wish the many dark rays which may later shine in here would at least not shine onto one particular event. In view of the difficulties of our negotiations, we should this time commemorate right at the start those dear theosophical friends of ours who have left the physical plane since the last time we were gathered here.

For years on end we have been speaking about our feelings and sentiments in such cases. So I do not need today specially to emphasize that for a properly sensitive theosophist the transition of a person from one plane to another is only a change of existential form. As we feel united through bonds which are not confined to one plane, so too these bonds with our dear theosophical friends also remain the same when they are obliged to exchange one plane for another. Just as those who have left us still retain us as their loving friends, so can we possess loving friends in them. We need only turn our thoughts wherever possible towards the persons to whom these thoughts were often directed when they were still working with us on the physical plane.

I am obliged to recall many dear and loyal friends, those we acquired recently before their death, and also those who for many long years tarried among us. Were I to express everything which lies on my heart this would become a very long speech. It only has any value if we create a loving attitude as the starting-point of our thoughts about friends who have passed over to the other side.

Steiner went on briefly to characterize various recently deceased members. Although most of them were German, he also mentioned one particular Englishman:

... Further, I have to recall a person who had much Theosophy in his cast of mind, but whom only few people came to know—Mr. Meakin, who left the physical plane in October of last year, after working with us over a long period of time with ever-increasing intensity...

The address ended:

My dear theosophical friends, we know that our bonds with those who have left the physical plane through death remain inextinguishable. We know that they have stepped into another sphere of life. If at this moment when we have come together you feel united in the given sense with these friends who have left us, let this be taken as a starting-point for feeling united with them in the future too. By rising from our seats we wish to express the loving feelings and thoughts which we send towards our separated friends.

*

In answer to a letter from Annie Besant which set out formal grounds for revoking the charter of the German Section, the gathering composed a reply stating that the Section was taking this revocation as expulsion.

On the next day there took place a General Meeting of the Anthroposophical Society, followed by the first lecture of a cycle on 'The Mysteries of the East and of Christianity.'

Besides many German members, those attending this cycle included Herbert and Mabel Heywood-Smith.

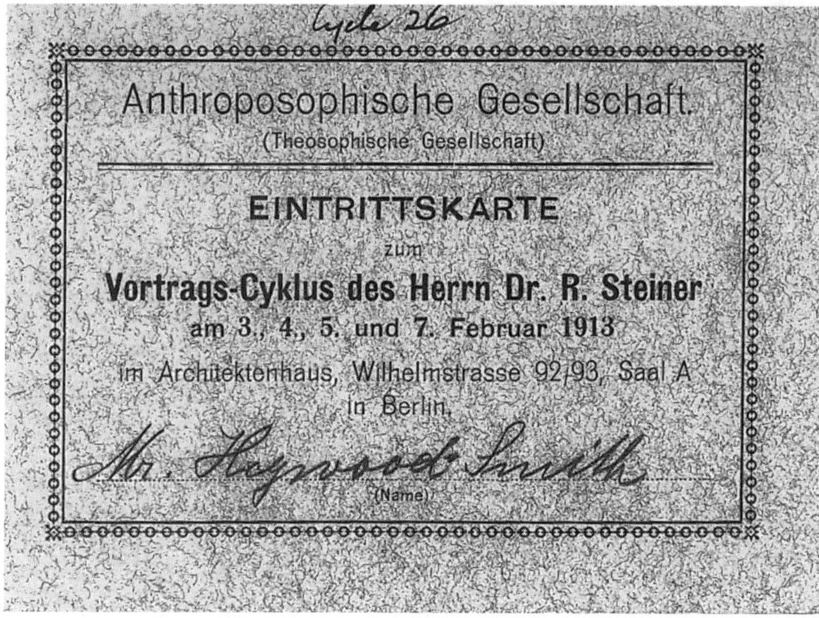

Cycle 26

Anthroposophische Gesellschaft.
(Theosophische Gesellschaft)

EINTRITTSKARTE
zum
Vortrags-Cyklus des Herrn Dr. R. Steiner
am 3., 4., 5. und 7. Februar 1913
im Architektenhaus, Wilhelmstrasse 92/93, Saal A
in Berlin.

Mr. Heywood Smith
(Name)

★

Baron Walleen must have been present at the cycle too, for in Berlin during this month he composed the preface to an English pamphlet, priced at a shilling: *The Turning-Point of Evolution*. By Baron C.A. Walleen. Based on the Unpublished Works of Dr. Rudolf Steiner.

The preface read:

> The content of this pamphlet represents in strongly condensed form the teachings on an all-important subject gradually given out by Dr. Rudolf Steiner during a period of about twelve years.
>
> It is therefore evident that many of the statements I have made want further explanation in order to be rightly understood. It will be the reader's concern to seek such further explanation, for this little book ought not to be considered as the last word upon the great questions treated therein, but as a condensed sketch giving an impulse contingently to further study.
>
> Hitherto it has not been considered expedient to publish so many and important occult truths within the restricted limits of a pamphlet. But times have changed, and the present moment is of such a character that in this direction the following attempt has been thought to be not altogether out of place.

The pamphlet gave a brief but careful sketch of Steiner's Christology, purely on its own terms. There was no mention or allusion whatever to that radically different kind of Christology which was being actively propagated within theosophical circles, chiefly in the English-speaking world, by the Order of the Star in the East.

★

Meanwhile, controversy between the different views was given further written expression elsewhere. *The 'Mitteilungen'* published a 'Letter from members of the West London Lodge about their retirement from the Theosophical Society':

> The undersigned members of the West London Lodge of the Theosophical Society, in resigning their membership of the Society, desire to express their complete agreement with the action taken by the German Section.
>
> H.N. Croxford, President; Maude M. Lee, Treasurer; Florence Franke, Ethel Blackmore, Alfred E. Mills, Jeanne Croxford.
>
> 10th February 1913.

★

On this same day, the 10th of February, Rudolf Steiner gave to Heywood-Smith's anthroposophical group the name 'Zarathustra'.

The naming of Collison's group is recorded in a letter dating from a week later:

> Windham Club,
> St. James's Square,
> SW
> 17th Feb. 1913
>
> Dear Mr. Heywood-Smith,
>
> I must congratulate you on your success in managing to prevail on the Doctor's coming over here. They told me before I left that it would have to be before Whitsuntide, from about the 30th April. There are so many engagements that follow Whitsuntide immediately—& at the end of May he is going to Helsingfors & on to Scandinavia.
>
> He has called my group the Myrdhin, after the early British initiation of King Arthur.
>
> I hope the Zarathustra & Myrdin groups will always work in harmony & in the recollection of the perfect ideal uniting such great names.
>
> Yours sincerely,
> Harry Collison

★

A week later, Edith Maryon wrote to Rudolf Steiner. (The initials F.M. stand for 'Freemasonry'—she was evidently unaware that the designation of rituals in the Mystica Aeterna had in 1911 been changed to M.D.)

58, Grove Park Terrace,
Chiswick, London.
25.2.13

Dear Dr. Steiner,

Rather unexpectedly to myself I find it will be possible for me to attend your course of lectures at the Hague, therefore when I see you there I shall ask you once again if I may be admitted to the F.M., if you think fit. Forgive me that I still must write in English, I have almost no time for study, it must wait until my return to Germany, then I hope there may be more opportunity to learn.

Believe me,

Yours sincerely,

L. Edith C. Maryon

At the Touch of Spring

The Vahan published a note from Winnifred Leisenring on '*The Path* Institute':

> *The Path* Institute opened a spring term of lectures and classes at Oakley House, Bloomsbury Street, W.C., on Monday evening, 27th January, when Mr. D.N. Dunlop began his series on Christian mystery-teachings. The Institute aims to promote systematic study of comparative religion, philosophy, science and art, and to assist in the application of the results of such study to life.
>
> Miss Charlotte E. Woods, Mr. W. Wroblewski, Mr. Frank J. Merry, Mr. F.S. Snell, B.A., and others are conducting classes which are held afternoons and evenings. A syllabus may be obtained from the Hon. Secretary at Oakley House, Bloomsbury Street, W.C.
>
> W.W.L.

★

The 'Mitteilungen' meanwhile published a letter from Harry Collison:

27 Clareville Grove,
Onslow Gardens,
S.W.,
28th February 1913.

To the President and members, *Light on the Path* Lodge, T.S.

I must preface my letter with the remark that it is with very greatest regret that circumstances force me to sever my connection with the *Light on the Path* Lodge. Apart from the friendship of those members I have the honour of knowing personally, and the many helpful discussions I have heard, I regard the *L.P.* Lodge as the one place in the Theosophical Society where freedom and tolerance prevail, and I had hoped that by its influence the Society might be purged of the sensationalism and dogma with which the name 'theosophist' has now become associated.

I was a member of the German Section, and therefore have now technically ceased to be a member of the T.S. If I desire to continue in your lodge, I would have to put myself under an obligation to the Adyar officials. This it is impossible for me to do, as I consider that it is they who are responsible for the trouble that has continued to befall the Society ever since Mrs. Besant took on herself the Presidency. I find her policy of the T.S. is the living example of an intensely overbearing personality which brooks no opposition. Of late I have had an unusually good opportunity of judging the T.S. as a whole, and have come to the regrettable conclusion that little good work of any independent kind can be done within it.

During the last few weeks I have been brought into touch with many T.S. officials, and can say with full conviction that in many cases they seem to regard their duty to Mrs. Besant as more important than their duty to the Society. And the members, having become blinded by a brilliant personality, are too indolent to bestir themselves and seek the truth independently. There is no limit to credulity when it is worked gradually. That this unhealthy state of things exists is also only too evident from the perusal of any theosophical newspaper, where flippancy on the one side, and adulation on the other, often take the place of serious investigation and sober fact. The recklessness with which false statements are cast into their columns and allowed to remain is appalling, and if one begs for a correction one is met by such an answer as 'It is not my affair', or 'You must be more polite', or to the effect that the President's memory must not be too much taxed.

The following is the statement of what has happened in Germany. It is untrue to say that the German Section declared that the Star in the East could not be in the T.S. What they said was: Owing to your untheosophic and hostile campaigning, you cannot join the German Section. More than this it had no power to do. Meantime, the Star in the East were getting charters direct from Adyar, and ought, if sincere, to have been satisfied with that.

By last December the continued policy of the Star in the East in Germany in its open hostility to the German Section had passed all limits, and as it was useless to appeal to a President who encouraged this policy, it became necessary that the appeal should be made to the General Council about to assemble at Adyar, and the only way to reach them in time was by cablegram. The facts were to follow. The German Section at the time declared that it was impossible for German members of the Star in the East in their present attitude to remain in the Theosophical Society, German Section. Anyone conversant with the methods of the Star President, Dr. Hübbe-Schleiden, and who reads his book attacking Dr. Steiner and the German Section, will at once see that the Star in the East in Germany has not the slightest claim to be called theosophic, if we judge the members by their actions.

The day before the Annual Meeting of the German General Section on 2nd February, the German General Secretary, Dr. Steiner, received a letter from the President demanding that he should cease his unconstitutional acts (presumably his action in protecting the German T.S. from the untheosophic methods of the German S.E.); otherwise she would execute the desire of the Adyar Council and cancel the German Section. She allowed the German General Secretary a fortnight to consider. The Adyar Council passed the resolution of expulsion without having waited to hear more. The German Section, at its meeting next day, brought face to face with what it held to be a glaring insult, unanimously passed a resolution declaring that it considered itself expelled from the T.S., though willing to re-enter when old theosophical ideals were restored. It has therefore ceased to exist, and the new Anthroposophical Society has been founded and has over 2600 members from various countries. An unjust attempt is made to show that the movement is only German, for the Secretary-General of Scandinavia and many other non-Germans have resigned in sympathy with Dr. Steiner, who is Austro-Hungarian.

Before the meetings it was discovered that Mrs. Besant had descended to a very cruel and subtle slander, and had repeated definitely in the *Adyar Bulletin* of January what she had previously prepared in other papers. Dr. Steiner in defence has been forced to make a public statement giving details of his life, which show conclusively that he was never 'educated by the Jesuits', and his life prevented him from ever coming in the slightest degree under what Mrs. Besant calls 'the fatal influence of the Jesuits'.

So we see how Mrs. Besant has at last succeeded in getting rid of a General Secretary inconvenient to her; and the T.S., having recently, I believe, lost about 700 members in India, and I know for a fact 2600 in Europe, now runs the risk of becoming the plaything of a Besant-Leadbeater faction.

I am sorry if my attitude is not to the liking of those people who prefer peace at any price. But if they have not forgotten their old teachings of karma, they will realize that it is a greater kindness to Mrs. Besant herself to speak the truth than it is merely to flatter her personality. It is never a pleasure to have to take up the disagreeable task of 'candid friend', but in conclusion I will quote the remarks of an Indian leader of the opposition to Adyar: 'It is a sacred duty if one is a theosophist to try all one can to purge the holy temple of the T.S. from all sellers and buyers of T.S. adornments, and put the T.S. once more above the psychical nonsense that has taken the place of its bygone spirituality.'

We would have stayed in the Society to accomplish this, but have been forced to retire. I hope the *Light on the Path* Lodge will have better fortune.

Thanking you all again for the very pleasant evenings and really helpful teaching I have had from your lodge, I remain

Yours theosophically,

Harry Collison.

★

A strikingly perceptive passage on the whole situation appeared in an editorial in the March number of *Theosophy in Scotland*:

> . . . In Germany the stress and strain of growth has made manifest a degree of tension that appears, so far as the German Section is concerned, somewhat critical. The ultimate issue of the tension is not yet apparent. The one thing clear is that there is a strain, severe and keen, but we feel that an optimistic view of the situation, whatever the result, is the one we must take. For is not this strain but an evidence of growth? And is it not ever the case that the swifter the growth the keener the strain? Has not the opening bud, at the touch of spring, to burst and discard the sheathing petals before the full beauty enshrined within can show forth? So let us try to take the view of the liberated flower and not the view of the discarded sheathing petals; for the sheathing petals represent the form, mortal and perishable, while the flower, that grows more and more beautiful as it expands, represents the life, immortal and enduring . . .

★

The last episode took place when on 7 March Annie Besant finally revoked the charter of the German Section.

It may further be noted that in the English-speaking world Besant was then publishing in book form a lecture she had given in Paris in 1911 on Giordano Bruno. But at the same time in the German-speaking world, Rudolf Steiner instructed that Bruno's name be dropped from the Cologne branch of the Anthroposophical Society.

★

The Vahan published a further announcement on a quite different matter:

The fifth International Summer School, organized by *The Path*, will meet this year at the Peebles Hotel-Hydro, Peebles, Scotland, from July 19 to August 2. An unusually interesting international gathering is anticipated and, by holding the school ten days earlier than usual, the organizers have been able to secure accommodation where the members of the school may be together.

Lectures and classes will be so arranged that more time will be given to study and discussions. The music will again be in excellent hands.

Early application for accommodation will be necessary, as bookings are already coming in rapidly. A circular giving complete information may be obtained from the Hon. Secretary, Fifth International Summer School, Oakley House, Bloomsbury Street, W.C.

Winnifred Leisenring, B.A.,
Hon. Secretary

Much Pleasure

In the middle of March, only six weeks before Rudolf Steiner's impending visit to Britain, Harry Collison wrote a letter to Herbert Heywood-Smith. (Since Collison too used the initials F.M., he cannot have attended the Mystica Aeterna class in Berlin on 16 December 1911, or subsequently have learnt that the designation of the rituals had been changed to M.D.)

Windham Club,
St. James's Square.
S.W.
17th March 1913

Dear Mr. Heywood-Smith,

Enclosed please find fifteen pounds for the F.M. decoration scheme. I have much pleasure in doing this.

Yours sincerely,
Harry Collison

★

Edith Maryon, attending in Holland the cycle on 'The Significance of Occult Development on the Sheaths of Man', wrote again to Rudolf Steiner:

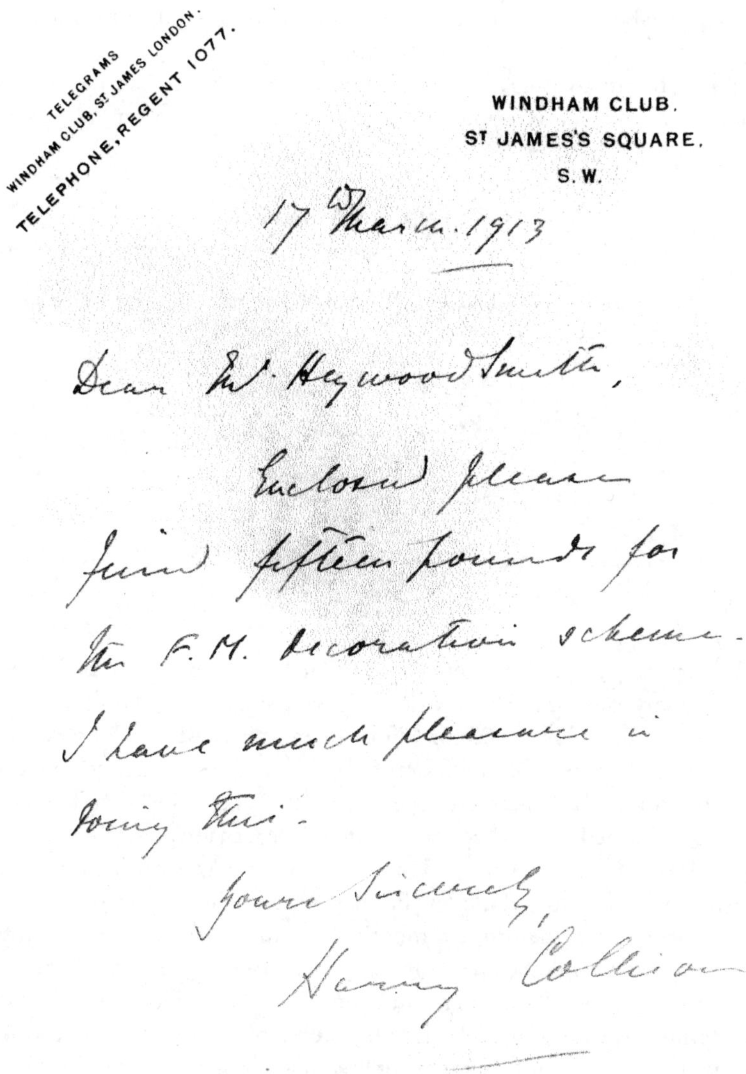

TELEGRAMS
WINDHAM CLUB, ST JAMES LONDON.
TELEPHONE, REGENT 1077.

WINDHAM CLUB.
ST JAMES'S SQUARE.
S.W.

17th March. 1913

Dear Mr. Heywood Smith,

Enclosed please find fifteen pounds for the F.M. decoration scheme. I have much pleasure in doing this.

Yours Sincerely,
Harry Collison

Prins Hendrik Straat 30.
The Hague.
22.3.13.

Dear Dr. Steiner,

I feel I must just write and thank you not only for your kindness in admitting me to the F.M. but for all you so unselfishly & ungrudgingly give to us. I am indeed grateful to you for many things; I am no longer terrified of the future as I used to be. Some day I hope through your teaching I may develop into a being who can be a little use to others, it is quite time I did do so.

Before I return to England perhaps you will be able to tell me if you consider I am carrying out your instructions regarding my exercises—correctly?

Believe me

Yours most gratefully & fraternally

L. Edith C. Maryon

I understand much more today than I feared I should, & Frl. Hollenbach is going to explain some more.

★

On her return to England, Maryon wrote to Steiner again just a week later:

58, Grove Park Terrace,
Chiswick, London
30.3.13.

Dear Dr. Steiner,

I think perhaps I ought to inform you that I have now quite definitely decided in my own mind that when I leave England in May it will be altogether, & with your permission I hope to entirely cast in my lot with the Anthros. Gesell. When I know more, I hope it may be possible for me do some work for it. Dr. Felkin returns on the 13th Ap. & I shall then tell him what I have decided, he has been most kind to me, & I am afraid he will not be very pleased as he only expected me to go away for a year or so. I think it better to tell you first, as doubtless he may refer to the subject when you meet in London. For the first few months in Munich I hope to give all my time to study, it worries me dreadfully not to be able to understand German, & one feels one must also be such a nuisance to other people. Then when I go to Berlin—as I unfortunately have no means of my own—I must look for some work to do, but I am not troubling myself unnecessarily about this, for I feel I have come to the right decision, & so when the proper time arrives the right work will arrive with it.

—I think you were a little surprised I have not been doing any definite thing for Neville Meakin, & feel I should explain. Dr. Felkin repeatedly told me he could not be contacted for the first six months & any effort to do so would only be harmful to him. I never could quite see how anything I should be likely to wish to do could possibly hurt him in any way, but as I thought Dr. Felkin must know much more than I—definite knowledge—I acquiesced & have done no more than try to send him some helpful thoughts & prayers—especially on Fridays. I do not think Dr. Felkin really does quite understand me or the position entirely, tho' I know he thinks he does, so now I shall just do as I wish myself. You may have thought we were engaged but we were not, & we should never have married, though I would have had he wished, because I thought he would have lived longer if he had had someone to look after him.

I am reading now to him every day, & have told him, if he knows of anyone else who would like to listen he may bring them too, that is, if they can understand me, I am not quite clear as to possibilities.

I forgot to ask you whether you received my letter addressed to Bauka Straat, but there was nothing in it except some of my thanks to you for all the help you have given me. I would have liked to tell you several things the other day, but they were too long & too difficult, & I do not like to tell anyone else too.

It makes me very happy to think I am coming to Germany.

Believe me,

Yours v. sincerely

L. Edith C. Maryon

I tried to find out from M. Schuré what your meaning was that 'Knowledge is a metamorphosis of death' but tho' he was rather illuminating about the meeting between man's higher & lower self, I do not think he explained the real meaning of your phrase to me; & my own is too vague.

Auf wiedersehen in England.

Readiness to Associate

By the beginning of April the outcome of the controversy in the Theosophical Society between Annie Besant and the German Section became known even in Britain. *The Vahan* published another note on 'Affairs in Germany':

> We have received a copy of the *Mitteilungen*, formerly the official organ of the Theosophical Society in Germany—now of the Anthroposophical Society. It contains a report of the Theosophical Convention held in Berlin at the commencement of February, from which we learn that the greater part of the German Section under Dr. Steiner has now definitely seceded from the Theosophical Society, having first by an almost unanimous vote of the delegates confirmed a resolution of the Executive Committee declining to admit to the Convention those members of the Section and of the T.S. who were also members of the Order of the Star in the East.

A subsequent report of the year's work in England and Wales further specified that

> . . . one lodge—the Rosicrucian, formed expressly for the study of Dr. Steiner's teachings—and about thirty Fellows left the T.S. in order to join the Anthroposophical Society.

Since the Theosophical Society in England and Wales numbered at the time some 2500 members, and that in Scotland another 300, those 30 Fellows were relatively speaking a tiny minority—not much more than 1 per cent of the sum total of theosophists in Britain.

★

The departure of the anthroposophical contingent from the Theosophical Society did not prevent Max Gysi from bringing out at this time in the Theosophical Publishing House in London another work by Rudolf Steiner: *The Lord's Prayer*, translated by A.M. Wilson.

The Vahan meanwhile printed a report of 'The Northern Federation at Harrogate', which contained further relevant matter:

> The seventy-fifth Conference of the Northern Federation was held at Harrogate at Easter in conjunction with various gatherings connected with the opening of the new Theosophical Hall of the Harrogate Lodge.
>
> At the business meeting of the Federation on Saturday afternoon the Baildon, Burnley, Hull and Ilkley Lodges were admitted to the Northern Federation . . .
>
> The usual discussion followed the business meeting. About seventy members were present, including Mrs Besant-Scott, the daughter of Mrs. Besant.
>
> A vote of condolence was passed to the widow of Mr. John Yarker, Hon. F.T.S., the celebrated Masonic author.
>
> The subject of discussion was 'The Main Work of the Theosophical Society. There has been a marked tendency recently to multiply Leagues, Orders etc. in the Theosophical Society. Does this strengthen or weaken the Movement?' A long and interesting discussion followed. The speakers were Messrs. Dunn, Dunlop, Bell, Hodgson Smith, Harrison, Outhwaite and Clarke . . .
>
> At this meeting Mr. Dunlop proposed and Mr. Bell seconded the following resolution, passed unanimously:
>
> 'The Northern Federation of the Theosophical Society in England and Wales regret the circumstances which have made it appear necessary to the members of the German Section under Dr. Steiner to resign from the Theosophical Society; and while confirming their loyalty to the Theosophical Society and its President, desire to express their readiness to associate themselves with their German comrades in all true theosophical activity under whatever name it may be conducted.'

On Sunday evening Mr. Wedgwood gave a public lecture in the theosophical hall (where all the meetings were held) . . .

The Conference concluded on Easter Monday with another public meeting, when Mr. D.N. Dunlop addressed about one hundred members and friends on 'The Drama of the Soul'. Taking the world-old drama, which has been retold in all the great religions but perhaps to Western eyes appears with special beauty in the story of the Christ, Mr. Dunlop showed how in feature after feature and by symbol after symbol this ancient story was the inner story of the individual and of the race. A long and interesting series of questions followed after the lecture.

*

The April issue of *The Path* opened with an article by Dunlop on 'Some Symbols of Magic', reproducing a lecture he had given on 30 January. There was also a fifth instalment of the shortened version of H.W. Percival's studies on the zodiac.

Further editorial notes commented on recent events, with analogies to the sinking of the *Titanic* in the previous year.

> The life of the present 'theosophical community' has been stirred by the secession from the parent body of the German Theosophical Society under Dr. Steiner. This had evidently been anticipated by the formation of a separate body called the Anthroposophical Society. At the critical moment this 'lifeboat' was 'lowered' from the larger vessel with all the followers of Dr. Steiner on board safe, sound, and rejoicing. Details of the controversy leading to this action have been circulated to some extent, but apart from deeper fundamental issues which have not been revealed, there does not appear to be any difficulty which could not have been overcome by a round-table conference of representatives of 'both sides' who were actuated by the spirit of brotherhood and endowed with a modicum of common-sense. Letters and telegrams between Adyar and Berlin afford little opportunity for the exercise of the necessary functions leading to adjustment. The business world is a 'school of occultism', in which many men have learned how to make the spirit of co-operation effective in the practical affairs of life. I think modern seers and prophets should call in tactful business men to adjust differences in matters of organization when they arise. It may be, however, that every teacher in the 'lesser mysteries' feels it necessary to build a special 'ark' in which his or her pupils may be safe from the 'blinding light' of the pure aether, majestic and star-decked. These special vessels may sail on the waters of life, bearing witness to the light, but they are not the light. In the midst of the icebergs of unbelief even a canoe may be safer than an Atlantic liner, but the wise man will learn to walk on the waters, poised, commanding the turbulent elements to be still and know that he is God.

The drift of these statements shows that Dunlop did not yet fully appreciate the doctrinal nature of the 'fundamental issues'. And indeed in all the published matter then available in English—whether in *The Theosophist*, *The Vahan* or even *The 'Mitteilungen'*—about the complex 'matters of organization' which formed the surface of the controversy, these underlying issues were in the English-speaking world not nearly so apparent as in subsequent years, after eventual translation of Steiner's relevant lecture-cycles, they finally became. The article by Mabel Collins in *The Occult Review* in March 1912, although briefly setting out Steiner's Christology, did not enter into details of controversial issues, nor did Walleen's pamphlet on *The Turning-Point of Evolution* draw attention to or indeed even mention the irreconcilability of Steiner's adopted doctrinal position with that widely promoted by the Order of the Star in the East.

In 1935 Dunlop summarized his situation by stating:

> I stood aloof from developments in the Theosophical Society, incurring the disapproval and often the firm opposition of orthodox followers of Annie Besant and C.W. Leadbeater, but opportunity for direct contact with Rudolf Steiner's teachings came only later.

The aloofness referred to was shown in his disinclination to join the Order of the Star in the East. But although Dunlop must have read such published works of Steiner's as *The Way of Initiation* and *The Education of the Child*, these had not made any particular impression upon him. He had heard something from Walleen about Steiner's Christology, but still had no 'direct contact' with Steiner's teachings through the then still restricted lecture-cycles.

★

The April issue of *The 'Mitteilungen'* published the addresses of all working groups in the Anthroposophical Society. Under 'England', beside the Zarathustra and Myrdhin groups was now listed a third group in Kensington: the Emerson Group,[28] led by Edith Cull.

In addition, names were given of two groups elsewhere in the country: the Ilkeston Group, led by Edith Lewis, and the Manchester Group, led by Fred Clarke (later joined by Edward Melland).

★

All the previous work for anthroposophy in Britain reached a culminating point on Tuesday, 29 April when Herbert Heywood-Smith received the following telegram, sent from Bruges:

> Arrive Wednesday Charing Cross five o'clock. Sivers.

Deep Inner Feeling

What Herbert Heywood-Smith related about Rudolf Steiner's 1913 visit to Britain is contained in one short paragraph of his account:

> Dr. Steiner remained with us for one week, and during that time gave two lectures for members, held other meetings and gave a great number of private interviews. We look upon that week as the most sacred of our lives, when we were privileged to shelter our beloved Leader and Teacher and Marie von Sivers in our house.

The house where Steiner lodged from 30 April to 7 May was that of the Zarathustra Group at 47 Redcliffe Square in South Kensington, where the Heywood-Smiths themselves were now living.

Steiner's lectures were held in the large room on the first floor. The Heywood-Smiths lived on the second floor, and probably gave Steiner a room above them, on the third floor at the top of the house, for Lawrence Edwards recalled:

> From Heywood-Smith himself I learnt that on Rudolf Steiner's visit the Heywood-Smiths were hosts to him, and had him living in their home. They would hear him moving round his room at 2 to 3 a.m. or later. He seemed to take hardly any sleep, being active almost all the 24 hours.

⋆

During his visit to London Steiner gave two lectures in this Kensington house to assembled members of the Anthroposophical Society.

The first was given on the evening of Ascension Day, Thursday, 1 May. It now bears the title 'Occult Science and Occult Development'.

Here is the opening:

> It gives me today great satisfaction to greet our friends in this country for the first time. I am sorry I cannot speak in your own language, but to overcome this difficulty our friend Baron Walleen will today translate sentence by sentence what I shall be saying. Tomorrow I shall give the lecture without any interruptions, and Baron Walleen will be kind enough to give a summary in English.
>
> Our dear friends in this country, who have often visited us on the Continent, have formed in the finest way an inner bond between our friends here and those on the other side. The beautiful home where we are gathered today gives evidence of the deep inner feeling with which our friends in this country have joined with us to work for the spreading of Anthroposophy. Those who have come over from the Continent to visit our English friends will truly rejoice to discover in this branch such a fine

space for what lies so close to our hearts, and is rooted so deeply in our souls.

Allow me today to address you for the first time and greet you most heartily, with the deep inner feeling of unity which belongs to Anthroposophy and in which all human beings on Earth should unite without difference of race, colour, or anything of that sort. To find that our friends have undertaken to work in this country with such great inner enthusiasm should be for us a good guarantee for work in the future.

The theme we want to discuss today leads us straight into a region belonging to the whole of mankind, completely separate from any differences.

We must first speak about a realm of human endeavour which in its true form cannot be described in any human language, but in its original form only in the language of thought. This is the field of occult science . . .

★

The second lecture, given a day later, now bears the title 'Christ at the Time of the Mystery of Golgotha and Christ in the Twentieth Century'. In his memoirs, Baron Rosenkrantz recorded his impressions of Steiner at this lecture, the very first one he gave concerning the Archangel Michael:

> I will never forget the deep impression he made on me when entering. Devoutness and a great inner concentration were shown when he mounted the platform. He spoke about the Archangel Michael being the guide of spiritual life from our century.
>
> The lecture was given in German and Baron Walleen translated it in three stages. These interruptions disturbed the experience one received from Steiner's fervent language when speaking about the great tasks of our time, which gave one directly the feeling of listening to an inspired orator.

Despite the interruptions for the actual listeners in 1913, readers of today may still sense the orator's inspiration in the continuous text of the published version.

The lecture ended:

> That is what can be said today about the relation of the Mystery of Golgotha, which took place at the beginning of our time-reckoning, to the Mystery of Golgotha as it can be understood at present. Let us make these feelings our own by recognizing that only in this way can we become true spiritual scientists. From time to time new revelations will arrive, for which we must hold our minds open. Should we not find it quite especially egoistic to keep these feelings exclusively as our own property? Let us rather feel it as our earnest duty, known to us through spiritual science, to make ourselves into ready instruments for such revelations. And although within the whole of mankind we are only a small society which is trying to

understand this new truth of the Mystery of Golgotha, this new revelation of Michael, let us nonetheless build up a new strength which does not in the least depend on our belief in this revelation, but only on the revelation itself, on the truth itself.

We shall then recognize quite calmly that only a few of us are ready to explain the following to the world, in so far as it wants to listen: there is from now onwards a new revelation of Christ. We want to be prepared to recognize it, and to belong to that small circle which desires to help it become greater and enduring. We want to build on the inner strength of this revelation, so that it may spread among the rest of mankind, for this knowledge will gradually be shared by everyone.

This is what we call wisdom, and what many might call folly. In order to stand firm, we need today only recall that this present time is that of Michael's second revelation, and also what was said by one of the old initiates at the time of his first revelation: What often appears to men as folly, is wisdom before God.

Let us attempt today to draw strength from such feelings, from such spiritual knowledge, which in many respects must appear to the world as folly. Let us gain courage to recognize that what appears folly to those who rely only on the senses can give us wisdom and light, and a clearer understanding of the supersensible, spiritual worlds, towards which we wish to strive with all the strength and conviction of our souls.

From the Luminous Heights of the Spirit

The reference made by Rudolf Steiner at the start of his lectures to 'those who have come over from the Continent to visit our English friends' indicates that it was not only British anthroposophists who were in the audience.

Among those present was for instance the well-travelled Dutchman Pieter de Haan, who mentioned the occasion in reminiscences published in *Medelingen voor leden van de Anthroposofische Vereniging in Nederland* in 1957:

> In 1912 my destiny brought me to Nuremberg, where I was working professionally in a big printing works. One of the leading personalities was an Englishman, who proved to be a theosophist with a philosophical cast of mind. We quite soon came into contact, and during lengthy conversations on evening walks he introduced me in a masterly fashion to the basic thoughts of Anthroposophy.
>
> In Zurich I came to know Ita Wegman, who smoothed the path to my first meeting with Rudolf Steiner.
>
> In 1913 my work brought me to London, where I had the fortune of

again being able to meet Rudolf Steiner and also coming to know Fräulein Marie von Sivers. Rudolf Steiner spoke here about the appearance of Christ in the ether-world. During lectures he revealed a side of his being which in normal dealings was not so apparent. When he was lecturing, it was as if the spiritual world opened up and the people present were no longer the chief matter; as if he were speaking for thousands of dead souls and at the same time for hierarchical beings. One felt united with what was happening in the world, part of it oneself, and also experienced all anthroposophical work as contained therein. Rudolf Steiner stood before us as the great initiate. This was again and again a tremendous experience with every lecture he gave. One felt taken up into a supersensible brotherhood, and at the same time called upon to take part in a great battle for the well-being of all humanity. One also felt united with everything which one had striven after and participated in through numerous lives. This gave strength and enthusiasm for the achievement of our earthly tasks both within the Society and outside it.

★

Mabel Collins published in this same month, May 1913, a further article in *The Occult Review*, entitled 'Some Views of Dr. Rudolf Steiner on Human Evolution'. It gave a detailed account of Steiner's booklet *The Spiritual Guidance of Man and of Mankind*.

Lawrence Edwards reported a connected social occasion:

Mrs. Stewart told me once of a dinner party she had attended at which two of the guests had been Rudolf Steiner and Mabel Collins.

★

Beside dinner parties, there were also personal interviews. In his memoirs, Baron Rosenkrantz recorded:

During my first conversation with Rudolf Steiner, which took place in London, he told me: 'You must let more light into your pictures'. I did not then realize or understand the extent of these words, but time showed me. I also received a meditation from him.

Rosenkrantz ended his memoirs by again recalling this first interview:

Finding my way and growing into Anthroposophy took place by means of artistic problems, and I wanted to show what great bliss for me it was to be able to carry this out under Rudolf Steiner's personal guidance and advice. His words at our first meeting, 'You must let more light into your pictures,' were not just advice for my art, but for the development of my soul as well. They helped me to find the light of life, which I would never have experienced without Anthroposophy.

When in London, Rudolf Steiner once said: 'I give the direction,' (he said 'duktus'), and pointed forward. I have taken care to follow that direction in life and in art.

★

Steiner also gave an interview to Edith Cull, leader of the Emerson Group. She received from him a verse for the opening of group meetings which has since become the most well-known verse for this purpose in English-speaking anthroposophical circles.

In English translation it reads:

From the luminous heights of the Spirit
May God's clear light ray forth
Into those human souls
Who are intent on seeking
The grace of the Spirit,
The light of the Spirit,
The life of the Spirit.
May he live in the hearts,
In the inmost souls
Of those of us
Who feel ourselves gathered together here
In His Name.

★

Steiner's visit may also have been connected with the formation of further anthroposophical groups in Britain. The June issue of *The 'Mitteilungen'* listed another in the North of England, the Harrogate Group, led by W.H. Wiffen (soon joined by Daniel S. Ward), and the July issue the first one in Scotland: the Glasgow Group, led by Arthur P. Imrie, a person who, as will be seen in a subsequent chapter, was to play several years later a rather tragic role in the history of anthroposophy.

Other Meetings

Now Herbert Heywood-Smith recorded that besides giving lectures to members and holding interviews, Rudolf Steiner on his 1913 visit to London also held 'other meetings'. It seems natural to deduce that these were the 'other private meetings' requested by Heywood-Smith himself in Berlin at Christmas 1912.

The specification of privacy indicates that these meetings were for restricted circles, almost certainly held behind locked doors at 47 Redcliffe

Square. Probably there were two such meetings, of which one would have been a meeting of the Esoteric School.

The other was without any doubt a meeting of the Mystica Aeterna. Although not a word on the subject survives in print, the content of Harry Collison's letter to Heywood-Smith only six weeks previously makes it virtually incontrovertible that such a meeting took place. In editorial matter in the volume *Zur Geschichte und aus den Inhalten der Erkenntnis-kultischen Abteilung der Esoterischen Schule* (GA 265) Hella Wiesberger states:

> Ritual events took place where suitable rooms were available: at anthroposophical centres in Berlin, Hanover, Cologne, Munich, Stuttgart etc., but also in other countries.

A footnote here adds:

> It appears from documents in the archives of the Rudolf Steiner Nachlassverwaltung that there must have been at least partial translations of Rudolf Steiner's ritual texts into English and French.

★

Here is such a ritual text of the Mystica Aeterna, used at the three altars from 1913 onwards. It was recorded by a participant.

East

In the service of Michael, my sisters and brothers, I am bound to admonish you to attend to his holy sign. The earthly time when you received its holy meaning is filled with significance. You know that it tells you how the sublime name of God resounds in your innermost being. Sublime mysteries of the world are contained in the sound of the holy sign.

What from the east has become your teaching will be strengthened inside you by Michael's power.

The spiritual word given to you in the holy sign should become the being of your own being.

The way of the holy sign was laid upon your heart from the altar of the east. Inscribe into yourselves the word which will then be spoken to you . . .

South

In the service of Michael, my sisters and brothers, I am bound to summon you to work. May my task be inspired by what the worker building the temple of humanity calls beauty. You should carry out work on the building, for which your hearts are the foundation stones, well-measured thoughts the links, and strength of will the cement. Look into the world around you: its life is moving your hearts, its wisdom is training your thoughts, its solar forces are nourishing your will. This is all a beautiful expression of a hidden spiritual essence. Take into yourselves the powers of this essence, and what is living inside you will flow outward as beauty.

The way to this beauty was laid on your heart through our great Master from the Altar at the East. Inscribe into yourselves the word which will then be spoken to you . . .

West

In the service of Michael, my sisters and brothers, I am bound to release you from work. May my task be inspired by what by the worker at the temple of humanity calls strength. When you leave the portal of this temple into external life you should bring the work you have learned into effect.

What can form hearts into foundation stones of the great temple should flow into humanity from your hearts. What can create links to this building should work from your thoughts. What can be the cement for the stones of this building should pour forth from your will. Do only what comes out of the sincerity of your hearts, what you are led to by the care of your thoughts, what you have been steeled for by the strength of your will.

You yourselves shall thus be likenesses of your archetype, and from you shall come the power which forms the world.

The way to this power was laid on your heart through our great Master from the altar of the East. Inscribe into yourselves the word which will then be spoken to you . . .

★

The cultic rituals of the Mystica Aeterna were not the only such ceremonies taking place in London in occult circles of the day. Letters of Robert Felkin held by the Nachlassverwaltung indicate that during this visit in 1913 Steiner also accepted an invitation from Felkin to attend a meeting of the Order of the Stella Matutina.

Meetings of the order's Amoun Temple were usually held at Felkin's home, 47 Bassett Road in North Kensington, a location not too far from the South Kensington centre of the Zarathustra Group in Redcliffe Square.

Whether W.B. Yeats was present on the occasion when Steiner attended is not known, but seems doubtful. While Yeats was probably a regular attender at meetings, the evidence of his letters shows that towards the end of April 1913 he was taken ill during a trip to Stratford and returned to London on 1 May 'very weak' and 'fit for little but sleep'. Although he remained in London until the 8th, he wrote a letter on the 3rd to his sister Lolly stating

> I have been kept out of Dublin by a bad cold—I am too shaky to stir I came back here from Stratford—I doubt if going at all now as I am rather out of sorts generally . . .

With the Uttermost Detachment

Another non-anthroposophist who met Rudolf Steiner during this visit to London was A.E. Waite.

There may be a reference to the interview between them in Waite's 1913 pocket-diary. The brief entry for Friday, 2 May reads:

> Left home by 1.27 train. R. 11.45, meeting R. & S. at S.C.

The entry seems to indicate that Waite left his South Ealing home in the afternoon, taking the 1.27 train into town, and only returned at 11.45 at night, having in the intervening period met at some location denoted by the initials S.C. two persons whose names began with R. and S.

One can of course only speculate as to what these initials denote. Waite stated that his conversation with Steiner was 'brought about by one of his women admirers and followers, who was also a member of the Golden Dawn'. Since Herbert Heywood-Smith in his letter of 10 July 1912 to Harry Collison listed among the latter's group the name 'Riddel', it is at least possible to interpret the last clause in Waite's diary entry as 'meeting (Beatrice) R(iddel, a member since 1908 of the Waite-led Independent and Rectified Rite) & (Rudolf) S(teiner) at (the) S(tudio of) C(ollison).'

★

In the last of his many books, his autobiography *Shadows of Life and Thought* (1938),[29] the octogenarian Waite recalled the meeting. During a discussion of the controversial cipher manuscripts which had played a key role in the foundation of the Order of the Golden Dawn, he described in turn his own association with Robert Felkin, Neville Meakin and Rudolf Steiner. (G.D. = Golden Dawn. Soc. Ros. = Societas Rosicruciana.)

> . . . According to a story which I and a very few others received from Westcott, there was a name and address found among the loose leaves of the ciphers, being those of Fräulein Sprengel, to whom it was affirmed that he wrote and from whom he attained a permit to work the grades of the Golden Dawn. By the hypothesis therefore he and his collaborators had their warrant from somewhere in Germany.
>
> Now all this is on one side of a most tangled subject; for it happens that there is another, and it is concerned with three persons whose depositions were made personally to myself and are shortly these.

(1) Dr. Robert W. Felkin, originally of Amen Ra Temple of the G.D. in Edinburgh and afterwards of Isis Urania, who subsequently to a grand bouleversement in 1900 and the expulsion of Mathers by an almost unanimous vote of the Second Order, including so-called Theorici Adepti Minores, and subsequent also to the period when the Mother Temple came into my own hands, bore witness to his personal acquaintance in Germany with a niece of Fräulein Sprengel, who was also one of his patients and belonged, like her aunt, to the Occult Association which had authorized Westcott to found a Temple of the G.D. in London. It will be observed that not only is Westcott corroborated apparently in this manner but that the entire G.D. claim is elevated into a realm of fact. What, however, about the good faith of Felkin? Having no axe to grind in respect of occult personalities and their depositions, all my metaphorical cards are invariably laid upon the table when a question like this arises. It must be registered in the first place that those who knew him well were the last to trust his statements because of congenital inaccuracy and recurring confusion of psychic dreams with events of daily life. On one occasion he is said to have caused great interest by an alleged discovery of the tomb of Christian Rosy Cross, and there was much subsequent dejection when it turned out to be one of his visions. Instead of dejection there should have been written derision, but it stood at that. Before this story happened to come my way, he told me concerning the mysterious tomb itself, saying that he could take me there, though he could not—when asked—reveal where it was.

It is imposed on me now to add that—at least on the faith of Felkin—Fräulein Sprengel's niece was neither a dweller in the astral only nor an 'airy nothing' bodied forth in the imagination of a dreamer. Felkin established communication, by correspondence at first apparently and afterwards on the spot in Germany, with the Occult Association to which the niece belonged, like the aunt before her; and later he appointed a representative to learn on his behalf all that they were willing to communicate.

(2) This representative was a much younger man than himself or me, and one in whom he had every confidence. He was and remained in a brief period that followed what is termed an 'advanced occultist', very seriously concerned, and with stories to tell of experiences when he cared and chose. As from the beginning of our fleeting acquaintance, so unto this late day, I am quite certain that Meakin was a man of honour who would scorn to palter with the point of fact, as he judged or knew concerning it; and I continue to accept as accurate what he told me of his German adventure as the ambassador of Robert Felkin. On the eve of his departure I conferred upon him the grade of Adeptus Minor, acting as Adeptus Exemptus in Felkin's Stella Matutina Temple at Bassett Road. In this manner he carried with him the fullest ritual advantage that was possible in his case at the time. There is nothing to suggest that he was received with open arms in the

German fatherland; but he won his way among those to whom he was accredited, and there witnessed things that were not of G.D. provenance, but had in his opinion a certain analogy therewith. He brought back his account of these, his impressions of things and people, and his moderately worded feeling that the clouded origin of the Golden Dawn had been substantially cleared up. Of the German brotherhood itself he had little to tell, and of Fräulein Sprengel I heard nothing at all. Meakin may have kept something to himself, or which he told to Felkin only. Its indirect and direct connection with a famous German occultist of that period was supposed beforehand. This was Rudolf Steiner, before proceeding to whom it will be well to dispose of the two other witnesses who have been cited in this memorial. Meakin died suddenly, aged about forty-five years, soon after his ambassadorial visit, and before this event Felkin himself, accompanied by his second wife, paid a visit to Germany and was there for some time. On their return I heard more concerning the later Fräulein Sprengel, but nothing that calls for record. They were present at certain ceremonies which again were like or recalled those of the G.D. Mrs. Felkin affirmed that she much preferred their own; and it stood at this, as her opinion did not signify. She was hopelessly hard of hearing and knew little or no German. Felkin was of opinion that he—if not both—had received a higher grade than that of Adeptus Minor; but the one and only certain thing is that they brought back Steiner's Anthroposophy, not especially in the sense of its metaphysical and metapsychical aspects, which might have been beyond their province, but in that of its rhythmic exercises and the best of those bits and pieces about which we used to hear and most of us have now forgotten.

A little later on I had unfortunately to break with Felkin over the question of an agreement between us, which he failed to keep. Not so long after he and his family left England for New Zealand, carrying their Stella Matutina Temple and—so far as he was concerned—a warrant of some kind for the foundation of the Soc. Ros. in the new country of his adoption. It remains only to add (a) that we parted good friends; (b) that to the last day of my life I shall always regard him as a first-class medical man and remember that I had his help in this respect; (c) that if I had called him from the antipodes as the only person who could save my life, I verily believe that he would have come to me at all costs, without money and without price. This is high praise. But in things occult we parted once for all: it was impossible that we should work together, for there was no sense in which we belonged to one another. The occult is a shifty business.

(3) Rudolf Steiner paid his visit to London, and I had a long conversation with him, brought about by one of his women admirers and followers, who was also a member of the Golden Dawn. She acted as intermediary also, for he could speak no English, while my knowledge of German was like my acquaintance with dead languages, which one reads but does not talk. I had

only a single object in view, to attain which the counsel was that I should avoid reference to the German Rosy Cross because it would prove to be *subjectum non gratum*. It was believed or known that Steiner held some kind of certificate, licence or warrant from that source in Germany but that he resented allusion thereto, almost as if he regretted the fact of its possession, much as he might do in regard to a diploma of the Theosophical Society, to which he had once belonged. Perhaps he felt towards the one as he most certainly did towards the other, that it was something from which he had come forth and that he put his past behind him in both respects. On the other hand, the counsel offered may have been based on some misconception; it does not signify, as after all the available time was short enough in which to attain my end: this was to verify the story that the Felkins had literally, and not in some astral journey, visited Germany and witnessed things—no matter what they were—of a ceremonial kind. As to this Steiner spoke quite frankly and with the uttermost detachment, saying (1) that he gave them nothing, (2) that he received them as Pythagoras received strangers and (3) that he showed them certain things. It follows that these were Rosicrucian rites, for there would be nothing else available, as it is fully evidenced from his writings that Steiner had connections of this kind. Meakin was therefore a faithful witness within his own measures, and the probability is that the so-called cipher MSS. came—in part at least—out of German archives . . .

If Steiner conferred nothing—in the sense, let us say, of Adeptus Major or some other G.D. grade—it is certain at least that he produced a ritual in spectacular form for the benefit of his English guests . . . Meakin and Felkin witnessed things which reminded them of G.D. Rituals but were not identical with these.

On a balance of probability, I conclude (1) that the G.D. Ritual Notes were produced well after 1870—perhaps even ten years later; (2) that they were not the work of Westcott, Woodman and Mathers; (3) that it is unsafe to challenge their remote German connections, as they were not challenged in Germany, while it is on record that Rudolf Steiner attended at least one Stella Matutina meeting on the occasion of his visit to London . . .

Another detail of Waite's conversation with Steiner about the Mystica Aeterna is found in an entry from a summary of his dealings with Felkin in the 'Ordo R.R. et A.C.' notebook. (The initials stand for 'Rosae Rubeae et Aureae Crucis'. Further abbreviations are: E.O.L. = 'Ex Oriente Lux', the motto of Neville Meakin. F.R. = 'Finem Respice', that of Robert Felkin, and Q.L. = 'Quaero Lucem', that of his wife Harriot.)

It is quite certain that there is a German Order, making Rosicrucian claims and working ritually; that it is a Steiner Order; that E.O.L. took certain degrees therein; that F.R. and Q.L. were allowed subsequently to witness certain ceremonies; and that, according to Steiner's personal testimony to me, they are not more than 30 years old, which may mean that they are not less than 10 years in their antiquity.

Meeting with Mr Meebold

The entry in A.E. Waite's 1913 pocket-diary for Saturday, 3 May, probably the day after his interview with Rudolf Steiner, states:

At home. Wrote Felkin, Meebold.

The second surname is that of the well-travelled German anthroposophist Alfred Meebold, and a previous diary entry shows Waite to have been already corresponding with him before Steiner arrived in Britain at all. The letter he wrote on 3 May must have been to arrange a meeting, which he later recorded in detail in the 'Ordo R.R. et A.C.' notebook. It took place on the 7th—probably the day of Steiner's departure from Britain.

(F.R. = 'Finem Respice', the motto of Robert Felkin; C.R.C. = 'Christian Rosy Cross'; 'Vigilate' was the motto of Helen Rand, a founding member in 1901 of the Independent and Rectified Rite; 'Per Deos' was part of the motto of Daniel Nicholson, a more recent member, and translator and editor of mystical texts.[30])

1. It should be stated that Mr. Meebold is an emissary of Steiner and an ardent worker in England of the spread of Steiner's views.
2. He belongs to the thing of which certain ceremonies were witnessed by F.R.
3. F.R. opened communications by correspondence with Steiner, as I had supposed.
4. Mr. Meebold was not present but knew of the facts.
5. His position is that F.R. did not understand what he saw.
6. His view is that F.R. could not carry on his group and therefore appealed to Steiner.
7. If F.R. has received MSS. from Germany they are those which are open to anyone under Steiner's teaching.
8. F.R. is correct in saying that C.R.C. belonged to the 13th century, but as this does not seem to rest on historical evidence, I conclude that it is a derivation from Akashic records.
9. So long as F.R. continues his Order, so long he will have no connection with Steiner. I forget how this arose and the end of the last sentence is approximate. The question may have been whether F.R. was an admitted channel of Steiner knowledge.
10. In any case his claim to be a link between English and German

Rosicrucianism, indeed the sole link, has gone by the board, on Steiner's own information, and the feeling is left that the said claim amounts to direct mendacity.

11. He has no doubt a mass of MSS., and one of our own members—I forget whom—connected with English Steinerism, says that they were bought in Germany in the ordinary way possible to Steiner's pupils.

12. The mathematical attributions of the Sephiroth are not likely to be Steiner's teachings. I feel that Meebold is right in saying that the old systems are cast aside as dead and useless for the present epoch.

13. I suggest that the attributions in question are those of E.O.L., who would have made no pretence about them. My recollection is that they were said to be chaotic and to require deciphering, a characteristic of E.O.L.'s writing.

14. Mr. Meebold told me that at an early stage of his Steiner experiences he was himself initiated into a form of Rosicrucianism at Rome and took his degrees, after which he smashed it up, to use his own expression, apparently by representing to the people concerned that they did not know what they were doing or the value of their own materials.

15. It was apparently an old form of Rosicrucianism; the people were of an emotional kind, but quite well-meaning and serious.

16. Mr. Meebold's position is admirable in its clearness. If I and those who are with me want the living reality, we should disband and join Steiner.

17. The position in respect of himself is almost enviable. The only living person who possesses the vital truth is Dr. Rudolf Steiner, whom he has not only the happiness of knowing but is in his confidence, and works with him and for him.

18. Mr. Meebold was most strong in his condemnation of emotionalism and on the need of being guided by reason.

19. Outside this, there is what he calls Inspiration, being the faculty possessed by Steiner.

20. Mr. Meebold is perhaps the most emotional man of my acquaintance.

21. I asked whether his people in Germany are concerned with discovering the material tomb of C.R.C. and were expecting so to do. Vide the information of F.R.

22. He laughed this to scorn.

23. I told him, as a story which had reached me, without naming the source, how it had been reported that Dr. Steiner was a German Rosicrucian of the old school originally, was sent into Theosophy by Rosicrucians to lead it into Christianity and was still under Rosicrucian direction of the old kind.

24. He accounted for this by saying that, in the past, a person who had been a Rosicrucian might reincarnate now and bring with him an element of interest in this direction. Such a person on meeting with Steiner would

conclude that he was a Rosicrucian, presumably on account of his knowledge along this line.

25. Mr. Meebold is staying with Mrs. Dally and yesterday Vigilate received her resignation on the stated ground that it was imperative, though she could not say why. Per Deos, however, tells Vigilate that it was laid down as a condition of her Steiner proposers.

26. Of two things one: either Meebold is exceeding his instructions—as he seemed to do from what he mentioned himself—or Dr. Steiner's statement to me, as recorded in other notes, does not represent his role.

27. I do not wish to take the latter view, but the alleged cover of Miss Maryon has to be borne in mind. She has been in Germany, and I have no official reason to suppose that she is taking instructions from Meebold.

This Ridiculous Fable

On 16 May 1913 *The Church Times* published the following editorial:[31]

A considerable number of people, presumably sane, in this country profess to accept Theosophy. Theosophy (or at least the English variant of it) endeavours to dupe people into supposing that an acceptance of its tenets is compatible with the retention of Christianity. The progress of which the Theosophical Society boasts is largely due to the propagation of this ridiculous fable. It can be refuted by a careful examination of the facts. But the theosophical teacher does not encourage a study of facts, and the theosophical pupil shows little anxiety for them. He is content to move in a haze of words, to find vague comfort in the use of a semi-oriental terminology with little idea of its meaning. Indeed, one of the chief difficulties in dealing with this nebulous creed lies in the fact that its chief exponents themselves appear uncertain as to the precise nature of its tenets. Their utterances are confused and contradictory, and seem to be varied in order to suit the views of the particular audience to which they happen to be addressed.

Investigation, however, shows that at the basis of Theosophy—which Mrs. Besant once defined as Hinduism in modern dress—lie three dogmas, each of which is in direct contradiction of the Christian faith. The theosophical concept of God amounts only to a misty form of pantheism. A mechanical and impersonal law of necessity, known as karma, is believed to govern the universe. And with this law of karma is combined belief in the transmigration of the human soul. Credulous persons are assured that they can reconcile such teaching with their Christianity!

Perhaps the one satisfactory feature of Theosophy and other such fantastic cults is the witness they bear against materialism. People who have broken adrift from Christianity find themselves driven to adopt some other form of at least quasi-religious belief. We may not be able to prevent foolish people from styling themselves theosophists. But it should not be difficult to make them realize that they cannot serve two masters, and that on the day when they accept Theosophy they renounce Christ.

★

Some weeks after his visit to England, Rudolf Steiner was travelling again to Helsingfors for lectures at the end of May and beginning of June, and on to Stockholm for further lectures and the foundation of the Anthroposophical Society in Sweden.

In reference to this trip, Harry Collison began another letter to Herbert Heywood-Smith:

Windham Club
St James's Square.
S.W.
19th May 1913

Dear Mr. Heywood-Smith,

I find I am wanted in Stockholm, so would prefer leaving here on the 31st or 3rd as I originally intended, unless you really need me.

Re the lectures & Mr. Franke, I saw him this evening. I do not understand his expression that you have purchased the rights. What I understood from you was that you would arrange for the translation of this & for the price at which it was to be sold, & whether printed or typed.

As regards the German version, that I will keep myself, as I had already arranged with the Doctor & Fräulein von Sivers.—I think I had better now state in writing what I had previously mentioned, that apart from the *Geheimwissenschaft* & the four brochures mentioned to you, the sole right of publishing any English translation of Dr. Steiner's works is vested in me.

Yours sincerely,
Harry Collison

★

Heywood-Smith replied:

47 Redcliffe Square,
S.W.
May 20th 1913

Dear Mr. Collison,

I am a little surprised at the content of your letter this morning. As the result of our conversation at the studio we agreed that after all I should have the whole matter of bringing out Dr. Steiner's two lectures in my hands. My first step was to engage Mr. Franke as stenographer and pay him for his services. It was not at all a question of purchasing rights but a matter of business in the ordinary way. The stenographer's report belongs to the one who engages his services & when paid for it ceases to be the stenographer's property. I was obliged to mention this to Mr. Franke as, on looking through the report, I found radical mistakes, & he contemplated sending a copy to Germany. It was said because it is necessary that a correct copy should be sent, in case it should be published out there; & the one to send it is the one responsible for its correctness over here.

Please do not think I wish to interfere with your publishing rights in any way, as I have not the smallest desire to do so. If you would still like to make arrangements to bring out those two lectures of Dr. Steiner's you are very welcome indeed to do so.

I paid Mr. Franke £4-4-0 for the reports, & now am busy revising the second of the lectures. The first is so bad—in three pages a 'nicht' & a 'niemals' had been omitted, giving exactly the opposite meaning, together with other inaccuracies—that I have sent it back to Franke to compare again with his original shorthand copy, but I hope to have it again by Wednesday.

Perhaps a chat will help to put matters right again. Can you come in for lunch one day—say tomorrow or Thursday? We shall be away this weekend.

Yours very sincerely,

H.J. Heywood-Smith

P.S. June 4th has been fixed as the date of the special meeting. We should be very glad if you could make it possible to be present.

H.J.H-S.

★

At the foot of his own copy of this letter Heywood-Smith subsequently added the note:

Finally, after much delay, with Dr. S.'s permission I published the two lectures myself. H.J.H-S.

★

Soon after the beginning of June, Edith Maryon, now in Munich, wrote to Rudolf Steiner:

Türkenstrasse 27 II,
München,
3. 6.13.

Dear Dr. Steiner,

I think you should see the enclosed cutting from the *Church Times* which my father has just sent me; the date is unfortunately cut off, but I expect it is last Friday's issue. The paper is practically read by all the clergy in Great Britain—certainly by all the English section, & through them reaches a very large section of the community; in addition it has many general readers.—It therefore seems to me to be of considerable importance, & to need a reply to the many erroneous opinions it expresses. Will you tell me if you think it should be answered?

It seems to me that any reply should be given by an English writer, as only an Eng. person would be quite in touch with and understand the English church, & to be of any use to the readers of the *Church Times* the answer requires to be written by as able a thinker as we can find.

The most suitable name which has occurred to me is that of Mrs. (Professor) Mackenzie. I think you met her at Dr. Felkin's; she has been a member of his Order for 7 or 8 years. She is Professor of Education at Cardiff University. (Her husband is Prof. of Philosophy there.) Both of them are members of the Anthros. Society. She is a personal friend of mine so that I could ask her if she would write a reply, but of course have no authority to speak on her behalf, nor do I know if you would approve. Perhaps someone else may have a better suggestion to make.

Mrs. Besant, you will see from the other cutting, is speaking in London.—I do not understand how she dares, now that the second case has gone against her.—We have had the telegram with the judge's finding, but not the newspaper report as yet. (The libel case I mean.) If an answer is to be written I suppose it should be as soon as possible. Perhaps you would tell me what you wish—& the line the reply should take? Or let me know thro' someone.

Believe me,

Yrs most sincerely,

L. Edith C. Maryon

Perhaps Prof. Mackenzie would be willing to collaborate with me—at least I could give her the facts, & she could incorporate them in an article. If she would undertake it, it would be well done; she is extremely clever.

⋆

Whatever Rudolf Steiner may have thought about the matter which Maryon brought to his notice, no reply or article by either Millicent Mackenzie or any other anthroposophist was printed on this subject in *The Church Times*.

It is Necessary to State

Herbert Heywood-Smith now sent a card to Harry Collison, who was still in Sweden:

18th June.

Dear Mr. Collison,

We are thinking of bringing out a little magazine for the use of anthroposophists in England. The principal idea in publishing it is that it be a means of keeping us in touch with the principal body in Germany and letting members know of Dr. S.'s movements and work. We should like to publish in it extracts from various of Dr. S.'s lectures, beginning with the one on 'Pfingsten', Whitsuntide, & also we think it would be useful to give the verses for meditation taken from the Calendar for the corresponding weeks. I have just heard through Mr. Meebold that we must first obtain your permission to do this. Would you therefore grant this & allow us to publish these in this way?

Yours sincerely,

H.J. Heywood-Smith.

P.S. I would also, with your permission, like to bring out the first course, 'Vor dem Tore', in instalments, giving one lecture in each issue.

H.J.H-S.

★

The correspondence continued:

47 Redcliffe Square,
London, S.W.
June 23rd 1913

Dear Mr. Collison,

Your wire of refusal has just arrived. As we are practically ready to go to press this is an unexpected set-back. No doubt you have good reasons for your action & I shall look forward to your letter of explanation within the next few days.

Yours sincerely,

H.J. Heywood-Smith

★

Poste Restante,
Marstrand,
Sweden
26th June 1913

Dear Mr. Heywood-Smith,

Your card dated 18th June, posted 20th, arrived on 23rd & I replied by telegram—for you seemed in a hurry—that I could not give my consent at present.

It is quite unnecessary for me to lay before you all my reasons. There was ample opportunity to have discussed the matter in London, but you did not think it advisable to take me into your confidence, & this card of yours is the first intimation from you that I have had.

Briefly put, were I to agree at this moment to your proposal, it would lead to difficulties. If later on I am able to arrange it, I will do so, but always on the distinct understanding that the proofs of the translations are first submitted to me for approval. I would also naturally insist on seeing your newspaper or the proof of it before giving my consent.

Yours sincerely,

Harry Collison

*

Heywood-Smith then decided to write about this whole matter to Marie von Sivers, who was not only the closest person to Rudolf Steiner but also the one to whom he had specially entrusted all arrangements concerning the publication of his works.

Anthroposophical Society
Wisdom is only in truth

47 Redcliffe Square,
London, S.W.
July 9th, 1913

Dear Miss von Sivers,

Many thanks for your letter which I was very glad to receive.

Immediately on hearing the Doctor's message through Mr. Meebold I wrote to Mr. Collison to obtain his sanction. Enclosed is the correspondence which has passed. We have come to a standstill with the magazine for the present, as we intended it to be a means not for the expression of personal opinions but of enabling the members to become acquainted with the Doctor's work which was not published in books in English: none of his courses or separate lectures are at present available to them. Now this project has been stopped, at any rate for the present. I am very sorry about it. When the Doctor left us I was under the impression that Mr. Collison was responsible only for the books that were to be issued to the public, and one of the courses, viz., the second, The Theosophy of the Rosicrucians. But now, since Stockholm, it seems Mr. Collison has been given jurisdiction over the whole of the Doctor's works in English, courses, books, &c. At any rate, Mr. Collison is evidently under that impression, or he would not have refused for the extracts from lectures & the first course. The whole difficulty may have arisen from some misunderstanding, however, and I am hoping that perhaps a little talk in Munich together with the Doctor will throw light on the situation, smooth out all difficulties & help to get matters straight.

If it is Mr. Collison's intention to publish the Calendar, the courses & odd lectures ('Pfingsten' &c.) himself shortly, & the courses in their consecutive order, so that English-speaking members may avail themselves of them, that will of course settle the whole matter quite satisfactorily. The thing is to make a good translation of the Doctor's various lectures available to members. It matters not who does it. In that case we should merely bring out an occasional news leaflet to keep members in touch with the Doctor's movements & with what is going on in the lodge.

H.J. Heywood-Smith

★

If any British anthroposophical magazine or even just news-leaflet came into existence at this time, no copy has yet come to light. Not until 1920, still seven years in the future, is any anthroposophical journal known to have been published in Britain.

Although the German original of the *Mitteilungen*, now a news-sheet for the Anthroposophical Society, continued until the outbreak of the First World War in 1914, the English translation came to an end in August 1913.

The last page carried this announcement:

With regard to the publications of Dr. Steiner's works, it is necessary to state that the rights of future translations are vested in Mr. H. Collison. He hopes to have *Christianity as Mystical Fact* in the hands of the public in September, and to follow up this volume with other translations at regular intervals.

With respect to works not for publication, it has happened that sometimes a whole course of lectures has been translated by someone unaware that it has already been done. To save unnecessary labour, Mr. Collison suggests that those wishing to translate should communicate with him, for as every lecture has to be translated, it is possible he may be able to supply the one desired. Further, Mr. Collison is always anxious to know of good translators who would be willing to help him.

7
INTERLUDE (1913–21)

Voice in the Wilderness

The difficulties which D.N. Dunlop was slowly coming to experience in the Theosophical Society were made evident in some 'Impressions of the Twenty-Third Annual Convention' which he published in *The Vahan*:

> According to the July *Vahan*, the programme of the twenty-third annual Convention of the English National Society began on July 3 with a meeting of the Temple of the Rosy Cross ('for members of that body only'). This was followed on the evening of July 4 with a meeting of the Order of the Star in the East ('for members of the order only'). On the agenda issued separately to F.T.S. at the Convention, the above meetings were put at the end of the programme and indicated as 'subsidiary activities' and 'unofficial'. As the Convention proper proceeded the effect of this confusion in the official mind became apparent...
>
> At 2.30 on Saturday the Business Meeting of the Convention assembled at the Small Queen's Hall, Mr. A.P. Sinnett, Vice-President of the Theosophical Society, in the chair. After the formal introductory business and the presentation of greetings from other National Societies, the usual reports of the General Secretary and Treasurer were taken as read and adopted. Mr. Wedgwood was heartily congratulated on his work as General Secretary, and Mrs. Sharpe was welcomed back to her old post. Her experience, tolerance and strength, if she will permit me to say so, inspire confidence, and everyone felt pleased, in view of Mr. Wedgwood's resignation, that she has hold of the reins once more. I was asked to present the resolution of the Executive Committee referring the reconstruction scheme arising out of the Incorporation Committee's report, to the new Executive Committee for careful consideration, and authorizing them to consult members as to details and if necessary call a special Convention of the National Society. In doing so I called attention to existing anomalies and to the need for a scheme of reconstruction on lines which would provide adequately for the increasing work of the Theosophical Society *as such*. The resolution was seconded and unanimously carried. Mr. Baillie-Weaver explained the principles which guided the lawyers in drafting the Articles of Association ... Mr. Whyte then introduced a resolution dealing with the report of the Sub-Committee on Ways and Means...
>
> Miss Rea introduced a 'discussion' on the advisability of founding a Theosophical School for children, but as there was no time to discuss a

subject on which there was likely to be a considerable variety of opinions the Chairman hurried us on, and we had to be content with a pious expression of opinion and hope that 'something' would be done.

Dr. Guest then appeared to present the resolutions of the Propaganda Conference, but there was hardly time to hear them read properly, and the Chairman wanted to put them to the meeting formally and dismiss them and close the Convention at the usual time.

I then rose and moved the adjournment of the Convention to meet again at 7 o'clock and continue the discussions on the resolutions of the Propaganda Conference and the work of the Society during the current year. This motion was supported by a large number of provincial delegates, but the London delegates defeated it by two votes, so that the official programme should have free course and be glorified. Mrs. Sharpe tactfully intervened and suggested that an opportunity should be provided somehow to discuss the resolutions affecting the important work of the Society. It was agreed that an unofficial meeting should be held at Headquarters on Sunday afternoon at 3.30 to discuss propaganda and the affairs of the Society...

The Chairman begged to be excused making the usual concluding remarks as proceedings had been unusually prolonged, and he had to lecture to members at 7 p.m. The Annual Convention then somewhat abruptly terminated and its official proceedings were at an end.

I have been like a 'voice in the wilderness' for the past few years urging the necessity for a complete change in the Convention arrangements, based on a recognition of the importance of the work of the Theosophical Society in the world. This year circumstances spoke more eloquently than I could ever hope to do, and Fellows of the Society from different parts of the country, most of them old and tried workers, declared that they hoped the lesson had been learned and that the arrangements for future Conventions would be made on a scale commensurate with the ideals and objects of the T.S.

Those who are interested in 'subsidiary' activities may arrange as best they may for whatever meetings they consider necessary, but such arrangements must not be allowed to overshadow the work of the T.S. Three days at least should be given to the T.S., and the time (say Whitsuntide) should be chosen to admit of this. Excepting the E.S., no F.T.S. should be excluded from any of the meetings arranged during the three days of Convention. The informal meeting held on Sunday afternoon made this clear. Although it was held under difficulties (it was postponed from 3.30 till 4.30 and held in a small room instead of the temporary building. The T.S. had to give way to a 'subsidiary' activity again, and the arrangements for tea seemed more important than the affairs of the T.S.), the room was packed. Dr. Guest took the chair and he performed the task with excellent spirit. Mrs. Sharpe was present as an inspiring presence to many, giving tactful advice and making useful suggestions at every point. Here was a T.S. meeting in the old spirit of freedom of utterance and friendly frankness. The future is to the cause whose adherents put into it the best work and the clearest ideas. Work is prophecy. If our future action is based on a few fundamental propositions which are always present as part of our being, like stars in the soul, we shall act wisely, and not try to be nice to everybody and succeed in helping nobody.

By changing the thought of humanity we best prepare 'the way of the Lord'. It is not to bask idly in His presence, or sit comfortably at His feet that we have committed ourselves. A number of people enthusiastic for the principles of *Theosophia* have not had their energies enlisted in the work of the Society, and are not likely to have while so few opportunities are presented to them for service. The way has been made smooth and easy for the 'joiners' of all the Orders and Leagues, and because of their novelty attention has been concentrated on them, and the work of the T.S. has suffered in consequence. In my opinion there should be no 'subsidiary activities'. The Leagues and Orders, being separately constituted, should be left in the hands of those interested; they will do justice to them all. Open the way for the T.S. workers who are interested in theosophical principles and are not particularly interested in the work of the other organizations. Loyalty to the 'subsidiary' activities should not be the only criterion of fitness for service in the T.S. Another reflection: the attendance of Fellows was probably not half what it was last year, due no doubt to the fact that the President had to return to Adyar, and the uninviting nature of the Agenda.

Surely it is a poor recognition of the cause to which the President devotes her life to fail to put in an appearance at the Annual Convention because she is unavoidably prevented from being present. The best way to sustain her hands is to work for the principles for which she makes so many sacrifices.

I end on a note of confidence. I have faith in Mrs. Sharpe's judgement. I believe she will enlist the services of all good workers on the broadest basis of service, by which the gifts of all have free play in the common cause. I believe our work is only in its infancy. If the 'lesson' has been learned, the service of all will be invited anew to the cause of Theosophy, and the work of the National Society will flourish like the cedars of Lebanon; in a few years, if this spirit is encouraged, the Annual Conventions of the T.S. will be of national importance and rival the work of the British Association.

It must only be added that James Wedgwood had resigned from the post of General Secretary because he had started to give priority to a quite different interest—the Old Catholic Church. A few weeks after this Convention, on 22 July, he was ordained to the priesthood in this Church.

Common Life

The 'Fifth International Summer School' was reported by M.M. Sharples in *Theosophy in Scotland*:

> When a number of people combine for the purpose of studying and trying to co-ordinate religion, philosophy, science and art, and thus through unity to find and express in social service the ideal human life, the characteristics of the gathering must of necessity be as varied as that life itself, and as the International Summer Schools follow each other during successive seasons it is interesting to notice the ever-differing form taken by the meetings according to the particular aspect of truth which is being emphasized at the time. Those who attended the first school five years ago still remember the force of the mental and spiritual impulse which they received, and each succeeding year has fed and fostered some side of that larger life.
>
> At the 5th International Summer School, held this year at Peebles during the last fortnight in July, the physical conditions (which in previous years have proved something of a 'test' to aspirants for knowledge!) were all that could be desired, for the Hydro is beautifully situated, well managed and comfortable, and in such fortunate surroundings members were able to concentrate without distraction on the mighty conundrums presented for consideration in the synthetic programme—the 'awesome questionnaire' as one paper called it! Religion, philosophy, science, art! What are they? Are they distinct and contradictory, or complementary and correlated? What is man, and what is his relationship to his present environment? How has that environment come about, and how best can he escape from it, or rather, how can he transmute the chaos of present conditions and return once more to the golden harmony of the dawn? These were, briefly, the vast problems suggested for study, and the cheerful courage with which the School settled down to consider them augured well for their ultimate solution. Each morning a lecture was given, which fell naturally under one of the four headings, while the afternoons were devoted to classes and the discussion of the various sections. The activities were carefully dovetailed into each other so that there was no overlapping, and it was thus possible occasionally to attend five different meetings during the day—which some enthusiasts did! The School owes a debt of gratitude to Mr. W.L. Hare for the accurate, patient way in which he conducted the discussions, sifting and sorting opinion and keeping debaters to the point, till one was at least convinced that if the various questions were not solved it was because no one present knew the right answers, and it would be well on leaving the school to do a little more study and try to find out. Besides helping so successfully to expose ignorance, Mr. Hare gave three lectures, and arranged readings from Dante's *Divine Comedy* and the *Bhagavad Gita*, which were much appre-

ciated. Dr. Anderson, Dr. Khedkhar and the Rev. A.B. Robb presented aspects of the religious question which gave rise to some illuminating discussion, and the School was honoured by a flying visit from His Highness the Prince of Kolapur, who offered some of his own beliefs as hypotheses worthy of consideration. Dr. and Mrs. Coomaraswamy, Miss Schlesinger, Miss Pagan and Mr. Wroblewski contributed to the art section; philosophy was presented by Mr. Dunlop, Mr. Hare and Miss Charlotte Woods; and Miss Dora Marsden gave her views on 'Woman'.

Of the four sections under discussion perhaps the one which suffered most was science, for the scientists who should have lectured were prevented from coming to expound their special branch of service, and it was voted after all somewhat 'dry bones' compared with the vivifying forces of philosophy, religion and art. Myths, under the able exposition of Mr. Lund, were considered much better worth study, as containing more of truth than the exactitudes insisted on as necessary by science. But after all, truth, whether in myth or in natural phenomena, is always shrouded. It must be sought for, and when revealed, whether by art, philosophy or science, stands serene and beautiful, for the wonders unfolded by dry (?) scientific research are as magical and miraculous as any fairy tale. The alchemist knew long ago the facts that the chemist is only just discovering, say some impatiently, and perhaps the mystic with his winged soul has seen visions that as yet science dreams not of. But if it be true that there are other centres of perception in the body still undeveloped, then as these unfold, the scientist will have more instruments with which to investigate.

In the meantime, he is constructing on a firm foundation a ladder by which the 'ordinary man' may climb towards truth, but who knows how soon the 'ordinary man', studying mathematics and observing natural phenomena through sceptical, accurate intellect, will use the carefully constructed ladder merely as a jumping-off place, and also trust his wings and soar beyond the stars?

At Peebles, however, the stars were for the moment ignored, and the School worried at the intellectual problems presented for discussion with a gusto that must have delighted those who were responsible for their presentation.

No record of the summer would be complete without a most appreciative mention of the beautiful music supplied at all the meetings by Miss Collier, Mr. Goosens and Miss May Muckle, and also of the recital of Indian music given by Ratan Devi, which alone would have made the School memorable.

In glancing back over the years as they have followed each other, one cannot but notice how very successfully the promoters, and those upon whom the brunt of the work has fallen, have managed to keep themselves in the background. People discuss the lectures and their fellow-members, the vibrations and the atmosphere (whatever those may be), they attend the classes of discussion, they appreciate the arrangements and the weather, and almost overlook, or at least take very much for granted, the work of the very able secretary and the unfailing carefulness of the unassuming chairman, who moves quietly in and out among the groups and classes, guiding and directing, and effacing his own personality so successfully that it is hardly realized till afterwards how much the School has owed to his tact and wisdom. One feels that the movement which Mr. Dunlop has started is growing in strength and vitality, for it was begun on the broadest basis and the widest lines, and is capable of unlimited expansion. Moreover, though necessarily watched over and fostered in the early stages, it is not *dependent* on any one person. Lecturers and audience alike must co-operate to ensure success, and that is undoubtedly the greatest testimony that any inaugurator and band of workers can desire.

The address by D.N. Dunlop at the end of the School was reproduced in *The Path*:

In this Summer School we have realized what it is to develop a kind of communal life. We have been able to get closely in touch with one another, to overcome some of the prejudices and inequalities and all the other peculiarities which each individual possesses, and to enter into a sort of common life in which we were *all equally interested*. This being so it should be possible, as has been suggested, to go back with joy to the work that lies before us. The end of one Summer School brings us nearer to the beginning of the next. (Laughter).

There are a great many things that have not been perfect, that might be considerably improved, and we cannot quite realize when in the midst of it what direction should be taken to effect improvements. But when we get away and look back on our experience it will appear a little more clearly what are the desirable changes. I see the possibilities to a greater extent than I have ever seen them before. But I believe a certain amount of sacrifice will be necessary to effect these possibilities. We need a 'building fund'. We shall have to create a place for ourselves. We shall have to have a revival of the mystical drama, to have other things besides music, which has been so excellently performed for us by our artist friends. We shall have to find a place of our own. I see that in some way or other there must be an opportunity for men and women to come together on a broad platform as we have had here without limitations, and I hope, even if I should have nothing to do with this movement in the future, that it will be maintained in that free and broad spirit in which at all events I can claim it has been started. We have refused no one. We have welcomed every contribution to the thought of the School. One temptation after another has been put in my way to limit in some way our platform and have our programme labelled 'official'. But I have refused, because I could see a little way into the future. Now we are ready to start a new session, and although we wish to have new elements come into the School we hope again to see the old elements and many of the old faces.

Further editorial matter about this Summer School at Peebles indicates that among those attending was Isabelle de Steiger, by now aged 77.

No further session of a Summer School was in fact to take place for another three years. But in August Isabelle de Steiger began to publish in *The Path* a series of articles on 'Superhumanity'. The series was continued for the next ten numbers, in every monthly issue until the journal itself ceased publication.

The Soul's Awakening

Rudolf Steiner spent most of the summer of 1913, from mid-July to mid-September, in Munich. His fourth Mystery Play, *Der Seelen Erwachen*, was due to receive its premiere performance, and rehearsals were in progress. The play was to be followed by an associated lecture-cycle on 'The Secrets of the Threshold'. Among those attending these events were several English members: Edith Maryon, Edith Cull, Ada Drury-Lavin, Harry Collison, Herbert and Mabel Heywood-Smith.

Another much younger Englishman, Arnold Freeman, also had his first meeting with Steiner at this time. In his booklet *Thou Eye Among the Blind* (1947) he recalled:

In 1913—aged 26—I was on holiday in Germany. I called upon Ernst Haeckel in Jena. He honoured me with his conversation for three-quarters of an hour. He autographed with the legend 'Anti-spiritist Monist' a picture-postcard of himself that I had bought in the town. I told him I was going to see Rudolf Steiner (whom he knew well) in Munich. He jocosely lifted his hand towards the ceiling and said: 'Tell him I am glad he has ascended into heaven!'

Dr. Steiner was in the midst of preparations for the production of one of his Mystery Plays. I waited in the vestibule of some hall and presently he came out to see me and we stood and talked for five or ten minutes. I carried away nothing in particular from the interview.

Round about that same time I read two of his books: *The Way of Initiation* and *Initiation and its Results*. They made next to no impression upon me. I only recollect a vague feeling that they seemed very woolly.

Another eight years were to pass before Freeman came into any further contact with anthroposophy.

★

At the premiere of *Der Seelen Erwachen* the new art of eurythmy was first publicly presented. In her biography of the first eurythmist, *Lory Maier-Smits* (1993), Magdalene Siegloch describes the course of events:

> When Lory arrived for the rehearsal in the Shwabinger Turnhalle Rudolf Steiner began to explain the second scene of the new play. 'There will appear some groups of elemental spirits, sylphs and gnomes.' He then informed the astonished people present that for about a year he had been quietly working out the beginnings of a new art of movement. This eurythmy would now 'be used for the first time' to present sylphs and gnomes. He also chose the persons to be involved in both groups.

These persons included Edith Maryon among the sylphs, and the naturally gnomish Harry Collison among the gnomes.

> Lory Smits herself was chosen for the gnomes. What the stage directions specify for the gnomes is as follows: 'They have steel-grey shapes, small compared to human beings, and are almost all head, but bent over forwards. They have long moveable limbs, inclined to gestures but unskilled in walking.' The way the gnomes were to move was so different from what Lory Smits had previously learnt and practised that Rudolf Steiner now demonstrated these special gestures himself. He 'took an umbrella in each hand and made rather harsh, characteristic movements with these elongated arms. Because of his head being stretched out forwards they had a very powerful effect: all vowels. From the very start he was also moving with bent knees in little triangles, emphasizing the angles by indications of his back, as if stumbling into every new direction. For the spectators it was astonishing, and even frightening. We had of course often experienced his matchless versatility, as in rehearsals when demonstrating Lucifer or Ahriman, standing beside the person then playing them. But this was still different. It was a grotesque being, utterly strange to our feelings, who was moving before us with a frightful insistence, knowingly mocking the stupidity of our human wisdom.'
>
> The painter Imme von Eckardstein eagerly made sketches of Rudolf Steiner's facial expressions. Later on she used these sketches as a stimulus when painting the faces single-handed onto wide oval stoles which these beings, 'almost all head', carry on their shoulders, while their heads are covered in gauze. After the dress rehearsal a beaming Rudolf Steiner came up to Lory Smits: 'You have really discovered all the characteristic movements of these gnomes—except one that these beings very often make, though it would have been too impertinent!' With a smile he then made a long nose.

The premiere of *Der Seelen Erwachen* on 22 August was followed on the 28th—Goethe's birthday—by the very first eurythmy performance, mainly consisting of threefold walking, 'Evoe', rod exercises, energy dance, peace dance, 'Halleluja', and some poems by Goethe.

> The initial appearance of eurythmy in the Munich festival weeks was wonderfully stage-managed, as appropriate for such an important stage art. Twelve hundred members of the Anthroposophical Society saw it first on the high level of its very own domain: in the presentation of supersensible entities—gnomes, Luciferic and Ahrimanic beings—in the novel drama of the Mystery Plays. Spectators at the eurythmy performance could learn the basic elements and the manifold ways they might be applied: hymns, lyricism and drama. Those allowed to take part in the eurythmy performance had already done an intensive course, and interested people could attend 'workshops', as orientation lessons in the art rooms were now to be called.
>
> When Rudolf Steiner's lecture-course had finished, the participants went home and spread around news about eurythmy, this new art of movement, in wide circles of the Anthroposophical Society.
>
> From Munich Lory Smits travelled directly to Stuttgart. There she gave introductory courses in eurythmy for children and adults during the whole of September.
>
> This was the start of a flourishing teaching activity which she pursued in the following years with enthusiasm and great diligence, whenever and wherever she was asked.
>
> She gave courses once a week in Cologne, and once a week in Düsseldorf. The zeal for work in Haus Meer' (the home of the Smits family in Düsseldorf) was strengthened even more when Lory was asked to prepare a 'proper', seriously festal eurythmy performance—without any demonstration of basic principles—to take place in Cologne in conjunction with lectures by Rudolf Steiner before Christmas.

Our Common Vocabulary

AE's *Collected Poems* came out in September 1913, in a print-run of 1000 copies. It was dedicated at the front:

TO
D.N.D.
IN MEMORY OF THE HOUSEHOLD

On the next page was a foreword, printed in italic type:

Collected here from Homeward, Songs by the Way, The Earth Breath, *and* The Divine Vision, *with such new verses as I thought of equal mood, this book holds what poetry of mine I would wish my friends to read. I have omitted what in colder hours seemed to me to have failed to preserve some heat of the imagination; but in that colder mood I have made but slight revision of those retained. However imperfect they seemed, I did not feel that I could in after hours melt and remould and make perfect the form if I was unable to do so in the intensity of conception, when I was in those heavens we breathe for a moment and then find they are not for our clay. When I first discovered for myself how near was the King in His beauty, I thought I would be the singer of the happiest songs. Forgive me, Spirit of my spirit, for this, that I have found it easier to read the mystery told in tears, and understood Thee better in sorrow than in joy; that, though I would not, I have made the way seem thorny, and have wandered in too many byways, imagining myself into moods which held Thee not. I should have parted the true from the false, but I have not yet passed away from myself who am in the words of this book. Time is a swift winnower, and that he will do quickly for me.*

AE

★

The first poem in the collection was also printed in italics:

Oh, be not led away,
Lured by the colour of the sun-rich day.
The gay romance of song
Unto the spirit-life doth not belong:
Though far-between the hours
In which the Master of Angelic powers
Lightens the dusk within
The holy of holies, be it thine to win
Rare vistas of white light,
Half-parted lips through which the Infinite
Murmurs its ancient story,
Hearkening to whom the wandering planets hoary
Waken primeval fires,
With deeper rapture in celestial choirs
Breathe, and with fleeter motion
Wheel in their orbits through the surgeless ocean.
So hearken thou like these,
Intent on it, mounting by slow degrees,
Until thy song's elation
Echoes the multitudinous meditation.

★

The author sent a copy to an old friend, who soon replied:

Coole Park,
Gort,
Co. Galway.
Oct 21

My dear Russell,

I was very glad for your book, which has brought back to me many memories. I conclude 'the household' of the dedication is the old Ely place one. You & I are alike in one thing that we must always have a 'household', a class, a circle, fellow workers, a party, though neither of us will have anything to do with the sort of party that founds itself on 'principles', & I hope we both will always measure our party's might not by its size but by its smallness. You have Plunket House now instead of the old Theosophical society & I have weeded out mine to three or four essential persons. I have little to say of the poems that I have not said years ago, & the old favourites remain undisturbed. I think our common vocabulary has suffered much from the collapse of the romantic movement but we may hope to be floated again next tide...

Yours sny

W. B. Yeats

The Path to the Heavenly City

At the very time when AE was bringing out his *Collected Poems*, a rather sensational event was happening on the Anglo-Irish political scene. There has been a whole collection of documents published about it: *1913: Jim Larkin and the Dublin Lockout* (1964).

This event stirred AE's political conscience to such an extent as to bring him once again during this year across the Irish Sea on a visit to Britain. In his biography *That Myriad-Minded Man* (1975), Henry Summerfield described the circumstances:

'... It was widely recognized that conditions in the Dublin slums were the worst in Western Europe: more than 100,000 people were packed in filthy, decaying tenement buildings with five, six, or even more often living in a single room.

The leaders of the workers and the employers in the great strike and lockout were James Larkin, a big, dark, passionate man, and William Martin Murphy, a handsome imperturbable capitalist. Both men were born fighters. It was probably some years before that AE had suddenly become psychically aware of the presence of a powerful personality while he was sitting on the top of a Dublin tramcar. Looking up, he saw a large man at the opposite end of the vehicle, and on being introduced to him a few days later he learnt that it was Larkin who had thus affected him. Surprisingly, the leader of the workers, though raised in poverty, appreciated art and beauty... Larkin, leader of the Irish Transport and General Workers' Union, was ably assisted by James Connolly, a fellow Catholic, socialist and Nationalist...

The strike began on the morning of 26 August 1913, when, at Larkin's bidding, the drivers and conductors of Murphy's trams abandoned their vehicles and walked home. Strikers' meetings and large-scale police violence followed, and Larkin and Connolly were briefly imprisoned. On 3 September, four hundred employers solemnly pledged themselves at Murphy's instigation not to employ workers who refused to forswear permanently any connection with Larkin's Union. In a leading article, AE blamed the capitalists for the police brutality, which had been directed at onlookers as well as strikers, and asserted that neither capital nor labour had a positive programme. He cited the fine examples of productive and distributive co-operation in Belfast and referred to the achievements of the Italian glassworkers, who had endured extraordinary hardships to escape from their masters and erect their own co-operative factories.

The four hundred employers retaliated by staging a giant lockout and triumphantly proclaimed that they themselves would continue to eat three good meals a day. AE was among writers who gathered at Liberty Hall to try to help the hungry men and women who queued there for food tickets, and he joined the Industrial Peace Committee, which after some weeks became the Civic League...

On 7 October, the *Irish Times* carried an open letter from AE denouncing the masters of industry as bad citizens, bad employers and bad businessmen. Having decided, not necessarily without just cause, on a lockout, they should have made tireless efforts to reach agreement, knowing that the fate of twenty thousand families hung in the balance. Instead of this, they 'determined deliberately, in cold anger, to starve out one-third of the population of this city, to break the manhood of the men by the sight of the suffering of their wives and hunger of their children.' Holding up to them an image of their own cruelty and arrogance, AE charged:

'If you had between you collectively a portion of human soul as large as a threepenny bit, you would have sat night and day with the representatives of labour, trying this or that solution of the trouble, mindful of the women and children, who at least were innocent of wrong against you.'

On 28 October, Larkin, convicted of sedition, was sentenced to seven months' imprisonment. Two days later AE decided to join the speakers at a protest meeting scheduled for 1 November in the Albert Hall in London. Meanwhile, he pointed out in an article in the *Irish Worker* that sedition was now no crime in Ireland—Unionists and Nationalists were openly preparing for civil strife. In his best vein of irony, he explained why Larkin deserved his sentence:

'He was preventing a sociological experiment of great importance to Ireland from being carried out. We have never accurately determined how little human beings can live on, how little air space is necessary for families . . . It is quite possible that after exhaustive experiments had been carried out . . . we might have found that human beings could be packed comfortably in rooms like bees in a hive, and generate heat to warm themselves by their very number, without necessity for coal . . . Nothing is more annoying to scientific investigators than the unscientific, humanitarian-like James Larkin, who comes along and upsets all calculations and destroys the labour of generations in the evolution of the underman, which was going along so well.'

At the Albert Hall, where James Connolly, Bernard Shaw and Larkin's sister Delia were among his companions on the platform, AE enlarged nobly on these themes . . . Describing the crisis in Dublin, he bitterly categorized his fellow-citizens:

'People are to us either human or sub-human. They are either on the side of those who are fighting for human conditions in labour, or with those who are trying to degrade it and thrust it into the abyss.

'Ah! But I forgot; there has sprung up a third party, who are superhuman beings. They have so little concern for the body at all that they assert it is better for children to be starved than moved from the Christian atmosphere of the Dublin slums . . .'

Summerfield at this point in his biography broke off AE's speech. But this loses the best part. For the quoted passage continued:

> . . . Dublin is the most Christian city in these islands. Its tottering tenements are holy. The spiritual atmosphere which pervades them is ample compensation for the diseases which are there and the food which is not there . . .

The account went on with the speech:

> '. . . A man has arisen who has lifted the curtain which veiled from us the real manhood in the city of Dublin. Nearly all the manhood is found among obscure myriads who are paid from five to twenty-five shillings per week . . . When the masters issued that humiliating document, asking men—on penalty of dismissal—to swear never to join a trades union, thousands of men . . . refused to obey. They would not sign away their freedom, their right to choose their own heroes and their own ideas. Most of these men had no strike funds to fall back on. They had wives and children depending on them. Quietly and grimly they took through hunger the path to the Heavenly City.'

AE knew well knew that he was jeopardizing his future in the Co-operative Movement—three days later he wrote to Weekes that he might soon be looking for new employment—but he declared in the Albert Hall:

'I am a literary man and not a manual worker. I am but a voice, while they are the deed and the being, but I would be ashamed ever in my life again to speak of an ideal if I did not stand by these men and say of them what I hold to be true.'

AE's letter to Charles Weekes was written on 4 November:

Dear Charlie,

I went on Saturday afternoon to your place of business but you work under good conditions of labour, I was told, and the Saturday half-holiday was your lot. I only made up my mind to go on Thursday and had no time to write. I would find it impossible to live in Ireland if there was no personal or intellectual freedom, and my conscience compelled me to strike a blow for what I conceived to be right. It is possible I may be looking for some other job in a little. But if the Church drives me out of the Co-operative Movement, it will liberate my pen to write on many things in Ireland I have refrained hitherto from touching on. I am sorry not to have seen you or Dan, but my visit was only for a day and I went back at once to find thunder and lightning waiting for me.

With kind regards,

Yours ever,

AE

★

It need only be added that after six months of widespread misery, the Dublin strike collapsed. The employers had won.

Nonetheless the strike also gave rise to the formation of the Irish Citizen Army, which lived on further, training its members in attitudes which three years later were to break out in violence at the Easter Rising of 1916.

Practical Work

During the year 1927 A.E. Waite wrote a preface to the *Memorabilia* of Isabelle de Steiger, published in that year soon after her death.

It began:

The passing of Isabelle de Steiger belongs to the first day of 1927, and she had reached the enviable age of ninety, retaining her faculties, so far as I am aware, even to the end. This itself is a great record for a moderately active worker, though it is mentioned more especially because these memoirs were begun, as will be seen, some fifteen years ago, but were laid aside and taken up from time to time, with long intervals between.

It will be obvious to all readers that the paramount influence on Madame de Steiger's life of thought was exercised by Mrs. Atwood. The phenomena of Spiritualism produced certain convictions, at least in respect of the facts, and the claims of Theosophy played no unimportant part during the lifetime of Madame Blavatsky. There came also a day when the Anthroposophy of Rudolf Steiner loomed large, a light of the first magnitude. But the acquaintance made with Mrs. Atwood under circumstances which are set forth at full length was like an abiding presence from its beginning even to the end, and long after the lady in question herself had passed away. It happens, however, rather curiously that an unversed reader will bring away only a vague impression as to the kind of influence, and that out of which it arose. To elucidate this point, it should be explained that the work entitled *A Suggestive Enquiry concerning the Hermetic Mystery* was published anonymously in London so far back as 1850, being described in the subtitle as 'An Attempt to Recover the Ancient Experiment of Nature'. When a few copies had been issued, it was not only withdrawn altogether but the edition was destroyed by the author, with the approval of Mr. South, her father, who was also a zealous student of Hermetic and alchemical literature. The reason was that in their opinion it revealed too much and might be open somehow to abuse, the 'ancient experiment' being no work in physics, but on the contrary seeking 'the conscious and hypostatic union of the intellectual soul with deity, and its participation in the life of God'. The alchemists, in other words, were not the chemists of their period, did nothing to lay the foundations of chemical science, and though it is suggested or implied that they could and did transmute metals, it was by the power of the liberated and divinely enlightened soul operating on matter . . .

One chapter in Isabelle de Steiger's *Memorabilia* includes the following passage:

The great souls, to my mind, have all gone to that bourne whence no traveller returns. My old friends Mrs. Atwood, Mrs. Kingsford, the kind and loving but saddened Countess Wachtmeister and others have all expressed the desire never to be sought for on any earthly matters. They felt that their lives were such that they had passed the 'Pass-Not' gate easily, and were henceforth in realms where sight and knowledge enable them to stand on that new rung of life, for which they had qualified by passing the test of the schoolmaster on lower planes. The lesser shortcomings have been rectified, and the troubles and difficulties alleviated by their trust in Christ.

The time has come when there is great spiritual movement, and the world which Anna Kingsford and others declared would come to an end has done so. The ways and doings of the world of 1825 have already come to an end, and we are able to look round in 1925 and see things to which in 1825 we were quite unaccustomed! Is not this a sure proof that more light will bring to our spiritual and indeed material sight more and more to see and know? As the Film of Life grows larger, do we not see that there has been no such thing as chance? That though we did not then see the cause, it existed all the time, although we did not know it? Is it not possible that some remain blind and in no wise educated by their own experience? Such souls, I fear, depart from their life on this planet little the better for the experiences which should have opened their eyes to the position in which they had been living when they came into birth.

After I left the Theosophical Society, the study of alchemy was revived, and Mrs. Atwood's book *A Suggestive Enquiry into the Hermetic Mystery* gave a very practical impetus to that study by a circle already formed in London . . .

This circle, named the Alchemical Society, was founded in 1912. In the following year it started to bring out *The Journal of the Alchemical Society*. The issue for November 1913 reported:

The seventh General Meeting of the Alchemical Society was held at 8.15 p.m. on Friday, November 14th, at The International Club, Regent Street, S.W. The chair was occupied by the Acting President, Mr. H. Stanley Redgrove, B.Sc., F.C.S.

A paper was read by Mme. Isabelle de Steiger on 'The Hermetic Mystery', which was followed by a discussion. (The paper and an abstract of the discussion are printed in the present number of the *Journal*.)

A vote of thanks was passed to Mme. I. de Steiger for her paper.

The Honorary Secretary announced the names of new members.

The Hermetic Mystery
by Isabelle de Steiger

In this paper I shall endeavour to give you, as far as I can, some idea of what is meant, or what I mean, by the title—'The Hermetic Mystery'. This word 'mystery' does not imply quite the same as 'doctrine', but practically, as you will see, the one is included within the other.

The Hermetic Mystery refers to the art of alchemy, 'The Royal Art', as this science is described.

The Hermetic Doctrine implies those connate philosophical and religious concepts, required to be held and put into practice by alchemists.

Broadly speaking, I may say I consider it that primitive heavenly doctrine underlying all formulated religions; but as alchemy comes more directly through Christian sources, I use the word 'Christian' as more especially explanatory of the religious views of Western alchemists.

In these days of the great expansion of knowledge concerning comparative religions, it will not be necessary to enquire as to the relation between the religion of the Western alchemists and of their Eastern brother-artists.

Please note the use of the word 'artist'. And I would like here explicitly to remark that I find Professor Bergson's idea of intuitive intelligence exactly covers much of the destined end. The ultimatum and demonstration of alchemy on the physical plane was in the mineral kingdom. By this I mean that the transmutation that reached the physical plane referred to metals only. The alchemists claimed that inferior metals could be raised to the superior or noble state, but never did they claim that the stuff of the cosmic ether could be transmuted into the next higher kingdom, that of the vegetable. Not a daisy can be made or created. The alchemists maintained that it was necessary to find the seed of each kingdom, and they declared that they had discovered that seed of metals, which would produce gold. This seed was 'the powder of projection', but here I cannot give details.

There is one point yet to mention, that the 'occult chemistry' of Mr. Leadbeater and Mrs Besant has I think no resemblance at all to the arch-chemistry of the alchemists.

I have given what I consider three strong clues, and a very important key to the labyrinth of alchemy, and lest you think my key is a poor and disappointing one, let me beg of you with that key to try to unlock therewith the old myths, classical and medieval, and to find out the meanings of the Kabala and of those great poems the *Iliad*, the *Odyssey*, the wonderful verse of Virgil, of Dante, and the cryptic stories relating to the Arthurian cycle, the Holy Graal, and much else of a like nature, as well as the hidden meaning of the Old and New Testaments. They all tend to one discovery and declare the same, and even in their inconsistencies will be instructive to him who has the key. And he who sets himself in this wise to the comprehension of the whole philosophy will be a competent judge of our labours, of how much assistance we have given to the recovery of lost wisdom, and with what sincerity we have opened the way permeating into those ancient abodes of light.

Abstract of discussion

Mr. D.N. Dunlop (Editor of *The Path*) said that he had listened with great pleasure to what he considered to be the best paper of its kind he had heard during the last twenty-five years. He considered that it had made plain an opportunity for the Society to undertake a great work for humanity, namely the practical work of alchemy, mystically understood. That was what was needed and should be attempted.

Mr. A.E. Waite said that he had listened to the suggestions of the last speaker with an interest only second to that with which he had listened to Mme. de Steiger's paper. The life requisite to the great alchemical experiment was the life of saintship, and could not be attempted by a Society other than a secret one. The ancient alchemists, he thought, were concerned with the same work as the mystics within the Church living the life of contemplation; but they had carried the experiment a stage further, and embodied the results of their experiences in symbolic texts. It was, he considered, the chief aim of the Society firstly to decode those texts, and thus gain the secret knowledge, which could then be practically applied.

The Chairman said that there was no necessity for him to point out that the meeting had listened to a very interesting and suggestive paper. It might in certain respects seem a departure from previous papers, which had been mainly historical or interpretative on the scientific side, but the founders of the Society had always intended that every side of the subject should receive attention, the mystical no less than the other. He agreed with Mr. Waite that the chief work of the Society must consist in decoding the alchemical texts. It was the business of the Society to get at the root of the matter, and produce a complete explanation of the origin and significance of alchemy. Mr. Dunlop's suggestions were also of much interest, but such practical work was the business of individuals, rather than of a Society as a whole; though were it possible to reveal it, the Society would be profited by an account of any such experiment. He was inclined to think, however, that there was something intrinsically secret in alchemy, mystically understood, something which was secret, not because it must not, but because it could not, be told to any but an initiate. Mme. de Steiger had spoken of this secret under many symbols—not all of which he understood—but to him the most beautiful and significant was that of the wonderful fairy-story of 'Sleeping Beauty and the Prince'.

Mme. de Steiger thanked the speakers for their gratifying expressions of approval of her paper. She hoped the suggestions she had made therein would be followed up by other members.

In her *Memorabilia*, Isabelle de Steiger recorded:

I was much pleased to find that my thesis, the Hermetic Mystery, was extremely well received. An interesting discussion followed, and many and valuable remarks in agreement with my theme were made by Mr. D.N. Dunlop, Mr. A.E. Waite and others, the dissenting voice being that of the Rev. J.J. Pool, D.D., who said that though his reason went with it as a whole, there was one of my expressions which he was inclined to query—'the Fall of man'. He did not think that nowadays one could believe in the 'doctrine of the Fall'. This point was taken up by Mr. D.N. Dunlop, who had the true understanding of that doctrine as esoteric religion knows it, so I will not now enter into the matter further.

I have now and then expressed sentiments on subjects which would seem entirely disconnected with the usual tenor of my life. The subject of alchemy and my connection with the Alchemical Society is a case in point.

> This may appear somewhat strange; but as I am writing my autobiography I cannot omit my fellowship with the Alchemical Society. I had already written my first two books, *The Cloud on the Sanctuary* and *On a Gold Basis*. My third work, *Superhumanity*, first appeared in parts in a very able periodical, *The Path*, edited by Mr. D.N. Dunlop, for whose abilities I feel much respect. It was full of good and rare matter, such as could not be found elsewhere.

An Air of Mystery

In editorial matter included in the volume *Zur Geschichte und aus den Inhalten der erkenntniskultischen Abteilung der Esoterischen Schule* (GA 265), Hella Wiesberger explains that exactly what happened during the cultic rituals of the Mystica Aeterna cannot be fully reconstructed even from the surviving ritual texts. But in view of the confusion caused in Britain by the Felkins' attendance in 1912 at one of these rituals, it may be appropriate to reproduce at this point an admittedly dubious but nonetheless undeniably vivid account which purports to describe such a ritual—the 'Initiation to the Grade of Rosicrucian Apprentice'.

The account is taken from an article by Robert Kuentz entitled 'Le Dr. Rudolph Steiner et la Théosophie actuelle', published in *Le Feu* in December 1913, and later republished in English translation by 'Inquire Within' in *Light-Bearers of Darkness*.

It must be emphasized that these sources were hostile, and for that reason alone the account—in contrast to the recorded ritual texts of the Mystica Aeterna previously included in this book—cannot be regarded as authentic or reliable, though it may be admitted that various single elements contained in it are indeed substantiated by the genuine ritual text for reception into the first grade. One more striking element, the skull, is however not substantiated. The present writer reproduces the whole account so-to-speak 'without prejudice'.

> . . . On the evening they begin by gathering together all new adherents, and after a little sermon from Steiner, vague and fraternal, you are told to sign a paper by which you acknowledge that Steiner is Grand Master of the Order of the Rose Cross. It is added that you must subscribe to the expenses of the Order, must consider your inferiors as your equals, and it ends with the formula of the oath . . . You are told beforehand to dress preferably in white. You enter, you recognize the theosophists. There is an air of mystery; all speak low . . . You are blindfolded, and all metal taken away from you—chains, rings, etc. An officer behind you places his hands on your shoulders, then the procession begins.

The first dialogue takes place before the Temple door. The Temple door opens, and you pass in, and circumambulate the room three times, sitting down three times, during which the Master of Ceremonies declaims in a religious voice, mysterious and sphinx-like, the well-known formulae of the rite used by the Grand Orient ... Then at last you sit down still blindfolded, and feel something happening at your waist and neck. Suddenly the bandage is raised by the guide, and you see in front of you a skull which Steiner holds under your nose. Steiner has a server, one on each side—a deacon and subdeacon—bearers of wax candles: the whole in dense obscurity. The bandage falls again. After a time it is taken away altogether: you begin to see light. This light comes from wax-candles placed on three altars. Black draperies hang everywhere, symbolizing the darkness which is always near ... Steiner, the High Priest, is completely clothed in red, with a red cap. He is before an altar, in the form of a cube, on which are a crucifix, a cup and a candle. The two servers, wearing Masonic aprons, are before another cube holding candles. The Master of Ceremonies is near to Steiner. (A woman of high Bavarian nobility, well known to the theosophists, at times took this office; she had a kind of alb and chasuble.) You glance at yourself and see the Masonic apron in front with triangle and trowel. You place your hand on the Gospel of St. John. Then you are told the password, and the sacred name which you can only stammer; it is JACHIN. Then with two extended swords curious signs are made in front of you. Then a sermon from Steiner on the legend of Hiram and Solomon ... Then the repast ... Second address from Steiner; he has taken off the red robe and now wears an alb of lace. He speaks on the triangle and the eye of God which is in the centre of the triangle and of man's being. Close of ceremony, which has lasted hours: ritualistic knocks with mallets on the three cubes. Candles extinguished and light switched on, the black draperies of burial are removed. You are surrounded with red. It is the light at last! ... Ite, missa est! ... You are initiated!

Nothing Could Be More Splendid

In her biography of Lory Maier-Smits, Magdalene Siegloch continued:

On the 17th of December 1913 Rudolf Steiner held the first of two lectures where he allowed tremendous pictures to arise of the life of Jesus of Nazareth. These were still echoing on inside spectators and performers the following afternoon, when in the middle of a eurythmy performance came the Christmas story according to Luke, with the 'Halleluja'.

The next performance—in expanded form—was taking place in January

1914 in Berlin. Lory Smits invited Annemarie Donath to work alongside her, and this work went on with much delight and exhilaration over the Christmas period.

The Anthroposophical Society's Annual General Meeting took place in Berlin from the 18th to the 23rd of January. Rudolf Steiner held four lectures on the theme 'Human and Cosmic Thought'. In these he showed a way for thinking, which is becoming in our time increasingly rigid, to rediscover a living mobility. By knowing and thinking from the twelve world-conceptions natural to the surroundings of the cosmos, thought can itself reproduce both their variety and their rightfulness, out of their origin.

During the afternoon before the first lecture, Erna Wolfram gave a solo eurythmy offering which stimulated the audience's mobility in the linguistic field. There were texts from four ancient languages, probably worked out with help from her mother Elise Wolfram, well-informed in this domain: the first psalm in Hebrew, texts from the *Odyssey* in Ancient Greek, various sayings in Sanskrit, and prayers in Latin and Old High German.

The performance by Lory Smits's group took place in the afternoon before the second evening lecture. Rudolf Steiner first gave an introductory address. Not once using the word 'eurythmy', he showed members how significant the new art of movement was in revealing a great perspective for the future of all human culture. In moving words he entrusted it to their own readiness to receive it.

He began: 'My dear friends! You will perhaps find a certain relation between what I said yesterday evening about intimate concerns of human thinking and what we are now presenting. Yesterday evening I put forward the fundamental demand that we should recover in our time both our thinking and our conception of the world. Can we bring human thinking and human thoughts out of their present rigidity and frozen condition into movement?' He then cited Fritz Mauthner, who in his book *Kritik der Sprache* expresses the whole despair in the spiritual condition of our time by envisaging how both thought and speech are dying. 'I was thinking about these things when I first discovered—now just over a year ago—a suitable person in Fräulein Smits. From the fount of our world's creative thinking and the sources in which the Logos or Word comes to activity in the world, I was then able to seek a special element in the human ether-body. This element calls up a gesture expressing the fact that life, not death, is impressed into the human body. You will see that the most sublime level to which human words can be raised is able to go over into movement.

By the laws of our world these forms of expression are connected with natural movements of the human ethereal body, and become movements of dance. Nothing could be more splendid than for as many anthroposophical friends as possible to try bringing these forms into flow, as a healing element in human culture.

'May anthroposophists perceive at the right moment that they have something here which they can really take out into life, and which will work in a healing manner!

The ensuing eurythmy programme began with some German pieces and continued with a few poems in Russian and French. Afterwards came the 'Ecossaises' by Beethoven and the Christmas story according to Luke.

Among those in the audience must have been Edith Maryon, who had arrived in Berlin the previous November, and was indeed staying in Motzstrasse 17.

On the afternoon of 23 January, two days after the eurythmy performance, Steiner gave an address about the architecture of the proposed anthroposophical colony at Dornach in Switzerland.

Co-workers are Very Welcome

On 28 January Rudolf Steiner himself arrived at Dornach. Edith Maryon arrived at Dornach too on the very same day.

Work on the planned Dornach building was now under way, with many helpers. Maryon remained involved into February, probably even into March, but also fell ill. Her presence is next recorded in Munich, which must have been for Steiner's lectures there from March 29 to 31.

After attending these Munich lectures she made her way back to England, but during the journey once again fell ill, quite seriously. When she finally arrived in London, she was completely out of action.

She could however still write letters, and by this time was able to do so in German. Her next letter to Steiner is here translated:

58, Grove Park Terrace
Chiswick London,
4. 4.14

Dearly beloved Teacher,

I feel I must say a word, because a very long time might perhaps go by before I can come to Dornach again. There is nothing I can do, nor do I have the German either, to clothe in words the great, great thankfulness I must feel for my teacher; but it is a feeling which is always there and I want for once to state it.

On the last evening you asked me whether I did not have much on my heart and my answer 'no' was not true, I only meant it was not the moment to ask the question.

Dr. Felkin is not in London, but I have written to him what you said; it is only, as I have sometimes said already, that you have so little time for letters, but perhaps, if one is not living in Germany, one does not understand it so well.

I hope my karma will allow me to work a little bit more for the building than up till now.

Please accept best greetings from

Your pupil

L. Edith C. Maryon

★

On the very next day Maryon also wrote a card to Marie von Sivers, sending it to Vienna. This however she wrote in English, though sprinkling in a few German words and names—without bothering about accents.

58, Grove Park Terrace,
Chiswick,
London.
5.4.14.

Dear Fraulein von Sivers,

Somehow I did not manage to say goodbye to you on my last evening at Munchen; it is however so unpleasant to say goodbye to people that in preference I will say 'Auf Widersehen' & hope it may be at an early date in Dornach; just when, however, that may be, at present I have no idea. I felt very jealous of Mr. Collison today; he is just starting off to Wien. His new home for the group is far nicer than the last, & ever so much more room too. B. Walleen is lecturing there 3 times in the week.

With kind regards,

Yrs sincerely,

L. Edith C. Maryon

★

Harry Collison was therefore on his way to Vienna to attend the course from 9 to 14 April on 'The Inner Being of Man and Life between Death and New Birth'—the last great lecture-cycle given by Rudolf Steiner before the outbreak of the First World War.

The new home found by Collison for the Myrdin Group was at 25 Hereford Square in Kensington, just round the corner from his studio at Clareville Grove. But although most of the original houses in this elegant square are still standing today, No 25 was among a small group destroyed by German bombing in 1940.[32]

★

On the day the course started in Vienna, Sophie Stinde—who had attended the Theosophical Congress in London in 1905—wrote to Herbert Heywood-Smith.

55, Adalbertstrasse,
Munich.
9 April 1914.

Dear Mr. Heywood-Smith,

Only now am I herewith sending you all receipts. Miss Bowles & Mrs. Abbott will get their membership cards from Dornach as soon as these are signed and issued. You will know from the *Mitteilungen* that the inauguration will in all probability only be towards Christmas. Even if the building is ready before, there will probably be so much preparation needed that we shall not be completely ready till Christmas. Our artists are now hard at work carving the pillars & architraves. Do you have anybody working in your group able to carve wood (even if only very little) who would like to work with us in Dornach? The work is of course unpaid, as it should be a voluntary contribution. But life in Dornach is not that expensive, as we have erected a restaurant for our artists where they can eat at midday for 70 cents, & even cheaper in the evening. Rooms cost about 25 or 30 francs. So co-workers are very welcome.

With heartfelt greetings,

Sophie Stinde.

★

In her biography of Lory Maier-Smits, Magdalene Siegloch continued:

The eurythmy performance arranged by Rudolf Steiner for the Anthroposophical Society's Annual General Meeting at Berlin in 1914—and his call to active members to include eurythmy in their activities—widened the ground on which this young art was to develop and expand.

Lory Smits herself gave various courses in Berlin and then in Cassel before returning again to Haus Meer. With Rudolf Steiner's advice and glad agreement, Harry Collison, representing the Anthroposophical Society in England, had already asked her during the General Meeting to give both eurythmy lessons and performances in London.

In mid-April he came to Haus Meer to make the necessary arrangements.

Collison must then have called in at Düsseldorf on his return journey from Vienna.

It was not always easy to translate into English Rudolf Steiner's special indications from the Bottmingen course. When Lory translated, Harry Collison found the English no good; and when he translated, she found no correspondence to what was eurythmically intended.

It was easier to find poems and verses as examples for instruction and for performance.

★

At the end of May Steiner was travelling westwards to lecture in Paris. An idea must have been mooted of his coming even further west and crossing over to England. Surviving correspondence about the matter includes an undated card:

Dear Heywood-Smith,

I know there are several who have reasons for being desirous of seeing the Dr. if he comes over & hope he will be able to accede to requests for an interview.

H. Collison.

★

Further details were given by Heywood-Smith in a letter which is also undated. (E.S. = Esoteric School. M.E. = Mystica Aeterna, the adjective being sometimes spelled Eterna.)

47 Redcliffe Square,
London, S.W.

Dear Miss von Sivers,

Many thanks for your letter and also for the Doctor's kind consideration for the work here in the midst of all he has to do in Dornach.

We shall be delighted to welcome you both here in England, but wish the Doctor to feel that if it will help him in any way to put off his visit until after the inauguration we are very willing to wait until next year; but if he is able to spare the time and it does not inconvenience him in any way we should prefer the beginning of June.

We should like, if it can be arranged, two or three lodge lectures on the subject of 'Christ Jesus', or some other subject the Doctor may choose, an E.S., and M.E. meetings.

I know there are several who are wishing for an audience from Dr. Steiner when he comes, and if he prefers to have no audiences this year it would be better to put off the visit until next year.

If you decide to come over in June I should be glad if you will let me know the dates and titles of lectures as soon as possible, that we may make arrangements.

With hearty greetings to you and Dr. Steiner from my wife and myself, I remain

Yours very sincerely,

H.J. Heywood-Smith

★

In the end Steiner must have considered that a visit to England of the type desired was not at the time feasible for him, and therefore deferred it.

The subsequent outbreak of the First World War, however, put any visit a year later completely out of the question.

The Grail Cup

The May number of *The Path* published a sixth instalment of the shortened version of H.W. Percival's studies on the zodiac.

There was also an article by Elinor Dunlop entitled 'The Grail Cup':

> I am sitting on Chalice Hill where, it is said, St. Joseph buried the Cup of sacred memories. The vale of apples (Avalon) lies all around, bathed in spring sunshine. Soon the countryside will be a drift of creamy white and pink blossoms, for the apple blossoming is in May, the Celt's earthly paradise. In the 'Avellenan' or song of apple-trees one of our bards describes his mystic tree as being seven and yet seven-score.
>
> Seven sweet apple trees, and seven score
> Of equal age, height, width and bulk,
> Out of one bosom of sweet mercy spring.
>
> The Mendips guard the far horizon, and at their feet gleams the mere into which the brave Sir Bedevere flung King Arthur's sword 'Excalibur'. Surely the past but slumbers in the present: what has been, is, and ever will be. The heart, a magic crystal, evokes whate'er it wills. In this crystal I can see Brigh, the radiant goddess of light and beauty, whose many-bowered chambers are in the Sun, and yet whose tender care is over all her children. We know her also as Dana, mother of gods and men. Swiftly she passes across the crystal, clad in rainbow glory, with a smile of transcendent sweetness on her lovely face. For a moment, all is white and clear, and then I see what looks like a crown of gold, which flashes with opal and ruby lights, rose, pale green, and blue, shot through with warmest crimson. A second glance shows it to be a circle of mystic fire, and in the centre plays a fountain from which melodies rise and fall—heartbeats of joyous life. Surely this glowing centre must be 'Brigh's Cauldron', the Grail Cup in which the precious brew of life eternal was distilled and offered free to every hero-soul who came to drink. 'Pair Dadena' was it called, 'Cauldron of Rejuvenescence'.
>
> Then the vision passed, and I saw an aged man stooping over a crucible, from which arose the fragrance of myrrh and cinnamon, olive and galangal. These, I was told, commingled to produce the golden oil, 'Elixir Vitae'.

With the mediaeval seer my visions passed. Alone, upon the green hill, I prayed. My prayer was answered. In a pine wood with no one near I saw the 'Grail'. Nearby the sound of running water, overhead the deep blue sky, and in the midst a pure white cloud, heart-shaped, appeared. I gazed upon this purity with deepfelt adoration, and then I saw a fount of rosy light rise up within its centre. The risen spray broke in a rose of perfect beauty which fell and touched my feet. Rosa Mundae, rose of love immortal, uniting with thy fragrance Earth to Heaven! So sweetly poignant was the fragrance of my rose that I knew not whether to rejoice or weep.

Then I bowed and raised the crimson rose first to my lips, then hid it deep within my heart, for I too had seen the Holy Grail, even as Blanchefleur in days of old. The ancient cauldron and the seer's golden oil are one with the Grail Cup of redemptive passion.

★

At the foot of the page where this article ended was printed a quotation:

Basing all his doctrines upon the presence of the Supreme Mind, Plato taught that the *nous*, spirit, or rational soul of man, being 'generated by the Divine Father', possessed a nature kindred or even homogeneous with Divinity, and was capable of beholding the eternal realities. This faculty of contemplating reality in a direct and immediate manner belongs to God alone; the aspiration for this knowledge constituted what is really meant by philosophy—the love of wisdom. The love of truth is inherently the love of good; and so predominating over every desire of the soul, purifying it and assimilating it to the divine, thus governing every act of the individual, it raises man to a participation and communion with divinity, and restores him to the likeness of God . . . It is the province of the discipline of philosophy to disenthral it from the bondage of sense, and raise it into the empyrean of pure thought, to the vision of eternal truth, goodness and beauty. 'The soul,' says Plato in the *Theaetetus*, 'cannot come into the form of a man if he has never seen the Truth.'—H.P. Blavatsky, *Isis Unveiled*, Vol I.

The Sphere of the Universe

The May number of *The Path* also published some 'Editorial Notes':

In these beautiful spring days it is good to find myself in the 'Isle of Avalon', associated with the legends of King Arthur and of the Holy Grail. In such moments of relaxation, one cannot readily sorrow for ought. The Sun becomes a source of understanding; the ecstasy of the Divine Intellect is over all. In such surroundings one finds no difficulty in realizing that trancelike yoga in which the operations of Nature proceed in silence. The visible world which appears so beautiful is realized as the manifestation of the One Divine Essence. Metaphysical difficulties disappear; every separate beauty is a jewel transformed from the gold of the Sun.

★

How can I do otherwise than give myself over to reflection? What to me are acts of merit or demerit, the results of good and evil? I extirpate them altogether. I turn my eyes to the trees. I realize that my body is a tree, with its seasons, nourished by sap, fostered by desires. This tree too has its branches. Is the mind not the trunk, the soul the root of the mind, the root of these the one great Cause of all? This garden in which I sit is the home of the quiet mind, and in this composure I witness the festival of life. In the cities and towns with their tumultuous life, man with unquiet mind gathers worthless treasure with as much delight as I gather these fragrant blossoms of spring, to make my offering to God in the holy shrine of my heart.

I believe I now understand what Nirvana is (I shall no doubt soon forget it again). I have lost nothing in reality in burying all separate possessions. Is this an 'empty space' in which I sit so silent? If so, it becomes the receptacle of all knowledge. How safe and secure is the soul in such a haven of rest. Having forgotten the separate forms, with their different names, I see the substance out of which they are all made. When the shadows cast by all these separate shapes are removed from my mind, then tranquility arises, the mirror of the soul is bright, the firmament is clear, the Sun of truth shines. Is it out of the essence of this felicitous spirit that these little hills, these trees and plants, these waters, and the fragrance of the flowers arise? Does it, like this widespread daylight, comprehend all objects and contain all worlds? Yes, I see now that the seed of all these beautiful productions of Nature is contained within me, that these countless worlds are the visible expression of myself. The sphere of the universe is my sphere; I behold myself in all objects and remain in peace. The butterfly dances before me in the sunlight, and under the shade of the tree I reach illumination. I see that where the Supreme Being is, He is accompanied by all these worlds of beauty and variety. He is present in everything—in the habitable Earth and the waters likewise; any word of mine will but misrepresent His true nature.

★

Outside my garden of peace there is tribulation. Am I to be disturbed thereby? Amidst the turbulent waters of life, will my soul retain the nature of its original, like the lotus rooted firmly in the midst of the lake however stormy its waters? Yes, if I remain steadfast in this consciousness. The human heart is tender, and soon affected by the network of feelings. It flows with affection, and murmurs silently in sorrow. But the 'aether' in the heart remains ever the same, the measureless reality, requiring no pillar for its support. Was it not the god Indra, who, when pursued by his enemies, took advantage of their having lost sight of him for a moment, and entered into the womb of an atom, like a bee entering the cup of a flower? Here he found instant rest, discovered the royal palace from which he had fled, and ruled over his imaginary realm. Moments of respite come to the most sorrowful heart, and wise is he who finds in such moments the necessary atom in the sunbeam which proves to be the doorway to peace and the celestial palace.

★

The people outside are returning from church where, no doubt, the Easter festival has been celebrated. I wonder if they have really seen the festival of resurrection as I have seen it under this tree in the garden. Have they seen the Christ with His hands stretched over all creation; His feet reaching to the end of the world; His face and eyes on all sides; His head piercing the spheres? Have they seen the Lord moving in and out of all things; the One Universal Ocean; the One Sun and Moon; the same land in all the Earth? However narrow the vision, He, the Lord, is in all the customs and manners of men, and in all their ways of thought. He resides equally in the parts of the atom and of the great Cosmos. A thousand images of Christ have gone by, and are going by still, but all these images vanish when Christ is seen everywhere. Is not the boundless heaven His Crown; the Earth his footstool; the whole universe His temple?

★

A bell rings and I leave the garden, but not before sending gifts and messages to the far-scattered children of the Kingdom who have from time to time shared with me this mystic vision. Is it not from visions such as these that we go forth equipped to fulfil our various destinies? The greatest spot on the Earth is the little hill of vision, far eclipsing the hanging gardens of Babylon. It is the ever-enduring hill, with ever-springing greenery, ever-living waters, where the mother raises her brood of heroic children. Today, perhaps, in some such quiet spot, making no noise at all, the good angel of mankind may be preparing the Saviours of the world. Be of good cheer all ye who dwell in isolation for a while.

D.N.D.

Much Appreciated and Enjoyed

On the very same Easter Sunday—it fell on 12 April—when the Dunlops were having their experiences at Glastonbury, Edith Maryon wrote again from London to Rudolf Steiner.[33]

58 Grove Park Terrace
Chiswick, W. London
Sunday

Dearly revered Teacher,

Forgive me for writing to you again, I did not intend to, but Herr Dr. Felkin does not know at all what treatment to give me, until you have said what you think it would be best to do. We do not wish to disturb your measures, and I myself think you know what I should do, and if you would give me your advice it could be a great help for Herr Dr. Felkin and for me too. Through this work (it is *hard*) my health has become somewhat worse and so tomorrow I am going out to friends in the country until the 4th of May.

In these last days I have learned something in the esoteric realm and today had an experience, and now no longer have darkness in the soul, and from this side I might wait with patience for an answer, but feel obliged to ask what it is best to do for Dr. Felkin, my family and also myself under these circumstances.

With the occult side of the matter we do not feel quite sure, to find the right way. It is always against my feeling if I ask you something, because it is always more work for you, but what else can I do? And this is really important.

So I ask you to send me a telegram, or to Dr. Felkin; his telegraphic address is Felskamm, London.

Miss Wilson can tell you more, it goes so much quicker in English!

I hope we can see each other again, my dear teacher! How can I thank you?

Your pupil

L. Edith C. Maryon

(Today Herr Dr. Felkin said that he has already said everything necessary about my health.)

*

Either Maryon did not yet go out to her friends in the country, or if she did she quickly returned to London, for her next letter to Steiner was written a few days later from the same address.

58 Grove Park Terrace
Chiswick, W. London,
18. 4.14

Dearly revered teacher,

On Easter Sunday I wrote you a letter, but sent it via Miss Wilson to Dornach, because I was not sure where you are. Perhaps you are now in Berlin, so I am writing a few words, as perhaps I do not have much time. Herr

Dr. Felkin says that when I was so ill at Dornach, I was quite near the gate of death and as a consequence my heart has now become very very weak etc. At Dornach I more or less knew this, and in my letter I asked what I should do after the 1st of May, if my work here is accomplished. After meditation and in the morning I feel there is perhaps more work for me, if my physical body can be saved, but the thing is, I have become so much weaker than I was at Dornach, all my surroundings here are so difficult, I feel like a plant without light and water. So I beg you to send me a word, I need some more strength to proceed further, or go through the gate of death. It is so very hard without you, but I wish to do what my destiny is, if I can find it. I once had the hope of helping a little later on, but now this hope is vanishing.

Until we see each other again, my dear teacher.

From your pupil

L. Edith C. Maryon

One line is enough for me, if you have so much to do.

Herr Dr. Felkin asks me to inquire whether I should eat meat. I want to know if it is necessary.

*

In the following month, the eurythmists arrived in London. Magdalene Siegloch continues:

> Beside Lory Smits, Harry Collison also invited Elisabeth Dollfus, Flossy von Sonklar and her younger sister Ada Smits, so it was possible to form a little eurythmy group. To relieve the strain on the hosts, Clara Smits' [Lory's mother] took along her housemaid. In London she could make herself well understood with her Low German.
>
> After these careful preparations Lory Smits ventured to give eurythmy courses in the English language in both London branches of the Anthroposophical Society. She was hard at work through the whole of May and also with the little group. A performance with English and German poems and Beethoven's 'Ecossaises' took place every week, to which invited guests also came. Everything was excellently arranged and lovingly cared for by Harry Collison.

Herbert Heywood-Smith reported that courses were given in the Zarathustra and Myrdin groups, but performances only in the latter—in the house in Hereford Square. He added: 'The visit was very much appreciated and enjoyed.'

*

While eurythmy performances were taking place for anthroposophists in Kensington, the customary lodge meetings were taking place for theosophists in Wimbledon.

At one of these on 8 May D.N. Dunlop's now 22-year-old daughter Edith met her future husband Gibson Young. In her autobiography *Inside Out* (1971), she described the occasion:

> . . . I considered theosophists people remote from me, and seldom attended the weekend meetings.
>
> Then I found that for which I had been almost unconsciously searching. Or rather, he found me. He fell in love with me at first sight—so he said. It was little Elsie who seemed to be the instrument of destiny.
>
> Her hand tapped at my bedroom door one warm evening.
>
> My father had asked her to find out whether I was at home. Did I know it was White Lotus Day? I said, what had that got to do with me? She knew the meetings bored me. But this was to be a special occasion. Mrs. Leisenring, my father's secretary, had invited a couple of musicians from the Royal College to play before and after the lecture. It might do me good, cheer me up, make me forget myself, if I came to the meeting, just for once, to please my father.
>
> Much against my inclination I said I would. I didn't know that the violinist would be standing with a fiddle tucked under his chin waiting for me to creep into the back of the meeting-room. I noticed that he nudged the pianist and whispered something in his ear that made him smile and turn his head in my direction. I presumed he was calling his attention to Cliff Thomson, buttoned into the uniform of the Officer's Training Corps, who had stood up to beckon me to a vacant seat next to his in the back row. Gibson couldn't know that Cliff, although ostensibly my brother's friend more than mine, had a crush on me. The faces of my father and his secretary were in shadow. Was my mother, seated in the front row knitting, listening to the music or to the telepathic communication that I felt there was between my father and the American lady? A dying chord vibrated into silence. My father rose to deliver his address. I seemed to know a lot of it already.
>
> 'Man,' he said, 'is obliged to share his intrinsic isolation with the rest of mankind. We in this room this evening not only share with one another our island, but share the adventure of exploring the uncharted seas which lie beyond the charted shores of our circumscribed human personalities. Even as Columbus had faith in the existence of America before he set out on his voyage, so we must have faith in the existence of a spiritual world before we can venture to explore its manifestations. Let us take heart. In this dark age—the *Kali-Yuga* of Hindu scriptures—H.P. Blavatsky has provided us with a chart to aid our exploration of the virgin lands that lay about us in our infancy, and to which we, as man, intrinsically belong. Evolution is a spiritual process; a process by which we have evolved from our simian ancestors to the stature of man. And man today is but an infant in comparison to that which he will eventually become. Becoming is the essence of man. It is this essence I speak of when I speak of spirit.'

Cliff nudged me. 'The violinist,' he muttered, 'has been trying to give you the glad eye ever since your old man started letting off steam.'

He was standing with his back to the window. I raised myself in the chair the better to see him, and was struck by the delicacy of his hand, by his long ash-blond hair swept back from a domed forehead to the nape of his neck. My father had finished. He smiled, nodded slightly and, cradling his fiddle as affectionately as if it were a girl, at a nod from the pianist he struck the strings with his bow.

As a round of applause greeted the close of a sonata which I afterwards learnt was by César Franck, Cliff hauled me to my feet. A cigarette at his lips, he edged me through members of the audience who were making for the door and out into the hall to the front steps. The smell of a syringa bush in flower at the gate mixed with that of tar and dust. I agreed that we should go for a stroll on the Common.

We had reached the brow of the hill when who should we see cycling rapidly towards us, his hand on the handlebar, wind ruffling his hair, but the violinist...

⋆

Herbert Heywood-Smith travelled over to Paris to attend Rudolf Steiner's lectures from 25 to 27 May. No doubt he told Steiner about the success of the eurythmists' visit to London.

Les Lundi 25 Mai et Mardi 26 Mai 1914,
à 8 heures ½ précises,
le Docteur Rudolf Steiner donnera deux Conférences
pour les Membres de la Société Anthroposophique
274, Boulevard St. Germain
Sujets des Conférences:
La clairvoyance et la révélation des Mondes spirituels.
Le progrès dans la connaissance du Christ.

Mr. Heywood Smith ....

Carte strictement personnelle.
Droit d'Entrée: 5 fcs.

★

Edith Maryon, meanwhile, was in the English countryside slowly recovering from her illness. She wrote to the railway bureau in Dornach.

The Grange,
Goudhurst,
Kent.
28.5.14.

Dear Sirs,

In March I purchased the enclosed ticket in your bureau. I have recently been very ill, and it is impossible for me to travel back on the 27th. I would be very grateful if you would tell me whether I can still use the ticket in a few weeks, when I am medically allowed to travel, if I pay something extra?

Yours faithfully

L.E.C. Maryon

★

The June number of *The Path* included an editorial note from D.N. Dunlop dated 31 May, stating that

> After careful consideration we have reluctantly decided to discontinue publication of *The Path* with this, the last number of the fourth volume.

A final supplementary number published in September contained a seventh and concluding instalment of the shortened version of H.W. Percival's studies on the zodiac.

★

British eurythmy was also discontinued. Siegloch's account ends on a rather sad note:

> In June a new training course was to begin in Haus Meer. But the political situation was so dark that English ladies who had enrolled did not want to risk the journey, and there was increasing hesitancy in starting.

★

Edith Maryon, however, having recovered from her illness, did risk the journey to Dornach, probably setting out on or just after June 28—the day when Archduke Franz Ferdinand was assassinated at Sarajevo.

Many Glimpses of Insight

The still complex relation of British theosophists to Anthroposophy was nowhere better shown than by the fact that even as late as 1914 the British publishing house of the Theosophical Society brought out not only a further reprint of Rudolf Steiner's *The Way of Initiation*, but also two other works of his: *Three Essays on Haeckel and Karma*, translated by Bertram Keightley, and, more importantly, *An Outline of Occult Science*. All were again edited by Max Gysi.

The last book was even reviewed in the July issue of *The Vahan*. The review was signed with the initials J.I.W., recognizable as those of James Wedgwood.

> *An Outline of Occult Science*. By Dr. Rudolf Steiner. (Theosophical Publishing Society, London. 7s. 6d. net.)
>
> This is a translation of *Die Geheimwissenschaft in Umriss*, which at the time of its publication in German was announced as Dr. Steiner's magnum opus. The translator has done well not to attempt a literal translation of the title, for German is a language richer than English in pictorial representation, and the full content of the German title could probably not be rendered into convenient English. We may say in passing that the general work of translation is done with exceptional ability, and the book is very attractively and substantially produced.
>
> The reader may gain some insight into the very interesting nature of the book, if we examine one or two points in detail, and then say a few words by way of general summary.
>
> The book contains seven chapters, together with a preface and concluding remarks by the author. It deals with the nature of occult science, sleep and death, human and cosmic evolution, the perception of higher worlds, present and future evolution, and details from the domain of occult science.
>
> In reviewing a previous work of Dr. Steiner some years ago in *The Vahan*, we pointed out that the interest of his writing lay especially in the fact that he approached occultism chiefly from the standpoint of consciousness, and a fresh angle of presentation is always valuable to the student. Writers such as Mrs. Besant, Mr. Sinnett and Mr. Leadbeater, while they certainly have not undervalued the study of consciousness, have chiefly adopted the scientific method of exposition, realizing that this is the special need of the age. Dr. Steiner is psychological rather than scientific, and if this sometimes renders his work vague and unsatisfying, it certainly reveals at times real depth of thought and much insight into the complex phenomena of life.
>
> We may cull a characteristic phrase from a paragraph where he is

warning us not to attribute to plants 'the same kind of consciousness as that of animals and human beings in the waking state':

'The sensitiveness of some plants is spoken of—for example, of those which contract their leaves when certain external things act on them. But the characteristic mark of consciousness is not that a being reacts in a certain way to an impression, but that it experiences something in its inner nature which adds a new element to mere reaction' (p. 25).

The student of occult science will notice with special interest that in Dr. Steiner's scheme great importance is attached to the double. This is natural amongst those whose path traverses the operations of ceremonial magic and intercourse with the intelligent forces of Nature. Probably much more knowledge will transpire concerning the double as occult teaching is more fully unfolded during the next few years.

Throughout Dr. Steiner's writings interesting and novel theories are elaborated, and the present book is far from being an exception to this rule.

One might, however, suggest by way of criticism that frequently these theories seem to step over into the region of the fantastic and improbable: a drawback which very seriously diminishes from the unusual attractiveness of much that Dr. Steiner otherwise writes.

We are impressed with the belief that Dr. Steiner in his investigations is brought much into sympathetic relation with the Hierarchies who stand behind the various kingdoms and groupings of Nature, and therefore explains things in terms of what he feels; for there are ever great streams of life playing from these Hierarchies as a cosmic urge upon all Nature. For those who are grouped upon the ceremonial ray of evolution, especially its occult side, the way of progress consists in the intelligent apprehension of the forces and laws of Nature; they work with scientific understanding of things, and must eventually have the technique of the whole system at their finger-tips. One discerns much of this tendency in Dr. Steiner, but the development seems to be psychological and mystic rather than scientific and occult.

But we may turn from these criticisms and endeavours to understand, to repeat our appreciation of the many glimpses of insight given to us by the great character who writes for our helping. Perhaps no modern writer on occult subjects is more akin to Novalis than Dr. Steiner; the two certainly belong to the same school of thought, and who knows but that there may be an even more intimate relation? Novalis's *Disciples at Sais* will appeal to the disciples of Christian Rosenkreutz as one of the most wonderful books ever penned; so rich in its imaginative power, so uplifting in its conception of all natural objects, formations and groupings of phenomena as the symbolical expression of the underlying noumenal concepts. We find much of the same characteristic idiom in Rudolf Steiner.

★

Herbert and Mabel Heywood-Smith, in answer to the letter from Sophie Stinde, decided to spend their summer holidays at Dornach working on the building, and daringly travelled out there towards the end of July, when the European political situation had become absolutely explosive. Scarcely had they arrived when in early August the First World War finally broke out, and they were quite unable to return.

Out of different circumstances from those of Edith Maryon the Heywood-Smiths therefore found themselves at Dornach in much the same kind of situation. They accepted this as indicating the further course of their own destiny, and remained there for the next twelve years.

With his move to Dornach, Heywood-Smith brought to an end his brief but historic account (written in December 1925) of the early days of anthroposophy in Britain:

> Other groups were gradually started in London and in July [1914] when we left, there were about 200 members in England. Since then we have remained in Dornach close to our beloved Teacher, and have been privileged to hear almost all the lectures he has given here.

In Sign Thereof

The story here related now enters the period of the First World War, from 1914 to 1918. It must be stated at the outset that for the limited purposes of the present work as indicated in the foreword this period will be examined largely from a British angle. In contrast to most anthroposophical accounts, attention will therefore only be paid to events taking place at Dornach during these years when related by or of specific concern to British people or to those who had by destiny a particular connection to Britain.

One matter of such concern is set out in a fragmentary draft by Marie Steiner for her article 'Was Rudolf Steiner a Freemason?' The article itself was published in the April–June 1934 number of the journal *Anthroposophie*.

> If anyone at the right time recognized and stated that the time for Freemasonry was over, it was Rudolf Steiner. Not only does his life-work—Anthroposophy—imply this, not only does he express it in his plays (the representatives of the occult society hand over their symbols and withdraw) [a reference to the 10th scene of the third play *Der Hüter der Schwelle*] 'but in the first days after the World War had broken out he tore up the document he had received, to signal and confirm his opinion that the times were past in which Masonry could still be recognized. In order to have before his conscience the right to such a rejection, he had a duty not to avoid contact

with it. And how short this contact was—dismissed as soon as its hollowness was revealed. Such statements should not affect the valuable members found in our ranks, who—

Here the text of this fragmentary draft breaks off. In the published article itself, Marie Steiner italicized the corresponding passage:

> ... The newly founded circle, which was completely independent and recruited from theosophists who harboured a longing to approach Western esotericism in this way as well, was made acquainted with the ancient symbols, at first in their pictorial significance, and then increasingly according to their inner essence, until the symbols were worked through in consciousness. These symbols were thus wrested from sensations of mystical twilight and made accessible to artistic and scientific life. *When the War broke out, in August 1914, Rudolf Steiner declared the working group founded in this manner, which had come together under the name 'Mystica Aeterna', to be suspended, and in sign thereof tore up the relevant document. Never did anyone come together in this manner again.*

★

There is very little to be discerned from available written sources during the period of the First World War about anthroposophy in Britain, apart from dates when a few works were published in English translation. The conditions of the time must have made the progress of anthroposophy in this island extremely difficult, and were no doubt also unconducive to the production of written news or other similar documents in British anthroposophical circles.

The following chapters therefore reproduce such few documents as have so far come to light, expanding the account to provide a fuller survey of the war years from a British angle with a selection of further miscellaneous material mainly concerning the life and writings of D.N. Dunlop.

With respect to Dunlop it is important to be aware that in Britain a quite different spiritual situation obtained from that in German-speaking lands as regards the Theosophical Society. Whereas on the continental part of Europe that Society, after the expulsion of the German Section in 1913, had lost all further relevance to the subsequent progress of anthroposophy, the corresponding position in Britain was not nearly so clear-cut. Here the Theosophical Society remained an active and powerful body which for many years continued to expand. But while on the one hand the long-established strength of theosophy in Britain may be held to have at first impeded the growth of a native British anthroposophy, as the years went by the Theosophical Movement on the other hand also supplied a small but steady stream of British defectors to the anthroposophical cause.

★

Translations of Steiner's lecture-cycles were still all in the form of duplicated typescript, circulated only among anthroposophists.

Harry Collison however brought out in 1914 a pamphlet by Steiner translated as *Spiritual Science*, Lotus Peralté's *The First Stages of a Spiritual Movement*, and three separate lectures by Adolf Arenson: *On the Study of Spiritual Science*, *The Interior of the Earth*, and *The Sermon on the Mount*. All were published by John M. Watkins.

In his later *Commentary on Rudolf Steiner's Four Mystery Plays* (1947) Collison recorded a further aspect of this work:

> After I had completed some translations, Dr. Steiner gave me his rights of translation, and in 1914 I went, at his request, to America to study the question of copyright, for which I had already qualified by many years as a practising English barrister.
>
> In America I found to assist me in my translations an old school friend, S.M.R. Gandell, and in England R.T. Gladstone from the same school at Uppingham.

Special Times

Eleanor Merry is a good example of a person who found her way towards anthroposophy through the Theosophical Movement. In her reminiscences she described her upbringing in Durham and Vienna, her subsequent marriage, and how she then entered onto a theosophical path:

> . . . A little later I became acquainted with a rather amateurish sort of spiritualism; and then, about 1914, with Theosophy. A friend sent me the *Secret Doctrine*, and from that moment I devoted myself to the study of it. Was this what I had been seeking all my life? I read many of Mrs. Besant's books too. From all I read, one outstanding realization began to colour my thoughts and feelings and actions. It was that there were actually 'Masters', elder brothers of humanity, seers and adepts, who had trodden the path I was longing to discover, and whom it was possible to meet—either in or out of the body. My childhood's capacity for hero-worship saw itself suddenly transfigured, lifted to spiritual heights undreamed of, and filled with all the romance of possible fulfilment in the everyday world. It seemed 'too good to be true'.
>
> The years of the War brought many sorrows, as was inevitable. They were not those of personal losses due to the War; but in any case, they would I think have been hardly bearable without the support of Theosophy, and the continued hope that some day eyes that had gazed deep into the mysteries of the world might look into mine.

A photograph of someone with precisely such eyes made a deep impression at this very time on a young man named George Kaufmann. (Many years later, during the Second World War, he dropped his father's German surname and substituted his mother's: Adams.) In his article on 'Rudolf Steiner in England', he described his own mixed cultural and linguistic background before recording his first meeting with anthroposophy at the outbreak of war in the summer of 1914:

> Like Rudolf Steiner himself, I was born, though not of Slavonic blood, in the Slavonic East of Europe. I think I owe to this the mobility in point of language which enabled me as a young man to become his interpreter. The speaking and hearing of several languages side by side is—or at least was at that time—part of the social structure of those countries on the Eastern fringe of Middle Europe; it belongs to the very air one breathes, the ethereal atmosphere of the landscape. My father, born in Australia of German and English immigrants, had come back to Europe shortly before my birth and was among the pioneers—mostly Irish Canadians and Poles in those early years—of the oil industry in the Carpathian foothills where we lived. It was a part of Poland (now incorporated in Soviet Russia as the 'Western Ukraine') belonging still at that time to the old Hapsburg monarchy; therefore I also felt the touch, though in a far outlying province, of the pervasive and rather fascinating qualities of Rudolf Steiner's Austrian home country. My own mother-tongue was English, and so was my upbringing; I had British citizenship by virtue of my father's birthplace. I learnt German as I went along.
>
> At the outbreak of the First World War I was an undergraduate at Cambridge—rather left to my own devices and dependent on my own decisions. That was the moment when I first heard of Rudolf Steiner. During an unforgettable holiday at a lonely spot on the Suffolk coast I read right through his *Outline of Occult Science.*

It was a friend in the Theosophical Movement who had first put this book into Adams's hands.

> The book impressed me deeply. Unlike some other theosophical works I had met, it made no attempt to come to terms with scientific orthodoxy, but the author did at every point state clearly and in a scientific spirit the ground on which he stood. You knew where you were; you felt the writer understood and shared the scientific outlook. As to its spiritual content—it was the English edition, with that impressive portrait where he is sitting with his hands half-folded, looking you straight in the eyes and yet far beyond—it made a 'timeless' impression on me. I cannot remember thinking, 'When did the author live, or is he living now?' Despite the modern style and context, he seemed to write from beyond all special times.

Quickly Disillusioned

One day at Dornach during this time, Edith Maryon opened her post and found herself reading an interesting letter. (The full text of this letter is still not available. Its first and last pages were reproduced in facsimile in Rex Raab's biography of Maryon, and Raab composed a paraphrase of the intervening pages.)

Windham Club,
St James's Square,
S.W.
13th Sept. 1914

Dear Miss Maryon,

Thank you very much for your letter and the kind and considerate way you put everything. It has really touched me very much & I am sincerely grateful; it has done a great deal to cheer me & encourage me.

Alas! One enters this Society thinking one is coming to an assembly of angels & one is quickly disillusioned. I cannot help being more sensitive to the actions...

(The letter goes on to describe conditions in England within the young Anthroposophical Society, especially at the start of the War.)

1. The leaders of the Anthroposophical Society in England have caused official alarm by instructing members that 'No communications should go beyond bounds.' The poor officials had never bothered about lectures from Dornach, but now they are of course asking what dangers might be hidden in such communications! It is absurd, but the officials cannot be blamed, for thereby the Society started to narrow down. And it is now reaping the reward.
2. My finances. I am not at all rich, as people believe. The Society receives everything which I possess.
3. My health. I have been in pain for the whole year, and travelling does not improve it.
4. The books and other translations must be brought out. And all this would come to a standstill, if I were unable to return to England.
5. The sick & wounded have to be looked after.

You can give Dr. Steiner all these reasons if you have an opportunity.

I hear you are doing wonderful work & congratulate you. I think in a letter to you of long ago I foretold this, but not to this extent & I claim no prophetic gifts.

Again thanking you for pouring a little oil on troubled waters,

yours very sincerely,

Harry Collison
Benedic anima mea Domino

★

The Latin phrase under the signature is the opening and closing verse of two psalms: Psalm 103, concerned with the soul itself, and more especially and famously Psalm 104, a glorious hymn celebrating the creation.

Collison had chosen this verse as his motto in the Order of the Stella Matutina[34]—in which Maryon had also been active during her English years.

★

In his book *Rudolf Steiners Erdenleben*, Guenther Wachsmuth described the origin of one of Steiner's lecture-cycles in the autumn of 1914.[35]

> From 3–6 October he gave at Dornach a cycle of lectures on 'Occult Reading and Occult Hearing'. Originally this subject had been chosen for the fortnight's lecture-cycle to have been given in Munich after the festival plays. The new Mystery Drama, which he intended to write as a supplement to the four already existing, fell victim to the War. (Rudolf Steiner wanted to compose it during rehearsals, and these no longer took place.) As he once said, it would have led us towards the Orphic Mysteries and then to the Castalian fount. By earnest request, especially from Herr Heywood-Smith, Rudolf Steiner now gave something in shortened form of what he had wanted to add to the festival plays.

Lawrence Edwards also recorded an anecdote about Heywood-Smith from the War years:

> From Heywood-Smith himself I learned that he spent a large part of those years working on the Goetheanum.
>
> One day he was high up on the scaffolding, carving at one of the architraves, when he became aware that someone was watching him from behind. It was Rudolf Steiner, who stepped forward, took the mallet and chisel from Heywood-Smith's hands and said very quietly, 'You see, you should hold them like this!'
>
> Heywood-Smith told me the story to illustrate Rudolf Steiner's striving for perfection, even in the smallest details.

The Dawning Light

Chapter XII of Isabelle de Steiger's *Memorabilia* (1927) opens as follows:

> I daresay most people, when they begin to reflect, note a similar experience to that on which I am going to touch. It is a fact that at a certain period of their lives their thoughts have taken a different turn, and subjects previously

unknown to them have become matters of deep thought and earnest enquiry.

On a survey of my life, I see without doubt that such was my case, and with me there have always been stated periods bringing changes; not, of course, unforeseen, but certainly not intended, or desired, still less aimed at. These changes, unsuspected by me, were mental ones, connected with my karma. I am not now inclined to explain the term to any readers to whom the word may be still unknown, and shall here state briefly that I use the word as standing for destiny, but not as synonymous with fate.

With regard to dates of changes, I had become a moderately known professional artist in London by the time I was forty-five; at fifty-five I was a recognized spiritualist, writing and lecturing on that subject. At sixty-five I was a recognized theosophist, doing the same and taking part in official work, but, as a Rosicrucian, my studies were restricted to the MSS of the Order. The next decade brought me to Liverpool, and further unforeseen moves and changes after my life in London, at orderly intervals of two or three years, in Edinburgh, Birmingham, Llangollen, Bournemouth, Rock Ferry and finally Liverpool again. Every experience was the opposite, so far as outward events were concerned, to what I hoped, for each change involved grave disappointment in places and people. I will just add briefly that my reasons for undertaking these continual changes were most complicated, depending on others and not on myself. I was swayed, and I yielded to what seemed to be my destiny, and so they have proved, but the events were handed out to me by Calamitas, the modern material goddess of Fate. I expect my next move will be to another world, and for this I have been trying to prepare more, and far more in detail, than I have for any of my earthly moves. Of course, these have always started with optimistic hope followed by pessimistic reaction.

I have noticed that the mental atmosphere of each town in which I stayed had a distinct individuality of its own. I found that each remained separate in my mind, and it seemed to me that Edinburgh was the most agreeable city for people with small incomes to live in pleasantly, the commercial atmosphere being little to the front. I liked it extremely, but the total absence of any feeling of warmth in the air, even in summer, kept my physical circulation at too low an ebb for me to bear it for many years. I suspect I live by the enjoyment of pleased nerves, i.e. by the harmonious state of my nerves, rather than by strength of muscle.

As I write now, in November 1920, I realize very distinctly that there is a feeling as of a flood of new thought clearing away the fog of material understanding; but I am not referring to that particular cult known as *New Thought*, though I once studied it.

Fog has obscured the vision of leaders such as were those Victorians who seem to me to have, *parti pris*, refused to consider the intellect of their predecessors as of any consequence. They accept the verdict of popular scientists as being too well recognized for dethronement, if ever their followers had the impulse to remove them from their posts. But they never attempt to dethrone them. I had, however, a dearly valued friend—my old teacher, Mrs. Atwood, of whom I shall make special mention in due course—who told me she was not a scientist in the orthodox acceptance of the word; and she certainly was unable to teach me any more science than what I might know from the popular works on science in which most girls had some little instruction during their schooldays, and what I might read in current science gossip.

One work which she recommended to me as being her chief guide was *Physio-philosophy*, translated from the German of Laurence Oken, and published by the Ray Society. I bought a second-hand copy in Edinburgh for 3s.6d. Not being a scientist, I had to grasp it by my own feelings. I conclude that it is even yet in advance of ordinary biology and psychology, for I have seen Laurence Oken's work noted by Dr. Steiner as an advanced thinker among European biologists, as a physio-philosopher of too advanced a grade for other researchers. Why did it interest me? I conclude that it was because it lifted a layer, like a piece of cotton-wool lying on a cabinet shelf, which layer, when removed, reveals the beautifully arranged shells to the admiring eye of the onlooker. Oken's *Physio-philosophy* may yet play a leading part in the mind of the coming man, whose knowledge fits him for the dawning light.

Isabelle de Steiger must have brought this work to the attention of D.N. Dunlop, for in October 1914 the latter started contributing to *The Vahan* a series of articles, entitled simply 'A Student's Notes', which paraphrased Oken's work. The series was continued until the following February.

Alchemical Transmutation

The Journal of the Alchemical Society reported a further meeting on Friday, 13 November 1914 at the Occult Club in 1 Piccadilly Place, when the owner of those premises, M.W. de Kerlor, read a paper entitled 'Some Notes on the Alchemical Researches of M. Jolivet Castelot'.

The paper was followed by an extensive discussion, which concluded with this speech:

Mr. D.N. Dunlop said that he was one of those persons who took an unbounded interest in the symbolism of alchemy. It seemed to him that whatever experiments were made on the physical plane by the ancient alchemists, greater interest attached to their works on the spiritual side. He thought, however, that a difficulty arose in that we were in danger of making too great a distinction between the spiritual and the not-spiritual—there was a tendency in most discussions to draw a very hard and fast line of division between spiritual interpretation and what might be called psychic and physical interpretation of these things. He suggested that there was no such division, and that the distinction was a purely artificial creation of our minds in their efforts to discover the truth. No state of spiritual consciousness, or consciousness in a spiritual condition as distinct from something more physical or psychic, could be experienced by a man or woman without a corresponding effect on the elements of the body, and the process was surely a reversible one.

In the light of the great symbolism of alchemy, the universe was conceived of as a precipitation from the pure ether, the primary substance from which all other elements derived their being. Everything we saw in the metallic or mineral kingdom was a precipitate from this primary substance. Now it did not require a very great stretch of the imagination to suppose that by a knowledge of the precipitation, the process might be reversed through the right bodily experience, and the minerals thus brought back to the primary substance, though we might not be able to convert this into gold in the ordinary understanding of that word. It seemed to him that here might be discovered something of alchemical magic, than which there was no greater magic. And to him personally such an experience would be at least more interesting than any chemical experiments which might yield a few golden coins—though these were certainly useful on occasion. It was the alchemical transmutation which could take place in a man's self that was really worthwhile. He was not prepared to dispute as to whether chemical transmutation had ever been effected; but even if a man succeeded in preparing a whole pot of gold, in the end he would probably come to the conclusion that after all it availed little in those moments when the greatest realities were concerned. Along the line of spiritual transmutation there was unbounded delight and happiness and magic, and when it was more generally traversed, somewhat of the glory that we read about as belonging to 'the Golden Age' would again return and be witnessed in the physical plane.

The chairman said that, bearing in mind the maxim that a tree is judged by its fruits, he could pay the present lecturer no greater compliment than by saying that his lecture had given rise to the most interesting discussion that had yet taken place at a meeting of the Alchemical Society.

The next meeting of the Society took place on 11 December. It was in the nature of a symposium with various contributions, including 'Some Notes on the Alchemist Alipili' by A.E. Waite and 'Principles and Symbols' by D.N. Dunlop.

★

Mention of Waite will perhaps recall the striking sentence in the notes of his meeting with Alfred Meebold in May of the previous year: 'If I and those who are with me want the living reality, we should disband and join Steiner.'

Waite had actually followed the first part of this advice. In the course of 1914, as a result of internal difficulties in the Independent and Rectified Rite, he finally disbanded the Order.

Some of its members, such as Ada Drury-Lavin and Edith Cull—maybe also Beatrice Riddel—had already long gone over to the Anthroposophical Society. But Waite himself, although wanting 'the living reality', was too set in his own ways, and did not follow their example. Rather than 'join Steiner', he went on in 1915 to found, together with a few other former members of the Independent and Rectified Rite, another nominally Rosicrucian Order of his own.[36]

★

Here are a couple of notices from the December *Vahan*:

The Theosophical Forum

A group, somewhat of the nature of a Debating Society, though differing from such in some important respects, has been formed at 19, Tavistock Square under the title of The Theosophical Forum.

Mr. D.N. Dunlop has been elected President, and the following have been elected to the Committee with power to add to their number: Dr. Haden Guest, Mr. Loftus Hare, Miss Dorothy Osmond, Miss Millicent Wadham, Mr. W.D.S. Brown, Captain A.E. Powell, R.E.

The purpose of the Forum is to hold discussions on any controversial subjects of general interest, as well as on topics of a purely theosophical character. It is hoped that the discussions will prove a stimulus to original thought and expression, and tend towards intellectual alertness and vigour.

The object is to discuss, not for argument's sake, but in order to arrive at truth.

It is proposed to hold meetings about every two weeks. The first will probably be held at 8 p.m. on Friday December 4, when Mr. Loftus Hare will open a discussion on 'The Root Causes of the Present War'.

Will all F.T.S. wish us well in our venture?

A.E. Powell, Hon. Secretary

Wimbledon Centre

The Saturday evening meetings continue as usual. The fact that I have been unable to take such active interest in other directions has probably increased the pleasure derived from meeting the few comrades who have gathered regularly round the fire to discuss the principles of Theosophy. The meetings are held at 8 p.m., at White Lodge, Sunnyside, Wimbledon, and a hearty welcome is extended to all. The book now under discussion is *Occult Science*, by Dr. Steiner.

Elinor Dunlop

★

It is noteworthy that the Dunlops had begun to study a work by Rudolf Steiner. But their fellow-students at this time came from a limited age-group. In her autobiography *Inside Out* (1971), Edith Young gave a description of the 'few comrades who . . . gathered regularly round the fire':

> The War crushed the hopes my father had cherished of establishing a flourishing theosophical centre at White Lodge. He had to content himself with an audience of elderly women with private means, who busied themselves while listening to him in helping the war effort by knitting comforters and socks for the troops. There was a sprinkling of men too old for military service.

With Mallet and Chisel

The memoirs of Arild Rosenkrantz record:

> With the outbreak of the First World War my artistic work was interrupted, so I devoted myself to massage, which at that time was not well known in England, and was able to assist in some hospitals tending the military.
>
> In the meantime other people were fully engaged at Dornach in Switzerland with the building of the Goetheanum, still called Johannesbau, which was to be a dignified setting for Rudolf Steiner's mystery dramas. Many of the artists helping with these works were called away because of the war, and thus in London I formed the opinion that I should go to work in Dornach. Several members gave financial support, and so my wife and I left shortly before Christmas 1914.

In an article included in the 1958 issue of *The Golden Blade*, Effie Wilson related a visit to Dornach at this time in the company of Edith Lewis:

> My first visit to Dornach with Miss Lewis was in order to spend Christmas 1914 there. One evening there was a social gathering in the Schreinerei, and after light refreshment we were expecting a Christmas lecture from Rudolf Steiner. Instead of that, he called all the children present to sit on such benches and stools as were near the stage.
>
> He then spoke to them of Him whose birth we were celebrating, pointing out that although Joseph and Mary had come a long journey, there

was no room for them in the inn. They were obliged to take refuge in the stable, and there Jesus was born. But, he said, each one of you can give him a place in your hearts.

I think Rudolf Steiner shook hands afterwards and spoke to each one present. Of me he asked if I had understood, and then added, 'That was sowing a seed in their hearts.'

Rosenkrantz continued:

The building was roofed at Christmas 1914. Now we could start to give both cupolas an artistic image on the insides. Shown in section, a sea of colours can be seen in the cupola vaults of the wax models done by Rudolf Steiner. To the north and south they are tinged with red, and continue in other shades towards the west. In this sea of colours certain motifs had to be woven in. Seven artists were to paint the large cupola, and five the small one. These cupolas were to be filled with colours in such a wonderful way, while the eight tripartite windows in the great hall were to cast their colourful light over the columns and hall.

In the inner part of the building a great scaffolding was put up to the height of the column heads. The artists whose task it was to deal with the carving of the columns could stand on the scaffolding, and likewise the painters of the cupola vaults. When we arrived, the surface of the cupola to be painted was being prepared.

At that time Rudolf Steiner had not given any directions for the central motif in the painting and on the statue that was to be placed into the niche on the stage. I will speak about these particulars later.

I at once made a start with the work expected from all newly arrived persons. This was to help in carving the upper part of the building, which was to be made all in wood. I was appointed a place in one of the arched-over gangways, where with mallet and chisel I tried, a bit desperately, to hew into the spiritual world.

Carving work did not suit my temperament; it asked too much of my patience. Fortunately a few days later Rudolf Steiner came along, while I was cutting away into the poor wood. He said: 'This work is not suitable for the hands of a painter. Come to me tomorrow and I'll give you other work.'

Apart from carving, there were all kinds of tasks others had chosen. I noticed a well-to-do English lady helping to deal with financial matters, and otherwise sitting in a modest room where day in and day out she would sharpen the many carving chisels. She had taken it upon herself to keep sharp the working parties' instruments and tools, being glad to serve the whole work in this way.

Another lady supervised the canteen in what used to be a very modest wooden house near the building. Here we all sat on rough benches at long wooden tables, and young ladies, many of whom were studying the new art of eurythmy, served our meals. Everyone was glad to contribute to the whole in his or her own way because we could listen to Rudolf Steiner's lectures and see the Goetheanum coming into being.

A young Russian Baroness kept our rooms in a tidy condition, since because of the demands of the large amount of work we could not look after them ourselves. My wife assisted with preparing the plates the artists needed for their studies, and for a time I joined the work of engraving the large coloured glass windows.

I had already made numerous windows for churches, composed of small coloured pieces of glass kept together by leaden panes, an old but unchanged artistic method. But the Goetheanum windows were huge sheets of one colour, three metres high, and had to be engraved with small stones—a quite different technique from what I was used to.

Once I showed Rudolf Steiner a sketch representing the crucified Christ surrounded by angels. I had in mind to paint this for a church in London, and wanted to get his advice about it. He thought my work too traditional, and explained how I should do it. Then following his advice I made another sketch, which I showed him. When he saw it he said: 'You must paint that in the small cupola. I'll correct your sketch. You can collect it tomorrow.' By the next day he had painted the small pastel hanging today with the collection of sketches at the Goetheanum.

It took me some months to transpose this into a gigantic composition, necessary as a base for execution in the cupola. This I did in the northern studio. When I had finished, Rudolf Steiner altered my work and the works of the other artists as well.

Voluntary Cooperation

In January 1915 D.N. Dunlop started to bring out a new quarterly, *The BEAMA Journal.* The first number opened with an unsigned article by himself on 'The Philosophy of Co-operation':

> The present European War has been termed a commercial war, and the causes are said by many to exist in 'economic conditions'. If war must come, there could hardly be any other immediate cause for it in this industrial age, and the fact that this life-and-death struggle of the nations can be so distinctly related to industry indicates that in our efforts to understand the problem we are indeed getting near the heart of it. We may observe in the history of the past few hundred years how wars have exercised increasing interference with the peaceful trading of the industries between different countries, even though the struggle may have been more or less local. Gradually science has brought inventions to assist industry which have

accelerated international exchange of commodities, so that a large industry may depend on several countries for its raw material or for half-finished goods. Sometimes it is merely a small item for packing that is required, but if one line of communication is cut, it disturbs the current of all others. The lack of one apparently insignificant chemical by-product, for instance, may hold up a huge industry. In a word, we obtain materials where they are most readily produced, either because of accessible and natural resources of a country or the idiosyncrasies of the people. Nations have become more and more interdependent and less self-sustaining, because they rely on this intercommunication. The world does not now consist of small self-contained communities as when agriculture and the various crafts and guilds of workers supplied local needs, and we can never return to these conditions; the problems of those days are not our problems. Wars, then as always, were initiated by ambitious leaders, but the provocative cause inheres in the conditions and problems of the time. Today the real problem in the western nations, but also in those of the East, revolves around industries, for through them the life of the people is sustained. It is now fully realized that 'the magic of industry' is the means by which natural resources are made available, and useful to men, and the underlying resource, the real asset, is human energy applied in a myriad ways.

There followed a section on 'How Nature Organizes':

It is very apparent today that there are laws governing the use of this energy which we do not understand, for without much imagination we can conceive of wiser, saner uses of energy than the present European imbroglio involves. This war has been forced on Europe by a nation which had very thoroughly organized the energy of its people, but with what object? Organization is a wonderful fact of life, and we have really underrated its infinite possibilities. But when man undertakes to co-operate with energy, he will always over-reach himself unless he follows the same principles by which Nature organizes. We say the Germans are 'materialistic' because they have not perceived the meaning of the very scientific facts on which they placed such confidence and reliance. Spontaneity, freedom, individuality (organic characteristics in Nature) they ignored in an overwhelming greed—'a national ideal'—and Germany as a tremendous machine has 'warped past the aim', for assuredly the aim of any race or nation is not at heart to create a mere machine and to change life into a mechanism. 'Government,' says President Woodrow Wilson, 'is not a machine, but a living thing. It is modified by its environment, necessitated by its tasks, shaped to its function by the sheer pressure of life. No living thing can have its organs offset against each other as checks, and live. On the contrary, its life is dependent upon their quick co-operation, their ready response to the commands of instinct or intelligence, their amicable community of purpose...'

After further sections on 'Individuality in Nature', 'Organization and Individuality', and 'Industrial Individuality', came one on 'Balance between Individuality and Co-operation':

> Industry in its broadest sense is the basis of any nation's life, and on its administration depend all other of its peoples' activities. In its various operations arise all the psychological, scientific, technical and even ethical problems of men, and therefore it is that today the two fundamental principles of evolution are challenging attention in the methods of industrial administration. In natural organisms, individuality and co-operation are as exactly adjusted as the most delicate balance, but in most organizations of men one is always threatening the other. We must then recognize that co-operation is necessary to give value to individual efforts. The co-operation of the heart and lungs and of all the other organs is the *sine qua non* of a healthy man, and only those men survive whose organs are fit for their functions. This is Nature's criterion of competition, a competition for quality. Thus intelligence exercises itself in Nature, we should say, without taking thought. But man *thinks*, and tries to regulate his competition. As yet we have not thought to great effect, it must be confessed. We have discovered (1) that unfettered competition means ruinous reduction of prices and consequent deterioration in quality, and (2) that quality is lowered also when corperate control becomes so strong that it completely minimizes individual enterprise. In both cases quality suffers, and there is no 'survival of the fit'. Large concerns then lose equally with the small in international competition.
>
> Thus to meet the present unprecedented conditions of industrial existence we must bring into operation a principle which has not yet been extensively tested by men, viz., the voluntary co-operation of individuals.

The final section was on this 'Voluntary Co-operation':

> Quality is always the result of individual competition protected by wise, corporate agreement against unnecessary 'cut-throat' competition. Co-operation is necessary to give value to individual efforts; but the real value, i.e. the quality, will deteriorate if the co-operation becomes compulsory in all directions.
>
> It is evident then that size, mere bigness, is not *per se* the characteristic of equipment required for the future. The essence of voluntary co-operation is in its quality, not entirely in the number of co-operating individuals. Today we are strirred by the wonders and ramifications of commerce circulating round the whole globe. All the world is before us where to choose, and we become hypnotized by 'size'. Big empires, big kartells, big territories—bulk, in a word, has deceived the Germans. The British Empire is big in extent, it is true, but once bigness became its essential characteristic it would surely

decline. It is not its size, nor any large trusts, nor corporations which constitute it an Empire, as is now quite clear. Nor is it held together merely by commercial compacts and trade agreements, valuable as these may be. It is united by trust, but not a Trust. The vitality and energy of billions of people of diverse races and national ideals constitute the British Empire, and they remain part of the Empire *voluntarily*, to support the principles of freedom and self-government. This is the greatest co-operative association in history, a voluntary union for a principle. But the principles of the German Empire stand condemned today before the whole world.

World-wide commerce as it now exists enforces the fact that the world is a unit, and war is suicidal to this unity. The unity of the world depends on the unity of nations, and the unity of each nation on that of its component parts. All unity is maintained by intelligent co-operation, not by blind and brute-like individualistic aggression. And all associations of men must recognize this principle if they are to be permanently successful.

★

At Dornach on 15 March, Rudolf Steiner stated in a lecture:

A few months before war broke out I was strangely moved when some of our ladies doing eurythmy went over to London to give a course. People enjoyed eurythmy. This is very good, as it ought to be enjoyed. But they do not notice that eurythmy is spiritual and the very opposite of materialistic sport. On one side Europe is being inundated by everything belonging to materialism. It is through sport that materialism is carried right into human movements. Sport serves people's amusement and their totally materialistic obsession with health. With us, on the other hand, every movement is an expression of the spirit . . .

The World-wide Aspect

On 22 May 1915, the Twenty-Fifth Annual Convention of the Theosophical Society in England and Wales held its opening session in the Portman Rooms in Baker Street. *The Vahan* reported:

Dr. Haden Guest, who had returned from Belgium only a few hours before, took the chair at 3 o'clock and called upon Mr. Sinnett, Vice-President of the Society, to open a discussion on 'The Occult Work of the Theosophical Society'.

Mr. Sinnett said that of late years so-called 'occult' work has chiefly been depriving occultism of its occult character. In the early days of the Theosophical Society no one knew anything of occultism, and in order to understand the growth of knowledge it was necessary to consider the beginnings of Theosophy, which date back to the beginnings of spiritualism. Spiritualism, he said, was definitely launched under the guidance of the great unseen leaders of the Theosophical Society. The whole drift of cultivated opinion had become, in the first half of the last century, so strongly materialistic, almost atheistic, that it was necessary to combat its influence by the introduction of spiritualism, by the provision of a scheme of information relating to another plane of consciousness and to a life after death. The purpose of spiritualism never aimed at more than giving evidences of another plane of existence, but later it was resolved that another experiment should be tried—in order to see if the time was ripe for a greater volume of teaching on the deeper realities of the higher life. That was what the Theosophical Society set out to do in 1875, in its early seedling days. The three objects were not composed at random by Colonel Olcott, but were definitely forecast as indicative of the work of the T.S., *if it should last.* For it was an important point that at first no certainty was entertained by the Great Masters that it would last...

Mrs. Powell and Mr. Bernard Old from the Northern and Midland Federations, Mrs. Windust and Mr. Scott emphasized different aspects of the question, and Mr. Dunlop spoke of a letter written by H.P.B. to Mr. Judge in which she definitely stated that she was herself the bearer of the teaching which was to change the whole of public opinion. He said: 'The occult work of the T.S. is to restore divine principles to life so that life may be regenerated, and to draw the attention of men and women to the most ancient doctines of the soul. It behoves us to study the three objects of the Society, which in themselves are strongly suggestive of what the occult work of the Society should be. Beginning with the third object, the first essential is to study the powers of one's own being, passing to the study of all the great philosophies and religions of the world, until finally brotherhood is the result of the change of consciousness brought about by an understanding of such religions and philosophies.'

After tea Dr. Haden Guest presided over a meeting of the National Council at which thirty-three members were present...

A fortnight later, the Scottish Convention was held, as reported by *Theosophy in Scotland*:

The Fifth Annual Convention was held at Headquarters, 28 Great King Street, Edinburgh, on Saturday 5th June 1915, at 2.30 p.m.

The General Secretary, in the name of the T.S. in Scotland, gave a hearty welcome to Mrs. Windust and to Mr. D.N. Dunlop, and had much pleasure in calling upon Mr. Dunlop to take the chair.

Mrs. Windust, in representing the T.S. in Holland, spoke of the very friendly feeling which exists between Holland and the Scottish and English Sections, and touched on the unity underlying the different kinds of theosophical work.

A telegram was received from the T.S. in England and Wales with good wishes for the Convention, and a letter from Dr. Haden Guest was also read by Mr. Dunlop, asking him, as representative of the English Section, to express most cordial greetings to the Convention . . .

There followed the main business part of the Convention, which ended:

In Mr. Dunlop's concluding remarks he said that the democratic methods of putting things before a body of people had many advantages. He hoped that in the near future England and Scotland would co-operate and hold meetings as a British Section of the Society. Especially at this time of crisis ought we to meet together on a larger scale, as there would be many problems to face. In years to come the work of the Society would be most important. He looked on Captain Graham Pole as a kind of international symbol, as he had been in touch with the movement in many different places, and had often assisted the President. Captain Pole's influence might be a factor in bringing us more closely together as a Society in the future. We should link up with our brothers in other countries. Speaking of *Theosophy in Scotland*, Mr. Dunlop said that personally he preferred it to *The Vahan*; but he thought it might be improved along propaganda lines. He thought there was a necessity for co-operation in research work between England and Scotland. We must not forget the world-wide aspect of the Movement, and we must begin a bigger movement that will come before men. Mrs. Besant was so busy in India that we must begin to offer something from our side. He proposed sending a cable of greeting to Mrs. Besant from the Convention, and this was unanimously agreed to.

Tea was served at four o'clock, and at half past five Mr. Dunlop addressed the members on 'The Three Objects of the Society'.

★

With reference to world-wide aspects of spiritual movements, Baron Rosenkrantz explained in his memoirs the problems being faced at this time over at Dornach:

In connection with the Goetheanum there arose many new artistic problems, especially that of how to handle wood. Rudolf Steiner was not content with the way the wood was being modelled. On one occasion we were all gathered round the artists involved in this work, waiting for Rudolf Steiner to come. When he arrived, we saw his disappointed glances. He then went on to explain how forms in sculpture came into being, and took up a tool to demonstrate. He led our thoughts back to the sharp divisions and surfaces of the world of crystals, in contrast to the smooth transitions of the world of plants. Although being helped by qualified artists, Rudolf Steiner was always obliged to show the way, for no one had gone into the problems of art so deeply as he had. This was also shown in his lectures. He always had to indicate the way to work, as well as how to treat materials. He was concerned with principles lying behind the different arts. Yet he would say to us: 'You are my hands.' He was the spirit who directed the work, but his 'hands' often disappointed him.

The texture of the colours gave us painters great difficulties. No one quite understood what Rudolf Steiner wanted. When the five painters had finished half of the small cupola, he had gradually to wash out everything they had done and paint it again himself, in order to show how colours were to be laid as a veil over each other. So here too was a quite new technique, a very difficult one, asking for profound ability and great patience. Rudolf Steiner said that technique is the artist's initiation.

The motifs up in the large cupola showed the Creation in space, those in the small cupola the Creation in time.

I still want to mention that on the same day when Rudolf Steiner gave me the sketch for the central motif of the small cupola, he handed the same motif to the English artist, Miss Maryon, as a sketch in crayon, and asked her to work it out in wood. The large wooden statue was to stand in a niche on the stage just underneath my equivalent painted composition. Rudolf Steiner wanted us to co-operate. He would often connect his pupils in this way, in groups of two.

Miss Maryon was an excellent sculptress who had left England to join Rudolf Steiner. She had previously been occupied in modelling forms for the wood-carving, but now began work on this great sculpture of the so-called 'statue' which showed first three, and later six figures. She started to make a design for Christ's head, which came out traditional, like my original sketch, so Rudolf Steiner corrected it in the same way as with me.

One day Rudolf Steiner came up to show me a small wax model representing Ahriman's head for the group statue, and I asked if he had done modelling before. He replied 'No. This is my first try.' He had previously just been modelling the column motifs and the gigantic architectural models of the building, but no figures.

An event to which we all looked forward was Rudolf Steiner's weekly lecture. It was most fortunate that all lectures at the time dealt with artistic themes. We gathered for this purpose in the woodwork shop behind the Goetheanum. The whole room was filled with long planks collected together in piles, which were to be put in the building in appropriate places designated for them. There were only a few chairs in this carpentry shop, and we mostly sat on the planks or the machinery. Rudolf Steiner would speak from a small reading desk, and at the start of his lectures would always remember with a prayer the soldiers who had fallen. It was wartime, and often when leaving the building we saw violent air-fights above Alsace. We felt deeply grateful to be spared these terrible horrors, and be able to work here for a great ideal. We listened in safety to Rudolf Steiner who was creating a home for a new culture, while a few miles away the cannons were thundering.

The Great Representative Man

As Baron Rosenkrantz described, Rudolf Steiner began work at Dornach together with Edith Maryon on a series of initial models for a planned wooden statue of large dimensions, to be named 'Der Menschheitsrepräsentant'—the Representative of Mankind.

*

In Britain meanwhile, *A Record of Higher Thought Work* reported a lecture given in London on 21 September 1915 at a 'Conference on Reconciliation and Reconstruction'.

> Mr. D.N. Dunlop kindly filled the place of Miss Maude Royden, who was most regrettably absent on Tuesday afternoon. He took as his subject 'Man's Evolution', and spoke in passing of the present awful cataclysm in the world and of the small place it took when viewed from the point of view of evolution, with all its gigantic processes.
>
> Starting from the early chapters in Genesis, he summoned before our eyes the chaos before the beginning, and the brooding of God upon the face of the waters, and the light of intelligence, which brought forth order, and set in motion those mighty rhythms of day and night, summer and winter, ebb and flow of tides, and the pulsations of an insect's wings. He spoke of the atom, which is a sphere as complete a system in itself as the whole universe. Then of man's sphere, divided into visible and invisible, and of the joy of those who have felt the thrill of infinite love in communing with that invisible self, which is ever united with infinite mind. We have in our progress reached the stage of thinking beings. Christ came forth from God as the great representative man. In Christ were represented all the attributes that will carry a being safely through the vast road of evolution. There may be seeming failure in our human affairs, but in the grand place of evolution there can be no failures. God said 'Let there be light!' and there was light. It is said every morning, *and it is so*. When God is uplifted in our hearts we shall see these things. When calamities overpower us, we know God is there. The darkest hour precedes the dawn—the Sun is always shining somewhere—and light in a mystic sense is always associated with spiritual life.
>
> According to certain writers who have made calculations, evolution is divided into periods and by this method of calculation we have arrived at Wednesday, 5.30 by the cosmic clock. We still have half a week to go . . .
>
> When we feel cross and nasty, *hesitate*, knowing, in view of the vast periods of evolution, it is foolishness. This will give you a sense of pro-

> portion. War in the light of evolution is a small thing. In the midst of all the splendour of the stars, what does it matter? We have wrought destruction and war for ages, forgetting all mighty and majestic thought. If we will do these mad, foolish things we must learn, until we co-operate with God. Sorrow will go on, and then, like the prodigal son, we will return to our Father.
>
> The story of evolution is the story of the prodigal son. The race is the human family—our family. Encourage moods that are great, encourage love for fellow men.

The report continued for Friday the 24th:

> In the evening Mr. Dunlop gave one of his lucid and convincing addresses on 'Reconciliation and Synthesis', showing the goal of the race to be a Divine Comradeship.

★

Towards the end of the year Dunlop republished in booklet form his 1914 editorial on *Symbols of Magic.* A note stated: '200 impressions of this booklet have been taken.'

Under the title 'The Promulgation of Theosophy', the November issue of *The Vahan* included a notice concerning other works:[37]

> *In the Light of Theosophy* is a book written some years ago by Mr. D.N. Dunlop. We have a remainder of this publication consisting of 500 copies; it is cloth bound, gilt top, and sold for 2s. each. We are prepared to distribute these copies to reading-rooms used by our soldiers if £15 is donated to cover part of the original cost and postage etc.
>
> The contents of *In the Light of Theosophy* are: What is Theosophy? First Principles; The Seven 'Planes and Principles'; Cycles of Evolution; The Days and Nights of Brahma; The Seven 'Principles' of Man; The Occult Teaching on Man's Evolution; The Higher Evolution of Man; Reincarnation; Karma.
>
> *Protean Man* is a little booklet also written by Mr. D.N. Dunlop several years ago; it is bound in heavy paper and sold for 3d. For every £4 contributed for the purpose we would distribute 500 copies of this booklet to reading-rooms in soldiers' camps, etc.
>
> We shall be pleased to send copies of these books to anyone who wishes to see them before giving the donation.
>
> The Path Publishing Co.
> W.W. Leisenring,
> Oakley House, Bloomsbury St., W.C.

★

The memoirs of Baron Rosenkrantz about work at Dornach continue:

We became aware that the building with its architecture, forms and colours, with eurythmy, mystery dramas and lectures should become a reflection of the spiritual world brought down into human experiences. One could meditate for many hours about what the thoughts behind the building expressed, without getting more than a partial understanding of what it really represented. Rudolf Steiner himself said he knew what objections could be brought forward against the building's architecture. It was just a first effort in this new way of art.

People should not however think that everything was so rosy in our small community which wanted to serve the building. On the contrary, it was like a little mirror of every human weakness and mistake. Sometimes when personal frictions became too much of a good thing, Rudolf Steiner warned us by saying: 'Awkward spirits are surrounding the building and trying to penetrate through you. Beware that this does not happen.'

On one occasion a lady artist had great difficulties with a colleague with whom she had to co-operate. She told me how she had gone in tears to Rudolf Steiner and told him that it was impossible to work with him any longer. 'Then you deprive me of my hands,' he said. She went back to work, but had a very difficult time.

One evening when we came into the carpentry-shop, a little platform had been made where eurythmy students could practice, and performances take place as well. It could also be used for plays. Eurythmists came up in white robes with a stole. Later on, coloured veils were added and at times the robes themselves were coloured.

At the same time as the stage was set up in the carpentry-shop Rudolf Steiner started rehearsing scenes from Goethe's *Faust*. Members formed a small drama group. My personal experience as an actor did not last long. A devil was needed in the funeral scene, and I was asked to help out. I was quite willing because I didn't think it right to refuse when Rudolf Steiner needed someone. Two groups consisting of different kinds of devils had to try to get hold of Faust's soul. One type of devil was tall and thin, the other small and thick. I had to join the tall ones, being 1.73 metres. But as my gestures were better suited to the thick ones, my first and only dramatic performance was as a thick devil! The appearance lasted hardly a minute, otherwise I stayed behind scenes.

Rudolf Steiner very much appreciated proper feelings in the members. For important work he often preferred laymen to accomplished artists. 'Talent alone' did not determine his decisions.

I often received indications for artistic matters, and these have given me a deep knowledge of life . . .

The Future Knowledge

Marie Steiner (as she now was) wrote a letter to Captain Beauclerk. (A.S. = Anthroposophical Society. H-S. = Heywood-Smith. D-L. = Drury-Lavin.)

Novr. 6th 1915

Dear Captain Beauclerk,

Dr. Steiner has received your letter. I am sorry that circumstances did not permit me to answer earlier. As a member of the Central Committee of the A.S. it is my duty to answer the business side of your questions. The various groups of the Society are autonomous, & it rests with the President of the group to arrange the affairs of his group. Mr. H-S., being President of the Zarathustra Group, has arranged with Mrs. D-L. for her to conduct the group during his absence. If any difficulties arise it is for him to deal with them.

So much for the business side. Dr. Steiner sends you his very best greetings & hopes that you won't mind too much Mr. H-S.'s long absence, when he'll be able to bring back the science he gets here. It would be a good thing if he could remain here as long as the War lasts, as he can deepen his knowledge & then let his friends partake in it. Meanwhile Mrs. D-L. will provide the group with lectures, & if you would help her by supporting her work, things will go well, no doubt.

The actual task should be to make a thorough study of all the material which has been given until now. Upon this, when thoroughly assimilated, we'll be able to build up the future knowledge. Mr. H-S. by being here will have the possibility of forming a link between the past & the future.

Yours very sincerely,

Marie Steiner

⋆

Gladys Meyer reminisced in an article 'The Initiate and the Teacher', published in the 1958 number of *The Golden Blade*:

> In 1915, among many other books of an occult nature, I read *The Way of Initiation* in the British Museum Library. This was the only one that made a lasting impression. I had a curious feeling as though I knew all its contents already; it was utterly familiar.

This experience was to be followed by a long gap, for the reader did not meet the author of the book for another seven years.

⋆

The initials D.O. under the notice published in September 1912 in *The Vâhan* concerning Charles Lazenby's final lecture in the '*Secret Doctrine* Group' must have been those of Dorothy Osmond, who by the end of 1914 was also taking part in 'The Theosophical Forum'. Her full initials, D.S.O., reappear under an article in the issue for December 1915 concerning 'The London, Home Counties and Eastern Federation'.

Mr. D.N. Dunlop presided over a crowded meeting of the London Federation on Saturday November 13th. The subject of discussion was: 'Can actions in the physical world which are the outcome of distrust, hatred and enmity be counteracted by means other than those which result in action on the same plane? If not, how can peace and goodwill be translated into positive action on the physical plane?'

Mr. Sinnett, Mrs. Ransom, Mr. Gardner, Mr. Loftus Hare and the General Secretary all contributed much of interest to an excellent discussion.

Mr. Dunlop, after briefly summarizing the speeches made, said in concluding that the forces of evil have no power on this plane except through man himself, and many other wars must of necessity arise so long as there exist false doctrines in the mind of man. 'If we are to have peace, we shall want militant armies for peace, and vague hosts of unformulated thought about goodwill and the like have little effective result so far as physical-plane action is concerned. The practical alchemist is the man whose consciousness is operative on the levels where the great Companions are to be found, where the presence of the Master is felt and His touch becomes the inspiration of life, as He contacts matter and stimulates its evolution. It is only by exercising energy in accordance with the love that is behind the universe that man can become conscious of how to array his divine powers against those forces which are inimical to human progress.

'Out of the heart of man, Babylons have arisen. But as the outcome of false doctrine, planetary cataclysms have come to pass. Therefore the destiny of the world can only lie in the hands of humanity itself, and humanity includes all the great ones who have clothed themselves in bodies provided by the human race. The gods war over us for ever; it is we ourselves who declare them victors or vanquished.'

A business meeting was held at 6 p.m. The reports of the Secretary and Treasurer were read and adopted...

The same issue contained a notice from George Arundale:

I am glad to be able to announce that Mr. D.N. Dunlop has kindly consented to give a Christmas Eve lecture at Headquarters on December 24th at 6 p.m. His title will be 'The Story of Jesus'.

There will be some good music during the evening. All Fellows of the Theosophical Society cordially welcomed.

★

During this year Harry Collison brought out as a pamphlet the lecture given by Rudolf Steiner in Berlin on 13 December 1907, entitled *Christmas*. It was again published by John M. Watkins.

Perhaps in Time

In January 1916 *The BEAMA Journal* opened with another unsigned article by D.N. Dunlop, entitled 'Protection for National Progress':

> What is a national policy? A national policy is never framed except by a strong, coherent nation, one that has become self-conscious of its national aims and ideals.
>
> A nation's ideals are formulated slowly by the people and are accepted often merely tacitly, until a crisis arises to threaten them, either from within or without. Then the nation may make its ideals articulate and declare that it will find means to protect its cherished traditions and to preserve its peculiar individuality. A nation will rise in this way as one man when danger threatens, just as an individual or a class will seek to protect himself or itself against aggression from others.
>
> Individuality is strengthened by such encounters. But no one who has reached any degree of intelligence will go out of his way to provoke a trial of strength. The natural laws of evolution will provide these tests. Bullies and professional fighters are of a low grade of intelligence. Fanatics and unbalanced 'reformers' view the world from a narrow angle of vision.
>
> Amongst modern nations, Germany has proved to be the bully, the professional fighter and fanatic *par excellence*. Great Britain with her larger understanding of individual freedom as an essential for progress has been content as a nation to let her ideals take care of themselves, not suspecting the danger to them from a determined fanatic among the nations. The fighter-nation has now come out into the open, and we know its method. But time and energy will be wasted if we spend them devising means of retaliation. No nation can teach another, none can learn for another. Each learns only by experience. Therefore methods of revenge will not promote our own national security. They will but perpetuate antagonism.
>
> Our ethical and moral standards are such that reprisals, merely as vindictiveness, cannot be used by any self-respecting man today. Neither can a nation such as ours stoop to methods of retaliation. We must not be anti-German. *We must be pro-British*!

There followed a section headed 'The Motive for Protection':

Our motive should be to develop our nation and the British Empire. It must not be to crush any other nation, not even Germany. Each nation may be left to reap what it has sown, and Germany will suffer the consequences of her ridiculous desire to dominate the world and to impose her standards on others. And we should suffer also if we violated the law that universally operates to give individuals the right to develop.

This war is being fought to preserve this principle—to prevent one nation from dominating others by efforts for 'supremacy'. It is very loose thinking, therefore, to advocate, as many do, 'a war for *commercial supremacy*' to follow the cessation of military hostilities. This would be only to fall into the same sin as Germany, and ultimately to become corrupted by greed and lust of power.

We maintain our navy as a means of *defence*, not for aggression; it *protects* commerce. But further protective measures are necessary if our commerce is not to be taken from us slowly and insidiously, along with standards of commercial conduct and of high-class products. The navy would then have nothing to protect and would soon perish for lack of maintenance.

Universal free trade is undoubtedly the ideal for the world, and it must be kept in view even while nations adopt methods of protection and security which are necessary among unequally civilized races. Each nation finds free trade within its different divisions beneficial. The rapid growth of the German Empire was assisted by the abrogation of tariffs between her various states. In the United States tariffs between them would make business very difficult, and hamper industry. But in Germany and the United States, as also in other countries, there is no antagonism in thought between the internal states and provinces to seek expression in obstructive tariffs. They are consolidated amongst themselves in national sentiment.

The nations of the world, however, do not yet feel the security against aggression from each other, and until they do they will not recognize the advantage of free international trading and be willing to adopt it as a national policy. It is indeed probable that they will enter upon a period of high commercial tariffs, almost in competition as to who can raise the highest wall. They would arrive at a point then when they would begin to bargain with one another to lower these barriers, and perhaps *in time* the nations would learn how necessary they are to each other; how they stand or fall together; and how humanity really requires mutual exchange and mutual toleration amongst its members if it is to advance to its high destiny.

In the meantime Great Britain would be in a stronger position to negotiate with other nations for reciprocal reductions if she could protect herself against unjust aggression, not only by her navy and army, but also by a tariff.

An army and navy are necessary at present to preserve and strengthen national interests. As the army and navy are supported by commerce a tariff is equally necessary in order to protect commerce, to preserve the navy and to strengthen the nation.

This is the true justification of protective tariffs which aim to *protect* national industries and to assist in maintaining a commercial balance amongst the nations, so that each will have an equal chance and none will crush others.

Every nation has a right to live, if it respect the same right for others. But the object and motive of Germany's high protective tariffs were far other than this. These walls were erected to build up the German Empire *in order to use its power for conquest.* Nevertheless the same weapon may be used with fundamentally different motives, even as our purpose in military execution is diametrically opposite to Germany's aim.

The Courage to Dare

During 1916 D.N. Dunlop collected his series of articles contributed in 1914/15 to *The Vahan*, and published them, slightly expanded, under the title *Studies in the Philosophy of Lorenz Oken.* The booklet, in the same format as *Symbols of Magic,* was 'set into type and printed by Winifred A. Parley at the Sunnyside Press, Wimbledon, London'.

Another work by Dunlop which appeared in this year was *The Path of Attainment*, brought out by 'The Path Publishing Company, Oakley House, Bloomsbury St., London, W.C.', but 'Printed by R. & R. Clark, Limited, Edinburgh.' It is possible that the latter firm was run by the Scottish family of Margaret Lazenby, herself now resident in Canada.

The book was prefaced by a foreword from George Arundale:

> The H.P.B. Lodge of the Theosophical Society is to be congratulated both on the publication of the addresses gathered together in the present volume, and on the choice of lecturer to deliver them. Mr. Dunlop asks us to remember in these times of stress and turmoil that the great Fathers of the world watch over us as they have ever done, that there is open to us the same ancient and narrow way to communion with them as has existed from time immemorial, testimony to the existence of which may be found in the scriptures of every world religion. We are told of the existence of Masters, our Elder Brethren, those who have learnt the lessons we are learning now, and who have dedicated themselves to the task of guiding us along the road their feet have already trodden. We are told of some of the conditions whereby we may become apprenticed to these Great Ones, so as to learn more swiftly the lessons appropriate to our class in the school of life in the world. We are told of the great expansions of consciousness—called initiations—marking our progress in apprenticeship, expansions of

consciousness which involve an ever-increasing, active understanding of the unity of all life.

Great truths these, and perhaps only for the few who dare to climb to the summit of the mountain by the rough, little-trodden path, rather than follow the well-beaten road of far longer—though easier—ascent. But some of us hope that the trials through which we are passing are giving to many the courage to dare. We are beginning to long to see the summit, at least to be reassured of its existence. We had indeed almost forgotten the goal. Now we are in the mists, that we may once again bethink ourselves of a summit whose attractive power depends upon its being veiled from time to time from constant though oft unseeing gaze.

Out of the mists comes the voice of one who tells us what has been known to the wise of all time, and reminds us of what all the world will some day realize. As one who also has seen the way, not unlike the path herein described, allow me to endorse his invitation to tread that path. The way is steep, the obstacles rough and piercing. The feet indeed do bleed, but the heart of the wanderer rejoices in all sacrifice that brings him to the radiant sunshine of eternal life.

George S. Arundale,
General Secretary of the Theosophical Society
in England and Wales.

★

On the next page was an author's note:

This book contains three addresses, originally delivered before the H.P.B. Lodge of the Theosophical Society at 19 Tavistock Square, W.C., in October, November and December 1915. I have been urgently requested to publish the reports made by a stenographer, and have therefore hurriedly revised them for press. The substance however remains unchanged, and I sincerely hope that readers will find suggestions in the ideas presented, and will pursue their investigations by studying the works of H.P. Blavatsky and examining their philosophical and scientific basis.

D.N.D.

★

The three addresses were entitled 'Adepts, Masters and Mahatmas', 'The Path of Discipleship', and 'Initiation'.

At the front of the book, at any rate in some copies, was also a list of 'Errata' stating that quotation marks indicating extracts from the *Commentary on the Comte de Gabalis* should precede and follow three designated passages—one in 'The Path of Discipleship' and the other two in 'Initiation'—and that the publishers regretted these omissions.

Recognition by Intelligent Individuals

The third work which D.N. Dunlop brought out in this year, again through the Path Publishing Company, was *British Destiny,* subtitled 'The Principles of Progress'.

It opened with an introduction:

> The contents of this volume consist partly of articles that have appeared during the past year in a quarterly periodical; all but one have been rewritten, and two entirely new chapters have been added. I feel, however, that the philosophical conceptions which are the basis of this brief examination of the principles operating in human life are worthy of a more leisured and careful treatment than my present business activities permit. But as ideas are important at the present moment, they are published forthwith for the consideration of all who have at heart the well-being of the British nation and of the Empire.
>
> The rise and fall of civilizations has always interested and puzzled historians; but the ordinary ethnological interpretation of races does not explain this phenomenon, nor give any hint of the meaning of human evolution. Races overlap and intermingle, and competent students of history have pointed out that no race is absolutely pure. The origin of races is obscure, and however far back we trace them, they are found to be blended. Political areas are always composed of more or less mixed races. Indeed, the ties of race are seldom as strong as love of country and civil rights. Fewer wars have been precipitated by racial passions than by other causes, such as political ambitions and desire for religious or political liberty. Race hatred is the result of war rather than the cause. Racial passions may be stirred up by political leaders for their own ends, but nations or empires that come under the dominance of such passions become dismembered and decline, unless a unifying principle be invoked and recognized in time. Men of different races associate in adherence to a political idea, and if the idea be a reflection of a pure ideal and be untinged by racial or class passions, it may include many races, as illustrated in the British Empire. The unity amongst the diverse races and peoples in all parts of this Empire has been realized through the power of an abstract idea, viz. voluntary co-operation for principles.
>
> At certain crises in its affairs a nation has the choice of two paths, and it is within its power to follow either. The fate of the nation depends on whether it take the path of its decline, or follow the direction that leads to the realization of its true destiny. On the downward path the disintegrating forces have full sway, and personal, class, or racial ambitions become stronger than national or imperial interest. The unifying principles depend for expression on their recognition by intelligent individuals. When understood they provide fully for individual freedom and initiative, and co-

ordinate all the diverse elements of the national and imperial life in a voluntary co-operation, so that they become the medium for the transmission of a higher intelligence. No nation has yet sufficiently fused the elements of antagonism within itself to enable it to completely fulfil its destiny. But as all the terrestrial elements may be a medium for the transmission of light, so the elements of man's complex life should be a medium for intelligence.

The co-operation of all minds, each exercising its own particular powers, renews the intelligence latent in the universe and available for each.

The 'antagonism' in Nature between earth, air, fire and water maintains the world. The 'antagonism' in man's body, between muscles, bones and nerves is necessary for his physical existence. But in Nature this individualizing antagonism does not destroy the unity. On the contrary, it emphasizes the interdependence of one part upon another.

The true function of any one class or type is maintained by the interrelations of all.

The prophet depends upon mystics to realize his message by personal experience in every environment, upon philosophers to develop its principles by thought, upon artists to universalize its appeal, upon scientists and inventors to provide the means to carry it into practical effect, upon executives to establish economic and political systems for making the spiritual life serve the day's work instead of being at odds with it, and finally upon men of action to shape the material world in conformity with the message and vision of the prophet. When man no longer disregards the truths which a study of Nature's laws reveals, he will recognize the necessity for co-ordinating all his affairs in conformity with these laws. He will recognize the spiritual unity of the race at one pole, and at the other his interdependence, as a physical being, on other men.

If the British Empire can maintain the unity so far realized, and extend the application of the principles it involves, it will fulfil its destiny and lead other nations to a recognition of the laws which must be observed for the creation of a world civilization.

D.N. Dunlop

March 1916.

★

Harry Collison too was engaged on further literary work. He wrote a pamphlet on anthroposophy entitled *The New Impulse and the New Era*, published again by John M. Watkins.

And during the same month when Dunlop was writing his introduction to *British Destiny*, Collison was composing a preface to the first translation of the work originally entitled in English *The Philosophy of Freedom*, to be brought out by Putnams:

The following pages are a translation of Dr. Steiner's *Philosophie der Freiheit*, which was published in Germany some twenty years ago. The edition has never been reprinted; copies are much sought after but very difficult to obtain.

The popularity of Dr. Steiner's later works upon ethics, mysticism and kindred subjects has caused people to forget his earlier work upon philosophy, in spite of the fact that he makes frequent references to this book, and it contains the germs of which many of his present views are the logical outcome. For the above reasons, and with the author's sanction, I have decided to publish a translation.

I have had the good fortune to secure as joint translators Mrs. Hoernlé and her husband Mr. R.F. Alfred Hoernlé, Assistant Professor of Philosophy at Harvard University, U.S.A., their thorough knowledge of philosophy and complete command of the German and English languages enabling them to overcome the difficulty of finding adequate English equivalents for the terms of German philosophy.

I am glad to seize this opportunity of acknowledging my indebtedness to these two, without whom this publication could not have been undertaken.

Harry Collison
March 1916.

★

In an article published in the *Basler Nachrichten* on 30 March 1932, the French anthroposophist Jules Sauerwein recalled:

> The wartime was very hard for Steiner. He suffered the same fate as always befalls those who tell the truth to a humanity torn by passions: he was attacked by both sides. A great number of Germans regarded him as a traitor, while many Frenchmen and Englishmen—headed by the significant mystic Schuré—indignantly announced their resignation from the Society.

Edouard Schuré's resignation took place on 30 March 1916.

For Discerning Students

In the April issue of *The Vahan* D.N. Dunlop published an article entitled 'The Master and His Pupils Celebrate the Easter Festival'. It was subtitled 'Part I'.

> On the first day of the Easter Festival, the pupils approached the Master and said to him: 'We desire to celebrate the Easter Festival with You. Where do You wish to go and make the necessary preparations?' He called aside two of His pupils and said to them: 'Go to the gate at the West and you will meet

there a man carrying a water-pitcher [A footnote stated: 'Symbolizing the Regent of Aquarius']. Follow him and say to the owner of the house he enters: 'The Master desires the use of a room in which He may celebrate the Easter Festival with His pupils.' He will show you a room on the upper floor which may be made ready [another footnote stated: 'The sign of Pisces']. The two pupils did as desired, and made the necessary preparations for the Feast.

In the evening, the Master went with His twelve pupils to the house at which the preparation for the Festival had been made. As they sat at table, the Master took a loaf of bread, and blessed it. Breaking the loaf in twelve pieces, He gave a portion to each of His pupils, saying: 'This is the symbol of My resurrection body, which I have portioned among you.' He then took the cup, and filled it with wine and held it up, saying: 'This is the symbol of My life in My eternal vesture. I shall not drink again of this wine until my final initiation.'

The Master then tasted the wine, and passed it to two of His pupils. Before they drank of the cup, they said to him: 'Master, grant us this favour: that one be seated on your right and one on your left hand, when You are crowned in Your glory.' The Master replied: 'Can you both pass through the ordeal which I am about to undergo?' On their answering in the affirmative, the Master continued: 'You shall drink of the cup which I drink, and take part in the psychic ritual with Me, but the places of authority on My right hand and My left hand are assigned to those for whom they have been prepared by My Father. In the Mystery drama there are two principal gates, the gate of Birth through which souls descend into generation, and the gate of Death through which souls ascend to the Heaven-world. You I have appointed to be the Wardens of these two gates, and I shall give you the keys both of the generative sphere and of the Heaven-world, and whatever soul you may seal with the inheritance of the Father in the Heaven-world shall descend to the Earth, and whatever soul you may set free on Earth shall ascend consciously to the Father's house.'

Then the two pupils drank of the cup, and passed it to the other pupils, who all drank of the wine of spiritual intoxication.

The Master continued His instruction concerning the functions of the twelve ruling Powers: 'Among you, My pupils, no one should seek to domineer over another. As brothers and sisters you are of equal rank, and I am in the midst as One who is Servant of all. When I become initiated into the final Mystery and enter the solar body prepared for Me, you shall sit on twelve thrones, and rule over the twelve great regions.' As they were reclining at table, He explained to them the solitude of the great ordeal through which He had to pass. 'This night one of you will, in fulfilment of your duty, hand me over to the final ordeal which is symbolized by this festival.' But the pupils did not understand that He referred to the complete abstraction of the highest of the sacred trances; they were sorrowful and each said to Him: 'I hope it is not I.'

The Master replied: 'It is one of the five: he who eats with me from the same bowl. And this very night you will all forsake Me.' One of the pupils, more impetuous than the others, said to Him: 'Although the others desert You, yet I shall not.' The Master replied: 'This night, before the cock crows twice, you will deny Me thrice.' [A footnote stated: 'The solar bird—the symbol of the higher self in man'.] But the pupil strongly protested, and declared: 'I shall never deny You, even if it is necessary for me to die with You.' All the pupils made the same declaration. And when they had chanted the parting hymn, they left the upper room, and went as usual to the olive-tree hill.

When they reached the sacred enclosure at the top of the hill, the Master said to His pupils: 'Sit here, while I go to the altar surrounded by the trees, for meditation.'

He took with Him two of His pupils, and they both observed that He was absorbed in contemplation. The Master said to them: 'Abide here, and do not sleep. My soul is isolated, as at the hour of Death.' He went to the altar and entered into deep meditation at the solitude. When He returned, He found both of His pupils asleep. He said to them: 'Awake! Could you not remain awake a single hour? Keep watch, lest you fail in this ordeal. The spirit is willing, but the physical body is frail.'

Again the Master went to the altar. When He returned He again found them asleep, and awakened them, repeating the same words. He went a third time, and on returning said to them; 'I have been in the consciousness of the Causal Body at the divine Centre; soon I shall be free from Death. My hour is fast approaching. Arise, let us be going; for he who hands Me over is near.' As the Master was speaking Judas came, followed by a crowd armed with swords and clubs, sent by the Chief Priest. Judas had arranged a signal with them. 'The one I kiss,' he said, 'is the man. Take Him and lead Him away safely.' And going up to the Master he said: 'Master, Master!' and kissed Him affectionately. The Master said to him: 'Judas, perform the duty assigned to you.' Then they laid hands on the Master, and arrested Him. He said to the guards: 'When I taught in the Temple day by day, you dared not raise your hands against Me. This is the hour when the Powers of Darkness reign.' He turned to them, and said gently: 'Lay aside your weapons. I am not a robber.'

All His pupils left Him and fled, save Judas, who tried to go along with Him. Judas, who handled the sacred objects, wore a linen cloth as his only garment. The guards tried to arrest him, but he fled naked, leaving the veil in their hands. The Master was led to the Council of priests, elders and scribes, to be tried. Simon, one of His pupils, had entered the court in advance, and was sitting with the officials, warming himself by the fire.

Meanwhile the High Priest and the entire Council was seeking evidence against the Master, to justify inflicting on Him the penalty of Death. Many witnesses gave false testimony against Him, saying: 'We have heard Him say: "I will pull down this temple made by human hands, and in three days I shall build another by supernatural means."' But even as to this, their statements were inconsistent. The High Priest became impatient, and said abruptly to the Master: 'You have heard the testimony against You. Have you no answer to make?' But the Master remained silent. The High Priest continued to interrogate Him: 'You claim to be the Son of God, and King of the star-strewn Universe, do you not?' 'You have said it,' replied the Master.

Rending his garments, the High Priest said to the Council: 'He asserts His divinity! What further proof is necessary? You have heard His blasphemous claim. What is your decision?' They answered unanimously: 'He deserves the death penalty.' The guards then blindfolded the Master, and struck Him with open hands, saying: 'Prove your power of psychic vision. Tell who it is that struck you.' Meanwhile, Simon was below in the quadrangle. One of the High Priest's servant girls came, and seeing Simon warming himself, she looked at him closely and said: 'You were one of His companions, were you not?' But he denied it, saying: 'What are you talking about?' Simon went out into the porch—into the shadow. Just then a cock crowed. The servant girl followed him, and said to the people standing by: 'This man is one of His pupils.' Again he denied it. Soon after, the bystanders approached Simon and said: 'Your peculiar speech betrays you. You are certainly one of His followers.' But he declared: 'I do not know the man.' When he had spoken, the cock crowed a second time. Simon, recalling the Master's words, 'Before the cock crows twice, you will deny Me thrice,' gave way to bitter tears.

I have consulted various authorities, and have written this for discerning students of the Christian Mystery.

D.N.D.

★

No further part ever followed, but the next issue of *The Vahan* recorded an 'Easter Meeting':

At the combined meeting of the Blavatsky, H.P.B., Union and Central London Lodges held on April 19th, Mr. Dunlop gave an address on 'Easter' which inspired all who were able to be present. He took the story of the Crucifixion and Resurrection as a great drama of initiation, describing the various acts and scenes with a power of mystical insight which we have learnt to associate with him, leading up to the final victory of spirit over matter as symbolized in the Resurrection on Easter Sunday. It was a sacred subject, treated with dignity and beauty, and music enhanced the devotional character of the meeting.

The Wider and More Transcendent Vision

The present chapter reproduces various items from 1916 issues of *The Vahan*.

The first one, in the May issue, was headed 'Theosophical Holiday School':

> Intending visitors are reminded that it *is absolutely necessary* to book at once. Owing to the situation and remoteness from the Zeppelin area the accommodation in Cornwall is very much in request and disappointment will be inevitable unless rooms are secured without delay.
>
> If an adequate number of bookings have not been returned by the middle of May the School will have to be abandoned.
>
> Further particulars may be had from the Hon. Secretary, Theosophical Holiday School, 19, Tavistock Square, London, W.C.

The same issue carried a notice on 'Brotherhood of Arts, Crafts and Industries':

> Public meetings will be held in the Temporary Hall, 10, Tavistock Square, London, W.C. (by arrangement with the Theosophical Society) at 8.15 on the following dates: . . .
>
> Tuesday, May 16. Lecture: 'The Theatre of Beauty', by W.B. Yeats.
>
> . . . All lectures are free, and a hearty welcome is extended to visitors . . .

Another notice was on 'H.P.B. Lodge':

> The H.P.B. Lodge has arranged a syllabus of lectures during the summer months on the Mystical Tradition in the West, following the plan adopted in the spring of one general heading under which the separate lectures fall. Mr. Stanley Redgrove, Chairman of the Alchemical Society, will appear, it is believed for the first time, at our Headquarters, speaking on 'The Mystical Basis of Alchemy', on May 17th, and we are very glad to welcome him. He will have much to teach us on a subject which of necessity has a great attraction for theosophists. Mr. D.N. Dunlop will speak on 'The Teaching of Jesus the Christ' and 'Mystic Masonry' on May 10th and June 7th respectively, and both lectures we hope will ultimately be published. Members would do well to arrive in good time for these lectures, for experience has taught us that whenever Mr. Dunlop's name appears on a syllabus the Hall is crowded to overflowing.

The Annual Meeting of the Northern Federated Lodges was held in Bradford on Saturday and Sunday, May 13th and 14th, when owing to the departure for India of the General Secretary, Mr. Dunlop of London was our distinguished visitor.

In order to bring the resources of the Federation into a more efficient organization, a new set of rules was discussed ... About eighty-five F.T.S. attended the Conference.

In the evening Mr. Dunlop gave a most stirring address on the three objects of the Society, dealing with his subject in his own charming and original fashion, and with a catholicity of sympathy which embraces all effort as well as recognizes all achievement.

In the afternoon a combined Lotus and Order of the Star meeting proved of intense interest, as did the evening lecture on 'Individualism and Co-Operation', delivered by Mr. Dunlop to an almost too crowded audience.

★

The June issue carried a notice on 'The London, Home Counties and Eastern Federation':

At a meeting of the above Federation held in the Temporary Hall on May 20th, Mr. Dunlop was unanimously elected President ...

Reports were received ...

After tea, during which some excellent music was provided by Mrs. Mann and Mr. Foulds, Major Graham Pole gave a most practical and inspiriting address on Theosophy in daily life ...

In response to a general request, Mr. Dunlop followed up Major Graham Pole's address. 'Brotherhood,' he said, 'exists in its fullest conception on the higher planes of consciousness, and whether it is made actual on the physical plane depends upon us. The unified state of consciousness which brotherhood implies is hindered in its functional expression by personal desires and distorted mental conceptions, and the eternal task before the race is so to polarize the conflicting elements of matter that the light of the wonderful unity of all life may flood the Earth with a new radiance.'

A few days after Dunlop had given his lecture on 'Mystic Masonry', the Society's Twenty-Sixth Annual Convention took place, on 10, 11 and 12 June. Here is a report of a meeting on the 12th:

On Monday afternoon Mr. Jinarajadasa presided over a meeting held under the joint auspices of the Theosophical Society and the Order of the Star in the East. Lady Emily Lutyens opened a discussion under the title of 'Assuming the coming of a World Teacher, how do we think that he will present his message?' ...

Mr. Dunlop: 'I believe that the Christ has never left the life of this planet from the moment He entered it, that every word of power is from Him, that every beautiful work of art which symbolizes some of the realities of the soul's life is inspired by His presence. I believe that Mrs. Besant is inspired by him, and that every sincere effort is an expression of His life. Great teachers will incarnate again among men, but we cannot tell by what mysterious ways the Lodge will prepare for their coming. Be certain that you know the marks of a Master, and that symbols of authority conferred from without do not lead you away from the reality, which may be developing in obscurity all the time. It is not probable that a Master will rise amid the seats of the mighty, but that in many village Bethlehems human hearts will begin to feel that sacred presence which cannot be described in terms of the senses. "Before man can find the true Master, he must lose Him. When He is lost to every sense then the One Flame arises, pure as before the beginning of worlds".'

A further meeting took place that same evening:

Major Graham Pole presided over the final meeting of the Convention on Monday evening, and for over two hours a spirited discussion took place on 'Theosophy and the World Crisis'.

Mr. Sinnett: 'Long ago in the history of the world, there were some in Atlantis who looked upward with desire towards the power they saw exercised by certain great beings guiding the progress of that early world. They craved such power for selfish purposes, and that was the beginning of the development of the Dark Host now combating the divine idea of evolution in this great struggle which is now going on in Europe. This war is not a war merely of soldiers or of nations, it is a war of principles, and that is why those of us who understand the thing have no doubt as to what the final result will be. For evil in the end must be vanquished by good. The Divine Power which presides not merely over this world, but over that mightier cosmos of which this solar system is a part, does not mean that this world shall be wrecked, but means to intervene, if necessary, in order to put the finishing stroke to the victory that must be won sooner or later.'

Mr. Dunlop: 'I welcome the majestic, satanic powers referred to by Mr. Sinnett, because only through the play of these pairs of opposites can man attain the power of individuality. I do not regard the Germans as being the sole agents of the Powers of Darkness. I think that men and women in every nation are agents for the exercise of such powers, if they give them recognition and the opportunities they seek. We all have our prejudices, imposed upon us by the particular bodies we happen to be using during this incarnation, but there is in the world another race of beings who are not labelled British or German or French or Austrian or Russian, but who look at things from the point of view of cosmic evolution. I believe that the best way to be a friend to your own country is to stand above its passions and racial enmities, and try to look at things with the wider and more transcendent vision of that keen-eyed Brotherhood who are above racial and national prejudices.

'An exercise of meditation, a little discipline develops within us the power to know for ourselves these things. I always suspect messages given through mediums, when through the vision of your own soul you can rise and come into contact with the Powers of Light about which you read. What good are we going to be to any Master if we have not developed the powers of our own being? The opposing powers are there to develop them, so that in the end we shall have a self to lay down in the service of Those who are standing as a guardian wall around humanity. Germany will have her place at the Round Table with the rest of us, and I am praying that England will take a sane, strong view of the situation, and that some of the Masters' influences will be felt at that Council so that a system will be built up which will do much to remove poverty and wretchedness and the limitations which hamper the true relation of men and women with each other. Peace must forge for itself a sword of strength if it is to build cosmos out of the chaos of the present crisis.'

The June issue contained a further notice on 'Theosophical Holiday School', subtitled 'Carbis Bay, Cornwall, July 29th to August 12th':

A sufficient number of applications have now been received to warrant the holding of the Holiday School and arrangements are being proceeded with.

Intending members are reminded that each week's delay in booking will add to the difficulty of procuring accommodation, as Carbis Bay, being in the Zeppelin-free area, is much sought after this year.

Particulars and application forms may be had from the Hon. Secretary, Theosophical Holiday School, 19, Tavistock Square, London, W.C.

On Different Lines

The story turns again to the surviving derivative of the Order of the Golden Dawn. For although the Alpha et Omega under 'Macgregor' Mathers and the Independent and Rectified Rite under A.E. Waite had as such closed down in 1914, the Stella Matutina under Robert Felkin continued its activities right through the War years. By November 1915 the number of members in this Order had risen to over 80.

In the following year, however, Felkin himself, now aged 63, decided to emigrate altogether to New Zealand. Before his final departure from Britain, he drew up a new constitution for the Stella Matutina. The main part of this document has of course no relevance to the present work, but one section does have some interest, namely, the last one, concerning 'The Daughter Temples'.

(R. = Rosicrucian; S.M. = Stella Matutina; R.R. et A.C. = Rosae Rubeae et Aureae Crucis; V.H. = Very Honoured; E.O.L. = 'Ex Oriente Lux', the motto of the deceased Neville Meakin; S.R. = 'Sacramentum Regis', the motto of A.E. Waite; T.A.M. = Theoricus Adeptus Minor.)

As you are aware, I can personally permit any Branch R. Societies to be started. But as I am leaving England, I naturally feel that such branches should be in close relationship with the S.M. and the R.R. et A.C. I propose before leaving England to form three such branches, and it will rest with you to make any arrangements you may wish with regard to their utilizing your rooms etc., or not. I think you would do well to do so, as it would help your financial position. The two I propose to form in London could pay you a yearly sum for the use of the Temple and Vault, on definite day to be settled by you, or you might arrange for them to pay half their initiation fees to you, which should be, I think, the Mother Temple.

With regard to a branch in Bristol which I am going to form, they can at present work their Outer entirely there, and make arrangements with you when they have any candidates for the Inner.

The conditions under which I should found these three branches are as follows:—

1. Each Branch must be absolutely autonomous and ruled by three Chiefs, who are at present time full 5–6 in the R.R. et A.C., and they must follow exactly the traditions of our Order.

2. The first three Chiefs I should appoint myself. If any one of them should relinquish office, the Ruling Chiefs and Three Adepti of the Mother Temple should confer with the remaining two Chiefs as to the appointment of a successor.

3. The Daughter Temples must finance their own Temples, and the Mother Temple is not responsible for their finance in any way, except in so far as above stated they should pay dues in some form if they make use of the Mother Temple's rooms.

4. The members of the Daughter Temples who are full 5–6 will belong to the College of Adepti of the R.R. et A.C. in Anglia, and as such will receive notice of the general meetings of the College, unless it should happen that the Daughter Temples become so strong that they can erect and work Vaults of their own. Until this happens, their responsibility to the Inner will be the same as that of the members of the Mother Temple.

5. With regard to the Bristol Branch, the first Three Chiefs will be:—

V.H. Sorores Lux Orta est, Magna est Veritas, Benedicamus Deo, the latter only acting until a Frater in that district is qualified.

6. The first London Daughter Temple will be confined to members of the Societas Rosicruciana in Anglia, who have taken at least Grade 4. I may mention here that the reason why I am obliged to form it is as follows:— When E.O.L. and I made our arrangements for recognition by our

Continental Fratres they stipulated and he agreed that the Masonic Rosicrucians, of whom there are large numbers, should be given the opportunity of being linked up with us. The first Three Chiefs of this Temple will be:—

V.H. Fratres Pro Rege et Patria, Fortes Fortuna Juvat, Faire sans dire.

With regard to the third Daughter Temple, there are some fifty or sixty members of the Temple which used to be ruled by S.R. and a number of members of the Anthroposophical Society who are seeking admission. It has been pointed out to me that as these people have worked on different lines from us it would not be well to admit them to S.M., as they would undoubtedly cause confusion in the S.M. Temple.

I therefore propose that they should form a Temple of their own, and that the first three chiefs should be:—

V.H. Fratres Cephas (probably, I have not got his definite consent, though he wishes to act), Benedic anima mea Domino and Non Sine Numine. This Frater you do not know, but he has been a member of the Society for 25 years, is a full T.A.M. and was for many years one of S.R.'s three Ruling Chiefs.

I take full responsibility for the formation of these three Daughter Temples, and it rests with you to do all in your power to help them be an added power to the Rosicrucian Movement.

Our password for the present six months is 'Achad', signifying 'Unity', and it is my great desire that all the scattered Rosicrucian forces within our reach should be gathered together into a harmonious whole, instead of drifting off into comparative uselessness, or into undesirable channels.

Finem Respice, Chief.
June 18th 1916

★

The first of these temples, in Bristol, was duly founded three weeks later, on 9 July, as Hermes Temple No. 28.[38] Two of its named chiefs were anthroposophists: 'Lux Orta Est' was Catherine Hughes and 'Magna est Veritas' her sister, Professor Millicent Mackenzie.

The third temple, in London, was to be known as 'Merlin Temple', a name obviously related to that of the anthroposophical Myrdin Group. Two of its proposed chiefs were again anthroposophists: 'Benedic anima mea Domino' was Harry Collison, leader of the Myrdin Group, and 'Non Sine Numine' Colonel Webber. There is however no record as to whether this temple was ever actually founded.

Deep Understanding and Earnest Devotion

Towards the end of July, Rudolf Steiner returned to Dornach after an absence of six months in Germany, mostly in Berlin. He found waiting for him Edouard Schuré's letter of resignation from the Anthroposophical Society.

A few days after his return, on the 30th of the month, Steiner gave a memorial address for the English member Ada Wilson, who had died during his absence.

My dear friends!

I was thinking yesterday how deeply satisfied I was to re-enter after a long time the place where our building is now standing. This satisfaction was mingled with a note of bitter sorrow, because among the dear friends who have worked faithfully and with ceaseless devotion to further our work at this site, Miss Wilson was no longer to be seen—is no longer to be seen—here on the physical plane. She belongs without any doubt to those beloved friends of ours the thought of whom on the part of such as remain behind on the physical plane cannot die away. These thoughts have been prepared by deep, proper and selfless work, by working with people who treat seriously this spiritual movement which is needed by the world, who treat it honestly and sincerely. Those who had close knowledge of Miss Wilson know what the Movement has lost—as far as the physical plane is concerned—by Miss Wilson having to depart from this physical plane. I feel bound to state that a deep sorrow entered the souls of all people outside who—thanks to communication from our friends here—learnt recently of Miss Wilson's departure from the physical plane. Miss Wilson stood inside our Movement in a manner which was always unassuming, but carried deep understanding and earnest devotion. This was not just because the Movement forms a stream of spiritual life which one's soul wants to take up. Miss Wilson also stood in our spiritual Movement with the deepest understanding for what it ought to be, wants to be, and has to be in the whole course of evolution, especially in the course of the spiritual evolution of mankind. Many of us will have known Miss Wilson as an exemplary person in our ranks for this kind of view of our Movement as a spiritual movement for the world. In this respect those who knew her will always find their way back to her in thoughts, but also rise up to her in feelings, since she now has to continue her existence in the spiritual worlds. Miss Wilson stood in our Movement in an active way, by giving help wherever she was able. Miss Wilson belonged to the people who take up our Movement with such a strong impulse that she was able to look beyond all the splits and divisions called forth among souls in our Movement by particular prejudices of our own times. Never ought or can such things happen if enough souls are present who, like Miss

Wilson, are aware of the priority of striving towards the spiritual impulse flowing through our Movement—striving towards it as something higher, uniting them in the face of all that comes divisively into our ranks from prejudices of the times. In this connection too, Miss Wilson is undoubtedly an exemplary person in our ranks. We want to hold firmly and loyally onto the thoughts which have started to bind us with Miss Wilson, to bind us in such a way that this link can never cease. A spiritual conviction can arise from our experience. We may say, and I hereby state, that we can count Miss Wilson, who is now working from spiritual worlds, among those souls to whom we shall always be able to look as to co-workers in the finest and most exalted sense. The sorrow felt by those who have known her is great, really great, because we no longer have her among us on the physical plane. Here on the physical plane we will no longer be able to live in that beautiful aura created by the loyal and friendly attitude with which Miss Wilson lived in our midst. But we want to build firmly and securely on thoughts which unite us further to her as a loyal, much-loved and highly appreciated co-worker from the spiritual world. We want to remain true to her, just as we are convinced that she will remain true to us, and that through our mutual respect and mutual discovery we shall remain united to this soul for all times for which human souls, once they have found each other, can remain united.

Dismembered with the World

During the First World War the 'particular prejudices of our times' touched on in Rudolf Steiner's address were in Britain especially hard for Germanophiles. Eleanor Merry, who already as a five-year-old child had in 1881 travelled with her family over to Germany to spend some months in Stuttgart, might justifiably be so described. She related:

> The strangest experience was to have lived, as a member of the English nation, having always taken Germany for granted not only as a close friend whom one visited frequently and joyfully, but as an indispensable fountain of beauty in her literature, her wonderful language, and above all her music, which was so inseparable and intimate a part of our national soul-life. And then to have it torn away, trampled upon and despised; to have thrust upon one a hideous caricature of that friend whose calmly beautiful features one had known for so long. And over the ruins of the friendship to find oneself carried along in a wave of national self-importance—seeing the urge of it pile up the vast majestic symbol of greatness: Britain's Empire. And everything else broken and suffering.
>
> During the War, and after, I could not feel myself really English. The frantic patriotism on all sides was disturbing rather than inspiring. It broke

the world into pieces; and the world should have been one. And as a human being one was dismembered with the world. One felt all the different nations suddenly emerging as separated, isolated entities out of a once slumbering wholeness. What was one's 'nationality' in reality?

A similar problem affected George Adams. He continued his reminiscences by describing the people with whom he was in contact during the war years:

In the summer of 1916 I joined the Emerson Group of the Anthroposophical Society in London. The meetings began with the verse 'From the luminous heights of the Spirit . . .', specially given by Dr. Steiner for this Group to its leader, Mrs. Cull, when it was founded a year or two before the War. She was a wise Scottish lady, daughter of Principal Tulloch of St. Andrews. In the mountains of Ceylon, before she met Rudolf Steiner, she made some acquaintance with Buddhist esotericism. She told me of the indescribable spiritual presence which she felt when she heard Rudolf Steiner in his lecture-cycles speaking of the Buddha.

To me as one of mixed descent (my father's father was German, my other three grandparents English) the War became a personal problem in a special sense. In my subjective feelings, however, my mixed descent played little part or none at all. Despite my German name I had no inhibitions in attending every conceivable kind of meeting, even those playing into political life. Everywhere I encountered the tolerance and good faith I inwardly expected—one of the good sides of English public life. If one opposed the leading stream in the midst of a war which was felt to be a struggle for life and death one certainly had trials to meet. And yet inner human convictions were respected and acknowledged. I was full of belief in the oneness and peaceful progress of mankind—an idealism no doubt far too easy, but sincere. It was a time when traditions of 19th century liberalism were still living. Lord Morley and others, believing the outbreak of war to have been avoidable, had resigned from the Asquith government. Bodies were formed, such as the 'Union of Democratic Control', with the resolve that methods of international intercourse should be so changed as to prevent the future occurrence of such catastrophes over the heads, as we thought, of the common people of either country. I myself naturally gravitated towards religious, pacifist and social-revolutionary movements, and was among those who refused military service. I mention these things because of the part they were to play in my first conversations with Dr. Steiner.

Through fellow-students at Cambridge I made the acquaintance of the family of Josiah Wedgwood, M.P. He, and also Mrs. Wedgwood (Ethel Bowen-Wedgwood—they were already separated at that time), received me with great kindness. Commander Wedgwood, as he then was, had been severely wounded in the Gallipoli campaign. He was an active member of the House of Commons, believing the War to be inevitable, yet not witholding sympathy and help from those who thought otherwise. He was the soul of chivalry, and had a deep and real belief in freedom. Like one of Rudolf Steiner's closest friends in Berlin in the 1890s, the Scottish-German poet John Henry Mackay, the Wedgwoods—though philosophic-anarchist rather than socialist in outlook—were followers of the social trend emanating from Henry George in America; they had some contact too with the Tolstoyan movement.

The connection between George Adams and Elizabeth Bowen-Wedgwood was to bear fruit for British anthroposophy at a later time.

★

A reminiscence of these years made by Rudolf Steiner in Norway in May 1923 belongs to the same atmosphere:

> The Anthroposophical Movement was founded from Berlin. It started out from Germany, and people joined it without any consideration of national or international connections, but purely out of the cause itself.
>
> During the War this already made for great difficulties. The English Society could only continue to exist during the War because the English simply did not say that they belonged to Germany; rather, they founded an English Anthroposophical Society...

Other than the pre-war notes about the Anthroposophical Society by Heywood-Smith, no record has survived in Britain about this foundation as such. Marie Steiner's letter of November 1915 to Captain Beauclerk tends to suggest that English anthroposophical groups were at that time still relatively independent from each other. Nonetheless, Rudolf Steiner's statement seems to imply that a national anthroposophical body, even if fairly nominal and loose in character, had come into existence in England during the course of the War, perhaps by about 1916.

The Revaluation of Life

The Vahan published in the autumn of 1916 a report of a 'Holiday School', signed by the initials M.S.

> Carbis Bay, especially when the weather is fine (and there was not one drop of rain from July 29 to August 12) is an ideal place for a Holiday School, and we were all most deeply grateful to Mr. Bibby for coming forward as guarantor and so making it possible to hold the School in this year of nervous and physical strain.

Miss Schlesinger's classes on the 'Occult Aspect of Music' were eagerly followed by an interested group of students, and Mr. Old's talks on astrology and his delightful personal reminiscences of Madame Blavatsky were greatly appreciated.

In grouping the lectures under the general title of 'The Revaluation of Life' it was thought that some ideas might be gathered from the various speakers which would be helpful, and perhaps lead to some practical action in the direction of reform in the future. Reform not necessarily along one particular line of service, but rather that those wishful to serve might be reinforced and bring an enlarged and vivified perception to their work.

Mr. Old in his lectures linked up cause and effect, showed part of the cosmic scheme of evolution as indicated in the teachings of alchemy and astrology, pointed out the path of development adopted by humanity (his remarks being enlarged and supplemented by Mr. Jinarajadasa) and showed the inevitable results of action.

Mr. Old strongly insisted that in spite of planetary conditions man was master of his fate. After the War he thinks there will be an opportunity for reform in many directions and it behoves us to think well, revalue life and its opportunities and be ready to go far in the direction of progress with the flowing tide.

The law of rhythm, expounded by Miss Pagan, also indicated that in accordance with another law advance will shortly be possible, and lamps should be trimmed and be kept burning so that, when the time comes, no chance will be passed by.

Fundamentally there is the control of thought. Most members of the Theosophical Society recognize the importance of the work and study of it, and Mr. Dunlop's careful notes were much appreciated, for he showed once again that thought might be made a much more potent force than it is at present. All actions begin in thought. All schemes that last begin in the mind, and in a humble effort on the part of one or two people. Gradually hard work, allied to thought, builds up something that is living and worthwhile. Madame Pogosky told us how her great work had been built up from very small beginnings.

But the soul of the artist is a living, burning thing, and the need for beauty is fundamental. We were told by Monsieur Delville, Madame Pogosky and Mr. Rawdon Briggs to create lovely things in colour, fabric and sound, and to tidy up the world that man has made so ugly and so untidy in various places. It is always worthwhile to make life beautiful, for it raises standards and feeds the soul.

Various methods of social and fiscal reform were touched on; Mr. Dunlop reviewed the commercial situation and pleaded for more co-operation and for competition for quality, instead of merely competition for gain. Each individual can practise co-operation in some direction, and if it were once a habit the illusions about rival interests and wars between classes and nations would soon cease.

Humanity will have to be saved very largely through its hands. For the mind's images of beauty must take concrete form, and the craftsman never mars or spoils the world. He loves all creative work, and the more skilful he is in his own line, the more he appreciates the work of others.

But besides the work of the mind and hand, the breath of the spirit must penetrate and consecrate all forms of matter. Mr. Jinarajadasa showed how the world of natural science obeys the law of the spirit and develops in accordance with it. Mrs. Despard in her exposition of *Prometheus Unbound* brought a breath of the 'divine fire', and Mrs. Baily and Mrs. Dunlop held up for us the benediction of love in life, that love which in its purity and selflessness is the greatest power of all.

Children of the great mother and father, we wander into Egypt and try all forms of pleasure, in order that we may gain that happiness which is the birthright of every human soul. We linger long, trying, testing, gaining experience in an infinity of ways, till like Parsifal we realize that love is the law and service is the only thing worthwhile. Once having realized that, we rejoice in nothing else. Out of the 'garden of desire' we bring that emblem of power the 'magic spear'. Possessing it, we can go forth to heal the wounds of humanity, and redeem the fallen. Once we turn our faces along that 'path which is retrograde', life is indeed revalued. It matters little what we do. All work is consecrated, all beautiful. Until the goal is won we fail and fall, but let us not watch our feet too closely. Keep the eyes fixed on the Grail, the Cup of Life that holds the mystic, purified heart of humanity, and when we come at last to add our own harmonized vibrations to that glorified whole 'the robe of glory' shall indeed be ours and the groping effort, the agony of striving and even the last sacrifice, which is losing life to find it, shall be well worth while.

Carbis Bay, where the Summer School was held, lies on the North Cornish coast far in the west beside St Ives, where the mainland narrows somewhat before the Land's End peninsula.

This spot is much further west than Tintagel, to which even Torquay lies nearer. Nonetheless the location on the north Cornish coast cannot but raise the possibility that if Dunlop did not visit Tintagel during the Summer School at Torquay in 1912 he may have done so on this occasion at Carbis Bay in 1916.

Take Hands and Promise Ourselves

Around this time, while in Britain the Theosophical Summer School was taking place in Cornwall, Albert E.S. Smythe in Canada wrote to H.W.

Percival in the United States, mentioning *inter alia* that he had noticed a (supposed) plagiarism by D.N. Dunlop from the *Comte de Gabalis*, and asking Percival whether he was bringing legal action against Dunlop and what his complaint was.

Percival replied in a letter dated 10 August 1916. He recounted to Smythe that several years previously he had noticed Dunlop's wholesale borrowings from his editorials in addresses published in *The Path* and had corresponded with him on the matter. He added:

> ... I will always be glad to have the editorials appearing in *The Word* made known but I did not intend that they should be changed as he saw fit...

After a brief mention of the shortened article series on the zodiac, he went on to discuss the 'literary burglary' in (the first half of) *The Basis of Friendship*. In the last few months Dunlop had sent him a copy of *The Path of Attainment*, where he noticed further 'mangled extracts' from his own editorials. He ended by stating that he would not bring legal action against Dunlop, but if the latter should continue to misrepresent and claim as his own articles from *The Word* he might take steps to make known in certain circles what Dunlop had done.

*

In Britain, *The Vahan* published some 'Reflections after the Summer School', signed with the initials N.P.

> In one sense we have not yet been sufficiently selfish. We have never had time to discover ourselves.
>
> Life might be compared to a long train journey which only rarely runs us into a tunnel. When it does so, then the lights are extinguished, the many passengers fade into darkness, and each is alone with his true self. And it is in order to familiarize man with his true self that the tunnels of solitude, illness and even death were built. At first there is darkness, but presently a glimmering, sympathetic glow reaches the traveller, and he realizes that it comes, not from the one sitting next to him, but from his own breast. Gradually the carriage fills with light, shining in soft synthetic vibration from all these fellow-voyagers. Now the train of life is, at present, passing through a long and terrible tunnel. It is cut deep, very deep, into the rock of self-existence. Our ears are deafened by the grinding roar of the wheels, the pulse of the engine seems one with the pulse of fate. Our eyes are blinded by the sparks that fly, but in the end, when we shall have succeeded in this discovery of ourselves, we shall come out of the tunnel and find ourselves in the terminus, where motion ceases.
>
> I am using these metaphors at present because one of these symbols of energy is rushing me further and further away from the Summer School at

Carbis Bay, away from a fortnight that was, to some extent, a reflection of what has been called the 'midsummer place of the soul'. It has been a reflection flung into some desert pool of that great land to which the soul is journeying; and though it is now behind us, I know that we are rushing on to the reality from which it was thrown, to that land of human fellowship of which our comradeship in Carbis Bay was only a foreshadowing. We have listened to words spoken by great hearts, and the question with which we are faced is this: shall we go back to the same old life of cramped deeds and words that was ours before the vision came? Did Pythagoras lead his pupils out into the silence, did Christ lead His disciples into the vineyards, for this? Nay, but the mirror of Heaven must be overflung on Earth, and it may yet be that with these words of strength and beauty there may have fallen a germ, a seed that will expand into a tree, whose leaves shall spread far into the outer spaces, till those who look up find the desert green! The law is that mind must precipitate itself into form, and where there have been great temples built with words shall there not be a crystallization into the shimmering arches of that city which all the poets have sought? How shall we begin? Perhaps by continuing this process of the polarization of our thought. During these summer days, we have been continually drawn and caught to beauty, love and truth even as the stars are caught in the great loving, comprehending arms of the ever-real.

Some of us may have seen visions, to others an aspiration deeper than sight may have been singing the song of true being. We have been taught to spell the fiery letters of the stars by those who have learned to turn the great blue leaves of the sky's scriptures, and we have been shown that man comprehends all these scriptures within himself. And so our thoughts have been continually polarized and drawn upwards.

Aspiration is the 'fearless eternal', spoken of in the 'Song of Life'. Thou art that Master which all the nations of the world go out to greet, but thou art so only when thou hast left thy life bound upon the altar, lighted by the blaze of worlds. Then the flame shall descend to the altar *from above* and unite thee with the one life. I do not know on what day it shall be given us, this knowledge of the one flame in ourselves, but if you have ever felt it in another, if you have watched the Universe behind the stars in another's eyes, and caught something of primordial gladness from his voice, then you will know that you are upon the way.

A deep and golden and ancient wisdom may have enveloped us where we little knew, or at most dimly sensed; the cliffs and the sands of Carbis Bay may have indeed been holy ground. We to whom this message was given must now arise and fight, bound as we are to the service of 'the golden gleaming genius, the Swan of Everlasting'.

Suggestions have been made as to the founding of a permanent Summer School. Shall we not call it the Earth? It is not too large, wherever there are dwellers; it is not too lowly, for it contains the Lord Himself. Shall we take hands and promise ourselves that this Earth shall be a permanent Summer School—ere we claim our peace?

The Human Race

The present chapter reproduces further notices from issues of *The Vahan* in late 1916.

The Autumn Conference of the London, Home Counties and Eastern Federation was held on September 29th, 30th, October 1st and 2nd, under the Presidency of Mr. Dunlop.

The meetings were held at the Temporary Hall, with the exception of the lectures on October 1st, which were given in the Small Queen's Hall, Langham Place.

The Business Meeting was held on Saturday afternoon, Mr. Dunlop in the chair... Brief reports of activities were given... The Council then discussed suggestions for the more efficient working of the Group system... In conclusion Mr. Dunlop strongly urged co-ordinated activity throughout London.

On Sunday morning Mr. Dunlop spoke to a large audience at the Small Queen's Hall, taking as his subject 'The Human Race'.

The effect of his address, which was full of breadth and vision, was heightened by the feeling of upliftment created by the extraordinarily sensitive and beautiful rendering of the music, which has become such a feature of our meetings. Mrs. Mann and Mr. Foulds are musical occultists whose influence is of deep and far-reaching importance, and the atmosphere created by them is but a forerunner of their achievements in the future. They are pioneers desiring and needing no advertisement of their work, but the gratitude of the Society is theirs.

Mr. Dunlop traced the gradual evolution of the human race from legendary time up to the present day. He described the beautiful appearance of the 'breath' race with their translucent spheres for bodies, a 'robe of glory' which surrounds the immortal being of man, and which may be seen even today by those who have spiritual vision. He spoke of the second or 'life' race, of the third or Lemurian, of the great fourth race and of Atlantis, until he came to the Aryan, our own race, the outcome of the others.

He reminded us that although we are in the fifth root race, yet we are only halfway on our journey back to the 'ancient green and imperishable land.'

'But what are mortal years to the brooding and eternal soul that has looked upon continents rising and falling since the existence of this star in space?'

He explained how skilfully consciousness has enshrined itself in the structure of the body, and stated that it required the deepest and most holy meditation to understand its mystery.

He said that all that would remain of these little civilizations of ours were great thoughts, great understandings and great conceptions, and that these would be our heritage 'because the universe itself exists for the purposes of the soul.'

Readers may think back eleven years previously, to 1905, when Rudolf Steiner was sitting in this very same hall listening to a lecture by Annie Besant:

> ... No one present will contradict me when I say that we spent together a time of deep theosophical life. One could take away a permanent impression both for heart and spirit ...

★

A very good attendance was secured for two public lectures organized by the Wood Green Centre. The first, by Miss Clara Codd on the subject of 'The Other Side of Death', was well received by a sympathetic audience ...

Mrs. Despard, who was advertised for the second lecture, 'Theosophy and the Problems of Life', had unfortunately lost her voice and was not able to be with us, but Mr. D.N. Dunlop at only a few hours' notice lectured to a large audience on the subject announced. The individual who acts as substitute has an unenviable part to perform, but Mr. Dunlop gave a most impressive address and dealt with questions with his usual ability. The Centre was exceedingly grateful to him for coming to the rescue at the last moment.

Altogether we feel that a very deep impression has been made locally, and we hope that great good will result from this work of propaganda.

★

It has long been a wish of many F.T.S. that at the great traditional festivals of the year, opportunity should be provided at Headquarters for meeting together, and as Mr. Baillie-Weaver has announced in his 'Outlook', the London Federation has arranged two meetings, one on Christmas Eve at 7 p.m. and the other on Christmas morning at 11.15 a.m., in the Temporary Hall. Mr. D.N. Dunlop will be the speaker at both meetings, and there will be appropriate music. Mr. Dunlop's title on Christmas Eve will be 'The Veils of the Mother', and on Christmas morning 'The Mind-born Son'.

Programmes will be sent to all members of the Federation early in December.

A Temple of Beauty

In January 1917 *The Co-Mason* published an article on 'Mystic Masonry', with a footnote stating 'Notes from a lecture delivered by Mr. D.N. Dunlop to the H.P.B. Lodge of the Theosophical Society'.

This then is the lecture which Dunlop had given on 7 June of the previous year.

> The Masonic Order is a link between the ancient Mysteries and the modern world. Its symbolism is related to a building which is proceeding, and the fact that those who enter the Order are called Masons indicates the object which was in the minds of the founders. They regarded the human race as in process of building, and man a being who was fashioning for himself something beautiful, something eternal which would be the embodiment of his highest ideals. It is the building of the human soul, of 'the Temple not made with hands, eternal in the heavens', which is raised without sound of hammer and without noise, silently, in the chamber of man's heart.
>
> The Order in its beginning was founded to overcome the prejudices which had been established between one religion and another, and to bring together in one human family the various communities of the world, and to some extent it has been successful. The prince and the peasant are, within the Masonic Lodge, on equal terms. The rich and the poor, the cultured and the uncultured are all there surrounded by those wonderful symbols of the life of the soul, very little understood but nevertheless true symbols, and they are seen shining through the darkness which often envelops the mind, bearing witness to that Ancient Wisdom which guides man while engaged on his character-building in matter.
>
> In recent times women have been readmitted into the secrets of Masonry in the Co-Masonic Movement, which was initiated in various countries with the assistance of women who had penetrated to some extent into the Mysteries. The 'legitimate' Order still discredits the Orders that admit women with men on equal terms, but I have no hesitation in saying that 'official' recognition will come in time. I do not mean to suggest that all during the dark ages through which humanity has passed it may not have been a very wise provision of some of the old Masters of Masonry that women should have been excluded. I do not think that men and women were ready to associate together in the close intercourse of the Lodge, but I believe that humanity is now approaching a state where men and women can enter the fold of the Mysteries with purity of heart and of desire, because they view life from the standpoint of the soul and not merely from the standpoint of phallic imagery. All true Lodges are in themselves Holy Ground, and you cannot enter a Lodge of true builders unless your desires are under control of the will.

The first stage in the Masonic system is marked by your desire to come into touch with the self within. You are seeking the light—the conscious principle within you. You have lost your way in the labyrinth of the world, you are weary, lonely, and you are always yearning for something different from that in which you find yourself engaged every day. You want to find reality and to dispel the illusion of ignorance. You thus seek the light which comes from the East where the Master is—a symbol of the Masters of Wisdom throughout the ages. In the First Degree you enact all the symbolism of the person who is ignorant. You are badly equipped, and you need assistance. You are met at the entrance of the Lodge by those who have looked upon the light with steady eyes, who have realized something greater than you have realized. They perform the necessary preparatory rites for you, and lead you through some of the stages that later you are able to take self-consciously for yourself. You find yourself being conducted through the symbolical journey, surrounded by the officers who at their posts symbolically represent great principles. You pass before them, and finally reach the place where you see the light. There you discover how little you possess, and before the Master at the altar you undertake your obligation to the service of mankind. You hear discourses which explain some of the things which you see around you. You see the canopy of stars above you, the symbols of the G. A. O. U. [Great Architect Of the Universe], the movable and the immovable jewels which represent the powers of the soul at different points in its evolution, and you are furnished with the working tools which you require in that degree to assist you in your labours. If your soul is awake at all, you will begin to see in the symbols far more than is told you. The whole secret is never revealed, only you yourself penetrate the arcana by your intuition, and begin to see into the meanings that underlie the particular symbolism with which you are surrounded. Finally you pass out, having dimly understood that you have become an apprentice in the eternal building of the Temple of God.

Then in due time you pass to the degree of Fellow Craft, where you see a little further, and other tools are given you. In this degree the symbolism indicates that you are making progress on the spiritual path, and in the building of the immortal vesture of the soul.

Having passed this degree you come to that in which you attain Mastership, and again tools are given you which indicate your achievement. The mystery of death is the principal feature of final attainment, as it has been in the making of all Masters who have ever lived in the world. The final triumph of that great Master Whom we name the Christ is associated with His death on the Cross and 'the Arhat is born at the midnight hour'.

When you have become a Master Mason and in due time a Past Master, you pass on to the Royal Arch degree, where you find the Lost Word and where you come into contact with the Great Companions, the Prince Adepts of the Order, who reflect the wisdom their souls possess.

Is it not clear, from the little of the veil which I have lifted, how great the possibilities are in an Order of this kind, in indicating the steps through which you must pass in your task of spiritual regeneration? If the Masonic Movement is going to play the part in the world that it should play, the Temple Courts will have to be cleared and the Lodges will have to be made into places of spiritual instruction where men and women may get some light upon the mysteries of their own being. And it is a very deep question indeed as to how far it is possible to revivify an old system, or put new wine into old bottles. I have often wondered how the Masonic Order could be vitalized, and those wonderful symbols made to glow again with some of the old magic which was associated with them in the minds of the first Masons of the Lodge of Light, where all humble hearts would feel the descent upon them of the Holy Ghost and would feel refreshed to take up the burden of life again, enthused with some of that wonderful mystery which surrounds every true symbol of the soul. I believe that anything is possible, if men and women have sufficient faith. Faith is one of the first things which you must acquire if you are going to make any progress in spiritual undertaking. It is 'the substance of things hoped for', and we should all exercise that faith which will enable us to build in our minds Lodges of beauty and righteousness, the very antithesis of the external life and all the ugly things that surround us today.

I am sorry to say that very few Master Masons have any real understanding of the meaning of the ritual and symbolism. There are those in the world who dislike ritual and regalia and all external symbols, thinking them of no real value. There are those, on the other hand, who find themselves wonderfully uplifted when they put on the symbolic robes, and feel that they are taking part in a ceremony linked with the rhythmical movements of the stars in the heavens.

There is no saying in what way you first touch that mysterious hand, or come into contact with that invisible presence which is always near you, seeking to make itself manifest. There is no saying when and where you will first feel the touch which alters your whole outlook, which enables you to see through the changing phantasms of life to that permanent reality which is the very core of your being, and which endures through every vicissitude. It is symbolized in the Lodge as the all-seeing eye, which is steady and unwavering, and watchful through all the tumult and danger of the symbolical journey.

You may wonder why the Masonic Order is a secret Order. I doubt very much if it would have held together at all if it had not been for its secrecy—for you will realize that it has not always been so easy to meet as it is now and discuss these mysteries. There were times when it had to be done secretly under the safeguard of passwords and signs. Now you do not penetrate to the heart of the mystery merely by joining a Secret Society. The only way to really understand is to live the life in your own heart and soul. The coming together of the brethren in this attitude of mind, surrounded by wonderful symbols, creates an atmosphere in which they can more readily realize what is the meaning underlying those symbols and the ritual used. I believe that in the coming years Masonry will grow to be a much greater force than it is at present, that it will manifest more life and vitality, and that the men and women who enter it will begin to understand to a greater and greater degree that the building is the building of the Temple of their own nature. The working tools are the powers of the soul which will have to be used in the building of the immortal nature, which will endure when this planet upon which we now live is rolled up again into its essence. When this is understood, men and women will enter the Lodge as loving labourers together for the raising of a superstructure of beauty, strength and wisdom, and their refreshment will be a true refreshment of the mind.

Gradually as you unfold the powers of the soul your life becomes a ritual, and an orientation of your whole nature takes place. Then you begin to understand the meaning of life in matter. You understand that the soul, impressing itself upon substance, charges every atom with an individual, immortal energy, and gains experience thereby. You have to make yourself into an individual immortal. Remember that. You as an individual centre have to secure for yourself, by effort and toil and struggle, the power to hold a form which you can use at will, and which is beyond the limitations of time and space as we now understand them.

These are not fancies of the mind only—they are realities. The heart of man, whatever outer conditions may be like, seeks to build the City Beautiful. Freemasonry is one of many Orders in the world preserving some of the ancient mystery-teaching in its symbols and ritual through the dark ages. I suggest that you begin in some way to introduce into your life a ritual of your own. Choose the symbols which you like best, and out of the imagination of your own heart build a Temple of Beauty in which the immortal virtues are represented by the jewels of character you wear. The wings of your imagination will carry you through all the aethers and bring you at last to your true home.

The end of your pilgrimage is marked by the most mysterious and sacred step of all. On the threshold of Nirvana the cry of humanity calls you back, and instead of donning the Dharmakaya robe, which means 'oblivion of the world and men forever', you don the glorious robe of the Nirmanakaya, and renew your pledge to human service.

Steiner's Philosophy

One of the most intimate but also most complex personal relationships of W.B. Yeats was that with the Irish patriot Maud Gonne. He first met her in London on 30 January 1889, when aged 23, and was at once profoundly affected.

A year later, in January 1890, the unmarried Maud gave birth to a son, Georges, fathered by the French Boulangist and journalist Lucien Millevoye. Yeats did not know about all this for another seven years. Georges however died in France, as a one-year-old baby, in July 1891.

Later in that year Yeats called on Maud in Dublin and made a proposal of marriage. Maud declined. She did however agree to Yeats's other proposition that she join the Order of the Golden Dawn.

Referring in his *Memoirs* to AE, Yeats continued:

> Russell had seen many visions, and some of them contained information about matters of fact that were afterwards verified; but though his own personal revelation was often original and very remarkable, he accepted in the main the conclusions of Theosophy. He spoke of reincarnation, and Maud Gonne asked him how soon a child was reborn, and if, where?

Peter Kuch in his study *Yeats and AE* (1986) observes at this point:

> Russell's reply, 'It may be reborn in the same family' is the answer a theosophist would give. He may even have taken it from Sinnett's *Esoteric Buddhism*:
>
> 'A child dying before it has lived long enough to begin to be responsible for its actions has generated no fresh karma. The spiritual monad leaves that child's body in just the same state in which it entered it after its last death in Devachan . . . A reincarnation of the monad therefore may take place immediately, on the line of its old attraction.'
>
> Yeats says in his *Memoirs*:
>
> 'I could see that Maud Gonne was deeply impressed . . .'

In August 1894, Maud gave birth to a second Millevoye child, a daughter named Iseult.

Full details and ramifications of these complex relationships are set out in the relevant biographies, and can of course not be reproduced in the present section. Suffice here to say that after another four years, in the spring of 1898, the 32-year-old Yeats visited Maud in Paris. During his visit Maud had a dream in which she was taken by a great spirit towards a whole throng of similar spirits, among whom was Yeats; her hand was put into his, and she was told that they were married. She then woke up. After relating this dream to Yeats in the evening of the following day, she decided also to unravel to him the complete story of her relationship with Millevoye.

Early in the next year, February 1899, Yeats travelled over to Paris again on another visit to Maud, and for a second time proposed marriage to her, but she again declined.

Four years later, however, in 1903, Maud—to Yeats's enormous dismay—went on to marry another Irishman, John MacBride. They had a son, Sean, known as 'Bichon', born in 1904. But the marriage itself foundered, ending by divorce in 1906.

★

Further years passed by. In 1911, the by now 46-year-old Yeats met another lady, the 18-year-old Georgie Hyde-Lees, whom he soon invited to an evening at his London flat in Woburn Buildings. Georgie—who besides English could speak French, German and Italian—was an avid reader of all kinds of occult literature, and like Yeats had marked spiritualistic tendencies.

In 1912 Yeats was lecturing to the Quest Society of G.R.S. Mead, who came about twice a month to the 'At Homes' in Woburn Buildings, while Georgie was attending Mead's weekly lectures in Kensington Town Hall.

Certainly by 1913 Yeats and Georgie were becoming friendly. Sometime after Rudolf Steiner's visit to London in May of that year, Georgie joined the Anthroposophical Society. Through her connection to Yeats she was however far more interested in the Order of the Stella Matutina, though since the latter had a minimum entrance age of 21, it was not until July 1914 that she could gain admission. Like Yeats, she came to play an active role within this Order.

★

In the spring of 1916 Maud Gonne's ex-husband John MacBride, as one of the leaders of the Easter Rising in Dublin, was condemned to death by the British and shot. In the summer, Yeats visited Maud at Colleville in Normandy, and for a third time proposed marriage to her, but once again she declined.

Moving in the same Parisian circles as Maud was the anthroposophist and musician Walter Rummel, often a guest in her home. This fact may explain one particular sentence in a letter from Maud to Yeats.

(The letter is lengthy, and only the relevant part is reproduced here. Although the year is not given, the part not reproduced indicates that it was 1917. Yeats was deeply involved in a legal controversy between the National Gallery in London and the Municipal Gallery in Dublin over the ownership of pictures left behind by his friend the distinguished art-collector Sir Hugh Lane, who in May 1915 had gone down on the *Lusitania* when that ship was torpedoed in mid-Atlantic by a German U-boat.)

20th Jany

My dear Willie,

I am leaving no stone unturned to return to Ireland for I know it is the best thing for Iseult & for Bichon but if I do not succeed it may be all for the best in the end as I may have more important work to do here—I am very philosophical . . .

You are making a splendid fight for the pictures & ought to succeed if you were dealing with people who really knew what honesty meant but—subject nations are meant to be robbed & small nations to be bullied.

Have you heard anything different from Meynal yet? Iseult is very anxious to know, as she would like to begin her translations.

By the way, when you write to her, ask her to send you the article she wrote on French Catholic writers & the earth—I think it is VERY good but she won't finish it, if you write for it she will have to, & I think you will like it.

She is just now very much taken up with Steiner's philosophy—I haven't read much but I think I should find him too dogmatic & assertive.

With best wishes for the success of your efforts for the pictures

Alwys your friend

Maud Gonne

⋆

At the time the present book went to press the author had not had access to *Letters to W.B. Yeats and Ezra Pound from Iseult Gonne* (forthcoming, 2003). Roy Foster in the second volume, *The Archpoet* (2003) of his authoritative biography of Yeats states that Iseult's letters to him at this time

> . . . had continued—lengthy, introspective, expressing ardent friendship and literary homage in between earnest discussions of Rudolf Steiner.

A Song of Rejoicing

The present chapter reproduces a report in *The Vahan*, entitled 'Without Distinction of Creed', and signed by the initials M.W.

> On Wednesday, January 31st, 1917, Mr. Collison lectured to the H.P.B. Lodge on 'The Occult Philosophy of Dr. Steiner'.
>
> In the quiet spaces of my heart I am singing a song of rejoicing about that Wednesday night, about the brotherliness of Mr. Collison and Mr. Dunlop

and the H.P.B. Lodge generally; about the value and joy of freedom of speech, as further exemplified by that evening and its happenings.

We do not realize what we lose in our fear of speaking freely and frankly to one another. We are painfully aware of our shortcomings as a Society, but we have not yet grasped the fact that it is this lack of frank and open exchange of opinion and criticism that throws us into the arms of mediocrity. For is it not true that any one of us can lecture, write, organize, or what we will, in a second or third or even fourth-rate manner, without ever having to run the gauntlet of wholesome and necessary criticism, openly expressed? The result is that those of us who are not suppressed run riot, and the rest of us suffer in silence (so far as our public life is concerned) until bursting point—and free speech—is reached. But by that time it isn't free speech at all, but a bomb, and the resulting explosion leaves us nothing to do after but collect and bury the fragments, more firmly convinced than ever in our minds of the disastrous results of freedom of speech.

If we want to improve matters, we must alter our methods. For pity's sake let us not attempt to check anything that wants to express itself, however bad it may be, for mediocrity has to grow to genius, and it will not do that by repression; but equally do not let us deprive it of half its nourishment: just criticism of its endeavours. Again take the other side; it is good for the mind to have things to criticize, but criticism too has to grow, and it suffers as much from mediocrity in its early stages as the things it criticizes. Obviously, then, the true adjustment of these activities is to give both of them free play and an equal share of the game; and what a splendid game it is, played that way! There is nothing finer for keeping us supple and generally brotherly; and as for the bruises and scratches, the rough and tumble of it, what is that compared to the good we gain? The game heartens and enlivens, where our present methods tend to refrigerate; and unless we change them we shall go on getting colder and colder in spite of all our good intentions, and more and more frozen until at last there we are, as fine a company of brother icicles as ever dripped from the same water spout; and there we remain, until the Sun—probably in the shape of a common catastrophe—thaws us down, and sets us free to trickle away together once more on our adventure seaward.

All of which leads me to this point, that whatever Wednesday evening was or was not, it was a grand thaw of theosophical and anthroposophical icicles. I shall not attempt to report the lecture; because I can't, any more than Mr. Collison could expound the occult philosophy of Dr. Steiner in an hour. Of course he couldn't do that and he knew he couldn't, and we knew it, and Mr. Dunlop said it, and then we all laughed together over it and thawed some more. We thawed so much that at last Mr. Collison dared to abandon the meticulous tactfulness of his lecture, and in response to a reminder that the Anthroposophical Society would not admit F.T.S. to its membership, stated roundly that our President had abused Dr. Steiner, whereat Mr. Dunlop replied that Dr. Steiner's followers had said pretty strong things about our President, and this exchange of opinions provoked no worse cataclysm than a chuckle from the audience at the *tu quoque*. Decidedly we were getting on; learning the game; and I would stake a good deal that had Mrs. Besant been there she would have been the first to laugh and approve.

Finally, Mr. Collison, as the result of various 'alarums and excursions', declared that membership in the Anthroposophical Group he represented (groups are autonomous) should be open to any F.T.S. who seriously desired to study Dr. Steiner's philosophy, and he wound up by reading a very interesting message from Dr. Steiner about the War, which we could listen to sympathetically without abating a jot of our belief in the higher ideals for which the Allies are fighting.

Then Mr. Collison thanked us and hoped to be allowed to come again, and we thanked him and invited him to do so and then we parted, some happy and some wrathful maybe, but at least no longer icicles, at least warmed and exhilarated with the game.

I don't suppose anyone's convictions 'suffered a sea-change', but at any rate the margin of disagreement and misstatement was considerably diminished, and as for the remaining differences, why shouldn't they be there? Didn't the Creator have to invent difference in order to manifest at all?

This teacher or that, Paul or Apollos? We've wrestled over it down the ages; but I suspect that the answer of Paul to his followers will also be the answer of Mrs. Besant and Dr. Steiner and every teacher, past, present and to come.

'Who is Paul, and who is Apollos, but ministers by whom ye believed, even as the Lord gave to every man? I have planted, Apollos watered, but God gave the increase.'

The lecture by Collison is all the more interesting since in this year, though he may have continued to translate Steiner's lecture-courses for the internal benefit of anthroposophists, he arranged no further publications.

The only anthroposophical work published in Britain in 1917 was a pamphlet on *The Mission of Spiritual Science and of its Building at Dornach, Switzerland*, translated from a lecture given by Steiner at Liestal on 11 January 1916, and with two illustrations. It was translated by A.M. Wilson and brought out by Herbert Heywood-Smith.

Upliftment of Spirit

The present chapter reproduces further items from *The Vahan* in 1917. The first is from the 'Outlook' by the General Secretary in the March issue:

> We had a very interesting discussion on propaganda at the meeting of the National Council on Saturday the 3rd ult.
>
> Miss de Normann and Miss Douglas Fox urged the advisability of consultation between Headquarters officials, Federation Secretaries, Group and Lodge Secretaries before new departures were made . . .
>
> Mr. Dunlop pointed out that concentration is the secret of success, and that too many interests spoil effective effort. If we could get experts to deal with many of the subsidiary branches of the work we have undertaken or are backing up in one form or another, many of our difficulties would disappear and better results would be obtained. He deprecated any suggestion that lecturing or other definite propaganda work is the only true method of furthering the cause of Theosophy for earnest F.T.S. to pursue, maintaining that every theosophist who in his own way genuinely strives to live the theosophic life and absorb and radiate out again the theosophic philosophy is doing propaganda work of a most valuable kind to further that cause. As I listened to him I thought of some words I once read which made a deep impression upon me. I quote from memory and I hope not too incorrectly. 'Remember the best work can be done without words. Those among whom you live, silent and unnoticed, may have the radiance cast upon them merely by your presence in their midst. So live that you may be the channel for higher things to descend to lower planes. It is not what we say or do but what we *are* that tells and that will leave its mark upon every character we meet as upon all time.'
>
> So work without words may be the best, but work with words is needed too, and I entirely agree with Miss de Normann and Miss Douglas Fox (as I know does also Mr. Dunlop) that such work, when it is undertaken, should be carried out in the best manner compatible with our resources . . .

> The ninety-first Conference of the Northern Federated Lodges was held in Sheffield on Saturday and Sunday, February 10th and 11th, when Mr. D.N. Dunlop was the distinguished visitor, and we were also favoured by the presence of the General Secretary, Mr. Baillie-Weaver . . .
>
> A discussion on lodge activities with a view to after-the-war problems was opened by Mr. A. Chappell of Sheffield, and contributed to by several speakers.
>
> After tea Mr. Dunlop gave a most interesting address to the Conference on 'He giveth His Beloved Sleep', explaining in very full detail the wonderful phenomenon of sleep . . .

The title of the address was quoted from Psalm 127:2. This is a psalm of Solomon, who was also named Jedidiah, 'beloved of Yahweh' (2 Samuel 12:25), and the verse may recall his dream at Gibeon (1 Kings 3:5–14), in which he asked Yahweh for an understanding heart.

... On Sunday, Mr. Baillie-Weaver addressed a meeting of the Order of the Star in the East, after which the Sheffield Lodge entertained the Conference to 'Tea and Music'. In the evening Mr. Dunlop lectured to a large audience of the public on 'Death and Resurrection'...

The Spring Conference of the London, Home Counties and Eastern Federation was held on April 6th, 7th and 8th, and the excellent attendance fully justified the experiment of an 'Easter Festival'.

On Good Friday there was a dramatic representation of nine scenes from the New Testament entitled 'The Crowning of Jesus', adapted from the New Testament by Mr. Loftus Hare...

On the Saturday the Business Meeting was held at 2.30 p.m...

The reports of Group Secretaries were of interest. Mrs. Cather (Central Group) stated that the H.P.B. Lodge had sent many parcels of books to the Fleet and that the work was still in progress...

The election of officers for the ensuing year then took place, with the following results:

President: Mr. D.N. Dunlop... Conference Secretary: Miss D.S. Osmond...

The Business Meeting was followed at 3.30 by a discussion on 'Spiritualism and Psychism in the Light of the Theosophical Philosophy'.

The discussion was rather warmly conducted at times, which perhaps was to be expected in view of the strong opinions held both for and against Spiritualism by the members of our Society.

On Easter Sunday the evening lecture was given at the Wigmore Hall to an excellent audience. Mr. Dunlop was the speaker and he took for his subject 'Death and the Resurrection'—treating it with that breadth of view and upliftment of spirit that we have learnt to associate with his lecture-work.

The General Secretary reported in the 'Outlook':

I left town on Saturday by a late train and consequently was not present at the public meeting on Sunday night, which was held at the Wigmore Hall and was addressed by Mr. Dunlop, but I rejoice to hear on all sides how successful it was. The audience was large and I gather that Mr. Dunlop's address was appreciated even more than his addresses usually are, and that is saying a great deal. The result confirms my conviction that our message will be listened to if only we present it properly and with sufficient boldness...

The meeting on White Lotus Day will be held at 8 p.m. in the

Temporary Hall, when there will be music, and readings from the *Bhagavad Gita* and *The Light of Asia* by Mrs. Betts and myself, and an address on 'The Life Everlasting' by Mr. Dunlop. It has been decided in future years to hold a commemorative meeting at which the usual readings will be given and an address will be delivered by a speaker who will, it is hoped, associate the commemoration with some branch of theosophical philosophy which specially emphasizes the life's work of Madame Blavatsky. In this connection an interesting suggestion has been made by Mr. Dunlop that we shall institute a 'Blavatsky Lecture' on the analogy of the Hibbert and Gifford Lectures, and appoint each year a 'Blavatsky Lecturer' who shall deliver it on White Lotus Day. The suggestion has found much favour.

The Theosophical Society's Twenty-Seventh Annual Convention took place on 25, 26, 27 and 28 May.

Here is a passage from the report of the 27th:

Mr. Dunlop said that human progress depends on the human hierarchy, and that there is no need to look for new fountains of knowledge when we have not used those we already have. If theosophists are to help to bring about an ideal civilization they must know, in whatever situation they may be placed, or whatever problems they may be called upon to face, *what standard they should apply*. What we want is the incarnation of a new idea out of which will grow a free democracy in which the free spirit of man will come into its own.

And here is a passage from the report of the closing meeting, in the evening of Monday, 28th:

Mr. Dunlop, Mrs. Sharpe and Mr. Baillie-Weaver were the speakers, and part songs, a solo, and a duet were exquisitely rendered by choristers from the London College for Choristers, under the direction of Dr. Harold Watts.

Mr. Dunlop: The closing meeting of Convention is the occasion for realizing the unity at the central heart of things, behind all the divergent views and ways of action which may be manifest in the paths of each individual. The light of the creative principle in the human heart burns without ceasing through the ages, and the ultimate perfection of humanity can never be doubted for one moment. Are the three objects of the Society going to stand the test of the changing world? Is the study of the nature of man, illumined by an understanding of the great religions and philosophies of the world, going to produce the flowering forth of that brotherhood of humanity of which mystics and seers have spoken? It is an individual matter, and the responsibility rests on each one of us. May it be ours at this Convention to renew our pledges in the light of the ancient wisdom, and to assist in the birth of this ideal in the world.

New Kinds of Combinations

An obituary of D.N. Dunlop written by Alice M. Callow for the July 1935 number of *New Thought* stated:

> . . . Though not present at the inaugural I.N.T.A. Convention in June 1914, which was so immediately followed by the Great War as to stop the activities which should have followed, he was with us at the First National Congress of New Thought held in 1917, when the work of the British Section of the International New Thought Alliance was resumed in that really wonderful gathering, which united fourteen different groups working for the one great cause of enlightenment and the spread of the truth of being. Mr. Dunlop spoke then as representing Theosophy, on 'Man—the Thinker'. From that time he has been almost invariably on the platform of the yearly Congress which followed this great adventure. He was also counted among our most valued Sunday morning speakers, whenever he could spare the time in his overcrowded life. For he united in himself two widely divergent capacities—he was at once scholar and true poet, and a brilliant man of affairs.

⋆

In July 1917 *The BEAMA Journal* carried an article on 'Voluntary Co-operation in New Directions', doubtless written by a man of affairs:

> The desire on the part of manufacturers to share their experiences and combine their efforts for the good of a particular industry and in the national interest is increasing. In many different industries manufacturers are consulting with one another as to ways and means of strengthening their industries. Some form of combination is always found necessary, and even when one firm feels strong and self-sufficient, its disassociation from the others does not last long, once its responsibility to the nation is realized.
>
> The strength of British Industry has hitherto been the element of individuality. So deeply is this engrained in the national character that the association of individual firms in this country will result in new kinds of combinations. Individuals will not sink themselves in gigantic combines regulated as a huge machine; instead, combinations of manufactures are being effected where individual experience is utilized and individual enterprise expanded by reason of association with others. The motive for combination is concentration and economy of effort, in order to raise the quality and quantity of output.
>
> The object is far other than that of the great German kartels, founded with a 'get-rich-quick' motive in order to dominate the world commercially. To that end Germans sacrificed individuality to a state scheme. Their methods were compulsory; ours are voluntary.

The voluntary co-operation of British manufactures to build up strong industries in order to preserve this country against German competition is one of the signs that Great Britain intends to mantain her ideals by means of industry as well as by military and political operations.

★

On 21 August 1917 Rudolf Steiner was in Berlin, giving a memorial address for three recently deceased anthroposophists.

One of these was Hermann Joachim. The lengthy printed text of what Steiner had to say about him includes the following sentences:

> Hermann Joachim was concerned at every moment about what could be done to lead the ideals of spiritual science directly over into life in one's own position. He was a Freemason who had gained deep insights into the essence of Freemasonry, but also into the essence of Freemasonic fraternities. He had put before himself the great idea of really achieving a spiritual penetration of Freemasonic formalism with the essence of spiritual science. Everything Freemasonry has stored up in the way of profound knowledge, but which has become formulaic, one might say crystallized, had been unveiled to Herman Joachim to a quite special extent through his high rank in Freemasonry. But in the very position he was placed, he could project in thought what was found there into the right relationship of mankind, and could penetrate what after all can only derive from the power of spiritual science with the traditions he wished to enliven. Whoever knows how Hermann Joachim was during these difficut times working in this direction, and is to some extent aware of the earnestness of his activity and the value of his thoughts in this direction, the strength of his will and the comprehensiveness of his work in this realm, will then know what the physical plane has lost precisely with him . . .

★

The musician Arnold Bax spent the months of August and September 1917 at Tintagel on the north Cornish coast, composing his *Tintagel Symphony*.

Did he perhaps incorporate into this work the strange music he had heard five years earlier while staying with AE in Donegal?

★

W.B. Yeats meanwhile had travelled back to Normandy, and in Colleville proposed marriage for a fourth time to Maud Gonne. But she once again declined.

The 52-year-old poet then made a proposal to Maud's daughter, the 21-year-old Iseult, with whom indeed he had been friendly ever since her birth. But her feelings were too mixed for her to be able to give him an immediate answer.

Both Maud and Iseult then travelled over to England in Yeats's company. In London on 21 September Iseult finally gave him her answer, which was negative.

Five days later, at 10 o'clock on the morning of the 26th, Yeats then proposed marriage to the 25-year-old Georgie Hyde-Lees. By 10.20 she had accepted his offer.

They were married within less than a month, on 20 October.

Breadth of Vision

No. 3 in 'The Path Series' was *The Masters* by Charles Lazenby, brought out in 1917 and like the others 'Printed by R & R. Clark, Limited, Edinburgh'. A 'Publisher's Note' stated:

> We have collected these studies from Volume II of *The Path*, and publish them in this series because they present the Masters as living men active in human evolution, and as such they may be valuable to many who at the present time are seeking a Master by means of spiritualistic phenomena.
>
> An understanding of the nature of the work of Masters is necessary in order to comprehend the events of history and the significance of the cyclic rise and fall of civilizations. Spiritual impulses and inspirations reach humanity through those of the race who have mastered the forces inimical to its progress, and have attained individual consciousness of the laws and principles governing evolution.
>
> No alteration of these articles, as they were written in 1911 and 1912, has been made, except a rearrangement of some paragraphs and the deletion of a few irrelevant passages consequent in a serial publication.

★

A further item from *The Vahan* read:

> The Autumn Conference of the London, Home Counties and Eastern Federation was held on October 26th, 27th and 28th, under the Presidency of Mr. D.N. Dunlop, and there was an excellent attendance, in spite of recent air-raids.
>
> The Conference opened on the 26th and 27th with two performances at the West Theatre, Royal Albert Hall, of a Mystery Play entitled *St Bride of the Mantle*...
>
> On Saturday afternoon, October 27th, the Business Meeting of the Federation was held... At the conclusion the majority of members partook of tea before attending the Mystery Play at Albert Hall.

The Conference concluded with a lecture by Mr. D.N. Dunlop, at the Small Queen's Hall, on 'The Vision of the Future', which proved to be one of his finest addresses. Preceded by beautiful music by Mr. Arthur Beckwith's Trio, he spoke with that eloquence and breadth of vision which always marks his best work, and brought the Conference to a close on a fitting note of harmony.

★

The Vahan further records that in November 1917 Dorothy Osmond was appointed the Society's Head Librarian. In the Summer 1978 issue of *Anthroposophical Quarterly*, Vera and Juliet Compton-Burnett published an obituary of her.

How vividly we recall that day in war-time London when we walked round and round Tavistock Square, summoning up our courage to enter the Headquarters of the Theosophical Society. Eventually we ascended the steps of the large corner-house and went into a room marked 'Enquiries', where a bird-like little lady was sitting at her desk.

We explained that we had been reading Theosophy for some years, and now wished to join the Society. The lady appeared very much perturbed by this direct approach, and replied that she hardly knew what to say: it was so important that the members of the Society should be quite perfectly sane. The situation was saved by the lady exclaiming in tones of relief: 'I think I had better fetch Miss Osmond.' She returned in a few moments followed by a tall slender figure, dressed in a becoming mole-grey velvet tunic, the uniform of the librarians. There was much of beauty in Dorothy Osmond's face, particularly in her large, dark brown eyes, and her manner was warm and welcoming. An immediate contact was established: this was friendship at first sight.

Dorothy did not talk much about her earlier life. The eldest of three children, two girls and a boy, her Exeter home was not a happy one, for her conventional mother failed to understand her, and her father's growing addiction to alcohol cast a shadow over the household. On leaving school she took a secretarial training course, and became private secretary to the Chilean Minister, acquiring Spanish with the feeling that she had known it before. We cannot remember how she met with Theosophy, but she was already head librarian.

★

In January 1918 *The Vahan* reported on 'The Inauguration of the Hampstead Garden Suburb Lodge':

Theosophists in 'the Suburb' and Golders Green District having long felt the need for a local lodge—the nearest being at Hampstead—on Monday evening realized their objective in the opening of the Hampstead Garden Suburb Lodge under most promising auspices. This desirable consummation was largely the result of theosophical work done locally by earnest members, with a final stimulus to action in the series of lectures given recently at the Institute by Mrs. Dorothy Grenside, which created a widespread interest in Theosophy.

The inaugural proceedings took place in the Library of the Institute, which overflowed with more than seventy well-wishers and members of the Theosophical Society, including a good percentage of the masculine element. In the absence of Mr. Baillie-Weaver (Gen. Secretary), Mr. D.N. Dunlop presided in his customary sympathetic manner. The Charter having been signed by the founding members, the new lodge was declared duly constituted, and Mr. Dunlop intimated that its activities would start on January 7th with a lecture by Mr. Loftus Hare. Suitable and eloquent addresses were then delivered by Mr. Dunlop, Mr. Loftus Hare (President of the Lodge), Monsieur Jean Delville (lately General Secretary of the Belgian Section), Mr. Hugh Gillespie (Hon. Secretary), Mrs. Grenside, Miss Clara Codd, and Miss Charlotte Woods. Numerous congratulations were received from the various lodges in the London Federation. A letter from the vicar of St. Jude's wishing the work 'God Speed' was read. The presence of representatives from the local Society of Friends and the Ethical Society all contributed to preserve the atmosphere of friendly toleration so characteristic of the Garden Suburb. Refreshments were then served, and an agreeable hour passed quickly amid the subtle charms of music, flowers and conversation, Miss Elsie Hamilton's superb command of the piano ministering to the intense delight of the company.

The proceedings then closed with a few wise and acceptable counsels from Mr. Dunlop to all who are seeking to tread the upward path.

The same issue also had a notice on 'H.P.B. Lodge':

The Spring Session will begin on Wednesday, January 16th, with a public lecture in the Steinway Hall, Lower Seymour Street, at 8.15 p.m., by Mr. D.N. Dunlop on 'The Path of Knowledge'. This is the first of a series of four lectures to be given by Mr. Dunlop at the Steinway Hall on January 16th, February 20th, March 20th, April 17th (third Wednesdays), two being under the general title of 'The Path of Knowledge' and two under the general title of 'Immortality'.

Guiding Us into Peace

During the year 1918 Harry Collison brought out translations of two books by Rudolf Steiner: *A Road to Self-Knowledge* and *The Threshold of the Spiritual World*. Both were published by Putnam's, London & New York.

And in the same year D.N. Dunlop brought out his book *The Science of Immortality*. It was the third in 'The Path Series' and once again 'Printed by R. & R. Clark, Limited, Edinburgh'.

A foreword stated:

The contents of this volume consist of addresses delivered at various times before lodges of the Theosophical Society, and selected for their reference to the subject of immortality. Some of them were published in *The Path*, Vol II. In order to make the chapters more or less coherent the matter has been slightly rearranged, but certain repetitions will be noticed which are unavoidable owing to the interrelation of the subjects discussed and to the fact that, having been addressed to different audiences, some explanation of the bearing of the part on the whole was necessary. I have not attempted to eliminate these redundancies, for the philosophy sketchily outlined herein is not easy to grasp, inasmuch as its fundamental data and principles are in contradistinction to much of the current thought of our time.

A completely systematized scheme of philosophy this book does not pretend to be. It contains only hints, upon which students may build for themselves a science of immortality.

Credit is due to Mr. H.W. Percival, editor of *The Word*, published in New York, for his original work on the philosophy of the Zodiac, and I acknowledge my indebtedness to him.

D.N.D.

January 1918

★

The book was reviewed in *The Vahan*:

A book of value on occult science appears only occasionally—perhaps once in ten years or so if one includes foreign publications. *The Science of Immortality* is one of these rare books, distinguished by the originality of the individual occultist who reinterprets the ancient arcane philosophy. The classical works by the great Kabalists, alchemists and Freemasons contain in various guises the doctrines elucidated by Mr. Dunlop, but the pith of these profound teachings has been extracted in the alembic of his own experience, and the essential factors of man's being are described in terms free from any especial techniques.

The will, breath, desire, personality, the soul, birth and death are terms we think we understand, but in this book we find their supersensible as well as physical meaning, just as the alchemists show us the metaphysical principles of earth, air, fire and water; their functions in the evolution of humanity through the seven root and sub-races are also indicated. The student is shown clearly the object of human evolution as distinct from that of the lower kingdoms, and the significance of the immortal soul contrasted with the ephemeral lower orders of souls. But in common with the writings of all real occultists, the teaching is that each man, since he has free will, must achieve his own self-conscious immortality. It is not a gift of Nature. All 'monads' or 'atoms' are eternal in essence, but are subject to the laws of Nature in whatever sphere they manifest. The monads can function consciously in the 'planes' of individuality and soul only as they conform to the law of self-conscious direction. In denser substances they are simply reflected, and their manifestations are subject to action and reaction, disintegration and death. But if physical incarnation be accepted as an opportunity and a focus for polar equilibrium—an aid to self-consciousness—the individual may begin to cultivate interior powers that will eventually culminate in mastery of the forces where consciousness is possible for humanity. The conditions of this discipline, the nature of the forces at our disposal, and the qualifications necessary for the recovery of the soul are indicated in the ten chapters of the book.

We know the author to be a very busy man engaged in applying theosophical principles in wide fields of business and departmental committees of the Government, and the fact that he was able to prepare and deliver these addresses and arrange the shorthand notes for publication suggests that the occultism contained in this most recent of the Path Co.'s notable publications is a practical, personal achievement and not merely a theoretical philosophy.

★

The credit which Dunlop gave to Percival in the foreword to *The Science of Immortality*, although no doubt genuinely intended, must also have been a precautionary measure. Percival's philosophy of the zodiac had ramifications over other subjects in editorials of *The Word*, and among addresses from Vol II of *The Path* which Dunlop incorporated into his new book were some for which he was not merely 'indebted' to Percival's editorials but which actually derived from them. Chapter IV, 'Individuality and Personality', reproduced with a new opening paragraph a large part of his address of that title from October 1911, which was paraphrased from Percival's editorial of January 1906, and Chapter VI, on 'Will', several paragraphs from the address in January 1912, the latter however developed with further material of his own in addition to what was taken from Percival's editorial of March 1906.

Over in America at this very time, Percival himself was after 13 years bringing publication of *The Word* to a close. Indeed the regularity of the journal had already begun to falter since the last two numbers, though dated August and September 1917, did not in fact appear until 1918. In the foreword to *Thinking and Destiny* (1946) Percival later recorded 'I ceased connection with all societies.'[39]

The final number concluded with a note:

To the readers of *The Word*:

No further issues of *The Word* will be published for the present. But this number, which ends the twenty-fifth volume, is not expected to be the last. For the present, publication of *The Word* will cease. The readers will be notified when *The Word* begins a new series.

Appreciation is due from all readers to the various contributors to *The Word*.

I have written an editorial for every published number of *The Word* since my message was written in October 1904, and have answered the questions in 'Moments with Friends', which appeared from time to time. The editorials written by me were not signed with my name. Information not before given, so far as is known, will be found in these editorials and in some of the 'Moments'.

The main object of my writings was to bring readers to an understanding and valuation of the study of consciousness, and to stimulate those who choose to become conscious of consciousness. To that end a system has been made known by me. I have called it the Zodiac.

I would not state these facts, as to purpose and authorship, except that it is advisable, so as to guard against misrepresentation by some persons who have claimed and some who may claim to have found these teachings elsewhere than in *The Word*, and by some who attempt to change, distort or obscure what is stated in these editorials. The information I have given in *The Word* is for those who will use it as a sacrifice to the plan of raising matter to consciousness.

If *The Word* is taken up again it is my intention to write other articles. They will lead some of the readers to know what it is to be conscious of consciousness.

Harold Waldwin Percival.

New York, April 15th, 1918.

★

The April issue of *The Vahan* reproduced a verse by AE:

> Fear not the stillness, for doubt and despair shall cease
> With the gentle voices guiding us into peace.
> Our dreams will change as they pass through the gates of gold,
> And Quiet, the tender shepherd shall keep the fold.

A Profitable and Stimulating Time

On 4 and 5 May the Southern Federation of the Theosophical Society in England and Wales held its Annual Conference in Bath—the town where the great debate had taken place on 12 October 1909.

The Vahan reported:

> A splendid gathering of Fellows was found in Bath on the occasion of the twenty-seventh conference, and the meetings proved that a vigorous life is welling through theosophical channels in these days. We were pleased to see our General Secretary, Mr. Baillie-Weaver, with us, as well as Mr. Dunlop, Mr. A. Burgess and others who by presence and addresses did much to assist our work, and to inspire our next efforts in expressing those truths we all hold vital.
>
> The address delivered to Fellows and friends by Mr. Dunlop, entitled 'Light and Shadows', will be long remembered, and will long stimulate us to search for as well as to express that light of truth which calls into being our many modes of activity and suggests all the settings to which we severally attach ourselves. Among the shadows ourselves, we shall nevertheless remember our great light-bringer, H.P.B., and strive for a greater tolerance, and a fuller expression of brotherhood in the world.
>
> The usual devotional meetings were held on Sunday morning, and in the afternoon Mr. A. Burgess spoke to us on the work of the T.S. Order of Service of the Blind. We gladly note the extension of this important service, and heard with interest of the many other ways than the provision of Braille literature (important as that part of the work is), by which the lives of our non-sighted brothers are made brighter and happier. Mr. Burgess took with him our sincere wishes for success in future endeavours.
>
> A public meeting on Sunday evening was addressed by Mr. Dunlop, on the theme 'The Life Everlasting', and the Conference terminated amid expressions from all that a profitable and stimulating time had been spent together.

The Society's Twenty-Eighth Annual Convention began on 18 May with the first Blavatsky Lecture, delivered by Edward L. Gardner. It was later published, with a foreword by H. Baillie-Weaver, which began:

> The idea of an annual Blavatsky Lecture emanated from Mr. D.N. Dunlop, whose devotion to Mme Blavatsky and her writings is well-known throughout the Theosophical Society, and the idea was so obviously an excellent one that prompt measures were taken by the Executive Committee to give it a concrete form.

Dunlop himself also attended the Convention, giving a lecture on the evening of Sunday the 19th.

★

From this time dates the first letter which Rudolf Steiner sent to Edith Maryon:

Berlin, 24th May 1918

Dear Fräulein Maryon,

My heartfelt thanks for sending the pictures of our sculptural works. I only request that I may be allowed to keep them still a little; I'll send them back later.

We'd like to be at Dornach in July. For the time being I hope the work can still go on further without me.

Heartfelt greetings,

Dr. Rudolf Steiner

Berlin W Motzstrasse 17.

★

In June, *The Vahan* had a note on

Classes in the New Library
(169, Piccadilly, W.)

A class on the theosophical philosophy is held by Mr. D.N. Dunlop on Friday evenings at 6 p.m. Owing to the very large number of applications, and the fact that accommodation is limited, admission will be by ticket only (for which application should be made to the Librarian) and the doors will be shut at 6.5 p.m.

D.S.O.

★

It was also in June that Esther Bright moved out of St James's Place and into Wimbledon—where the Dunlops lived. Eleanor Dunlop had now succeeded her husband as President of the Wimbledon Lodge.

Esther Bright's new residence was called 'the Old House'. In her *Old Letters and Memories of Annie Besant* (1936), she recorded this anecdote:

I remember Mr. A.P. Sinnett's surprise once when lunching with me at the Old House in Wimbledon. I was speaking with enthusiasm of Dr. Steiner's gifts and personal charm.

'Why, I thought you were devoted to Dr. Besant!' he remarked.

'I am,' I said.'

Eternal Beauty Wandering on Her Way

The August issue of *The Vahan* included an article entitled 'The Spheres of the Soul—Notes of an address by Mr. D.N. Dunlop'.

This globe with which our lives have been for so long associated has four atmospheres, physical, psychic, mental and spiritual. In the physical atmosphere with which we are most familiar, we recognize that every breath nourishes our body if the air is pure, and indeed, roughly speaking, three-quarters of the nourishment of our bodies is derived from it. This atmosphere is only the sediment of other atmospheres which are of a purer and more subtle quality. The psychic atmosphere is like a spherical ocean, a transparent water in which the physical atmosphere is as sediment to the eye of spiritual vision.

The mental atmosphere is subtler still and so important that if we were without it we would be mindless beings. The breath of the mind in the mental atmosphere is the cause of all our operations in the psychic and in the physical worlds.

Behind, penetrating and including them all is the spiritual atmosphere, from which all the others emanate. It is the eternal dwelling of the spirit of man, from which he views all the kaleidoscopic activities of his life in the three worlds. The ideals of the spiritual world become ideas in the mental world, desires in the astral world and objects in the physical world. All these are the outbreathing of the spirit of man.

In the spiritual atmosphere there are potential spirits as well as progressed planetary spirits. There are those living in that world who have passed consciously through all the other atmospheres, are living there fully conscious of their divine powers, and are in a position to exercise them through all the atmospheres of our globe. They have the power from that level to direct their energies for the good of every living entity in the life of this planet. They stimulate the potential spirits who have not yet entered upon the great adventure we call life, and are still only feebly conscious of the existence of the spiritual world.

Let us now consider the mental and astral atmospheres. The thought of man at present is a reflection of true thought, which is the energy of the mental atmosphere in its purity and is rather the result of reaction. We think indirectly, and much of our thought is but a feeble reflection coloured by desire and emotion, leading us hither and thither. Those who are clairvoyant can see the currents, whirling eddies and storms set up in the astral body by the emotions and desires of man, which cloud his thought and render him today subject to great inspiration, and tomorrow to an impulse which carries him into the elemental world. There is little clear thought with definite purpose. We are always looking for leaders, because we have no leading thought or guiding principle. We do not allow the eternal Spirit to shine upon our thought. The Spiritual Sun is darkened in our world. The clouds in the mental atmosphere obscure the radiance of the true Sun of our being. Darkness falls upon us, and the sediment of selfish emotional life discolours the clear translucent waters of the true life of the soul.

Circumstances around us are the result of our own thinking, and its objects are the fate-forms which bind us and make us slaves rather than free men and women. The various elements of Nature which are used by man for destruction at the present time are evidence that he has used his thought in a purely selfish way, and that Nature has responded to the selfishness of his thought. Nature always responds to the thought of man, and he has been able to take of her most precious substances and use them for the purposes of the destruction of form. That is the result of thinking, and a concrete expression of the fate-forms which man has made.

If therefore we are to change the order of life, we will have to still the waters of personal desire. We will have to calm the lower astral elements, and raise emotion to the plane of ecstasy, where the meditations of the soul from the spiritual atmosphere can be entered. That is why it has been suggested by the Wise Teachers of men that it is necessary to withdraw from the turbulent waters of the astral atmosphere, and enter into conditions where this ecstasy will be experienced and will, ultimately, from the spiritual atmosphere, reflect itself into physical life.

Every single thought and vibration of energy in man passes out and in perpetually through the four atmospheres of his being, finding pasture and in turn affording nourishment to other souls.

Let us assume that we recognize the virtue of discipline, and the necessity for the attainment of the true peace 'which passes understanding'. That peace has its home in the spiritual atmosphere of man's being and by 'modification of the thinking principle', by stilling the thought in meditation, some of that spiritual light floods itself upon the mirror of man's mind and thought, reflects itself in true images of the spiritual world upon the translucent waters of his soul, and then all Nature responds and obeys the commands of the Master Consciousness. The body, beautiful and pure as the substance of it is in essence, responds immediately to the subtler vibration under these conditions. Along that silver thread which runs through all the atmospheres there is a vibration of the immortal peace, and divine understanding which changes the whole consciousness. Such a man has tasted of the divine wafer, and drunk of the divine blood. His bodies have been given to drink of 'Amrita's sweet waters'.

I am quite sure that the Masters of Life can use every possible energy in Nature to convey their messages to sensitive ears. The Masters who are concerned in the realization of any ideals to which men and women have pledged themselves use the elements of Nature to come into contact with them. They send vibrations which nourish and stimulate the inner life, and their presences hover continually around the souls of men.

We must begin to realize the truth of these things, that the Spiritual Sun shines in the spiritual atmosphere for ever, and our consciousness must be quickened to perceive it in all its glory. A passage has to be made for its rays down to the heart of the physical atmosphere. These bodies which we possess have ultimately to reflect the image of the King in His beauty, and in all our acts His loveliness should be mirrored. And this is the purpose for which consciousness is associated with form—that every organ of the body and pulse of the heart should give forth the fragrance of the consciousness which men have named God.

All our images of the Master are for the purpose of reminding us that we ourselves are of the same essence, and that we must ourselves become the bearers of the Robe of Glory. The emotions have to be purified, and the waters of astral life stilled to reflect the true image of the soul. A way will then be prepared for the Master, who will come to command the riotous elements of life into obedience to the divine will.

When you are moving in the physical atmosphere, remember that it is penetrated by all the subtler atmospheres, and that as spiritual, mental and psychic beings you are moving in them, and breathing their magical airs at every moment. I know of no other magic which will reveal to you 'Eternal Beauty wandering on her way' through a world grown beautiful for love of her.

D.N.D.

⋆

The quotation in the final sentence is from the poem by W.B. Yeats 'To the Rose upon the Rood of Time', printed in italics at the front of the section headed 'The Rose' in his *Poems.*

Red Rose, proud Rose, sad Rose of all my days!
Come near me, while I sing the ancient ways:
Cuchulain battling with the bitter tide;
The Druid, grey, wood-nurtured, quiet-eyed,
Who cast round Fergus dreams, and ruin untold;
And thine own sadness, whereof stars, grown old
In dancing silver-sandalled on the sea,
Sing in their high and lonely melody.
Come near, that no more blinded by man's fate,
I find under the boughs of love and hate
In all poor foolish things that live a day,
Eternal beauty wandering on her way.

Come near, come near, come near—Ah leave me still
A little space for the rose-breath to fill!
Lest I no more hear common things that crave;
The weak worm hiding down in its small cave,
The field-mouse running by me in the grass
And heavy mortal hopes that toil and pass;
But seek alone to hear the strange things said
By God to the bright hearts of those long dead,
And learn to chaunt a tongue men do not know,
Come near; I would, before my time to go,
Sing of old Eire and the ancient ways:
Red Rose, proud Rose, sad Rose of all my days.

At the foot of the page containing Dunlop's address a further two lines of space were filled with another quotation:

> All true triumphs are triumphs not of force, but the conquest by a superior beauty of what is less beautiful. AE

With Reserve and Balance

Vera and Juliet Compton-Burnett, after describing in their obituary of Dorothy Osmond how they had joined the Theosophical Society, continued:

> It was not long before we too were working at Headquarters, where we found a situation both complicated and inharmonious. Various extraneous movements had grown up alongside the main stream of Theosophy. It must be confessed that Dorothy Osmond's melancholic temperament, coupled with that unique sense of humour which sometimes goes with it, took a certain delight in imparting these disharmonies to us. There was also a strong 'Back to Blavatsky' movement, and her sound judgement in occult matters led her to join the Blavatsky Lodge, the leader of which was D.N. Dunlop . . .

The reference is actually to the H.P.B. Lodge, in which Dunlop was active since 1915 and of which he was briefly President in 1918. Dorothy Osmond was its Secretary from 1915 to 1918.

> . . . She told us that when, feeling somewhat strange and shy, she went to her first group meeting, D.N.D., as his friends called him, and whom she had never met, immediately came up to her and said 'You are all right, Dorothy'. With these words began the closest personal contact of her life.[40]
>
> The Theosophical Library specialized in occult writings of all kinds, and

among them Rudolf Steiner's books naturally had their place. These she read as librarian, and they completely changed the direction of her thoughts. Printed at the back of these books was the address of the Anthroposophical Library, and there we all three gained access to the first English translations of the lectures.

The address was in a quite different part of London from the Theosophical Headquarters in Tavistock Square. For the Anthroposophical Library was over in Kensington, in Hereford Square at the house of Harry Collison used by the Myrdin Group.

Having ventured over to Kensington and discovered Steiner's lecture-cycles on Christological and other subjects—at this time still only available in typescript—Dorothy Osmond must have passed them on to Dunlop. But as the latter recalled in his autobiographical sketch, his initial reaction was rather circumspect:

> The manifest absurdities and trivialities filling theosophical literature, above all from the year 1907 onwards, gave rise to a natural caution when Rudolf Steiner's works first came into my hands. They were utterly different in tone and content, but I felt they must be approached with reserve and balance.
>
> I had always longed to hear of the cosmic mysteries connected with Christ and His incarnation, and here, in Anthroposophy, was the first indication that rang true. But I confess quite frankly that, at the beginning, earlier prejudices arose in strong reaction to these new teachings. Was Anthroposophy, after all, based merely on the assertions of psychic faculties as yet unproven?

★

As noted in *The Vahan*, Dunlop had also become by this time 'a very busy man'. Probably it was for this reason that he composed a letter published in the issue for September 1918.

> Dear Sir,
>
> For the information of my many friends in the Society, I hereby state that I have resigned membership of the National Council and Executive Committee, the Presidency of the London Federation and the H.P.B. Lodge.
>
> I thank you for the courtesy of inserting this letter.
>
> Yours fraternally,
>
> D.N. Dunlop

★

Dunlop had however already committed himself to an event at Michaelmas, as reported in *The Vahan*:

The ninety-sixth Conference of the Northern Federation was held at Harrogate on Saturday and Sunday, September 28th and 29th, at which Mr. D.N. Dunlop presided over a large gathering of delegates and members from all parts of the Federation area.

At the Council Meeting on Saturday afternoon a resolution was passed... A brisk discussion, the subject being 'Hierarchy and Democracy', was opened by Miss Patterson, and summed up by Mr. Dunlop, who commented on the harmony prevailing throughout the discussion.

In the evening Mr. Dunlop's address to F.T.S. on 'What is more real than a Wish in the Heart of Man?' was followed with close attention. He said his intense wish was that the T.S. should become a perfect organization in the world, and while emphasizing personal discrimination, recognized that the Society is wide enough for all to share in lifting the burden of the world.

He showed that if we feel that the T.S. corresponds to the real wish in our hearts, and if that wish be of sufficient intensity, it must come true, for the desire in the heart of man so quickly impresses the world.

Thus the T.S. will through its members fulfil its work in the world, and show itself worthy of those great leaders H.P.B. and Mrs. Besant, and become the body the Masters desire.

On Sunday afternoon the Harrogate Lodge entertained the Federation to tea, and the musical programme was much appreciated.

The Conference closed with a public lecture to a large audience by Mr. Dunlop on 'Theosophy and Human Destiny'.

The Pilgrim of Eternity

In October 1918, AE crossed once again over the Irish Sea. The context was set out by Henry Summerfield in his biography *That Myriad-Minded Man* (1975):

AE... would continue, he told his friends, to serve the I.A.O.S., and after the announcement of conscription he wrote to St. John Ervine dissociating himself from the optimism of Plunkett's renewed attempt to secure a compromise settlement, and adding exultantly:

'MacMillan and Co are bringing out a book of mine this year I think, which will finally make it impossible for me to take part in politics in Ireland, as it is full of religious heresies and will give me a bad name.'

Before the book appeared, he found time to take his usual holiday in Donegal, where he enjoyed for a time the company of James Stephens, and to make one more attempt to influence the political situation. On 11 October he joined James Douglas and the Irish labour leader Thomas Johnson in pleading Ireland's cause before the British Labour Party

Executive and the Parliamentary Committee of the Trades Union Congress. He stayed with Sidney and Beatrice Webb, and the latter was fascinated by his conversation, though her outlook was too far removed from his for real understanding. She noticed his ambivalent attitude to science, which he valued for its practical utility and as a form of intellectual training, but feared as a threat to faith in the unseen. 'Personally,' he had written in the *Homestead*, 'we believe that there are no natural explanations of anything in Nature, and that is the reason why science is so continually wrong.'[41]

On 22nd October, *The Candle of Vision* was published, and AE was pleasantly surprised by its success—it was reprinted five times within two years—though he attributed its popularity to the style: he had rewritten the individual chapters seven or eight times to make them as readable as possible, despite their difficult content. It gave him great pleasure to correspond with an elderly clergyman who was interested in a possible relationship between his book and St. John's Revelation.

In *The Candle of Vision* AE surveyed the mystical experiences of half a lifetime, seeking to convey the wonder and awe which his encounters with realities so far transcending those of bodily existence aroused in him. He felt that in using his skill as a professional writer in this way he was fulfilling a duty . . .

The first chapter, 'Retrospect', includes this passage:

I was aged about sixteen or seventeen years, when I, the slackest and least ideal of boys, with my life already made dark by those desires of body and heart with which we so soon learn to taint our youth, became aware of a mysterious life quickening within my life. Looking back, I know not of anything in friendship, anything I had read, to call this forth. It was, I thought, self-begotten. I began to be astonished with myself, for, walking along country roads, intense and passionate imaginations of another world, of an interior nature began to overpower me. They were like strangers who suddenly enter a house, who brush aside the doorkeeper, and will not be denied. Soon I knew they were the rightful owners and heirs of the house of the body, and the doorkeeper was only one who was for a time in charge, who had neglected his duty, and had pretended to ownership. The boy who existed before was an alien. He hid himself when the pilgrim of eternity took up his abode in the dwelling. Yet, whenever the true owner was absent, the sly creature reappeared and boasted himself as master once more.

That being from a distant country who took possession of the house began to speak in a language difficult to translate. I was tormented by limitations of understanding. Somewhere about me I knew there were comrades who were speaking to me, but I could not know what they said. As I walked in the evening down the lanes scented by the honeysuckle, my senses were expectant of some unveiling about to take place. I felt that beings were looking in upon me out of the true home of man. They seemed to be saying to each other of us, 'Soon they will awaken. Soon they will come to us again.' And for a moment I almost seemed to mix with their eternity. The tinted air glowed before me with intelligible significance like a face, a voice. The visible world became like a tapestry, blown and stirred by winds behind it. If it would but raise for an instant, I knew I would be in Paradise. Every form on that tapestry appeared to be the work of gods. Every flower was a word, a thought. The grass was speech; the trees were speech; the waters were speech; the winds were speech. They were the Army of the Voice[42] marching on to conquest and dominion over the spirit; and I listened with my whole being, and then these apparitions would fade away and I would be the mean and miserable boy once more. So might one have felt who had been servant of the prophet, and had seen him go up in the fiery chariot, and the world had no more light or certitude in it with that passing. I knew these visitations for what they were and named them truly in my fantasy, for writing then in the first verses of mine which still seem to me to be poetry, I said of the Earth that we and all things were her dreams:

She is rapt in dreams divine.
As her clouds of beauty pass
On our glowing hearts they shine,
Mirrored there as in a glass.

Earth, whose dreams are we and they,
With her deep heart's gladness fills
All our human lips can say
Or the dawn-fired singer trills.

The Outlook

In the volume *Zur Geschichte und aus den Inhalten der Erkenntniskultischen Abteilung der Esoterischen Schule 1904–1914* (GA 265), Hella Wiesberger included the following editorial matter:

Describing the cognitional-cultic institution in his autobiography *The Course of My Life*, Rudolf Steiner states that it fell asleep on the outbreak of war in summer 1914 because it would have been taken as a secret society, though nothing of the sort obtained. In her essay 'Was Rudolf Steiner a Freemason?' Marie Steiner states that he declared the institution suspended and in token thereof tore up the relevant document. This action was obviously taken because the outbreak of war made it clear to him that Freemasonry as an 'originally good and necessary thing', intended to serve the whole of humanity without distinction, had been placed through certain Western secret societies in the service of 'folk egoism and the selfish interests of particular human groups'.

It was this misuse for special political purposes which he held responsible for the catastrophic development introduced by the World War in 1914, and which he strongly condemned. This is expounded in detail in lectures during the war years 1914 to 1918. He was extremely concerned to contribute as much as possible towards forming a judgement on the occult background which had led to the outbreak of this War, and above all to an open explanation of the question of war-guilt. On this account he also wrote a foreword to the work *Entente-Freimaurerei und der Weltkrieg* (1919) by Karl Heise, when asked by the latter to do so. However good or bad this work may be, it was at any rate the first attempt to verify by external documents the tendencies which Rudolf Steiner had sketched.

His sharp condemnation of the special political interests of certain Western secret societies did not of course refer to the Masonic cause as such. This is confirmed by the fact that soon after the end of the War he advised a member of his 'slumbering' symbolic-cultic institution (Johannes Geyer, then a minister in Hamburg) to be admitted into Freemasonry. This emerges from his letter of the 25th of February 1919 to Rudolf Steiner, which among other things states: 'Following your advice, on the 13th of February I had myself admitted into Freemasonry. To be precise, I joined the Johannine 'From the Rock to the Sea' Lodge which belongs to an Association of the Grand National Mother Lodge in the Prussian State called 'To the Three Cosmic Globes'. This is the same lodge to which our friends A.W. Sellin and Kurt Walther belong, as well as Hackländer in Wandsbeck. In course of time I hope to awaken and maintain an interest for anthroposophically oriented occultism in this circle. It is from that point of view that I have taken this step. May the gatherings in our own occult Society soon also be resumed!'

★

In November 1893 D.N. Dunlop published in *The Irish Theosophist* an 'Interview with Mr. W.B. Yeats' relating the poet's memories of H.P. Blavatsky.

The interview included this passage:

> 'On one occasion, too,' said Mr. Yeats, continuing, 'she referred to the Greek Church as the church of her childhood . . .'

In December 1935 Walter Johannes Stein published in *The Present Age* his 'Appreciation of Daniel Nicol Dunlop' which stated:

> Mr. Dunlop joined the Greek Church as a member about the year 1920. He wished—in this connection—to travel in Russia, and he really started,

but unforeseen circumstances intervened and he got no further than Norway . . .

The date of the journey, and its resultant effect on the traveller's mind, can be gauged from a statement in 'The Outlook' by H. Haden Guest, General Secretary of the Theosophical Society in England and Wales, dated 15 March 1919 and appearing on the front page of the next issue of *The Vahan*.

> I am busy getting ready to leave for Paris next week.
>
> I have thought for some months past that it was highly desirable that I should meet Capitaine Blech, the French General Secretary, and discuss with him the resumption of theosophical relations and propaganda on the Continent, and the calling together of a general assembly of Fellows of the Theosophical Society as soon as possible . . .
>
> My view on the subject has been much strengthened by the news that Mrs. Besant contemplates paying us a visit sometime in May or June. If she can carry out her intention—and there is, I believe, a good chance that she can do so, despite the shortage of ship room—she will be able, and I hope willing, to preside over the general assembly . . .
>
> My view on the subject has been strengthened by yet another piece of news, i.e. the report of Mr. Dunlop on the situation in Norway, which I had the pleasure of hearing from his own lips a few days ago upon his return to this country.
>
> Mr. Dunlop told me that he found in Norway that the followers of Dr. Steiner and the members of the American Theosophical Society, the organ of which is the *Theosophical Quarterly*, were in the aggregate more numerous than we were, and that both possessed good headquarters which our Society lacked . . .

★

While Dunlop had set out towards the north with the intention of travelling further east, Harry Collison was making a journey in a completely opposite direction—to the west! Referring in *A Commentary on Rudolf Steiner's Four Mystery Plays* to his school-friends, he continued:

> . . . We finished our work on the Plays during the War of 1914–1918, and in the following year [1919] I returned to America to arrange publication on a legal and workable basis with the well-known firm of Messrs. Putnam. This closed my legal career.
>
> With the printer's proof of the Plays I went round the world lecturing and reciting—and I established groups for study in America, New Zealand and Australia . . .

Rudolf Steiner's *Four Mystery Plays* were first published in English in 1919, with an introduction which finished:

> ... In conclusion I should like to express my gratitude to my friends and fellow students R.T. Gladstone, M.A., Cantab., and S.M.K. Gandell, M.A., Oxon., for their most valuable help in the very difficult task of translating the plays into English verse. Only a translator can appreciate the difficulties involved in preserving both the sense and rhythm of the original, and it is no exaggeration to say that without their aid the production of these works in English would not have been possible at the present time.
>
> I should also like to take the occasion of thanking Dr. Steiner himself for permitting me to attend the rehearsals and assist in the performances of the plays. It was a great privilege and pleasure for which I can never feel sufficiently grateful. And last but not least, I have to thank him for his ever kind and patient attention to all my questions on the subject of these plays and of spiritual science in general.
>
> H. Collison.
> New York, 1919

★

The Vahan reported on the 'London Federation':

> The Spring Conference and Annual Business Meeting was held at the Mortimer Halls on Saturday April 12th, at 3. p.m. and was well attended ...
>
> At 6.30 a debate on the subject of 'Theosophy and the League of Nations' began, with Mr. Hare in the chair. The subject was opened by Mr. Howell ... Mr. Dunlop then spoke at some length, expressing his belief that the real League of Nations would spring out of the present Paris Conference, and giving voice to his opinion on several other subjects ...

The Needs of the Times

In April 1919 Rudolf Steiner travelled into Germany to involve himself as fully as possible in the campaign for the Threefold Social Order. He did not return to Switzerland until August. During his long absence from Dornach, an extensive correspondence developed between himself and Edith Maryon, who had started to translate into English his latest book *Die Kernpunkte der Sozialen Frage.*

A large part of this correspondence also throws indirect light onto anthroposophical affairs of the time in England. This part is here reproduced.

Villa Rosenau,
Arlesheim bei Basel.
29th of April 1919

Dear Teacher,

Frau von Heydebrand has taken two shots of the Christ figure, and I'll be sending them to Berlin as soon as I get some copies. At the moment everything in the studio is going reasonably, if rather slowly, forwards. I've already sent to England the translated foreword, 1st chapter and appeal, and am now asking you to correct the (enclosed) paper.

The weather in Dornach is dreadful, snow, rain and cold, only 2 degrees temperature in the studio.

Frau Stein read me out today a letter from her husband in Stuttgart. It was most interesting to hear something of the work there; we're falling a little to sleep again here!

With heartfelt greetings,

Edith Maryon

★

Stuttgart,
10th of May 1919

My dear Fräulein E. Maryon,

Many thanks for the letter. I'm so overworked here that I can't look through the paper you enclosed or return it for a few more days, if it's to be done properly. Giving at least one lecture every day with a discussion following is demanding too much from the old organism, and with artistic work at Dornach I'd be glad in between to exert other bodily members than only the larynx as here. And yet so it all has to be. Since the day before yesterday it seems I might be better understood than previously. But it can always still change. Naturally I'm thinking a great deal about work at Dornach and will be pleased when conditions again allow me to share in it. Work here will still last some time.

Heartfelt greetings for today,

Rudolf Steiner

Stuttgart, Landhausstrasse 70 (c/o Kinkel)

★

Villa Rosenau,
Arlesheim bei Basel,
21st of May 1919

Dear Teacher,

I've been spending two days in Zurich. At the Women's Congress on Saturday Herr Dr. Boos sent me an urgent telegram, saying my presence in

Zurich was urgently needed for discussion with the delegates. I found a lady friendly enough to promise to take papers along, so gave her two copies of 'The Kernel' etc., the letters and the translation of the book's first chapter—hopefully they'll arrive all right. (I hadn't received any news about the previous letters.) Listening to the speeches was for me most interesting. A deputation is being sent to Paris to protest against the blockade and the peace conditions. They can speak well and quite reasonably, but I fear very little will be achieved.

A very nice letter has arrived from Collison—now in California. The appeal was forwarded to him in New York and he made use of it both there and in England.

The four translations of the plays are now being printed, and he hopes to send you copies in autumn at the latest. Unfortunately—he continues—they still cost such a frightful amount that I never have anything to send our dear Teacher. He says the translation of 'Social Question' should be sent to a Dr. Connor in Chicago. But it has to wait for everything to be ready and properly worked through, as it's terribly difficult!

Everything in the studio is slowly making progress, with great longing for your help and correction, and hope that a time for this will soon be coming? I'd be very glad to hear that lectures are only necessary every other day and not daily.

With heartfelt greetings,

L. Edith C. Maryon

No Duty May be Evaded

Ten days later, on 31 May, D.N. Dunlop gave an address to the Second Annual Conference of the Braille and 'Servers of the Blind' League, a theosophical foundation of the time.

He chose the subject 'Duty', and drew part of the substance of his address from an article of that title, headed by an epigraph from the *Bhagavadgita*, which was published in *The Word* in December 1915 by H.W. Percival's friend and ammanuensis Benoni B. Gattell. Dunlop's address was brought out as a pamphlet, and comparison reveals that for almost three quarters of his text he made intermittent borrowings from Gattell's article of certain ideas, phrases, even at times whole sentences, around which however he also developed thoughts of his own on the subject. The final quarter of his address was entirely original.

There follow Dunlop's own portions from this address, with gaps indicated for the parts adopted from Gattell's article. The discussion of the word 'karma' is also largely drawn from an editorial on that subject published in *The Word* in August 1908, showing the extent to which Dunlop had absorbed the contents of this journal.

> In considering the subject of duty I found that the root of the word brought me to the idea of debt . . . Every single man in the world at any given moment knows what his duty is. There is, moreover, no need to spend any time in regretting duties omitted in the past, because every moment spent in regret of past sins of omission or commission is wasted, giving less efficiency for the present moment. Therefore spend no time in regret. Be, in each moment, ready to perform the duty of that moment . . .
>
> I personally cannot treat a subject in any other way, to be true to myself, than from the standpoint of Theosophy, which to me, and probably to many in this hall, is not a belief or religion, but a life. It includes all religions, all points of view, all philosophy, all science; everything in fact, that interests man as a thinking being.
>
> It is stated, not only by theosophists, but by thinkers of all schools . . . that there is a fundamental unity or harmony at the root of all manifested worlds. The physical universe is but a small part of the universe *in toto* . . . Mind is a principle in operation in every department of Nature. In all the kingdoms of Nature some degree of intelligence is in operation. This intelligence, although it has reached a higher degree of individualization in man than in the lower kingdoms, is not yet fully manifested or incarnate in physical man, but only partially so . . . The five senses . . . delude the mind. They lead the being astray, they deceive him, they lead him to believe (because of their limited range of perception) that the physical world is the only world of reality, that matter is just as 'solid' as it appears to be, but even the work of so-called materialistic science proves this to be an erroneous conception, and one only has to consider the phenomena of the penetrating radium rays to realize how thin a veil is offered by the seeming opacity of physical matter.
>
> Since the substance of the universe is fundamentally a unity, it follows that every disturbance of its harmony necessitates a reaction to restore harmony, and this action and reaction, constantly in operation, is called by theosophists by a Sanscrit word, *Karma*. Karma is a curious term, which, to people who have not studied the subject, suggests Kismet—Fatalism. But let us look at it for a moment. It is built up of certain Sanscrit roots, 'Ka' and 'Ma', bound together by the letter 'R'. 'Ka' is the first and most elementary sound produced in the throat. Therefore with the ancients it was a symbol of Brahma as creator of the universe. The 'word' or 'sound' is always associated with creation, as a study of the first chapter of Genesis will remind you. Then there is 'Ma'. Its root is Manas, mind, thought. 'R' signifies action, motion, vibration. So we have the word *karma* representing desire or will, and mind, in action. Three principles, therefore, in man are included in the word *karma*, which is rightly 'the law of action and reaction' operative through all the worlds in space . . .

The wise men of the ages have taught us, and some of us have proved its truth in experience, that man's true life extends beyond the circle of his present limitations and beyond his personal memory, and duty is an obligation to which man is held... Whatever his occupation in life, whatever his environment, though they always entail action of some sort for the sake of others, yet fundamentally man is always performing his duty to himself... Death provides no release, for duty is an imperative backed up by all the forces of the universe. It may be postponed for a time, but it always rises again with all the weight of the past behind it, with reactions from an ever-widening circle.

Everything in the physical world is the expression of something which has its root in the worlds of more subtle matter—the invisible worlds. There is nothing that may be said truly to originate in the physical world. It is true that man is subject to impacts from without which are real, but his response to them is modified and affected by his own karma, and by his understanding of life and sense of duty. This world in which we now find ourselves is the most important of all the worlds in which man's consciousness operates, because it is the point of balance, the realm of synthesis and of complete crystallization. Physical life determines all destiny and karma. It is *here* that the work must be done.

The physical matter in which our consciousness manifests reveals the effects of the invisible, impersonal laws which are immanent and transcendent through the universe. In man the physical body is, as I said before, only one aspect of the expression of the invisible—it is the small portion which can be made manifest at a given time and in a given place, and only a very small portion of the total karma of any individual acts at one time, namely that which relates directly to the environment in which he finds himself at the moment. The invisible past is focused in the visible present, and from the present radiates the future. Here and now in this physical world of crystallization, there is worked out second by second, hour by hour, the intricate design and order of that Archetypal Plan which converges from the ends of the Earth, connecting all things and everyone together 'in mystic brotherhood'. That process is going on eternally.

It appears to me that this, when properly understood, will induce in the mind an attitude of reflection and of worship... All duties are noble if performed faithfully, however trifling they appear to be, and their fulfilment is the only way to attain complete individual freedom. Our duties are assigned to us by that divine portion of ourselves which is variously named Christ, the Master, the higher self, the 'Light which lighteth every man coming into the world'.

Every neglected duty has to be faced again under different conditions, because only so can man bring about that equilibrium between himself and the universe which is necessary to his evolution and development. It is only by the performance of his duty that man merits assistance from those who are able to serve the race on a wider scale of usefulness, and with wider range of understanding and knowledge. No Master, no priest, no bishop can perform our duties for us, for we must learn at some point of our evolution to perform them for ourselves.

I do not believe that any of us here would willingly give a burden to another to bear, but it is quite true that when we fail to perform a duty it devolves upon someone near to us. We make their burdens a little heavier, and it is only a temporary release from our own obligations.

I expect the idea of the redemption of the world by the saviours of the race will present itself to your minds in this connection. It is true that every saviour is an embodiment of the life of the Logos, and possesses a power which makes it a little easier for us to perform our duty. In that sense there may be redemption, but it is none the less an individual matter. 'And I, if I be lifted up, will draw all men unto Me,' but that does not in any sense imply that man's efforts should be lessened.

Through the two thousand years that have elapsed since the birth of the Christian Master, there stands the figure of Jesus who became Christ, unique and splendid, who has helped men through the centuries to strive a little more zealously in the performance of duty. The stimulus has never departed from this Earth, and men and women, when they feel unable any longer to bear the burden of life, have by the very intensity of their mood risen to the plane where the Christ is with them 'even unto the end of the world.' But no external saviour, be he ever so mighty, can attain freedom for another.

We have seen then that the precipitation from the invisible past in the form of duty has to be met faithfully by every man, if he would set himself free for greater work. By the performance of duty we call upon that Light which never dies from the beginning to the end of the manifested universe, which man in his true being really is. It is this Light which radiates upon all the problems which beset the soul and is the solvent in which all doubts are ultimately destroyed. With this consciousness the future can be looked into with perfect confidence, and the soul can stand unafraid and untroubled before 'a million universes'. Do not brood upon your ignorance or failings or limitations. I remember once when I felt the skies were as brass, the world empty, and everything seemed to conspire against me, that a little child in trouble came across my path. In trying to make that little child happy the skies became clear blue, and the joy of life broke over me again like the rising of the Sun over grey hills.

So in conclusion I would say to you that in moments of complexity you can find the magical solvent for all doubts by invoking the Divine Being which is your real self and that the simplest duty, faithfully performed, takes you forward on 'the path to glory', to the kingdoms where, in the imagery of an ancient Egyptian scripture, the soul is weighed against the feather of Truth in the Halls of Osiris, and is not found wanting.

⋆

A few days after Dunlop gave his address on duty, Rudolf Steiner included a small observation on the same subject in his next letter to Edith Maryon:

Stuttgart,
4th of June 1919

Dear Fräulein E. Maryon,

Many thanks for the letter. I've been wanting to reply for a long time, but am weighed down by much work which really needs everything to be considered at length. It would all of course be much easier if on top of everything else one were not confronted by misunderstandings which are still continually arising. Everything one says, when further related, at once becomes something totally different. I see that people are fighting against me on all sides through being misinformed. They try to shove everything into a party-political stereotype, and if it's something which has no connection with any party at all, then they make out of it something utterly different. It's not only opponents who are doing this, but also people who are kindly disposed towards the cause I represent. So all the actual work is very difficult.

I'm very satisfied to hear the sculptural work in Dornach is progressing and will be very pleased when I can again do artistic work there, far from the daily bustle of the moment. But one has to serve the needs of the times. No duty may be evaded. I hear my book on the social question has now come out in Switzerland; I hope people see from it what I really want, and numerous things perhaps abate which only arise from tittle-tattle by opponents—and beginners too.

However, I'm pleased there are people who properly understand me and with this thought

send heartfelt greetings in unchangeable attitude,

Dr. Rudolf Steiner

Stuttgart, Landhausstrasse 70, (c/o Kinkel)

A Protest

The Twenty-Eighth Annual Convention of the Theosophical Society in England and Wales took place on Saturday, 7 June 1919. *The Vahan* reported the initial Business Meeting:

The General Secretary took the Chair at 11 a.m. and opened the Convention with the joyful news that the President was now in London and would attend and speak at several meetings during this Convention . . .

The Chairman then explained that he had not himself proposed any agenda because he thought it better to leave the meeting entirely free to select its own subjects for consideration . . .

Mr. D.N. Dunlop then rose to make a protest against the nature of the programme for this Convention. He expected something very different after what had been said last year: he hoped for a programme on a fine theosophical scale, and this was nothing of the sort. He protested against the Union Lodge being given the privilege of receiving Mrs. Besant, and in spite of what the Chairman said, he thought a little guidance might have been afforded as to what to discuss. He particularly objected to the absence from the programme of any provision for the general public, to which none of the meetings were open. He then proposed for the consideration of the meeting the following subject in the form of a resolution:

'This Convention of the T.S. in England and Wales heartily welcomes the President of the T.S. on her return to England after a prolonged absence due to the War, and seeks to strengthen her hands in all work which she undertakes for the good of humanity.

'This Convention confidently relies on the President to protect the best interests of the T.S. in any change of its objects which may be proposed by anyone, so that no alteration will be made involving members of the Society in the acceptance of any form of dogma.'

This proposal was seconded by Mr. C.S. Best, and after taking a vote upon it, the Chairman declared it open for discussion.

One or two amendments were proposed with a view to dividing the resolution into two parts, and ultimately it was decided so to divide it.

The Chairman then put the first part of the resolution as follows, viz.:

'This Convention of the T.S. in England and Wales heartily welcomes the President of the T.S. on her return to England after a prolonged absence due to the War, and seeks to strengthen her hands in all work which she undertakes for the good of humanity' and declared the same carried unanimously. In moving the second part of the resolution in the following words, viz.:

'This Convention confidently relies on the President to protect the best interests of the T.S in any change of its objects which may be proposed by anyone, so that no alteration will be made involving members of the Society in the acceptance of any form of dogma.'

Mr. Dunlop said that we ought to declare quite frankly that, whatever alterations were made in the objects of the Society, we will not impose a dogma upon anyone who wishes to enter the Society. He was opposed, for instance, to the inclusion of any declaration as to the existence of Masters in the objects of the Society, not because he himself did not believe in them; on the contrary, he knew of their existence of his own knowledge, but because the whole tradition of the Society is that it is intended to be a free unsectarian body, welcoming all persons who wish to join it, without making such persons feel that they have to accept any dogma before being admitted to membership.

An interesting and animated discussion ensued . . . and Mr. Dunlop then expressed the wish not to ask for a vote on the resolution . . .

One may recall here further questions which Dunlop was at this time considering, as listed in his autobiographical sketch:

Would room be left in Rudolf Steiner's teachings for the exercise of that 'healthy human reason' which now seemed to have deserted so many thousands of theosophists? Was this new spiritual teaching capable not only of theoretical but of practical application to human life and activity, to art, to science in all its branches, to therapy, education, religion, economics, industrial and social life? Would it speak as a reminder and revealer of knowledge already hidden in the soul, and not as another body of doctrine to which there was no inner assent?

The Vahan gave further details of 'H.Q. Timetable':

On Sunday June 8th, the Public Lecture will not be held at the Mortimer Halls but at the Royal Institute of Painters in Water-Colours, 195, Piccadilly, when Mr. D.N. Dunlop will speak on Theosophy and the Theosophical Society.

This lecture—unreported—was held on Whit Sunday.

Available to English Readers

On the very same day as D.N. Dunlop was giving in London his lecture on 'Theosophy and the Theosophical Society', Edith Maryon was writing from the Dornach neighbourhood to Rudolf Steiner:

Villa Rosenau,
Arlesheim.
Whitsun morning.

Dear Teacher,

Your letter's very welcome, though I'm sorry about the content: hearing how many hindrances and misunderstandings must be fought against if such hard work is to make progress. I can only recommend every person to study the book thoroughly, as there'll then be no need to bring in all conceivable things which have nothing to do with the matter at all. I'll finish the translation this weekend, the first time, that is. It then has to be worked through critically. I still have nothing to report about the printing; at the moment I'm corresponding with Fräulein Franklin (the ground first has to be a bit prepared), but hope things are now so far that she'll visit the publisher this week. It seems paper is now very expensive and the price of books has risen very high. She also finds the book hard to understand. So I've no idea how far our luck will hold. I've had a favourable review of the first chapter from Miss Hughes, but not yet from the Professor. I'd like to read the most recent book if a copy were available, but perhaps one has to wait till it's no longer dangerous to send. Is there any hope that Stuttgart work will be far enough by the end of the month for you to resume work here? Everything is moving slowly forward; the scaffolding between pillars and windows on the south side of the Goetheanum has been removed, so the vault and pillars are standing free and the capitals can be seen. It's really wonderfully beautiful, and allows one to foresee what the effect will be when completely freed from the forest of scaffolding poles. I did a casting of the (plasticine) head of the 2nd Ahriman in the big studio, so the model can stand beside it when working out the wooden head in the small studio. But the original will of course be spoilt. May I have it done, or would you prefer us to wait a bit with this?

I hope the letter about Collison and the photographs arrived all right? Otherwise everything here is unchanged.

With heartfelt greetings,

L. Edith Maryon

★

Steiner replied:

Stuttgart,
28th of June 1919

My dear Fräulein E. Maryon,

I was very pleased to receive the letters and packet of pictures. The work here still has to go on for some time. But this time I don't believe it'll be too long. I'm longing very much to be at work in the sculpture studio at Dornach. After a time I can probably once more be there, and then return again here to found a school being planned for Stuttgart. But about the next period of time nothing can be said for sure. The conditions of our times don't allow that kind of certainty.

It's very difficult to find any understanding for what's most needed in the conditions of our times. It's becoming hard for people of our time to understand these needs out of a spiritual background. The influence of materialistic habits of thought has estranged them from any understanding of how spirit is also at work in matter. They believe material things can only be improved through material things, and don't see that every attempt to improve matter just by matter leads to further confusion. To many people my book is incomprehensible just because it contains different things from what they were hitherto accustomed to think. If people already find it hard to get rid of other habits, they find it hardest to rid themselves of habits of thought. But there's no help for our time except by rethinking and relearning.

I'm thinking a lot about our work in the Dornach sculpture studio and would like to be there. It's just that work must be done which there's a duty to do, and only my thoughts can be there.

With heartfelt greetings,

Dr. Rudolf Steiner

Currently at Landhausstrasse 70, Stuttgart (c/o Kinkel).

★

Maryon had by now completed her translation of the *Kernpunkte*. She was however not the only English person to have been so impressed by this book as to have thought of translating it. George Adams recalls the powerful effect of the book on his Cambridge friend Ethel Bowen-Wedgwood:

Towards the end of the War, while I was her guest, Mrs. Wedgwood heard of Rudolf Steiner's work through me. She read with deep interest his lectures on the Apocalypse, in which the spiritual-scientific conception of human history and evolution is set forth. Then in the spring of 1919 came his newly written book on the Threefold Social Order. Mrs. Wedgwood had always taken an active part in public life. In her girlhood she had known the aged Gladstone, a personal friend of her father's. Her lifelong interest and belief in a renewal of the body politic in the true human spirit of the time was quickened and enhanced by the terrible events of the War, to which her generous nature responded with intense human sympathy and with indignation against any falsehood or injustice. With all the enthusiasm of her choleric temperament, she now entered into the solution which emerged from Dr. Steiner's masterly analysis, in which all her experience appeared confirmed and her ideals realized, not with Utopian proposals, but with a practicable and progressive path to their fulfilment.

We wrote to Rudolf Steiner: it was important that this book be made available to English readers as well. We offered to translate it.

Greatly Significant

The offer by Elizabeth Bowen-Wedgwood and George Adams to translate the *Kernpunkte* was first noted in a further letter from Edith Maryon to Rudolf Steiner:

Villa Rosenau,
Arlesheim bei Basel,
6th of July 1919

Dear Teacher,

I'm sending you herewith the most recent photo of Christ's head, it's also the best so far. Then I'd like to know if I might call the book's title 'The Roots of the Social Question within the Vital Needs of the Present and Future'. I don't like 'Germs', it sounds rather funny and doesn't satisfy anyone. I'm now waiting for a reply from Messrs. Routledge (instead of the National Labour Press; they've no office in London, and Miss Franklin applied to the other publishers.)

I'm really very sorry the work is made so difficult by so little understanding. Herr Dr. Boos was here today and seems very satisfied with progress in Switzerland. A very nice letter has come from a lady in England; she seems to have some understanding of the matter and is offering to do the translation. Herr Dr. Boos introduced me today to an American lady, now English, and she's promising funds and other help. She was very nice. She wants to win over Bernard Shaw and Wells to our cause, if she could, they could do a lot for the cause. The last blocks are coming into the studio this week; it'll all then be arranged, but the work is longing very much for its foremost sculptor, especially the figure of Christ.

A dreadful housing shortage has broken out; many houses have been sold. A wealthy Swiss lady has offered double for Fräulein Clason's room, more than triple for services etc., so Fräulein Clason is now on the street. My own life here will probably be short too; double is already being asked for heating etc., and I've already been asked if it wouldn't be better to find other rooms! But I'm (still) staying a bit longer. I've had much discussion with Herr Bay about the possibility of building small houses to provide rooms at about 30–35 francs, and he's now considering the matter. I thought my mother might perhaps lend me the money for a three-roomed house, if land could be rented near the canteen or the office (because of plumbing etc.). Herr Bay thinks some rich members from Bern would like to build these sort of houses. But I'm waiting first for your opinion, till you come. The plan is for 2 rooms and 2 kitchens but I'd like 3 rooms and 1 kitchen, and thought it might perhaps be something for Kisseleff, Clason and myself, if the price is within possible reach. I first have to know your opinion; we're waiting till you come, and just hoping the wait won't last too long. Correction of the book's final proof is going very slowly; my head seems to have become rather tired!

A small committee has been formed in England for work on the social question. Herr Dr. Boos is suggesting I travel to England and give lantern-lectures on the Goetheanum!!

There's a lot of work here too, Stuttgart has already had very much.

With heartfelt wishes,

L. Edith C. Maryon

★

Maryon's next letter to Steiner is undated, but was presumably also written in July 1919:

Studio Villa Rosenau,
Arlesheim,
Sunday

Dear Teacher,

I've now received news that Messrs. Routledge would rather not take the book, as they're not in agreement with such questions. If they were to bring it out, it would only be at our risk, and the costs £100—1000 copies, afterwards £12–£13 per 1000. Mr. Courtney went to the National Labour Press and was sent from there to a very well-known Labour person, who has dealings with a publishing firm. He speaks very favourably about the book, and will give us a reply within a week. They work with Messrs. Allen and Unwin and publish all the Fabian literature. We don't seem to have lost any time, as it's now holiday time and very unfavourable for books; those published now almost without exception go wrong. The book could appear in October and they say the best time is from 1st Oct. to Christmas.

A small committee has now been formed in England for work on the social question, and Mr. Kaufmann has given 4 lectures on the book for members and friends. He seems to have spoken very well, and his audience was very enthused and showed great interest in the ideas. He thought it would be good to write an article for a newspaper, to herald the book in. What d'you think?

Please address letters to me in the studio; I shan't be in Rosenau any more after the 1st Aug.—my room has been let to someone else at a much higher rate. I have Miss Maquet's room till 1st Oct., afterwards uncertain.

I've many things to ask—and hope you can soon return; it's now very long since you've been away. On Thursday we celebrated a topping-out ceremony for the group. The final block was set up in place and we were photographed on top, some of the workers and woodcarvers, that is—as a co-worker you were there too, but unfortunately just metaphorically! I don't yet know how it'll come out, as Frau von Heydebrand almost had to float in the air with her camera!

There's a concert today in the Arlesheim church for the benefit of holiday children from Munich. Herr Schuurman is playing, so I believe many of us will be going, despite the fact that money is much more important than our presence.

I'm hoping for a reply to my last letter!

With heartfelt greetings,

L. Edith C. Maryon

I'd like to give the book to a German to read, so that all semantic errors could be spotted, but who? If you return as soon as possible, perhaps Frau Dr.?

★

Steiner replied:

Stuttgart,
25th of July 1919

My dear Fräulein Edith Maryon,

It was nice to receive the two letters and the picture of our artistic work. I'm sorry to hear such difficulties have arisen with housing. But perhaps something can be arranged to moderate the difficulties. My own work here hasn't lessened at all. These last few days, for instance, I've been giving lectures here on Sunday, in Heilbronn on Monday, in Ulm on Tuesday, here on Wednesday; on Thursday I was speaking here for the eurythmy, and today had many interviews and so on. In between, a lot to discuss—and to write.

How much I'd like to be at our artistic work again! Our plan at the moment is to proceed to Dornach in the first half of August. At present all is uncertain. But I'm definitely hoping this will happen. However, I have to be in Stuttgart again during the second half of August, to give a course for the teachers of a school to be founded according to my intentions. And yet, if all goes as I'm thinking now, I'd be at work again in the sculpture studio for a short time.—Boos has meanwhile done good work in Switzerland.

The train of ideas, however, is too little understood. There are certainly few who show comprehension. There's a lot of misunderstanding and people are coming forward much too slowly for the conditions of the times. You too are having difficulties translating my book. But it'll be greatly significant for this translation to come out.

Besides the other sort of lectures I have in the last few days also given anthroposophical ones. People can now even be said to be more obliging towards these than towards the others.

In the time left over from work I'm thinking a lot about the sculptural work in our studio. I'll be pleased to be there again. We'll see if it'll be in the first half of August.

Heartfelt greetings for today from

Rudolf Steiner

Stuttgart, Landhausstrasse 70.

Fruit in Practical Life

AE's *Collected Poems*, first published in September 1913, was reprinted in November 1913, December 1914 and April 1917, each time in a print-run of 1000 copies. A further edition appeared in July 1919, with the same print-run, but with new poems added. The dedication remained unchanged.

A recent work by the dedicatee had meanwhile been translated into another language, as seen from a book review in the August issue of *The Vahan*:

> *La Science de l'Immortalité.* By D.N. Dunlop (traduit de l'anglais). (Paris: Publications théosophiques.)
>
> We were pleased to receive this translation of Mr. Dunlop's last book, and congratulate the French Section of the T.S. on having obtained the co-operation of Mlle. Marcelle Senard, to whom, only a few years ago, was entrusted the rendering into French of Edward Carpenter's *Towards Democracy*.
>
> We think it would be hard to select a passage more indicative of the high standard of Mlle. Senard's work than the following, which, beautiful as it is in English, is so beautiful in French that it is almost difficult to believe it a translation:
>
> 'L'homme quitte les eaux ténébreuses, il entre dans la voie qui, depuis le commencement du monde, invoquait la trace de son passage, ses pieds sont encore humides de l'écume de la mer, et son regard pénètre à peine la brume qui l'enveloppe encore. Mais son âme est ainsi faite qu'elle ne peut cesser de lutter, jusqu'à ce que le tumulte de ses éléments ait fait place au calme qui réfléchit la beauté parfaite, comme les eaux tranquilles d'un lac réfléchissent l'image du soleil.'

⋆

The Electrical Development Association was founded in 1919. It is referred to in the press notice circluated by the BEAMA straight after Dunlop's death, parts of which were incorporated into obituaries in *British Industries*, *The Electrical Review* and *The Electrical Contractor and Retailer.*

Mr. Dunlop was perhaps most widely known as Director of the BEAMA. The original conception of that organization was his; and after it was firmly established, he was inevitably carried by its success into all the ramifications of the electrical world, and he seized every opportunity afforded by the rising tide of electrical science and industry of advancing the common cause. Many of his most brilliant conceptions are perhaps not now generally recognized as such and many possibly forgotten. The BEAMA itself was the most successful of them, but the early days of the Electrical Research Association [to be founded in 1920], when co-operative effort was almost unknown, saw him in the van of progress; and he should be given (for he never took it) full credit for the creation of the Electrical Development Association, a branch of activity which was particularly attractive to him as a trained publicist. He had the Scot's *nous* to perceive that 'business' always comes first, but that those valuable instruments of electrical progress, education, research, standardization etc. should be put into motion concurrently; and they received their impulse from him. The committees on which he found himself, either as Chairman (always a willing one) or member, were as the sands of the sea in number, some of them, perhaps (as is not unusual) rather shifting sand. Much has been said in disparagement of the committee method of arriving at action; but in his case there were some fundamental principles behind. He *believed* in committee meetings as a means of settling rivalries. A case in point is the Fair Trading Council, an attempt to reconcile very many conflicting views within the home industry. Several such enterprises, originated by him, will occur to everyone. Talk, conciliation, reconcilement: those were his methods, and in many cases they brought everyone into final agreement. His patience was endless, his suavity acknowledged by all; he might not ineptly be called 'the great conciliator'.

And how, after all the talk, were the original conceptions brought down to bedrock fact in action and work? The answer seems to be that he had the priceless gift of choosing the right men and winning their loyalty. His time was always at their disposal at any hour of the day or night, without notice. He was rarely known to reprimand anyone for haste or error resulting from over-enthusiasm; and nothing that he said left a sting behind. He would have heartily agreed that, as with Nature, there are no punishments but only consequences. A vivid personality, almost baffling description, he has been described as a Scotch metaphysician; and undoubtedly his private philosophic studies engendered in him a detachment of mind enabling him to face delays and opposition with patience and equanimity in the sure belief that he was endeavouring to create something that would meet with approval in the future even if the present did not receive his proposals with enthusiasm.

Dunlop's address on *Duty* was brought out by the Theosophical Publishing House, 1, Upper Woburn Place, W.C.1, with a note on the title-page stating that 'All profits on the sale of this pamphlet go to the service of the blind.'

The address was prefaced by a foreword:

> In the midst of many business concerns and at a certain inconvenience, I consented to give the public address to the Second Annual Conference of the Braille and 'Servers of the Blind' League, because I could not fail to have sympathy with the objects of such a league, and appreciation of the selfless spirit shown by many of its workers.
>
> A faith that really lives always bears fruit in practical life, and I chose the subject of 'Duty' because I thought it would have a close relationship to the ideal of service for those who suffer from the great physical disadvantage of blindness.
>
> I wanted to lift the idea of duty away from the rather pious atmosphere with which it is often associated, and to restore some of the ancient inspiration which saw in the daily round of tasks accomplished the fulfilment of divine law, and which revealed the truth that 'faithfulness in little things', according to the saying of the wise old Chinese Master, is the only way whereby further opportunities may be earned for service worthy to be offered in the fellowship of the Three Kings.
>
> D.N.D.
>
> August 1919

★

(The last reference is probably connected to a small society for the furtherance of occult and literary interests, 'The Fellowship of the Three Kings', organized by W.B. Yeats and others in London in 1900 and 1901—though this was a very long time previously. A few meetings were reported in *The Lamp* when Dunlop was associate editor. Among other members was the occult publisher and bookseller John M. Watkins.)

Dunlop's foreword was followed by a page of epigraphs. The first, although taken from the *Bhagavadgita*, was a quite different one from that used by Benoni B. Gattell.

> Men being contented and devoted to their own proper duties attain perfection. Hear now how that perfection is attained by devotion to natural duty. If a man maketh an offering to the Supreme Being, who is the source of the works of all, and by whom this universe was spread abroad, he thus obtaineth perfection. The performance of the duties of a man's own particular calling, although devoid of excellence, is better than doing the duty of another, however well performed; and he who fulfils the duties obligated by Nature, does not incur sin. A man's own natural duty, even though stained with faults, ought not to be abandoned. For all human acts are involved in faults, as the fire is wrapped in smoke. The highest perfection of

> freedom from action is attained through renunciation, by him who in all works has an unfettered mind and subdued heart.
>
> From the *Bhagavad Gita.*

> It (the Tao) is that great crown of acts by which man might escape from bondage. Therefore it has remained the greatest thing in the world, acting without design, capable without making a business of it, finding the great in what is small, the many in the few, repaying injury with kindness, effecting difficult things in their beginnings. This is the way of Tao.
>
> From a Chinese scripture.

Faithful to the Original

Rudolf Steiner finally returned to Dornach in the first half of August. It may have been then that he wrote to Elizabeth Bowen-Wedgwood and George Adams, as reported in the latter's account:

> In his reply Dr. Steiner put us into touch with the sculptress Edith Maryon, who was helping him with the Goetheanum building and above all with the great wooden sculptured group—the Christ-like figure of the 'Representative of Humanity' between the adversary powers, Lucifer and Ahriman—which was to occupy the central position between the pillars at the eastern end of the completed building. Miss Maryon throughout those years was one of his closest collaborators in other respects too, for the studio in which the work was going on became his study for a great part of the day. Here he received his visitors and she was acting very largely as his secretary. Now he himself had been anxious for an English edition of the book, and as no one else was at hand, Miss Maryon had undertaken to translate it. She too now wrote to us and eventually sent us her draft. In style, however—like many of the attempted translations of Dr. Steiner's works in those early days—it was impossible, certainly for a work that was to reach a wider public, and we said so frankly. We were then invited to Dornach to go into the whole question.

★

As indicated in his last letter to Maryon, Steiner was back in Stuttgart again from the second half of August onwards. Their correspondence resumed:

Villa St. Georg,
Arlesheim bei Basel.
24th of August 1919

Dear Teacher,

I'm sending you herewith a letter from my brother-in-law, I've marked in red pencil his criticism of the translation of your book 'The Kernel of the Social Question'; so far the other translation hasn't yet come. I learnt from Fräulein Sharp that the lady who translated it is the one who offered Herr Dr. Boos her services for this work, and have given her Mrs. Drury-Lavin's address. My translation arrived afterwards. She was dissatisfied with it and then made her own with help from Herr Kaufmann and compared it sentence by sentence with mine. Fräulein Sharp also says people weren't entirely pleased that I'd turned to a friend instead of to members, but actually I knew only Collison; Drury-Lavin and Cull I saw a couple of times at lectures in Munich in 1913, and I knew nothing of Herr Kaufmann's existence!

I've finished modelling the forestage; it's to be cast tomorrow. The studio now seems very empty and still. Not being allowed to help with work in Stuttgart, I'm quite envious of Fräulein Waller! This week I'm starting to carve again at Ahriman's head and Lucifer's hand, so am holding myself in balance. Herr K. Ballmer has written an article on the Goetheanum for the Arlesheim paper: I'm sending a copy—it's a rejoinder to a criticism of the artistic forms in the Goetheanum.

With heartfelt greetings,

Edith Maryon

⋆

Stuttgart,
4th of September 1919

My dear Fräulein E. Maryon,

I've received the letter, and it's given me much pleasure. I'm thinking a lot about work in the sculpture studio and will be pleased when I can once more take part. There's much work to be done here to establish the school. We start every morning at 9 o'clock with a lecture on general pedagogy, which after quarter of an hour's break is then followed by a second lecture on special methodology and teaching. After these two lectures it's half past 11. In the afternoon the seminar begins from 3 to 6. Then there are mostly some meetings. It's therefore so-to-speak lecturing the whole day. In between, I'm thinking about work in Dornach, especially about our sculptural group.

As for the translation of my book, it'll be a question of one person finding good what to another seems less good. We certainly won't be able to decide till we have another translation in front of us. The opinion on the completed translation is in fact already enough. So the only result will be to delay publishing this translation, as has already often been the case with my books, with one translator always being dissatisfied with another. People ought to be satisfied with the translation we've already done—which I've been involved in, after all—and see to getting it published by the committee, instead of criticizing it so much. But we'll see what'll happen when I'm back again in Dornach.

On Sunday is the opening here of the school. The preparatory lectures and seminar exercises should finish this week. Then on Tuesday or Wednesday of next week I'd like to go to Berlin; I have to give lectures in Dresden from the 18th to the 21st of September; then here once more on the 24th of September and soon after that I should be on my way again to Dornach.

It'll be very satisfying for me to work again in Dornach and be again in the sculpture studio.

With heartfelt greetings,

Rudolf Steiner

at the moment Landhausstrasse 70, Stuttgart.

*

Villa St. Georg,
Arlesheim bei Basel,
14th of September 1919

Dear Teacher,

The second translation of the 1st and 2nd chapters of your book has at last arrived, but I find it infinitely difficult to form any judgement about it. At first I read the two chapters purely from the viewpoint of an English book, and found it well written, in quite modern and suitable English, and the pictures in an entirely English manner, without any trace of their German origin (as with my poor creation!). Only here and there did I find a sentence which seemed to me like modern 'slang', but probably isn't felt like that in present-day England. It reads fluently and interestingly, and if properly published I certainly think it might even become a popular book. One of the translators is already a practised and well-known authoress, and has already a lot of influence in these circles, and could help considerably for the book to be published by the National Labour Press.

I then read it and compared it with the original. It here transpired that the two translators have allowed themselves a lot of freedom with the sentence-division, without in my opinion having any good reasons for it, except in one or two places. I mean they've made two or three sentences out of one, and one out of two etc. This happens on average twice or more per page.

But this could be quickly corrected and made good; it would I think be desirable, as there comes out a different nuance.

And then three quarters of the words which in the original are in italics they've written normal, so an emphasized word has only the same value as others. I also think they've often translated too freely, which means they've tried to understand the meaning and then reproduce it freely in their own way, so it's rather as if a person had seen a blue picture and from memory then made a green one! It's the same with the paragraphs: they make completely new ones, in an arbitrary way.

Finally, I compared the 1st chapter in the two translations and find the other one on the whole reads more fluently. It's easy to understand, as one of the translators has already done a lot of writing and I haven't! I find my sentences often clumsier, but perhaps more faithful—in some respect—to the original; others are even like a different version, many are better. (Is that presumptuous?) But in the end I think it best for our cause to take the other translation, as these people have some influence in England and I don't have any, and they have to work there and will have more interest in doing so if they can create tools of their own. I would only insist that italicized words be also italicized in English and different sentence-divisions not arbitrarily introduced. If time is not too pressing and the others allow it (which they perhaps won't, being convinced that their translation is totally faithful to the original) I'd like to see some things a bit different. This opinion has been formed from the first chapter; I've only skimmed through the second, but my criticism is roughly the same. In the next few days I'll give the matter further study, but probably won't think very differently.

So I'm writing now, to save perhaps a little time. The lady and Herr Kaufmann are intending to be in Dornach at the end of September. The question is whether the Nat. Lab. Press should be given a translation at once, so that we can get a reply?

When the others come and if they allow me, I'd like to go through the work and compare it. It might perhaps be improved, but it would take time. Is it perhaps better and more important to make a start quickly now? I'm awaiting your opinion on everything and haven't said anything of this to the two persons concerned.

I have various letters from the committee etc. to present you with later.

I'd very much have liked to support this work as well, only it seems to me that in this regard life wants to push me out, and for the sake of our cause I have to let this happen.

It'll be so nice when you're able to work here again. Times are really hard and the weeks very long. I received the letter all right and it gave me much pleasure.

With heartfelt greetings,

Edith Maryon

For the English-speaking World

The visit to Dornach of Elizabeth Bowen-Wedgwood and George Adams in the autumn of 1919 was the first such visit by British persons since the end of the World War. It is understandable that in his reminiscences Adams gave it more extensive coverage than any other episode.

> We arrived in Switzerland at the end of September 1919. Dr. Steiner was away in Stuttgart, where the first Waldorf School had just been opened. We were received in the most friendly way by the Dornach members and above all by Miss Maryon herself. She gave us mallet and chisel and let us help with parts of the sculptured group where there was much superfluous wood and our unskilled hands could do no harm. One day we were thus engaged when Rudolf Steiner appeared at Miss Maryon's side, up the steep steps of the scaffolding. Miss Maryon introduced us, and he talked with us in the most natural way. He was very simple, courteous, friendly—and happy. That was my first impression—his delight in telling of the school and of the children. These are the first words that have stayed in my mind: '*Die Kinder toben*!' ('The children are romping!') '*Wenn ein Kind nicht toblustig ist, wird's nachher kein tüchtiger Mensch.*' ('A child that's never rampageous won't grow up into a capable person.' An approximate translation! The word *toblustig*, I am told, is in no orthodox vocabulary. That too is characteristic.) I thought a little ruefully of my own rather subdued and melancholic childhood.
>
> My impression even in those first few days was, so to speak, of many Rudolf Steiners. There was the simple, friendly gentleman whom we had seen at this first meeting. We were able to see him in numerous later gatherings. He made me think of stories about great initiates, who went around quite unknown. There was Dr. Steiner lecturing—deeply impressive and stern, vivid in characterization, then often moving into anecdote, good-natured satire, rollicking fun and humour. And there was Dr. Steiner speaking in a more esoteric meeting—more as you see him in that portrait in the old editions of *Occult Science*—the initiate from timeless realms. Moreover, there was Dr. Steiner as you might see him during a personal interview, when you told him of your life's difficulties and ideals and he answered your questions—the deep, silent look in his eyes, the warm kindness and encouragement at some moments in his whole manner, and at others the absolute quiet, so that it was left entirely to you to come out with what you had to say and how to say it, with seemingly no help from him, but silent waiting.
>
> Mrs. Wedgwood and I saw Dr. Steiner several times during those days. We had to tell him why and how we thought Miss Maryon's translation inadequate. She herself was present in the studio, busying herself with sundry other things. I remember when Mrs. Wedgwood, as tactfully as she could in her forthright, choleric way, had explained how impossible the

translation was, I assenting, Dr. Steiner's matter-of-fact and kindly answer: '*Das ist ihre Überzeugung.*' ('That is your conviction.') There was no pointed emphasis in the sentence, no implication for or against—it was a simple statement of the fact: we start from here. Presently he asked for examples, which we began producing. '*Maryon, kommen Sie einmal her,*' he called out, and explained to her the disparities we had been pointing out. Impersonal, unselfish and detached, in the end she said that she had only offered to do the translation because no one else was at hand; she did not really feel competent in this realm and gladly withdrew her work.

In the course of his biography of Edith Maryon, Rex Raab related a memorable anecdote which may suitably be inserted at this point:

Charles Gaze, who at the front during the World War worked through the English translation of Rudolf Steiner's *Die Geheimwissenschaft im Umriss* no less than five times, was well-known to the author. He vouches for the correctness of what Gaze told him twenty years after these events.

When the *Kernpunkte* was going to be published in English, Rudolf Steiner had already been asked how best to undertake the translation. He replied that the book should be written completely afresh for the English-speaking world out of conditions which obtained there. But no one was confident of being able to capture faithfully his train of thought in so bold a way.

Rudolf Steiner then suggested: 'If you don't want to, then please take the text of the book page by page, and rewrite at least these . . .'

When no one could envisage a page-by-page free rendering either, but again asked the author of the *Kernpunkte* if he had any wishes regarding publication, he replied: 'Yes. Do me the favour of rounding off the book's corners, so that British workers can draw it more easily from their pockets during tea-break!'

A Problem to His English Friends

Publicational matters were not the only subject discussed on this visit, as George Adams made clear in the further course of his account:

In those autumn days of 1919 each of us also spoke with Dr. Steiner alone. I remember as he sat there in his studio beneath the great figure of the Christ on which he was still working, with manifold sculptures and clay models all around, there on his shelves were the books I had known so well in the war-time years in England, where the questions of the outbreak of the War and the economic and political background of warfare generally in the modern world were thrashed out—controversial books by E.D. Morel, C.H.

Norman and others. It was typical of Rudolf Steiner. However deeply he might see into the supersensible background of events, he spared no pains in getting to know the precise details of outer happenings, the prevalent opinions and the thoughts of others. We naturally came to speak of my war-time experiences: he took seriously and acknowledged on my behalf the movement with which I had been associated. He valued the fact that there were men and women who in the last resort had the moral courage to follow their own individual conscience, and that there was a country in which one was able to play an active and fruitful part in public life. The system of separate nation-states, each with its citizen or conscript army—a heritage from Napoleonic times—however comforting for the nineteenth-century sense of bourgeois honour, cannot go on for ever. Face to face with the appalling lethal powers which modern technical science has conjured up, Rudolf Steiner saw a time approaching when the Spirit of mankind will give individuals the courage to take upon themselves quite different and far-reaching decisions, in the face of all prevailing powers and conventions.

Of her conversations with him during those days, Mrs. Wedgwood told me something which reveals again how he was wont to see a question from many sides, and I will relate it, though at second-hand. It concerns his attitude during the War of 1914–18, about which a few words more may here be said, for it presented a problem to his English friends. He certainly did not see in that War a straightforward issue of right and wrong, brought about by aggressive military designs on the part of the Central Powers. Rather he seems to have been convinced, especially in the initial stages, that Germany and Austria were fighting in self-defence. In the Wilsonian conception that underlay the peace-treaties of 1919—the setting-up of many smaller nation-states—he recognized a profound mistake. Let your political principles, he says in effect (in *The Threefold State* and other writings) guarantee the rights and liberties of man as such—individual man—and the freedom of nationalities will follow; it cannot be achieved the other way round.

He saw the War in a far deeper and wider context; to quote the title of one of his war-time lecture-cycles, it was the inexorable 'Karma of Materialism'. He composed meditations addressed to the guardian angels of those who were at the front or had been killed, and to the souls of the nations—the archangel-beings 'in the choirs of the spheres of peace'. Of such a kind that they could equally well be used in all the warring countries, these meditations quickly reached us through friends in Switzerland and elsewhere. They were translated—more easily perhaps than some of his other verses—and in the anthroposophical groups one heard them regularly.

During those years Dr. Steiner spoke again and again about the spirit of the time and the souls of nations. Some of his deepest and most loving characterizations of the English, French and Russian peoples were given in his lectures at Berlin and Dornach a few weeks after the War had broken out, and in the years that followed. His own people he kept calling to their true spiritual task, exposing the perilous sources of illusion which were unhappily to prevail not many years after his death.

Mrs. Wedgwood, ardent in her wish for truer international relations, had been resisting the one-sided and often extravagant propaganda of her own country, and at that moment she was incensed by the harsh provisions of the Versailles Treaty. Rudolf Steiner's answer was to temper her indignation. Yet after all, he said in effect, perhaps it is as well that victory was not on the other side. And he went on, thinking perhaps of Ludendorff and others like him: we have to bear in mind the kind of militarist mentality which gained control in Germany towards the end of the War. These people would not have treated a defeated enemy with magnanimity or made a wise peace-settlement in the true interests of human progress.

A Deed of Purest Freedom

George Adams went on:

I asked Dr. Steiner for his spiritual guidance, and he gave me a fresh appointment. When I came again a few days later he had written out for me an evening and a morning meditation, based on the opening words of St. John's Gospel. He explained in detail how it should be done, and then continued: this is only half of what is necessary. The other half is, you must be aware that the regular doing of your meditation in the evening and morning is the one entirely free deed of the day. However much the other things you do spring from your own resolves, the circumstances that lead up to them are determined by your particular destiny in this present life. But nothing is obliging you to do regularly the meditation. That is entirely the outcome of your own free decision.

I think this, too, was typical of Rudolf Steiner. What in the spiritual schools of former times would have been a binding vow, he would translate into a deed of purest freedom. This metamorphosis—this inversion, one might almost say—he practised in ever so many ways, not always equally explicit; and we, his pupils, were often slow to perceive it. We thankfully received the new content of his teaching and poured it too often into old bottles of would-be piety and sheltered 'goodness', not really true to the spirit of the time. Or else we took the new freedom too lightly. One sometimes had the impression that this, more than anything, saddened and made him lonely.

★

Adams ended his account of this visit by describing more personal matters:

Straightaway in my first interview Dr. Steiner entered with great kindness into the question of my future life and career. I had ambitions in scientific research and had made a promising beginning. But in 1919, as an outcome of the War and the upheavals in which it ended, the social needs of mankind were in the foreground, and I was wondering in which way to turn. In answer to my question, Rudolf Steiner said: 'These issues are more urgent now than purely scientific work.' At that moment I had been offered a job in Berlin which would have brought me into close contact with social events. During the War I had enjoyed the friendship of the distinguished journalist Michael Farbman. A warm-hearted and highly intelligent Russian Jew, he had been working at a book in which he vainly tried so to influence Allied policy that his war-weary country would not be driven, as in fact it was, into the arms of the Bolsheviks. His command of English was not perfect. I loved the Russian language and was deeply interested in all that was going on in Russia. During the last years of the War I helped him in London to put his work into good English. Farbman was now about to become Russian correspondent of a leading English daily, with his headquarters in Berlin to begin with, and wanted me to go with him as his secretary. I told Dr. Steiner of this. Our conversation naturally turned to the Russian revolutionary leaders. 'Lenin himself,' said Dr. Steiner in reply to my question, 'I hold to be an honest man and an intellect of no mean order.' '*Lenin selbst halte ich für einen ehrlichen und geistig nicht unbedeutenden Menschen*' were his exact words. I only remember the gist of what follows, not the exact words: 'What he is doing, however, is ruthlessly to exploit and destroy the old civilization. This civilization, it is true, is inexorably dying out, including the old confessions. Be under no illusions about that. But one should not play fast and loose, destroying it the more quickly' ('*Raubbau treiben*' were the words he used). 'Rather should one be sowing seeds for what is new, what is really fruitful for the future.'

Speaking of the possibility of my being active in Berlin, he went on to say: 'Of course you might go there, but do not imagine that the future lies there. It was in the later 19th Century that it attained its recent greatness. That was a time of spiritual void'—here he took pencil and paper and sketched an empty hole—'a time when the old spirituality was no more and the new was not yet born. Vienna may now seem utterly broken, suffering far worse starvation, but its roots are true and it will rise again.'

In the late autumn of 1919 I went on from Switzerland to Germany, and shortly afterwards to Poland—to the south-eastern borders of that country, where my home had been. Everywhere there was only destruction to be seen: the towns and villages were laid waste; famine and typhus were raging.

For our work there, my wife and I joined the War Victims' Relief Mission, organized by English and American Quakers.

Emergency Business Meeting

The Vahan now reported a significant meeting:

> An emergency Business Meeting of the H.P.B. Lodge was held at the Mortimer Halls on Monday, November 10th, at 7 p.m., at which the President of the Society was present. Also in attendance were Capt. Gauntlett, President, Mr. Warden, Treasurer, and the following members of the Council: Mrs. R. Graham Pole, Miss Dorothy Osmond, Messrs. Kingsley Bayly, Digby Besant and R. Graham Pole. Capt. Gauntlett in opening the proceedings referred to the circular letter which had been sent to all members of the lodge, suggesting the final closing of the lodge owing to its inanition, but said that since that circular had been sent arrangements had been made whereby it had become possible to obtain a fresh lease of life. He referred to an opportunity which had been put in their way to make their headquarters at 169 Piccadilly, and said that Mrs. Besant would then speak to them on the subject.
>
> Mrs. Besant, rising, spoke of the affection she had for the H.P.B. Lodge, of which she was one of the Founders, and said that she was very anxious to save it. She spoke of an interview she had had with Mr. Gauntlett, during which he offered to take charge of 169 Piccadilly on behalf of its present owner, and in which he further said he proposed, if this were permitted, to let the H.P.B. Lodge use the said library as its headquarters. She was glad to tell the members that she had acceded to this request and that 169 Piccadilly was now to be handed over to Capt. Gauntlett, and the lodge, having at last a home of its own, might look forward to reconstruction, and a period of usefulness to the cause of Theosophy.
>
> Mr. Slater wished to know if this lodge had to consider itself under an obligation to Captain Gauntlett, and said he felt sure that were this lodge in financial difficulty it would find sufficient support from its members, on the position being defined. He said further that he would be pleased to contribute £5 or £10, if necessary, as the lodge in all fairness should at least provide the funds to justify its existence.
>
> Mr. Kingsley Bayly, the ex-Treasurer, said the lodge was *not* in difficulties, and Mr. Warden, the Treasurer, stated that the bank balance was £36 at the moment.
>
> Capt. Gauntlett, rising, said that the lodge was not under any obligation to himself in the matter. That, as a private member of the Theosophical Society, he had stepped forward with an offer intended to save 169 Piccadilly from the closing which was apparently intended by the Executive

Committee, and that offer had been accepted. Now, in turn, he offered to allow the H.P.B. Lodge the use of those premises, at a rental to be arranged, and in so far as the lodge appeared willing to consider this offer, he was to that extent benefited and helped to carry out the arrangement he had made with Mrs. Besant.

Other speakers offered a few remarks and the proceedings appeared to be coming to a harmonious close, when Mr. Dunlop rose and said that he wished to move that the resignation of Capt. Gauntlett and the members of the Council be called for on the grounds that their inaction during the past five months had given cause for offence to the members of the lodge, and that in particular Capt. Gauntlett's circular to the members had contained a number of inaccuracies which he wished to take this opportunity of rebutting. Mr. Dunlop spoke of the difficulties he had had in carrying on the lodge during the War and said that, far from being an active lodge at the commencement of his association with it, only a very few members indeed had helped him in his work.

This resolution was seconded by Miss Dorothy Osmond.

Capt. Gauntlett, responding, tendered his resignation to the lodge and said he was specially willing to do this, owing to the fact that Mr. Digby Besant had suggested before the meeting that it might be desirable, in order to give the lodge an entirely free hand.

Mr. Digby Besant, rising, said that Capt. Gauntlett had evidently misunderstood him and he had not suggested such a course, but merely said that if the suggestion to give 169 Piccadilly to the care of Capt. Gauntlett in his capacity as President of H.P.B. Lodge were made, it would more or less force the lodge to retain him as President, whether they wished or not.

Mrs. Besant made it clear to the lodge that the offer of 169 Piccadilly was to Capt. Gauntlett personally, and that the H.P.B. Lodge could take it or not as they liked, and that this would be possible whatever official position was or was not held in the lodge by Capt. Gauntlett. Mrs. Besant inclined to the opinion that the resolution proposed by Mr. Dunlop was uncalled for, and asked for further expressions of opinion.

Mrs. Whyte moved an amendment that 'this meeting affirms its confidence in Capt. Gauntlett and the members of the Committee and requests them to withdraw their resignations'. This was seconded by Baroness de Kuster and carried unanimously.

On this Mr. Dunlop resigned his membership of the lodge and left the Hall, followed by Miss Osmond, who also resigned. More desultory talk followed, largely of a constructive character, and Mr. Slater, on ascertaining that there was great difficulty in this connection, offered his services as Hon. Secretary, and these were tentatively accepted by the President of the lodge, pending Mr. Slater's election by the Council at its next meeting.

Mrs. Besant expressed her satisfaction at the arrangement which had been come to, and kindly offered to give the lodge its first lecture in its new premises at an early date. She then declared the meeting closed.

Rupert Gauntlett,
President, H.P.B. Lodge

An Entirely New World of Thought

Towards the end of the year Rudolf Steiner returned for another fortnight in Stuttgart. Edith Maryon wrote to him again:

Sculpture studio,
Goetheanum,
Dornach,
21st of December 1919

Dear Teacher,

Life has become quite different here; my time is divided between the big and small Lucifers. (Hopefully I'm not thereby developing all sorts of fantastic thoughts and qualities?) The small Lucifer's head is bent so far forward that it's hard to carve him. Already I nearly hit off a bit too much from his nose—but it can be put right. Our studio looks very empty and abandoned, as if no work had been done there for a whole month.

I had a long talk with Mrs. Wedgwood about the people concerned.—She judges much less severely than I do, and says whoever hasn't lived through it themselves can scarcely have any idea of how unbelievably hateful and difficult it was in present-day England, and the couple of hundred people who more or less perceived the actual significance of this war went through a really ghastly time. The whole atmosphere there is poisoned and polluted with lies. Human beings who had to stay upright in such an atmosphere without any help or support—right amongst a mass of people who turned hostile as soon as anyone was known to be a pacifist—felt depressed when they sensed how atrocious this war was, and had to go through a really horrible time. Had they seen all through it, she thought many would have been unable to survive. She has some hope for people who at least want to listen, while others are blind, deaf and hostile to all other thoughts. Even without actually being there, however, I think one can well understand how things over there looked.

22nd Dec. Today I attended the Threefold Commonwealth working group in the reading-room. It was actually quite interesting, chiefly a little speech by Mrs. W., clearly expressed, with a bit of humour, etc. Theme: capital. The questions were sometimes amusing. Mr. Monges wanted to know whether a dentist sold his work in exactly the same way as any other worker and could hardly grasp the difference, and thought he must feel like a slave.

Mrs. Drury-Lavin spoke of the contentedness and piety found in England among those who work on the land, and couldn't quite see that they actually belong to a period of time which is past and can't be continued any further. Both questions were very characteristically put.

I'm looking forward to the public lectures in Basel.

With heartfelt greetings,

Edith Maryon

★

In a typescript entitled 'My Meeting with Rudolf Steiner (A Testimony to the Spiritual Guidance of Destiny)', Eleanor Merry recalled her first encounter with anthroposophy:

About 1919 I came across Rudolf Steiner's *The Way of Initiation*, and a friend who was a member of the Anthroposophical Society lent me the lectures on the Gospel of St. John. These books, in spite of some resemblances to the content of Theosophy as I knew it, opened up an entirely new world of thought. Though Steiner's terminology was different and the essential content was different, yet quite naturally what I had learnt through Theosophy passed over into the other through a sort of balance of contrasts. I did not then feel that Rudolf Steiner was a 'Master'. In fact I felt a good deal perturbed by much that I read in his books. There was a portrait of him in the beginning of *The Way of Initiation*, and I used to gaze at it, puzzled and fascinated. 'What is he? Who is he?', I thought. 'Can I trust him? I cannot possibly know unless I meet him face to face. And then I shall know finally and completely.' I longed to meet him. But all the circumstances of my life seemed to point to that as being utterly out of the question.

★

It may also be mentioned that during the year 1919 Charles and Margaret Lazenby crossed over the Atlantic and reappeared in Britain. They now had a five-year-old daughter, dedicated by her father to the service of humanity and named Petrovna, after Helena Petrovna Blavatsky.

The family both renewed old friendships and made contact with new audiences all over Britain. Introducing articles about Lazenby in the November-December 1988 issue of The *Canadian Theosophist*, the editor wrote:

In England a few years ago, a member approached me at the end of a meeting and asked if, as a Canadian, the name of Charles Lazenby meant anything to me. Encouraged by my enthusiastic reply, she went on to say that more than sixty years earlier her mother had taken her as a child to hear a lecture by Lazenby in a northern English city. She said the strong impression he had made on her at the time had never diminished, and his message had continued to inspire her throughout her life.

In the next issue, another old member reminisced:

The articles on Charles Lazenby were delightful. They revived a host of memories of the first time I saw and heard him. It was a long time ago—over seventy years ago . . .

He was not a *breath*, but a *gust* of fresh air . . .

His platform manner was easy and relaxed, and he sure had a way with words. And his voice! I shall never, ever forget his declamation of the opening stanzas of *The Secret Doctrine* at a small private meeting that was held. Magnificent!'[43]

New Book

At the beginning of January 1920 *The Vahan* carried a large advertisement, taking up half a page:

New Book by Mr. D.N. Dunlop.

THE PATH OF KNOWLEDGE

Contents

1. Awakening Mind.
2. The Four Worlds.
3. The Cycle of Evolution.
4. Incarnate Mind.
5. Via Lucis.
6. Spiritual Alchemy.
7. The World of Knowledge.
8. Fiat Lux.

Published by request, and printed privately by
The Three Kings Press, 8, Carlton Hill, London, N.W. 8.

Price 5/-; postage 3d. *Limited Edition*

★

On the first printed page at the front of the book was a dedication:[44]

TO MY FRIEND
AE

After the title-page and the contents, the main text ran to 66 pages. Apart from the chapter titles, epigraphs and a few variants and additions, this text was entirely drawn from a series of editorials on 'Consciousness through Knowledge' which H.W. Percival had published in *The Word* some twelve years previously, from December 1907 to May 1908. At the end of the book Dunlop provided an 'Appendix' of his own notes.

The first chapter, 'Awakening Mind', included a footnote. A reader who turned to the 'Appendix' at the back was supplied with a quotation from John Locke.

The second chapter, 'The Four Worlds', contained two such footnotes. The first as given in the 'Appendix' made a comparison to Plato's *Timaeus* and to 'the teaching of Empedocles, Heracleitus and other Greek philosophers . . .' The second read:

> Cp. again the teaching of Heracleitus and the *Anthroposophia Theomagica* of Thomas Vaughan.

This last work, published in London in 1650 under Vaughan's pseudonym of Eugenius Philalethes ('Lover of truth'), bore the lengthy subtitle 'A Discourse of the Nature of Man and his State after Death; Grounded on his Creator's Protochimistry, and verifi'd by a practicall Examination of Principles in the Great World'.

It was the very first work in any language to use the term 'anthroposophy'.

★

The third chapter of *The Path of Knowledge*, 'The Cycle of Evolution', included a footnote referring to Chapter XV of the *Bhagavadgita.*

The fourth chapter, 'Incarnate Mind', began with an epigraph, the last clause of which was in this instance italicized:

> Then the builders, having donned their first clothing, descend on radiant Earth, and reign over men, *who are themselves.*'—Stanzas of Dzyan, VII. 7.

> We must now study the functions and faculties of the mind in closer detail.
>
> Let us consider Universal Mind under the symbol of boundless space, and that space to be in the form of a crystal sphere. I select a crystal sphere because the human mind, although it can place no limit to abstract space, naturally conceives it to be in the form of a sphere, and transparence is the attribute of crystal. Let us then symbolize the Universal Mind as such a boundless crystal sphere of space in which there were no objects or beings, but only shadowless light, in the state which existed before any effort at creation or emanation of the worlds was willed by Divine Mind.
>
> Let our next conception be that of perpetual motion, or energy inherent within Universal Mind, and that through its agency there appeared in

outline within this boundless crystal space many crystal spheres, as miniature reflections of the all-inclusive parent sphere. Those individual crystal spheres are the individual minds within Universal Mind, the Sons of Mind, also called 'Sons of God', each differing from the other according to the state and degree of perfection which each respectively had attained in a previous period of manifestation or manvantara. When that period had ended and all had returned into the bosom of Universal Mind, there came the period of pralaya, or 'Night of Brahma', spoken of in many of the ancient scriptures. In the language of the ancients, after 'seven eternities' had passed, this transparent space or Universal Mind took on a different appearance. As a cloud may gradually appear in a cloudless sky, so the finest matter condensed and solidified within the Universal Mind, and the worlds came into existence. Each potency within the Universal Mind becomes active at the appropriate time.

Here came a footnote. A reader who referred to the 'Appendix' at the back was informed that

> This is a very condensed statement of an immense range of spiritual philosophy, and I can only advise students to turn to Madame Blavatsky's *Secret Doctrine*, Volume I., for further elucidation and guidance.—D.N.D.

The main text of the fourth chapter continued:

> We can speak of the individual minds as being crystal spheres, of more or less brilliance and glory according to their development. These individual minds or crystal spheres were not all at the same stage of development. Some had attained to a full and complete knowledge of themselves and their relation to their parent sphere, the Universal Mind. Others were ignorant of the Universal Mind as their parent, hardly conscious of themselves as individual beings. Those minds who were in perfect attainment were and are the rulers, the great Intelligences, the celestial hierarchies or Sons of Wisdom and are the agents of the Supreme Logos controlling and regulating the affairs of the world according to divine law.

Here came another footnote, and a reader who once again referred to the 'Appendix' at the back was told:

> See *Dionysius the Areopagite*. Parker. Vol. II. Also compare *An Outline of Occult Science*, by Dr. Rudolf Steiner, chap. iv.

In the Interests of Truth

The same January issue of *The Vahan* which carried the advertisement for the new book by D.N. Dunlop included in its correspondence columns the following letter:

Dear Sir,

We, the undersigned, write to protest against the misleading report of the meeting of the H.P.B. Lodge published in your last issue over the name of Captain Gauntlett. The remarks attributed to Mr. Dunlop, the ex-President, are so inaccurately and incompletely reported that we cannot allow the matter to pass in silence. The report states that Mr. Dunlop called for the resignation of Captain Gauntlett and the Council on the ground 'that their inaction during the past five months has given cause for offence to the members' and suggests that this speech was the one inharmonious note in the meeting. Captain Gauntlett does not mention the fact that the Treasurer of the lodge made a far more serious implication when he said that a large number of members had lately refused to pay their subscriptions because they felt that the lodge had ceased all activity. It struck us as strange at the time that an Honorary Member who had not for many years attended a single meeting should have felt able to move a vote of confidence in the Council, immediately following this most disquieting statement by the Treasurer.

Why is no mention made of Mr. Dunlop's report of lodge activities during his term of office? Of the public and private lectures which were arranged, the distribution of literature to every ship in the Grand Fleet, etc., but only his criticisms quoted? Why is no report made of his constructive proposal that a fresh Committee should be appointed with an absolutely free hand, to consider how the lodge could most effectively be revitalized?

The report bristles with inaccuracies. For instance, Miss Sharples seconded Mr. Dunlop's motion, not Miss Osmond. Mr. Dunlop withdrew his motion and left the Hall *before* Mrs. Whyte's amendment was put to the meeting and voted on, not after. The amendment was not 'carried unanimously', it was carried *nem. con.*, and so on. It must inevitably have produced a completely false impression in the minds of those who were not present at the meeting, and in the interests of truth, let alone of the most elementary courtesy to our ex-President, we wish to express our deep regret that Captain Gauntlett should have seen fit to publish such an account.

Yours faithfully,

G. Christie.
G.E. Hart
M.M. Sharples.
J. Conigrave.
D.S. Osmond.

★

The February issue continued this correspondence with two further letters:

Sir,

In your January issue of the *Vahan* under the heading of Correspondence, I notice a letter signed by five ladies commenting on the report of the H.P.B. Lodge, and drawing particular attention to the remarks made by the new Hon. Treasurer of the lodge, who stated 'that he had not communicated with the members regarding outstanding subscriptions, as the continuance of the activities of the lodge was so uncertain, and casually mentioning that some had raised an objection to pay their subscriptions as the activities of the lodge had been suspended'. At this point my remarks ended, and I was under the impression that these members referred to the activities during the entire period of the War, as I personally was able to attend but few of the lodge meetings; so my remarks were quite innocently expressed, and in no way wished to convey a wrong impression.

It seems a great pity that these unfortunate incidents are allowed to mar the work which I am sure one and all of us feel we must proceed with as quickly and harmoniously as possible.

May I in conclusion say we welcome all members to co-operate with us in again making the H.P.B. Lodge what some of us older members recall with pleasure.

I am, Sir,

Yours faithfully,

A. Warden
Hon. Treasurer, H.P.B. Lodge.

★

Dear Editor,

With reference to the letter appearing in the January issue of the *Vahan*, signed by five F.T.S. (some of whom, by the way, are not members of the H.P.B. Lodge), may I quote from the minute-book of the lodge kept whilst I was in France. 'Owing to the very poor attendance at the lodge lectures during the last session it was decided to discontinue temporarily the lodge lectures.' The meeting at which this resolution was passed took place on November 25th, 1918, Miss Dorothy Osmond in the chair, and effectively disposes of the contention that the lodge has in any way suffered under the present Council.

I greatly regret if I mistook Miss Sharples for Miss Osmond as seconder of Mr. Dunlop's motion. I apologize to both ladies.

Faithfully yours,

Rupert Gauntlett,
President, H.P.B. Lodge.

Members having had an opportunity of expressing their views on this subject, the correspondence is closed.—Ed.

★

In their obituary of Dorothy Osmond, the Compton-Burnetts continued by describing the consequences of their joining the Anthroposophical Society:

> Now we were faced with the question of membership. Could we be members of both Societies? We soon realized that this was not the real answer and resignation from the Theosophical Society became inevitable. For Dorothy Osmond this also entailed giving up her position as librarian. 'D.N.D.', deeply imbued as he was with Celtic and Oriental wisdom, found difficulty in Rudolf Steiner's Central European approach, and for him the change came somewhat later.

Although Dunlop had in a footnote drawn a comparison to one of Steiner's published works, he had indeed not yet drawn on the content of anthroposophy as such.

A New Birth All Over this Planet

Neither the date when Isabelle de Steiger came across anthroposophy and joined the Anthroposophical Society nor how this came about seems to be recorded, but it must have been at the very latest by around this time.

Scattered throughout her *Memorabilia* (1927) are several passages referring to the teachings of Rudolf Steiner. In the present chapter these passages are extracted from her book in the consecutive order in which they are found.

> I have referred in the early pages of this memoir to my original literary hero, Count Albert of Rudolstadt in George Sand's famous book. There is one item in Count Albert's history which I must recount. It refers to the part in George Sand's marvellous novel *Consuelo*, in which she describes the mysterious underground grotto with its strange 'well' scenes, and the powerful secret order of which Count Albert was the leader and head. The name of that secret order, said the author, was embodied in the mystic initials of three Latin words of what I believe was the name of an order existing mysteriously at that time, *L.P.D.* I never tried to translate them! It was the mystery that enthralled me. I ought to have been a little more inquisitive. Desire for true knowledge is a godlike quality; but a lack of enquiry, as it were, as to what is mystery, is a weakness, a fear of light.
>
> One day when I was about fourteen, I was standing at our nursery window looking up Canning Street, when suddenly I saw coming round the corner from Percy Street a new strange vehicle with a complete hood of green canvas, and on the canvas in large black letters three separate letters, *L.*

P. D. Count Albert's sign! Nobody in the house knew anything about Count Albert. How could they? I was the only one! I nearly fainted, and could not speak. I did not know what was going to happen to Liverpool. I could feel nothing but an overwhelming haze of some awful coming event. I ran upstairs to a large empty room to be alone—a room given to us children by my papa ('father' was never said), and called 'the top room', where we did what we liked, or nothing at all. Here I climbed onto the high, broad window ledge, where there was room to sit and think, and gaze down onto the cemetery, and the distant view of Liverpool and the Mersey, and far away to the Welsh hills. I realized that nobody seemed at all affected, and I can remember the shock of disillusion when I overheard one of the passing servants on the staircase speaking to another, saying: 'Did you see that there new cart going down Canning Street? I'm told it's a new sort, for people to send their things about to other people's houses. Them letters mean the Liverpool Parcels Delivery.'

Yes, it was the inauguration of a most useful service, but my feelings had received a shock. However, my interest in the secret society idea, the germ of which George Sand implanted in my nature, never died out, and it has had in my later years most active fulfilment, when I came to life by joining first the Spiritualists' Society, then the Theosophical Society, after that the Rosicrucian, and finally the Anthroposophical Society of Spiritual Science. I am now studying with vivid interest the teachings of Dr. Rudolf Steiner . . .

★

Can there be any doubt that these shuddering days are only the trembling of man's soul in the throes of the new birth, the heralding of the higher evolution of humanity? It is the process before the birth of the superman—it is not the new life itself that man fears! As I tried to point out in my books *The Cloud on the Sanctuary*, *On a Gold Basis*, and *Superhumanity*, with the approach of humanity to the next sign of the zodiac—that of Aquarius—a further step forward in man's evolution will take place. It is believed by all mystic thinkers and philosophers that the coming spiritual evolution will gradually lighten the gloom cast by the receding sign.

Modes of coming thought, however, become more and more entangled with the present and past, although this entanglement may cause deep trouble; by degrees the skein will grow less tangled, until gradually the strands separate easily and singly, and the new work will run smoothly. New and able writers will soon appear, until a new world of thought arrives, and the era of a more complete humanity gradually attains maturity. That event is drawing nearer and nearer, but for the present I must confine myself to my own position. I am able to write my own, but not anyone else's experiences. Each thread may be alike, but occupies a different place in the finished fabric.

There are specially valuable words of Dr. Steiner, in direct answer, almost, to the dumb question of certain loyal souls, which I should like to quote.

In his pamphlet on *Occult Science and Occult Development* (p. 10), he says:—

'In the depths of his own soul, every man possesses the possibility and the power, before he becomes a seer, of recognizing the truths of occult development. Occult truths can, it is true, be discovered only by the seer, but when they have been discovered and expressed in ordinary normal language of the human reason, they can be understood by every human soul who will remove the obstacles to such understanding from within himself.'

★

Several years passed after the death of William Sharp; and I heard nothing further from or of his widow; but just lately I have had a letter from her, telling me that she is one of the travellers on the same road as myself!

★

I believe that humanity is undergoing a new birth all over this planet, according to the degree of advance of the various races of the human kingdom, and that further evolution is rapidly working. We are, as nations, like a woman in travail, but we have the hope, nay the certainty, that these pains will be forgotten for joy when a better humanity is born. We must remember the microcosm is the pattern or forerunner of the macrocosm, and young and growing children have their growing pains when they disobey the counsel of wise teachers.

By degrees, to every nation will the Christ and His disciples be known. The Christ has never been absent. I must here say that I *am not watching for any Eastern ray or prearranged Star in the East.* The new man will, according to Dr. Steiner, be the developed ethereal body. Christ is already here, in His ethereal body; for it is thus that the universal great work was first accomplished by a man heralding the redemption of the flesh from weakness and corruption.

I certainly think that Mr. Sinnett in his last book (*The Early Days of Theosophy in Europe*) narrates his story with much vigour, but I regret that he dwells so much on the disaffection between the leaders of the Society. Such had long been clear to me, though it was not mentioned outside . . .

★

I must here digress in order to refer to a more remote subject; that is, the recovery of the ancient knowledge regarding the Sybils. Their epoch and position in the world's history is obviously recurrent in the present day. The idea of Spiritualism is reminiscent of a historic period when a Sybil dominated the mind of the Roman king, Numa Pompilius, as his Egeria.

The Greek gods were then gradually vanishing; king and people seemed to fear that they were left without any god or goddess. It was to refute this idea that the Sybils came out of their empyrean retirement to help mankind. In the lapse of centuries it has come about that mankind is again in need of some connecting link with the old spiritual world; hence Spiritualism. The pre-Christian reincarnated Sibyl teachers were, as Dr. Steiner's doctrine leads us to see, reincarnated souls who had lived on earth at a certain period of the world's history and were, under their personal forms, known as Sibyls, or people of similar character. These souls required still further lives to arrive at the great climax of spiritual attainment, when, it is said, they gained 'liberation' or freedom from the necessity for rebirth—that which Christians really mean by the term 'salvation'. Dr. Steiner places the teachings of Spiritualism on a level with the doctrine in Sibylline books, because the Sibyls, having only attained to the first grade in Jacob's ladder, were not able to take their followers any higher than the point which they had reached themselves. Spiritualism, like the Sibyls, although it points to higher planes, does not give the full itinerary of the path to final deliverance. This, spiritual science alone seems able to give.

★

In theosophical circles, after Madame Blavatsky had fulminated in the early days against the 'spooks' of Spiritualism, a great deal of real mystic and spiritual knowledge on all these subjects was formulated in the various societies. However, for many reasons I finally withdrew my allegiance to the Theosophical Movement and from all those leaders who had separated the Society into the large number of lodges scattered all over the country, and thus rent the Society in twain. It has been left to a seer like Dr. Rudolf Steiner to connect it all cosmically, and to keep on solid ground that Ancient Wisdom which has within the last half century greatly illuminated us.

★

I feel no inclination to dwell upon this Adyar manifesto of Mrs. Besant and her party beyond expressing a strong disbelief that the Saviour of the World (and I use these words in the inner meanings of the words) will ever come again in the flesh. As a follower of Dr. Steiner, I deliberately take his mystic teaching that the special part of the 'work of the Christ' when he came in the flesh *has been done*. 'It is finished' were His words, which are ringing out over the world.

What that work was, how it was accomplished, whether the teaching of it is finished, and its application to experience, is for every follower to prove. As such teaching is part of the mysteries, it is not for a neophyte like myself to speak . . .

Englishmen's Houses

Towards the end of February 1920, Rudolf Steiner left Dornach again for a further visit to Stuttgart. Another letter from Edith Maryon dates from this time:

Villa St. George,
Arlesheim,
7th March 1920

Dear Teacher,

So far no letter has arrived; it takes a long time from Stuttgart—perhaps it'll come tomorrow.

We had a visit yesterday from Dornach, the court president and seven or eight high-up beasts. They were friendly and had some understanding for our cause; afterwards they bought various books. Some even carved a little at the big Lucifer, which they found most enjoyable. They liked the models for the houses. I told them it was an attempt to alleviate the housing shortage and the houses were intended to be equipped very simply, without any luxuries, in an architecture rather adapted to the building. They were very interested. We all tried to make a good impression. The court president seemed to me particularly well disposed, if it was genuine.

Today the weather has broken, it's cold and raining; few visits to the building.

The plasterer has finally arrived, but we'll hardly be finished with the alterations before you return.

Mrs. Drury-Lavin has written. She visited my brother, and was very pleased: he and Miss Word (the fiancée) are going to visit Mrs. D.L. next Sunday, and then she'll see if it'd be possible to give a lecture in the university. Today she had to give news to the group in London. Old Gatey has unfortunately donated £1000 to found a *British* Society or (a British) centre. She's given it to the Myrdin Group. Collison will be in London soon after Easter. The four Mystery Plays are appearing in London in May or June; I have a letter from Putnams, as I wanted to know the title for the poster.

Mrs. Drury-Lavin writes that she feels as if she's only just left the spiritual world and not yet got used to this incarnation; it was too nice a time in Dornach—she drew fresh courage for life there and is infinitely thankful. I wrote to her today.

Monday. Deep snow!

With heartfelt greetings,

Edith Maryon

★

In his biography of Maryon, Rex Raab wrote:

Steiner returned to Dornach in mid-March and remained until the end of the first week in June. On the 9th of April he founded a 'Goetheanism Union', which was not just a local affair but a plan conceived on a large scale to present an exemplary measure against the world-wide shortage of housing.

The purpose of the union was expressed by Rudolf Steiner as follows: 'The new union must take on everything related to the installation of enterprises leading to what is to be done *in* the building.'

In the building! The word 'in' presupposes the building's adaptation to man and the activities he undertakes therein, which is precisely what there is generally so little feeling for.

Steiner went on: 'The first thing which has become necessary is to construct a number of houses for people working here, on the basis of a small fund. The undertaking must be done in such a way as to be carried out *strictly through me*, because that is the condition under which the money has been given.

. . . Construction of the houses has already begun. Payment will have to be made every fortnight, in instalments. In the next few days I shall make further relevant announcements . . .'

It appears from these statements that plans from a model had meanwhile been drawn up, necessary costings made, tenders requested, builders engaged and last but not least, sufficient sums of money promised. The architect Paul Bay, with whom Maryon had negotiated in the previous summer, became—without a contract—building contractor. A large sum of money was made available, above all from England. Miss Edith Lewis, owner of a factory in the Midlands, with whom Maryon had evidently formed a connection, provided the basis of the building costs with an amount of about the value of SFr. 200,000. Possibly Louisa Maryon senior also helped, as her daughter had hoped. These multiple connections to England were the reason why the emergent buildings were first known as 'Englishmen's houses', as attested by Daniel von Mutach, formerly active in the Dornach building bureau, in a letter to Rudolf Steiner directly after Maryon's death. Only later on was the name changed to 'Eurythmy houses' because eurythmists came to predominate among the occupants.

When a year later this trio of stylistically similar but in detail differentiated houses to the immediate west of the Goetheanum was completed, Edith Lewis moved into the middle one, and Edith Maryon into the lower one.

★

George Adams concluded the story of the translation of the *Kernpunkte*:

Soon afterwards, in the spring of 1920, Mrs. Wedgwood's translation (for it was very largely hers—I only gave incidental help) was published in London by Allen and Unwin, entitled *The Threefold State*. The book was well received in press reviews. Mrs. Wedgwood afterwards retranslated it for a new edition, which we renamed *The Threefold Commonwealth*.

The Destiny of this Planet

On 22 May, during the Annual Convention of the Theosophical Society in England and Wales, D.N. Dunlop delivered this year's Blavatsky Lecture, stated in *The Vahan* to have been 'closely followed and greatly appreciated'. The Theosophical Publishing House brought it out as a booklet, headed *Nature-Spirits and the Spirits of the Elements*.

The booklet runs to 36 pages. In the first seven-and-a-half, Dunlop began with his own original presentation of the subject. But halfway down page 8 he started again to make wholesale borrowings from an extensive series of editorials which had appeared some years earlier in *The Word*. This series began in January 1915 under the title 'Ghosts', and although the title was successively varied to 'Nature Ghosts', 'Prophecy', and 'Ghosts That Never Were Men', it went on running regularly for the next three years until the journal's discontinuance with the number for September 1917.

Almost all the remainder of Dunlop's lecture, from page 8 to page 35, was extracted without acknowledgement from the majority of the editorials between May 1915 and December 1916. A close comparison shows that he systematically skimmed through the series, searching for the essential or important, and lifting out particular sentences or at times even whole paragraphs, which he simply then linked together into a shorter account, always however changing Percival's term 'Ghost', and sometimes 'Elemental', into 'Nature-Spirit'.

At certain points he also added to Percival's argument a supplementary remark of his own, as follows:

> ... This is the explanation of the legends that Michael, Gabriel and the other Archangels rule over respective periods of time. They become the Regents, for the time being, of cycles of time and of human history.
>
> ... This is the basis of the science of homeopathy.
>
> ... Some of the modern experiments made with radium and the application of X-rays are a striking example of this.
>
> ... For instance, Westminster Abbey is built upon the site of an ancient Temple of Apollo.
>
> ... They knew of the special times connected with the phases of the Moon, the position of the planetary bodies in the Zodiacal signs etc.

> [Dreams are caused] ... in the cases of men of some degree of occult development, by Celestial Intelligences of a higher order.
>
> ... Exorcism, however, may have no effect whatever on epilepsy of another origin.

The most substantial of Dunlop's additions comprises two paragraphs towards the end of his text:

> In the case of a person who is to some extent developing occult powers, dreams occur which convey information of various kinds to the personality. Such dreams are a faint echo of the direct spiritual knowledge which the man of Atlantis for instance had at his command. Enlightenment in philosophy, science, art and the past and future progress of the Earth and its races may come in this way. Records of the past may be brought before the dreamer, hidden process of Nature may be shown to him, or symbols may be illustrated and their meaning explained.
>
> Such instruction through the means, always, of Elementals and Nature-Spirits is given in dreams where the Higher Mind cannot reach the personality directly. A sufficiently strong tie has not been established between the incarnated portion of the Mind and that higher portion which is not as yet incarnated, and man should aim at creating that which in *waking life* will be a connection enabling him to be directly in touch with his Higher Mind.

Having paraphrased much of the substance of Percival's last series of editorials, Dunlop then ended his lecture:

> It will be realized from what I have said that the subject of Nature-Spirits and elemental forces is intimately related to real life, and not remote from human affairs as one may at first be inclined to suppose. The elemental world is around and within every single department of life. The structure of physical objects is made up of elemental beings; in and around all physical phenomena heave the oceans of the four occult elements. Their spirits, temporarily embodied or bewitched into physical objects in the mineral and vegetable worlds and in animal and human bodies, I have referred to as 'Elementals' or 'Elemental Intelligences', and those in external invisible Nature as 'Nature-Spirits', because it was necessary to make a distinction. It is man's task to redeem these beings which are imprisoned into matter. By means of his senses he constantly receives into himself hosts of these beings, and through spiritual activity he either changes and frees them back into their own element, or makes their imprisonment still more secure. Moods of depression, of idleness, of pessimism all have the effect of binding these bewitched Nature-Spirits or Elementals more closely into matter. Optimism, cheerfulness, kindness have exactly the opposite effect. Those elemental beings which a man has not released during his life remain within his soul-sphere and return with him at his next incarnation as 'skandhas'

until he is able to free them into their element. There is constant action and reaction between man and the ocean of elemental life around him, which Rosicrucian wisdom poetically named 'the waters under the Earth'. Man has the destiny of this planet in his keeping, to make or mar as he will.

A Visit by the Artists

In early June Rudolf Steiner travelled yet again to Stuttgart, this time for three weeks. Correspondence with Maryon was once more resumed.

Goetheanum Sculpture Studio,
Dornach,
10th June 1920

Dear Teacher,

A letter has just arrived from Baron Rosenkrantz. Among other matters he says the 10th or 15th August would be a good date for a visit by the artists, and wouldn't it be better to suggest they stayed here ten days, rather than four or five? After such a long journey four or five would be rather short. What d'you think? Can lectures, eurythmy etc. go on so long? He also asks if the invitation can be extended to non-practising artists, as he thinks there are many people who aren't actually artists but are very interested in a spiritual movement in art, and would have a lot of understanding for the Dornach work. My reply was that I think there's nothing to prevent the invitation from being extended to such people, but I'd ask directly. He says many people will show great interest in eurythmy. There are now many movements in England for the furtherance of dramatic art: all sorts of old customs are being revivified (can one say this?) and old mystery plays are surfacing. There's a liking for mystical things rather than anything occult, as that demands too much intellectual effort. D'you think it might be possible (if there are enough people available, of course) to give a little performance from the Mysteries? Or if that seems impossible, from *Faust*?

Mrs. Drury-Lavin has written too, quite inspired by the Walleen idea, and says people will certainly arrange for him to come; she's also written directly to you. She doesn't feel enough is happening in England in the interests of the building; they're suffering there from a great lack of people capable of giving lectures, and of the two they have, one, Mrs. P., can perhaps be considered, but her sister doesn't at the moment stand deep enough in our cause.

Once again people are displeased with my article, as they prefer to write something themselves. She wants to write more about this in a few days' time.

Yesterday I visited Herr Hamel. There's little change in his condition,

31. *The First Goetheanum under erection*

32. *Arild and Tessa Rosenkrantz at Dornach*

33. *Mabel Heywood-Smith (Oil painting by Nellie Heath)*

34. *Isabelle de Steiger*

35. *Elizabeth Sharp (widow of Fiona Macleod)*

36. *Edith Lewis*

THE

THREEFOLD STATE

THE TRUE ASPECT OF THE SOCIAL QUESTION

BY

RUDOLPH STEINER

Author of 'The Philosophy of Freedom,' 'Von Seelenrätseln,' etc.

LONDON

GEORGE ALLEN & UNWIN, LTD.

RUSKIN HOUSE, 40, MUSEUM STREET, W.C. 1.

37. Title-page of first English translation, published in spring 1920

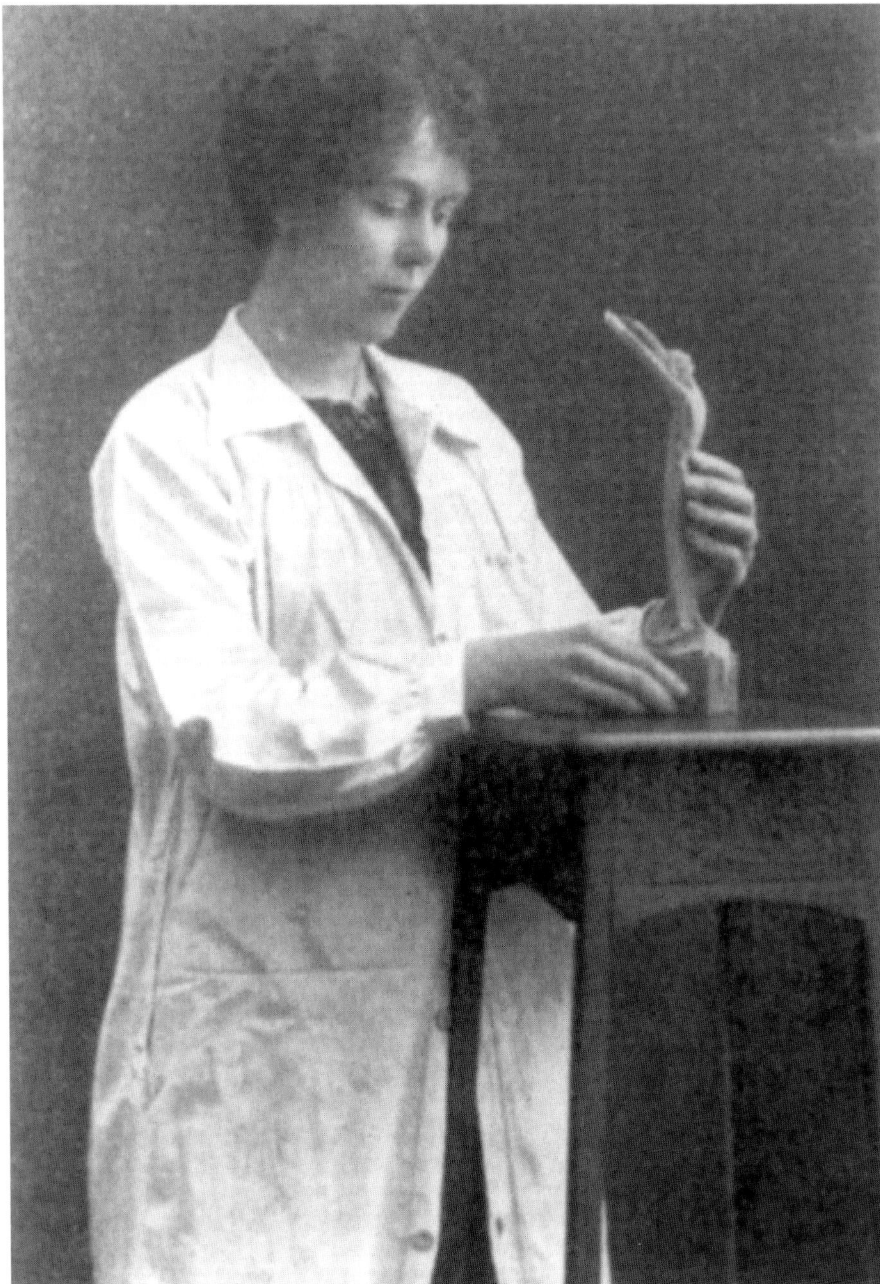

38. Edith Maryon modelling an early eurythmy figure, circa 1920

39. The three Englishmen's Houses, viewed from the terrace of the First Goetheanum

40. The lower two Englishmen's houses, with the First Goetheanum in the background. (Edith Maryon lived in the house on the left, facing the building, Edith Lewis in the middle house on the right.)

41. *Montague Wheeler*

42. *Eleanor Merry*

43. *Harry Collison*

44. *George Adams*

No. 1. Price 1/-

ANTHROPOSOPHY.

NOVEMBER, 1920.

THE GOETHEANUM.

CONTENTS.

	PAGE
THE BOUNDARIES OF NATURAL KNOWLEDGE ...	1
THE ART OF EDUCATION	3
INTERIOR OF THE GOETHEANUM	5
THE SCIENTIFIC COURSE IN THE GOETHEANUM AT DORNACH. FIRST REPORT	6
THE LIFE OF MAN FROM THE STANDPOINT OF SPIRITUAL SCIENCE	8
THE GOETHEANUM AS A NEW IMPULSE IN ART	11
WHAT CAN ANTHROPOSOPHY OFFER TO MODERN NATURAL SCIENCE?	12
ANTHROPOSOPHY AND THE SOCIAL QUESTION ...	13
ANNOUNCEMENTS	15
PUBLICATIONS BY DR. RUDOLF STEINER ...	16

The Boundaries of Natural Knowledge.

RÉSUMÉ OF LECTURE BY DR. STEINER.
DELIVERED AT THE AUTUMN COURSE, 1920.

WHAT we need for the coming development of mankind is a type of ideas which will, when realized, give to all men the social conditions in which they can feel that they are living worthily as human beings.

So much is being said to-day about the need for spiritual impulses in social reconstruction; but people do not generally ask from whence those spiritual ideas are to come, by whose help a new social order can be founded, wherein humanity can find a worthy place.

For the past three or four centuries educated people have been brought up on ideas which have grown out of the modern mode of scientific observation. It is easy to see that scientific conceptions have forced their way even into modern theology, history, jurisprudence, and elsewhere. On the other hand, the old *instinctive* relations of social life have gradually lost their elasticity. In the place of these instincts, on which even our present parliamentary institutions are founded, it is necessary to

45. Front page of first issue

46. D.N. Dunlop in the early 1920s

and not much hope for a complete recovery. Otherwise his room and food are good, and the nurses nice.

Dr. Boos says there's really nothing new. Yesterday's lecture was very long, and afterwards an outsider spoke. After the lecture by Herr Schremp there was a lively discussion. Otherwise there's nothing new to report.

I'm trying to become wise in my loneliness here, and am greatly reproaching myself.

I hope lectures today and the day before yesterday were well attended; and things are proceeding calmly? I'm still worried by events in Germany.

With heartfelt greetings,

Edith Maryon

★

Stuttgart,
15th June 1920

My dear Edith Maryon,

I'd like to have written long ago. But so far there's been an extraordinarily great deal to do; and as I also have a public lecture this evening, I can't write more than a couple of lines. Heartfelt thanks for your letter, which I've received. I think matters with Baron Rosenkrantz can be arranged according to his own opinion. People who aren't practising artists can come too. Whether we can offer anything from the Mystery Plays depends on what's possible. We can certainly try.

I'll write tomorrow or the day after about everything else. Apart from other lectures, I also gave last Saturday a lantern-lecture here on the building.

Heartfelt greetings for today and my assurance that all worries are unfounded. I probably won't yet be back on Monday; but soon afterwards.

Heartfelt greetings,

Rudolf Steiner

Stuttgart, Landhausstrasse 70

★

Sculpture Studio,
Goetheanum,
Dornach bei Basel,
19th June 1920

Dear Teacher,

Many thanks for your letter, which I've received. Baron Rosenkrantz writes that he'll now get into action and make a provisional announcement, and as soon as he gets a more definite programme, issue another one. I'm sending you herewith his suggestions; he asks for criticism and corrections.

He thinks eurythmy will awaken great interest, precisely in the spiritual form as taught at Dornach. The Dalcroze method is purely emotional and easily exciting, but is now having great success.

Might it perhaps be possible for certain members to invite for these two weeks a couple of the best eurythmy-children from Stuttgart? It would for this somewhat strengthen our forces.

Should only British artists be thought of, or the invitation extended to other countries?

Mrs. Drury-Lavin writes that £150 has been collected for Walleen and Miss Pethick thinks we should wait for her to arrive at Dornach, so as to write to him once and for all. She wanted to invite him for Oct. and Nov., so that she can make preparations in London at the end of Sept. But I want him to come at the beginning of August (if we can find someone to invite him as a guest), so that we've a competent translator for the August lectures.

With most heartfelt greetings and hoping you'll return soon,

Edith Maryon

★

Provisional Programme

10th–20th August 1920

1.) A series of 3 or more lectures on art from Herr Dr. Steiner (ask for number and theme, so that we can make an announcement.)
2.) Shall we say about 3 eurythmy performances?
   A. A performance to show the entire domain of eurythmy.
   B. Performance of *Faust* or something else already worked out.
   C. A performance of a part of the Mysteries.
3.) Could Frl. Vreede give shall we say 3 lectures on spiritual science, purpose of the building (different working groups) or some other theme stated by Herr Dr. Steiner and Frl. Vreede?
4.) Might I show and explain building and studio? (Answer: I believe you'll do this).
5.) If the programme is still longer, might the three lantern-lectures be given?

★

Stuttgart,
23rd June 1920

My dear Edith Maryon,

As circumstances have turned out, I can't be at Dornach before Sunday. It's not right for me at all; but there's no other way.

In regard to the programme suggested by Baron Rosenkrantz I can only say that I'll make every effort to do it like that. I'm of course prepared to show visitors round the building and studio, and talk about them in detail myself.

I can hardly say anything else from here except that in spite of everything I'll be leaving much work undone. What's lacking are purposeful people, capable in their own subject. Today they're hardly to be found. Such a great work as is begun here weighs heavily on the soul. Compared to such a weight, whether I'm somewhat more or somewhat less tired has little consequence. Certain things just had to happen.

I'm very much longing to be at work again in our studio. It'll be soon.

For today

heartfelt greetings,

Rudolf Steiner

currently at 70 Landhausstrasse, Stuttgart

It Could Easily Be Too Late

Rudolf Steiner came back to Dornach for a few weeks, but then returned once again for another fortnight in Stuttgart.

The next two letters between Maryon and himself probably crossed:

Sculpture Studio,
Goetheanum,
Dornach bei Basel
25th July 1920

Dear Teacher,

There seems to be a direct train on Wednesdays via Lille and Calais, so Paris can be avoided. I got the visa without any difficulties. The vice-consul even fetched the second visa for me from the French consul, for which I was really grateful, as some 30 people were already waiting in the street under a burning sun. The Arlesheim municipality also issued straightaway a permit for the return journey, so if nothing better (or less bad!) takes place, the journey should be on Wednesday evening at 10.50 (4th Aug.).

Two English ladies and three English men have arrived. They say that Rosenkrantz has so far had little success for our art-course, and people there are simply going to sleep, though there are many who'd willingly accept what we have to give. But they don't perceive it, and nobody can make them understand it. Today they're visiting the Group.

Dorothy Pethick is in Linthal, Glarus, and is forwarding a copy of a letter from Mrs. Drury-Lavin to Walleen asking that it be given to him, in case the letter hasn't arrived in Copenhagen. She promises to pay for his stay here etc.

I very much hope Dr. Boos's lecture on Tuesday will go off calmly and he doesn't have any disturbance.

The day has gone calmly here, though roundabout-music can still be heard from early morn till late evening. There've been many visitors in the building, but behaving properly.

I hope work in Stuttgart will soon be finished, so you can arrive in Dornach on Saturday. We've now removed the scaffolding from part of the Group (Lucifer).

With heartfelt greetings,

Edith Maryon

★

Stuttgart,
26th July 1920

My dear Edith Maryon,

Straight after this we're having a rather lengthy meeting of our administrative council; so I just want to send off a couple of lines before travelling out to Dischingen tomorrow to our well-known experiments. So far everything non-official has gone well. But officiality is causing ever more worry. Business-mindedness, of which we now have so much need, is unfortunately little available today. The couple of people we have are overburdened. No others whatsoever are to be found. The Göttingen lecture can't take place at all, as resistance there is too great.

I'll only arrange the concert for Baron Rosenkrantz's people when I return. There'll be plenty of time, and I wouldn't like anything to be said about it before.

I'll be pleased to be back at work again in our Dornach studio. I'll return at the scheduled time. For today

heartfelt greetings,

Rudolf Steiner

70 Landhausstrasse, Stuttgart

★

Steiner returned to Dornach on 3 or 4 August, probably just in time to see Maryon again before her departure for England in the late evening of the 4th.

Their next communications must again have crossed, as both were written on the following Monday, 9 August. Maryon's was a brief card:

48, Norfolk Road,
Seven Kings,
Ilford,
Essex.
England.
Monday.

Dear Teacher,

I'm writing these lines at a highly awkward post-office counter! I arrived fine, without getting too tired. Please open the little window in our studio at night, otherwise the air's too stuffy. I'll write a letter tomorrow or the day after. All I'm saying now is: see you again. I'm longing for Dornach already, and find London dreadful!

With heartfelt greetings,

Edith Maryon.

★

Dornach,
9th August 1920

My dear Edith Maryon,

Baron Rosenkrantz has written to Frau Doctor that his efforts have had no success. So the artists' visit to Dornach seems unable to materialize. It's a pity. We've been postponed till next year. If everything goes like this, it could easily be too late.

I'm writing these lines from the deserted sculpture studio, which is longing for its manageress, but not wanting her to shorten her stay to the point of inconvenience.

Apart from Rosenkrantz's cancellation, nothing special has happened here. The lectures went off according to programme. All is fine, apart from the usual distortions of our cause. So at the moment I have nothing other to report

than heartfelt greetings from

Rudolf Steiner

Burn with the Holy Flame

In his biography of AE, *That Myriad-Minded Man* (1975), Henry Summerfield described events in Ireland during this summer:

> The condition of the country did not prevent AE from taking his usual holiday in Donegal in the summer of 1920. Soon after his return it became clear that the wrecking of creameries had been made part of a deliberate

though unofficial policy, and the pleadings of the I.A.O.S. proved of no avail. Plunkett, Anderson, AE and other pioneers of the Irish co-operative movement were almost helpless in the face of this wanton attempt to destroy their life's work. The coming of the Co-operative Commonwealth, AE declared, would be delayed for at least a generation, though from time to time he tried to console himself and his readers with the thought that persecution would eventually refine and strengthen the spirit of the societies. He advised creameries to extend the range of their business by engaging in less vulnerable activities, to put all the evidence about an attack into the hands of solicitors, and to insure their premises even at the present extraordinary rates. What most alarmed him was the fear that the newly emerging spirit of enterprise and hard-won technical competence would be lost.

In August, writing to E.H.W. Meyerstein, the eccentric Anglo-Jewish novelist and poet, AE lamented the havoc being wrought on the one movement in Ireland free from sectarian and party passions. He would not, he said, blame the individual Englishman unless he approved of his Government's conduct, and went on to detail British actions:

'It is not only policemen are shot here, but civilians in far greater number are killed or imprisoned. Half a dozen trains have been wrecked by the military, dozens of factories burned, and there have been over thirty thousand raids by military on private houses, in many cases involving looting and destruction of property as well as brutal treatment of civilians. This has been going on so long I have lost the power of being angry.'

During this month Terence MacSwiney, the imprisoned Lord Mayor of Cork, embarked on a heroic hunger-strike, and AE, his admiration kindled as the prisoner held out week after week, wrote a powerful sonnet lauding this manifestation of an inflexible Promethean will:

See, though the oil be low, more purely still and higher
The flame burns in the body's lamp. The watchers still
Gaze with unseeing eyes while the Promethean will,
The Uncreated Light, the Everlasting Fire,
Sustain themselves against the torturer's desire,
Even as the fabled Titan chained upon the hill.
Burn on, shine here, thou immortality, until
We too can light our lamps at the funereal pyre;
Till we too can be noble, unshakeable, undismayed;
Till we too can burn with the holy flame, and know
There is that within us can conquer the dragon pain,
And go to death alone, slowly and unafraid.
The candles of God already are burning row on row:
Farewell, light-bringer; fly to thy fountain again.

Reading this tribute on its appearance in the London *Times*, MacSwiney was deeply touched and sent a message to AE through a mutual friend. His fast ended in death on 25 October, and the Lord Mayor's martyrdom not only strengthened the fervour of the Irish who were fighting for their freedom, but helped many Englishmen to understand the intensity of their neighbours' convictions. Reading his posthumous book *Principles of Freedom*, AE came to feel that MacSwiney had been a man of philosophical depth akin to Emerson and Epictetus.

The Epoch-making Decision

It is important to remember that the many letters passing at this time between Rudolf Steiner and Edith Maryon were all written in the German language, and are reproduced in the present work only in translation. Maryon had long since gained fluency in German, and through permanent residence at Dornach since 1914 had become a well-known figure in the anthroposophical circle around the Goetheanum. This was where her commitment, interests and sympathies were now centred.

Naturally the geographical readjustment also brought its consequences. Maryon's letter of 7 March clearly betrayed her annoyance, perhaps even envy, on learning that Elizabeth Gatey had donated £1000 to found a *British* Society—rather than giving this nice sum of money to the Goetheanum. And her remark in the postcard from England of 9 August that she found London 'dreadful'—the same adjective as used by AE to Clifford Bax in 1913—may have expressed an understandable distaste for the noise and pollution existing in any large European metropolis, but also shows the extent to which she had inwardly distanced herself from the spiritual atmosphere of the British capital, where she had formerly grown up and lived.

Interesting as Maryon's letters may be, therefore, they do not give any picture of how a native English person with little knowledge of the German language would have approached for the first time the Dornach phenomenon in the immediate post-war years. In order to visualize this completely different scenario a reader must now pick up the threads of the story related by Vera and Juliet Compton-Burnett.

In their article 'Memories of the First Goetheanum', published in the Winter 1976 issue of *Anthroposophical Quarterly*, the Compton-Burnetts described the situation then obtaining in Britain in the Anthroposophical Society:

> During the First World War and the years succeeding it, Anthroposophy was represented in England by a very small group of elderly members,

earnest and cultured people, who had been in close contact with Rudolf Steiner from the early days of his work in the Theosophical Society. Towards the end of the War a new impulse showed itself through the fact that a number of young people, mostly in their early twenties, suddenly appeared and began to throw themselves wholeheartedly into the Movement, attending whatever then existed in the way of study groups.

At this time work on the First Goetheanum was nearing completion, but the inevitable separation between Dornach and England caused by the War had prevented the significance of this fact being realized by younger members. The curtain was first lifted by Miss Newcomb, an elderly lady who gave a lantern-lecture, giving descriptions and showing pictures both of the building as a whole and many details of its forms. In spite of the strangeness caused by lack of understanding we were somehow strongly attracted.

The next step had to be Dornach itself, for there we should be in the actual presence of Rudolf Steiner.

In their obituary of Dorothy Osmond, they credited to their deceased friend the initiative for taking this next step:

Dorothy Osmond came to the epoch-making decision that we should go there ourselves, so we arranged our visit to fit in with the time of her holiday, September 1920.

The article continued the tale:

Early on a September morning, three young people, ourselves and Dorothy Osmond, now well known for her translations, arrived at Basel station weary from the discomforts of a post-war journey. We found our way to the Dornach tram and got down to Arlesheim where rooms had been booked for us. In the afternoon we set out to find the Goetheanum. We had not gone far before we caught our first glimpse of the grey-green slates of its cupolas shining in the sunlight and a little further on we saw on a sign-post the word 'Goetheanum'.

At last we were there; the building stood before us. All around was a scene of intense activity and haste. Dismantled scaffolding was being carried away, planks were being stacked in piles and there was every sign of preparation for some great event. Only afterwards did we learn that a fortnight later the Goetheanum was to be used publicly for the first time. The doors of the west entrance being open, we found ourselves quite free to enter the building, and ascending one of the two great staircases stood spell-bound looking down the vista of the two cupolas.

What met our gaze? Colour, weaving, ethereal colour. As we ascended the main gangway we felt ourselves caught up into another world. Gradually we became aware of the great pillars which surrounded the auditorium, and the forms of the pedestals and architraves, their surfaces shimmering with colour. Each plane of the six-sided pillars glowed with pink, green, violet or whatever was reflected upon it. After sitting awhile, ourselves bathed in a sea of colour, we ascended a few steps into the small cupola. Here again was another world, solemn and mysterious, the only colour being the brilliant paintings on the dome. The pillars surrounding this space were slender, but our attention was caught by the strangely carved majestic seats on either side of an empty space in which we later learned the statue was to have been placed.

During the week that followed, the beauty and power of the Goetheanum gradually gave us the assurance that here we should not meet the disappointments we had experienced in the Theosophical Society, so we decided to return after spending a few days in the mountains and attend the conference where we knew Dr. Steiner was to give a course of lectures.

The mention at precisely this point of the disappointments which Dorothy Osmond and the Compton-Burnetts had experienced in the Theosophical Society is significant. For although these three English visitors to Dornach were overwhelmingly impressed by the architecture and paintings of the First Goetheanum, it will become apparent that as human beings they were not at first made very welcome. And the main reason for the hostility which they encountered—from persons whom they did not name—was their theosophical background.

All through the preceding summer months, opposition to anthroposophy from various quarters in German-speaking lands had been given substantial verbal and written expression, often in a manner in which anthroposophy was categorized as 'Theosophy'. Seen from the viewpoint of the circle of Dornach residents, therefore, the unannounced appearance at this very moment of persons with a theosophical background must have seemed at best suspicious, and at worst positively alarming!

It is highly probable that one of the unnamed persons who gave Dorothy Osmond and the Compton-Burnetts a less than welcome reception was the Swiss anthroposophist Roman Boos, at the time enormously active in everything to do with the Anthroposophical Movement. Boos had recently taken charge of the Dornach Secretariat, and was not only the initiator and organizer of the 'Highschool course' about to be given at the unofficial opening ceremonies of the First Goetheanum, but also very involved in defending Anthroposophy against its detractors. Certainly fluent in both German and French, and probably with some command of English as well, he was an extremely powerful speaker with a great formulatory capacity, and if necessary a verbal contestant whose tongue could become devastatingly sharp.

Readers will have noted from several of her letters that Edith Maryon was on friendly terms with Boos. It is ironic that at first she too showed unmistakable hostility towards at least one of her English compatriots, and revealing that there seems to have been an immediate reflection in her own dream-life. For by now she had returned from England to Dornach, and as Steiner had left again for another week in Stuttgart, she wrote him a letter:

Villa St. George,
Arlesheim bei Basel.
17th Sept. 1920

Dear Teacher,

Not much has happened here. Apart from a theosophical lady arriving with two lady friends. She's not in my belief very recommendable.

Mrs. Wedgwood has apologized and taken back what she said. But what's dissatisfying is that she understands nothing at all about it, and doesn't want to listen to anything. She says it's all a matter between her and Herr Dr. St. It seems to me as if she still believes I'd blackened her name!

I'd be very glad if our work were continued at the end of next week; there's rather a sad mood here, and yesterday I had a bad dream.

Otherwise work here goes on and I'm busy with Lucifer's ribs!

I very much hope work in Germany has gone quite quietly.

With heartfelt greetings,

Edith Maryon

*

The Gesamtausgabe volume of Maryon's correspondence has an editorial note on Dorothy Osmond which includes the following remark:

> In E. Maryon's negative assessment lay no doubt a misunderstanding. No one acquainted with D. Osmond's sacrificial activity over decades on behalf of Rudolf Steiner's work could uphold the characterization of her by E. Maryon.

It would be hard to find such an embarrassed editorial comment in all the volumes of the Gesamtausgabe. But what divided Edith Maryon from Dorothy Osmond may perhaps have been not so much a misunderstanding as rather the kind of tension liable to arise in a meeting between two members of different spiritual streams.[45]

The Situation Which Had Arisen

The opening festivities of the Goetheanum took place just over a week later, on 26 September. They are described by the Compton-Burnetts, who by then had returned from their few days in the mountains:

When we came back the entire scene had changed. The Dornach hill, which had been so empty, was thronged with members assembling from far and wide. Now when we entered the Goetheanum for the inaugural meeting and took our seats, the great auditorium where we had spent so much time alone was filled to capacity. Full of expectation we awaited the entrance of Rudolf Steiner.

He came in at a side entrance, a slight, erect figure, dark-haired, and walked with a quick, firm step to his seat, turning before he sat down to cast a penetrating glance over the audience. Only a confused recollection remains of the programme. Frau Dr. Steiner recited and we saw eurythmy for the first time. Everything seemed bewildering. Even when we heard Rudolf Steiner himself speak, it was only the power of his delivery that made an impression, for owing to our slight knowledge of German most of the content of the lectures was lost to us.

Even during our first week in Dornach we had been distressed by an unfriendly reception and the distrust which our previous connection with the Theosophical Society had aroused, but now our sense of loneliness was intensified. Three unknown English members, we were surrounded by a surging throng and what seemed to us a babel of foreign tongues.

They were not however the only English members present. George and Mary Adams, returned from Poland, were also there. The former related:

In the autumn of 1920—*The Threefold State* having in the meantime been published—we decided to return to England, hoping to build up a movement for the Threefold Order. There was a public conference at Dornach—the first opening of the Goetheanum building—so we made the detour, receiving unforgettable impressions in the great auditorium, with ever-varied lights and shades from the coloured windows playing on the rough-hewn wood, the unending life and variety of sculptured forms. This time I did not ask to see Dr. Steiner personally. But a not very respectful friend, wanting to reach me quickly, had sent a telegram with the rough and ready address: c/o Dr. Steiner, Dornach. To my no small embarrassment there was Dr. Steiner making his way to us through the crowded ranks to the middle of the hall where we sat, just before one of his lectures. 'Why, you are not to be recognized,' he said laughingly as he handed me the telegram. (I had been growing a beard in the meantime.) This was the first time Mary Adams met him. He was very good to her, and gave her much spiritual help in the years that followed.

The Compton-Burnetts too narrated their meeting with Steiner:

After one of the lectures, as we were standing forlornly near the south entrance, we heard a footstep approaching and a voice said in German: 'If you will have a moment's patience I will come to you.' It was Rudolf

Steiner. When he came back the gaze of his dark eyes concentrated so intently yet so kindly upon us, and his carefully articulated answers to our questions dispelled any remaining doubts. We returned to England certain of where we belonged.

★

In their obituary of Dorothy Osmond the Compton-Burnetts again referred to this memorable first visit to Dornach in September 1920, but added another small detail:

> ... Here Dorothy experienced her first personal contact with Rudolf Steiner, and the indescribable beauty of the building. On our return we were met at the station by Mr. Dunlop ...

Readers may then imagine, after the lengthy return journey all the way back from Switzerland to England, the scene on the platform of the London railway terminus, with Dorothy Osmond and the Compton-Burnetts at long last stepping out of the train, and being greeted by their theosophical friend.

Now Dunlop recorded that of all the questions which were alive in him at this time '... Rudolf Steiner himself was the greatest question of all!' He must have been extremely curious to hear what his friends now had to relate, and have listened with interest to their glowing descriptions of the First Goetheanum and of the strange but impressive events at the conference they had attended, and above all to the account of their meeting with 'Rudolf Steiner himself!'

But since Dunlop was still an active member of the Theosophical Society, one may perhaps wonder whether Dorothy Osmond in particular might not also have thought fit to mention that British visitors with known theosophical backgrounds would not be made at all welcome by certain other Dornach residents ...

★

'Yet another impression of this time in Dornach may be recalled,' stated Marie Savitch in her biography of Marie Steiner, after also relating the visit of Dorothy Osmond and the Compton-Burnetts:

> One day there appeared in the carpentry-shop a grey-haired, very distinguished-looking gentleman. There he sat in one of the artists's rooms, perched on a table otherwise used for setting out make-up for performances. He supported himself on an arm resting on one of his legs, cocked up high. The other leg he rocked to and fro. He stared to the front with astute blue eyes. When one of the eurythmists asked him what he was doing there, he replied: 'I have already been waiting here some time for an interview

with Marie Steiner.'—Later, at the founding of the English Society, Rudolf Steiner welcomed this man as its General Secretary. During the War, however, he had fallen into extreme nationalism. Marie Steiner took such deviations very seriously. She would withdraw from such people. So when he returned to Dornach after the War he had to wait in the eurythmists' make-up room until Marie Steiner, who had still not given him any appointment, would receive him. His outstandingly active commitment to Rudolf Steiner's work and his understanding of the situation which had arisen then soon healed this war-time estrangement.

Nothing further has yet come to light about Harry Collison's alleged lapse into nationalism. But it may be noted that this biography by Marie Savitch was first published in German in 1965, and the translation into English—undertaken by Juliet Compton-Burnett—which appeared two years later was prefaced by a publisher's foreword stating that 'the author has kindly allowed a few emendations, omissions and additions to this English translation'.

By comparing the German and English versions of the biography a reader may discover at what points these changes occur. Where the quoted passage stated that 'During the War he had fallen into extreme nationalism', the English version substitutes for the simple pronoun 'he' the magniloquent phrase 'this significant personality'.

Such a little alteration would scarcely seem worth mentioning but for another interesting change in the final sentence of the passage. Here Juliet Compton-Burnett—who undoubtedly had a far better knowledge of her fellow-countryman Harry Collison than had Marie Savitch—simply excised the entire phrase 'and his understanding of the situation which had arisen'.

Almost Unnoticed

On 16 September 1920 a certain H. Wilson Harris contributed to *The Daily News*, which had at the time a circulation of some 260,000 (a paper later incorporated into *The Daily Mail*), an article entitled 'How to treat Capital: A Book Europe is discussing':

> On the Continent everyone who thinks is discussing a remarkable book published in the early part of this year by a remarkable man. Dr. Simons, the German Foreign Secretary, has spoken of the plan it outlines as the one practicable alternative to Bolshevism. Dr. Benes, the Foreign Minister of Czecho-Slovakia, and one of the ablest and most effective of the builders of small States, had it on his table at Spa. Mr. Venizelos has been reading it. Everybody who is anybody has been reading it.

Here, oddly enough, it has passed almost unnoticed. It has been translated—under the title *The Threefold State*—and published by Messrs. Allen and Unwin at five shillings. But, apart from a handful of cursory reviews, it appears so far to have left the British public cold. If it has been merely overlooked for the past month or two to be studied in earnest now, that is no bad thing, for the more vivid the signs of revolt against the old order of society the more pertinent do Dr. Rudolf Steiner's arresting proposals become.

Dr. Steiner is not unknown in this country. Primarily he is a mystic, and a course of lectures on his exaltation of the spiritual life attracted considerable attention in the West End a couple of years before the War. Now the Munich philosopher has turned from abstract to applied mysticism. The spiritual he insists is paramount, but the spiritual and the material cannot be dissevered. Failure to apply the spiritual to the practical has stultified the visionaries through all ages. Forthwith, therefore, he sets himself, like a long line of predecessors, to outline the ideal commonwealth for his times.

Space precludes any comprehensive survey of Dr. Steiner's doctrine. His threefold state is the political, the economic and the spiritual. The distinction between the several spheres thus defined would take too long to elaborate here, and it is more to the point at this particular moment to examine the very interesting proposals put forward for the control of the use of capital. It is enough to say that while the political state will be concerned generally with defining and safeguarding the rights of each member of society, the spiritual state will be the directing authority in the sphere of religion, of education and of justice, and—a far wider conception—will be responsible for seeing to it that no man's abilities are prevented from bearing fruit for the community from lack of the opportunity of exercising them to the full.

That is the starting-point of the provisions as to capital, capital consisting in the main of the means of production. In regard to that Dr. Steiner is no nationalizer. His gospel is freedom, the unfettered play of individual effort and ability, and he sees in socialization petrification when what is essential is elasticity. But no capital, whether it be money or factories or land, must serve any other purpose than the good of the community. The man competent to use capital, in the wide sense, for the public benefit must have capital to use. No man, on the other hand, can be allowed to make access to capital the means of piling up gains for himself and his descendants. Under the copyright laws the fruit of a man's brain reverts to the community on his death or shortly after. Likewise the capital which enabled him to produce must be transferred, when he can no longer use it beneficially, to someone else who will continue the production for the public good.

There will, then, be no confiscation. The political state will own no capital. It will merely see that no man retains capital of which he is not making proper use. It will not necessarily regulate the transfer. The user of capital may nominate his own successor, subject to a right of veto by the spiritual state, which will nominate users for capital improperly employed or for capital voluntarily submitted to it for allocation. Increments of capital earned by production may be retained so long as they are employed for the further development of production, but they, like the original capital, must in due time be passed on to a new user. Savings out of salary for management and labour will of course have their due remuneration and in certain cases a percentage of the increment earned by capital can be retained as private property and lent at interest during the owner's lifetime, but even here there will be severe restrictions on bequest, which must, for example, be to producers for use, not to non-producers for the support of idleness.

I have not attempted in this most incomplete summary to present at all adequately even the one section of Dr. Steiner's book which seems to me most to the point at the moment. Neither am I for an instant committing myself personally to the advocacy of his proposals. His scheme is by no means clear-cut. At points it is distinctly obscure. His processes of separation and liaison are often perplexing and inconclusive. But a living and arresting idea runs through the book. What it needs is to be discussed and argued about and classified and elaborated. Personally I want to argue about it a lot. I cannot, because so far I have found no one in this country who has read the book. Hence this article.

The Step Must Be Taken

If no one in Britain could be found who had read *The Threefold State* it may partly have been because the activity of British anthroposophists at this time was still wholly confined to internal group meetings. A passage in the obituary of Dorothy Osmond by the Compton-Burnetts is here of great relevance:

> In the Theosophical Society Dorothy Osmond had had the experience of a large and well-organized society, and this now stood her in good stead. She realized that the step must be taken from the intimate readings of lecture-courses in private homes to what could lead to a centralized Anthroposophical Movement. This aroused a certain opposition from members, who feared that expansion would lead to loss of depth, and it must also be said that Dorothy's very zeal made it extremely difficult for her to see other people's points of view, a trait which lasted throughout her life.

Problems relating to the idea of centralization are indeed recorded in a circular letter sent to members of the Myrdhin Group by its Secretary:

27 Clareville Grove,
London, S.W.7.
Sept, 1920.

Dear Sir, or Madam,

The Committee calls the attention of members to the following resolution passed at the General Meeting Feb. 17/20:

Resolution. That Miss Gatey's offer of a gift of £1000 should be gratefully accepted.

(Miss Gatey expressed a wish that this gift should be devoted to the purpose of forming a joint Headquarters in London of the English groups.)

In accordance with that offer, the Committee approached the other groups on the subject of forming a joint Headquarters, & discovered that they were not willing to co-operate so long as the Myrdhin Group was known as the Anthroposophical Society of Great Britain, for the reason that they regarded this as breaking away from the Parent Society.

The Committee feel that the formation of the British Society was a War measure, the necessity for which has passed away, & suggest that with a view to a closer co-operation with the other groups & the formation of a joint Headquarters, the Myrdhin Group should resume its old connection with the Parent Society.

Apprehension is still felt by some that adhesion to the Parent Society denotes German control. Any such control is contrary to the professed principles of the Society, which expressly state that each group is perfectly free.

A postcard is enclosed, & an expression of opinion is requested as soon as possible.

Yours faithfully,

Rae Acton,
Hon. Secretary

★

The idea of closer co-operation between the existent groups must have found sufficient approval, for an agenda survives of a 'General Meeting of Anthroposophical Society':

To discuss ideas and methods for spreading knowledge of our Movement, and to facilitate and co-ordinate work for the winter, there will be a General Meeting of all groups at 47 Redcliffe Square on Monday the 27th Sept. at 8 p.m.

Agenda:—

(1) Organizers for Activities.
(2) Central Headquarters.

(3) Speakers and Readers.
(4) Methods for creating interest in Anthroposophy.
(5) Need for Publishing Dept.
(6) Financing.

There is great need for efficient individual workers in each of these activities.

Your attendance and help is earnestly requested.

One practical result of this meeting was a communication sent out to all members from 'the Publicity Secretary' at 47 Redcliffe Square:

> It has become evident for some time past that we are expected to do our very utmost in making Anthroposophy known in this country. Since we are not in a position to conduct courses of lectures, the only method, and one which is obvious, in order to gain publicity is to produce a periodical which will send forth the work of Anthroposophy.
>
> The first number of a monthly magazine is to appear in November. In it will be a report of the autumn course being held at the Goetheanum, where lecturers of different nationalities show how spiritual science is being brought to bear on every branch of human knowledge and endeavour, as well as on the inner life of the individual. This wide-reaching object is one which, as members of Dr. Steiner's Society, we must now put forward publicly, and it is hoped that every effort will be made by members to distribute the magazine as widely as possible. In it will appear articles bearing on the work and teaching, articles on science, art, education, social science, and also translations of Dr. Steiner's recent public lectures.
>
> The magazine is to be called 'Anthroposophy' and will cost sixpence without postage. Please send a postal order before the 15th of October for as many copies of the first number as you can distribute.
>
> Three extra copies will be given for every six copies ordered.

Although no permanent Headquarters had yet been found, it was decided as an interim measure to rent a small library-office and the use of a lecture-hall from the Royal Asiatic Society at 74 Grosvenor Street.

These premises are still standing today, though the Royal Asiatic Society has long since departed from them. Before the First World War the same rooms had sometimes been used for meetings of the Alchemical Society, of which the anthroposophist Isabelle de Steiger and interested theosophist D.N. Dunlop were both members.

*

In November Rudolf Steiner was spending another three weeks in Stuttgart. Edith Maryon wrote him a couple of letters:

Sculpture studio,
Goetheanum,
Dornach bei Basel,
9th November 1920

Dear Teacher,

Everything here is proceeding in order, except that the studio is looking very waste and empty. I've been carving at Lucifer, and with great effort have finished the 3 eurythmy posters, though only at the last moment—when Miss Melland had to leave.

A Mr. Gaze has arrived today, sent to me by Mrs. Cull, and it appears Frl. Vreede was to smooth his path so that he could travel for a few days to Stuttgart. He told me he was to take over the books from Courtney; probably he wants to talk about it, if an opportunity is offered him.

Felkin arrived all right and has now received good news from her mother. She writes that she's trying to preach threefolding to her acquaintances, and says that when she explains it to people they grasp what the thing means much better than she does herself, and she supposes they understand through the intellect, because she only understands through intuition. Rather funny, isn't it? There's nothing exactly amusing here otherwise.

I very much hope affairs in Stuttgart can be put in good order, more according to your wishes, as before, and you're not overworking too much.

With heartfelt greetings,

Edith Maryon

★

Sculpture studio,
Goetheanum,
Dornach bei Basel,
14th Nov. 1920

Dear Teacher,

I'm sending herewith a review of the *Threefold State* by a respected newspaper in the North of England, and as it seems to me pretty good I've also ordered some extra copies.

Mr. Gaze was unable to get a passport through shortage of time and has already left. He says a second edition of the *Threefold State* will probably have to be published in the spring, and thought it might be joined with some or all of the articles from *In Ausführung der Dreigleiderung des Sozialen Organismus*. I told him it'd be best to write directly to the publisher about this and ask what he wants. Today I visited the Sharps (Herr and Frau) and congratulated them: the wedding was on Thursday. On Friday I'm going to visit little Schmiedel; the proud father has already been showing around a picture of the first birthday (8 days).

On Saturday we have a lecture from Dr. Boos in the Bernoullianum.

No news has come from Stuttgart; I can only hope all is making progress and send

heartfelt greetings,

Edith Maryon

Will Dr. Unger be able to get stoves for the houses?

Through All Her Powers

In his biography of AE, *That Myriad-Minded Man*, Henry Summerfield continued with his description of the Irish crisis:

> On 21 November, Lloyd George summoned AE to London, and three days later, over breakfast at 10 Downing Street, they discussed possibilities for a settlement. AE had a low opinion of the Prime Minister, regarding him as a glib talker without ideas other than those he picked up from the conversation of people less shallow than himself, and during the interview he observed 'cunning in every wrinkle' of his face. As he left the official residence, he remembered a point that had slipped his memory and turned back to mention it, but was told that the Prime Minister already had another visitor. At the time, he thought that he had made a truce possible (apparently by recommending that Sinn Fein be induced to accept Commonwealth membership in return for the inclusion of Ulster), but events in Ireland moved so swiftly that his plan came to nothing. It may have been on this trip that he called on Lord Northcliffe, the newspaper magnate, who, being Irish, asked what he could do for the cause. AE requested that he publicize it in the United States, and he did this to such effect that substantial pressure was brought to bear on Great Britain by her most important ally.

The Irish political situation had by now become acutely sensitive. Another of AE's friends, Monk Gibbon, stated that for a time AE refused to set foot in England at all, and this visit to London in November 1920 proved to be the last occasion when he crossed over the Irish Sea during Rudolf Steiner's lifetime.

★

The first issue of *Anthroposophy*, a bi-monthly publication serving as both general journal and news-sheet for British members, appeared in that same month, November 1920. It was edited by Baroness Rosenkrantz.

The issue contained a résumé of one of Steiner's lectures, various articles by George Adams, W.B. Paton and Baron Rosenkrantz, and at the foot of one page a quotation from the famous exordium to Book III of *Paradise Lost*:

> Celestial light
> Shine inward, and the mind through all her powers
> Irradiate, there plant eyes, all mist from thence
> Purge and disperse, that I may see and tell
> Of things invisible to mortal sight.

★

Despite—or perhaps just as a result of—the previously publicized remark that 'we are not in a position to conduct courses of lectures', the titles were announced of several lectures to be held over the next couple of months at the Society's premises. As well as the anthroposophists Harry Collison, Wilfred Norton, Baron Rosenkrantz, Harriet Newcomb, George Adams and George Francis, the list of lecturers also included a prominent member of the Theosophical Society: D.N. Dunlop.

Dunlop's lectures were scheduled for 9 and 16 December. These dates are of especial interest since it was right in between, on the 14th, that he finally applied to join the Anthroposophical Society—for administrative purposes British groups at the time had come to form part of the Society in Switzerland—with Collison as his sponsor.

The lectures were reported in the next issue of *Anthroposophy*:

> Mr. D.N. Dunlop gave two lectures at 74 Grosvenor Street on 'The Story of Creation'. In addressing an audience of strangers he drew attention to the deep wisdom in the books and lectures by Dr. Steiner, and advised his hearers, in order to enlarge and fructify their studies, to become members of the Anthroposophical Society. Mr. Dunlop then gave an account of man's development. While natural science declares man to have evolved out of the mineral, vegetable and animal world, as the youngest kingdom, we are, in reality, the oldest kingdom. The other kingdoms have been thrown off by man—left behind, as it were, in the process of evolution. All life is related to cosmic forces, and until this is realized we cannot have harmony in the world nor in our thoughts. Without knowledge of cosmic creation we cannot hope to reconstruct social systems. We must have co-operation with the beings of the cosmos. What these beings have done we must also do. Students of spiritual science have a great responsibility, for their work in the world is of great positive importance. Consciousness of the spiritual world has been lost, and it must be regained consciously. By inward culture we can open ourselves up to the divine beings and realize the cosmic forces. By sacrifice and co-operation we can accomplish what they have accomplished. We must vivify material things; it is our business to transform the Earth. The expression of our work is to attain earthly freedom.

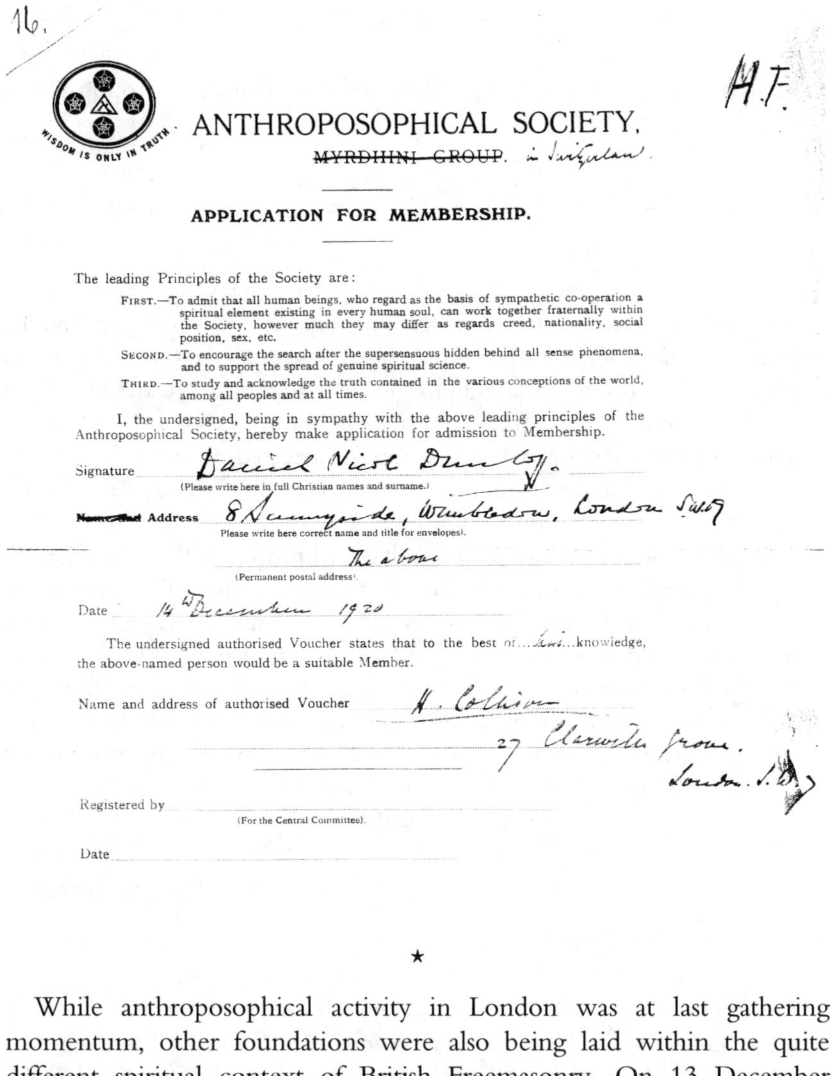

16.

H.F.

WISDOM IS ONLY IN TRUTH

ANTHROPOSOPHICAL SOCIETY,

~~MYRDHINI GROUP~~. in Switzerland.

APPLICATION FOR MEMBERSHIP.

The leading Principles of the Society are:

FIRST.—To admit that all human beings, who regard as the basis of sympathetic co-operation a spiritual element existing in every human soul, can work together fraternally within the Society, however much they may differ as regards creed, nationality, social position, sex, etc.

SECOND.—To encourage the search after the supersensuous hidden behind all sense phenomena, and to support the spread of genuine spiritual science.

THIRD.—To study and acknowledge the truth contained in the various conceptions of the world, among all peoples and at all times.

I, the undersigned, being in sympathy with the above leading principles of the Anthroposophical Society, hereby make application for admission to Membership.

Signature Daniel Nicol Dunlop.
(Please write here in full Christian names and surname.)

~~Name and~~ Address 8 Sunnyside, Wimbledon, London S.W.19
Please write here correct name and title for envelopes).

The above
(Permanent postal address).

Date 14th December 1920

The undersigned authorised Voucher states that to the best of his knowledge, the above-named person would be a suitable Member.

Name and address of authorised Voucher H. Collison
27 Clarendon Grove.
London. S.W.

Registered by
(For the Central Committee).

Date

★

While anthroposophical activity in London was at last gathering momentum, other foundations were also being laid within the quite different spiritual context of British Freemasonry. On 13 December 1920—the day before Dunlop's application for membership of the Anthroposophical Society—Grand Lodge granted a warrant to found the Old Uppinghamian Lodge No. 4227.

It was three Old Uppinghamians who had translated Rudolf Steiner's Mystery Plays into the world-language. And the petitioners for the foundation of the Old Uppinghamian Lodge included one of these very translators, namely Harry Collison, also now Steward of the Leathersellers Company.

Millions for Mediums

Early in the new year, a letter was circulated to all British anthroposophists:

74, Grosvenor Street,
London, W.1.
January, 1921.

Dear Fellow Members,

The library has been built up in order that it may be maintained by members themselves. We have the privilege of the combined libraries placed to our use, but all replenishings must be kept going if we are to have a library at all. This necessitates our calling your attention to the matter, so that each member may make such contribution towards it as he or she can afford. The cost of material has considerably increased, and therefore we feel obliged to make a yearly minimum membership subscription of 2/6 from January.

It having been brought to Mr. Collison's knowledge that a great many lectures are still unreturned, he begs to remind members that lectures are only on loan, and he cannot afford to continue an unlimited supply. Unless members are more careful in the custody and proper return of the lectures, Mr. Collison will be compelled very reluctantly to withdraw from the Society what remains of his library. The total cost of the production of a course of lectures is on the average £25. Members borrowing lectures will in future, in case of loss, be liable for the cost of production.

Yours faithfully,

E. Engert.
Hon. Sec. and Librarian.

★

On Wednesday 26 January *The Daily Telegraph* published an article entitled 'Occultism in Germany', with further subtitles of 'Spirit-rapping Craze' and 'Millions for Mediums'. It was 'From our Special Correspondent, Berlin, Tuesday'.

The correspondent of the *Berliner Tagblatt* points out that the profligate pursuit of materialistic pleasures which astonishes visitors to the German capital has its counterpart in an unprecedented interest in occultism. He says that if Cagliostro could pay another visit to Berlin he would no longer write in his diary: 'Disgusting town; no one will believe anything.' A large section of the population is seeking consolation for the disillusionments of the War in attempts to peep behind the veil which hangs between us and the beyond. Card-readers and clairvoyants minister to the needs of the more humble in purse and mind. For those with greater educational and pecuniary advantages there are innumerable more or less serious spiritualistic, occultistic, astrological, theosophical and psychical research societies, most of which are of quite recent creation. Many classify themselves as 'lodges' and bear esoteric names, such as 'Armadora' and 'Ohm-Rahms-Johjiyjah'. An 'Order of Occultists' was established only a year ago, but already has a thousand members. It holds periodically 'evenings for the selection of mediums' when 'nervous ladies and gentlemen form a chain round a big table, sigh, tremble, fall into swoons, or get convulsions' and so demonstrate their stance for communication with the spirits. The order issues a paper, in which hand-readers, clairvoyants and 'medium-curers' advertise their consulting hours. It is said that the president intends to found a 'popular school of occultism'.

In 'Armadora' the dominating personality is a medium who is known among the initiated as 'Queen of the Stars'. This society has an 'archive for revelations from the other world' in which one of the members has recorded, with illustrations, life in the star 'Agfa'.

On a rather higher plane stands the 'Anthroposophic Society' founded by Dr. Steiner on his secession from the theosophists in 1913. It now has altogether 8000 members, and is building at Dornach a 'Goetheanum' in which four millions of marks have already been sunk. Another of its developments is to be a 'limited company for the production of scientific and spiritual values'. For this enterprise fifteen million marks have already been subscribed, but apparently the work is not to begin till twenty-five millions have been secured.

Among the unincorporated circles which are devoting themselves to similar pursuits, the writer mentions that of an engineer who claims to have weighed on a 'phantom scale' the 'teleplasma' which streams from a medium's body when a spirit materializes itself. The weight of the emanation was found to be three kilogrammes (about $6\frac{1}{2}$ lb).

Three days later, the correspondence columns on the 29th included a letter:

To the editor of *The Daily Telegraph*

Sir,

In an account sent by your correspondent in Berlin—taken from the *Tagblatt*—of spiritualistic crazes rampant in that city, the name has been included of Dr. Rudolf Steiner. As an artist with a clear appreciation of the difficulties now besetting a world which has outgrown what is old and is unsure about what is new, I would be grateful for this opportunity of saying that Dr. Rudolf Steiner is one of the most powerful forces living for bringing an entirely wholesome and new impulse into the world of art.

Traditions of the Renaissance being dead and realism exhausted, a return to what is spiritual is absolutely necessary. And this return is the very thing advocated, insisted on, and urged by the whole teaching of Dr. Steiner, who has dealt, in over 1000 public and private lectures, on all branches of human creative activities, and is doing so much to rescue art from its present deplorable conditions.

Believe me, Sir,

yours truly,

Arild Rosenkrantz

The Mystery of Matter

At the end of 1920 the 30-year-old *Vahan* was discontinued and replaced by a new journal with the same title as the weekly newspaper supplement of 1909–10 edited by D.N. Dunlop—*Theosophy*.

For the first number in January 1921, Dunlop contributed an article on 'The Mystery of Matter'.

> There is a significant tendency among students of occult philosophy in our modern days to overlook the importance of the consideration of the nature and constitution of matter, and concentrate all their attention upon so-called 'psychic' phenomena and abstract psychical speculation. This fact is indeed far more significant than is usually thought, and it suggests a curious reaction, leading to much false mysticism and unproductive philosophy.
>
> The nineteenth century produced such a tremendous development in the realm of science that *man himself* and his relation to matter was almost lost sight of in the intricate labyrinth of evolutionary theories. At the end of the century emphasis again began to be laid upon the ancient doctrines of a spiritual origin of man and of the universe, and it is easy to see how a natural reaction came to pass among those who misunderstood the mystery of the reality of consciousness, or spirit, on the one hand, and of matter on the other. Just as it was false fifty years ago to deny the factor of divine intelligence in the realm of biology and zoology, so it is false in the twentieth century to imagine that the investigation of matter must be left to the scientists, and that with close study of atoms, molecules, elements and substances occultism is not concerned. But scientists themselves are finding that their minute investigations are bringing them back to a mystery which they cannot describe in scientific terms, and occult philosophy, if it is to be a light in this darkness which confronts science at the boundaries of physical nature, must prove itself applicable in the minutest detail to the discoveries of the human intellect in the realm of matter. Records of psychic experiences and vague theories of reincarnation are quite inadequate in this connection. The gates to the mysteries of matter are obdurate before thought that is not of the keenest and clearest, and speculations of nebulous, emotional phantasy will lead nowhere but to illusion.

Intimate consideration of matter as the outermost expression of substance leads to the conclusion that it is graded in states or distinct degrees of development. In the primary unformed states, that of *fire*, or *warmth*, all the later developments are contained 'in solution'. Matter in this condition corresponds in theosophical literature to the First Round. The second stage is that of the condensation of warmth into *air*, and the period is named the second, or Sun Round. After a further process of condensation *water* (as the ancients understood this term) appears during the third or Moon period; and finally, in the Fourth Round, the 'dry land', or physical matter in a *molecular* state, crystallizes into the concrete solid form of the mineral kingdom. At this stage the process of involution becomes one of evolution, so far as the Earth is concerned.

Out of the molecule develops the *cell*—matter is in its vegetable or cellular condition. The cell enters organic existence, and *animal life* in all its complexity is the next stage. The next degree is the human mind, individuality—'I AM I'. Into this high state of matter the one consciousness is reflected as the microcosm. An individual emerges, having under its guidance an organized animal body, impelling each organ to perform a particular function. Molecules, cells and organs are all under the direction of *self-conscious* matter, and the ego is able to take upon itself the task of conscious evolution. There are yet two higher stages, difficult to circumscribe in human speech, because they correspond to realms which can be consciously known only after initiation, and the race as a whole is far from understanding the 'mystery' language capable of describing them. A faint conception may be suggested by Emerson's term 'oversoul'. The knowledge of 'I am I' widens to the realization of 'I am Thou', 'Thou art I', and finally Divinity itself embraces in god-like consciousness men, animals, plants, minerals and elementary kingdoms.

It will be seen from these few suggestions how essential it is to bring fundamental principles of spiritual philosophy to bear on the consideration of subjects such as this. The possibilities of an atom are not exhausted by mathematical analysis, however far-reaching, nor are conglomerations and collections of molecules and the behaviour of the electrons disposed of by the periodic law of modern physicists and chemists. Furthermore, there can be no true therapeutic science without knowledge of the various degrees of matter and the correlation of the elements to the organs and functions of the body. Man as a fourfold being is compounded of the matter of the worlds or 'Rounds' of fire, air, water, earth, and the agencies to be used by the functions of these elements in his bodies are to be found by logical sequence in the four different degrees of matter corresponding to them in the manifested world. Thus mineral agencies are adapted to ills of a purely physical nature; vegetable agencies to diseases of the ethereal (pranic) body; animal agencies to diseases of an organic origin; human agencies, consisting of the right use of words of power, to diseases of the ego. But this is a vast subject, connected with the study of the inner elements and earlier Rounds of our planetary incarnation, and can only be hinted at here.

In a book written only last year by a scientist of great reputation in this country, I find these words: 'From this world mystery in any real sense has been banished.' It is a significant indication of the attitude of the human intellect of our time, but it is a danger signal. Science may be justly proud of many of her achievements, but it will be forced upon her sooner or later that her present methods are inadequate in many of the problems with which humanity is faced. If science could but realize that she must join hands with occult philosophy in its investigation of matter, then much of the materialism typical of present-day thinking would disappear, and the real relation of man to the universe would no longer prove a Rubicon around the achievements of human consciousness. It is possible for man to build a bridge from the physical world to the spiritual world by following the path indicated by the ancient symbols of the zodiac. But the laws of that great starry scripture are no longer applied to the problems of consciousness and matter, which cannot and will not be solved without an understanding of the principles it embodies, and which are reflected into matter in all its degrees.

It is obvious that all men cannot have access to the training which a scientist requires, but it is absolutely essential that every student of occultism should have some instruction in simple, natural phenomena. Science, with all its limitations, should be more fascinating than a séance, especially when its discoveries are considered in the light of even an elementary knowledge of occult philosophy. A study of the elements should be more suggestive than sensational tales of psychic manifestations or life on other planets! To know how a crystal is formed, how gold is precipitated, how a seed grows into a tree, how food is transformed into bodily tissue, how a physical human body is built up from a germ smaller than a grain of sand, and recapitulates all evolutionary life in its embryonic state, would lead of itself to a truer understanding of the Secret Doctrine of the ages than plausible descriptions of the astral and devachanic planes.

It was Novalis who wrote with the intuition of a true spiritual seer of the mysteries wrapped up in matter: 'Celestial ambassadors alone have let a few syllables of this sublime science fall. Its territory is still unexplored—a Holy Land.'

Such a Lot to Discuss

In the article reproduced in the last section D.N. Dunlop used three times the phrase 'occult philosophy', reminiscent of the title of the lecture given to the H.P.B. Lodge exactly four years earlier, in January 1917, by Harry Collison—'The Occult Philosophy of Dr. Steiner'.

By 1921 Collison no longer had any further concern with theosophical lodges. But he was certainly concerned with a Masonic lodge, for when on 7 February the consecration took place of the Old Uppinghamian Lodge, he was installed as Junior Warden.

★

For the first time since the World War, Rudolf Steiner now began to revisit non-German-speaking countries. On 18 February he travelled to Holland.

Correspondence with Edith Maryon was again resumed:

Sculpture Studio,
Goetheanum
26th Febr. 1921

Dear Teacher,

I've received a letter from Miss Felkin asking me to write to you saying that a meeting of her friends is taking place next Tuesday at 6 o'clock in the evening, and things seem to be getting very difficult and be dissolving—and she wants to be thought about at this time. (She's coming here again for a short period.)

It'd probably be quite good if it came to an end, wouldn't it?

This week very bad news was received of a dramatic sketch, performed by students, in Basel casino in the evening, a caricature (under assumed names of course) of the Anthroposophical Society. It went into every detail, without any joking, but very, very nasty. In places it even went over into blasphemy. But it was quite according to Basel taste, great applause and a large public. Some things were highly clever and devilishly thought out. (Herr Ith, Frau Dr. Boos, Beatrice and others were present. I hope you bring better news from Holland and people there are less offensive than they are here.)

I'm busying myself with a boxful of puppets and posters for St. Gallen.

I think of your birthday tomorrow and again send many good wishes,

Edith Maryon

Greetings for tomorrow from Frl. Geck.

★

Amsterdam
28th February 1921

My dear Edith Maryon,

Heartfelt thanks for your greetings on February 27th. I'm right in the middle of lecturing. In the evening of the 19th I spoke in Amsterdam, then each day according to programme. Both yesterday and today Mrs. Drury-

Lavin, Miss Woolley, Mr. Neal, Mr. Kaufmann, Mr. and Mrs. Franklin were here, and today Mr. Collison too. When there's such a lot to discuss and so much lecturing, little time is left for coming to oneself.

Apart from what was on the programme, there was a lecture on the 25th for teachers and students in the technical college in Delft, and this evening I have to speak in the college here.

Tomorrow is the public lecture in Rotterdam. On 3rd March, for extremely important reasons, I'm speaking in Hengelo. I travel to Stuttgart on the 4th and hope to be in Dornach on the 6th or 7th. I'm heartily looking forward to the time in the Dornach studio.

Some things have gone very well here; other things might have gone better. We're just lacking really practical people.

I was only able to give one group lecture, in the Hague on 27th February. There was a eurythmy performance in the afternoon, and the public lecture in the evening.

I've so far managed with my voice. I had to be very careful. But having to speak all too often is still tiring.

Today is just an evening lecture.

Heartfelt thoughts and greetings

from

Rudolf Steiner

★

One episode at his lecture that evening was recalled by Steiner on 15 June 1923, while reminiscing about earlier theosophical days:

> Leadbeater, whom you will have heard much about, has now in his old age become an Old Catholic bishop, and one of his comrades, who was also at the Munich Congress, has even become an Old Catholic archbishop. One should not be at all surprised about these things. No sense of direction now existed and everything was going crisscross and awry. Why should this not happen too?
>
> There was no particular need to alter one's personal relationship to these people, a direct social relationship, I mean. I believe it was two years ago that I was lecturing in Amsterdam. After the lecture one of those gentlemen who had given a lecture at the Munich Congress in 1907 came up to me in the old friendly way. He still looked exactly the same, but had meanwhile become an Old Catholic Archbishop. He was not wearing his robes, but that is what he was!

The reference is to the British theosophist James Wedgwood, whose life had taken a turn for the worse. In June 1915 he accepted an invitation from Annie Besant to travel out to Australia, where he fell completely under the spiritual infuence of Charles Leadbeater.

Returning to Britain in early 1916, he was then consecrated a bishop in the Old Catholic Church. He went all the way back to Australia, and passed on the consecration to Leadbeater.

In 1917 he came back again to Britain, where however he was disowned by the Archbishop of the British Old Catholics. Leadbeater and Wedgwood thereupon changed the name of their Church to 'Liberal Catholic Church', and simply continued their activities as before.

The range of these activities was especially shown in 1919 when Wedgwood became implicated in London in a sexual scandal. He quickly moved away and over to Holland, where he went on to establish the European headquarters of the L.C.C.

He makes no further appearance in the present story.

Grafted onto the Old

The interview in Holland between Rudolf Steiner and Harry Collison covered several different subjects. Elsie Armour reported:

> Acting on Rudolf Steiner's recommendation, alongside his work for Anthroposophy Harry Collison maintained his connection with the City, with art, with the Masons and with the Church of England. Thus he maintained a harmonious balance between the outer and the inner. And through him the new was firmly grafted onto the old.

This last sentence is recognizably adapted from Steiner's statement in Chapter XXXVI of his autobiography that he was '. . . in favour of linking, whenever possible, what is coming into being with what exists historically.'

The reference was to the link between the Mystica Aeterna and the existent tradition of historical Freemasonry.

★

Another result of the interview was Collison's editorial note to the book which now reappeared under the title *The Philosophy of Spiritual Activity*:

> In 1918 Dr. Steiner published a revised edition of the *Philosophie der Freiheit*. For the translation of the new passages added to, and the incidental changes made in this revised edition I am indebted to Mr. Hoernlé, now Professor of Philosophy in the University of Durham.
>
> At the author's request I have changed the title to *Philosophy of Spiritual Activity*, and throughout the entire work 'freedom' should be taken to mean 'spiritual activity'.
>
> H.C.
> March 1921

★

Steiner, meanwhile, travelled once more to Stuttgart. Maryon wrote to him again.

Her letter contains the first reference to the British naval officer E.H. Grafton, who after a career at sea became Captain of the Chatham Dockyard, and in 1915, on taking early retirement from the Navy at the age of 50, was promoted to Rear-Admiral.

Sculpture studio,
Goetheanum.
19th March 1921

Dear Teacher,

I hope during your stay in Stuttgart you can somewhat straighten the matter out? I'm giving it a very great deal of thought and hope people in the right places will see how terribly mean these attacks on you are, and how offensive to all truth; they're unbelievably nasty, and one really asks where the truly understanding people in Germany are hiding, and whether those with broad horizons are totally lacking.

I've received a letter from Mrs. Drury-Lavin. D'you remember she once wrote about an admiral? The one who was studying your books for many years without knowing if you were still alive; and on the bridge of his ship, when he had to be on watch, always had extracts of books to read in his pocket. He's now become a member, is coming to the course at Easter, and bringing his young daughter, as he says she should at least hear something sensible before the world talks all sorts of rubbish into her head! He's made a book for her too—extracts from your books, and she reads this every evening. He's hoping for a few minutes talk with you, just to express his gratitude for all he's learnt from Anthroposophy.

I hope your voice is all right? And you're not overtired?

Most heartfelt thoughts,

Edith Maryon

★

On 21 March a meeting of leading members of the Anthroposophical Society was held at 74 Grosvenor Street in London, at which the first officials were appointed. Miss E.M. Engert became Secretary and Montague Wheeler Treasurer.

Wheeler was a former colonel in the Berkshire Regiment. During the First World War he had been stationed in Salonika, and through his experiences there emerged as a convinced pacifist who could never send anyone into war again. He was now working in an architectural firm in London. Exactly how, when or where he had come across anthroposophy seems nowhere recorded, but he soon became one of the most active British anthroposophists of his day.

No Reasonable Person

On his departure from Britain in 1916 Robert Felkin[46] had left as Chiefs of the Stella Matutina in that country William Hammond, Librarian at Freemason's Hall, and Christine Stoddart, a former neighbour in Bassett Road in North Kensington. In 1919 Stoddart moved to South Kensington, to 56 Redcliffe Square, only a few doors away from number 47, the headquarters of the anthroposophical Zarathustra Group.

Stoddart now wrote to W.B. Yeats.

(G.H. = Greatly Honoured; F.R. = 'Finem Respice', the motto of Robert Felkin; Q.A. = 'Quaero Altissima', that of his daughter Nora; Q.L. = 'Quaero Lucem', that of his wife Harriot; A.B.S. = the discarnate medial contact 'Ara Ben Semesh'; C.R.C. = Christian Rosy Cross)

London
18 March 1921

Care G.H. Frater,

I have just received the following information thro' Collison from Steiner. It plainly shows that Steiner knows nothing about this supposed continental centre or F.R.'s claimed authority & also does not think much of F.R. as an occultist & of Q.A. he thinks nothing. This information is for the Order so we can use it as we think fit. Collison also said that Q.A. called upon him to ask if he thought she might use Steiner's name in dealing with the trouble in the Order. He said she must judge for herself.

I honestly do not believe that F.R. has the authority he claims & probably the grades are not sound. It almost looks as if he had again been deceived.

Yours fraternally,

C.M. Stoddart

★

Notes of Mr. Collison's interview with Steiner re F.R. & the Order.

F.R. he says cares mostly about getting higher grades. He is spiritualistic and mediumistic.

Q.A. is of no account, purely a church-woman with strong leaning towards Rome.

Q.L. is the only one who could be made anything of. She is clairvoyant but hopeless under her present influences. She is as it were on one side of a veil & calls for say Lloyd George who she supposes is on the other side, gets an answer without making sure that it is Lloyd George, writes it down & even then may not write it down correctly.

A.B.S. he knows nothing about & I presume does not wish to trouble about him.

C.R.C. may be invoked in the vault. He does not think that C.R.C. himself comes, probably someone under his influence, but on the other hand any evil spirit may come, it depends on who wishes.

Ceremonies are not evil in themselves even under present circumstances in our Order & are all right as long as one takes them as symbolism, tho' evil can come in according to who is invoking. These ceremonies are in fact necessary to some people according to their stage of development.

F.R. was permitted to be present during his (Steiner's) ceremonies (3 grades, 1,2,3, the only ones he gives) but he gave him (F.R.) no grades.

He gave him no introductions to anyone. He thinks they (F.R. & Q.L.) may possibly have got some Masonic grades somewhere in Germany, possibly Rosicrucian Masons. He knows nothing about it & apparently does not think that he or Q.L. received any recognized grades at all. He knows nothing of this claim to sole continental authority put forth by F.R.

Details given to me by Mr. Landrieux & given to him by Mr. Collison who saw Steiner in Holland & asked specially for information for us.

★

Stoddart soon wrote Yeats a further letter:

London
2 April 1921

Care G.H. Frater,

Mr. Landrieux wrote to me last night saying he had seen Mr. Collison again & after much persuasion Collison has promised to write a signed letter to Mr. Landrieux giving details of his conversation with Steiner in Holland. His one condition is that the previous statement must be considered non-existent, to be destroyed, & the knowledge not to be used in any way. This because he wishes to leave out all personal references to F.R. & his family. He will however give all the really important information re F.R.'s connection with Steiner & Steiner's statement re continental connection. Also he is to answer certain questions I asked re Q.A.'s interview with Steiner at Dornach. It is interesting to know what Steiner thinks of the Felkins but we don't want to use such information. Will you either destroy the notes you have or let me have them back as I have promised to see that they are destroyed. I will send you a copy of Collison's letter with information.

No further developments.

Yours fraternally,

C.M. Stoddart

★

Collison did not write the letter until over a month later. It was addressed to Dr. Hammond at Freemason's Hall:

27, Clareville Grove,
S.W.7.
8th May 1921

Dear Brother Hammond,

Having had the advantage of an interview with you, I am now in a better position to be able to write the letter which I promised Mr. Landrieux. I told him that in order to clear the ground of misconception, I would write the letter only upon the condition that any other report I have made or am supposed to have made be cancelled, & this letter be substituted.

The following then is what I gathered from an interview with Dr. Steiner in Holland last March:—

(1) Dr. Felkin was a spectator at one of Dr. Steiner's 'ceremonies' in Munich several years ago. No grades have been given him by Dr. Steiner. No grades were given to him in Munich. But Dr. Steiner gave Dr. Felkin a great deal of instruction, such as he gives to other pupils who desire it.

(2) Several visits have been paid by various enquirers into Rosicrucianism to castles & other places in Austro-Hungary, but there has never been any true & practical result from these researches.

(3) Dr. Steiner said he had told Miss Felkin he would be glad to see any reasonable person whom her friends chose to send; but no reasonable person had so far arrived.

(4) Dr. Felkin was anxious to get a charter from Dr. Steiner & made many attempts to gain this, and be appointed his sole representative in England. Dr. Steiner, in a letter to Dr. Felkin, of which I was the bearer & which I read, said that he was unable to grant this request, for though ready to admit that Dr. Felkin's Order was beneficial & useful, his way of working was quite different.

(5) Dr. Steiner cannot say that the forces in the Order are good or bad, but in all spiritualistic practices under the old form of clairvoyance which is resorted to in the Felkin Order, self-deception is very possible; & forces may enter which are beyond the power & understanding of those physically present.

(6) The Order is decorative, & useful for those who need it and are able & willing to distinguish between mere ornament & reality. The Order has the capacity to be made extremely serviceable if rightly used.

Yours sincerely,

H. Collison

P.S. As I have no typewriter or facilities for copying, might I ask you to send me a copy; it would be extremely kind of you.

★

On the very same day when Collison was writing this letter, Yeats, who was also in London and had just interviewed both Miss Stoddart and Dr. Hammond, wrote to his wife Georgie stating:

> I think if we want to get rid of our followers—about four in all—in the Order we can put them into Steiner's care & they will do their ceremonies, with his motherly care in the background. But this is all too complicated for a letter...

As Widely as Possible

The May 1921 issue of *Anthroposophy* carried an announcement about the forthcoming Summer Art Course at the Goetheanum, postponed from the previous year:

> The object of the Art Course is to arouse in the hearts of artists and art-lovers a realization that art springs from the world of spirit, and that its true mission is to manifest that world.
>
> The course has been arranged for the first week in August, and English-speaking artists, art students, and others interested in art are especially invited.
>
> Programme: lectures on art and spiritual science; eurythmic performances; scenes from Dr. Steiner's Mystery Plays, and a concert.
>
> Arrangements have been made with the Polytechnic, Regent Street, W.1, to take out parties, and to provide hotel accommodation. All particulars to be obtained from the Polytechnic.
>
> Members of the Anthroposophical Society in England are cordially invited.

★

On 30 May, the Central Committee had a meeting at 74 Grosvenor Street, of which part of the minutes read:

> Report from Mr. Francis of his visit to Dornach, propaganda, etc.:
>
> Dr. Steiner emphasized the necessity now to spread anthroposophical knowledge as widely as possible, and said members should study as many lectures as possible and introduce them to friends and associates. Dr. Steiner promised to furnish a list of lectures suitable for publication in England, and suggested that titles of lectures be first submitted to him, before being given to the public. The introductory lecture to the 'Apocalypse' and the lectures on 'Bible and Wisdom' would be good to put into the hands of the public.
>
> With reference to the name of the Society the Dr. advised no alternative to 'Anthroposophy', but suggested we should try and popularize it.[47]

★

By mid-June Rudolf Steiner was on another week's visit to Stuttgart. Edith Maryon wrote to him:

Sculpture Studio,
Goetheanum
14th of June 1921

Dear Teacher,

I'm actually still sitting at home, while a worker is bringing the drainage pipe into order; it's a very boring job which should have been avoided. Today I'll probably be able to give Herr Bay the sketch.

The weather is cold and unfriendly. Yesterday Frl. Vreede gave a lecture on the history and development of mathematics—quite interesting. Afterwards Wachsmuth, Storrer, Pfeiffer and Herr Stadlin asked questions. Wachsmuth spoke about sound-figures. Pfeiffer wanted to know to what extent ancient Egyptians erected their astronomy on mathematics. He's not a bad speaker, but too monotonous. There were quite a few members present, in spite of very rainy weather. Unfortunately only three or perhaps four outsiders. Dr. Boos wasn't there; I haven't seen him at all. His mother and wife were present at the lecture on Saturday, but I haven't any news.

I've received a letter from Miss Franklin. She's inviting me again on a little journey. If only it could be arranged, it would perhaps be the cheapest way for me to have a little holiday while you're away.

Rosenkrantz has written and sent the summer programme; I sent you three more and hope they're in your hands. Prices in England for electro-galvanic reproductions are even higher than in Switzerland, so I'll try out how the man in Locle works. The samples I saw were faultless, but not cheap.

I'm thinking a lot about the work in Stuttgart and wishing I were there doing it. Hopefully the eurythmy performance was well received? I'm very interested to know how things there proceed further—the work and the hostile attacks. I hope the situation has somewhat improved through your public lecture; such a success should gain a number of people.

If only you didn't need to overexert yourself, is what I'm thinking.

With heartfelt greetings,

Edith Maryon

★

The June number of *Theosophy* contained a paragraph headed 'European Federation':

Mr. D.N. Dunlop and Mrs. Beatrice Ensor, with the General Secretary, were appointed members of the General Council of the European

Federation for the present year, and Mr. J. Krishnamurti was appointed to act for Mr. Dunlop at the forthcoming meeting of the Council to be held in Paris in July during the World Congress, as Mr. Dunlop will be unable to attend that meeting.

★

Theosophical activity was also taking place in Yorkshire. In his booklet *Thou Eye Among the Blind* (1947) Arnold Freeman, who in 1913 had had that strange meeting with Steiner in Munich, continued his reminiscences:

> In 1921 Mrs. Besant was in this country, willing to give lectures. I helped to arrange a visit to Sheffield. We gave her hospitality at The Sheffield Educational Settlement of which I am warden.
>
> Mrs. Besant took for her subject 'The Reconstruction of a Shattered World'. I was disappointed in her lecture. I hinted at my dissatisfaction as we drove to the Settlement in a taxi. 'There wasn't much Theosophy in your lecture,' I said. She replied: 'It was all Theosophy.' But it wasn't. It was nothing but the threadbare platitudes I had heard a hundred times over at socialist meetings.
>
> Very shortly afterwards I came across an article of Dr. Steiner's in the *Hibbert Journal*. It was a translation of an essay that originally appeared in the *Soziale Zukunft* in Switzerland. It bore the bleak title 'Spiritual Life: Civil Rights: Industrial Economy'. This article made an immediate and profound impression upon me. I underwent something like an instantaneous conversion. Here was a thinker altogether greater than the Shaws and the Webbs and the Wellses. Here was somebody who saw all round the social problem. What Steiner had to say in this connection led me to consider what he had to say in other connections. It swiftly came about that for me there was now only one question in my life: 'How can I help that man?' For me and others like me this question knocks insistently at their hearts.

The article in *The Hibbert Journal*, a wide-ranging theological magazine edited by L.P. Jacks, Principal of Manchester College, Oxford, appeared in the number for July.

The Nature of the Imagination

The July issue of *Anthroposophy* opened with an article by Baron Rosenkrantz on 'The Power of Art'. This was followed by two paragraphs extracted from chapters on 'The Many-Coloured Land' and 'The Mingling of Natures' in AE's *The Candle of Vision.*

> I have always been curious about the psychology of my own vision as desirous of imparting it, and I wish in this book to relate the efforts of an

artist and poet to discover what truth lay in his own imaginations. I have brooded longer over the nature of the imagination than I have lingered over the canvas where I have tried to rebuild my vision. Spiritual moods are difficult to express and cannot be argued over, but the workings of imagination may well be spoken of, and need precise and minute investigation. I surmise from my reading of the psychologists who treat of this that they themselves were without this faculty, and spoke of it as blind men who would fain draw, although without vision. We are overcome when we read *Prometheus Unbound*, but who, as he reads, flings off the enchantment to ponder in what state was the soul of Shelley in that ecstasy of swift creation? Who has questioned the artist to whom the forms of his thought are vivid as the forms of Nature? Artist and poet have rarely been curious about the processes of their own minds. Yet it is reasonable to assume that the highest ecstasy and vision are conditioned by law and attainable by all, and this might be argued as of more importance even than the message of seers. I attribute to that unwavering meditation and fiery concentration of will a growing luminousness in my brain as if I had unsealed in the body a fountain of interior light . . .

To move a single step, we must have power. To see, we must be exalted. Not to be lost in vision, we must learn the geography of the spirit and the many mansions in the being of the Father. If we concentrate, we shall have power. If we meditate, we shall lift ourselves above the dark environment of the brain. The inner shall become richer and more magical to us than the outer, which has held us so long. How may I allure to this meditation those who see only by the light of day, who, when their eyes are shut, are as cave-dwellers living in blackness beneath the hills? The cave of the body can be lit up. If we explore it, we shall there find lights by which the lights of day are made dim . . .

★

After a further article on 'Goethe's Theory of Colour' came a full-page announcement on 'The Summer Art Course at Dornach', which was not after all taking place in the first week of August, but in the last. Details of the programme, costs, and other arrangements were followed by another notice:

We address this appeal to make the Summer Course at the Goetheanum a success. The work can only grow and feed modern life if there is a proper response to its activities, and if signs are forthcoming that these are understood. We hope earnestly that those who can possibly do so will visit Dornach in August, and that every member will assist in making this Summer Course as widely known as possible. By an attitude of sympathy towards what is being accomplished at Dornach, we can largely influence the culture of the future. Even a small group of persons going there this

> summer can, if they work earnestly with the principles they will assimilate there, infuse a new spirit at home. Co-operation is sadly needed to bring to realization in the world the profound significance of the art movement at Dornach, which stretches far beyond the mere realm of what interests artists. The eurythmy performances on the stage and the musical recitals are gaining in beauty and scope. They contain qualities which are astounding and which will affect, in a vital manner, the spiritual culture of the future.

Readers of this appeal must have sent invitations to various press organs. But the reaction was not exactly positive. On 16 July *The Architect* published under 'Notes and Comments' a paragraph on 'A College for Spiritual Science':

> A College for Spiritual Science has been erected under the name of the 'Goetheanum' at Dornach, Basle, Switzerland, and the building itself illustrates a new conception of art which has been initiated by Dr. Rudolf Steiner. It is proposed to organize a visit to Basle to see it, and Dr. Steiner has promised to personally instruct the party during a visit of ten days, which is to take place in August. Allowing for four days spent in travelling, this will allow for nearly six days in which the party should be able to recover from the first shock caused by the appearance of Dr. Steiner's creation. In order that no one who is able to go should miss what we anticipate should be an interesting experience we give an illustration of what they will see at the end of their pilgrimage, and if any of our readers go we hope they will give us the benefit of their impressions on their return.

Another invitation must have gone to the editor of *The Daily Express*. The result appeared in the editorial column of that paper on 22 August, in a passage entitled 'More Uplift'.

> I have received an invitation to take the Summer Art Course at the Goetheanum at Dornach, Switzerland. The Goetheanum is a building which has 'grown out of the conception that Art must give aesthetic form to spiritual realities'. In this case Art has given something the like of which was never on land or sea, and rather resembling the worst kind of provincial free library topped by two immense and bulbous domes. If this is the 'new orientation of Art' I prefer to grovel in the darkness of the Renaissance and the spiritual night of the Gothic.
>
> However, I should like to hear the lectures by Dr. Rudolf Steiner, Dr. Vreede, Baron Rosenkrantz, Dr. Steffen, Dr. Uehli, Director-General Benkendörffer, and the rest. The greater part of the Summer Art Course is in German. That seems to explain the gem of architecture to which I have referred.

★

In the event the Summer Art Course, though chiefly English in intention, attracted a widely international audience. Participants came not only from Britain but from France, Belgium, Italy, Austria, Czechoslovakia, Denmark, Norway, Sweden, Holland, Greece and even the United States.

The September issue of *Anthroposophy* carried a report:

> The Summer Art Course which took place at the Goetheanum in August marks an important step, for this was the inauguration of the international spirit which is of such vital consequence to the progress of what the Goetheanum stands for. We may be sure that, since English has now made its entry into the curriculum, other subjects besides art will be dealt with in English. Indeed, it is gratifying to learn that as an outcome of this initial art course other courses are being arranged, notably one for educationists at Christmas time.
>
> Among visitors whose interest was aroused by the announcement that a new and spiritual interest in art was emanating from Dornach, there were artists to whom the teaching of Dr. Steiner was quite unknown. It is much to be regretted that owing to the limited powers of the Anthroposophical Society in England the Summer Art Course was not made more widely known, for despondency among artists and the intensity of their longing for right guidance in the present period of chaos is an assurance in itself of widespread interest. Great Britain is a country where the spiritual depths of life are never forgotten, and it can be confidently believed that here is fertile ground for what is being given out at the Goetheanum.
>
> The whole programme of the week, the continuous lectures carrying on in a positive direction the thoughts awakened in the listeners, the performances of eurythmy, varied, finished, and full of stimulus to the imagination, the energy and vitality of the assembled people—all this was arresting and suggestive . . .

The eurythmy performance on 24 August opened with an item from Steiner's Mystery Play *Die Prüfung der Seele*. Then came Thomas Moore's 'Evening Bells', for performance in blue dress with red veil.

> Those evening bells! Those evening bells!
> How many a tale their music tells,
> Of youth, and home, and that sweet time
> When last I heard their soothing chime!
>
> Those joyous hours are past away!
> And many a heart that then was gay
> Within the tomb now darkly dwells,
> And hears no more those evening bells!

And so 'twill be when I am gone;
That tuneful peal will still ring on,
While other bards shall walk these dells
And sing your praise, sweet evening bells!

There followed a poem by Soloviev, a verse from Steiner's *Seelenkalender*, Willam Watson's 'April', further poems by Goethe, Rameau, Steiner and Longfellow, some music by Max Schuurman, and in conclusion various pieces by Giraud and Morgenstern.

> ... Apart from lectures delivered by Dr. Steiner, which were repeated in English by Baron Walleen, Dr. Fräulein Vreede gave three lectures in English on Anthroposophy, collecting together with well-versed skill the numerous threads which together make an idea of the whole subject possible. Baron Arild Rosenkrantz lectured twice on art, the first time showing how the development of ego-consciousness is one with the history of art, and in the second an attempt was made to suggest how, in the Goetheanum itself, forces upon which art and evolution depend are to be found expressed in the arts of architecture, painting, and sculpture.
>
> Dr. Steiner conducted a vast concourse of people round the building on two occasions, and perhaps the most prominent feature in his discourse was his exposition of the doctrine of metamorphosis, showing the absolute necessity for one phase to develop into another, be it in plant growth, in art, learning, or human life. Nothing must stand still.
>
> The impressiveness of the building, so impossible to convey by photographic reproductions, was forcibly felt by those visitors who had never seen it before. Besides what it contains as the expression of a definite knowledge, the massive grandeur of the Goetheanum and its extraordinary completeness give a feeling of satisfaction, even to those to whom the originality of style offers an obstacle.
>
> Another point which stood out prominently during the course was the unquestionable necessity before the world to bridge over difficulties of nationality. Without injuring the healthy feeling of patriotism, a fellow-feeling with all humanity must now begin to be inculcated. No doubt but that such an attempt at union was frankly made and carried out by this first Summer Course for the English at the Goetheanum.

Deep Satisfaction

The course 'for educationists at Christmastime' mentioned in the report of the Summer Art Course was initiated by Professor Millicent Mackenzie, who had attended the Art Course along with her husband, Professor John Mackenzie. A brief sketch of their lives may here be given.

John Stuart Mackenzie was born at Springburn, near Glasgow, in 1860, as the younger of two sons. He was brought up in Scotland until the age of eight, when his parents decided to emigrate to Argentina. The sea-voyage to South America on which the family embarked took in those days over seven weeks.

When the Mackenzies at last arrived in Buenos Aires, they found themselves in the midst of an epidemic of cholera. The mother succumbed very quickly and died, and a few months later the father as well. So relatives arranged for the two orphaned boys to be reshipped on another seven-week sea-voyage all the way back to Scotland.

John then attended Glasgow High School, and in due course went on to study philosophy at Glasgow University. Becoming especially interested in German philosophy, he travelled over to the Continent and completed further studies in Berlin, from where he retained vivid memories of the deaf Heinrich von Treitschke, who was also to feature in the autobiography of Rudolf Steiner.

Returning to Britain, Mackenzie gained a fellowship at Trinity College, Cambridge, and soon afterwards took on a succession of academic posts in various British universities. Finally he settled down as Professor of Philosophy in the University of South Wales in Cardiff. Here he met and married an enterprising colleague: Millicent Hughes, Professor of Education.

Although for many years the Mackenzies were largely absorbed in university teaching, they also wished to extend their horizons by travelling over the world, and in 1915 took early retirement from their academic posts. Their travelling plans were deferred by the continuance of the First World War, but eventually in November 1920 they set off on what was to become a series of lengthy journeys over different parts of the globe.

The first journey took them to India, where *inter alia* they met George Arundale at Adyar and Bertram Keightley at Benares. They had just returned from this Indian journey in the spring of 1921 when Millicent's friend Edith Maryon invited them to the Summer Art Course at Dornach.

★

Steiner himself wrote an appreciative description of these two unusual British academics and their writings:

> During the summer, workers at the Goetheanum made the acquaintance of Herr and Frau Prof. Mackenzie. A visit by these two people could not but fill all these workers with deep satisfaction from the viewpoint of the Anthroposophical Movement. Prof. Mackenzie is a person in whom a significant note of English philosophical life comes to expression. His

> *Constructive Philosophy* is independent both in content and style of thought when compared in this sphere with other currents of our time. With the assurance given by an intuitive grasp of reality, it apprehends in this independence the realm which activates a human being's true philosophic sense. Mackenzie, I would say, begins his constructive philosophy where a beginning has to be made if any firm basis is once more to be gained for the unstable realms of metaphysics, psychology and epistemology around us. His literary and philosophic activity is thus spread over many fields in the history of culture and in social and educational matters. This is especially borne out by his books on humanism and social life.
>
> While staying here at Dornach in the summer, Frau Prof. Mackenzie, who has herself also been a university teacher (Prof. of Education, University College, Cardiff), handed me her highly interesting book *Hegel's Educational Theory and Practice*. The extensive activity of this wise and practical woman finds literary manifestation in this book.
>
> Hegel is easily misjudged. His books have an abstract effect. But the strange thing is that behind these abstractions stood a man who held with a firm grip onto reality. Basically his thoughts form a lively if seemingly abstract reflection of a practical life saturated by passion. Frau Mackenzie has perceived this as clearly as can be. 'What I mean is that these two philosophers (Plato and Hegel) are constantly endeavouring to see not merely—like all other philosophers—what the truth is, but also how it is to be reached and appropriated by a mind to which it is naturally remote and foreign; and they both believe that the process by which this is done is dialectal.' This is what she says in the preface to her above-mentioned book, and she tries to show what this philosophical self-education thinks about the education of both children and youth. In regard to Hegel, she comes to this opinion: 'On the whole I venture to claim for Hegel that he supplies us more than any other educator (more even than Herbart, because his educational ideas are based upon a deeper philosophy) with just those things that we are most in want of in our time and country.'
>
> We may observe in this relationship of hers to Hegel what a closer acquaintance with Frau Mackenzie fully confirms: in her we have before us a fine head-thinker, who unites philosophic profundities with far-reaching interests in the educational and social questions of mankind.

These last remarks about Millicent Mackenzie may have been perfectly true. It has to be said, however, that the two quotations which Steiner attributes to her preface are not actually found there, but are taken from an 'Introductory Note' to the book, composed by her husband John.

Arousing Greater Interest

When the Summer Art Course was finished Rudolf Steiner returned for another fortnight to Stuttgart, and then travelled on to Berlin.

Edith Maryon, meanwhile, went on holiday to the south of Switzerland with her friend Jeanette Franklin. From here she wrote some further letters to Steiner.[48]

Hotel San Salvatore,
San Salvatore,
Lugano.
Saturday afternoon, on the mountain.

Dear Teacher,

I haven't received any news from Stuttgart today and would dearly like to know how things now are with the wound on your hand, and your voice? It's uncertain whether or not we stay here beyond next Wednesday; anyway I'll make sure at the post office that I receive letters all right. Unless we find anything better on Monday or Tuesday we'll be staying here. The food is excellent; I've nowhere found better vegetarian cooking.

Mrs. Mackenzie has written to me from London with all sorts of thanks to you for hospitality etc. Dr. Mackenzie expresses himself very enthusiastically about his stay in Dornach; he'll be writing to you in a fortnight, when you arrive at Dornach, and be sending a book. They both feel properly recuperated in body and soul. She's now preparing her plans for Christmas.

Miss Franklin too now seems again to be getting more interested in Dornach. At the moment she's having a long walk in the surroundings, while I'm writing and thinking about today's outing to Stuttgart. Afterwards we want to drink tea outside, but I don't know what she'll say when she comes back and finds both of us have forgotten the water. I don't dare enter the hotel to fetch the water, as cows are wandering around and will certainly eat our cake.

Mrs. Mackenzie has translated some of Hegel's speeches; they're towards the end of her book. She also translated Fichte's speech and wanted to have it printed at the start of the War, but at the time everyone said nobody would read it, so she waited with it and probably it'll now at last be printed. It seems she prefers my translation to Wedgwood's, which she finds more like a report of a book that's been read than an actual translation, so perhaps mine wasn't so dreadful after all! Though of course I don't mean it was first class, as I know too well it can't be.

I hope no plans have been made for the theological and Christmas course times and you're taking a holiday for your voice from the 7th Sept.

onwards??? It'll certainly be needed. How's your voice now? And are you very tired? Or d'you perhaps try to have a little rest every day?

Till we see each other again!

Heartfelt greetings,

Edith Maryon

★

Pension Eugenia,
Ruvigliano,
Lugano,
12th Sept. 1921

Dear Teacher,

I'm travelling back to Dornach again on Wednesday. I think my stay here has really done me good, and Jeanette too finds her nerves improved. It's become very hot again, but not so oppressive as before. I haven't heard when you arrive in Berlin, but hope it'll be Sunday, because of proofreading etc. What will the date of your arrival at Dornach be? We very much need you in the studio from Monday onward, before the theological course begins, as your time will then be so taken up that everything else must step back. I'll be prepared for Monday, hoping you'll be coming.

We've done all sorts of little excursions in the surroundings. I've been very lazy; I thought this would be good preparation for a lot of work in the winter. Mrs. Mackenzie writes that she's preparing her plans for the teachers' course at Christmas. Was anything said or done about it at Stuttgart? I'm longing to see if we succeed this time in arousing greater interest in our cause, and already hope some suitable helpers might in this way be found, as we need them so urgently. Once we had them, things could grow and spread like a snowball.

I'm sending all sorts of good thoughts and wishes for Thursday to be a success and your voice to get better.

Jeanette has a friend who's made various interesting inventions, among others a machine allowing blind people to hear printed letters: they sound. Another machine rings if a person's shadow falls on it. She'll send me the document he wrote about the first machine.

Is there anything in print I could send him about the scientific research-work in Stuttgart?

With heartfelt greetings,

Edith Maryon

★

In Britain the September number of *Anthroposophy* published a detailed lecture-list for the next three months. The lecturers from the previous year were joined by four others: Montague Wheeler, Irene Groves, W.B. Paton and Kathleen Schlesinger.

As well as the Society's own premises at Grosvenor Street a larger venue was engaged for outreach to the general public, as stated in an announcement:

> Five public lectures will be given at the Essex Hall, Strand, on five consecutive Thursdays, beginning on November 17 at 8 p.m. Admission will be free. Particulars can be obtained at the Society's offices, and it is urgently hoped that no member will fail in using some of the energy so desperately needed in the world today in order to get friends to attend one or more of these lectures, which are calculated to bring the teaching of Dr. Steiner within the reach of those who up to now have had no opportunity of benefiting from it. The lectures will be on Anthroposophy, and its effects on education, industry, and social subjects.

A further announcement was included about a 'forthcoming training course for teachers':

> An interesting educational course will be held at the Goetheanum this winter from about December 23 to January 7.
>
> The course will include lectures by Dr. Steiner on education, and other educational experts will take part. Although the course is primarily arranged for British and Americans, parties of teachers from Holland and Scandinavia are joining, and other countries are expected to be sending teachers. The new conceptions underlying the 'Waldorf' Free School at Stuttgart are arousing so much interest on the continent that British and American teachers, and all interested in education, are strongly recommended to take this opportunity of gaining some insight into Dr. Steiner's theory and methods.
>
> A knowledge of German will not be necessary, as the lectures will be repeated in English and ample opportunity for English discussion provided.
>
> For those who desire it, a specially conducted travel party will be arranged.
>
> Fee for the course: four guineas.
>
> This fee will give admittance to all lectures, demonstrations of eurythmy, and dramatic entertainments.
>
> Boarding accommodation at moderate rates.
>
> Early booking is essential. The first instalment of 10/6 should be paid as soon as possible.
>
> For further particulars send addressed and stamped envelope to Mrs. Mackenzie, 56 Russell Square, London, W.C.1.

★

The October number of *Theosophy* included a notice stating:

A series of 'Talks on Books' will be given in the Theosophical Library, 23 Bedford Square, every Tuesday during the winter months from 6 p.m. to 7 p.m. The speakers for October will include Mr. Loftus Hare, Mr. D.N. Dunlop and Mr. L. Bosman.

Mabel M. Sharples
Hon. Librarian

New Light on 1914

On 5 October *The Pall Mall and Globe* (a paper later incorporated with *The Evening Standard*) published an article entitled 'New Light on 1914: What the Kaiser Believed'. The main part of this article was also reprinted the next day in *The Manchester Guardian*.

Paris, Wednesday.

Under the heading 'A Light on the Origins of the War', the *Matin* today publishes an interview with the well-known Austrian sociologist, Dr. Steiner, who was an intimate friend of General von Moltke, head of the German General Staff, in the course of which Dr. Steiner detailed to M. Jules Sauerwein what von Moltke related to him concerning his memoirs, the publication of which was prohibited in Germany.

Von Moltke wrote his memoirs for his family circle, and it was after his death that his widow asked Dr. Steiner to publish them. They were to have appeared on a certain date in 1919, but just previously the Prussian diplomatic representative at Stuttgart visited Dr. Steiner to tell him that publication was impossible, and had been forbidden at Berlin. Later a general, who had been aide-de-camp to General von Moltke and then to William II, came to deliver the same message.

'I protested,' continues Dr Steiner, 'and wrote to Count de Brockdorff-Rantzau, then at Versailles, but received no reply. These efforts were the more useless, as at the time pressure was brought to bear on Mme. von Moltke, which she could not resist.

'Von Moltke's memoirs are not an indictment of the Imperial Government, though they show it up in a way perhaps that is worse—*in very great confusion, directed with feebleness and inconceivable ignorance*, so that one can apply to the men responsible in these days the tragic phrase which I have written in my preface—"it is not this or that act of theirs which has contributed to bring about the catastrophe, but the very essence of their personality".'

Proceeding to relate what von Moltke told him, Dr. Steiner continues: 'At the end of June 1914, von Moltke, who had been Chief of the General

Staff since 1905, visited Carlsbad on account of his health. He knew nothing up to the time of his death of what passed at the famous Potsdam Council of July 5 or 6, for he only returned to Berlin after the ultimatum had been presented to Serbia.

'From his arrival he said he was persuaded that Russia was going to attack, and foresaw clearly the tragic development of the affair; that is to say, he believed it certain that France and England would intervene in a world conflict. He wrote a memorandum for the Emperor detailing his plan of operations. The plan of the German General Staff had in its broad outlines remained unchanged since it was drawn up more than fifteen years previously by von Schlieffen—overwhelming forces against France, to ensure a rapid result at any price, and against Russia a weak army of defence, which later would be brought up to strength after the anticipated success of the Western operations.

'Von Moltke really only modified one important point of his predecessor's plans. *Whilst von Schlieffen provided for the simultaneous attack on Belgium and Holland* (this revelation doubtless supplying the reason why the publication of the memoirs was prohibited) *von Moltke omitted Holland, so that Germany, in case of a blockade, might have a breathing space.* When he reached the Palace on July 30, von Moltke found himself surrounded by bewildered men, and his impression was that he alone could take a definite decision. He asked the Emperor to sign the mobilization order, which in Germany is practically a declaration of war, since from the time of its issue the initial operations are proceeded with according to timetable with inexorable precision. Wilhelm satisfied himself on that day with announcing the threat of war.

'On Saturday July 31, at four o'clock in the afternoon, von Moltke returned to the Kaiser. He found him with Bethman-Hollweg, who was literally trembling, Falkenhayn, the Minister of War, and Generals von Plesson, Lynker and others. The Kaiser was denouncing the plan of his Chief of Staff, and said he had received better news from England. *Not only would England remain neutral, but would prevent France from taking part in the war.*

'In these circumstances the logical plan was to throw all his forces against Russia. He was deaf to the objections raised, and refused to modify his plans. The marching orders must be given, he declared, without delay.

'Von Moltke had no faith in the news from England, and as he held the mobilization order signed by the Kaiser, withdrew at the first opportunity, leaving the rest in confusion.

'On the road halfway between the Palace and the military headquarters his carriage was overtaken by a fast car, and he was asked to return to the Palace. Before turning back von Moltke gave the mobilization order to his A.D.C., and said to him: "Order the advance of the troops."

'The Kaiser showed the General a telegram from England which, he said, made it certain that England and France would be neutral. "We must," he concluded, "immediately countermand the order you have given for the advance of the troops."

'The General refused, whereupon the Kaiser, on his own authority, ordered his aide-de-camp to telephone to General Headquarters the order for the German Army to stop at least at an hour's march from the French and Belgian frontiers.

'Von Moltke returned to his quarters and sat down at his table, declaring he would not sign the order confirming the Kaiser's telephone message. Until ten o'clock he remained at his table in a kind of prostration.

'Then the Kaiser sent for him again. The Emperor had received fresh news from England which counteracted all he had said. "Now do as you wish," he told von Moltke. War began the following morning.'

Dr. Steiner adds that on August 26, 1914, he saw von Moltke at Coblenz. The battle of the Marne struck the imagination of the General. In time of peace he had thrice executed a march on Paris, and each time von Kluck, commanding the right wing, had marched too quickly.

In the stern reality when he learned that von Kluck was turned, he said 'Germany has lost the War.'

On September 13, when he returned to General Headquarters, he gave the impression of being ill, and at that time it was actually Falkenhayn who, without the official title, commanded the army.—Exchange.

A Laboratory Technician

Rudolf Steiner's work in the medical field was now well under way. Not only had he started giving doctors fundamental principles and specific curative indications, but he had also been suggesting quite new types of medicine. These medicines of course had to be produced, and the person who began this task—from which the later Weleda eventually developed—was the anthroposophical chemist Oscar Schmiedel.

Schmiedel's reminiscences, first set down in 1943, were not published until 1992. The present section reproduces a particular part which starts at the point of his thirty-fourth birthday in October 1921.

> ...As I felt myself too young (thirty-four) and too inexperienced in commercial matters, I explained to the Futurum administration that I was unable to take on the laboratory's commercial management. They also believed that legal regulations needed an apothecary registered in Switzerland for managing a pharmaceutical business. (As it later turned out, this was incorrect. A chemist, as I was myself, would have been able to manage just as well.) The administration made the following division: firstly: the

'Futurum Chemical and Pharmaceutical Production Laboratory' under the management of a very old (about seventy) apothecary (Heim), and secondly: the 'Futurum Chemical and Pharmaceutical Experimental Laboratory' under my management. Right from the start this was an unfortunate and impossible arrangement. The foundation or rather takeover of the experimental laboratory took place in the summer of 1921. Work went on as before in the Goetheanum hut. (Work could only be taken up in the new house in Arlesheim in winter 1921/2, when the most essential fitting-out work had been completed.) In the summer and autumn of 1921 a lot of medicaments were already being produced, as Frau Dr. Wegman (who had opened her clinic in Arlesheim on the 16th of June 1921) and other doctors too required them. Since the takeover of the laboratory by the Futurum, there were meanwhile continual battles with the administration, against whose petty bureaucratic measures and regulations I constantly had to defend myself. My former style of life and work in the laboratory hut, where I was also working with only one assistant, was of course different from what it would have been, and later also was, in a proper 'business'. The administration did not wish to perceive this self-evident truth, and required the observance of a proper business standard.

As I have mentioned, I was working in the laboratory with only one assistant. This had previously been my wife. When through the birth of our child she was unable to help in the laboratory any more, I had to find another assistant. The Futurum administration suggested I should take on an English chemist, A.M. Imrie . . .

Arthur Imrie, as already indicated by his name, was not in fact English, but Scottish. He was the former leader of the anthroposophical group in Glasgow.

. . . Since I needed for assistance a laboratory technician and not a chemist of my own age, I feared that I would not in Imrie obtain any real help. I was therefore against him being employed. As the administration told me his employment would be taking place at the wish of Dr. Steiner, I spoke to him about it. I explained the reasons why I was against it, but said I would agree if it really was his express wish. He saw my reasons, but told me he would like to see Imrie employed. Thereupon I declared myself in agreement. Subsequent developments were to prove how right my fears had been, in particular since Imrie gradually became ever more peculiar. There would be no point in providing details, since after a few years he himself resigned from our work and left.

The period now following was on one hand very pleasant, a period rich in work on the constant new tasks Dr. Steiner was giving. New medicaments had to be produced, which he either gave me directly or often had given to me through Dr. Wegman. On the other hand this period was also a very difficult one by reason of everything connected with the Futurum. Frau Dr. Wegman too had great difficulties in getting on with the Futurum administration. At Dr. Steiner's wish the Clinical-Therapeutic Institute was to be incorporated into the Futurum. Frau Dr. Wegman was frequently obliged—with good reason—to resist the administration's various arrangements, and it often came to sharp disagreements between herself and them. As the Futurum administration was becoming ever more difficult, Dr. Steiner finally asked Herr Emil Molt to take over its management. I do not wish here to touch further on what Herr Molt carried out by way of reorganization, but only to mention what affected the laboratory. The first thing was that he had a 'director' employed, to be present for commercial matters. The technical management of the laboratory fell to me.

The division between experimental laboratory and production was now dropped. The apothecary Herr Heim became 'bookkeeper'. The newly employed commercial director was a Herr Denzler. Herr Molt had actually intended him to direct his tobacco wholesale business in Zurich, which the Futurum had taken over as well. The reasons why he had not employed him for Zurich are unknown to me. Herr Molt took him on without having asked Dr. Steiner or introduced Denzler to him. When I then asked Dr. Steiner to allow me to introduce Herr Denzler, he curtly declined with the words: 'No, I don't know him.' Nor could he in future be moved to receive him. Denzler was Swiss, son of a respected doctor in Zurich, and was not an anthroposophist. He had a curious history behind him. He had gone out to Canada and there had every conceivable sort of employment. He had for instance even been in the Canadian mounted police. As I said, he was rather distant from Anthroposophy, and had no interest in it either. Sale trials arranged on a big scale were set up through his activity and swallowed up a lot of money. In England, for instance, a big campaign was started for Biodoron ('Bidor'). Every possible sort of advertisement was made through a wholesaler. Over thirty thousand francs were soon spent on this, and nothing achieved. At this time was also begun the American business with Mme. Ricardo. In the laboratory itself there was a peculiar situation. There were only a few workers, male or female, but to make up for this the 'bosses' were relatively numerous. Denzler and I were directors; Imrie now wanted to become a director too. Rudolf Steiner sharply rejected his wish, stressing that he was only employed as a laboratory technician and was further to remain as such.

The tale of Imrie's subsequent activities on the Dornach scene will be resumed in a later section.

No Time Must Be Lost

In the late autumn a document was circulated to British anthroposophists under the title 'A brief report of transactions of the Annual General Meeting of members held at 74 Grosvenor Street on Thursday, October 20th 1921':

> The Committee feel that members will be interested to hear of some of the more important transactions of this meeting.
>
> In presenting the General Report of the Committee, Mr. Neal mentioned that the Society now numbered 245 members, 60 of whom had joined during the past year.
>
> Members were reminded that it was essential the Society should have a good permanent address, and the new quarters be accessible and central. If our present capital of £1000 could be increased, it would be possible to secure a longer lease and larger premises.
>
> A sum of £400 was guaranteed by the 37 members present. As the matter is of extreme urgency, any member willing to guarantee a sum of money for this purpose is asked to communicate with the Treasurer, Mr. Wheeler, at above address.
>
> Miss Beverley gave a report upon the autumn work, and quoted Dr. Steiner's words at the recent Art Course—'The future will indeed depend on a sufficient number of people finding the way to this inner clarity and knowledge.'
>
> The educational course of lectures at the Goetheanum this Christmas, organized by Mrs. Mackenzie, will provide a great opportunity of bringing to the notice of English educationalists the practical value of Dr. Steiner's teaching, and also the spiritual work at Dornach.
>
> Members are informed that a new group, 'The Human Freedom Group', has been opened at the Studio, Campden Mews, W.8. with Mr. Dunlop as Leader and Miss Osmond as Secretary.[49]
>
> Public addresses are given every Sunday at 7 p.m.
>
> The Fellowship Meetings will be renewed on November the 6th at 5.15 p.m. at 75 Harley Street.
>
> With reference to publications, Mr. Collison brought out *Investigations in Occultism* last autumn. *The Spiritual Guidance of Man and Mankind* is being reprinted, and a new edition of *The Education of Children* is expected at Christmas. Mr. Collison is now publishing *The Origin and Nature of the Arts*, and a work entitled *Fruits of Anthroposophy* (2/6) is being prepared for publication by Miss Osmond and Mr. Kaufmann. A retranslated edition of *The Threefold State* is in the hands of the printer.
>
> A stirring appeal on the need of support for the Goetheanum was made by Miss Groves. It was of tremendous importance, because if the building

cannot be completed the whole work must consequently suffer. One of the London members is trying to collect £5 from every member of the Society.

The Committee feels that it is the attitude of mind accompanying the spiritual impulse which makes it possible to carry on anthroposophical work, and appeals to every member to do all in their power to assist in the various activities and thus help the Committee in the difficult tasks confronting them.

Signed on behalf of the Committee,

E.M. Engert
Hon. Secretary

★

A further notice about the 'Christmas Course on Education at Dornach, December 22 to January 7' appeared in November in *Anthroposophy*:

Widespread interest not only in this but in other countries has been aroused in this course, and many representative educationists hope to be present. The full programme of lectures by Dr. Steiner and the Waldorf teachers is now complete, and in addition to public demonstrations in eurythmy, private lessons are arranged for those who desire them.

Considerable reduction in fares is arranged for parties of not less than twenty-five. Second-class return to Bale, £5.10s, lasting twenty-five days. One such party will leave Victoria at 2 p.m. on Thursday December 22, reaching Bale at 6.20 a.m. on Friday, in good time for Dr. Steiner's first lecture at 11 a.m. Applications must be made immediately, as seats on the French trains have to be secured. On the return journey travelling can be independent.

It is hoped that every reader will try to persuade some teacher, settlement worker, member of an education authority, &c., to attend this first course. If Anthroposophy is to have any say in the reform of education in England no time must be lost. We hope to raise the number of persons attending to a hundred. All information to be obtained from Mrs. Mackenzie, 56 Bassett Road, W.10.

★

Meanwhile, *Theosophy* gave details of 'Talks on Books, Tuesday, 6 to 7 p.m., in the Library, 23 Bedford Square'.

Nov. 1st. *The Philosophy of Freedom* (Steiner)—D.N. Dunlop.
,, 8th. Psychological Difference in Subtle Bodies in Cultured and Uncultured Man. Definition of Cultured and Uncultured Man.—P.D. Ouspensky. (Author of *Tertium Organum*)

„ 15th. The Awakening of Faith of Acvaghosha (Suzuki)—J.E. Ellam (Editor of the *Buddhist Review*).

Nov 22nd. The Stanzas of Dzyan—D.N. Dunlop.

★

On 9 November, W.B. Yeats wrote a letter from Oxford to his wife Georgie. (FR = 'Finem Respice', the motto of Robert Felkin.)

> . . . A Miss Imrie . . . came to see me about the order. She had one new fact she had been to Switzerland with, or at the same time as Miss Felkin. She says the idea of passivity, Miss Felkin has been teaching it, has been spreading from Steiner, whose later teaching is full of it. His followers stand round a large wooden image of Christ-Adam-Lucifer, & adore it with carefully emptied minds. She came to see me because she had received from the enemy a typed announcement of Miss Stoddart's suspension by FR. She was at my 'Guest' lecture & was told as she came away by Miss Stoddart that I belonged to the order. So far as I could judge by a very short conversation she was intelligent & sensible . . .

And that was the end of the matter. It was probably in 1922 that Yeats himself—who had joined the Golden Dawn as far back as 1893 and was therefore one of the longest-standing members—finally withdrew from the Stella Matutina. He later stated that his connection with the Order 'ended amid quarrels caused by men, otherwise worthy, who claimed a Rosicrucian sanction for their fantasies'.

Yeats's departure was the last straw. In 1923—the year of the foundation of the Anthroposophical Society in Great Britain—Christine Stoddart dissolved the Amoun Temple of the Order of the Stella Matutina.

A First-class Contribution

On 11 November a leading article appeared in *The Daily Telegraph*.

> This is the Day of Remembrance. It is the third anniversary of the signing of the Armistice which brought to its end the most devastating and desolating war of which history, with its full chronicle of violence, holds any record. We are prompted to forget all the events which have occurred since the ink began to dry on the instrument which brought silence to the battlefields and opened the seas once more to their lawful traffic. The three years seem a lifetime, so difficult has it proved to take up again the broken threads of our disordered and shadowed lives. This is a day of mourning and rejoicing; we think of the dead, and are warned by our consciences, even if Field Marshal Earl Haig had not issued his appeal not to turn our backs on the living. We

also count the blessings which have come to us as a result of the sacrifice of human life—husbands, sons and brothers—which was made that we might enjoy a larger freedom. On this day of days for this nation, tears and laughter may mingle before the night closes, but first we have our tribute to pay to those who 'passed through Glory's morning gate'. Most of them were at the threshold of life, with all its unplumbed possibilities. They counted every promise which it held as of little account, and for our sakes went forth as the champions of a great cause, which was at last to mobilize most of the nations of the world. Not only in London this morning, but throughout the wide realms in which the peculiar phase of liberal civilization in which we take pride has rooted itself, the bustle of everyday existence will be stilled for two minutes. Memory will retrace her steps down the corridors of Time, and call up half-forgotten incidents in the lives of those who have this in common—that they all passed through one of 'the thousand doors that lead to death'. They form a great communion with which we are linked by ties of heartfelt gratitude. As the hour of eleven strikes this morning men and women—even those who hide no wounds in their hearts—will recall that the Angel of Death has been abroad throughout the world, and they will almost hear the beating of his wings. In all the calendar of the year, this is for us, as a community confronted with Fate, the most solemn moment. It says a good deal for the character of the British peoples, here and overseas, that they should have consorted to make this day one of Remembrance. It points to a fine sensibility—an awakening to the reality of things spiritual and material. It is a recognition that there is a debt to be paid to those whom 'no pain shall wake . . . till joy shall overtake her perfect peace', as well as to the living. We dare not turn our backs on those who have been broken in body or estate by the ordeal of those four years of war any more than we can shut our mind's eyes to all the lonely graves that constitute enduring monuments to the loftiest instincts and achievements of our race.

This is Poppy Day, when we shall wear the flower of Remembrance. It is the flower that sheds its radiance over the torn and riven fields where thousands of our dead rest in quiet content. One of them, while the world was still rocking with the violence of war, left us, as a legacy for all time, a warning: 'If ye break faith with us who die, We shall not sleep, though poppies grow in Flanders's fields.' That is the charge which comes to us today from the graves, not only of Flanders, but of France, Salonika, Gallipoli, Egypt, Mesopotamia, Palestine, and all the other theatres in which three years ago the clarion was still sounding its call to sacrifice. These men were not only patriots in the narrow sense of that word; they fought not that we might have dominion over other nations, but that the world might be saved from the oppressions by which it had suffered so long. General Sir Alfred Knox has told us that most of the Russian peasants who were led to the slaughter did not know why they went. That was not so in any of the

> armies we raised. Our men went forth as to a Crusade. Have they died in vain? That is a question that will rise to many minds as wreaths are laid on Cenotaph or other monument to the dead and hymns of prayer and praise are sung. These men 'passed over' that the world might be a sweeter place. Against the background of history their courage, endurance, and patience will stand out with unfading lustre. Fighting was not in most cases their profession, but a high sense of duty made them combatants. They were not thinking of themselves as, in alien lands, they reached, full early, their journey's end; their thoughts were of the New World which they were helping to purchase with their last fitful breath. Remembrance Day, with its poppy, 'a drowsy balm for every bitter smart', is therefore an occasion when the nation may fittingly review, in the presence of a great company of witnesses, the uses which it has made of the new freedom which these men conferred on it. What has been done in the three years which have intervened since the war closed to realize the dreams which these heroes nourished? The record is not altogether good, but it is not altogether bad; some progress, it may be hoped, has been made. Tomorrow delegates of the great States of the world will meet at Washington. If they find a common ground of agreement, to banish suspicions and quieten fears, as find it they must if they are not to break faith with the dead, posterity, whatever material burdens we may be forced to pass on to it, will keep the Day of Remembrance with a deeper sense of gratitude than even we must feel as we marshal once more, in sorrow and yet in joy, our memories of the Great War.

In the very next column came a report, sent the previous day 'from our special correspondent' in Berlin, entitled 'Before the Great War: Kaiser and the Staff':

> A first-class contribution to the history of the outbreak of the War appears in an obscure Stuttgart paper. It is an extract from Count Moltke's memoirs, which have been printed in book form but withheld from publication. The editor of the paper mentioned procured a copy of the work and transcribed certain passages, which he now gives to the public. Describing the council of war in the Berlin Palace on Aug. 1, 1914, Count von Moltke, then Chief of Staff, writes:
>
> 'The Imperial Chancellor who, as already indicated, saw the most important aim of his policy in the establishment of a good relationship to England, and who strange to say, even till that day still believed that a general war or at least England's participation in it could be avoided, was obviously joyfully excited over the contents of the despatch received from the German Ambassador in London, Prince Lichnowsky, and so was His Majesty, the Kaiser. The despatch announced that Secretary of State Grey told the Ambassador that England would assume the obligation that France

would not enter the war against us if Germany, for her part, would bind herself to take no hostile action against France. I should remark, in passing, that in France mobilization had been ordered the same day as here, and this was known to us.

'There prevailed, as has been said, a joyful tone. "Now we only need make war against Russia," the Kaiser said to me. "You see, we simply concentrate the whole of our army in the East." I answered His Majesty that this was impossible. The concentration of an army of millions could not be improvised. It was the result of years of laborious work, and once arranged could not be altered ... The Kaiser insisted on his demand, and was very angry. Among other things he said to me "Your uncle would have given me a different answer," and this hurt me greatly ... My objection that France was already engaged in mobilization, and that it was impossible that mobilized Germany and mobilized France should peaceably agree not to touch one another, remained without success. The discussion became ever more excited, and I was alone.

'I finally succeeded in convincing His Majesty that our dispositions, which provided for strong forces against France and weak defensive forces against Russia, must be carried out according to plan if fatal confusions were not to ensue ... In accordance with this there was then drafted a reply despatch to London, that Germany accepted the English offer very gladly, but that the existing mobilization plan must, for the present, for technical reasons also take its course against France. We would, however, do nothing to France if under the control of England she would remain quiet. More I could not attain. From the outset the senselessness of the whole of the English proposals was clear to me ... I demanded as a guarantee that France would not strike on the temporary transfer to us of the fortresses of Verdun and Toul. This proposal was rejected as a vote of no confidence against England. In the course of this affair my state of mind had become almost desperate. I foresaw the greatest mischief in the war confronting us from this diplomatic action, which threatened to interfere with our mobilization.

'I must interpolate here that our plan provided for the occupation of Luxemburg by the 16th Division on the first day of mobilization. Whatever happened we had to ensure the Luxemburg railways against a French coup, as we needed them for our deployment. Thus it was all the more severe a blow for me when the Chancellor now declared that Luxemburg must under no circumstances be occupied, as that would be a direct menace to France and render illusory the proffered guarantees. As I stood there the Kaiser, without asking me, turned to the aide-de-camp on duty, and ordered him to telegraph immediately to the 16th Division at Trèves and command that it should not enter Luxemburg. I felt as if my heart would break ... I tried in vain to convince His Majesty that we needed the Luxemburg railways and must secure them. I was dismissed with the remark that we could use instead other lines. The order stood.'

Count Moltke relates that he left the council chamber 'shaken by the isolation' in which he found himself with his demands 'as against the Kaiser and all responsible quarters'. It was only in the evening, when the later news from London had shown that the 'intervention of England in favour of Germany was quite out of the question', that the Kaiser, with the words 'Do as you like,' gave Moltke a free hand to carry out the General Staff plans.

Of Special Importance

In mid-November Rudolf Steiner left Dornach on a journey via Stuttgart and Berlin to Norway. Several letters again passed between himself and Edith Maryon.

Sculpture Studio,
Goetheanum
18th Nov. 1921

Dear Teacher,

I'm sending you a copy of the programme for the teachers' course, in case you haven't yet received one. Mrs. Mackenzie writes that she's bringing at least 25 people with her. For various reasons some have cancelled, but others are coming. How many from England are able to come will probably only be known at the last moment. She's getting a price reduction from the railway of £2.00 per person for a group of 25 people, and that'll help. She says others will probably be able to come. On November the 24th she's giving a lecture to the Anthroposophical Society on 'Education from a Spiritual Standpoint', and on December the 7th in the Bloomsbury Club on 'Education as a Fine Art'.

I'm very occupied with ordering rooms, clearing up rooms etc. Today I visited Frau Dr. Grosheintz for rooms and found her in bed, with a cold (and a very unbecoming rash in her face!), but otherwise in very friendly mood.

Mrs. Mackenzie writes that Flossy is doing good work in London and will be giving a little demonstration on December the 10th.

Otherwise there isn't much to report. We still haven't got the stoves in our studio.

I'm thinking very much about Berlin, and soon I'll be thinking about the journey to Kristiania, and wish it had been granted me to be present as well. I very much hope you won't catch cold. I'll be glad when Berlin is past. Hopefully no lectures have to be given in Munich?

With best wishes,

Edith Maryon

★

Berlin,
19th November 1921

My dear Edith Maryon,

The journey has so far gone well. My stay in Stuttgart was quite short and in consequence filled with work. I haven't caught any cold. So the lecture I announced will be this evening.

Departure for Norway is arranged for early Monday. I hope everything is going all right in our studio. I'll be pleased to be there again. Just these lines and heartfelt greetings for today,

Rudolf Steiner

Motzstrasse 17, Berlin W.

★

Sculpture Studio,
Goetheanum
21st Nov. 1921

Dear Teacher,

I'm very pleased that everything has so far gone well, and especially that you haven't caught any cold. Hopefully things also stay that way. No news so far of how the lecture and eurythmy performances went; I'm hoping for a quiet but big success.

I received the enclosed letter from Herr Fadum; it seems I didn't meet the right person who would be interested in selling eurythmy souvenirs! I had sent him one, and twelve through Frau Clason; perhaps it would be best if Frau C. simply brings them all back, as none of our people have time to deal with it, and if Norwegians don't want to...! In my opinion they were suitable for Norwegians, but these sort of things no one can foretell!

If you have no objection, two rooms in the school will be arranged after 20 December for participants in the course, where they can stay between the various events.

With heartfelt greetings,

Edith Maryon

★

Sculpture Studio,
Goetheanum

Dear Teacher,

I've heard there was a thick snowstorm on the 21st–22nd and very much hope you've arrived all right in Kristiania, without catching any cold? I also hope the Norwegians didn't arrange a lecture in the station waiting-room on your arrival. They would certainly have used the time, had they learnt soon enough you were coming a day early!

The stove arrived today in the studio; it heats very well but looks like a monster; otherwise it isn't unpleasant, when one has recovered from the first shock.

There's still a lot to do in the houses. I've now become clerk, painter, seamstress and various other things and won't be displeased to have everything in order by the end of next week.

Two of the most important men from the people Mrs. Mackenzie wanted to bring have too much work at Christmas and so are unable to come, but will come later. Would it be possible to give another course at Easter or Whitsun? I don't know how much holiday they have at Whitsun in England; at Easter it's usually from 10 days to 3 weeks, it all depends; at Whitsun certainly not longer.

No news from Kristiania has yet arrived in Dornach.

I hope the people there aren't placing too many demands on you?

With heartfelt greetings,

Edith Maryon

★

10 Oskarsgate
Kristiania,
24th November 1921

My dear Edith Maryon,

I just want today to express heartfelt thanks for the letters I've received, and also the one with the programme. The journey was fine, and so far everything is in order here too. Hopefully all is going fine with you as well, despite the strain in finding accommodation for the Christmas course. I'm hoping in this course to elaborate much educational material of special importance for the kind of audience who are coming. For now, heartfelt greetings in our studio from

Rudolf Steiner

Staying at:
Anthroposofisk Sels Kap.
10 Oskarsgate, Kristiania

NOTES

1. This was first published in 1956 in the collection *Wir Erlebten Rudolf Steiner*. In his biography *Willem Zeylmans van Emmichoven* (1979), Emanuel Zeylmans noted: 'The book had a difficult birth, for some of the contributing authors felt that they had to watch as censors over the articles of the others.' In the following year, 1957, the whole book was translated into English as a special number of *The Golden Blade*. It is apparent that Adams himself was the translator of his own contribution, for the English version altered or omitted several passages in the original of his text, but more than compensated for this by adding other sections which had not appeared in the original at all. In the course of the present work the writer has therefore used sections, sometimes conflated, from both the German and English versions.
2. Charles Weekes was born in Dublin on 11 June 1867. He was educated at Erasmus Smith High School from about 1878 to 1885, where his contemporaries included W.B. Yeats, W.K. Magee (John Eglinton) and Charles Johnston. In 1886 he went on to enroll at Trinity College Dublin, studying arts and law.

   Weekes was introduced, probably through Johnston, to AE, and it was he who then introduced AE to John Eglinton. But although AE interested Weekes in Theosophy, the latter never actually joined the Theosophical Society. On a visit to London he did however meet H.P. Blavatsky, who laughingly called him 'ever a doubter'.

   After graduating from Trinity College in about 1892 Weekes travelled with John Eglinton to Göttingen in order to learn German. In 1893 he moved to London and, although returning to Dublin in 1894, moved back to London in 1896, where he worked as a reader for the publisher George Allen. He married in 1901, and in 1902 was called to the Irish bar.

   It must have been through Dunlop that Weekes in 1905 entered the Westinghouse Company, as assistant to the British General Manager Newcomb Carlton. In 1911 he followed Dunlop into the BEAMA, as Secretary to its Council and legal adviser, in which post he remained for the rest of his working life. He died on 6 January 1946.
3. The title *Das Christentum als Mystische Tatsache* itself contains an English borrowing, namely, the word *Tatsache*. Peter F. Ganz in a glossarial entry to his monograph *Der Einfluss des Englischen auf dem Deutschen Wortschatz 1640–1815* (1957) records that this compound—literally 'Tat', deed, + 'Sache', matter—derives from the English expression 'matter of fact'. The borrowing was first made in 1756 by J. Spalding, translator into German of Butler's *Apology of Religion*. Initially the new term met with purist disapproval: J.C. Adelung in his *Versuch eines grammatisch-kritischen Wörterbuchs der hochdeutschen Mundart* (1774–86) described it as *unschicklich*. But since Immanuel Kant himself went on to use

it in his *Kritik der Urteilskraft* (1790), another disapproving entry which it received a few years later in J.F. Heynatz's *Versuch eines Deutschen Antibarbarus* (1796–7) had no further effect. Under the influence of Kant and others the term was soon popularized into normal German usage, and by the twentieth century its foreign origin had long since ceased to be felt.

The English expression 'matter of fact', originally a legal phrase, is first recorded in 1581. Among early attestations is one from *The Advancement of Learning* (1605) by that 44-year-old lawyer Francis Bacon—who when the phrase came into being in 1581 had been a 20-year-old barrister at Gray's Inn standing at the beginning of his legal career. It is a revealing paradox that Steiner incorporated a term with Baconian colouring into the very title of his book on Christianity!

4. The notes are held today by Thomas Meyer, who kindly let the present writer have a copy. Although Stein wrote at the head the exact place and date—Westonbirt on 27 August 1934—when Dunlop recounted to him something about his life, a reference which the notes contain to an obituary of AE in July 1935 shows that they were not written at Westonbirt at the time but composed from memory almost a year later, evidently as preparatory jottings for Stein's article 'An Appreciation of Daniel Nicol Dunlop', which appeared in *The Present Age* in December 1935. By the time the article appeared Stein would have read Dunlop's own article 'Rudolf Steiner and the Fulfilment of a Quest', posthumously published in July of that year in *Anthroposophical Movement*. Since Dunlop dated the occasion when he had previously seen Steiner to 'about the year 1906', Stein in his article simply repeated this indication. It is clear from the notes, however, that the year which he remembered Dunlop mentioning at Westonbirt was 1902.

   The separate paths of Steiner and Dunlop crossed on several occasions in the first decade of the century: in London in 1902, there again in 1903 and just possibly in 1904, certainly in Amsterdam in 1904, in London once more in 1905 and in Paris in 1906. At Westonbirt Dunlop seems to have recalled the first of these occasions. The one which had impressed Steiner's face and bearing so unforgettably into his memory was however by his (approximate) dating one of the later ones—probably in London in 1905. It was this one to which he referred in his 1935 article, though without saying that it was the *only* previous occasion when he had seen Steiner.
5. Geoffrey Tillett in his biography *The Elder Brother* (1982) records that in August 1902, shortly after his appearance at the Convention in London, Leadbeater left Britain for America. Here he stayed for the next three years, when he travelled on to Australia. He only returned to Europe in 1906, and then anyway resigned from the Theosophical Society. The 1902 occasion was therefore the only one when Steiner actually saw Leadbeater.
6. There is no contemporary evidence as to precisely when the statement was made. Lindenberg in his *Chronik* dates it to 5 July. But in the text of his reminiscence Steiner's phrase 'zum ersten male' is clearly referring to his own presence in London rather than actually qualifying 'sprach'. It seems most

likely that he made the statement at the further meeting concerned specifically with this subject, on 7 July.

7. Peter Kuch in his study *Yeats and AE* (1986) gives a vivid description of how the two figures first met at this school:

'When William Butler Yeats first enrolled in the painting class at the Art Schools in Kildare Street, Dublin, in May 1884, his attention was captured by the manner and work of one of the students. This student appeared to be something of an oddity. He was tall and thin. He wore wire-rimmed pince-nez, and had an unruly shock of hair that gave him a dishevelled appearance. He was conventionally but carelessly dressed in a well-worn Donegal tweed suit—so carelessly in fact that one of his closest friends used to quip that his clothes always looked as if they had been put on with the aid of a shovel. His manner seemed kind, gentle and dreamy. He was quiet, with the quietness of self-absorption. Though he could become animated in discussion, he rarely spoke; not in deference to the many 'Silence is Requested' notices posted around the classroom, but because he had a very bad stammer. Yet even when he spoke, his thoughts were so profuse and clotted that what he said was largely unintelligible. Some of the members of the class thought that he was inspired, others that he was pixilated. Yeats learned that the student's name was George William Russell. He also discovered that Russell had been coming to the art classes irregularly since he had moved to Dublin from the small northern town of Lurgan about six years before, and that he had gained a reputation for remarkable promise.

'What interested him most were Russell's paintings. While other members of the class, with their vocations as art teachers firmly in mind, dutifully laboured to capture an acceptable likeness to the assigned model, Russell would paint effortlessly, without preliminary sketch or working diagram, representations of the images that apparently rose spontaneously before his imagination. Sometimes there were scenes depicting the spiritual history of other worlds and other incarnations, but mostly his canvases were peopled with radiant spirit-beings caught in a moment of light-hearted blitheness in some dappled natural setting such as a lake, a seashore or a forest. At times these paintings displayed a talent for composition which amazed both students and masters. "I can remember," Yeats recalled over 30 years later, the "half-whisper of a student, now a successful sculptor, who said, pointing to the modelling of a shoulder, 'That is too easy, a great deal too easy!' For with brush and pencil he was too coherent." To some, this fluency was further proof that Russell had access to a form of supernatural power.

'At first, Yeats shared their awe for this odd Northerner. "I used to listen to him at that time," he later wrote, "mostly walking through the streets at night, for the sake of some stray sentence, beautiful and profound, amid many words that seemed without meaning; and there were others too, who walked and listened, for he had become, I think to all his fellow-students, sacred, as the fool is sacred in the East ... We derided each other, told absurd tales to one another's discredit, but we never derided him, or told tales to his discredit. He stood outside the sense of comedy his friend John Eglinton has called 'the social cement' of our civilization; and we would 'gush' when we spoke of him, as men do when they praise something incomprehensible. But when he painted there was no difficulty in comprehending. How could that ease and rapidity of composition, so far beyond anything that we could attain to, belong to a man whose words seemed often without meaning?"

'Yeats, who was still deciding whether to be a poet or painter, immediately divined a kinship of purpose in these fluent, vision-inspired paintings . . .'

8. With reference to Steiner's several early visits to the Kensington vicinity mention may be made of the old wooden seat in Kensington Gardens, on the east side of the Longwater, with a metal plaque 'In loving memory of Rudolf Steiner, who loved this spot'.

9. This story is related in a tribute by Alfred Heidenreich published in 1953 in *The Christian Community* on the occasion of Coleman's ninetieth birthday.

George Coleman was born in 1863. At the age of 14, he was apprenticed to a London printer. A friend of his father's then enabled him to travel as a journeyman in this trade to America. For some years he undertook further training in New York—long before the first skyscrapers began to appear on the Manhattan horizon.

In 1889, aged 26, he returned to Britain fully proficient in the printing trade. He married in 1893, but his wife died only three years later. The bereavement opened his sense for the unseen, and he found his way to the Theosophical Society and became closely acquainted with leading personalities, especially G.R.S. Mead, to whom he lent financial support for his translation of the *Pistis Sophia*, first published in English in 1896. He was also a lifelong friend of Max Gysi and it was in this connection that he narrowly missed a meeting with Steiner at the London Congress in July 1905.

Coleman's father had lived a long time in India, and in about 1906 he left Britain again and travelled eastwards in his father's footsteps. He found employment as a printer for the *Times of India*, and stayed in this post for several years. Although in 1913, at the age of 50, he retired from printing for reasons of health, he still continued on the board of the *Times of India*. One precious memory from this period was of standing in Agra before the sixteenth-century tomb of the Emperor Akbar and deciphering its Arabic inscription: 'God is great. Through me may His glory shine!'

After the end of the First World War, in about 1919, Coleman returned again to Britain. Now in his late fifties, he decided to make a completely fresh start, and enrolled in an art school. He became proficient in woodwork and leatherwork, and also a keen watercolour painter; by the early 1920s he even had paintings exhibited in the Royal Academy. But he did not come across anthroposophy, though this was the very time of Steiner's later visits to Britain.

Many more years passed by. In 1940, during the Second World War, Coleman and his second wife were bombed out of London, and moved to Minehead on the north Somerset coast, where the anthroposophical 'New

School' had also been evacuated. One day he noticed in Minehead Post Office a striking poster designed by Isabel Wyatt. This was his first encounter with Anthroposophy. He was now aged 77, and no less than 35 years had passed since that far-off time in 1905 when he narrowly missed meeting Rudolf Steiner at 'The Apple Tree' on London Wall.

Coleman's second wife died in 1949, and Isabel Wyatt herself looked after the octogenarian widower during his last years. These were spent—still at his easel—at Torquay in Devon, where Steiner had given the famous course in 1924.

10. In an article about AE published in February 1943 in the *Atlantic Monthly* his son Diarmuid Russell reminisced:

'It is difficult to talk or write of Father, for in a sense his chief work was himself, and the things for which he was known seemed a by-product...

'I don't think it would be wrong to say that what he would have liked most to do would have been to paint. Summer after summer he would depart for Donegal to bring back twenty or thirty canvases sufficiently finished so that he could work on them during the winter at his leisure. He told me at one time the urge to paint was so strong that he had contemplated doing nothing else, but had been restrained by some feeling that a single pursuit would be bad for him. In a similar fashion, years before, he had been obsessed by mysticism, and the same austerity had made him relegate that to being just a part of his life.

'He must have had considerable strength of will to relegate painting to being just a hobby, for he not only found pleasure in painting but competent people thought he could have been a great painter...

'His prices for paintings must have infuriated other artists, for Father felt he had no right to make money out of a hobby, and so had calculated carefully the cost of the materials—canvases and paint and oil and brushes. Adding a small charge for his time, which couldn't have amounted to more than fifty cents an hour, he had arrived at the figure of five pounds for a small canvas and ten pounds for a large one. This figure was revised upwards a little as costs increased over the years, but other Irish artists may have felt aggrieved at the unfair competition. Maybe Father felt there was something in this, for he stopped showing his pictures and kept them in the house, where only friends could see them.'

AE exhibited his paintings in Dublin every summer from 1904 to 1915, when he ceased doing so because full-time painters objected that his desire to bring art to the comparatively poor was interfering with their livelihood. Thereafter, annually from 1917 to 1934, he assembled his recent canvases instead in a room at Ballymore in Donegal, where he invited certain local residents and others to view them. But these private shows were only for friends and personal acquaintances. After 1915 his paintings were no longer publicly exhibited in Ireland during his lifetime.

11. This cannot refer to the 1902 Convention, as stated in the footnote to GA 185, for as pointed out by Lindenberg in his *Chronik* the 'Entente Cordiale' only came into existence in April 1904. Steiner's statement must refer to the

1905 London Congress; indeed, in the programme Jinarajadasa is listed among the lecturers.

As it stands, however, the statement is erroneous. By this time Steiner had given numerous speeches in the Theosophical Society in Germany, and several in England too. Why he made this misleading assertion—assuming it was correctly reported—is hard to say. Maybe he simply meant that it was his first speech at this particular Congress.

12. An error. This took place on 7 July, as is clear from the Congress programme and the 'Report of Proceedings', and as Steiner himself had correctly stated in his letter to Günther Wagner.
13. Sharp had indeed met Blavatsky in Paris. Mead eventually published Sharp's notes on the Stanzas of Dzyan in 1909 in the opening number of *The Quest.*
14. See Gotthold Deile: *Goethe als Freimaurer* (1908), and in general Irene Diet *Die Wahre Freimaurerei und ihre Gegenbilder* (1997).
15. Another pseudonym later used by Dunlop was 'Bryan Stuart'. This is of interest in relation to the notes about him by Walter Johannes Stein, which state: 'Dunlop himself is an illegitimate Stuart through Flora Macdonald who helped Bonnie Prince Charlie to escape.'
16. In his study *Es Werde Licht und es Ward Licht* (1976), Karl Friedrich Althoff wrote:

'On a papyrus leaf found in Egypt among the collection of Oxyrynchos papyri are found these words as a statement by Christ:

῾Οπου εἂν ὧσιν δυο,	Wherever they may be
οὒκ ἒισιν ἂθηοι.	They are not without God;
και εἰ που εἰσ ἒστιν μονos,	And where one is alone
ἰδου ἒγω εἰμι μετ′ αὖτου.	Behold, I AM with him.
᾽Εγειρον τον λιθον,	Lift up the stone (or: awaken the stone),
κακει εὖρησεις με;	And you will find me there;
σχισον το ξυλον,	Split the wood,
καγω ἒκει εἰμι.	And I, I am there.

'Only a short-sighted intellectual thinking could dismiss such a statement as "pantheistic" or "panentheistic" and thereby "inauthentic"! Do not rather these words of Christ, which remained hidden until their discovery in the desert sand of Egypt at the very turn of the 20th century, sound like a message shaped by Him into meaningful signs for our present isolated and God-forsaken humanity? The verse anyway points towards proximate statements by Christ as transmitted through John the Evangelist. It is certainly significant that such discoveries be placed before the astonished world of our time, which threatens to lose all spiritual contents from former ages. This verse by Christ is like a call: seek for a path on which to practise finding the light in an environment of technology, industry and civilization dedicated to death. "Awaken the stone!"—within the spiritless environment of dispiriting science. "Cleave the wood!"—in order to learn how to see in the downfall of a shattered world the glimmering light of a new beginning, and with one's own new light help to bring about the emergence of a new Earth! This would mean nothing less than searching in the modern world of machinery for traces of the light of Christ, and with one's own enlightened entity laying down those tracks of light out of which the Kingdom desires to arise.'

17. In 1940 Collison nonetheless went on to form a link with Winchester College by presenting to this ancient school his unique collection of a hundred English watercolour paintings, ranging from Turner to Wilson Steer.

    The timing of his gift was curiously fortunate, for shortly afterwards his own home in Kensington was completely destroyed.

18. Rex Raab's statement that 'as barrister Collison was already a Freemason' puts the cart before the horse. Collison was well into Freemasonry before even starting on his legal studies at all. The supposition that he studied law at university is anyway erroneous.

19. This was incorrect: his wife Mabel was also a member of the Society, having joined the H.P.B. Lodge in December 1908, soon after their discovery of Steiner's writings.

    It may further be mentioned that in later years Mabel Heywood-Smith was among the first persons, perhaps indeed the very first—at any rate in the English-speaking world—to transcribe Steiner's lectures into Braille.

20. This was Mabel Heywood-Smith's sister, who lived with their brother and another sister at Blackheath.

21. Lawrence Edwards gave information about Madeline Stewart, and added an anecdote about one of her friends:

    'Mrs. Stewart was a New Zealander—in her young days had been a stewardess on one of the old clipper ships. She must have been one of the earliest English followers of Rudolf Steiner. I did not see her after I joined the army in 1939. I heard she returned to N.Z. and died there soon after. From little things she let drop, I suspect that in her younger days she had been somewhat outspoken and perhaps had played a rather—shall we say?—resolute role in some of the troubles; I don't know. When I knew her she had become tranquil and mellow; just occasionally the old fire showed through.

    'One day, in the early years, she had given a copy of *The Way of Initiation* to an artist friend, who was an invalid. Within a few months this friend was having clairvoyant experiences, which she then painted. Mrs. Stewart showed me the paintings, which she had kept all those years. They were in transparent water-colour, but there their similarity to traditional anthroposophical painting finished. They were on postcard-sized pieces of paper, and were almost wholly geometrical—regular patterns of cubes, spheres, cones, tetrahedra & other pyramids, and star-like forms, with a very occasional little fairy-like being interposing—painted with hard sharp edges, and no attempt at merging or mixing colours.

    'Mrs. Stewart showed them to Rudolf Steiner at one of her interviews with him. He studied them carefully and then said:

    "These are good. But they are not pictures of the spiritual world. They are imaginations of her own thought-forms. And they were good thoughts—strong and clear." '

22. Quotations from Percival's writings are made with permission from The Word Foundation, which he established in 1950 to continue their promotion. John L. Coiro, the current President, also kindly supplied Percival's letter to Smythe of 10 August 1916.

It is notable that the absorbing but also questionable relationship which Dunlop formed to these writings later gave rise to a series of misunderstandings by Thomas Meyer incorporated into the successive versions of his Dunlop biography—the claim in the 1987 version that the zodiac editorials in *The Word* were written by Dunlop, the suggestion in the 1992 version that Percival was a pseudonym, and the assertion in the 1996 version that the editorials derived from collaborative work were all misconceived.

Only after publication in 1992 of the English version did the present writer, who was by then very familiar with Dunlop's characteristic literary style and had become somewhat uneasy about not quite so usual passages in *Duty* and even more puzzled by the content of *The Path of Knowledge* and *Nature-Spirits and the Spirits of the Elements*, uncover the truth of the matter. For the relation with Percival still seemed to require further exploration, and on browsing through *The Word* he noticed editorials with the same titles as some of Dunlop's articles. On comparing the texts and dates with Dunlop's writings it became clear what had been happening. Over quite a number of years Dunlop had made use of *The Word* as an important quarry for ideas, and since this American journal probably did not have in Britain more than a very small circulation was able to present these ideas to his largely British readership as if they were his own, with little risk of anyone realizing their original source. Indeed, there is no record that anyone in Britain at the time ever discovered it. But over in America Percival himself did.

It was therefore necessary to make a systematic examination of every single number of *The Word*, a process which revealed the extent and variety of the borrowings, as well as the different ways in which they had been made. The present writer passed on the information to Meyer, who however would not accept that Dunlop was plagiarizing, and on the basis of the latter's allusion to Percival in October 1912 as 'my friend' put forward a different explanation by inserting into the German text of his 1996 edition a completely fictional account of Percival and Dunlop, impliedly in America, having discussions together! The expression 'my friend', however, is more likely to have been used by Dunlop in late 1912 in an attempt to establish good relations with Percival after his previously unacknowledged borrowings in 1911–12 had been discovered, and scarcely constitutes a secure basis for projecting their whole relationship back to the nineteenth century. This hypothesis, increasingly elaborated in the successive versions of Meyer's biography and subsequently also put forward in his entry on Dunlop in *Anthroposophie im 20. Jahrhundert* (2003) as if it were established fact, is in reality entirely speculative, and seems extremely doubtful. A charge of plagiarism founded on the close comparison of documents whose separate authorship and date are readily ascertainable cannot justifiably be dismissed as 'superficial' merely because it may be possible to devise as an alternative some far-fetched and quite unsubstantiated fabrication! The superficiality can be seen rather to consist in having supposed that everything bearing Dunlop's name actually emanated from him. Both Meyer and the present writer originally made this mistake. But Dunlop's whole modus operandi was altogether more mercurial, and sometimes in a sense risky. One obituarist described him as 'a complex personality', and even if the full story of his relationship with Percival is not contained in the surviving documents, it is clear that a problematic element was involved. The exact position of the line where literary borrowing ends and plagiarism begins may be hard to define, but the evidence suggests that in regard to Percival's writings Dunlop at various times dangerously overstepped that line, and by a fair margin. His adoption of the vast majority of relevant passages from *The Word* was not 'almost' verbal, but entirely so, even over sequences of paragraphs. And the notion that Percival was 'wholly indifferent' to the matter is sufficiently refuted by the content of his statements. There is no documentary evidence of a meeting or other contact of any kind whatever between him and Dunlop before the year 1911, nor of their collaboration in any context or on any subject at all other than the help given by Percival on the zodiac articles of 1912–14 in *The Path*.

The first sentence in the motto which Meyer placed at the front of Part 2 of his biography actually derives from Percival, only the second sentence from Dunlop. The motto at the front of Part 7 is also a slightly reworded version of a statement by Percival.

23. According to Lindenberg's *Chronik*, though with a question-mark indicating uncertainty—Steiner was at the time in Munich.
24. Heywood-Smith had natural healing faculties, which however he ceased to use on learning that anthroposophical healing went through full consciousness.
25. The reference to Parsifal—however the name may be spelt—is problematic, for as far the present writer is aware Steiner did not allude to this figure in any lecture in December 1911, in the whole of 1912, or in January 1913. The Heywood-Smiths were present in February 1913 at the cycle in Berlin on 'The Mysteries of the East and of Christianity', but Steiner's discussion on 6 February of Parzival as a representative of the consciousness soul is embedded in an elaborate context and can hardly be what was meant. Whether in the following month the Heywood-Smiths also attended the cycle in the Hague on 'The Significance of Man's Occult Development…' is unknown, but anyway the examination on 26 March of differences between Amfortas and Parzival also does not fit the given description.

    The reference, although stated (in 1925) to have been 'a little later' than 5 December 1911, is almost certainly to a lecture given over two years later, at Leipzig on 1 January 1914, in which Steiner read out some 40 lines from a modern German translation of Chrétien de Troyes's *Perceval.* The Heywood-Smiths were indeed present at this Leipzig cycle on 'Christ and the Holy

Grail'—which also made an extremely deep impression on the two Russians Andrei Belyi and Assya Turgeniev.

26. 'Inquire Within' (pen-name of Christine Stoddart) made use in her chapter on the Stella Matutina of historical notes by Felkin which have not survived. Meakin's letter was further republished—with various mistakes and unstated omissions—by Francis King in *Ritual Magic in England* (1970).

    Ellic Howe in *The Magicians of the Golden Dawn* (1972) stated that the abbreviation 'S' in the letter referred to a certain 'Sandrieux'. But this character never existed, being invented by Howe from misreading in Stoddart's correspondence the name of René Landrieux; capital L and capital S are hard to distinguish in her handwriting.

27. The Rudolf Steiner Nachlassverwaltung has kindly supplied the present writer with a photocopy of this letter from October 1912, the very first one written from Maryon to Steiner. The letter presents a curious problem, for it was written in German, though all subsequent letters which Maryon wrote to Steiner over the next year were then in English. Not until November 1913 did she consider her own German good enough for her to write again in that language.

    How then is the first letter to be interpreted? In his biography of Maryon, Rex Raab suggested that she composed it herself and copied out a translation made by another person who had some knowledge of German.

    Although certainly plausible, this solution still remains inferential rather than testified fact. Since the letter is only extant in German, it is misleading to label it *Übersetzung*, as is done in the Steiner-Maryon correspondence volume (GA 263/1). *Übersetzung* would only be a justifiable label if an English 'original' were also extant, which is not the case.

    Moreover, as the present writer was surprised to discover, Maryon's letter is noticeably different in regard to grammar and syntax from what is presented in the Gesamtausgabe volume. Here is the *actual* text of this historic letter:

58, Grove Park Terrace,
Chiswick, London.
16.10.12.

Dear Dr. Steiner,

Dr. R.W. Felkin (F.R.) hat mir gesagt dass ich Ihnen dieses schicken soll, und Ihnen bitten dass Sie mir eine Unterrednung gestatten möchte. Wenn ich es arrangieren kann hoffe ich einige Wochen in Köln zu zubringen und wenn Sie mir schreiben würden wann Sie in Köln sein werden werde ich versuchen zu der Zeit mein Besuch dort zu machen. Ich muss zu erst irgendwo finden wo ich 'au pair' wohnen könnte, und Englische Unterricht geben könnte.

Ich kann nur sehr wenig Deutsch sprechen, vielleicht könnten wir aber Franzosiche zusammen sprechen.

Hochachtungsvoll
Ihre
(Miss) L. Edith C. Maryon

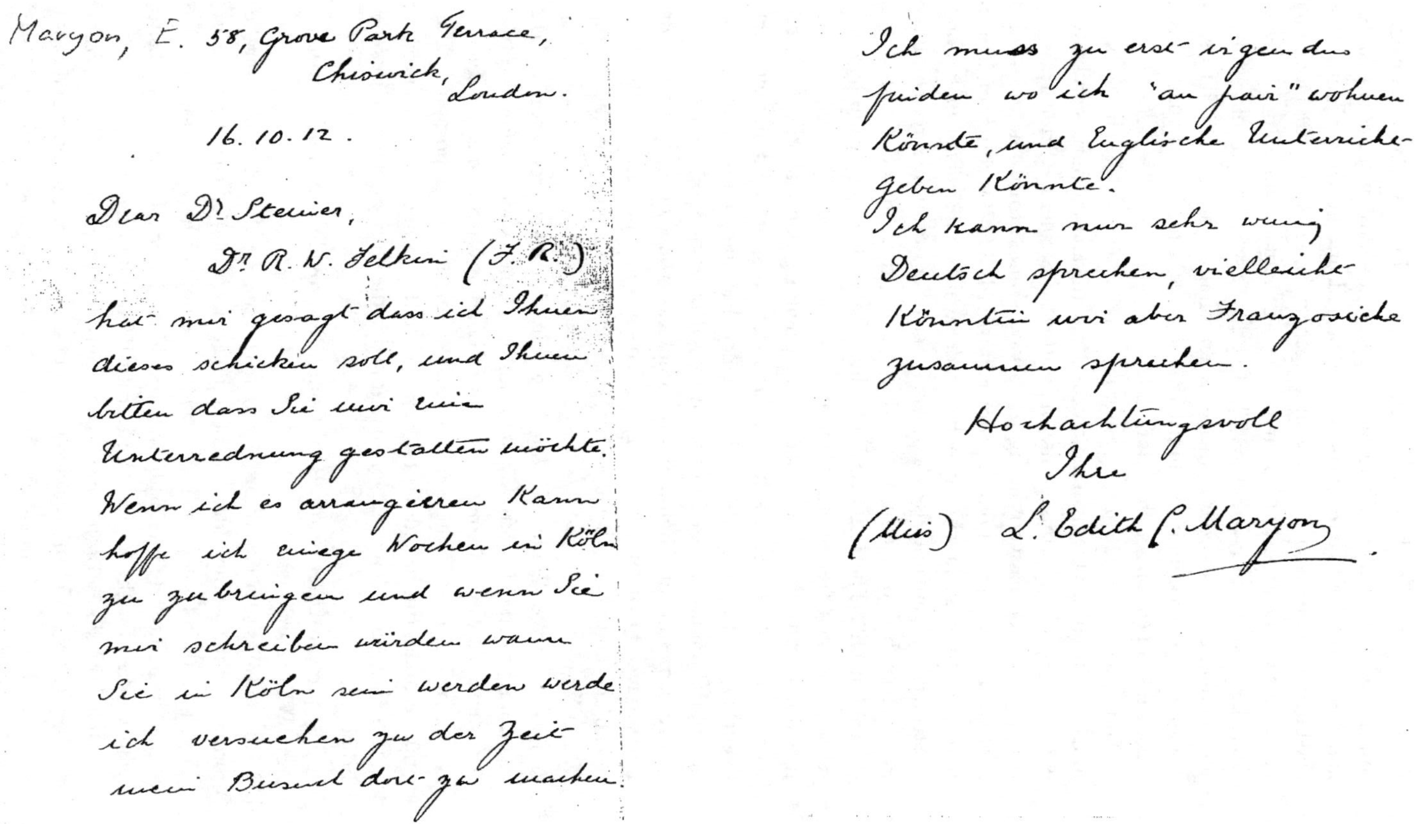

Maryon, E. 58, Grove Park Terrace,
Chiswick, London.

16. 10. 12.

Dear Dr Steiner,

Dr R. W. Felkin (F. R.)
hat mir gesagt dass ich Ihnen
dieses schicken soll, und Ihnen
bitten dass Sie mir eine
Unterredung gestatten möchte.
Wenn ich es arrangieren kann
hoffe ich einige Wochen in Köln
zu zubringen und wenn Sie
mir schreiben würden wann
Sie in Köln sein werden werde
ich versuchen zu der Zeit
mein Besuch dort zu machen.

Ich muss zu erst irgendwo
finden wo ich "au pair" wohnen
Könnte, und Englische Unterricht
geben Könnte.
Ich kann nur sehr wenig
Deutsch sprechen, vielleicht
Könnten wir aber Französische
zusammen sprechen.

Hochachtungsvoll
Ihre
(Miss) L. Edith C. Maryon.

It is clear that the German of this letter, although quite comprehensible, is formulated in a style which betrays an underlying English idiom. But even if someone else also had a hand in the rendering, it seems much more genuine and characteristic of Maryon's entity than the pedantically 'correct' but lifeless and bogus version given in the Gesamtausgabe volume. Raab in his biography perceptively stated that with Maryon Steiner 'could at once, as he always desired, speak an artistic language. The fact that to start with she did not have such perfect command of German was almost an advantage . . .' Her determination in overcoming her initial ignorance of a foreign language was a remarkable aspect of her character.

To transpose the text of such a historic—and essentially delightful—letter into formally correct German merely for the gratification of purist sensibility is effectively to obscure this point. In relation to Steiner's written texts, by contrast, the Nachlassverwaltung has always claimed to promote so-called *Authentizität.* Not to uphold the same editorial ideal for his correspondents is in practice to pursue a schizoid policy under which *Authentizität* applies only to Steiner, while anyone else's lexical or syntactic creations are forced onto the Procrustean bed of German prescribed usage, there to be chopped and changed at will. The result seriously distorts the character of the linguistic relation between Steiner and Maryon.

28. It is noteworthy that Steiner named an English group after the American writer Ralph Waldo Emerson. This inspiration was revived under quite different circumstances in 1962 when Francis Edmunds founded an anthroposophical training centre in England named Emerson College.

    The names of the English anthroposophical groups given by Steiner did not survive the turbulent history of British anthroposophy in the mid-twentieth-century as played out against the background of the Second World War.

29. As Raab observed, Waite in his autobiography misdated the occasion to 1912, an error repeated in later studies of the history of the Golden Dawn. A further statement that it was Steiner's first visit to London was also misconceived.

    In a later chapter Waite reminisced about another anthroposophist, Dorothy Osmond. But he did not fully appreciate the significance of his meeting with Steiner, though it was even mentioned in the blurb on the dust-jacket of his book!

    The present writer thanks R.A. Gilbert for providing the further material from Waite's archives.

30. Nicholson was later co-editor (together with the Revd A.H.E. Lee, another former member of the Independent and Rectified Rite) of *The Oxford Book of English Mystical Verse* (1917), and while assembling this collection in 1916 struck up an intimate friendship with the then 30-year-old Charles Williams, who worked for the Oxford University Press. Until his death in 1933 he remained the closest of the latter's confidants. In the preface to *The Descent of the Dove* (1939), Williams recalled the friendship by stating that the dedication of his book 'to the Companions of the Co-Inherence' was 'meant generally;

but in particular for all those who have, in one place or another, cared to study with me "the half-read wisdom of daemoniac images", and most especially for D.H.S.N., who nobly and happily disputed on the Nature of Love:

What make ye and what strive for? Keep ye thought
Of us, or in new excellence divine
Is old forgot? and do ye count for nought
What the Greek did and what the Florentine?
We keep your memories well; O in your store
Live not our best joys treasured evermore?'

31. In his Maryon biography, Rex Raab supposed this to be 'an article with erroneous statements about the Anthroposophical Society'. The editorial indeed contained erroneous statements, but none of them directly concerned the Anthroposophical Society, which in 1913 was still hardly known in Britain at all, whether in ecclesiastical circles or elsewhere.

32. Collison was away from home when the bomb fell, but another anthroposophist, the painter Margaret Wansey, who lived in nearby Chelsea, happened to be in the house at the time and was killed instead.

Wansey was a well-known painter of animals, gardens, and especially mountain scenery, who would travel every year to either the Alps or the Pyrenees. Between 1913 and 1938 she had 17 paintings exhibited in various English art galleries.

33. The letters numbered 17 and 18 in GA 263/1 make better sense if taken in the reverse order. The allusion to Ada Wilson as mediator is surely decisive. Admittedly there are still small difficulties, but it seems easier to explain these than to solve the problems presented by the order in the text.

34. For decades the identity of Frater Benedic anima mea Domino remained unknown to Golden Dawn researchers. Only the publication in 1993 of Rex Raab's *Edith Maryon*, where the first and last pages of this letter were reproduced in facsimile (pp. 134–5), at last revealed that it was Harry Collison. It is ironic that Raab himself, although befriended with Collison, failed to decipher the motto and informed the German readers of his book (p. 76) that 'We do not know . . . which motto he chose'!

The assertion by Ellic Howe in *The Magicians of the Golden Dawn* (1972) that Collison 'had joined the Order with a watching brief from Steiner' was assessed by Raab as follows:

'I have great difficulties with this idea, and detailed inquiries have not justified the misrepresentation. Collison was a freedom-loving person, and it was his own business if after joining the Anthroposophical Society he also wanted to interest himself in the Golden Dawn as a quite differently operating esoteric group. "Watching brief" has a flavour both of spying and of bondage to another person, which in this case is completely ruled out. Golden Dawn historians, as also Waite, evidently lack any feeling for the honesty of Rudolf Steiner's being and work. The most it could have been is that Steiner, who had nothing directly to do with the Golden Dawn, did not disadvise Collison from his notion of joining the Order.'

35. This passage was shortened in the English version *The Life and Work of Rudolf Steiner* (1955). The book's American co-translator Olin D. Wannamaker stated in a preface: 'Upon suggestion of the author, the English translation has been somewhat compressed.'
36. This was the Fellowship of the Rosy Cross, which flourished from 1915 until the outbreak of the Second World War in 1939, in its original form finally petering out on Waite's death in 1942.

    The Order's members came to include Charles Williams, who first became acquainted with Waite in 1915. Probably their connection was furthered by D.H.S. Nicholson, though the latter did not join the new Order. Williams however did so in 1917, and over the next ten years played an active and prominent part second only to that of Waite himself. He chose the motto 'Qui Sitit Veniat', taken from Christ's words at the Feast of Tabernacles in the autumn of the year 32:

    'On the last and greatest day of the festival, Jesus stood there and cried out: "If anyone is thirsty, let him come to me. Let whoever believes in me come and drink. As scripture says: From his breast shall flow fountains of living water." He was speaking of the Spirit which those who believed in Him were to receive; for there was no Spirit as yet because Jesus had not yet been glorified.' (John 7: 37–9)

    In 1927 Williams ceased to participate any further in the rituals. Although staying in contact with Waite until 1931, he could not be persuaded to resume his former role in the Order, which in effect he abandoned. But its practices and the associated Kabbalistic terminology and symbolism set out in Waite's study of *The Secret Doctrine in Israel* (1913) left a lasting impression on Williams's mind, the effects of which are easily discernible in the multifarious writings he went on to compose during the period of his great literary productivity from about 1930 until his death in 1945.
37. Despite all the seemingly positive evidence—*Protean Man* was also serialized under Dunlop's name in *New Thought* from June to October 1931—the present writer has come to feel great difficulty in accepting Dunlop as the actual author of both or even either of these works. Apart from the fact that their content is not mutually compatible, neither of them are written in his very characteristic and recognizable literary style. The matter remains problematic, but on the basis of how Dunlop borrowed from Percival's editorials, it does not seem entirely inconceivable that one or other or possibly even both of these works were composed by some person or persons unknown whose writings he later felt free to promote under—or at any rate largely in association with—his own name.
38. The Mackenzies maintained contact in subsequent years with W.B. Yeats, who on 24 October 1929 wrote from London to his wife Georgie stating:

    'I have had a very pleasant afternnon at the Mackenzies—I like both of them greatly. The philosopher Broad is in the order—a 5–6. They seem to have got something about the sources of order through Steiner. I go to Bristol (not Cardiff) tomorrow & return on Sunday...

The present writer thanks Dr. John Kelly for kindly providing material in this work from Yeats's letters.

Meetings of the Hermes Temple were held at first in the home of Catherine Hughes in the Bristol suburb of Redland. But when in 1936 her brother Donald bought a house in the neighbouring suburb of Cotham, meetings were then transferred to these new premises at 6 Hillside. In course of time the teaching became entirely anthroposophical, and when in 1968 the temple was finally closed down Donald Hughes sold the premises to the Bristol congregation of the Christian Community, of which they have ever since formed the centre.

39. Since Percival also wrote a book on Freemasonry, Thomas Meyer labelled him a Freemason. But this conclusion is erroneous, as shown by relevant statements on the matter made by Percival himself.

He ended Chapter XI, 'The Great Way', of his book *Thinking and Destiny* (1946) by stating:

'A chapter on "Freemasonry" was to follow this last section of "The Great Way", in which that subject was treated in the light of what is stated in this book. It was shown how the history of the conscious self in the body is depicted in the ritual of Freemasonry . . .

'On presenting the manuscript to the publishers, it appeared that an interpretation of the "dogma and ritual" of Freemasonry by a layman not a member of the Order might give offence. That was not intended. Therefore the chapter is withdrawn; it will not be published, unless so desired by Masons.'

Six years later, in 1952, Percival then brought out *Masonry and its Symbols*—his last work. The preface stated:

'The subject-matter of this little book was originally one of fifteen chapters of a manuscript entitled *Thinking and Destiny*, publication of which was delayed owing to the paper situation during the Second World War. As time went on it was deemed advisable to delete this chapter from the manuscript, and publish it at some future time under separate cover and with the assurance that it would not be disapproved by the Masonic Fraternity. It is now published on the suggestion of Masons who have read the manuscript.'

The final section of the book ended:

'Masons who have read the foregoing approved it, and it is now published with the hope that all readers will see its application to "The Great Way" described in *Thinking and Destiny*, and which preceded this work in the original manuscript. It is addressed to all human beings, and the author, though not a member of the Masonic Fraternity, wishes especially to remind all Masons, of whatever lodge or rite, that entrusted to their care were the plans for the rebuilding of their second temple . . .'

40. Dorothy Osmond stands immediately behind Dunlop in the large photograph of participants at the Westonbirt Summer School in 1934 reproduced in Thomas Meyer's *D.N. Dunlop* (1992). The (in the English version) 'unknown' persons in the centre are Montague Wheeler, Pieter de Haan and Margarete Hauschka.

41. As time went on AE's antipathy towards science seems to have diminished, for in a later chapter of his biography Summerfield wrote:

'A careful study of the *Irish Statesman* shows that AE, despite his essentially pre-scientific outlook, made a considerable effort to come to terms with the intellectual life of the modern world. Calling for the reopening of the Dublin College of Science, temporarily occupied by the Government, he argued: "The teaching in the College, with its insistence on precision of method, on careful experiment, and proof by investigation, is the best antidote which could be provided against the sloppy idealism whch passes for thought in Ireland." At a deeper level, he tried to persuade himself that science was an ally, not an enemy of spirituality...'

42. A term taken from the Stanzas of Dzyan in *The Secret Doctrine*. Stanza IV begins:

'1. ... LISTEN, YE SONS OF THE EARTH, TO YOUR INSTRUCTORS—THE SONS OF THE FIRE. LEARN, THERE IS NEITHER FIRST NOR LAST, FOR ALL IS ONE: NUMBER ISSUED FROM NO NUMBER.

2. LEARN WHAT WE WHO DESCEND FROM THE PRIMORDIAL SEVEN, WE WHO ARE BORN FROM THE PRIMORDIAL FLAME, HAVE LEARNT FROM OUR FATHERS...

3. FROM THE EFFULGENCY OF LIGHT—THE RAY OF THE EVER-DARKNESS—SPRUNG IN SPACE THE RE-AWAKENED ENERGIES; THE ONE FROM THE EGG, THE SIX, AND THE FIVE. THEN THE THREE, THE ONE, THE FOUR, THE ONE, THE FIVE—THE TWICE SEVEN THE SUM TOTAL. AND THESE ARE THE ESSENCES, THE FLAMES, THE ELEMENTS, THE BUILDERS, THE NUMBERS, THE ARUPA, THE RUPA, AND THE FORCE OF DIVINE MAN—THE SUM TOTAL. AND FROM THE DIVINE MAN EMANATED THE FORMS, THE SPARKS, THE SACRED ANIMALS, AND THE MESSENGERS OF THE SACRED FATHERS WITHIN THE HOLY FOUR.

4. THIS WAS THE ARMY OF THE VOICE—THE DIVINE MOTHER OF THE SEVEN...'

In her commentary on the fourth sloka H.P. Blavatsky stated:

'The "Army of the Voice" ... a term closely connected with the mystery of Sound and Speech ... is the prototype of the "Host of the Logos", or the "WORD" of the Sepher Jezirah, called in the Secret Doctrine "the One Number issued from No-Number"—the One Eternal Principle.'

43. Since all through 1920 *Theosophy in Scotland* published a series of articles by Charles Lazenby headed 'The Servant', then brought out in book form, it seems natural to suppose that the Lazenbys spent their time in Britain largely in Scotland, where Margaret would have had relatives. During this year Charles also travelled over to Switzerland to study psychology at the school of Carl Jung in Zurich. His instructor, Dr. Baines, later stated that Lazenby taught him more than the other way round. The Canadian did not however

meet anthroposophy; indeed the fact that he studied with Dr. Baines might perhaps suggest that he did not learn much, if any, German.

The Lazenbys then returned to the American continent, where for the next three years Charles lectured on theosophy and organized Summer Schools in Canada and the United States.

In 1923 the family took ship again, this time westwards to Australia. They lived for two years in Sydney, at a time when Annie Besant came into conflict with the Theosophical Society's Sydney Lodge and cancelled its charter. The Lazenbys were among those involved in then founding in Sydney an Independent Theosophical Society.

In 1925 the family returned again to the American continent, staying for some time in Mexico, then Texas, and finally back in Canada, where they settled at St Thomas, a few miles north from Lake Erie. During the summers of 1926, 1927 and 1928 they went camping in the region of the Georgian Bay, and it was here too that Charles Lazenby suddenly died from an ulcer, on 2 December 1928, aged only 50 years old.

In 1930 his widow Margaret, a quiet lady who remained largely in the background, republished *The Servant* in a memorial edition. She lived on for only a few years, but wrote down some recollections of her husband before her own death in 1933. These recollections formed the basis for a biographical sketch which their daughter Petrovna Cosgrove eventually published in the November-December 1988 issue of *The Canadian Theosophist*. The present writer thanks the editor, Ted Davy, for his help and also for supplying the letters which Charles Lazenby received from Daniel and Freida Dunlop.

44. The high regard in which AE was held by his friends is well illustrated by the sheer number of works dedicated to him—

    1. W.B. Yeats: *Fairy and Folk Tales of the Irish Peasantry* (1888)
    2. Charles Weekes: *Reflections and Refractions* (1893)
    3. W.B. Yeats: the first section, 'Crossways', in *Poems* (1895)
    4. Charles Johnston: *From the Upanishads* (1896)
    5. W.B. Yeats: *The Secret Rose* (1897)
    6. Paul Gregan: *Sunset Town, and Other Poems* (1901)
    7. Susan and John Varian: *Cuchulain, A Cycle of Irish Plays* (n.d., *circa* 1906)
    8. Padraic Colum: *Wild Earth: a Book of Verse* (1907)
    9. James Stephens: *Insurrections* (1909)
    10. Dermot O'Byrne: *The Sisters and Green Magic* (1911)
    11. (Dedicated to AE and W.B. Yeats) W.Y. Evans-Wentz: *The Fairy Faith in Celtic Countries* (1911)
    12. St. J.G. Ervine: *Sir Edward Carson and the Ulster Movement* (1915)
    13. Darrell Figgis: *The Mount of Transfiguration* (1915)
    14. (Dedicated to AE and John Eglinton) Susan Mitchell: *George Moore* (1916)
    15. Katherine Hinkson: *Late Songs* (1917)
    16. D.N. Dunlop: *The Path of Knowledge* (n.d., 1919/20)
    17. L.O'D. Walters: *Irish Poetry of Today: An Anthology* (1921)

18. J.M. Pryse: *A New Presentation of Aeschylus' Prometheus Bound* (1925)
19. Simone Téry: *L'Isle des Bardes* (1925)
20. Fritz Bennicke Hart: *Deirdre in Exile*, Opus 66 (written in 1926)
21. Seumas O'Sullivan: *Common Adventures* (1926)
22. James Stephens: *Collected Poems* (1926)
23. F.R. Higgins: *The Dark Breed: a Book of Poems* (1927)
24. Lady Gregory: *Dave*, the second of *Three Last Plays* (1928)

After AE's death in 1935 some further works were also dedicated to his memory—

25. P.G. Bowen: *The Occult Way* (n.d., 1936)
26. Austin Clarke: *Collected Poems* (1936)
27. (Dedicated to AE and Robert Bridges) H.E. Palmer: *Post-Victorian Poetry* (1938)
28. Constance Sitwell: *Seek Paradise* (1948).

45. In this connection Rex Raab included the following passage in his Maryon biography:

'There are also people, however, who remembered another side of Edith Maryon. She was repeatedly given the scarcely enviable task of going to the studio door and deciding whether insistent visitors to Rudolf Steiner were to be let in or not.

'She had taken it upon herself to shield Rudolf Steiner as much as possible, and give him some rest for his work. This was certainly not easy, and evidently she did not always succeed in leaving an impression of friendliness on those who were turned away.

'The Dutch doctor Willem Zeylmans van Emmichoven describes how on his first Dornach visit in 1920 a talk which he had arranged with Rudolf Steiner was almost prevented:

'"Since I had now been introduced, I also wanted to put particular questions ... and asked if I might be allowed to speak with him.

'" 'Please come tomorrow about three o'clock to my studio,' he said.

'"On the next day I came punctually into the anteroom of the studio, where a lady was carving at a wooden sculpture. She asked what I wanted, in a not very friendly manner.

'" 'I have an appointment with Dr. Steiner.'

'" 'Herr Dr. Steiner is not having visits today.'

'" 'But, if you please, he told me.'

'" 'No, today he is not receiving anyone.'

'"This was just too much for me.

'" 'Please be so good as to announce me to him.'

'"Before any further refusal came, the door was opened and a lady came out who proved to be Dutch and said:

'" 'Do come in, Herr Doctor is waiting for you.'

'"So I went in. Dr. Steiner was sitting by a red-hot stove, and there was an empty chair, just as near to the stove as his own. Fortunately I too am fond of warmth, and so felt very well ..."

'No, it was certainly not easy—especially in particular cases when she had perhaps not been told about forthcoming visits.'

46. In New Zealand Felkin had a high reputation as a doctor, and made use in his medical practice of a colour light therapy for which he may well have received indications from Steiner. As soon as he heard at the beginning of 1924 about the burning of the Goetheanum he wrote to Steiner to express his regret.

Until his death in 1926 he continued as Chief of the Stella Matutina, being succeeded by his widow Harriot, who in time also became an anthroposophist. During these years the Order continued to flourish, membership in Havelock North growing by 1930 to about two hundred. A heptagonal room decorated with mystic sigils where ceremonies were held is still preserved in a basement in Felkin's former house. In 1938, together with the Australian anthroposophist Charles McDowell, a new centre was formed near Taupo. But after the Second World War the situation gradually changed, and by the time Harriot Felkin died in 1959 the Order was in decline, though it was not until 1979 that the temple was finally closed down.

The beginnings of anthroposophy in New Zealand, which centred on the early figure of the remarkable Emma Richmond (1845–1921) and her son-in-law Bernard Crompton-Smith, later joined especially by Edna Burbury and Ruth Nelson—see relevant entries by Hans van Florenstein Mulder in *Anthroposophie im 20. Jahrhundert* (2003)—took place alongside the initially thriving but later moribund Stella Matutina, and gained various members from it.

47. In the course of his article 'An Impression of Dr. Rudolf Steiner' published in October 1922 in *The Occult Review*, William Loftus Hare was later to write: 'Theosophia, first used, I believe, by Porphyrius, and Anthroposophia by Thomas Vaughan, do not endow those who adopt them with Divine Wisdom and Man Wisdom respectively. Dr. Steiner's movement is now doomed to go forward wedded to a word which will always sound strange to English ears, and I can only hope—and indeed suggest—that it will be quietly dropped overboard in favour of one of its really English synonyms.'

Similarly, a review of *Fruits of Anthroposophy* in the November 1922 *Journal of Education* opened:

'We have come to the conclusion that the worst thing about Anthroposophy is its name. Etymologically the word is, of course, more than respectable, and its begetter makes a good case for it, especially when he differentiates his use of it from his use of the term anthropology. But it will remain hard for a convert to Anthroposophy to escape the suspicion of being a crank.'

48. It is evident that the letters from 1921 numbered 68–72 (not reproduced in the present work) in GA 263/1 have been misordered. The correct ordering is as follows: letter 69 from Maryon sometime in late August was answered by letter 68 from Steiner on the last day of the month; Maryon's reply, from the same address as before, was letter 72, written immediately on receipt of his in the first days of September; Steiner answered with letter 71 on the 5th, to

which Maryon at once replied with letter 70, from a new address. A few days later, on the 12th, she wrote letter 73 from this same address.

49. In his biography of Dunlop, Thomas Meyer misdated his entry into this study group to 1918, three years before it had even been founded. What is most striking about Dunlop's approach to anthroposophy is precisely the deliberate retardation, as Meyer elsewhere emphasizes.